T3-BNS-219

Soil and Water Conservation

Second Edition

Frederick R. Troeh
Professor of Agronomy
Iowa State University

J. Arthur Hobbs
Professor Emeritus of Agronomy
Kansas State University

Roy L. Donahue
Professor Emeritus of Soil Science
Michigan State University

Prentice Hall, Englewood Cliffs, New Jersey 07632

Library of Congress Cataloging-in-Publication Data

Troeh, Frederick R.
Soil and water conservation / Frederick R. Troeh, J. Arthur Hobbs, Roy L. Donahue: editorial assistance, Miriam R. Troeh. — 2nd ed.
p. cm.
Rev. ed. of: Soil and water conservation for productivity and environmental protection. 1980.
Includes bibliographical references and index.
ISBN 0-13-830324-X
1. Soil conservation. 2. Water conservation. I. Hobbs, J. Arthur (James Arthur). II. Donahue, Roy Luther. III. Troeh, Frederick R. Soil and water conservation for productivity and environmental protection. IV. Title.
S623.T76 1991
333.7'2—dc20 90-38945
CIP

Acquisitions Editor: **Robin Baliszewski**
Editorial/production supervision and interior design: **Lillian Glennon**
Cover design: **Bruce Kenselaar**
Manufacturing buyer: **Mary McCartney / Ed O'Dougherty**

Printed in the United States of America

10 9 8 7 6 5 4 3 2 1

ISBN 0-13-830324-X

Prentice-Hall International (UK) Limited, *London*
Prentice-Hall of Australia Pty. Limited, *Sydney*
Prentice-Hall Canada Inc., *Toronto*
Prentice-Hall Hispanoamericano, S.A., *Mexico*
Prentice-Hall of India Private Limited, *New Delhi*
Prentice-Hall of Japan, Inc., *Tokyo*
Simon & Schuster Asia Pte. Ltd., *Singapore*
Editora Prentice-Hall do Brasil, Ltda. *Rio de Janeiro*

Contents

Preface

Soil and water have always been vital for sustaining life, and these resources are becoming more limited and crucial as population increases. The importance of conserving soil productivity and protecting the quality of both soil and water is becoming clear to more people than ever before. Declining productivity and increasing pollution could spell disaster for all residents of the earth. The soil and water resources of the planet are finite and are already under intensive use and misuse. Environmental degradation is becoming painfully evident, and increasing numbers of people are demanding that steps be taken to not only reduce the amount of current degradation but also to amend some of the previous damage.

Soil and water conservation deals with the wise use of these important resources. Wise use requires knowledge, understanding, and value judgment. The hazards posed by erosion, sedimentation, and pollution, and the techniques needed to conserve soil and maintain environmental quality are all treated in this book. Situations and examples are drawn from many places constituting a cross-section of the soils, climates, and cultures of the world. The scope includes agricultural, engineering, mining, and other uses of land. Soil and water are recognized as essentials for everyone's life.

This second edition will be easier for United States students to read because the authors decided to use foot-pound-second units as the principal units of measurement. Metric units are usually included in parentheses and are presented as the principal or only units where they are the units generally used in the United States. The second edition has been thoroughly updated with many citations to the literature published since the first edition was printed. The authors also made a strong effort to shorten the book by condensing the wording while still retaining easy readability.

Much of this book can be read and understood by anyone with a good general education. Some parts, however, necessarily assume an acquaintance with basic soil properties such as texture, structure, water-holding capacity, and cation exchange capacity. These topics are covered in any introductory soil science textbook and one of these should be consulted if the reader lacks this background. The system of soil taxonomy used in the United States is followed in this book. An explanation of that system can also be found in modern introductory soils textbooks.

The authors have a broad collective background in soil science and soil conservation in the United States and abroad. This experience has been supplemented by extensive use of excellent libraries to locate appropriate literature including journals, books, and publications from government agencies. Many colleagues have also contributed valuable suggestions and some have thoughtfully reviewed the manuscript of one or more chapters dealing with subject matter in which they were especially well qualified. The helpful assistance of the following persons is gratefully acknowledged:

Julian P. Donahue, Assistant Curator, Entomology, Natural History Museum, Los Angeles County, California

Gustave Fairbanks, former Professor of Agricultural Engineering, Kansas State University, Manhattan, Kansas (retired)

George R. Foster, SEA-USDA, Purdue University,

Harold R. Godown, SCS-USDA (retired)

Robert Gustafson, Botanist, Natural History Museum, Los Angeles County, California

Lawrence J. Hagen, ARS, Manhattan, Kansas

Walter E. Jeske, SCS-USDA, Washington, D.C.

Rattan Lal, Agronomy Department, Ohio State University

Leon Lyles, SEA-USDA, Kansas State University

John Malcolm, USAID, Washington, D.C.

Harry L. Manges, Professor of Agricultural Engineering, Kansas State University

Gerald A. Miller, Professor of Agronomy, Iowa State University

John A. Miranowsky, Professor of Economics, Iowa State University

Basil Moussouros, former Minister for Agriculture, Government of Greece

Gerald W. Olson, former Professor or Soil Science, Cornell University (deceased)

G. Stuart Pettygrove, Department of Land, Air, and Water Resources, University of California at Davis

William L. Powers, Professor of Agronomy, University of Nebraska

Kenneth G. Renard, ARS, Tucson, Arizona

Frank W. Schaller, SEA Extension, Iowa State University (retired)

E. L. Skidmore, SEA-USDA, Kansas State University

Gene Taylor, U. S. Congress from 7th District of Missouri

D. Keith Whigham, Professor of Agronomy, Iowa State University

C. M. Woodruff, Professor Emeritus, Department of Agronomy, University of Missouri

Frederick R. Troeh
Ames, Iowa

J. Arthur Hobbs
Winnipeg, Canada

Roy L. Donahue
Forsyth, Missouri

1

Conserving Soil Productivity

Soil is a vital resource for the production of food, fiber, and other necessities of life. Food and fiber are renewable resources—a fresh crop can be grown to replace what is consumed. The soil that produces these renewable resources is essentially nonrenewable.

Strong reactions occur when there are shortages of food products or other consumer items. Prices of coffee and sugar, for example, have increased dramatically when a significant part of the world's crop was damaged, temporarily decreasing the supply. Such situations arise suddenly and require adjustments in the lives of many people. The more gradual changes resulting from persistent processes such as soil erosion may escape attention despite their fundamental importance. The long-term loss of productivity caused by soil erosion should be of greater concern than temporary shortages.

The purpose of soil conservation is not merely to preserve the soil but to maintain its productive capacity while using it. Soil covered with concrete is preserved, but its use to produce crops is lost in the process. Intensive cropping uses the soil but often causes erosion on sloping land. Land needs to be managed for long-term usefulness as well as for current needs. Scarred landscapes, as shown in Figure 1-1, tell a sad story of waste and ruin where long-term principles have been sacrificed for short-term gain.

Soil erosion is often more detrimental than might be supposed from the amount of soil lost. The sorting action of either water or wind removes a high proportion of the clay and humus from the soil and leaves the coarse sand, gravel, and stones behind. Most of the soil fertility is associated with clay and humus. These components also are important in microbial activity, soil structure, permeability, and water storage. Thus, an eroded soil is degraded chemically, physically, and biologically.

Figure 1-1 The amount of soil eroded by gullies eating their way into a landscape is spectacular but is often exceeded by sheet erosion around the gullies. (Courtesy USDA Soil Conservation Service.)

1-1 NEEDS INCREASING WITH TIME

The demand for plant and animal products increases with time as population increases and standards of living are raised. People now consume more food than do all other land animals combined (Deevey, 1960). Their needs place an increasing load on soil productivity—a load that can severely strain the ecosystem (Wöhlke, et al., 1988). Plants can be grown without soil by hydroponics and sand or gravel culture, but the expense is high and the scale is small. Even seafood is used on a much smaller scale than are soil products.

Until recent decades, production increases came mostly by using more land. New frontiers were opened, forests were cut, prairies were plowed, and deserts were irrigated. It was suggested that one hectare (2.5 acres) of cropland per person was needed to maintain a satisfactory standard of living. A continually expanding land base maintained approximately that much area for a long time. Of course, the best land is chosen first, so the average suitability of the land declines even if the area per person is maintained.

The one-hectare-per-person rule is no longer supported. Many countries now have more people than hectares of cropland. Production depends on soil, crop, climate, and management as well as land area. One hectare per person may not be enough in some places, but it is more than adequate in others.

In recent decades, the land base has been relatively constant. Most of the good cropland is already in use. Irrigation has been increasing and may continue to increase, but much of the newly irrigated land comes from nonirrigated cropland. The small areas of new cropland being added each year are offset by new roads and buildings on former cropland. Ryabchikov (1976) estimates that people already are using 56% of earth's land surface, 15% of it intensively. Much of the rest is not suitable for human use.

Increased production is now obtained mostly by using present cropland more intensively. New crop varieties and increased fertilization are important factors producing higher yields. More intensive cropping systems increase row crops and grain crops at the expense of forage crops. Multiple cropping has increased, and the rest period in the slash-and-burn system has been reduced or eliminated in some tropical areas. The effect of these changes on soil erosion has been mixed. Fertilization and multiple cropping increase plant cover on land and reduce erosion. The replacement of forage crops with row crops and grain crops and the shortening of rest periods in slash-and-burn tend to increase erosion.

1-2 EROSION PROBLEMS

Erosion occurs in many forms as a result of several causes. Anything that moves, including water, wind, glaciers, animals, and vehicles, can be erosive. Gravity pulls soil downslope—either very slowly as in soil creep or very rapidly as in landslides.

1-2.1 Intermittent Erosion

Erosion can be uniform and subtle. Sheet erosion, for example, removes layer after layer a little at a time until a lot of soil has escaped almost undetected. Most erosion, though, is intermittent and spotty. Surface irregularities concentrate the erosive effect of either wind or water in certain spots. Cavities may be blown out by wind or gullies cut by water. The pattern is usually spotty, as illustrated in Figure 1-2.

Half or more of the annual soil loss in most places probably occurs in only a few days during which rain and wind are intense and plant cover is at a minimum. Weeks, months, or even years may pass without much soil being lost. The loss from a single ferocious storm sometimes exceeds that of an entire century.

The spotty and intermittent nature of erosion complicates the interpretation of erosion measurements. A field with an average soil loss of 4 tons/ac (9 mt/ha) annually is within the accepted tolerable rate for most deep soils if the loss is evenly distributed. But if most of the loss comes from part of the field eroding at 40 tons/ac, that part of the field is being ruined by erosion. Furthermore, crops on adjoining areas may be suffering damage from sedimentation, as shown in Figure 1-3. An average over time is equally deceptive. The benefits of having only small soil losses for nine years are wiped out if severe loss the tenth year completely destroys a crop.

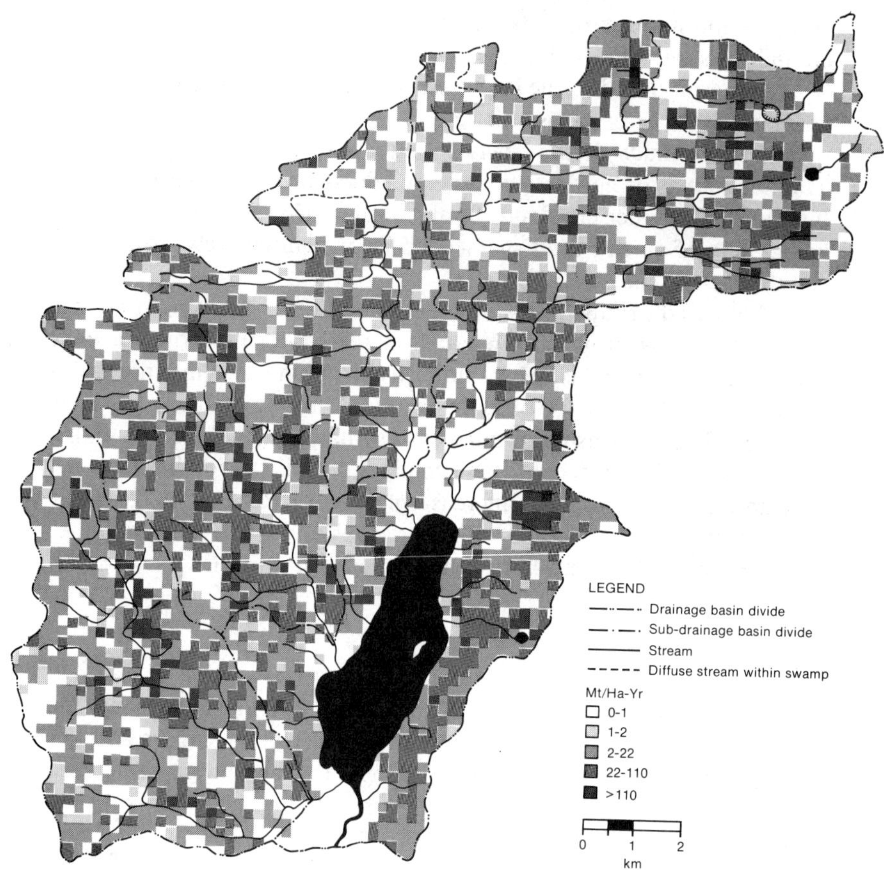

Figure 1–2 Estimated annual soil-loss rates by 10–acre cells in the Lake Canadarago drainage basin, New York. (From Kling and Olson 1975).

1–2.2 Accelerated Erosion

The normal rate of erosion under natural vegetation is in approximate equilibrium with the rate of soil formation. A particular set of conditions maintains sufficient soil depth to insulate the underlying parent material from weathering just enough so that soil is formed as fast as it is lost. Deviations from equilibrium cause the soil to get either thicker or thinner until a new equilibrium is established. Precise data on rates of geologic (natural) erosion and soil formation are difficult to obtain but are thought to average about 0.5 ton/ac (1 mt/ha) annually (see Section 3–7).

Tilling cropland, grazing pasture or rangeland, or cutting trees nearly always increases the rate of soil erosion. Loss of soil cover reduces protection and may accelerate soil loss by a factor of 10, 20, 50, or 100 times. Formation of new soil cannot keep pace with greatly accelerated erosion rates, so the soil becomes progressively thinner, sometimes until little or no soil remains.

Accelerated erosion reduces the amount of plant growth a soil is able to support. The productive potential is reduced even if the actual production is main-

Figure 1–3 Sediment from the higher areas covered and killed the crop in the foreground in this Iowa field. (Courtesy USDA Soil Conservation Service.)

tained or increased by the use of fertilizer and other management techniques. A shallower soil, with its reduced capacity for storing water and plant nutrients and its generally poorer structure and aeration, cannot match the productive potential of the uneroded soil.

1–2.3 An Old Problem in a New Setting

Cultivated fields, overgrazed pastures, and cutover forestlands have suffered from erosion since the dawn of civilization. The eroded soil becomes sediment that covers bottomlands and sometimes becomes so thick that it buries both fields and cities. The result becomes an archaeologist's treasure when a famous city such as Babylon is uncovered centuries after its inhabitants lost a frustrating battle with sediment eroded from nearby hills.

Gullies, sand dunes, and other obvious signs of erosion have caused concern since the beginning of agriculture. Impressive terrace systems were built thousands of years ago to stop erosion. Even so, entire soil profiles have been lost by sheet erosion, gullies have dissected hillsides, and sand dunes have drifted across anything in their path as, for example, the sidewalk shown in Figure 1–4. Many millions of acres of formerly productive land have been abandoned because of erosion damage.

A new concern has been added in recent years in addition to the age-old problems of erosion and deposition. Dust clouds and muddy water signify air and water pollution. Soil particles carry plant nutrients and other chemicals that contaminate water. Erosion has become an environmental problem that must be remedied for the sake of clean air and water. This new concern has added an urgency to erosion control that should have been recognized earlier.

Figure 1-4 Sand from a nearby beach drifted into the city and blocked this sidewalk in Montevideo, Uruguay. (Courtesy F. R. Troeh.)

An increasing part of the impetus for soil conservation, especially that which is legally mandated, stems from environmental concerns. The early stages of pollution control concentrated on point sources such as sewage systems and smokestacks. Current efforts are beginning to include nonpoint sources such as soil erosion. Soil conservation practices must be used along with other pollution controls to protect the environment.

1-2.4 A Concern for All People

Eroded soil and the chemicals it carries are matters of concern because a degraded environment harms everyone's health and enjoyment. Polluted water, for example, is unsafe for drinking, swimming, and many other uses. It can kill fish; moreover, the surviving fish may impair the health and reproductive capacity of birds that eat them. Both the fish and the birds may be made unfit for human food.

Erosion adds to the cost of producing food and other soil products and thereby increases the cost of living. Taking ruined land out of production places a greater load on the remaining land and drives up production costs. Installing expensive erosion control practices also adds to production costs, but these practices help assure that production will continue.

Soil conservation legislation should be of concern to all voters, even those not directly affected by it. Government may provide too little, too much, or the wrong kind of control to bring about effective soil conservation. Tax funds are used to pay the public's share of conservation costs. Everyone is affected; the public needs to understand and support the principles of soil and water conservation and environmental protection.

1-3 OBSTACLES TO CONSERVATION

Conservation is difficult to oppose, yet easy to overlook or ignore. Too many people give lip service to conservation but leave the application to someone else. Reasons for inaction include economic and aesthetic obstacles, insecurity and uncertainty, ignorance, and apathy.

1-3.1 Economic Obstacles

Major decisions are usually based largely on economic considerations. How much will it cost? What returns can be expected? Will the cost be repaid in a short time, in a long time, or not at all?

Conservation practices vary greatly in costs, returns, and effectiveness. The easiest practices to promote are those like a good fertilizer program that will both conserve soil and return a profit within a short time. Longer-term practices such as liming and soil drainage may be recognized as desirable for some time before any action is taken. The time lag is still longer for terracing and other practices whose high investment costs require many years to repay. Least popular of all are practices such as changing to a less intensive land use with lower probable returns.

1-3.2 Aesthetic and Cultural Obstacles

A great deal of pride can be involved in certain agricultural traditions. Straight rows, for example, are considered a mark of skill. Years ago, young farm workers were instructed "Don't look back!" because a tug on the reins would turn the horses and make a crooked row. Straight rows are appealing, but they cause erosion on hilly land by providing channels for runoff water to erode. Contour tillage is often the solution, but it must overcome tradition.

Many farmers take pride in plowing so that crop residues are completely covered. Unfortunately, this practice exposes the soil to the impact of rain, runoff, and wind. Conservation tillage reduces erosion by leaving residues on the surface, but it must overcome tradition before it will be adopted.

1-3.3 Insecurity and Uncertainty

Many people in developing countries can barely eke out a living from their land by hard work such as the hand tillage shown in Figure 1-5. They know that traditional management has kept them and their predecessors alive, and that they have nothing to spare for gambling on a new method. It is difficult for them to change their techniques even for immediate benefits such as higher yields and/or less soil loss. It is still more difficult for them to adopt a practice that requires an investment, especially if the benefits are delayed or distributed over several years. The establishment of conservation practices under such conditions requires a reliable guarantee that these people will not starve to death if the new practice fails.

Short-term tenancy prevents the adoption of many desirable practices. A one-year contract, or even a five-year contract, does not give the renter enough time to

Figure 1-5 Much hand labor is used in areas where people are barely able to subsist by tilling the land. (Courtesy F. Botts, Food and Agriculture Organization of the United Nations.)

benefit from the sizable investment of money and labor required to install many long-term conservation practices. Theoretically, the landowners should be willing to invest in sound long-term practices, but many owners are too far removed from the land to realize what practices are needed. Short-term tenancy makes it easy for both tenants and owners to overlook problems even when those problems reach critical stages.

1-3.4 Ignorance and Apathy

Most erosion occurs so gradually and subtly that its effects are easily overlooked until long after preventive action should have been taken. Even rills (small erosion channels) in a field are often ignored because tillage operations can smooth the surface again. Unproductive subsoil exposed on the shoulder of a hill is overlooked if the rest of the field remains productive. Even people who work with land often are unaware of how many tons of soil are being lost each year, of how costly these losses are, and of how short the useful life expectancy may be for a rapidly eroding soil.

Many people are apathetic about future needs and have short-term viewpoints regarding the use of soil and other resources. Land that was ruined in the past is unavailable now, and land that is ruined now is lost to future generations. Reduced productivity of eroded but usable land is even more important because it is more widespread.

Erosion control practices needed to prevent environmental pollution often are not installed or are long postponed because of indifference. Some landowners claim the right to use their land as they please even if it is being ruined and even if the sediment is damaging other people's property. Public opinion and environmental considerations have provided the impetus for laws restricting the rate of soil erosion allowable under certain conditions.

Much reluctance to protect the environment is based on economics. The people who must spend money to conserve their soil are not the only ones who suffer if the soil is eroded or benefit if it is conserved. Often the persons most affected live someplace downstream or downwind or will live at a later time. People are commonly reluctant to spend their money for unknown beneficiaries; some are unwilling to spend money to conserve soil for their own future benefit.

1-4 CONSERVATION VIEWPOINT

The need for soil conservation has been clear enough to catch the attention of both modern and ancient people. For example, the people of ancient Rome, India, Peru, and several other places valued soil enough to build terraces that still stand today such as those shown in Figure 1-6. Terrace walls were built of stones left on eroded hillsides; then laborers carried soil in baskets on their backs from the foot of the hill up to the terraces to make level benches. The Chinese still carry out similar laborious projects, but most modern conservation structures are built with the aid of machines.

Concern for the land is the most important characteristic of a soil conservationist. Those who have such concern will find a way to conserve their soil and water; those who lack it often neglect to use even the most obvious and inexpensive

Figure 1-6 These terraces in Bolivia were built hundreds, or perhaps thousands, of years ago and are still protecting the soil from erosion. (Courtesy F. R. Troeh.)

means of conservation. Conservation efforts therefore include education and persuasion aimed at convincing more people to care for their land.

Several organized groups now exist to promote soil and water conservation. The Soil Conservation Service of the U.S. Department of Agriculture helps people install conservation practices; several other agencies assist their efforts. The Soil Conservation Service works in cooperation with local Soil Conservation Districts that have their own national association. Interested individuals can become members of the Soil and Water Conservation Society, and there are many other groups at national, state, and local levels that advocate conservation of natural resources.

Conservationists take a long-term view regarding the use of resources. Some land has been used for several thousand years and is still productive. All land needs to be used in ways that will maintain its usefulness. The objective of soil conservation has been stated as "the use of each acre of agricultural land within its capabilities and the treatment of each acre of agricultural land in accordance with its needs for protection and improvement."

1-5 CONSERVATION TECHNIQUES

The practices used for conserving soil and water are many and varied. Some practices are expensive and some only require new habits; some are permanent and some are temporary; some are limited to very specific conditions whereas others are widely useful, although none have universal application. The amount of erosion reduction varies from one practice to another and from one set of circumstances to another.

1-5.1 Land Use and Management

One of the first items a soil conservationist considers is the use of land within its capabilities. Some land is suited for intensive cropping, especially where the soil is deep, level, fertile, and well drained and has favorable texture and structure. Other land is so steep, shallow, stony, or otherwise limited that it is suitable only for wildlife or other nondisruptive uses. Most land is suitable for some uses but unsuitable for others.

Land use can be broadly classified into cropland, pastureland, woodland, wildlife and recreational land, and miscellaneous use. Each broad class can be subdivided several times. For example, cropland may be used for cultivated row crops, small grain crops, or hay crops. The soil exposure to erosive forces declines from cropland to pasture and woodland and then to wildlife land. These latter uses are therefore considered to be progressively lower intensity. Nonagricultural classes may also be provided paralleling the agricultural ones. For example, lawn grasses, as shown in Figure 1-7, might be roughly equivalent to a similar growth of pasture grasses.

Management can alter the erosive effects of land use. Row crops, for example, can be grown in wide or narrow rows that may or may not follow contour lines. The time of exposure to the elements between the harvesting of one crop and the

Figure 1–7 A dense growth of bluegrass in this lawn provides excellent protection against erosion. (Courtesy F. R. Troeh.)

protective growth of the next varies considerably. The soil may or may not be protected by crop residues or by special cover crops during periods when the main crop is not on the land. These variables have considerable effect on the amount of erosion that is likely to occur.

Variations also occur with other types of land use. Pasture, for example, may have selected grasses and legumes that provide good ground cover and forage, or it may have whatever happens to grow. The number of livestock may be limited to what the pasture can readily support, or overgrazing may kill much of the vegetation. Both extremes may occur in the same pasture if the animals spend too much time in one area. Also, both soil and vegetation may be damaged by trampling if livestock are allowed to graze when the soil is too wet.

1–5.2 Vegetative and Mechanical Practices

Conservation techniques are often divided into vegetative and mechanical practices. There is no good reason for always favoring one type over the other; both include a wide variety of methods of protecting soil against erosive forces. The best approach in many situations requires a combination of vegetative and mechanical practices.

Vegetative practices include techniques that provide denser vegetative cover for a larger percentage of the time. Changing to less intensive land use usually reduces erosion considerably. The problem is that less intensive land use is usually less profitable. A crop rotation provides a compromise using a series of different crops with some providing more income and some giving more soil protection.

Crops grown for the purpose of protecting soil between other crops are known as cover crops.

Choices of land use, crop rotations, and cover crops need to be accompanied by good management practices that help each crop grow well. Good seed planted at the right time in a proper seedbed helps get the crop off to a good start. Adequate fertilizer and lime where needed promote vigorous growth. Narrow row spacing allows a row crop to provide better soil cover sooner. These management techniques generally improve both yield and erosion control.

Special vegetation is needed in critical places. Grassed waterways can prevent the formation of gullies. Windbreaks can direct the wind away from erodible land. Various forms of strip cropping reduce water erosion, wind erosion, and pollution. Appropriate plantings in odd corners, steep slopes, or other problem areas provide food and cover for wildlife as well as erosion control. Disturbed areas such as roadbanks and mine spoils need special plantings.

Vegetation can limit erosion to geologic rates—the rate of erosion under native vegetation defines the geologic rate for a particular setting. Grasses, trees, and other plants are nature's tools for controlling erosion. Although geologic rates are usually quite slow, they occasionally are as sudden and rapid as a landslide. Sometimes the rate of erosion should be reduced below the geologic rate by providing more than the natural amount of protection. More often, some increase above the geologic rate is allowable.

Mechanical methods broaden the choice of vegetation and allow higher-income crops to be grown even though the crops provide less soil protection. Contour tillage, for example, often reduces erosion to half that resulting from straight-line tillage. Tillage systems that leave more crop residues on the soil surface reduce erosion markedly. Further reductions can be achieved by building terrace systems such as those shown in Figure 1–8 to hold soil in the field. Soil movement may occur between terraces, but the soil caught in terrace channels will not pollute a stream. Of course, the channels must be cleaned periodically as a part of terrace maintenance.

Various structures made of concrete, wood, metal, or other sturdy material limit erosion by controlling water flow. Critical points occur where water must drop to a lower elevation. The water may be conducted through a pipeline, down a flume or chute, or over a drop structure. Pilings, riprap, or other bank protection may be used to keep a stream from meandering to a new location.

Mechanical methods of erosion control tend to be either very inexpensive or very expensive. Conservation tillage saves fuel, time, and money by reducing the number of trips and the total amount of work done on the soil. Contour tillage may require more planning and layout and add the inconvenience of short rows, but it normally costs no more than conventional tillage. The fuel requirement for working across the slope is usually slightly less than that for up and down the slope.

Tillage changes require no new investments unless new equipment is needed. However, these inexpensive practices are short-lived and must be repeated for each new crop. Most long-lasting mechanical methods of erosion control involve expensive structures such as terraces, dams, and drop structures. The earth-moving and

Figure 1–8 Terraces such as these hold the soil on the field rather than letting it erode away. (Courtesy USDA Soil Conservation Service.)

concrete work required are costly. Expensive structures are usually justified by many years of usefulness and increased flexibility of land use.

1–5.3 Conserving Soil and Water Together

Soil and water conservation are so interrelated that they must be accomplished together. There are very few techniques that conserve one but not the other.

Both soil and water can be conserved by protecting the soil from raindrops that would puddle the surface and produce a crust. Plant material intercepting raindrops helps maintain permeability so that water can infiltrate instead of running off. The soil acts as a reservoir that conserves water; reducing both splash and runoff conserves soil.

Contouring, contour strip cropping, rough surfaces created by tillage, and terracing all increase infiltration by holding water on the land. Any runoff that occurs is slower and carries less soil. Streams fed by seepage and slow runoff have more uniform flow and lower flood peaks than would occur from unprotected watersheds.

Reducing erosion keeps streams, ponds, and lakes from filling as rapidly with sediment. Reservoir capacities are thus maintained for recreation, flood control, power generation, and irrigation. Keeping sediment out of the water also lowers the supply of plant nutrients in the water and thereby reduces unwanted growth of algae and other vegetation. Soil particles absorb pollutants that are best kept out of water by keeping the soil on the land. The control of nonpoint sources of water pollution therefore centers on conserving soil.

Wind erosion control is more closely related to water conservation than it might seem. Water conservation is very important for plant growth in dry climates. Anything that slows runoff and helps get more water into the soil or keeps it there by reducing evaporation provides more water for plant growth. Improved plant growth in turn helps reduce wind erosion as well as water erosion.

1-6 CHOOSING CONSERVATION PRACTICES

Soil and water conservation is too complex to be solved by only one approach. Each situation needs to be analyzed to determine what problems and potentials exist and what alternatives are available.

1-6.1 Soil Properties That Influence Conservation

Many soil properties influence soil and water conservation, but a few deserve special emphasis because they strongly influence erosion control. Soil topography, depth, permeability, texture, structure, and fertility are worth consideration in relation to conservation.

Topography includes the gradient, length, shape, and aspect (direction) of slopes. These features control the concentration or dispersion of erosive forces such as runoff water and wind. Topography also influences the practicality of erosion control practices such as contouring, strip cropping, and terracing. These practices may be very helpful on long, smooth slopes but impractical on rolling topography with short, steep slopes.

Soil depth, the nature and thickness of soil horizons, and the underlying rock material all affect the rate of soil formation. The tolerable rate of erosion is much lower for shallow soils over hard bedrock than for deep soils underlain by loess or other unconsolidated material. Subsoils with high clay contents or other unfavorable properties need a covering of topsoil to support plant growth. Deep soil is favorable for water storage and plant growth. Where the soil is shallow, it may be impossible to smooth the land for drainage and irrigation or to move soil to build terraces and ponds.

Soil permeability helps determine how much water will run off and cause erosion. Soil permeability is most commonly limited by a soil surface puddled by raindrops or traffic, plowsoles or other compact layers, heavy subsoils with small water passages, frozen soil, and bedrock or cemented layers. Restrictive layers near the soil surface require little water to saturate the overlying soil and cause runoff to begin. Soil permeability also influences the functioning of subsurface drainage systems and septic tank drain fields.

Soil texture and structure influence soil permeability and erodibility. Clay can bind soil either into a solid mass or into structural units with pore space between them. Individual clay particles are difficult to detach from soil but can be moved long distances after they are detached. Sand particles are easily detached from sandy soils, but fast-moving water is required to transport them. Silty soils are often the most erodible by water, because the silt particles are too large to stick together well and are small enough to be transported readily. Silt particles are small enough, however, to resist detachment by wind unless they are knocked loose by something else, such as moving sand particles.

Soil fertility is important to soil conservation because plant cover helps protect the soil. Vigorous growth produced on a fertile soil provides more complete cover and better protection than sparser growth. Fertilizer and lime are therefore important for soil conservation.

1-6.2 Maps for Conservation Planning

Most of the soil properties discussed in the preceding section can be mapped. Topographic shapes and elevations are shown by contour lines. Soil depth, texture, structure, and many other properties are considered in naming the soil series shown on soil maps along with slope gradient and past erosion.

Conservation plans are based on soil maps. The soil mapping units are classified on the basis of the intensity of land use for which they are suited and the treatment they need. Soil maps are often colored to make important features stand out for planning. The soil maps are published along with descriptions of the soils and interpretations for various uses in soil survey reports such as those shown in Figure 1-9.

Figure 1-9 Soil survey reports such as these contain soil maps, descriptions, and interpretations for various uses such as soil and water conservation. (Courtesy F. R. Troeh.)

1-6.3 Considering Alternatives

Any piece of land could be used and managed in a variety of ways. Some ways would cause disastrous damage or monetary loss, but several satisfactory ways usually remain after unsatisfactory uses are eliminated. For example, a field might be used for pasture or hay production without any special practices, or it might be used for a crop rotation without excessive erosion if contour strip cropping and conservation tillage were used, or it might be used for intensive row crops if terraces were built and conservation tillage used. Increased intensity of use normally requires additional conservation practices to protect the land. Economic factors and personal preference are usually considered when a choice must be made from alternatives such as these.

Many choices depend on the type of agriculture being practiced. Growing hay or pasture on part or on all of one's land implies an operation that includes livestock. Building terraces to permit more row crops fits a cash-crop operation. Cover crops can be used to protect the soil between the trees in an orchard. Irrigation makes it possible to grow a wide variety of crops in arid climates, and soil drainage permits previously wet areas to be cropped.

1-7 CARING FOR THE LAND

Conservationists see the possession and use of land as a stewardship. The land that one person has now was previously someone else's and will soon pass to others. Its condition should be as good when passed on as when it was received. The owner has a responsibility to society for the way the land is used and the care it receives. The authority of governmental units to tax land, to place restrictions on its use, and to require that access and some other rights be granted to others indicates that ownership is not absolute.

Soil and water conservation attitudes and practices are needed everywhere. Even the best land is subject to damage it if is abused. Good land, fair land, and poor land are all useful if they receive proper care. People need constant reminders not to choose short-term exploitation over long-term productivity.

The use and care of agricultural land are stressed throughout this book, but the conservation needs of nonagricultural land must not be overlooked. Erosion on a construction site is often more rapid than in any nearby field. Excess traffic, especially by off-road use of motorcycles, 4-wheel drive, all-terrain, or other vehicles, can start a gully. Modified versions of agricultural practices may control erosion in these and many other circumstances. Vegetation and mechanical structures can be adapted to a wide variety of situations.

Population growth makes good land stewardship more crucial. "How many people can the earth support?" is a pertinent question. Increasing pressure from higher population densities makes the conservation task both more important and more difficult. The need for population control has become obvious enough to cause many programs to be developed for that purpose, such as the family planning

Figure 1–10 Family planning centers such as this one on Mauritius, an island in the Indian Ocean, are helping reduce birth rates and control population. This island has 850,000 people living in an area of 720 mi² (1865 km²). (Courtesy P. Morin, Food and Agriculture Organization of the United Nations.)

center shown in Figure 1–10. These programs and soil conservation practices are both needed, literally, for the salvation of the world.

SUMMARY

Erosion of the soil resource often goes unnoticed. The loss in productive capacity is usually worse than the tonnage indicates because erosion sorts the soil and removes the most fertile part. Soil conservation seeks ways to use the soil without losing it.

Production increases formerly came mostly by cultivating more land. Now, increased production must be obtained by increasing yields and intensity of land use because new cropland is hard to find.

Erosion is so intermittent and spotty that averages fail to reveal much of the serious damage done to soil and crops. Cultivated fields, overgrazed pastures, and cutover forest lands have suffered from erosion since the dawn of civilization, and sediment has been polluting streams and burying fields and cities. Erosion control efforts such as terrace systems have been in use for thousands of years but have been inadequate to prevent the loss of millions of acres of land. The contribution of erosion to air and water pollution has become a major concern in recent years. Erosion, pollution, and soil conservation are costly to everyone.

The installation of conservation practices is costly, and people are reluctant to abandon traditional methods. Subsistence agriculture, short-term tenancy, ignorance of erosion problems, and apathy are additional obstacles, but people who care about the land find ways to conserve their soil.

Many different techniques are available for conserving soil and water. The first requirement is to select an appropriate use within the land capability. Good management and conservation practices come next. Protective practices may be vegetative, mechanical, or a combination of the two. The effectiveness of vegetative practices depends on the density of the vegetation and the percentage of time it covers the land. Permanent vegetation, such as grassed waterways, windbreaks, or other plantings, can provide protection for vulnerable sites. Mechanical methods such as conservation tillage and water-control structures permit the growth of higher-income crops.

Soil and water conservation must be accomplished together. Contouring, terracing, and protecting the soil surface against crusting all increase infiltration and conserve both soil and water. Keeping sediment out of water reduces pollution and lengthens the life of reservoirs. Water conservation in dry climates increases plant growth and reduces wind erosion.

Soil properties such as topography, depth, permeability, texture, structure, and fertility influence the erodibility of soil and the best choice of conservation practices. Topographic maps and soil maps identify many of these properties and are useful for conservation planning.

Good stewardship of land requires passing it on to others in good condition for continued productivity. Both agricultural and nonagricultural land need soil and water conservation. Population growth makes land stewardship increasingly important.

QUESTIONS

1. In what ways can average rates of erosion be misinterpreted?
2. Why should a factory worker living in an apartment house be concerned about erosion?
3. Why do people fail to adopt new methods of erosion control?
4. Why would one build expensive terraces to control runoff and erosion that could be controlled by inexpensive vegetative methods?
5. What influence has increased environmental concern had on soil conservation?
6. Why are different techniques needed to conserve soils of sandy, silty, and clayey textures?
7. What information useful for conservation planning can be shown on maps?
8. Why do some people do a much better job of soil and water conservation than others?

REFERENCES

Barnett, A. P., 1972. Agriculture and a quality environment. *J. Soil Water Cons.* 27:104–108.

Brink, R. A., J. W. Densmore, and G. A. Hill, 1977. Soil deterioration and the growing world demand for food. *Science* 197:625–630.

Committee on the Role of Alternative Farming Methods In Modern Production Agriculture, Board on Agriculture, National Research Council, 1989. *Alternative Agriculture.* National Academy Press, Washington, D.C., 448 p.

Davis, R. M., 1985. Conservation: A matter of motivation. *J. Soil Water Cons.* 40:400–402.

Deevey, E. S., jr., 1960. The human population. *Sci. Am.* 203(3):195–204.

Frye, W. W., and R. L. Blevins, 1989. Economically sustainable crop production with legume cover crops and conservation tillage. *J. Soil Water Cons.* 44:57–60.

Kling, G. F., and G. W. Olson, 1975. Role of Computers in Land Use Planning. *Information Bull.* 88, Cornell Univ., Ithaca, N.Y., 12 p.

Kraft, S. E., P. L. Roth, and A. C. Thielen, 1989. Soil conservation as a goal among farmers: Results of a survey and cluster analysis. *J. Soil Water Cons.* 44:487–490.

Loehr, R. C. (ed.), 1977. *Food, Fertilizer, and Agricultural Residue.* Proc. 9th Annual Cornell Agric. Waste Mgmt. Conf., 1977. Ann Arbor Science Publishers, Ann Arbor, Mich., 727 p.

Nowak, P. J., 1988. The costs of excessive soil erosion. *J. Soil Water Cons.* 43:307–310.

Olson, K. R., and E. Nizeyimana, 1988. Effects of soil erosion on corn yields of seven Illinois soils. *J. Prod. Agric.* 1:13–19.

Owens, H. B., 1973. The public's responsibility to the American landscape. *J. Soil Water Cons.* 28: 195–196.

Ryabchikov, A. M., 1976. Problems of the environment in a global aspect. *Geoforum* 7:107–113.

Stamey, W. L., and R. M. Smith, 1964. A conservation definition of erosion tolerance. *Soil Sci.* 97:183–186.

U.S. Department of Agriculture, 1974. *Our Land and Water Resources.* Misc. Pub. No. 1290, 54 p.

Wischmeier, W. H., and J. V. Mannering, 1969. Relation of soil properties to its erodibility. *Soil Sci. Soc. Am. Proc.* 33:131–137.

Wohlke, W., G. Hengyue, and A. Nanshan, 1988. Agriculture, soil erosion and fluvial processes in the basin of the Jialing Jiang (Sichuan Province/China). *Geojournal* 17:103–115.

2

Soil Erosion and Civilization

The earliest cultivated fields were small, with tillage likely restricted to more level, productive soils, and with short periods of cultivation followed by long periods of fallow (shifting cultivation). Erosion losses were not serious until population multiplied and the cultivated acreage increased to meet the need for food. More intensive and widespread cropping caused increased erosion, decreased soil productivity, destroyed considerable land, and added sediment to streams, lakes, and reservoirs.

2-1 ORIGIN OF AGRICULTURE

Human beings were hunters and gatherers until relatively recent times. It is impossible to determine where crops were first cultivated, but relics from old village sites indicate the location and age of early tillage.

Archaeologists in 1946 uncovered an ancient village at Jarmo in northern Iraq (Braidwood and Howe, 1960). One relic found in the "dig" was a stone hand sickle. Other stone implements found at the village site could have been used for tilling the soil and for weeding growing crops. This village was occupied about 11,000 B.C. and is considered the earliest site of cultivated agriculture. Other prehistoric villages were found in the same general area dating from 11,000 to 9500 B.C.

These villages were located on upland sites with friable, fertile, easily tilled, silt loam soils. The progenitors of modern domestic wheats and barleys are believed to have been among the grasses native to the area and wild beans, lentils, and vetches among the indigenous legumes. Rainfall probably amounted to 18 to 20 in. (450 to 500 mm) annually.

Villages that were occupied during the period 9500 to 8800 B.C. were also excavated on lowland sites in the southern part of Iraq, near the Tigris and Euphrates rivers. The climate of this area is considerably drier than that farther north. Crop production by dryland farming methods was nearly impossible so irrigation had to be invented and used. The record is clear that water from the rivers was used to produce crops. An abundant food supply enabled large cities, such as Babylon, to develop.

2-2 EROSION IN THE CRADLE OF CIVILIZATION

The Sumerians of Mesopotamia at the peak of their power and prestige numbered about 25 million; by the 1930s, Iraq, a major part of ancient Mesopotamia, had a population of about four million. Something happened to cause the area to lose its one-time large population. The prehistoric village sites so far discovered were excavated from under many feet of erosional debris, suggesting that soil erosion was partly responsible for this loss of population.

Lowdermilk (1953) believed that water erosion around the upland villages began as soon as relatively large fields on sloping land were opened and used continuously. Soils in the area are now badly gullied, and much of the original soil is gone. Lowered productivity reduced food production and the large population could not survive.

Irrigated fields of the southern, lowland region were not damaged by soil removal, but were ruined by sediment from eroded land. Demand for food forced cultivation higher up the steep slopes in the watershed to the north. Sheep and goats overgrazed the hill pastures, and trees were felled indiscriminately for lumber and fuel. These practices denuded the watershed, causing severe erosion and erratic river flow. Large sediment loads carried by the rivers in the sloping areas where flow was rapid settled out in the more level areas. Much sediment was deposited in the irrigation canals and ditches. In time, human labor was insufficient to cope with removal, so sections of irrigated land were abandoned. Drifting soil from the sparsely covered, abandoned lands filled the remaining irrigation structures. In addition, salts from the irrigation water accumulated in the soils. Eventually, the whole irrigated area was destroyed. Large urban populations could not be supported. Cities were abandoned, and the area became a virtual desert. This was the first of many failures to develop a permanent, productive, cropland agriculture.

2-3 EROSION IN MEDITERRANEAN LANDS

Peoples on the trade routes between Mesopotamia and Egypt developed systems of arable agriculture shortly after tillage was invented. It is probable that the knowledge of cultivation and irrigation was carried from Mesopotamia to these countries by traders and other travelers.

2-3.1 Soil Productivity in Egypt

Egypt had a dry climate. Only the narrow Nile River floodplain could be cultivated. A type of irrigation developed, with natural flooding and no canals. Level lands were involved so little soil eroded.

The Nile River rises in the mountains and tablelands of Ethiopia far to the south of the irrigated Egyptian floodplain. Extensive forest cutting and cultivation of steep slopes in the upper reaches of the watershed caused considerable erosion. The coarser sediments were deposited mostly in the Sudan where the river left the high country and entered the more level plain. Sediment carried into Egypt was fine textured and fertile. The annual deposit helped maintain soil productivity. The system developed in the lower Nile valley was the first successful attempt to develop a permanently productive, cultivated agriculture with irrigation.

2-3.2 Erosion in Israel, Lebanon, Jordan, and Syria

The ancient lands of Palestine, Phoenicia, and Syria have long had sedentary populations and established cultivated agricultures. Cultivation was restricted initially to gently sloping lowland areas, with flocks and herds utilizing the steeper-sloping lands as range. Cultivation gradually encroached on the steeper lands. This and the reduction of protective native cover by overgrazing and timber harvesting increased runoff, erosion, and sedimentation.

The Phoenicians were among the first people to experience severe erosion from steep cultivated slopes. They found that bench terraces made by constructing stone walls on the contour and leveling the soil above them reduced water erosion and made irrigation on steeply sloping land possible. These ancient terraces are still being cultivated successfully in Phoenicia and the surrounding countries. Large soil losses have occurred from nonterraced sloping land through the years.

Extremely severe erosion has occurred on over a million acres of rolling limestone soils between Antskye (Antioch), now in Turkey, and Allepo, in northern Syria. From 3 to 6 ft (1 to 2 m) of soil has been removed. Half of the upland soil area east of the Jordan River and around the Sea of Galilee has been eroded down to bedrock. Much of the eroded material was deposited in the valleys, where it is still being cultivated. Even these floodplains are subject to erosion, and gullies are cutting ever deeper into them. Archaeologists have found the former city of Jerash buried on a floodplain under as much as 13 ft (4 m) of erosional debris.

Some arid regions, such as the Sinai Peninsula, have been so severely overgrazed that the land is cut by extremely large gullies, despite low rainfall. Winds severely eroded the soil between the gullies, but as stones of various sizes were exposed, a closely fitted desert pavement formed which now prevents further wind damage. The productive capacity of the soil has greatly deteriorated. As a result, population in many sections has been drastically reduced by starvation and emigration. Some areas that formerly produced food for export to the Roman and Greek empires now cannot produce enough to feed the small indigenous population.

Some authorities blame the decline in productivity, particularly in the drier sections, on a change of climate, but agricultural scientists are convinced that the climate has not changed sufficiently to account for this decline. They believe that soil loss due to water and wind erosion is the root of the problem (Le Houerou, 1976).

2-3.3 Erosion in Southern Europe and in Northern Africa

Knowledge of cultivation spread westward from Egypt and the Middle East to Greece, Italy, and northern Africa and on to other parts of Europe.

Erosion in Greece and Italy. The Greeks originally were a pastoral people. The upland areas of their country were covered with forests and the productive lowland soils were used for grazing. Farming gradually replaced flocks and herds. Productive valley soils were cultivated first, but as population increased, food needs demanded production from land higher up the hillsides.

Old Greek agricultural literature describes a few special soil-management practices, such as multiple cultivations, fallowing for one to several years, and deep plowing, which help to maintain productivity or at least reduce the rate of its decline. Soil erosion and soil deterioration, however, were rarely mentioned. Apparently they used no special erosion control practices. More than three feet (1 m) of soil was washed from the surface of extensive areas, in places the soil was removed to bedrock; severe gullying occurred on the steeper slopes; and lower-lying fields were buried under unproductive erosion debris.

Increased food needs and declining production from their soils caused the Greeks to exploit the grain-producing potential of their colonies in Italy, in northern Africa, and on islands in the Mediterranean. The cheap grain imported from the colonies caused Greek farmers to shift to the growth of more profitable olives, grapes, and vegetables. Some areas that had not been too seriously impoverished continued to produce food grain because of frequent loss of overseas grain shipments by acts of war, piracy, and bad storms.

Italy was a colony of Greece for several centuries before Rome established its own empire. Initially, little land was cultivated, but when tillage was introduced both dryland and irrigation farming methods were used. Italy eventually became a granary for Greece.

When Rome first became independent of Greece, it produced all its food needs locally. Agriculture was a prominent and respected vocation. Many Roman authors assembled knowledge of successful farming methods used at home and abroad. Widespread use was made of fallow; the legume crop, alfalfa (lucerne), was highly recommended, not only as a valuable forage but also as a soil-fertility-improving crop. Other legumes were recommended and used also.

As Roman population increased, demands for food also increased, and the level bottomland areas were insufficient to produce what was needed, so cultivation moved farther up the hillsides. Erosion from the uplands accelerated and became even more serious as forests were felled to supply timber for ships and for fuel.

Denuded soils and huge gullies resulted. Dedicated and industrious farmers terraced and contoured much of their land to reduce erosion. Figure 2–1 shows some terraces currently in use in northern Italy.

Sediment still washed into streams and was deposited in irrigation works, making regular removal necessary. When the empire deteriorated as a result of wars and invasions, labor for sediment removal became scarce and irrigated fields were progressively abandoned. Sedimentation of the major river channels caused frequent and destructive floods. Swamps developed close to the streams and malaria and other diseases increased in severity, forcing people to move to higher ground and to intensify farming on the steeper slopes. This caused still larger soil losses.

With growing populations, deteriorating soils, and smaller yields, Rome had to depend on imported grain from other countries, particularly Carthage, Libya, and Egypt. Cheap imported grains and declining soil productivity forced farmers to abandon some fields and to switch to the production of olives, vegetables, and grapes on others, as shown in Figure 2–2.

Italian soils, despite severe damage, were more durable than those of Greece, and recuperated after the fields were abandoned. Reasonable yields can be produced with modern technology on most soils, but erosion is a continuing threat.

Erosion in Northern Africa. Northern Africa (Tunisia and Algeria) was a very productive area in the early Roman era, along the coast of the Mediterranean Sea where the rainfall was approximately 40 in. (1000 mm) annually and inland for a considerable distance where rainfall was considerably less.

Carthagineans were excellent farmers; cultivation techniques were advanced for the times, and yields were good. They used very careful water conservation

Figure 2–1 Numerous terraces help to control erosion on this cropland near Miniato in northern Italy. (Courtesy F. R. Troeh.)

Figure 2–2 This vineyard near Florence, Italy, has widely spaced rows that allow room for soil-conserving grain and hay crops. Hillside ditches provide drainage below each row of grapes. (Courtesy F. R. Troeh.)

methods and had extensive irrigation works. Water-spreading techniques were employed in many of the drier regions. Relics of grain-storage structures and olive-oil presses attest to farmers' expertise and to the region's productivity. Grain in excess of local needs was exported.

Serious deterioration took place over the centuries despite the high initial productivity of the soils. Winter rainfall caused erosion on bare soils, and wind erosion often destroyed soils left without cover during drier parts of the year. After the fall of Rome, Carthage was attacked by desert dwellers (herders mostly) from the south and their agriculture declined. Vegetative deterioration caused by neglect and overgrazing further reduced soil productivity. Much formerly productive land lost all of its topsoil as it was eroded down to a stony desert pavement. Desert encroached onto productive cultivated fields and the potential for feeding a large human population was drastically reduced.

Soils in many areas that once supported large populations now provide food for only a few hundred people. Lowdermilk (1953) mentioned the ruined city of El Jem on the plains of Tunisia whose amphitheater could accommodate 65,000 people. He stated that in the late 1930s there were fewer than 5000 inhabitants in the whole district surrounding the city's ruins. El Jem's cultivation agriculture was destroyed after only a short period of successful production. Local wars and invasion played a part in the massive decrease in production but soil erosion was the main cause of the deterioration and ultimate demise of a system.

2-4 EROSION IN EUROPE

Western Europe, north of the major mountain ranges (Alps, Jura, and Pyrennes), has a forest climax vegetation. Rainfall is abundant in most areas. Local agriculture was generally improved when Roman methods were introduced.

2-4.1 Erosion in the British Isles

The Celts, pre-Roman inhabitants of Britain, had a well-developed arable agriculture. They cultivated fields across the slope. Gully erosion was not a serious problem because the rainfall was gentle. Washed sediment gradually built up on the downhill side of each field as a result of sheet erosion and of tillage-induced downhill movement (Bennett, 1939). The Celtic agricultural methods were altered but not replaced by Roman techniques.

The Saxons, who came to Britain from mainland Europe, introduced a system of long, narrow, cultivated fields, mainly on the more level lowlands. Most of the old Celtic fields were then abandoned, many permanently.

Soil erosion was more severe in Scotland than in England because a shortage of level land caused more steeply sloping soils to be cultivated. The detrimental effects of erosion were recognized in Scotland, and conservation practices were developed. Contour ridges were recommended and used, and a predecessor of the graded terrace was developed.

2-4.2 Erosion in France, Germany, and Switzerland

Erosion became extremely severe in many hilly areas of central Europe as steep slopes were cleared of forest cover and cultivated. The farmers in what is now France developed bench terraces and returned some cultivated land to forest over a thousand years ago. Some terraces were constructed on slopes as steep as 100% (45°). The soils on the benched areas were turned deeply every 15 to 30 years as the soils became "tired." These terraced areas are still being used. Lowdermilk (1953) suggests that the Phoenicians were responsible for these developments. Appropriate land use and careful husbandry reduced erosion losses over most of the region. The steep land at high elevations is now used only for forest and pasture, as shown in Figure 2-3. Grain crops are grown on moderate slopes at lower elevations, as in Figure 2-4. Level bottomlands are used mainly for truck crops, as shown in Figure 2-5.

Wind erosion is a serious menace in Europe also. Sandy soils subject to wind damage are found along seacoasts and inland where water-laid or glaciated coarse deposits occur. Systems of revegetation have been developed to hold the sands and prevent drifting in most areas where wind erosion poses a threat. These sandy soils are generally used for pasture or forest and are rarely cultivated.

Figure 2-3 Steep areas in the Swiss Alps are either left in forest or grazed judiciously. (Courtesy F. R. Troeh.)

Figure 2-4 Upland areas in Switzerland are cropped where the soils are favorable and the slopes are not too steep. Pasture and woodland are interspersed with the cropland. (Courtesy F. R. Troeh.)

Figure 2-5 Level alluvial soils in Swiss valleys are used for vegetables such as the lettuce in this field and other high-value crops. (Courtesy F. R. Troeh.)

2-4.3 Erosion in Eastern Europe

Considerable sheet erosion occurred in Hungary, Czechoslovakia, and Poland; gully erosion was not severe. Most of the rains were gentle, and a type of agriculture was developed that was uniquely adapted to forest soils. It improved rather than destroyed soil productivity (Jacks and Whyte, 1939). The system involves use of adapted crop rotations, return of animal manure and crop residues to the soils, and recently, judicious application of lime and fertilizers. Cultivated crops in much of the area are produced only on gentle slopes. Grain and other agricultural products are imported when local production is not sufficient to meet national needs. The main conservation needs of these soils are the maintenance of soil fertility and the improvement of drainage.

Severe erosion in the Soviet Union has a long history. Excessive tree cutting on forested slopes and overgrazing and cultivation of steep and semiarid lands have caused serious water and wind erosion in both European and Asian regions. Cultivation of "new lands" in southern Siberia after World War II increased the extent of submarginal, cold, and dry farming areas. Severe wind erosion occurred. Some of these areas proved so erodible that cultivation was abandoned.

2-4.4 Soil Reclamation in the Low Countries

The Low Countries include the Netherlands and a part of Belgium. They occur on a generally flat plain with little land more than 150 ft (50 m) above sea level. Instead of losing land by soil deterioration, arable area has been increased by reclaiming land from the sea. The new land is obtained by building dikes such as that shown in Figure 2–6, pumping the salt water out, originally with windmills, such as the one in Figure 2–7, and using river water for irrigation and reclamation (Note 2–1). Much of this new land is a mixture of sandy soils, clayey soils, and peat. Water erosion was never serious on these lands, and wind erosion has been well controlled by protective

Figure 2–6 A dike protecting lowlands in the southern part of The Netherlands. (Courtesy F. R. Troeh.)

Figure 2–7 A windmill near Kapelle, The Netherlands. Windmills were the original power source for pumping water to reclaim the polders. (Courtesy F. R. Troeh.)

vegetation on sandy sites. The soils in this area are generally more productive now than they were when first reclaimed.

NOTE 2-1

RECLAMATION OF THE POLDERS

The people of The Netherlands and Belgium have been reclaiming land from the sea for hundreds of years to help meet the needs of dense populations. Most of the reclaimed land was near sea level and much of it was reclaimed in relatively small tracts. The polders form a much larger and better-known reclamation project than any of the others.

The general plans for large-scale reclamation were drafted about 1890 by Cornelius Lely, but initiation was delayed until the 1930s. The Zuider Zee, an arm of the North Sea that reached deep into the Netherlands, was cut off and converted into a body of fresh water called Lake Ejssel. Five polders covering 220,000 ha (about 545,000 ac) have been reclaimed within Lake Ejssel by the following procedures:

1. The *Afluijdijk* barrier dam, 30 km (20 mi) long and nearly 100 m (325 ft) wide, was completed in 1932 to form Lake Ejssel. River inflow gradually converted it to a freshwater lake (excess water is emptied into the ocean by sluice gates).
2. An area within Lake Ejssel was surrounded by an inner dike, and the water was pumped out to form a polder.
3. Rushes were planted in the freshly drained polder to control weeds, use up water, and help aerate the soil.
4. Trenches, ditches, and canals were dug for drainage and irrigation. The reeds were burned and a crop of rape was planted the first year and wheat the second year. Both rape and wheat tolerate the initial saline conditions and are good soil conditioners.
5. After three to five years the land was dry enough to replace the trenches with drain tile. Farmsteads were built, and the units leased to selected farmers.

2-5 EROSION IN ASIA

China, countries of south-central Asia (India, Pakistan, Bangladesh, and Sri Lanka) and of southeastern Asia have suffered catastrophic soil erosion. Cultivation began in China and India soon after the Sumerians developed it in Mesopotamia. This long history of land utilization is responsible for very severe erosion damage, although extreme population pressure has caused severe exploitation and considerably increased soil losses.

2-5.1 Erosion in China

Erratic but intense rainfall and relatively steep land slopes in northern China combine to cause severe sheet and gully erosion when cultivation moves upslope. Gullies as deep as 600 ft (185 m) have eaten back into the deep loess hills of Shenhsi and surrounding provinces. Erosion has so damaged the soils of the area that only isolated patches of more level land are now fit for cultivation, but because population density is higher in this gullied area than anywhere else in China, cultivation continues on much of the land.

Although erosion threatens the existence of the Chinese in the hilly lands, millions of people on the plains of China suffer more. A number of major river systems traverse China from west to east. They collect water and vast quantities of eroded sediment and carry it eastward. In the west, the river headwaters have relatively steep gradients; in the east, they level out and sediment is deposited. The deposits elevate the streambed, reducing channel capacity and causing periodic flooding. This is particularly true of the Hwang (Yellow) River. About 4000 years ago, the Chinese started constructing levees along the river. A system of double dikes about 400 mi (600 km) long has been built. The inner dikes are close to the river channel and the outer ones are about 6 mi (10 km) on each side of the inner levee system. Sediment has raised the river channel within the levees, in many places making the river flow more than 40 to 50 ft (15 m) above the floodplain and delta. Floodwater still breaks through the levees occasionally laying waste to cultivated fields and homes, drowning thousands, and causing hundreds of thousands more to die of starvation. The sediment deposited by a flood may be a long-time benefit to soil fertility, but it is a short-time disaster.

Wind erosion has also been severe in many sections of northern and western China where semiarid and arid climates prevail. Soil drifting has been most severe in desert areas and on cultivated fields during droughts in semiarid areas.

Despite more rugged terrain and greater rainfall in southern China, water erosion has been less than in the north because of less pressure on the land for food production, better protection by native forest vegetation, more assured crop cover on cultivated fields, and less erodible soils. Bench terraces are used extensively on the steeper cultivated slopes; contouring is employed on less steeply sloping land.

2-5.2 Erosion in South-Central Asia

South-central Asia is a very old and geologically stable area with very diverse soils on topography ranging from very steep slopes in the mountains and hills to level alluvial plains. Most soils are Oxisols and Ultisols in the higher rainfall sections, but basalt rock has formed a large belt of Vertisols on the Deccan Plateau. Aridisols and Entisols are found in drier areas. It is a tropical and subtropical region with rainfall ranging from less than 4 in. (100 mm) in the northwestern desert to over 400 in.

(10,000 mm) annually in the western Ghats and along the border between Bangladesh and Assam. The region has monsoonal wet summers and dry winters.

Native vegetation of the region, except in the desert and some semiarid areas, controlled erosion well. Under cultivation the land is much less protected, and soils become less permeable, making erosion common.

Soil erosion and deterioration were negligible in this region when tillage was first used because shifting cultivation with the recuperative periods ten or more times as long as the cultivation periods was employed. As population increased, especially over the last 150 years, fallow periods have been shortened. Continuous cropping is now normal, giving the soil little chance to recuperate. Larger contiguous areas of cultivated land increase the potential for erosion also.

The most severely eroded area in south-central Asia is in the hills south of the Himalaya Mountains in what is now Pakistan. Livestock herders, woodcutters, and farmers combined to denude the slopes. As a result, torrents of water rushed downhill during the rainy season, causing severe sheet erosion and forming deep gullies. Deterioration was not restricted to land from which soil was removed; floods inundated fields and villages, and transported sediments were deposited on good soil, causing severe crop and soil damage.

Fields on more level plains and alluvial soils have not eroded seriously, but many have been ruined by excessive salt buildup. Plantation crops such as tea and coffee have produced little erosion. Major obstacles to erosion control in this region are the tremendous demand for food, excessive livestock numbers, the general abject poverty of the people, and the great difficulty of communicating effective conservation information to millions of small farmers.

2-6 EROSION IN THE AMERICAS

There are two major areas in the Americas with long histories of continuous cultivation, Peru and Mexico. In other areas of the Americas, population pressure did not force the people to use continuous cultivation until after the European settlers arrived. With increasing immigration, the number of fields and their sizes increased. Farm implements and animal power made it possible to cultivate larger fields and to incorporate crop residues thoroughly into the soil. Erosion increased and soil deterioration followed.

2-6.1 Erosion Under Prehistoric Civilizations

In Peru, the Incas were expert soil and water conservationists. They developed bench terraces to control water and soil loss when the population became too large for adequate support from the level bottomland soils. Relatively large areas were covered with these terraces. The face of each bench was a stone wall generally 3 to 15 ft (1 to 4.5 m) high, with some as high as 50 ft (15 m), as shown in Figure 2-8. Rocks, gravel, and other nonsoil materials were placed behind the wall to within a few feet (about a meter) of the level surface of the bench. This last meter was filled with good soil, which was carried from the level bottomland, or more frequently from a considerable distance. Many terraces are still being cultivated. They also installed much broader terraces in the stream valleys to prevent flooding and soil erosion.

The Incas probably had the world's most effective erosion-control structures. Modern-day farmers are unwilling to pay the price in money, energy, and labor to emulate them. Peruvian farmers recently have cut the forests, overgrazed the range, and greatly reduced the length of the recuperative fallow between periods of cultivation. They are farming on exceedingly steep slopes, as shown in Figure 2–9. They are short of fuel, and use manure and even excavated tree roots for cooking fires. These have all combined to increase erosion greatly in a relatively short time.

The Maya of Central America specialized in corn production, initially grown only on the level lowlands. Eventually, it became necessary to cultivate the forested slopes also. Many unprotected sloping sites were damaged so severely that the soils lost much of their productive capacity, and the streams, which were necessary to the continued existence of the population, were filled with sediment. Recently, archaeologists (Matheny and Gurr, 1979) found a complex system of Mayan bench terraces, dams and other water-diverting devices, and underground water-storage cisterns and walk-in wells in southeastern Mexico. These practices and structures apparently reduced soil and water losses. Modern-day Maya have reverted to shifting cultivation, taking two or three crops, then abandoning the field for long

Figure 2–8 Rock-faced bench terraces constructed by the Incas at Machu Picchu, Peru (the "Lost City of the Incas"). The dark channel in the foreground carried irrigation water to the terrace. (Courtesy F. R. Troeh.)

Figure 2-9 Peruvian fields on a steep mountainside south of Cuzco. Hand tillage is used to raise grain crops on these steep slopes. (Courtesy F. R. Troeh.)

periods of recuperation. This system cannot support a large population such as that of the Mayan civilization at its peak. Here again a system of continuous cultivation failed largely because of erosion.

2-6.2 Erosion in the Amazon Rain Forest

Much of the uncultivated arable land of the world is located in tropical areas. One large block of this land is found in the Amazon Valley. Many consider that this land can be cultivated without difficulty. Not true; soil deterioration from fertility loss and erosion is a constant threat.

Until relatively recently, the populations of most tropical regions have remained in balance with food supplied by a system of shifting cultivation. This is permanently productive. Such a system was common in the Amazon Valley.

Over the last few decades, the local population in the region has increased, and in addition, entrepreneurs have acquired large blocks of forested land for cultivation or for mining or other commercial activities. Too often these efforts are undertaken with little concern for long-term effects they have on soils or on other phases of the environment. Extensive denuded areas, from whatever cause, generally erode rapidly and spectacularly. In addition, valuable hardwood logs are burned or otherwise destroyed, and climax vegetation is lost, perhaps forever.

To date, the Brazilian government appears not to consider the situation serious. Steps need to be taken to control these losses before it is too late.

2-6.3 Erosion in the United States

The influx of new settlers from all over Europe and population buildup in the United States, particularly after 1800, provided labor and the market for expanded cultivation. Crops were grown as monocultures, not as mixtures. These crops, particularly those grown in widely spaced rows, left the fields open to the beating action of the rain and to the force of runoff water for long periods each year. Cotton and tobacco production in the southern states permitted extensive erosion. Corn grown in northern states was nearly as destructive. Rainfall intensity was much greater in the new land than it was in Europe, and far greater damage was done to the soil. With little knowledge of how to reduce the losses and with an abundance of new land available, a philosophy of unconcern was adopted. A few individuals developed new techniques to reduce erosion losses and to maintain productivity. Several of these innovations are still in use. Most landowners tried to cope with land deterioration, without much success, or moved west to start again.

The western frontier vanished at the end of the nineteenth century; since then the nation has had to depend on existing farms. The productive capacity of many eastern farms has been greatly depleted; severe soil deterioration has occurred on many "new" farms in central and western parts also. Water erosion was the major hazard in the humid sections; wind erosion a serious menace in drier regions.

Loss of fertility was serious also. Limited applications of nutrients were made in humid areas; essentially no fertilizer or manure was applied in the drier regions. Summer fallow helped to stabilize crop production in semiarid areas, but it increased soil exposure to erosive rains and winds, and contributed to soil salinity (saline seeps).

Erosion surveys in the middle 1930s showed the following: 12% of the total cropland essentially ruined, 12% severely damaged, 24% with one-half to all of its topsoil lost, another 24% with measurable erosion loss, only 28% unaffected by erosion. The survey showed that 3 billion tons (2.7 billion metric tons) of soil was washed off the fields, pastures, and forests of the United States annually. This is equivalent to the loss of the furrow slice 7 in. (17 cm) thick from 3 million ac (1.2 million ha) of land each year. The severe dust storm of May 12, 1934, which started in southeastern Colorado, southwestern Kansas, and the panhandles of Texas and Oklahoma, carried an estimated 200 million tons (185 million metric tons) of soil about 2000 mi (3000 km) to New York City and Washington, D.C., and out to sea.

Gradually, progressive farmers and research and extension personnel realized the importance of reducing soil losses. They pressured Congress in the late 1920s and early 1930s to establish government agencies to combat erosion. These agencies are discussed in Chapter 19. National awareness prompted the passage of the Soil Conservation Act in 1935. This established the Soil Conservation Service as a research and promotional body. Soil conservation activities in the United States have done much to reduce soil degradation, but erosion is still serious in many areas.

2-7 EROSION IN AUSTRALIA

Australia was thinly populated prior to European immigration. The aborigines did not grow crops and had no grazing livestock (Hallsworth, 1987).

Cultivation and introduction of western-style livestock began approximately 200 years ago. These changes caused erosion to increase. Water erosion became especially severe in southeastern Australia, where precipitation falls mostly in the summer and where intense thunderstorms are common. Forest cutting in Queensland also increased water erosion. Overgrazing dryland vegetation in southern and western Australia increased wind erosion.

After about 150 years of exploitive agriculture, concern about soil deterioration surfaced and development and promotion of conservation measures were started in the early 1930s. Individual farmers began to develop and adopt soil improvement practices and state and Commonwealth governments initiated research, promotion, and financial programs to control soil losses.

Soil erosion and other forms of soil degradation continue to plague the nation, but soil productivity losses are being halted and practices for improvement continue to be promoted.

2-8 EROSION IN AFRICA

Africa has a very wide range of climates and soils. In more temperate regions animal agriculture was dominant with few and scattered fields. In tropical regions animal agriculture was restricted by parasites, mainly trypanosomes carried by tsetse flies, so crop agriculture developed. Arable agriculture always involved shifting cultivation.

Until recently, populations in most African countries have been in balance with the food supplied by animals and by shifting cultivation. This system broke down when population increased dramatically. A much larger cultivated acreage is now needed and the fallow period is greatly curtailed.

2-8.1 Erosion in Southern Africa

Erosion was not a serious problem in southern Africa until gold discovery accelerated European immigration in the late nineteenth century. Prior to that, population density was low, and livestock numbers were moderate. Native forage plants and forests thrived, cropping was not intense. Even in the deserts and on the desert fringes, wind erosion was serious only intermittently. Immigration and rapidly increasing native population expanded the need for cultivated land. Erosion quickly became severe in many areas, and was exacerbated by steadily increasing numbers of livestock owned by native populations. Rainfall in the region is generally erratic. This increases erosion potential.

Most countries in this region have dual farming sectors—a commercial sector dominated by Europeans, and a communal sector operated entirely by native peoples. Erosion was apparent and became serious first on the commercial farms.

With increasing native populations and enlarged flocks and herds confined to relatively small, poor-quality areas erosion soon became very serious on the communal lands, too. In many communal areas overgrazing by livestock was responsible for more erosion than was cultivation. Serious consequences of erosion were first recognized in the 1920s and efforts were made by individual commercial farmers to initiate control programs. By the 1930s government assistance was being demanded and provided. Quality of land, density of population, availability of capital, control over resources, and production of food and export revenue clearly favored the commercial sector in the battle against erosion and in getting the assistance and direction provided by government. Native sectors were left largely unassisted. With independence from European political dominance some redresses are being made, but erosion losses from communal lands continue at very high levels. The developing countries in this region will have great difficulty funding suitable control programs without external assistance (Whitlow, 1988).

2-8.2 Erosion in Eastern Africa

Many east African countries have extensive areas with temperate climates due to high elevation. These and more tropical areas were occupied and farmed by native peoples without serious erosion taking place. European immigrants took over much of the arable lands in the temperate regions in late nineteenth and early twentieth centuries, leaving drier and more tropical areas for the native population.

Erosion incidence increased after this partition, first on the "white" farms, but soon on communal lands also. Production of corn and cotton on more sloping land, overgrazing, and unrestricted felling of forest trees caused the increases in Kenya. Increased cotton production was primarily responsible for erosion in Uganda. The desert enlarged in both countries in the early 1930s. This resulted from expanded cultivation on marginal land in the semiarid, desert fringes and from overgrazing due to increased livestock numbers.

Ethiopian highlands form the upper watershed of the Nile River. The original forest cover protected this area from erosion. Excessive forest cutting and overgrazing denuded the land over the last several centuries. Whereas 75% of Ethiopia was forest covered, now only about 4% is protected in this way. This change caused rapid runoff and soil loss; the highlands, particularly the Amhara Plateau, are now very severely eroded.

2-8.3 Erosion in Sahel Region

The remarkable destitution brought about by drought in the Sahel region in the 1970s is well known. Conventional wisdom blamed this on a long-term change in climate; in reality the root cause was overgrazing by domestic animals and excessively expanded cultivation of marginally arable land which bared the soil and promoted severe wind erosion. Desert expansion is occurring as a result. Here, too, desert expanded not because of irreversible climatic change, but because of land abuse.

2-8.4 Erosion in Western Africa

In the rain forest and forested areas of western Africa cultivated fields were small and shifting cultivation was used with long fallow periods. In drier regions fields were larger; fallow periods were shorter. Erosion was limited in the whole region. During the last half century or slightly longer population has increased rapidly, cultivated acreage has expanded, and fallow duration has decreased to the point that continuous cultivation is practiced in many areas. As a consequence, soil productivity decreased, erosion increased, and huge gullies developed (Osuji, 1984).

Large cities in many of these countries have made continuous cultivation even more widespread. Lack of roads from farms to markets and from villages to cities demands that vast areas in the vicinity of the cities must be cultivated every year. Local farmers cannot let land lie idle long enough to replenish its productive capacity, and productivity and production go down.

It is not enough to add fertilizers to continuously cultivated land in this region. Fertilizers are scare and very high priced. Nitrogen fertilizers cause soil acidification. This can have very serious consequences on the fragile soils in an area where lime is scarce.

Another cause of productivity loss in moister regions of west Africa and of other tropical areas is the irreversible dehydration of hydrous iron oxides. When forest cover is removed for extended periods, the temperature and moisture regimes of the soils change and soft iron concretions in the soil harden into an ironstone that reduces or prevents water and root penetration. The resulting poor plant cover allows the friable soil above the ironstone to be washed away (see Figure 2-10).

Figure 2-10 Ironstone (hardened plinthite) in a tropical soil in Ghana exposed by the erosion of about 6 in. (15 cm) of overlying soil. (Courtesy Henry Obeng.)

Soil erosion is a serious problem wherever relatively large populations of people and animals occur and where rainfall and wind are conducive to soil detachment and transportation. If appropriate techniques were selected and used worldwide, excessive soil losses could be reduced to tolerable levels and soil productivity could be maintained indefinitely for the benefit of all the world's people. This is not being done, even though the tools and methods to do the job are at hand. More than knowledge is necessary. "Human desires, motives, and emotions, including greed and the drive for self preservation, are as crucial to the cause of soil erosion as rainfall (and wind) erosivity and soil erodibility." (Miller et al., 1985, p. 25).

SUMMARY

Accelerated erosion is older than recorded history. It has been a common cause of soil deterioration all over the world. Soil erosion has been severe from the earliest civilizations in the Middle East to the most recently cultivated lands in the Americas, Australia, and southern Africa. Soil deterioration has often been so great that the land has been abandoned because it is no longer productive.

People have frequently failed to develop effective cultivation systems that maintain soil productivity over long periods. Soil deterioration resulting from erosion has caused the decline of many civilizations. A few civilizations have developed and used conservation measures that reduced soil deterioration and maintained soil productivity at satisfactory levels for many centuries. In many "new" lands, colossal productivity losses occurred in very short periods and emphasized the urgency for conservation measures.

QUESTIONS

1. Point out where soil deterioration and sedimentation have played a major role in the decline of early civilizations.
2. What positive and negative effects did the Romans have on soil-conservation methods in Europe?
3. How and why have people reclaimed land from the sea?
4. Explain why most European settlers in the United States failed to take adequate precautions to reduce soil erosion and deterioration as they moved into and across the country.
5. Describe the forces that have impinged on the stable farming systems found in many tropical countries and caused the systems to break down.

REFERENCES

BALDWIN, M., J. L. BUCK, H. GREEN, A. B. LEWIS, T. C. TSIANG, S. B. SHOW, T. B. CHAMBERS, J. G. STEELE, C. E. KELLOGG, and R. L. PENDLETON, 1948. *Soil Conservation: An International Study.* FAO Agric. Stud. 4, FAO, Washington, D.C.

BEASLEY, R. P., 1972. *Erosion and Sediment Pollution Control.* Iowa State Univ. Press, Ames, Iowa, 320 p.

BEAUMONT, P., and K. ATKINSON, 1969. Soil erosion and conservation in northern Jordan. *J. Soil Water Cons.* 24:144–147.

BENNETT, H. H., 1939. *Soil Conservation.* McGraw-Hill, New York, 993 p.

BLOOMFIELD, N. J. T., 1977. *An Evaluation of Soil Erosion in Southern Brazil, and a Proposal for an Integrated National Program of Soil Conservation and Soil Survey.* M.S. thesis, University of Wisconsin, Madison.

BRAIDWOOD, R. J., and B. HOWE, 1960. *Prehistoric Investigations in Iraqi Kurdestan.* Univ. of Chicago Press, Chicago, 184 p.

BUIE, T. S., 1964. After thirty years. *J. Soil Water Cons.* 19:93–102, 147–152.

HALLSWORTH, E. G., 1987. Soil conservation down under. *J. Soil Water Cons.* 42: 394–400.

HELMS, D., 1987. Soil conservation is an old-time religion. In *Our American Land* Yearbook of Agriculture USDA, Washington, D.C. p. 175–180.

HUBERT, P., 1970. The soils of Cyrenaica (Libya). *Pedologie* 20:285–338.

JACKS, G. V., and R. O. WHYTE, 1939. *Vanishing Lands.* Doubleday, New York, 332 p.

KELLOGG, C. E., 1957. We seek; We learn. In *Soil,* Yearbook of Agriculture. USDA, Washington, D. C., p. 1–11.

KORELESKI, K., 1975. Types of soil degradation on loess near Krakow. *J. Soil Sci.* 26:44–52.

LAL, R., 1974. Soil erosion and shifting agriculture. In *Shifting Cultivation and Soil Conservation in Africa,* Soils Bull. 24. FAO, Rome, p. 48–71.

LE HOUEROU, H. N., 1976. Can desertization be halted? In *Conservation in Arid and Semiarid Zones.* FAO Conservation Guide 3. FAO, Rome, p. 1–15.

LOWDERMILK, W. C., 1953. *Conquest of the Land through Seven Thousand Years.* USDA, SCS Agric. Inf. Bull. 99.

MATHENY, R. T., and D. L. GURR, 1979. Ancient hydraulic techniques in the Chiapas Highlands. *Am. Sci.* 64(4):441–449.

MILLER, F. P., W. D. RASMUSSON, and L. D. MEYER, 1985. Historical perspectives of soil erosion in the United States. In *Soil Erosion and Crop Productivity.* R. F. Follett and B. A. Stewart (eds.). Am. Soc. Agron., Madison, Wis., p.23–48.

OSUJI, G. E., 1984. The gullies of Imo. *J. Soil Water Cons.* 39: 246–247.

WHITLOW, R., 1988. Soil conservation history in Zimbabwe. *J. Soil Water Cons.* 43:299–303.

3

Geologic Erosion and Sedimentation

Geologic erosion processes are natural—they exclude accelerated erosion resulting from tillage, traffic, overgrazing by livestock, cutting of trees, or other human influence. But naturally caused catastrophic events such as glaciation, landslides, and floods are included. Understanding geologic erosion improves one's comprehension of erosion processes and underscores the importance of controlling accelerated erosion.

3-1 THE GREAT LEVELER

Erosion is known as the "great leveler" because it wears down high places and fills up low places. Valleys are created and the hills between them are eroded. The end result of long-continued erosion theoretically is a rather featureless plain.

Geologic erosion is very old and very persistent. It has worn mighty mountain systems down to stubs. Entire sea basins have been filled with sediment, then lifted and eroded into new forms. The shapes of earth's landscapes are determined by the action of geologic forces, especially erosion and sedimentation.

The nature of sedimentary deposits depends on the source of the material, the transporting agent, and the environment of deposition. Geologists learn much about the climate, vegetation, and landscapes of the past by studying sediment and rock layers.

3-2 ROCK TYPES

The earth's original crust was formed of igneous rocks that solidified as the earth cooled. Weathering forces caused the surface of the early rocks to crumble into small particles. The leveling action of erosive forces has been active ever since. Sedimentary and metamorphic rocks now cover about 85% of the land surface, but the underlying "basement" rocks are igneous (Note 3–1).

NOTE 3–1

ROCK TYPES

Rocks are broadly classified as igneous, sedimentary, or metamorphic depending on how they were formed. Igneous rocks form by solidification when a magma (molten rock material) cools. The rate of cooling determines the grain size. Magma forms a fine-grained rock when it erupts to the surface as a lava flow that cools quickly. Lava rocks are extrusive in contrast to the slower-cooling, coarser-grained intrusive rocks. A simple classification of four important igneous rock types is as follows:

	Extrusive (fine-grained)	Intrusive (coarse-grained)
Rocks containing quartz crystals	Rhyolite	Granite
Rocks lacking quartz crystals	Basalt	Gabbro

Basalt and granite are the most common igneous rocks. Several other types are defined as intermediates or extremes of the above types or as having special mineral contents.

Sedimentary rocks form where transported material is deposited. Soft sedimentary rocks are classified by transporting agent and grain size. Some important examples are:

Alluvium: material deposited by water
Colluvium: material moved downslope by gravity
Glacial till: material deposited by glaciers
Loess: silty material deposited by wind

Hard sedimentary rocks include a cementing agent or process in their formation. Some important examples are:

Sandstone: cemented sandy alluvium
Shale: clayey material compressed enough to bond together
Limestone: primarily precipitated calcium carbonate

Heat and pressure change other rocks into metamorphic rocks by making them recrystallize and form new, usually larger, crystals. The material does not melt—that would result in an igneous rock. Metamorphism may be either low grade (relatively small changes produced) or high grade. Some low-grade metamorphic rocks are easily related to an earlier rock type, but some are more general. The metamorphosed rock is often harder than the original:

Marble: metamorphosed limestone

Slate: metamorphosed shale

Quartzite: metamorphosed sandstone with a high quartz content

Schist: low-grade metamorphic rock high in small flakes of mica

Gneiss: high-grade metamorphic rock with elongated grains and a general banded appearance

Many sedimentary deposits have accumulated to thicknesses of several miles. The pressure and heat of deep burial change the deposits into metamorphic rocks that later may be reexposed at the surface by uplift and erosion.

3-3 PROCESSES THAT ELEVATE LAND

Erosion has worked long and persistently. It would have eliminated all dry land long ago, but fortunately, there are equally potent and persistent counteracting forces. The net result is a balance that maintains a nearly constant amount of land. The processes that elevate land masses can be classified into three groups: deposition, lava flows, and uplift.

3-3.1 Deposition

Sediments that gradually fill a pond, lake, or other basin often produce fertile level land. Gray colors are common in sediments deposited in water. Some of these sediments include organic layers where the residues of lush vegetation fall into shallow water and are preserved. Bogs are formed where thick layers of organic materials fill a low area. Low, wet areas can become part of a smooth valley floor by the combined action of erosion and deposition.

Much of the material removed by young, actively eroding streams is deposited downstream where the stream floods across a valley. Small streams entering a large valley often deposit sediment in alluvial fans that slope down to merge with the valley floor, as the one shown in Figure 3-1. Sediments deposited in valleys are commonly several feet thick, but some accumulate to thicknesses of a few miles. A large deposit can cause the area to sink and continue receiving sediment.

Figure 3–1 An alluvial fan is formed where a small stream flowing on a steep gradient enters a large valley and is slowed by the flatter slope. Orchards are grown on alluvial fans in this Idaho scene because the fan soils are well drained, but the bottomland soils are wet. (Courtesy F. R. Troeh.)

3–3.2 Lava Flows

Molten rock flowing out on the land as in Figure 3–2 is an obvious way to increase elevation. Lava flows several feet thick are common. Most lava areas have multiple flows resulting in cumulative thicknesses ranging up to thousands of feet. Some lava rock is covered by or layered with ash that spewed out of a volcano and was spread across large areas by wind. Loess layers and alluvial deposits may also occur on or

Figure 3–2 The edge of a basalt lava flow in Oregon. This flow is about 50 ft (15 m) thick. (Courtesy F. R. Troeh.)

between lava flows. The largest area of lava rock on land is the Columbia River Basalt, covering large areas of Washington, Oregon, and Idaho in northwestern United States.

The ocean basins are lined with basalt (the most common type of lava rock). Undersea lava flows have built up mountains that reach miles above the seafloor and form islands where they protrude above sea level. The Hawaiian Islands are an outstanding example of thick lava accumulations surrounded by deep ocean.

3–3.3 Uplift

Slow persistent uplift is the principal process that elevates land masses and offsets erosion. Both upward and downward movements occur, resulting in the warping and twisting evidenced by contorted rock layers, but the upward movement is dominant in land areas.

Uplift is an expression of *isostasy* (the tendency to equalize pressure). Even solid rock is able to flex and move across dimensions of many miles. Pressure inequalities produced by erosion are balanced by internal shifts in the earth's crust. Eroded areas are lifted up again, and depositional areas gradually sink. Thus uplift and erosion continually reactivate each other and produce stresses in the earth's crust. Sometimes the stresses are released suddenly in an earthquake.

Density differences in rock types cause unequal elevations to produce equal pressures. Basalt dominates in ocean basins and has an average density of about 3.0 g/cm^3. Granitic rock in the cores of large mountain ranges has an average density of about 2.7 g/cm^3. The 10% difference in density permits the lighter-weight rocks in the mountains to "float" above the denser rocks. Like an iceberg, the mountain exposes only about 10% of its total mass. The other 90% is submerged and provides buoyancy, as shown in Figure 3–3.

Continental masses are believed to be shifting slowly around the globe in a process known as plate tectonics that is widening the Atlantic Ocean at the expense

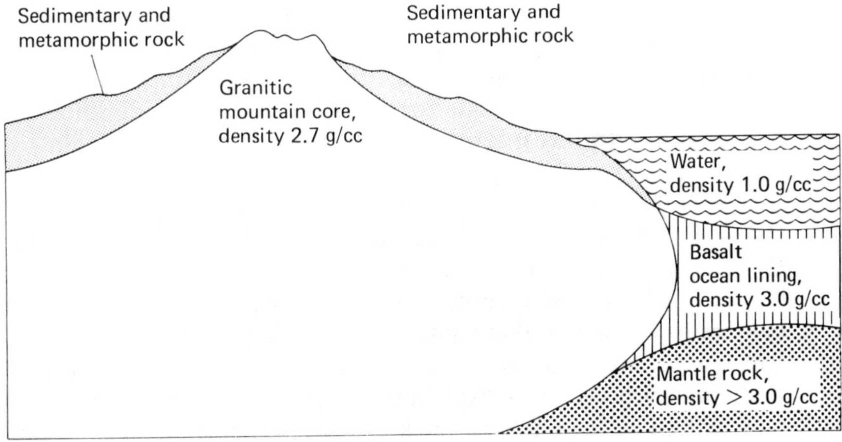

Figure 3–3 Land areas, especially mountains, protrude above sea level because they are formed of rock with a lower density than that lining the oceans. (Courtesy F. R. Troeh.)

of the Pacific. The subcontinent of India illustrates a dramatic type of uplift deduced within this framework. India appears to have split from Africa and drifted across the ocean to its present position. The "collision" of India with Asia produced the highest mountains in the world, the Himalayas (Frank et al., 1987).

3-4 LANDSCAPE DEVELOPMENT

Erosion, deposition, lava flows, and uplift play major roles in shaping landscapes. The results are seen as hills and valleys, mountains, plateaus, and plains. All landscapes, whether simple or picturesque, have been affected by these age-old forces. While the geologic history of some landscapes is fairly easily interpreted, that of others is very complex.

Some landforms are controlled by single agents of erosion or deposition in ways that produce close approximations of geometric shapes. River floodplains, for example, come close to being plane surfaces. The flow of a small stream into the side of a larger valley produces a nearly uniform slope profile in every direction it moves. The result is a fan-shaped area with contour lines approximating segments of concentric circles. The effect continues even though the slope gradient decreases with distance.

Erosional surfaces resembling alluvial fans are called *pediments.* A classic example of a pediment is located in the area of Gila Butte, Arizona. As shown in Figure 3-4, the pediment surface comes close to fitting a mathematical equation. The floodplain and other adjoining landforms do not fit the equation.

3-4.1 Geomorphology

"The study of the Earth's surface forms, and of the processes that shape them, constitutes the field of geomorphology" (Butzer, 1976, p. 7). Geomorphology and soil science are so interrelated that neither can be understood without some consideration of the other. As Butzer says, "Soils modify the gradational process and, in turn, the external agents of erosion and deposition affect the soil mantle and its development." Some principles of geomorphology are included in this section to help clarify the subject of landscape development.

3-4.2 Uniformitarianism

Credit for the early development of modern geomorphic principles is given to James Hutton. Hutton presented his ideas in a paper in 1785 and in his book, *Theory of the Earth,* in 1795. The underlying theory that Hutton developed and used to explain how the earth received its form is called the principle of uniformitarianism. Previous theories had supposed that landscapes were shaped primarily by sudden nonrecurrent events. Hutton argued that past processes are still at work and that one can study present processes to explain past events. Uniformitarianism is summed up in the statement, "The present is the key to the past." Due allowance must be made for variations in rates and importance of various processes, but strange and unknown processes need not be invoked.

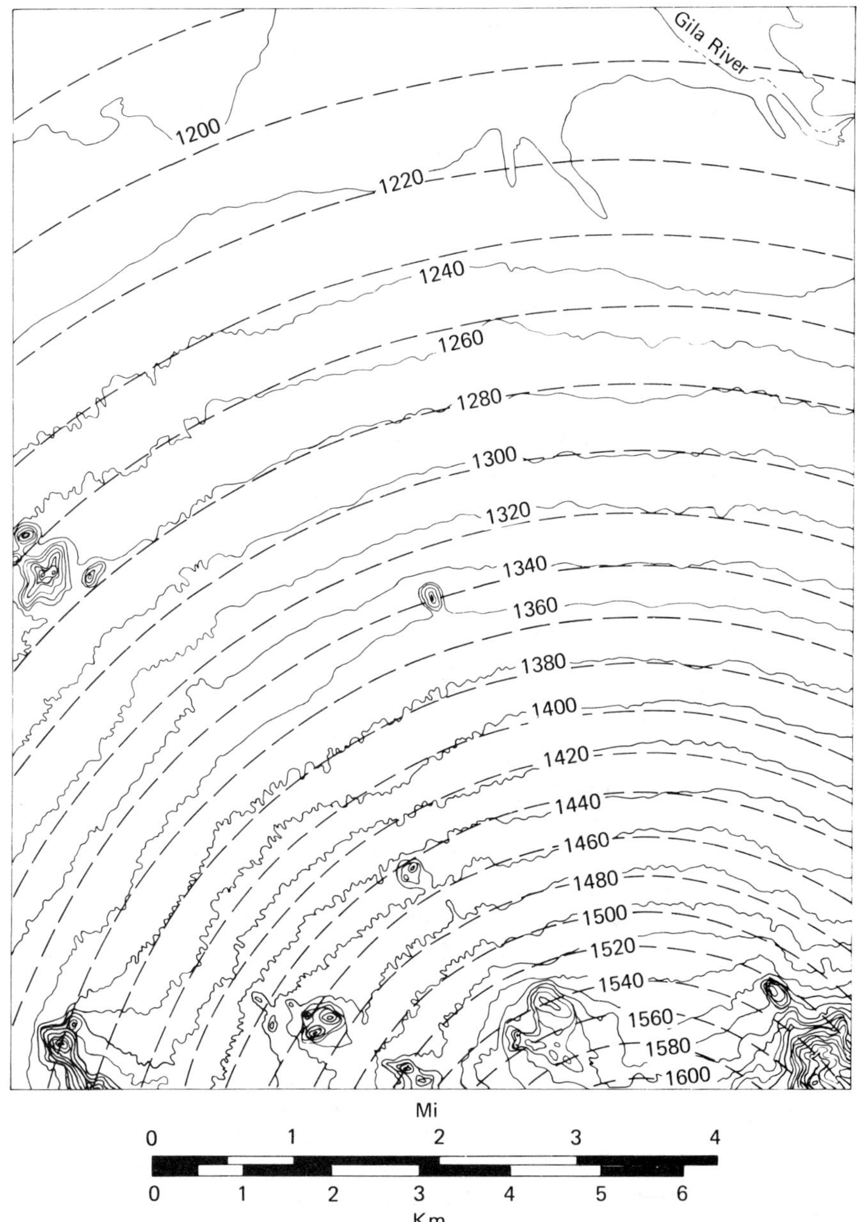

Figure 3-4 The contour lines of the area around Gila Butte, Arizona, are closely approximated by a series of concentric circles drawn to fit the equation $Z = 1707 \text{ ft} - 0.0192R + (0.000{,}000{,}176/\text{ft})R^2$ with R equal to the distance in ft from the center of the circles. The elevations (z) are in feet above mean sea level. (Courtesy F. R. Troeh.)

3-4.3 Structure, Process, and Stage

The principles of geomorphology were further clarified by W. M. Davis in the 1890s. Davis theorized that erosion phenomena resulted in a "geographical cycle" of landform development. According to Davis, the nature of any landform is a function of structure, process, and stage of development in the geographical cycle.

Structure. Structure includes all aspects of the physical nature and arrangement of the rocks in which the landscape formed. The hardness of each rock material, the presence or absence of layers, and any tilting, folding, or faulting are part of structure. Grain size, degree of cementation, and permeability are also included because they influence the rate and pattern of erosion. The shape of erosional landscapes depends largely on structural factors that determine which rocks are most erodible.

Process. Process refers to the combined action of the agents building and eroding a landscape. Water erosion, wind erosion, and mass movement remove material from some areas and deposit it elsewhere. Glaciers add their own dramatic touch. Soil movement by plants and animals should not be overlooked. Human activity, however, causes accelerated erosion and is excluded from geologic erosion.

Rock weathering and soil formation are vital predecessors of the erosion process because they help produce fragments small enough to be moved. Erosion rates are limited in many places by the rate of production of loose material.

Erosive agents sometimes leave identifiable impressions on the landscape. A hillside scar and debris in the valley mark a landslide long after the event. Scratches on the bedrock of central Canada remain today as evidence of glacial scour thousands of years ago. Moraines and other glacial features in northern United States show how far the glaciers reached. Old bison trails show conspicuously on aerial photos of certain areas in the Great Plains (Clayton, 1975).

Climate. Climate exerts a strong influence on the geomorphic process. Arid regions typically have angular topography (Note 3–2), and humid regions usually have rounded features because of the combination of weathering, erosion, and deposition working on their landscapes. Cold climates with heavy snowfall produce glaciers and glacial landscapes. A trained observer can learn much about the climate simply by observing landscapes (see Figure 3–5).

NOTE 3–2
ARID LANDSCAPES

It is often assumed that arid landscapes are shaped by wind. Wind is an active agent in arid regions, but other factors such as the sparse vegetation and the distribution of water in both time and space should not be overlooked.

Arid regions have bare soil exposed to the direct impact of rainfall because the bunchgrasses, shrubs, cacti, and other native plants cover only a fraction of the area. Also, the relatively low organic

Figure 3–5 The shape of a landscape tells much about the climate of the area: (a) an angular arid landscape in Arizona (Courtesy F. R. Troeh.); (b) a semiarid landscape on the island of Kauai, Hawaii (Courtesy USDA Soil Conservation Service.); (c) a rounded humid-region landscape in New York (Courtesy F. R. Troeh.).

matter contents produce weaker soil aggregates, slower permeability, and less resistance to erosion than would be likely under more humid conditions.

Rainfall in arid regions can be intense even though it is infrequent. Runoff can accumulate quickly and cause a local "flash flood" because there is not enough vegetation to slow the water flow. A literal wall of water comes rushing down a streambed that was dry only a moment before. The stream may empty onto a broad flat area where the water spreads out and infiltrates into the alluvium deposited by countless flash floods of ages past. These flats are a marked contrast to the adjacent steep angular hills. Some flat areas completely surround one or more hills.

Local runoff gives the flats more water than adjacent hills (nearby mountains may receive more precipitation than the lower areas). Rock material within a few feet of the flats is often moist enough to weather and erode faster than the drier rock above. Wind and water erode these softened lower rock layers and produce angular topography with unique landforms such as natural bridges and balanced rocks. Wind erosion abrades most at low levels because the wind carries more and heavier particles at low levels than at higher levels.

Stage. Landscapes pass through stages of *youth, maturity,* and *old age.* When water erosion first cuts a set of steep, narrow valleys in an upland, the landscape is said to be in youth even though the relatively undisturbed areas between the valleys represent an older stage of a preceding geomorphic process. Maturity is reached when the new cycle has molded the entire area. Maturity is a long stage that is often divided into early and late substages. A mature landscape typically has many valleys and is very hilly. Old age is reached when the hills are nearly worn away and erosion has slowed.

Multiple Cycles. Landscape development is often interrupted by environmental changes before old age is reached. Any of several factors such as climatic change, uplift, or the cutting of a barrier by erosion may initiate a new cycle of landscape development. A landscape may show the effects of two or more cycles of development long after such changes occur.

Climatic changes have caused glaciers to come and go several times during the last million years across vast areas of North America, Europe, and Asia as shown in Figure 3-6. Each glacial and interglacial stage had marked effects on landscapes both within and beyond the glacier-covered areas. Glacial deposits have been cut by valleys, filled by a later glacier, and then cut by new valleys in different directions. Associated water and wind erosion and deposition combined with the glacial processes to produce very complex landscapes.

Climatic changes can produce dramatic differences in landscape development even without glaciation. A small change in precipitation or temperature might

Figure 3-6 Glacial ice still covers major areas between 60 and 90° North and South latitudes and once covered much more extensive areas in Europe, Asia, and the Americas. (Courtesy F. R. Troeh.)

influence the rate and pattern of erosion by altering the vegetation. Major climatic changes may cause an angular topography to shift toward roundness, or vice versa.

Renewed uplift rejuvenates old landscapes. Greater elevation differences result in faster erosion and deeper valleys with steeper slopes. Uplift in one area may be accompanied by downwarp (sinking) in another area that will then receive deposits. The intervening area is tilted to a new angle that shifts the position of streams and their erosional and depositional areas. The record of such changes is often preserved in buried surfaces, sloping and dissected terraces, and other landscape variations.

3-4.4 Stream Systems

Streams cut valleys in all but the most arid landscapes. Most streams are integrated into river systems that carry runoff water to the ocean. Exceptions occur where the water all infiltrates and flows underground and where the water accumulates in a low area such as the Dead Sea or Great Salt Lake and escapes by evaporation. Such exceptions are called closed drainage systems in contrast to open systems that drain to the ocean.

Some streams originated from water flowing down the initial slope the area had when it was first exposed to erosion. Such streams are called *consequent streams* because they are a consequence of the original slope.

Tributaries flowing into consequent streams are called *subsequent streams* because they developed later. Subsequent streams flow down the sides of consequent valleys, and headward erosion cuts their valleys across the original slope of the area. Tributaries to subsequent streams are called *secondary consequent* if they flow in the same direction as the consequent stream and *obsequent* if they flow in the opposite direction.

The preceding terminology works well on *rectangular* stream patterns where all streams tend to meet at right angles. Tilted rock layers of varying erodibility can produce such a pattern. Most of the streams are subsequent streams flowing in valleys cut into the softest rock strata and are parallel to each other. The connecting links are consequent streams that flow down the tilt-produced slope. Parallel fault lines are a less common cause of rectangular patterns. A *trellis* pattern is a rectangular pattern with a large preponderance of streams in one direction.

Dendritic stream patterns are the most common type. Directional terminology is not very useful in describing dendritic systems because the branching streams may flow in any direction. Dendritic stream patterns on a map resemble the branching of a tree, as illustrated in Figure 3–7. They develop where there are thick rock masses with uniform degree of erodibility.

Other patterns also occur. For example, a mass of rock may be pushed up in the form of a dome and develop a *radial* drainage pattern from the water running off on all sides. *Complex* patterns include elements of several patterns.

Streams may also be classified into orders. *First-order streams* are the first identifiable channels formed where runoff water begins to concentrate into streams.

Figure 3–7 A dendritic stream pattern is one that "branches like a tree" and has streams flowing in all directions. (Courtesy F. R. Troeh.)

A *second-order stream* is formed where two first-order streams meet, a *third-order stream* is formed by the union of two second-order streams, and so on.

3-4.5 Development of Valleys

Stream erosion produces valleys. Valleys are the growing parts of a landscape, whereas hills are remnants that have not yet been worn away. Observers may see the hills, but they need to study the valleys to understand how the landscape formed.

A valley begins where water collects from a large enough area to form a stream. The stream cuts a channel in a low part of the landscape where the soil and rock material are relatively erodible. The early development is often so rapid that a gully forms, eroding its way toward the source of the water.

A stream is a dynamic entity that does three things as it forms its valley:

1. It erodes downward toward a *base level* determined by the elevation of the stream or area into which it empties.
2. It erodes headward toward its main source of water, thus lengthening the valley.
3. It picks up tributaries as smaller streams enter the sides of the main valley and produce their own smaller valleys.

3-4.6 Mass Wasting

Much material that a stream removes from its valley reaches the stream by mass wasting. This broad term includes all processes by which gravity moves soil downslope. The movement may be rapid and dramatic as in landslides and mudflows or it may be measured in fractions of millimeters per year as in soil creep (Troeh, 1975). Water promotes movement by lubricating and weakening the mass but is not the actual transporting agent. The slope need not be very steep, because saturated soils on gentle slopes can become almost fluid. Saturated soil is especially common where wet springs follow winters that freeze the soil to a significant depth. Two different theories, often called downwearing and backwearing, describe how mass wasting progresses with time.

3-4.7 Downwearing

W. M. Davis developed the downwearing theory in the 1890s as part of his geographical cycle idea discussed in Section 3-4.3. Davis suggested that the hills in a landscape are gradually worn down by erosion and the steep valley slopes of youth gradually become more gentle as the landscape ages. The end result, if the landscape remained stable long enough, would be such gentle slopes that erosion would cease. The landscape would then be a nearly featureless, poorly drained surface called a *peneplain*. Some argue that present-day landscapes are not old enough to be called peneplains, but surfaces such as the Pampas of Argentina certainly are "almost a plain."

3-4.8 Backwearing

Davis delivered a set of lectures in Germany challenging the leading European geomorphologist, Albrecht Penck. Albrecht's son, Walther, answered Davis in his book *Die Morphologische Analyse,* published in 1927. Walther's untimely death prevented him from seeing his book in print and from developing his concepts further.

Penck's lengthy development of the concept of backwearing (also called *parallel retreat of slopes*) made geomorphologists realize that the subject of slope retreat deserved more study. Penck argued that a valley develops two kinds of slopes as shown in Figure 3-8—a relatively steep backslope (the valley wall) and a flatter footslope between the backslope and the bottomland along the stream.

Penck reasoned that after an equilibrium is reached, the slope gradients should remain constant as the hill gradually wastes away. Flat hilltops would not wear down as Davis had suggested but would be worn away from the sides. The end result is similar to the peneplain concept but is called a *pediment* to distinguish between the two theories. The term "pediment" can be used to describe a smaller area than is appropriate for peneplain and is useful at an earlier stage.

The pediment surface begins as an enlarging footslope. It is normally mantled with soil material that is slowly moving across the pediment from the backslope area to the stream. The soil on the pediment is considered to be moving *en masse* as a form of mass wasting in addition to any water transport occurring at the soil surface.

Many efforts have been made to combine the ideas of Davis and Penck. Some have suggested that the rounded topography of humid regions may best fit Davis' downwearing concept, whereas backwearing better explains the angular topography of arid regions.

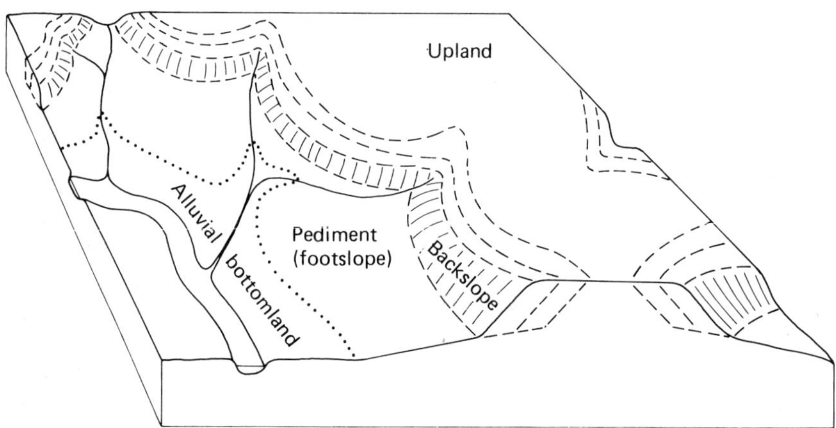

Figure 3-8 A backwearing landscape gradually erodes an upland as the backslope recedes in a manner described by Penck as "parallel retreat of slopes." A sloping pediment surface forms between the backslope and the bottomland. (Courtesy F. R. Troeh.)

3-4.9 Soils on Eroding Landscapes

The concepts of downwearing and backwearing have important implications for soil development. Downwearing implies constant erosion of the entire landscape with the highest areas eroding fastest so that the landscape becomes smoother. The soils on hilltops should therefore be less developed than those in lower areas.

Because backwearing leaves the hilltops undisturbed until removed by eroding slopes, this theory predicts stronger development in the hilltop soils than elsewhere. The shallowest and least-developed soils, apart from floodplains, should occur on the backwearing slopes. Material accumulating on footslopes should produce deep, moderately developed soils.

Soil scientists usually favor the backwearing theory because the soil development pattern outlined in the preceding paragraph occurs on many landscapes. A composite theory dominated by backwearing but with some loss from the hilltops might have the most support. Most hilltops lose some soil by water erosion, and wind erosion can occur anywhere. Furthermore, chemical erosion leaches material from hilltop soils in humid regions.

3-5 SEDIMENTARY LANDFORMS

Material eroded from one place is deposited elsewhere, so the wearing away of one area causes another to be built up. Deposition sometimes converts water areas into land by filling lakes or ponds. Even a shallow sea may become land through deposition and uplift. The many gray-colored limestone, sandstone, and shale formations composed of materials that accumulated on seafloors are evidence that vast amounts of erosion, deposition, and uplift have taken place. The term "sedimentation" as used in this book includes the depositional process and related factors as they influence the nature of the deposited sediment.

3-5.1 Water Deposits

Water sorts materials by particle size as it transports them. The coarsest materials are either left in place or occasionally moved for short distances. Progressively finer particles are deposited as the water flow reaches lower, flatter areas and moves at slower velocities (see Chapter 4 for more details).

Alluvium. Deposits left by flowing water are called *alluvium*. Alluvial deposits occur in floodplains, terraces, fans, piedmonts, and deltas. Alluvial land is desirable for many purposes because it tends to have smooth topography, deep, fertile, permeable soils, and more readily available water than most other land. Such land is in demand for farming, road building and other construction activities, and many other uses.

Floodplains are narrow or nonexistent in young valleys but become broader and flatter as the landscape ages. Heavy runoff floods across these areas and deposits a fresh layer of alluvium. The deposition produces a nearly flat surface except where stream channels cut the floodplain. Of course, each flood may rearrange material deposited earlier and cut new channels while filling old ones. The stream channel itself meanders gradually across its floodplain, occasionally making sudden major shifts. Although natural, these shifts are distressing and costly to landowners.

Flood hazard should be taken into account whenever construction on floodplains is considered. Protective works such as levees and channel dredging may prevent small floods but are often inadequate to protect against major floods. In fact, flood-prevention efforts cause rivers to raise the level of their beds by depositing sediment that should have been deposited on floodplains. The result is an ever-increasing flood hazard such as that experienced by the Chinese along the Yellow River and the Americans along the Mississippi River. There is no known way to control a major river permanently.

Alluvium in river valleys is usually only a few feet thick, although some very thick exceptions exist. Thick alluvium occurs mostly in downwarp areas. The weight of the sediment helps cause the area to sink, and the lowered position increases the likelihood that the area will trap more sediment. The magnitude such deposits can reach is illustrated in Note 3–3.

NOTE 3–3
SEDIMENTARY DEPOSITS

Some sedimentary deposits become very large. The Idaho Formation will serve as an example. This body of sand and silt occupies an area 100 mi (160 km) long and 30 mi (50 km) wide in southern Idaho and eastern Oregon. Sediments washed from the Rocky Mountains were deposited in a gradually sinking area that has been called the Snake River Downwarp. A well drilled to a depth of 5000 ft (1500 m) was still in the formation; in fact, it penetrated only 30% of the formation's probable thickness as estimated from the slope of its layers. Samples taken from the well indicated that the sediments were all deposited on dry land even though most of the formation is now below sea level.

Sedimentary deposits are common in most parts of the world, though most are smaller than the Idaho Formation. Some deposits remain loose, but many are cemented into sandstone and shale. The nature of the rock indicates the depositional environment. Red colors characterize land deposits where oxidizing conditions prevailed; gray colors and fossils of water creatures indicate that the sedimentation occurred under water.

Terraces are formed when the base level of a stream changes and its channel is cut too deep for normal flooding to occur. The stream may have cut through a barrier to a lower base level, or uplift may have increased the slope of the stream channel. Either cause leaves the former floodplain higher than the stream and its new floodplain. The old floodplain becomes a terrace, but its origin is recognizable by its flat surface bordered by a slope down to the new floodplain on one side and a slope up to another terrace or the upland above on the other side. Terraces are subject to erosion as the new floodplain enlarges and to dissection where tributary streams cross them.

Alluvial fans, also called *alluvial cones,* are named for their shapes. They line the sides of many valleys where tributary streams erode the adjoining uplands. Suddenly free to spread out, a stream slows down, loses energy, and deposits much of its load of sediment. The deposit forms the shape of a fan radiating downward from the point of entry into the main valley. The depositing stream often disappears by soaking into highly permeable fan deposits. The upper part of the fan is normally the steepest and coarsest textured. The gradient decreases and the texture becomes finer with distance, until the fan blends into the terrace or floodplain below.

A *piedmont* is a plain formed at the base of some mountain ranges. It forms in a manner similar to that of alluvial fans but on a grander scale. Many streams blend their sediment and form a smooth surface sloping away from the mountains. A piedmont surface is shaped like a pediment but has a great thickness of accumulated sediment in contrast to the thin covering of soil characteristic of a pediment. Similar depositional surfaces in arid regions where the coalescing alluvial fans merge into the level area of an undrained basin are called *bajadas.*

Deltas form where streams empty into bodies of standing water. Their shape as seen on a map normally resembles the Greek capital letter delta, △. Deltas have nearly level surfaces that are partly above and partly below water level. A small delta may be only a few feet across, but some large ones continue for hundreds of miles. Small deltas formed in lakes are quite sandy because the finer sediments are carried farther into the lake. Rivers flowing into the ocean produce finer-textured deltas because salt water flocculates clay particles and makes them settle out. Such sediment represents the richest part of the soils from the source area and produces a fertile soil. The internal drainage is poor because of the delta's low elevation. Much rice is grown on deltas in warm climates.

Bottom Deposits. Sand and gravel are seldom carried far into a body of water, but fine sediments and chemical precipitates may cover the entire area and gradually form deposits on most lake bottoms and seafloors. Sediment is sometimes dominant, but chemical precipitates dominate at other times and places.

Lacustrine deposits, also called lake-laid clays, are composed mostly of fine sediment carried past deltas into the main body of water. The texture of the deposit may vary from silt or sand during seasons of high runoff to fine clay during cold or dry seasons, thus producing a layered effect such as that shown in Figure 3–9. These layers are called *varves* and are sometimes counted to estimate the age of the deposit. The depositional process usually levels the surface, so the varves lie horizontally.

Glaciers crossing hilly topography produced many small lakes whose locations are marked by deltas and lacustrine deposits. Deltaic deposits high on hillsides show the former water level and have been used as sources of gravel for road construction. The lacustrine deposits are at lower elevations and produce fine-textured soils that

Figure 3–9 A varved clay deposit in Michigan. Each varve is about 1 mm thick and is composed of a thin sandy layer deposited during the summer thaw and a coating of silt and clay deposited while the glacial lake was frozen. The scale is in centimeters. (Courtesy Roy L. Donahue.)

are poorly drained. They are erodible and, when wet, subject to small slips and even landslides.

Limestone is the most common sedimentary rock. It normally contains some silt and clay sediments but is composed mostly of a consolidated chemical precipitate of calcium carbonate triggered by the growth of algae and other plant and animal life. Conditions that result in the formation of limestone are common on the floor of shallow seas, as seawater and some lake water is nearly saturated with calcium carbonate. Large formations of limestone have been uplifted and converted into dry land. Limestone rock is gradually dissolved away in humid regions but is quite resistant to weathering in arid regions. Chalk and marl are less consolidated calcium carbonate deposits (and less resistant to weathering) than limestone, chalk being a saltwater deposit and marl a freshwater deposit.

Evaporite deposits form where salts are concentrated by evaporation. An ideal situation for evaporites occurs where a warm, dry climate evaporates water from a shallow bay that receives an input of salty seawater. Another evaporite situation occurs where rainfall in mountain areas seeps down into dry, closed basins such as Death Valley, Great Salt Lake, or the Dead Sea. Large deposits of sodium chloride have been formed as evaporites. Other salts also precipitate, sometimes in relatively pure form. Potassium chloride from evaporite deposits in western Canada, southwestern United States, and elsewhere is the principal source of potassium fertilizer. Borax deposits in Death Valley provide much of the world's commercial boron. Sodium nitrate from the Athabasca Desert in Chile was an early source of nitrogen fertilizer. All of these salts are too soluble for their deposits to form in humid environments.

3-5.2 Wind Deposits

Wind sorts materials by particle size even more effectively than water does. Wind deposits are relatively free of layering and of textural variations in any particular vicinity. Wind deposits are widespread, but much of their area is not very thick. A few deposits attain thicknesses of 600 ft (200 m) or more, but even these thin to less than 100 ft (30 m) thick within a short distance and continue to thin with increasing distance from the source until they become too mixed with other materials to be identified. Thick wind deposits bury the underlying landforms and have a steep topography of their own resulting from a combination of depositional and erosional effects. Most of the area is mantled with a silty deposit averaging only a few feet thick and conforming approximately to the shape of the buried surface.

Aeolian Sands. Wind normally does not move large particles, so stone fragments are left in place. Desert areas often accumulate a surface layer of gravel one pebble thick as the wind carries away the finer soil particles. This gravel layer, called *desert pavement,* prevents further wind erosion. The sand component of the soil is deposited nearby, often in the form of dunes.

The difference between a stable surface and one that can be blown into sand dunes is largely a matter of vegetative cover. Droughtiness and blowing sand make it difficult to maintain and more difficult to establish vegetation on sand dunes. Climate is also a factor—additional precipitation increases the likelihood of stabilizing vegetation being established. Thinner, smoother deposits of aeolian sands are easier to stabilize than sand dunes, especially if they have a water table within reach of plant roots so they can support a thick stand of vegetation.

Loess. Loess is wind-deposited material dominated by silt-size particles. Loess deposits are the most extensive form of wind deposits because silt particles are more detachable than clay and easier to transport than sand. Most wind deposits change from aeolian sands to loess within one or a few miles of the source.

Guy Smith (1942), in his classic study on Illinois loess, found three distinct trends:

1. Loess deposits are thickest near the source and become thinner with increasing distance.
2. The average particle diameter decreases from coarse silt to fine silt and the clay percentage increases with increasing distance from the source.
3. The calcium carbonate percentage decreases with increasing distance from the source.

The decreases in deposit thickness and in particle size are direct results of the additional energy required to transport particles longer distances. The decreased calcium carbonate content is attributed to the thin portions being deposited more slowly and leached more thoroughly than the thicker portions during the period of deposition.

Soils formed in loess resist wind erosion because they lack the sand particles that would move first and knock silt particles loose. But loess deposits and the soils formed in them are susceptible to both water erosion and mass movement. Falling raindrops and flowing water can readily detach silt particles which are easily transported in runoff water. Gully erosion is relatively common in loess materials, and the gullies often cut straight down to the bottom of the deposit. The nearly vertical sides and flat bottoms of such gullies are described as U-shaped. U-shaped gullies help to identify loess deposits because most other gullies are V-shaped.

When an exposed loess surface becomes saturated with water, it is subject to mass movement ranging from small slumps to large landslides. Landslides were a common problem in loess roadbanks until road builders learned to make vertical banks in loess. Loess has a natural tendency to cleave along nearly vertical planes that are more stable than sloping surfaces, as shown in Figure 3-10. Friction between the flat silt particles and cementation by calcium carbonate have been suggested as reasons for vertical stability. Also, while vertical surfaces stay relatively

Figure 3-10 A nearly vertical loess bank in western Iowa. (Courtesy F. R. Troeh.)

dry in a storm, sloping surfaces may become saturated with water—an unstable condition for loess.

Windblown Clay. Wind deposits contain less clay than silt and sand. Clay particles stick together and are hard to erode, but bouncing sand particles knock loose some clay, much of which is mixed with silt in the downwind portions of loess deposits. Clay also may be picked up and carried with drifting snow.

Wind formed extensive clay deposits in southern Australia during the Pleistocene. More recent clay deposits occur near the Gulf coast of Texas and Mexico, and in Senegal and Algeria (Bowler, 1973). In an arid environment, material containing 20 to 77% clay can become strongly aggregated and so loose between aggregates that the wind can cause it to drift like sand. Bowler (1973) indicates that clay dunes form only on the downwind side of seasonally exposed mud flats around shallow bodies of saline water.

Volcanic Ash. Volcanoes occasionally spew out large quantities of ash that blanket the landscape. The ash is much like a thin loess deposit but has more angular particles and more clay. Some ash layers can be traced to a specific event and thus become a geologic time marker. The explosion that formed Crater Lake in Oregon by blowing the top off Mount Mazama is a prime example. The resulting layer of volcanic ash can be identified across much of Oregon. The ash from the 1980 eruption of Mount St. Helens in the state of Washington is a more recent example of the same phenomena (Karowe and Jefferson, 1987). Volcanic ash soils have high clay contents and are very sticky when wet and hard when dry. Some of them have wide cracks during dry seasons along with the self-swallowing action characteristic of Vertisols.

3-6 GLACIAL LANDSCAPES

Glaciers produce dramatic effects on landscapes. Moving ice picks up soil and stones, then deposits them far from their source. Stony material held in the ice at the bottom of a glacier scratches and gouges the bedrock. Areas such as central Canada were scoured by the ice. Glacial movement following the length of valleys deepened the Finger Lakes in New York so their bottoms are below sea level. The fjords of Norway, Greenland, Canada, and Alaska had a similar glacial origin in coastal areas and are flooded with seawater. The moving ice also steepened valley walls near the lakes and fjords.

Much material picked up by glaciers crossing Canada was dumped in hilly areas where they melted away in the United States. Ice margins were marked by *terminal moraines,* forming irregular ridges a few feet or tens of feet (several meters) above the adjacent landscape. A thinner *ground moraine* (also called a till plain) extends back over the glaciated area and is commonly marked by lines of low arcing hills. These hills represent end moraines formed by brief advances of the ice during its waning phase. Many former valleys were filled with glacial deposits, so present landscapes may be quite different than the preglacial ones.

Glacial influence extended beyond the area actually covered by ice. Valleys leading away from glaciers were enlarged by torrents of meltwater laden with debris that was deposited as sediment on broad, flat floodplains. Some of these floodplains remain today as oversized floodplains for present streams; others are terraces or outwash plains on upland areas completely separated from major streams. The broad floodplains of major rivers such as the Missouri and Mississippi became source areas for some of the world's major loess deposits.

3-7 RATE OF GEOLOGIC EROSION

Measured or estimated geologic erosion rates can serve as an important reference for evaluating rates of accelerated erosion. Ruhe (1969) gives examples of Iowa landscapes that eroded at rates ranging from 2 to 222 mm per 1000 years before agriculture entered the area. One area changed from a presettlement rate of 150 mm per 1000 years to 1500 mm per 1000 years after settlement. Each millimeter of soil depth represents 5.8 tons/ac (13 mt/ha) of soil with a bulk density of 1.3 g/cm^3. Thus Ruhe's sample data are equivalent to 0.01 to 1.3 tons/ac (0.03 to 2.9 mt/ha) of geologic erosion per year and 8.7 tons/ac (19 mt/ha) of accelerated erosion per year.

A rate of 0.5 ton/ac (1 mt/ha) may be considered typical for geologic erosion from gently sloping soils. Actual rates vary widely from essentially zero for thousands of years in the most stable areas to catastrophic events such as a landslide that moves thousands of tons of soil and rock in a moment's time. Water and wind have caused remarkable geologic erosion that is more puzzling and only slightly less sudden than a landslide. For example, the origin of the "channeled scablands" in the state of Washington (Figure 3-11) was unknown for a long time. Finally, it was explained on the basis of a sudden release of water from glacial Lake Missoula in northern Idaho and eastern Montana (Baker, 1978). Torrents of water crisscrossed hundred of square miles of land, eroding channels to bedrock but leaving scattered islands of soil. This event was brief but its effects, including gravel bars 100 ft (30 m) high and soil islands surrounded by channels of bare rock, are still conspicuous.

Except for occasional catastrophic events such as those mentioned, geologic erosion rates are determined by such factors as climate, vegetation, slope, and soil material. The effect of precipitation is of interest because the lowest rates of geologic erosion are from moderate precipitation. The rate is higher in very wet climates because high precipitation has great erosive force. Arid climates also have relatively high rates because there is too little vegetation to protect the soil against wind erosion and the occasional heavy rains that occur in such areas.

SUMMARY

Erosion, "the great leveler," persistently removes material from uplands and fills low areas with sediment. The process is usually interrupted before it can reach the end result—a featureless peneplain. All land would have been worn down to sea level if

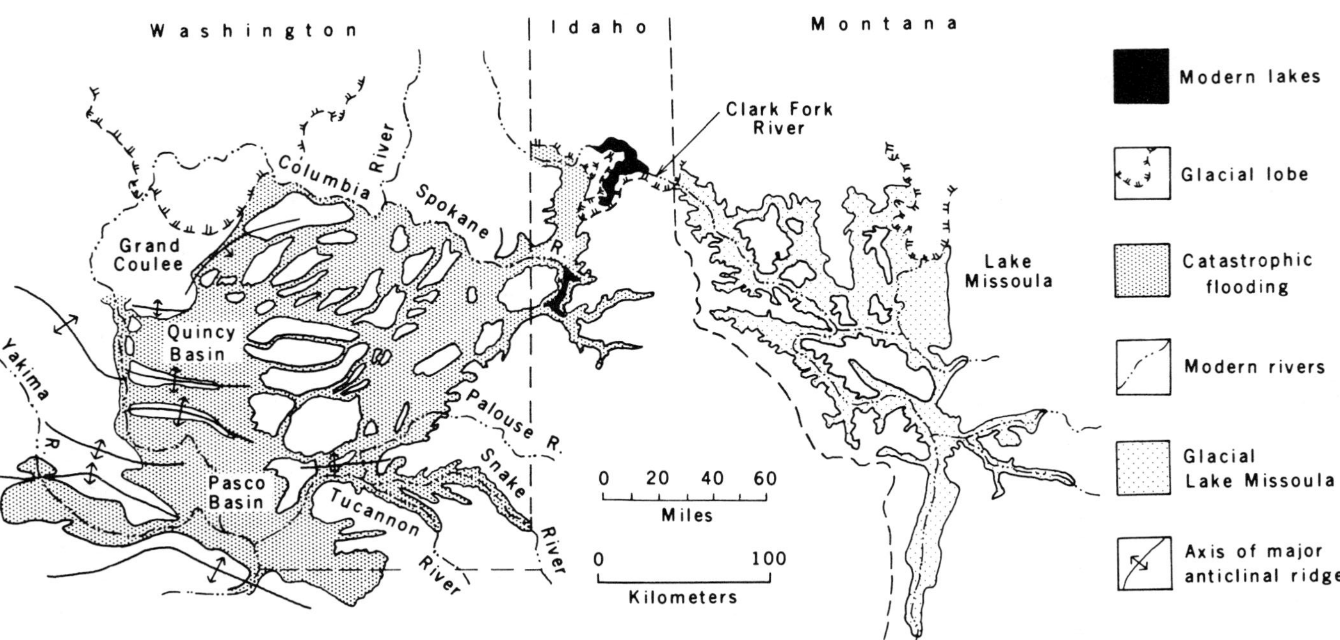

Figure 3–11 The channeled scablands were formed when an ice blockage broke in northern Idaho and released the water from Lake Missoula in Montana as a torrent that raged across eastern Washington. (Courtesy Victor R. Baker, *Science* 202:1255, Dec. 22, 1978. Copyright 1978 by the American Association for the Advancement of Science.)

not for the opposing forces—deposition, lava flows, and uplift. The most important of these forces is uplift caused by isostatic adjustments.

Geomorphology is the study of landforms and the processes that shape them. Geomorphologists apply the principle of *uniformitarianism* to landscapes and consider the effects of *structure, process,* and *stage.* Much landscape development occurs as streams cut downward, lengthen headward, and pick up tributaries. Streams cut valleys that gradually enlarge as the hills erode. Two theories have been developed to explain erosion by mass wasting. The *downwearing* theory supposes that higher areas wear down and slopes become less steep until a peneplain is formed. According to *backwearing,* a parallel retreat of slopes erodes the hillsides but not the hilltops. The surface formed as a slope retreats is called a *pediment.* Most soil scientists favor the backwearing theory because older soils are usually found on hilltops and younger soils on hillsides.

Water deposits *alluvium* in fans and on floodplains; remnants of former floodplains become terraces when a new floodplain forms at a lower level. Water sorts sediment by particle size—coarse material settles near the source and finer material is carried into quieter waters. *Deltas* form where a stream enters a lake or sea. *Lacustrine deposits* high in clay accumulate on lake bottoms. Calcium carbonate precipitates as limestone, chalk, or marl on the bottom of many bodies of water, especially on shallow seafloors. More soluble salts precipitate from briny lakes in arid regions.

Wind also sorts the material it erodes. Sand is deposited in nearby dunes, but silty *loess* deposits blanket larger areas. Volcanic ash also blankets large areas but in a much shorter time.

Glaciers scour soil and rock in their source areas and deposit the material where they melt. Glacial margins are marked by hilly *moraines* and the area between is covered by *ground moraine.* Much of the area covered by glaciers is smoothed as the hills are eroded and the low places filled.

A rate of 0.5 ton/ac (1 mt/ha) per year is considered typical for geologic erosion from gently sloping soils.

QUESTIONS

1. Discuss the relative importance of erosion and deposition in forming steep and level landscapes.
2. Why is the principle of uniformitarianism important to geomorphologists and soil scientists?
3. What combinations of structure, process, and stage produce hilly landscapes?
4. Why are some hills angular whereas others are rounded?
5. What difference does it make whether the dominant process of landscape development is downwearing or backwearing?
6. Why is an alluvial fan steepest near the top and flatter in its lower parts?
7. What evidence is there that wind is able to sort particles by size?
8. Why did glacial action deepen some valleys and fill others?

REFERENCES

ANDREWS, J. T., and W. E. LEMASURIER, 1973. Rates of quaternary glacial erosion and corrie formation, Marie Byrd Land, Antarctica. *Geology* 1:75–80.

BAKER, V. R., 1978. The Spokane flood controversy and the Martian outflow channels. *Science* 202:1249–1256.

BOULTON, G. S., 1987. Progress in glacial geology during the last fifty years. *J. Glaciol.* Special Issue: 25–32.

BOWLER, J. M., 1973. Clay dunes: Their occurrence, formation, and environmental significance. *Earth Sci. Rev.* 9:315–338.

BULL, W. B., 1968. Alluvial fans. *J. Geol. Educ.* 16:101–106.

BUTZER, K. W., 1976. *Geomorphology from the Earth.* Harper & Row, New York, 463 p.

CLAYTON, L., 1975. Bison trails and their geologic significance. *Geology* 3:498–500.

DAVIS, W. M., 1922. Peneplains and the geographical cycle. *Geol. Soc. Am.* Bull. 23:587–598.

FRANK, W., A. BAUD, K. HONEGGER, and V. TROMMSDORFF, 1987. Comparative studies on profiles across the northwest Himalayas. In *The Anatomy of Mountain Ranges,* J. P. Schaer and J. Rodgers (eds.). Princeton Univ. Press, Princeton, N.J., 298 p.

KAROWE, A. L., and T. H. JEFFERSON, 1987. Burial of trees by eruptions of Mount St. Helens, Washington: Implications for the interpretation of fossil forests. *Geol. Mag.* 124:191–204.

MCKERROW, W. S., and R. ST. J. LAMBERT, 1973. Deep earthquakes, surface subsidence, and mantle phase changes. *J. Geol.* 81:157–175.

MCMEEKING, R. M., and R. E. JOHNSON, 1986. On the mechanisms of surging glaciers. *J. Glaciol.* 32:120–132.

PENCK, W., 1927. *Die Morphologische Analyse.* J. Engelhorns Nachf., Stuttgart, 283 p.

ROY, R. N., and A. B. BISWAS, 1975. Use of grain-size parameters for identification of depositional processes and environments of sediments. *Indian J. Earth Sci.* 2:154–162.

RUHE, R. V., 1969. *Quaternary Landscapes in Iowa.* Iowa State Univ. Press, Ames, Iowa, 255 p.

SMITH, G. D., 1942. *Illinois Loess: Variations in Its Properties and Distribution.* Ill. Agric. Exp. Sta. Bull. 490, p. 139–184.

SPARKS, B. W., 1972. *Geomorphology,* 2d ed. Longman, London, 530 p.

THOMAS, W. A., 1983. Basement-cover relations in the Appalachian fold and thrust belt. *Geol. J.* 18:267–276.

TIPPER, J. C., 1988. Techniques for quantitative stratigraphic correlation: A review and annotated bibliography. *Geol. Mag.* 125:475–494.

TRINGHAM, M. E., 1985. Tectonic deformation of a channel sandstone. *Geol. J.* 20:247–255.

TROEH, F. R., 1965. Landform equations fitted to contour maps. *Am. J. Sci.* 263:616–627.

TROEH, F. R., 1975. Measuring soil creep. *Soil Sci. Soc. Am. Proc.* 39:707–709.

VAN HOUTEN, F. B., and R. B. HARGRAVES, 1987. Paleozoic drift of Gondwana: Palaeomagnetic and stratigraphic constraints. *Geol. J.* 22:341–359.

4

Water Erosion and Sedimentation

Movement of soil by water occurs in three stages. Individual grains are detached from the soil mass; detached grains are transported over the land surface; and soil grains fall out of suspension and are deposited on new sites. Soil removal and deposition occur to some degree in nearly all locations, but detachment and transportation are of major concern on uplands, and deposition is most important on lowland sites and in streams and lakes.

Dense vegetation reduces erosion; fire, cultivation, overgrazing, logging, mining, and construction activity destroy vegetation and promote erosion. Sparsely vegetated, arid regions may suffer severe erosion from infrequent, intense rainstorms.

4-1 TYPES OF WATER EROSION

Water erosion is classified as sheet erosion, rill erosion, gully erosion, or streambank erosion. The classification is based on the nature and extent of soil removal.

4-1.1 Sheet Erosion

Sheet erosion is the removal of thin layers of soil over the whole soil surface. Raindrop splash and surface flow cause sheet erosion, with splash providing most of the detaching energy and flow providing most of the transporting capacity. Sheet erosion is insidious because it is difficult to see. The first sign is when subsoil color begins to show, as cultivation mixes surface soil and subsoil. It is most apparent on upper portions of convex slopes (see Figure 4-1).

Figure 4-1 The hilltops in this Iowa field are light-colored because the dark-colored topsoil has been lost by sheet erosion. (Courtesy F. R. Troeh.)

4-1.2 Rill Erosion

Rills are channels small enough to be obliterated by normal tillage operations (Figure 4-2). Rill erosion occurs when runoff water concentrates in streamlets as it passes downhill. This water has greater scouring action than sheet flow; it removes soil from the edges and beds of the streamlets. Rills frequently occur between crop

Figure 4-2 Rills in a cultivated Vertisol in India. (Courtesy Roy L. Donahue.)

rows and along tillage marks. Cultivation smooths the surface so the long-term effect is similar to that of sheet erosion.

4–1.3 Gully Erosion

Erosion channels too large to be erased by ordinary tillage are called *gullies* (Figure 4–3). Deep, relatively straight-sided channels develop where the soil material is uniformly friable throughout the profile. The channels in deep loess soils are U-shaped with almost vertical walls. Broad V-shaped channels often develop where friable surface soils overlie cohesive, tight, nonerodible subsoils. Gullies are *active* when their walls are free of vegetation, and *inactive* when they are stabilized by vegetation. Gullies are also classified as small, medium, and large according to depth, with medium-sized gullies 3 to 15 ft (1 to 5 m) deep.

4–1.4 Streambank Erosion

Removal of soil material from the sides of running streams is called *streambank erosion.* It is usually greatest along the outside of bends, but inside meanders often are intensively scoured during severe floods. Streambank erosion affects relatively small areas, but damage is done to very productive soils.

Streams that are "unloaded" pick up sediment from their beds and banks. Thus streambank and bed erosion are increased by reducing the sediment load brought into the streams with conservation measures on uplands or by catching upstream sediments in reservoirs or other traps.

Figure 4–3 A gully eroding uphill from a cultivated field into a grassed area near Bruxelles, Manitoba, Canada. The equipment in the background is smoothing the gully to make it into a grassed waterway. (Courtesy Manitoba Department of Agriculture.)

4-2 EROSION DAMAGE

There are many ways in which water erosion causes damage. Soil is lost; plant nutrients are removed; texture changes; structure deteriorates; productive capacity is reduced; fields are dissected; and sediments pollute streams and lakes and pile up on bottomlands, in stream channels, and in lakes and reservoirs. Recent estimates of the annual damage caused by water erosion in the United States are: on-site damages—$500 million to $1.2 billion; off-site damages—$3.4 billion to $13 billion (Colacicco et al., 1989).

4-2.1 Soil Loss

The most apparent damage caused by water erosion is the removal of soil from eroding surfaces. While erosion from land covered with perennial vegetation, either grass or trees, amounts to only a fraction of a ton per acre annually, that from bare cultivated fields may exceed 200 tons/ac (450 mt/ha). Grant (1975) reported that many newly cropped fields in all areas of the eastern half of the United States lost in excess of 40 tons/ac (90 mt/ha), some losing as much as 140 tons (314 mt) in 1974.

Surface soil is generally more friable, more permeable to water, air, and roots, and higher in organic matter and fertility than subsoil, so loss of surface soil is critical.

4-2.2 Plant Nutrient Losses

Bennett and Chapline (1928), in one of the earliest reports on erosion, stated that over 43 million tons (40 million mt) of N, P, and K were lost in the soil washed each year from the fields, grasslands, and forests of the United States. Only a small proportion of this quantity was immediately available to plants, but this amount of available and potential nutrients was nearly 65 times the fertilizer N, P, and K applied in the United States in 1934 (Bennett, 1939, p. 10). Since World War II, U.S. fertilizer use increased rapidly and consistently until 19 to 22 million tons (17 to 20 million mt) of N, P, K per year were applied in the 1980s (Vroomen, 1989). These applications have not counteracted erosion losses because they have not been large enough to replace nutrients sold off the farm in crops and those lost in erosion. Thus losses of plant nutrients in solution and in eroded sediments still are very important.

4-2.3 Textural Change

Water erosion makes sandy soils even sandier by moving the finest particles considerable distances and leaving the coarser particles close by. Medium- and fine-textured soils are usually well aggregated. Their textures are not altered seriously because the water sorts aggregates, not individual soil particles. Generally, small and large aggregates have similar textural compositions.

Erosion may remove the entire surface horizon. The new surface soil, really the exposed subsoil, is generally finer textured. This makes seedbed preparation more difficult and poses problems at other stages of crop production.

4-2.4 Structural Damage

Water erosion affects soil structure in three ways. Loss of surface soil generally exposes a less granular and less permeable subsoil; raindrops disintegrate aggregates on the surface and produce a compact surface crust; and percolating rainwater carries suspended soil grains through the soil surface, plugging pores, and reducing permeability and infiltration rates. These changes cause increased runoff which increases erosion and reduces the amount of water stored.

4-2.5 Productivity Loss

Losses of soil material and nutrients, and deteriorating structure reduce productive potential. The magnitude of this reduction depends on properties of surface soil and of subsoil. Losses are largest when subsoil is shallow and infertile, or fine textured, compact, and intractable. Often the reduction in productive potential is masked by increased inputs and better management. Early studies showed that grain and cotton yield losses on artificially truncated profiles averaged 77% on several soil conservation stations when no fertilizer or manure was used. Where adequate fertilizer was applied, corn yields were reduced by about 80% in years with poor rainfall distribution, but comparable yields were obtained on truncated and normal soils when rains were adequate. In another study crops were grown on farmers' fields on soils which had experienced differing erosion severity. Yields were superior where little or no erosion had occurred and were reduced progressively as erosion was more severe (Table 4-1). Larson et al. (1985) set up a mathematical model to calculate indirectly the effect of erosion on soil productivity index by including soil properties which influence productivity and which are known to be affected by erosion. Seventy-five important north-central U.S. soils were examined. The study predicted that loss of 25 cm (10 in.) of soil will reduce the index for one-third of the soils by more than 10%, and one-eighth by more than 20%; a 50-cm (20-in.) loss will reduce the index for one-half the soils by more than 10%, one-third by more than 20%, and one-sixth by more than 30%. The index of four soils (5% of the total) will be reduced more than 40%. Current rates of erosion for these soils range from 0 to 105 mt/ha-yr (0 to 50 tons/ac-yr).

TABLE 4-1 EFFECT OF EROSION SEVERITY ON CROP YIELD

			Crop yield (bu/ac)		
Crop	State	No. of farms	Slight erosion	Moderate erosion	Severe erosion
Corn	Wisconsin	8	80	67	60
Grain	Wisconsin	11	65	50	43
Grain	Minnesota	5	36	30	23

Source: Hays et al., 1949.

4-2.6 Field Dissection

An eroding field can be farmed as a unit as long as erosion channels are small enough for ordinary machinery to cross. Reduced cultivatable-land area, lower yields, and higher production costs combine to reduce farm net income when a field is cut by larger gullies.

4-2.7 Engineering-Structure Damage

Erosion damages buildings, roads, bridges, and other engineering structures. Foundations are undermined by washing, landslides, and soil creep. Road ditches and culverts can cause gullies that affect road safety (Figure 4-4). Bridge approaches, footings, pilings, and supports are structurally weakened or destroyed.

Figure 4-4 Erosion damage to the ditch along a roadway in Kansas. (Courtesy USDA Soil Conservation Service.)

4-2.8 Water Pollution

Soil sediment is the greatest single pollutant of surface water, on a volume basis. The muddying of streams and lakes reduces their value for home and industrial use, for recreation, and for fish and wildlife. Erosion also contaminates streams when fertilizers and pesticides are dissolved in runoff water or adsorbed on eroded soil.

4-2.9 Sedimentation

Rich bottomland soils owe their productivity to sediments eroded from the surface of upland soils, but they can be harmed if subsequent erosion deposits subsoil or other less productive material on them. Lower-lying uplands can also be damaged in this way (see Figure 4-5). Sediment is also deposited in stream channels, lakes, and reservoirs. This changes the aquatic environment and affects plant and animal life. For example, sediment in fish spawning areas may ruin these sites for fish propagation. Sedimentation raises streambeds, reducing the depth and capacity of the channels. This causes navigational problems and severe flooding. Sedimentation of lakes and reservoirs reduces their capacity, value, and life expectancy. In extreme cases, sedimentation changes an aquatic habitat into a terrestrial one.

Figure 4-5 Sediment deposited at the foot of a slope in a cultivated field near Alexander, Manitoba, Canada. Several rills and a small gully were subsequently eroded through the sediment. (Courtesy J. A. Hobbs.)

4-3 AGENTS ACTIVE IN WATER EROSION

Two major agents are active in water erosion: falling raindrops and running water. Both derive the energy needed to detach and transport soil grains from the force of gravity. Water also acts as a lubricant as gravity causes soil to roll or slide downhill. While spectacular and significant where it occurs, this type of movement is much less important overall than that caused directly by water movement.

4-3.1 Falling Raindrops

In the early years of erosion-control activity it was assumed that overland flow caused water erosion. Now a substantial part of soil movement is credited directly to raindrops.

Energy of Falling Raindrops. The kinetic energy of a falling body can be calculated from the equation

$$E = {}^{1}/{}_{2}mv^2$$

where E = kinetic energy, ergs (ft-lb)
m = mass of falling body, g (lb)
v = velocity of fall, cm/s (ft/s)

Air friction limits drop fall to a maximum known as terminal velocity that is related to drop mass. Laws (1941) and Gunn and Kinzer (1949) studied the relationship between drop diameter from 0.2 to 6.0 mm and *terminal velocity.* Figure 4–6 presents a graphic form of their data as developed by Wischmeier and Smith (1958). These data show that larger drops have higher terminal velocities. Thus larger drop size affects kinetic energy in two ways—by larger mass and faster fall. Laws (1941) found that smaller drops reached terminal velocity in a shorter distance but that all drops are at terminal velocity after falling 30 ft (9 m) or less.

Rainstorm Intensity and Energy. Laws and Parsons (1943) found that average drop size increased as storm intensity increased up to 6 in./h (150 mm/h), but a range of sizes from 0.25 to 7 mm was present in each storm. Hudson (1981) and McGregor and Mutchler (1976) found an increase in drop size up to about 3 in./hr (75 mm/h). Above that the median drop diameter decreased with increasing intensity.

Wischmeier and Smith (1958) used Laws and Parsons' data to develop the relationship

$$e = 916 + 331 \log_{10} I$$

where e = total energy, ft-ton/ac-in. for each inch of rainfall
I = rainfall intensity, in./hr (up to 3 in./hr)

A table, developed from this equation, is presented in Chapter 6.

Wind and Raindrop Energy. Strong winds add a horizontal-velocity component to raindrop fall. Wind partially reduces air resistance by moving air horizontally away from the drop. This reduced resistance and the actual force of the wind combine to accelerate the drop. Smith and Wischmeier (1962) suggested that the velocity of wind-driven rain can be estimated by multiplying the drop's terminal velocity in still air by the secant of the angle between vertical and the direction of fall in the wind. They calculated that 3-mm median-drop-size rain falling in a wind at a 30° angle of inclination has a velocity 17% greater and kinetic energy 36% greater than the same rain falling vertically. Lyles (1977) calculated the kinetic energy of a 2-mm drop in a 20-mi/h (32-km/h) wind was 2.75 times that of a similar drop falling in still air. Wind tends to break larger drops into smaller ones, but windblown drops are much more erosive than drops falling in still air.

Vegetation and Raindrop Energy. Wollny in 1890 first reported that vegetative cover affected rainfall and that growing crops intercepted up to 45% of

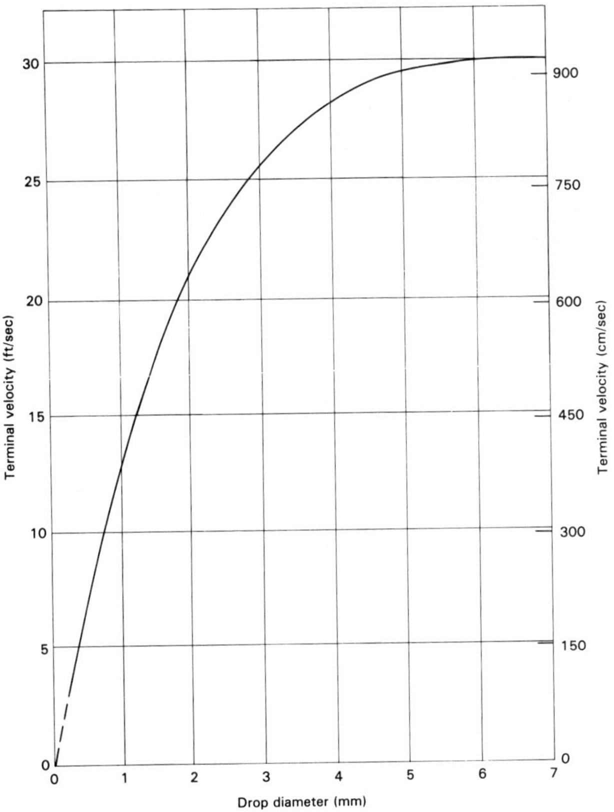

Figure 4-6 The relationship between drop diameter and terminal velocity of falling raindrops. (Modified from Wishmeier and Smith, 1958.)

the raindrops (Baver, 1939). Shaw (1959) showed that a growing corn crop intercepts and holds 0.13 to 0.19 in. (3 to 5 mm) of moisture from a storm that exceeds 0.3 in. (7.5 mm) of rainfall. This water never reaches the ground. Drops that are temporarily intercepted by plants have much of their energy dissipated at the plant surface. Some break into smaller drops that have reduced energy also.

Work of Raindrops. Raindrops release energy when they strike a surface. This energy does three kinds of work. It breaks aggregates and clods into smaller aggregates and individual particles; it moves soil grains to new locations as water splashes back into the air; and it compacts and puddles the surface layer of soil. The first is the basis for the detaching capacity of the raindrops; the second is the source of the transporting potential; and the third reduces the soil's infiltration rate, causing more water to run off the soil surface.

Raindrops and the Erosion Process. Ellison (1944, 1947a, 1947b) showed that the falling raindrop is the main detaching agent in sheet erosion. Roose (1977) demonstrated that raindrops are more responsible for sheet erosion than is sheet flow. Ellison showed that raindrops break many aggregates into smaller aggregates and particles and detach them from the soil mass.

A wide range of grain sizes is loosened by raindrop splash. Certainly, all material 2 mm in diameter and smaller can be detached directly. Ellison (1944) found that 10-mm pebbles, when partly submerged in surface flow, were moved by raindrops. He also found splashed particles 2 ft (60 cm) or more above the land surface. They moved horizontally as much as 5 ft (1.5 m). Heavy rains can splash more than 100 tons/ac (225 mt/ha) on bare, highly detachable soil (Ellison, 1947a).

Raindrops falling on level, bare soil, in the absence of wind, splatter equally in all directions; soil carried out of any area is matched by movement into the area. Although there is a lot of soil movement, there is no net soil loss and no measurable erosion. When raindrops fall on sloping land more of the splash of each raindrop goes downhill than up, and the distance individual splashes travel is greater downhill also, causing soil movement even if no runoff takes place. Ellison (1944) found 75% of the splash was downhill on a 10% slope. Wind causes a similar directional splash even on level surfaces. Wind-driven raindrops hit the soil at an angle and water and soil are carried downwind by splash.

Duley and Kelly (1939) noted the development of a thin compacted layer at the surface of the soil where unimpeded raindrops beat on bare soil. Crop residues on the soil surface eliminated or greatly reduced the compacted layer. When compact layers developed, the soil's infiltration rate declined rapidly during the storm and runoff increased. They proved that it was the thin compacted layer that produced the reduction in infiltration rate.

4-3.2 Running Water

Runoff is recognized as an important cause of erosion. The most common cause of runoff is rain falling faster than soil can absorb it. Other causes are snowmelt and irrigation.

Runoff is classified as prechannel or sheet flow and channelized flow. The depth of sheet flow seldom exceeds 0.1 or 0.2 in. (3 or 4 mm) unless surface vegetative mulch causes it to be slightly deeper. Channelized flow depth varies from about 0.2 in. (5 mm) in small rills to 10 ft (3 m) or more in large streams. Erosiveness of runoff water is controlled by its depth, velocity, turbulence, and abrasive-material content.

Energy of Running Water. Kinetic energy and erosive force of running water is related to the quantity and velocity of flow the same as raindrop energy is controlled by mass and velocity of fall. The velocity generally increases with the depth of the water layer but seldom exceeds 5 ft/s (1.5 m/s) even in a gully. Runoff water moving at this speed has only $^1/_{28}$ of the energy of an equal mass of raindrops falling at a terminal velocity of 26 ft/s (8 m/s). Very slow flows are essentially nonerosive.

Energy of Transported Material. Clear water has limited erosive energy. Soil grains saltating (jumping along the bed) in the stream are about 2.65 times as dense as water and carry about 2.65 times as much energy as an equal volume of water traveling at the same velocity. Energy differential is greater when grains move faster than water in contact with the streambed (the common case). Thus a stream carrying abrasive material has greater power than clear water to break up aggregates and clods on the bed and put them into motion.

Stream Depth and Energy. Depth of water moving across a field is controlled by rainfall intensity, soil infiltration rate, and type of flow. No runoff will occur from a 0.1 in./h (2 or 3 mm/h) rain because almost all soils can absorb the water. Runoff commences when rainfall intensity exceeds soil infiltration rate. Greater rainfall intensity increases thickness of runoff films, runoff velocity, and erosive energy.

Water films at the top of a slope are thin even in intense rainstorms because there is little water movement from above. Water films are thicker farther down the slope because of water accumulating from above. However, with increasing thickness, the water moves at a faster rate and this limits increases in flow thickness. Water is more likely to flow in channels farther down the slope. Runoff from relatively broad areas is funneled into rills and gullies, causing appreciably thicker layers, higher velocities, and more energy to erode soil than sheet flow has.

Turbulence and Energy. Fast-flowing fluids move in an irregular manner with random oscillations in direction and with small to large changes in both horizontal and vertical velocity. This irregular motion is called *turbulence.* Water passing across the land in very thin films moves in laminar flow at relatively low velocity. It is generally incapable of initiating soil movement. Turbulence develops as depth of flow and velocity increase until the whole flow becomes turbulent. Kinetic energy of a stream and its erosive capacity are both increased dramatically by full-flow turbulence.

Slope and Runoff and Erosion. Four features of slope affect velocity and amount of runoff and hence erosiveness: slope gradient, slope length, slope shape, and slope aspect.

Slope gradient (steepness) is measured in units of vertical fall either per single horizontal unit (decimal fraction) or per hundred horizontal units (percent). Increasing slope gradient increases the speed of water moving downhill and the erosive force of the flowing water, as explained in Note 4-1.

NOTE 4-1

SLOPE STEEPNESS AND FORCE OF RUNOFF

Force of a body moving on a frictionless inclined plane is defined by the equation

$$F = mg \sin \theta$$

where F = force, dynes

m = mass, grams

g = force of gravity, cm/s^2

θ = gradient angle, degrees

Increasing the gradient angle increases $\sin \theta$ and therefore increases the value of F.

If land slope is measured in units of vertical fall per unit of distance along the land surface, rather than along the true horizontal, the slope so determined is numerically equal to the sine of the gradient angle, or

$$F = mg \times \text{gradient}$$

where "gradient" is a decimal fraction. Thus a unit volume of runoff water exerts twice the force on a 10% (0.1) frictionless slope as on a 5% (0.05) slope.

When friction is considered in calculating the force, the equation becomes

$$F = mg \sin \theta - fmg \cos \theta$$

where f is the coefficient of friction (dimensionless). Sin θ increases but $\cos \theta$ decreases as the gradient, θ, increases. Consequently, the force of the water, taking friction into account, increases proportionately faster than $\sin \theta$ increases, or faster than the gradient, expressed as a decimal fraction, increases.

Runoff from medium- and fine-textured soils usually increases with increasing slope; runoff from sandy soils does not always increase on steeper slopes. Erosion, however, always increases with slope steepness.

Slope length is the distance from the crest of a knoll or hill to the point where deposition of transported material starts, or where runoff enters a natural or prepared waterway. Slope length in a terraced field is the distance from the ridge top of one terrace to the center of the channel of the terrace immediately below. Slope length has a variable effect on runoff and erosion. Runoff losses per unit area are usually (though not always) greatest on short slopes. There is generally more erosion on longer slopes in spite of less runoff per unit area. Longer slopes increase the amount of erosion when rainfall intensity is high or the permeability of the soil is low or both.

Slope shape across the slope (along the contour lines) can be straight, concave, or convex, and the downhill direction also can be straight, convex (increasingly steeper gradient downhill) or concave (gradients progressively less steep downhill). Many slopes are convex at the top and concave at the bottom (complex). Convex slopes (in either the contour or the slope direction) cause water to flow away from an area so that the site is drier than it otherwise would be, whereas concave slopes cause water to accumulate and make the soils wetter (Troeh, 1965). Slope-shape effect on runoff and erosion is complex. Runoff velocity is slow and soil movement is minimal near the top of convex slopes because runoff volume is small and slope is gentle. Water movement is faster lower on the slope because the gradient is steeper and more runoff water accumulates. Soils tend to be shallow on convex slopes; soil replacement from the flatter slope above is slower than loss to steeper slopes below.

Runoff is usually slower on concave slopes because at the top (where slopes are steepest) there is little accumulated water and lower down (where there is lots of water) slopes are flatter. Nearly all natural slopes in humid regions are complex, having convex slopes at the top and concave slopes at the bottom. Meyer and Kramer (1968) studied the effect of four slope types on erosion using a computerized program. Smallest losses were predicted for the concave slope and greatest from convex slope. Complex- and uniform-slope losses were intermediate, with complex slope losing less than the uniform one.

Slope aspect is the direction the slope faces. A limited study on the effect of slope aspect on runoff and erosion was conducted by Wollny and his associates in Germany about a century ago. They found smaller runoff but greater erosion losses on south-facing slopes (Baver, 1939). The major effects of aspect apparently result from its influence on the angle at which the sun's rays strike the land. Aspect has minimal effect at the equator, but the influence increases toward the poles. South- or west-facing slopes in the northern hemisphere are warmer and have higher evaporation during the growing season. Water storage is reduced and there is less plant growth, especially in dry climates. Reduced vegetation usually results in increased erosion. North- and east-facing slopes are usually noticeably cooler, more moist, and better vegetated.

Surface Condition. Micro-topographical depressions and plant material, living or dead, reduce runoff volume and velocity. This reduces the energy of runoff water and the amount of erosion. A smooth, bare surface offers the least possible frictional resistance; a pitted soil covered with dense vegetation presents the ultimate in resistance to water movement. Manning's formula (see Note 4–2) predicts quantitatively the effect of surface roughness on flow velocity.

NOTE 4-2
MANNING'S FORMULA

The most common method for estimating flow velocity in an open channel employs *Manning's formula:*

$$V = 1.5 \frac{R^{2/3}S^{1/2}}{\eta}$$

where V = average velocity of flow, ft/sec
R = hydraulic radius, ft
S = land slope, ft/ft
η = coefficient of surface roughness

Hydraulic radius (R) is related to depth of flow, but is not depth, not even average depth. It is defined as

$$R = \frac{A}{P}$$

where A = cross-sectional area of flow, ft^2
P = wetted perimeter, ft

The method for calculating the hydraulic radius is shown below:

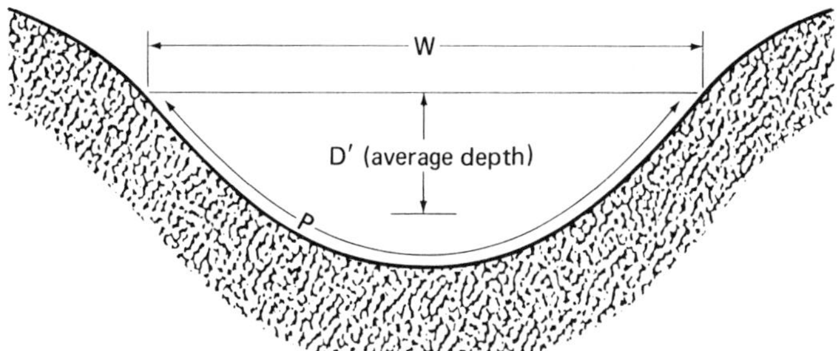

The value of R is equal to average depth in sheet flow but is less than average depth in channel flow.

Surface roughness coefficient (η) ranges from 0.017 for a smooth, straight, bare, earthen ditch to 0.300 for a dense, uniform stand of grass such as bermudagrass more than 10 in. (25 cm) tall. Selected values of η are shown in Table 4-2.

Runoff and the Erosion Process. Both detaching and transporting capacity of runoff are small when the flow is in thin films and the velocity is low, but they increase as the runoff becomes channelized and depth and velocity increase. Prechannel flow by itself has little or no capacity to detach and transport soil particles. Raindrops that fall into prechannel flow detach large numbers of soil grains. Falling

TABLE 4-2 SELECTED VALUES FOR COEFFICIENT OF SURFACE ROUGHNESS (η) FOR USE IN MANNING'S FORMULA

Surface condition	Values of η		
	Minimum	Design	Maximum
Ditches			
Earth, straight and uniform	.017	.022	.025
Winding, sluggish ditches and gullies	.022	.025	.030
Ditches with rough, stony beds, and vegetated (weedy) banks	.025	.035	.040
Earth bottom, rubble on sides	.028	.032	.035
Natural stream channels			
Clean, straight banks, no rifts or pools	.025		.033
Clean, straight banks, some weeds and stones	.030		.040
Winding, some pools, but clean	.033		.045
Winding, some pools, some weeds and stones	.035		.050
Sluggish river channels, either weedy or with deep pools	.050		.080
Very weedy channels	.075		.150
Vegetated waterways (prepared)			
Dense, uniform bermudagrass, 10 in. tall[a]	.040	.040	.300
Dense, uniform bermudagrass, 2.5 in. tall	.034		.110

[a]Other sod grasses slightly less rough.
Source: SCS Engineers' Handbook.

drops also cause sheet flow to be turbulent, thus increasing its carrying capacity. Soil grains detached by raindrops can be transported long distances by turbulent pre-channel flow.

Raindrops cannot easily detach grains deep below the surface of running water, but velocities of such streams give them detaching and transporting powers. Erosive energy of soil particles carried in runoff must be added to the energy of clear water. Erosiveness of the particles generally exceeds that of the clear stream. A stream's carrying capacity is related to the third power of its velocity and to its turbulence. Even when a stream carries its maximum burden, the composition of the sediment load constantly changes. Gravity causes some soil particles to drop out of suspension; other particles are picked up. The larger and heavier grains drop out quickest; the smallest remain in suspension for long periods.

Sand can be deposited on land from fast-moving waters; silt will settle out in quantity only as the stream's velocity is markedly reduced, such as when the stream gradient levels off; and clay settles out in quantity only when the water is still or when it is flocculated as the stream enters a body of salt water.

4-3.3 Gravity

Gravity moves soil directly. Soil movements caused by gravity are known as landslides, mudflows, slips, slumps, soil creep, and surface creep. An avalanche (strictly speaking) is a mass of moving snow, but it may strip all vegetation and soil down to bedrock and deposit them in a heap at the bottom of the slope.

In most cases of gravity-induced movement, the topography must be steeply sloping. Soil creep, which occurs on slopes of only a few percent, especially in foot-slope positions, is a notable exception.

Land in native vegetation, even on steep slopes, is ordinarily in equilibrium with its environment; soil movement is usually extremely slow. If soil cover is destroyed or greatly reduced by fire, overgrazing, logging, cultivation, surface mining, or construction, and if an excess of moisture develops due to heavy rains or rapid snowmelt, normal friction between the semiviscous soil mass and the underlying material is reduced and the mass slowly or rapidly slides downhill. Sometimes the soil slumps down and out, forming a hump above the former surface at the bottom, and a depression at the top. This sort of movement occurs on the north sides of hills on the steep cultivated fields in the Palouse region of eastern Washington and northern Idaho.

Along the Pacific slopes of the Cascades and the Coastal Range, in the Intermountain Region, and in other hilly and mountainous areas of the United States and of other countries, a watery soil mass called a mud flow may pass down a valley like a very slowly moving river. Mud flows also occur in permafrost regions when upper soil layers thaw and become saturated by rain or snowmelt. There the mud flows move either downslope or vertically into solution caverns where ice has melted.

4-4 SOIL PROPERTIES AND SOIL ERODIBILITY

Differences in soil erodibility are obvious and were noted in the early years of the conservation movement. It has been difficult though to determine what soil properties actually make soils erodible.

Middleton (1930) and Middleton et al. (1932, 1934) analyzed soils from the soil erosion stations and from other sites. Many chemical and physical analyses were made and results compared to an assessment of erodibility made by scientists in the field. Properties and combinations of properties related to aggregate size, structural stability, and soil permeability appeared to be most closely related to soil erodibility.

Wischmeier et al. (1971) developed a nomograph to predict soil erodibility using texture, organic-matter content, soil structure, and soil permeability. If these four soil properties can be used to predict soil erodibility they must be responsible for making soils erodible.

Erosion detaches individual soil grains from the soil mass and carries them away in raindrop splash or running water. Soil erodibility therefore must be related to the soil's detachability and transportability. Any property that prevents or makes difficult soil detachment or soil transportation reduces soil erodibility. Texture and structure certainly affect the size of grains exposed to erosive elements. Runoff must occur for rapid erosion to take place, so soil properties that affect infiltration rate and permeability also affect the rate of erosion. Therefore, texture and structure must control a soil's erodibility to a very large degree.

4-4.1 Soil Texture

Sand particles are easy to detach but difficult to transport because of their size and mass. Clay particles tend to stick together and are difficult to detach, but are easily carried great distances once separated from the soil mass. Silty soils are frequently well aggregated, but the aggregates break down readily when wetted, and the individual particles are easily transported.

Infiltration rate and permeability to water are related in part to texture. Water moves rapidly through macropores; it moves only slowly through micropores. Large pores between sand particles permit rapid water movement. Fine to very fine pores common in medium- and fine-textured soils such as the loams, clay loams, and clays restrict water movement. While total porosity of the fine-textured soils is nearly always greater than that of coarse-textured soils, the individual pores in the fine soils are usually much smaller, and both infiltration and permeability are slower. Therefore, a moderate storm generally produces more runoff and erosion from the finer-textured soils than from sandy ones.

4-4.2 Soil Structure

Large, stable aggregates make a soil difficult to detach and transport and make it more permeable to water. While soils high in clay usually have low permeabilities and low infiltration rates, a well-aggregated clay soil permits faster water movement than a poorly-aggregated clay.

Factors that influence the size and stability of aggregates include texture, cations on the exchange complex, type of clay mineral, organic-matter content, cementing materials other than clay and organic matter, and cropping history.

Texture. Sand has a weakening and loosening effect on structure. Clay is a cementing and aggregating agent. If the cation-exchange complex is occupied mainly by H^+ or di- or trivalent cations, the colloid will be flocculated, and individual soil particles will aggregate. Large stable aggregates resist both detachment and transportation. The higher the clay content, up to about 40%, the larger and more stable the aggregates. Clay contents above 40% promote development of very small aggregates that erode easily, especially where surface soils freeze and thaw frequently during winter. Soil colloids with large amounts of Na^+ and K^+ or with very large amounts of Mg^{++} on the exchange sites will deflocculate. Deflocculated colloids prevent aggregate formation, cause low permeability and high erodibility.

Some soil aggregates, particularly those high in silt and very fine sand, are relatively unstable. Raindrops destroy these aggregates and the fine grains flow into and plug surface pores to produce a dense compact layer at the soil surface. Slow infiltration into this compacted layer causes increased runoff and erosion.

Type of Clay Mineral. Aggregation of soils is influenced by the type of clay mineral. Tropical and subtropical soils, which are high in hydrous oxides of iron and aluminum and in 1:1-type lattice clay, kaolinite, tend to be better aggregated than soils high in the 2:1-type lattice clays, montmorillonite and illite.

Organic-Matter Content. Soil structure improves and the individual aggregates become more stable as organic-matter content increases. This is accompanied by increased permeability and decreased runoff and erosion. Too much organic matter may cause soils to be very erodible because of the small size and low density of granules formed.

Cementing Agents. Secondary lime is a cementing agent and helps to hold particles in aggregates. Some iron compounds bond clays and other soil grains together in stable forms in many strongly leached, temperate-region soils and in numerous tropical soils. These soils may be quite resistant to erosion.

Cropping History. Soils plowed from native vegetation, cultivated pasture, or meadow resist erosion. They tend to have excellent structure and relatively large, stable aggregates. Roots permeating the aggregates and large amounts of incorporated crop residue add to stability. Actively decomposing plant materials help to develop resistant structure, whereas humus, which resists further decomposition, is less effective. Aggregates become less stable and more subject to breakdown and erosion increases as the native plant residues are broken down by continued cultivation.

4–5 VEGETATION AND WATER EROSION

Vegetation limits the erosive action of raindrops on soil. Plant material intercepts raindrops and slows down runoff. An historic early erosion study at Columbia, Missouri, showed clearly that crops differ significantly in their effect on water erosion (Table 4–3). These results show that runoff and erosion are most severe on bare soil (fallow). Continuous corn, planted in intertilled rows, was the next most erosive cropping system, followed by continuous wheat, and then by the rotation of corn, wheat, and clover. Continuous bluegrass gave the most protection of any system tested.

Kramer and Weaver (1936) demonstrated conclusively that plant top growth was significantly more effective than roots in reducing water erosion. Duley and Kelly (1939) showed that dead plant material on the soil surface is as effective as thick perennial vegetation in maintaining infiltration rate and in reducing runoff and erosion. The concept of *stubble mulch tillage,* an early conservation tillage practice, developed from this early research finding.

TABLE 4-3 EFFECT OF CROPPING SYSTEM ON RUNOFF AND EROSION AT COLUMBIA, MISSOURI, 1918-1931

Cropping system	Average runoff		Average annual erosion (tons/ac)	Time to erode a 7-in. layer (yrs)
	Inches	Percent		
Continuous fallow	12.3	30.5	41.4	24
Continuous bluegrass	4.8	12.0	0.3	3043
Continuous wheat	9.4	23.3	10.1	100
Continuous corn	11.9	29.4	19.7	50
Corn, wheat, clover rotation	5.6	13.8	2.8	368

Source: Modified from Miller and Krusekopf, 1932.

4-6 WATER EROSION AND POLLUTION

Major concern about erosion in the past has centered on damage to the soil and its productivity. More emphasis is now placed on pollution that erosion sediments cause on land and particularly in water. Concern about agricultural chemicals in runoff and eroding sediments is growing. Pollutants from agricultural activities entering streams in diffuse patterns over wide areas constitute *nonpoint source* pollution.

Soil conservationists are concerned about soil loss above a "tolerable limit" of 1 to 5 tons/ac-yr (2 to 11 mt/ha-yr); many people view even "tolerable level" erosion as excessive. They are deeply concerned about fertilizers, pesticides, and animal wastes that enter streams and groundwater. Water pollution and its control are discussed in Chapter 17.

4-7 WATER EROSION AND SEDIMENTATION

Sedimentation is a part of the erosion process. Repeated detachment, transportation, and deposition move soil from the highest uplands to ocean beds. Not all sediment comes from cultivated lands or upland sites. Bottomlands, even stream banks and beds, lose material to erosion. Using every practical means to control erosion on cultivated land, range, and forest will reduce but not prevent sedimentation. For example, the Mississippi River in central United States was given the name "Big Muddy" by the western pioneers at a time when there was little or no cultivation along its banks.

Sedimentation is both beneficial and harmful. Alluvial soils are among the world's most productive soils; they developed on rich surface soil eroded from uplands. Accelerated erosion removes surface soil initially, but soon carries less productive subsoil. Subsoil deposited on fertile bottomland soils reduces their productivity. Serious floods in midwestern United States in 1950 deposited 2 ft (60 cm) or more of coarse, unproductive sand on thousands of acres of highly productive alluvial soil. Erosion from denuded mountain slopes often deposits several feet of soil, rocks, and other coarse material on the land at the foot of the slopes.

Sedimentation damages all types of vegetation. Even large trees may be killed. Highways, railroads, commercial buildings, and residences may be covered or inundated by flood-borne sediment.

Sedimentation is a continuing process. Sediment from upland areas and streambeds is deposited on the bed when flow velocity decreases. This raises the level of the river bed and reduces channel capacity so that subsequent floodwater overtops the banks and causes increased damage.

Levees have been built to control river flow. These are seldom effective permanently because sedimentation raises channel beds in the levee systems so much that many river beds are actually above much of the surrounding land. Severe storms eventually cause overflow and extreme losses on the alluvial plains the levees were built to protect.

Siltation of stream channels forms shallow areas and sandbars which must be cleared from navigable streams. Dredging operations are expensive and may be needed at frequent intervals.

Most alluvial soils have water tables close to soil surfaces. As sediments raise river beds, water tables also rise. Higher water tables reduce crop growth by reducing depth of well-aerated soil. Some of these areas become swamps with no commercial value.

Sedimentation of reservoirs is costly also. Silt and coarse clay carried by streams are deposited when velocity slows as they enter lakes and reservoirs; finest clay passes through the lake and out the spillways. Excessive sedimentation and short useful life are likely where stream gradient is steep, where catchment area soils are erodible, watershed area is small (less than 100 mi^2 or 250 km^2), and the ratio of watershed area (mi^2) to volume of storage (ac-in.) is less than 80:1 (200:1 km^2/ha-cm). When a reservoir is filled with sediment, its value is gone forever. Figure 4–7 shows a reservoir destroyed by sediment.

4–8 PRINCIPLES OF WATER EROSION CONTROL

Water erosion occurs when conditions are favorable for the detachment and transportation of soil material. Climate, soil erodibility, slope gradient and length, and surface and vegetative conditions influence how much erosion will take place. A method for predicting the effect variations of each of these factors has on erosion loss is presented in Chapter 6.

Many different practices have been developed to reduce water erosion. Not all

Figure 4–7 This reservoir in Kansas originally had a surface area of 20 acres (8 ha) but has been filled with sediment that has changed most of the area into mud flats. The remaining water is only about 3 ft (1 m) deep. (Courtesy USDA Soil Conservation Service.)

practices are applicable in all regions. However, the *principles* of water erosion control are the same wherever serious water erosion occurs. These principles are:

1. Reduce raindrop impact on the soil.
2. Reduce runoff volume and velocity.
3. Increase the soil's resistance to erosion.

Management practices that effect one or more of these principles will help to control water erosion. These practices are discussed in later chapters.

SUMMARY

Water erosion occurs wherever rainfall strikes bare soil or runoff water flows over erodible and insufficiently protected soil. The principal forms of water erosion are sheet erosion, rill erosion, gully erosion, and streambank erosion. Erosion damages the upland areas from which soil and plant nutrients are removed and also the bottomland on which sediments are deposited. It washes out crops on uplands, buries them on depositional sites, pollutes water, fills in river channels and reservoirs, and contributes to flooding.

The erosiveness of rainfall is influenced by the total amount of rain, the size of the drops, and their velocity of fall. The erosiveness of runoff is influenced by both the volume and the velocity of flow. Flow volume is directly related to rainfall intensity and duration and inversely related to soil infiltration rate and permeability. Flow velocity is related to flow thickness, slope gradient, and surface condition.

Water also acts as a lubricant, aiding gravity in mass soil movement. Landslides and mud slides occur in some areas with steeper topography. Mud slides are most common in winter rainfall areas where cultivated soils are nearly saturated and lack adequate anchoring roots.

Soil properties, especially texture and structure, influence the ease or difficulty with which soil grains are detached and transported, and also influence infiltration and percolation rates. Vegetation, both living and dead, intercepts raindrops and reduces the energy they release at the soil surface, and it slows the passage of runoff water over the soil surface, thus reducing its energy.

Erosion removes valuable soil from the uplands, and reduces the productive potential of the soils. Eroded materials are deposited on lower-lying lands. Sedimentation is both beneficial and harmful, and part of it is natural. Sedimentation is most damaging when it raises the level of a stream channel or fills a reservoir with soil material. Eroded soil is an important nonpoint-source water pollutant because of its large bulk and the chemicals it carries.

Water erosion and sedimentation can be controlled by reducing the energy of the erosive agents, usually rainfall and runoff water, or by increasing soil's resistance to erosion.

QUESTIONS

1. In what ways is water erosion important to the nonfarming segment of the world's population?
2. How do raindrops cause soil loss?
3. Describe briefly how runoff depth, land slope, and surface condition affect the erosiveness of running water.
4. How does soil structure influence the amount of soil lost by raindrop splash and runoff water?
5. How does vegetation reduce soil loss that is caused by water erosion?

REFERENCES

BAVER, L. D., 1939. Ewald Wollny—A pioneer in soil and water conservation research. *Soil Sci. Soc. Amer. Proc.* (1938) 3:330–333.

BENNETT, H. H., 1939. *Soil Conservation.* McGraw-Hill, New York, 993 p.

BENNETT, H. H., and W. R. CHAPLINE, 1928. *Soil Erosion a National Menace.* USDA Circ. 33.

COLACICCO, D., T. OSBORN, and K. ALT, 1989. Economic Damages from Soil Erosion. *J. Soil Water Cons.* 44: 35–39.

Duley, F. L., and L. L. Kelly, 1939. *Effect of Soil Type, Slope, and Surface Condition on Intake of Water.* Nebraska Agr. Exp. Sta. Res. Bull. 112.

Ellison, W. D., 1944. Studies of raindrop erosion. *Agric. Eng.* 25:131–136, 181–182.

Ellison, W. D., 1947a. Soil erosion studies: II. Soil detatchment hazard by raindrop splash. *Agric. Eng.* 28:197–201.

Ellison, W. D., 1947b. Soil Erosion studies: V. Soil transportation in the splash process. *Agric. Eng.* 28:349–351.

Grant, K. E., 1975. Erosion in 1973–74: The record and the challenge. *J. Soil Water Cons.* 30:29–32.

Gunn, R., and G. D. Kinzer, 1949. The terminal velocity of fall for water droplets. *J. Meteorol.* 6:243–248.

Hays, O. E., A. G. McCall, and F. G. Bell, 1949. *Investigations in Erosion Control and the Reclamation of Eroded Land at the Upper Mississippi Valley Conservation Experiment Station near LaCrosse, Wisconsin, 1933–1943.* USDA Tech. Bull. 973.

Hudson, N., 1981. *Soil Conservation,* 2nd ed. Cornell Univ. Press, Ithaca, N.Y., 324 p.

Kramer, J., and J. E. Weaver, 1936. *Relative Efficiency of Roots and Tops of Plants in Protecting the Soil from Erosion.* Cons. Dept. Bull. 2, Univ. Nebraska, Lincoln.

Larson, W. E., F. J. Pierce, and R. H. Dowdy, 1985. Loss in long-term productivity from soil erosion in the United States. In *Soil Erosion and Conservation.* S. A. El Swaify, W. C. Moldenhauer, and Andrew Lo (Eds.). Soil Cons. Soc. Am., Ankeny, Iowa, p. 262–271.

Laws, J. O., 1941. Measurements of fall velocity of water drops and raindrops. *Trans. Am. Geophys. Union* 22:709–721.

Laws, J. O., and D. A. Parsons, 1943. The relation of raindrop-size to intensity. *Trans. Am. Geophys. Union* 24:452–459.

Lyles, L., 1977. Soil detachment and aggregate disintegration by wind driven rain. In *Soil Erosion: Prediction and Control.* Soil Cons. Soc. Am., Ankeny, Iowa, p. 152–159.

McGregor, K. C., and C. K. Mutchler, 1976. Status of the *R* factor in northern Mississippi. In *Soil Erosion: Prediction and Control.* Soil Cons. Soc. Am., Ankeny, Iowa, p. 135–142.

Meyer, L. D., and L. A. Kramer, 1968. *Relation between Land-slope and Soil Erosion.* Paper No. 68–749. Am. Soc. Agric. Eng., St. Joseph, Mich. (Abbreviated paper in *Agric. Eng.* 50:522–523.)

Middleton, H. E., 1930. *Properties of Soils Which Influence Soil Erosion.* USDA Tech. Bull. 178.

Middleton, H. E., C. S. Slater, and H. G. Byers, 1932. *The Physical and Chemical Characteristics of the Soils from the Erosion Experiment Stations.* USDA Tech. Bull. 316.

Middleton, H. E., C. S. Slater, and H. G. Byers, 1934. *The Physical and Chemical Characteristics of the Soils from the Erosion Experiment Stations, Second Report.* USDA Tech. Bull. 430.

Miller, M. F., and H. H. Krusekopf, 1932. *The Influence of Systems of Cropping and Methods of Culture on Surface Runoff and Soil Erosion.* Missouri Agr. Exp. Sta. Res. Bull. 177.

Roose, E. J., 1977. Use of the universal soil loss equation to predict erosion in West Africa. In *Soil Erosion: Prediction and Control.* Soil Cons. Soc. Am., Ankeny, Iowa, p. 60–74.

Shaw, R. H., 1959. Water use from plastic-covered and uncovered corn plots. *Agron. J.* 51:172–173.

SMITH, D. D., and W. H. WISCHMEIER, 1962. Rainfall erosion. In *Advances in Agronomy,* Vol. 14, Academic Press, New York, p. 109–148.

TROEH, F. R., 1965. Landform equations fitted to contour maps. *Am. J. Sci.* 263:616–627.

VROOMEN, H., 1989. *Fertilizer Use and Price Statistics, 1960–88.* USDA-ERS Stat. Bull. 780.

WISCHMEIER, W. H., C. B. JOHNSON, and R. V. CROSS, 1971. A soil erodibility nomograph for farmland and construction sites. *J. Soil Water Cons.* 26:189–193.

WISCHMEIER, W. H., and D. D. SMITH, 1958. Rainfall energy and its relations to soil loss. *Trans. Am. Geophys. Union* 39:285–291.

5

Wind Erosion and Deposition

Wind erosion is the process of detachment, transportation, and deposition of soil material by wind. It occurs in all parts of the world and is a cause of serious soil deterioration. Chepil (1957) said:

> *The basic causes of wind erosion are few and simple. Wherever (1) the soil is loose, finely divided, and dry, (2) the soil surface is smooth and bare, and (3) the wind is strong, erosion may be expected.*
>
> *By the same token, whenever (a) the soil is compacted, kept moist, or made up of stable aggregates or clods large enough to resist the force of the wind, (b) the soil surface is roughened or covered by vegetation or vegetative residue, or (c) the wind near the ground is somewhat reduced, erosion may be curtailed or eliminated.*

Wind erosion is usually considered a problem of dryland regions, but humid area sandy soils, particularly along seacoasts, muck soils, and medium- and fine-textured soils that are laid bare can suffer severely from soil drifting. It can be a serious problem on irrigated land (Mech and Woodruff, 1967). It is a worldwide problem, particularly serious in the United States and Canada, in the drier parts of Argentina, Bolivia, and Peru, in parts of the USSR, in Middle East countries, and in China, India, and Pakistan, both north and south of the equator in Africa, and in Australia.

In North America, wind erosion has been most damaging in the Great Plains states and in the Canadian Prairie provinces, but it is also important around the Great Lakes, in eastern Washington and Oregon, in southeastern coastal areas, and along the Atlantic seaboard.

Serious widespread wind erosion occurred in the 1930s. Research has provided a better understanding of this phenomenon, and better techniques for its control have been developed. Efforts by the Soil Conservation Service, the Canadian Prairie Farm Rehabilitation Agency, agricultural universities, and local Conservation Districts have promoted conservation measures on farms and ranches, and governments have subsidized some conservation practices to promote their adoption.

Increased use of conservation measures has reduced the effect of severe droughts and strong winds so that soil losses, although often serious, have not again reached the levels encountered in the 1930s. The U.S. Department of Agriculture estimated in 1984 that wind erosion causes excessive soil losses on over 61 million ac (24 million ha) in the 10 Great Plains states, and over 89 million ac (36 million ha) in the entire United States (private communication from L. J. Kuder, SCS). Over 75% of this is on cropland, over 20% on pasture- and rangeland, less than 1% on forestland, and about 2% on "other" land.

Hagen and Woodruff (1973) found that the number of hours of dust storms per year at various locations in the Great Plains ranged from 0 to 250, with an overall average of 45 hours. The average duration of single dust storms was 6.6 hours, and the average dust concentration was 4.85 mg/m^3.

5-1 TYPES OF SOIL MOVEMENT

Soil is carried by wind in one of three ways:

1. *Suspension.* Soil particles and aggregates less than 0.05 mm in diameter (silt size and smaller) are kept suspended by the turbulence of air currents. Suspended dust does not drop out of the air in quantity unless rain washes it out or the velocity of the wind is drastically reduced.
2. *Saltation.* Intermediate-sized grains, approximately 0.05 to 0.5 mm in diameter, move in a series of short leaps. The jumping grains gain a great deal of energy and may knock other grains into the air or bounce back themselves. Saltating grains are the key to wind erosion. They drastically increase the number of both smaller and larger grains that move in suspension and in surface creep.
3. *Surface creep.* Soil grains larger than 0.5 mm in diameter cannot be lifted into the wind stream, but those smaller than about 1 mm may be bumped along the soil surface by saltating grains.

Aggregates, clods, and particles larger than 1 mm in diameter remain in place on the eroding surface and form a covering called desert pavement or lag gravel, as shown in Figure 5-1, that protects against further erosion.

5-2 EROSION DAMAGE

Wind-erosion damage includes loss of soil, textural change, nutrient and productivity loss, abrasion, air pollution, and sedimentation.

Figure 5-1 Desert pavement in New Mexico. The finer soil particles have been blown away, leaving a heavy, continuous gravel cover. (Scale is in inches and centimeters.) (Courtesy F. R. Troeh.)

5-2.1 Loss of Soil

Annual losses higher than 300 tons/ac (700 mt/ha) have been estimated for highly erodible, bare, sandy soils. An entire furrow slice (about 1000 tons/ac) could be blown away in three or four years at this rate if soil was removed uniformly from the entire surface. Loss from less erodible, bare soils (noncalcareous silt loams with less than 20% clay) ranges up to about 55 t/ac (125 mt/ha) (Lyles, 1977). A furrow slice could be lost in about 18 years at 55 tons/ac-yr. Actual losses are usually less than these figures because land is seldom left bare and unprotected for a whole year, but greater losses have occurred. Plow layers from many farm fields in the Great Plains were blown away in single dust storms in the 1930s. Some fields in western Canada, such as the area in Figure 5-2, lost 1 ft (30 cm) of soil in a single year.

5-2.2 Textural Change

Wind winnows soil much as it sifts chaff from threshed grain. Fine soil grains are carried great distances in suspension; saltating grains move to the fence rows or other barriers at the edges of the fields; coarser grains stay where they are or move relatively short distances within the eroding field.

The winnowing action coarsens texture in soils developed from glacial till, mixed residuum, and other materials having a wide range of particle sizes. Texture changes were reported during the erosion period of the 1930s in North America (Chepil, 1946; Daniel, 1936; Moss, 1935). Lyles and Tatarko (1986) confirmed

Figure 5-2 More than a foot (30 cm) of soil was removed by wind erosion from this fine sandy loam in southwestern Manitoba. The concrete structure on the left is a geodetic survey marker. (Courtesy Canada-Manitoba Soil Survey.)

texture coarsening of western Kansas soils between 1948 and 1984 with largest changes in the more erodible sandy soils.

Medium- and fine-textured soils suffer less from texture change. The coarser grains left in eroding fields and the finer grains in dunes are generally aggregates rather than particles. These have the same texture as the whole soil had before erosion. Many silt loam "dunes" were deposited around buildings in the Great Plains during the 1910–1914 erosion period. The texture of these old dunes and of associated cultivated fields are the same.

5-2.3 Nutrient Losses

Colloidal clay and organic matter are the seat of most of the soil's fertility. Colloidal material lost in dust storms contains a lot of fertility. Lyles and Tatarko (1986) showed that ten soils in the western half of Kansas had lost an average of one-fifth of their 1948 organic-matter content by 1984. Fertility loss is particularly severe in coarse-textured soils that become coarser as erosion progresses, but it is also important in medium-textured soils that lose surface soil but do not change texture.

5-2.4 Productivity Losses

Soils become less productive as winds erode them. Soils developed from glacial till and other mixed-textured material lose productivity mostly because of lowered nutrient content and reduced water-holding capacity. Soils developed from loess or other relatively uniform material lose productivity because of loss of friable, productive surface soil and the exposure of more clayey, less permeable, less fertile subsoil material.

Productivity losses have been measured. Finnell (1951), for example, found that average wheat yields in the southern Great Plains were lowered progressively with increasingly severe wind erosion. Lyles (1977) suggested a method for estimating productivity decline from the prediction of surface soil loss and the known relationship between depth of surface soil and crop yield.

5-2.5 Abrasion

Soil grains carried by wind have etched automobile windows and sandblasted paint on houses, cars, and machinery. Soil particles sift into bearing surfaces in machinery and accelerate wear. This type of damage is costly, but is insignificant compared to the damage done to young, growing plants.

Plants seldom suffer permanent damage solely from the flogging action of high winds, but severe damage is done, especially to young plants, when the erosive wind carries abrasive soil material. Damage ranging from delayed growth and reduced yield to actual death has been inflicted on cotton, sorghum, wheat, soybeans, sunflower, alfalfa, a number of native grasses, and several vegetables. A relatively short exposure to soil blast will reduce final yields; plants are killed when the exposure is long enough. Figure 5-3 shows a field of wheat in southwestern Kansas destroyed by severe wind erosion.

Figure 5-3 The wheat crop in this field in southwestern Kansas was destroyed by a windstorm on February 10, 1976. (Courtesy USDA Soil Conservation Service.)

5-2.6 Air Pollution

The presence of soil particles in the air has long been noted (Free, 1911). Early Greek writers mentioned dust storms which probably originated in the Sahara Desert. Most dust originates in deserts or in dryland areas temporarily bared of vegetative cover by overgrazing, cultivation, or fires.

Atmospheric dust causes discomfort some distance from its source; near the source, discomfort is much greater and a dust storm can be fatal to travelers caught in it.

Dust caused by farming activities seldom is the direct cause of death, but it can and does cause accidents and respiratory ailments that sometimes prove fatal. Hagen and Skidmore (1977) report that dust in the air can reduce visibility dangerously on highways and at airfields. Dust may also carry pathogens that cause skin disorders.

5-2.7 Deposition (Sedimentation)

Suspended dust is carried long distances and deposited as a thin film over everything, doing no great physical damage. Some soils may even gain from added nutrients and organic matter, but the all-pervasive dust has a tremendous demoralizing effect on rural families.

Saltating soil material does not travel far but it causes considerable physical damage. Many farm fences were buried during the 1930s by soil that settled behind tumbleweeds trapped by the fences. Sometimes two fences had to be built on top of the original one to keep livestock confined and cropland protected, or to control soil and snow drifts (see Figure 5-4). Drainage and irrigation ditches have also been

Figure 5-4 Wind erosion sediments have buried three snow fences erected to protect the road at the right of this picture. The surface of the dunes over the snow fences is 3 to 10 ft (1 to 3 m) above the former ground level. (Courtesy USDA Soil Conservation Service.)

plugged with blowing soil. Land leveled for irrigation as well as ordinary farm fields have been made hummocky by drifting soil.

Crops can be buried by drifting soil, particularly when they are planted in furrows. Young plants are most likely to be damaged, but even mature plants on the windward edges of fields next to eroding areas can be completely covered. Sand dunes can move into windbreaks and tree shelterbelts, eventually killing them if the drifts get too deep, and highways and other engineering works can be covered with blown soil. Huszar and Piper (1986) surveyed off-site costs of wind erosion in New Mexico and reported annual costs of over $465 million. This dwarfs the $10 million on-site costs claimed annually for the state.

Sand deposits are expensive to remove. The Santa Fe Railway found this out when the John Martin Dam was built in eastern Colorado. The mainline track had to be relocated from the river valley to the uplands south of the river, passing through a very sandy region. Blowouts were common during the 1930s and sand frequently covered the right-of-way. Soil drifting was controlled only after livestock numbers were reduced and the area revegetated with large government input.

5-3 EROSIVENESS OF SURFACE WIND

Moving air possesses energy. The higher the velocity of the wind, the higher the energy level and the more erosive the wind.

5-3.1 Velocity of Wind near the Ground

Standard wind velocity is measured at a fixed height, usually 30 ft (9 m), above the ground. Height is important because velocity of even a steady wind increases dramatically above the ground surface. The height of measurement therefore must be specified along with wind velocity.

Wind velocity over a bare surface is zero at a height (Z_0), slightly above the average height of a bare soil surface but below the tops of soil irregularities (see Figure 5-5a). Velocity approaches zero considerably above the soil surface in a vegetated area, as shown in Figure 5-5b. Here D represents the zero plane displacement caused by the vegetative cover and Z_0 is the roughness parameter. The velocity gradient behaves as if velocity was zero at $D + Z_0$ (top dashed line in Figure 5-5c), but air still moves slowly and erratically through the crop below this point as indicated by the lower dashed line. The velocity gradients over all surfaces plot as straight lines on a semilog graph within 15 ft (5 m) of soil surfaces as shown in Figure 5-5d, if $(z - D)$ is used for height plotted on the log scale.

Measurement of wind velocity profiles shows that the height Z_0, where velocity becomes zero, is the same on a specific bare surface for all wind speeds. Similarly, the height $(D + Z_0)$ is constant for a specific vegetated surface as long as the crop is not bent over by stronger winds.

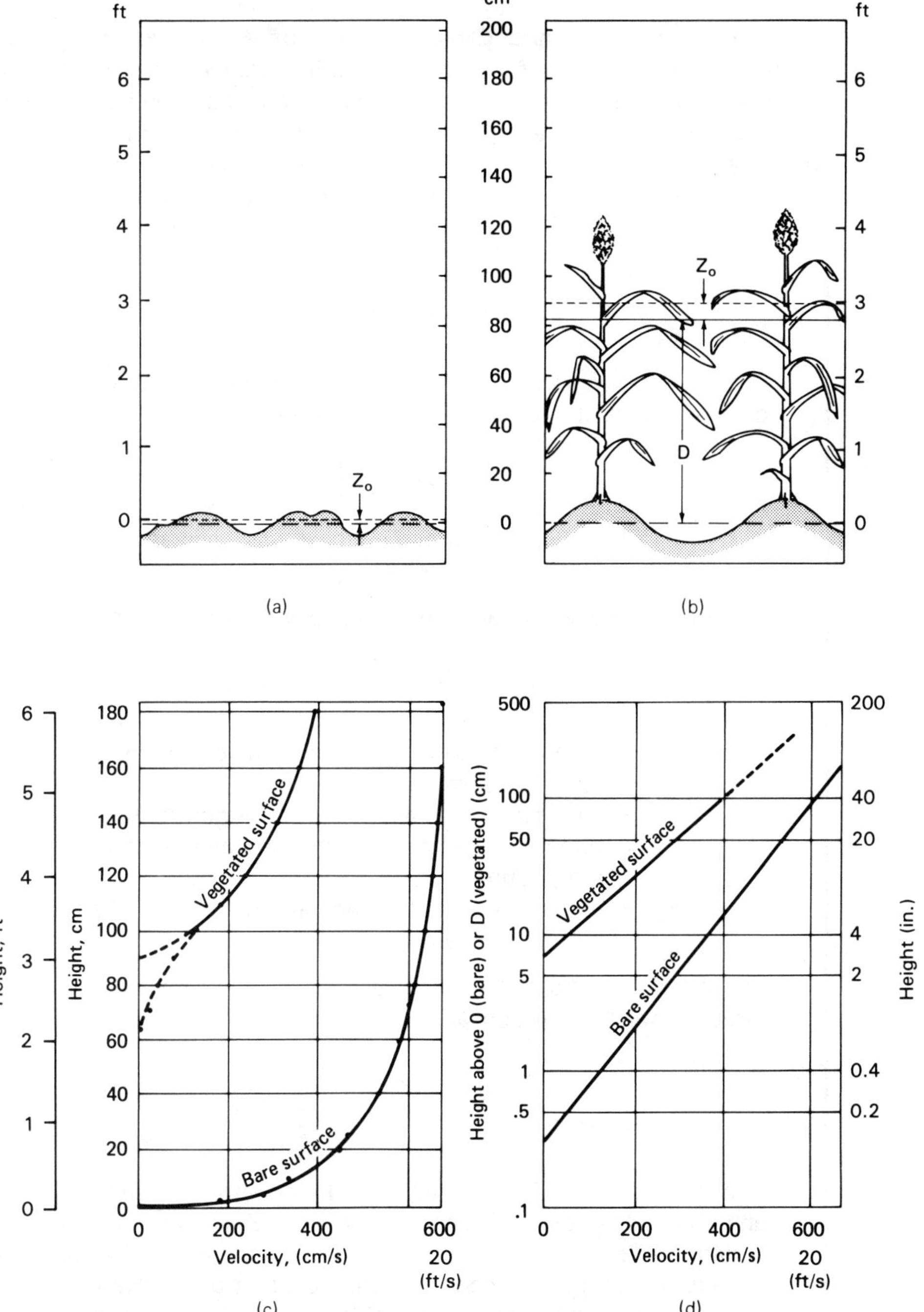

Figure 5–5 Wind velocity near a soil surface. (a) Zero wind velocity occurs at a height (Z_0) above the average height of the soil surface but below the high points. (b) A crop or other vegetative cover raises the level where wind velocity extrapolates to zero by a distance $D + Z_0$ equal to about 70% of the height of the vegetation. (c) Velocity profiles above a bare surface, as in (a), and above and within a vegetated surface, as in (b), under the influence of the same "free" velocity wind [same velocity at 1600+ ft (500+ m)]. (d) Velocity gradients plot as straight lines when a logarithmic scale is used for the height.

Friction Velocity and Erosive Power of Wind. Friction velocity (u_*) controls the erosive power of wind (Note 5–1). It is related to the velocity profile and to the drag exerted by wind on the soil surface. Over a bare soil it increases in direct proportion to the wind velocity measured at a specific height until the drag on the soil surface (surface shear stress) begins to cause erosion. As soil starts to erode, some of the wind's energy is used to transport soil grains so velocity decreases.

NOTE 5–1
FRICTION VELOCITY OF WIND

Friction velocity, u_*, is not an actual velocity, but it has the same units as velocity, l/t. It is defined by the equation:

$$u_* = \frac{\tau_0^{1/2}}{\rho}$$

where τ_0 = surface shear stress, dynes/cm^2
ρ = air density, g/cm^3.

Friction velocity is related to wind velocity by the equation:

$$u_z = \frac{u_*}{k} \ln\left(\frac{z - D}{Z_0}\right) + \phi_0$$

where u_z = mean wind velocity, cm/s, at height z, cm
k = von Kármán's constant $\cong$ 0.4
D = zero plane displacement, cm (Figure 5–5b)
Z_0 = effective roughness height (roughness parameter), cm (Figure 5–5a)
ϕ_0 = integral adiabatic influence function (usually zero for highly turbulent flow)

The above equation can be solved for u_* under conditions of fully turbulent wind (for which $\phi_0 = 0$):

$$u_* = k \frac{u_z}{\ln\left(\frac{z - D}{Z_0}\right)}$$

Friction velocity, u_*, is proportional to the mean wind velocity, u_z, over any noneroding surface because k, D, and Z_0 are constant for each surface (unless vegetative cover height is reduced by bending with increasing wind) and z can be made constant by always measuring wind velocity at the same height. Friction velocity will be different for bare and vegetated surfaces because vegetation changes values of Z_0 and D. Movement of soil grains changes u_* by absorbing wind energy.

For a given friction velocity, shear force is greater over rough surfaces, which therefore should be more erodible than smooth ones. Actually rough surfaces usually reduce erosion because surface roughness elements absorb much of the drag and leave only a small residual force to strike erodible soil grains.

5-3.2 Wind Turbulence

Wind strong enough to cause erosion is always turbulent, with eddies moving in all directions at a variety of velocities. Turbulence increases with increases in friction velocity, with increasing surface roughness, and with pronounced changes in surface temperature. It is also more pronounced close to the soil surface than higher in the wind stream (Chepil and Milne, 1941).

Air turbulence was once considered the major factor initiating movement of grains in saltation, but other factors are now known to play a more significant role. Turbulence is important in keeping soil grains suspended in air.

5-3.3 Wind Gustiness

Wind velocity fluctuates widely and frequently. Wind-tunnel studies show that soil composed of a mixture of erodible and nonerodible components will stabilize if wind velocity is constant. Nonerodible components eventually blanket the surface and protect it from further loss. Variable wind velocity prevents the soil surface from stabilizing completely. Higher-velocity gusts start a stabilized surface eroding again, with erosion continuing until gust velocity drops below that required to cause erosion.

5-3.4 Prevailing Wind Direction

Winds from any direction can cause erosion. Changing wind direction affects the erosion process in two major ways. Change of direction may cause a stabilized surface to erode again because the pattern of nonerosive clods and grains that established stability is directionally effective. A shift in direction, as little as 30°, will allow soil movement to start again.

If erosive winds are predominantly from one or both of two opposite directions, it is possible to reduce soil losses by placing barriers, such as furrows, crop strips, and windbreaks, perpendicular to prevailing wind direction. For example, the prevailing direction of wind at Dodge City and Wichita, Kansas, is from the north for six months and from the south for six months. Each month, over twice as much erosive wind force occurs parallel to the prevailing direction as occurs perpendicular to it. East-west directional barriers are therefore quite effective. Douglas, Arizona, has prevailing winds from the east for three months, northwest or north-northwest for two months, southwest and south-southwest for six months, and south for one month, and in no month is much more than half the erosive wind from the prevailing direction. Barriers are not very effective against such variable winds.

5-4 INITIATION OF SOIL MOVEMENT BY WIND

Some winds do not cause soil movement. Chepil (1945b) found that for each soil and surface condition there is a minimum wind velocity necessary to start soil movement. This *threshold velocity* varies from 8 to 30 mi/hr (360 to 1350 cm/s), measured 6 in. (15 cm) above the soil surface.

5-4.1 Saltation

Soil drifting usually starts when medium-sized grains start moving in saltation. The first American agricultural authors to discuss wind erosion (King, 1894; Free, 1911) also mentioned saltation. Considerable study was required, however, to explain the mechanism for saltation initiation.

Chepil watched sand grains on the smooth, wooden floor of his wind tunnel, and observed that they started to roll along the bed. After a relatively short distance, without contacting other grains or striking any irregularity, the particles suddenly jumped almost vertically into the air. The angle of ascent generally ranged between 75 and 90°. By this time they had a very significant spin, later measured at 200 to 1000 revolutions per second (Chepil, 1945a). Ascending grains were carried downwind by the increasingly rapid velocity of the wind currents through which the grains rose. They continued downwind with increasing velocity even as they fell back toward the tunnel surface. Acceleration brought about by the wind seemed to match the acceleration of gravity, because the path back to the bed, as shown in Figure 5-6, was nearly a straight line with an impact angle generally between 6 and 12°.

Chepil observed that grains ascended for about one-fourth to one-fifth of the length of the leap. Grains reaching a height of 2 in. (5 cm) or less traveled about seven times the height. Grains leaping higher than 6 in. (15 cm) traveled about 10 times the height of the leap. About 57% of the load carried in saltation by an erosive wind moves in leaps less than 2 in. (5 cm) high, 93% in leaps less than 12 in. (30 cm), and 99% in leaps less than 3 ft (1 m).

Bagnold (1937) suggested that sand particles rise into the air in saltation because stationary particles lying on the soil surface are knocked into the air by the impact of descending particles, or that saltating particles returning to the soil surface carom back into flight. Neither of these suggestions explains how particles first get into movement. Free (1911) suggested turbulence was responsible for starting soil grains moving in saltation. Chepil also believed this at the beginning of his study of

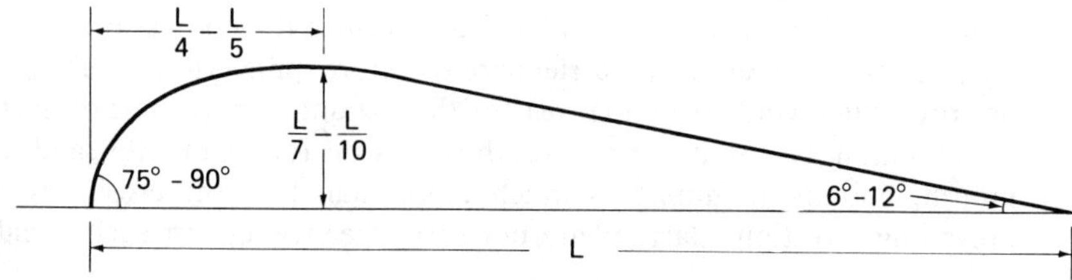

Figure 5-6 The path of a sand grain in saltation.

wind erosion (Chepil and Milne, 1939). His calculations showed that a velocity in excess of 10.4 mi/hr (465 cm/s) would be necessary for its turbulence to lift a soil cube 0.5 mm on a side. His measurements showed, however, that sand grains larger than 0.8 mm diameter were saltating in a wind with a velocity of only 5 mi/hr (225 cm/s) at 1/4 in. (6 mm) height. He concluded that some factor(s) other than turbulence must be responsible for initiating saltation.

Chepil (1945a) studied the possibility that soil grains might be bounced into the airstream by irregularities on their surfaces or on the ground. He decided that the near-vertical takeoffs he observed could not be explained by this mechanism. He then examined the possibility that particle spin and the steep velocity gradient close to the soil surface might initiate saltation. Differences in velocity of fluid flow over the top and bottom surfaces of an object set up pressure differences on these surfaces. A zone of lower pressure develops where flow is more rapid; higher pressure develops where flow is slower.

Sand particles rolling along the bed of a wind tunnel increase the flow velocity of air on top of the grain and decrease it on the bottom. The rapid increase in wind velocity with height close to the surface contributes to a large velocity differential between the top and bottom of the spinning grains, as shown in Figure 5-7. Chepil felt that the pressure differential was sufficient to force the particles steeply upward into the wind stream.

Bisal and Nielsen (1962) did not believe soil grains roll on the soil surface prior to lifting into the air stream. They showed, in a wind tunnel, that air blowing across a small vertical tube caused soil grains inside the tube to vibrate and leap upward (*Venturi effect*). They believed this was the phenomenon that initiated saltation. However, this cannot be the case on a smooth surface where there are no "tubes."

Saltation in field conditions is probably the result of combined actions of spinning particles, Venturi effect, and bouncing of irregularly shaped particles moving across rough surfaces. Saltating soil particles and aggregates increase movement of all grain sizes. The number of saltating grains and their erosive effects increase progressively across an eroding field.

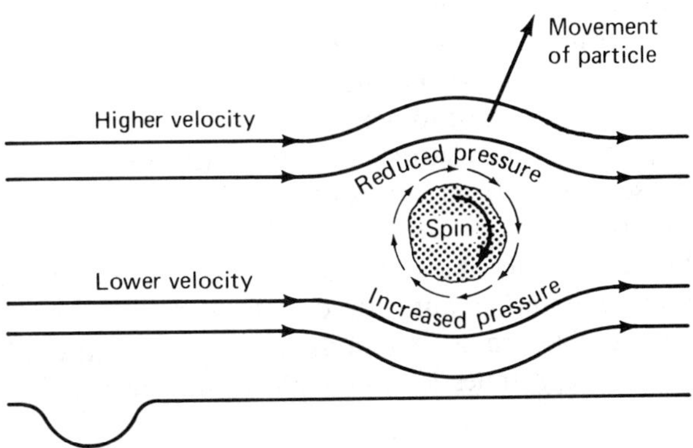

Figure 5-7 A spinning sand grain in a moving airstream is lifted by increased air pressure below and reduced pressure above.

5-4.2 Avalanching

The increasing rate of erosion as the wind blows farther across a field is called *avalanching*. Chepil (1946) suggested there are three major reasons for avalanching: accumulation of eroded material from previous storms, increasing quantity of saltating particles, and smoother surfaces.

Erosion often results from successive high winds coming from the same prevailing direction. Soil farther downwind in such fields is likely to be more erodible simply because it has been eroded previously and deposited there. The farther leeward the wind moves, the more abrasive material it is likely to carry. Saltating particles constantly drop back to the soil surface and in the process detach new soil grains and abrade clods and aggregates. Abrasion, and consequently erosion, accelerates as these new materials are added to the wind stream. Wind moving across a field smooths the surface by cutting humps and filling hollows. Wind flows faster across smoother surfaces, and faster winds are more erosive.

5-5 WIND AND THE EROSION PROCESS

Wind has power to detach and transport soil grains. After transportation, particles and aggregates come to rest short or long distances from their origin.

5-5.1 Detaching Capacity of Wind

The detaching capacity of wind is related to its friction velocity or shear stress and to the size of the erodible grains

$$D = f(u'_*)^2$$

where D = detaching capacity, g/cm²-s
u'_* = friction velocity over an eroding surface, cm/s

A sharp velocity gradient near the soil causes grains that protrude higher into the wind stream to be struck by stronger wind force. Larger particles stick up higher, but their larger mass requires more force to detach them. Any particle from 0.05 to 0.5 mm in diameter can be detached if the wind is strong enough, but those from 0.1 to 0.15 mm are the easiest to detach of any grains that move in saltation. Silt- and clay-sized grains (<0.05 mm) and very coarse sand and gravel sizes (>1.0 mm) cannot be separated from the soil mass by even strong winds that are free of saltating particles.

Winds containing abrasive material can detach both smaller and larger grains. These abrasive materials not only detach erodible grains from the soil, they also abrade nonerodible grains and clods, detaching small erodible grains from them, and if the wind continues long enough, disintegrating the whole clod (see Figure 5-8).

Figure 5-8 Abrasion of soil cylinders 3 in. (75 cm) in diameter and 2.5 in. (62 cm) tall by dune sand carried in a wind blowing from left to right with a friction velocity of 2 ft/sec (61.5 cm/s). Soils from left to right are fine sandy loam, loam, light silt loam, heavy silt loam, and silty clay. (Courtesy USDA, AES Soil Erosion Research Unit.)

5-5.2 Transporting Capacity of Wind

Transport capacity of wind is related to wind velocity, but not to soil-grain size. Greater numbers of smaller-sized grains can be picked up, but the total weight of material a specific wind can carry remains relatively constant.

Early work by Chepil (1945a) showed the proportion of material in suspension, saltation, and creep depended on the aggregate- and particle-size composition of the soil. Minor quantities of suspended material were found over very coarse-textured soils and over strongly aggregated, fine-textured soils; quantities of creep were relatively large. Suspension was greater and creep noticeably smaller over dusty, silty, and fine sandy soils. In every soil Chepil studied, the amount of material in saltation was always greater than that in suspension and creep combined. Amounts in suspension ranged from 3 to 38%, in saltation from 55 to 72%, and in creep from 7 to 25% of the moving soil.

Bagnold (1941) and Chepil (1945c) noted that rate of dune sand and soil movement by wind, or the wind's transportation capacity, was related to the third power of the friction velocity:

$$q = f \frac{\rho}{g} u'^{3}_{*}$$

where q = rate of soil movement, g/(cm width)-s
ρ = air density, g/cm^3
g = gravitational constant, 980 cm/s^2
u'_* = friction velocity over an eroding surface, cm/s^2

The relationship between amount of soil removed from a unit area and erosive wind force probably has greater significance than that between rate of loss and wind force. Chepil and Woodruff (1963) suggest that

$$X = \text{f}(u'_*)^5$$

where X is the transportation capacity, g/cm^2.

This relationship is influenced by a number of factors, but the carrying capacity appears to be proportional to the fifth power of the friction velocity.

5-5.3 Soil Deposition

The distance soil is transported from its original site depends on wind velocity and on size and weight of particles and aggregates. Lag materials are not moved by wind, but they may lose some bulk by abrasion. Surface creep travels a very short distance. Saltating grains usually remain in the vicinity of the eroding field, deposited behind cultivation ridges, as small dunes behind clumps of vegetation in the field, or in vegetation of fence rows. Coarser saltating grains are deposited on the windward side of the dunes, finer ones to the leeward ("leesands"). Dust, which is kicked up by saltating particles and carried in suspension by the wind, is moved far away from the original location. This cloud of dust, however spectacular it may be, contains only a small part of the full soil load. Nevertheless, it is a very important loss because it contains the finer, more fertile elements from the soil—the clay and the humus.

5-6 FACTORS AFFECTING WIND EROSION

High-velocity winds do not always cause soil drifting; erosive winds do not cause the same amount of erosion in all situations. Factors which influence the amount of erosion that wind will cause are the soil's resistance to erosion, surface ridges, rainfall, land slope (hummocks), length of exposed area, and vegetative cover.

5-6.1 Soil Resistance

The major factor that makes soil resist wind erosion is size (mass) of individual soil grains. If the mass is sufficient, particles, aggregates, or clods are nonerodible. Large grains also protect and stabilize erodible grains in their wind shadow. Chepil (1950) called this "the governing principle of surface roughness." This is roughness caused by soil cloddiness, not by mechanical ridging.

Dry Aggregate Size Distribution. Grains larger than 1 mm in diameter are nonerodible; those between 1 and 0.5 mm are erodible only in very high velocity winds; those less than 0.5 mm in effective diameter are highly erodible. The more nonerodible grains the surface contains, the less erodible the soil is.

The proportion of nonerodible grains present on or near the soil surface affects the ease and speed with which soil starts to move, how long erosion will continue before a nonerodible blanket forms to halt it, and the total amount of soil that will blow. A relatively smooth soil containing nonerodible clods may become rough as it erodes and thus reduce erosion losses. The likelihood of a field forming a protective surface condition can be assessed by determining the size distribution of stable clods in the top inch (2.5 cm) of soil. The relationship between proportion of nonerodible clods and soil erodibility is shown in Figure 5-9. A smooth, bare, infinitely wide field with 2% nonerodible clods would permit 250 tons/ac (560 mt/ha) to erode in a year, whereas a similar field with 40% nonerodible clods would lose only 56 tons/ac-yr (125 mt/ha-yr) under the same conditions.

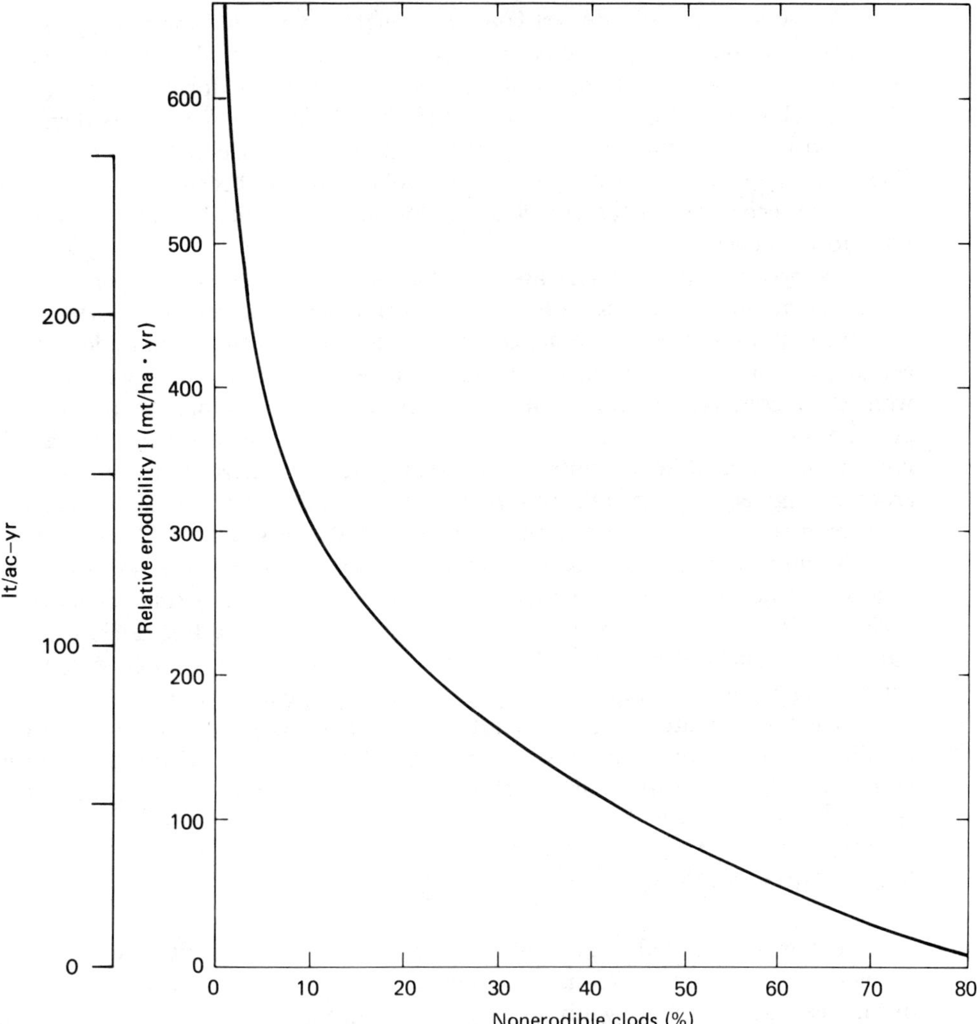

Figure 5–9 Relationship between percent nonerodible clods in a soil and its relative erodibility (I). [Modified from Soil Science Society of America Proceedings, Volume 29, p. 602–608, 1965 (Woodruff and Siddoway), by permission of the Soil Science Society of America.]

Mechanical Stability of Structural Units. Presence of nonerodible structural units does not, by itself, prevent soil erosion. Aggregates and clods that are easily abraded do not resist erosion for long. Accordingly, aggregate stability is an important attribute also.

Factors Affecting Aggregate Size and Stability. Soil properties such as texture, organic matter, exchangeable cations, and free calcium carbonate influence aggregate size and stability.

Coarse-textured soils do not contain enough clay to bind the sandy particles into structural units; clayey soils develop aggregates and clods, but weathering, especially freezing and drying while frozen, breaks them down. Chepil (1953) claimed a clay content of about 27% was best for clod development. Less than 15% clay almost precluded a good cloddy condition. The presence of large amounts of fine and very fine sand influences soil erodibility directly because these sizes can saltate. Very coarse sand and gravel help reduce soil erodibility because they are too large to be moved by most winds.

Soil organic matter is often associated with high levels of aggregation and with structural stability, but soils with really high organic-matter levels are often more erodible than those with moderate contents. Chepil (1955) found that additions of cereal straw and legume hay increased nonerodible dry clods and reduced erodibility while the materials were undergoing active decomposition (about six months). As decomposition slowed down, initial cementing materials lost their aggregating ability, and microbial fibers disintegrated. Nonerodible-clod size decreased and soil erodibility increased, especially on high residue treatments. Often a high proportion of medium-sized, water-stable aggregates developed. These are highly erodible.

Applications of lime to acid, humid area soils often improves soil structure. This is not true for arid and semiarid region soils. These are rarely calcium deficient; surface soils have an abundance and subsoils invariably contain free calcium carbonate. In fact, shallow calcium carbonate horizons in drier areas may be mixed with surface soil by cultivation. Chepil (1954) showed that the presence of as little as 1% free calcium carbonate in a soil generally caused clod disintegration and increased erodibility. Despite this relationship, when calcareous B or C horizons are exposed by erosion, surface crusts often develop that effectively protect soils from further erosion.

5-6.2 Surface Ridges

Surface ridges produced by tillage also reduce erosion. Effectiveness of ridges depends on height, lateral frequency, shape, and orientation relative to the direction of the wind. Ridges reduce wind velocity near the ground and they trap eroding soil grains in the furrows between ridge crests. Armbrust et al. (1964) showed, in a wind tunnel, that ridges from 2 to 4 in. (5 to 10 cm) high reduced wind erosion. Shallower ridges did not reduce wind velocity or trap soil grains as effectively. Ridges higher than 4 in. actually increased erosion in higher winds because the friction velocity increased over the crests of the ridges and there was more wind eddying.

5-6.3 Rainfall

Rain moistens surface soil, and moist soil is not eroded by wind. Studies show soil erodibility decreases—slowly at first, then more rapidly—as a soil is moistened from the air-dry condition to the wilting point. Chepil (1956) worked with four Great Plains soils and found they became nonerodible at moisture contents ranging from 0.82 to 1.16 times the water content at 15-atm tension. Bisal and Hsieh (1966) studied three Canadian soils and found moisture contents from 0.32 to 1.46 times that at 15-atm tension prevented soil drifting. Unfortunately, the direct effect of moisture on soil erodibility is transitory; it takes only a very thin layer of dry surface soil to permit erosion to start, even if moisture is abundant immediately below. Wind soon reduces the moisture content of surface layers. Erosion of some sandy soils can begin 15 or 20 minutes after an intense shower.

Rainfall can increase wind erosion by breaking exposed wind-resistant grains, detaching erodible grains, and smoothing soil surfaces so they are less resistant to erosion. Rain also reduces erodibility indirectly by increasing plant growth. Crop response to rainfall is extremely important, because plant cover controls wind erosion best.

5-6.4 Knoll Slopes

Over long slopes, short slopes not exceeding 1.5%, and level land, the velocity gradient and friction velocity are reasonably constant for a given wind. Over hummocky topography, where slopes are relatively short, layers of higher wind velocity move closer to the soil surface as they pass over knoll crests (see Figure 5-10). Z_0 is a relatively constant height above the surface, so the shorter vertical distance to the higher-velocity flow makes the friction velocity greater over the knolls. This makes the wind's erosive force much greater on the crests than on level land or on long slopes. Chepil et al. (1964) calculated probable increases in erosion on the crests and upper slopes of relatively short 3, 6, and 10% slopes, assuming that the zone of 14 mi/hr (625 cm/s) wind was found at 12, 8, 4, and 2 in. (30, 20, 10, and 5 cm) above the crests of knolls with side slopes of 1.5, 3, 6, and 10%, respectively. Their calculated values are presented in Table 5-1.

5-6.5 Length of Exposed Area

Soil drifting increases substantially with increasing length of the eroding strip. Wind starts to pick up soil grains close to the windward side of an erodible field. It continues to add to its load as it passes over the field until it can carry no more. Traveling farther it may continue to pick up other soil grains, but must drop some of its load, because the carrying capacity is finite.

A wind's transport capacity at a specific friction velocity is similar for all soils, but the distance the wind must travel across a field to pick up its full load depends on

TABLE 5-1 RELATIVE AMOUNTS OF EROSION FROM LEVEL (1.5% SLOPE) AND SHORT SLOPING (HUMMOCKY) LAND

	Relative amounts of erosion	
Slope (%)	Crests	Upper slopes
0–1.5 (level)	100	100
3.0	150	130
6.0	320	230
10.0	660	370

Source: From the Journal of Soil and Water Conservation, Volume 19, p. 179–181, 1964 (Chepil et al.).

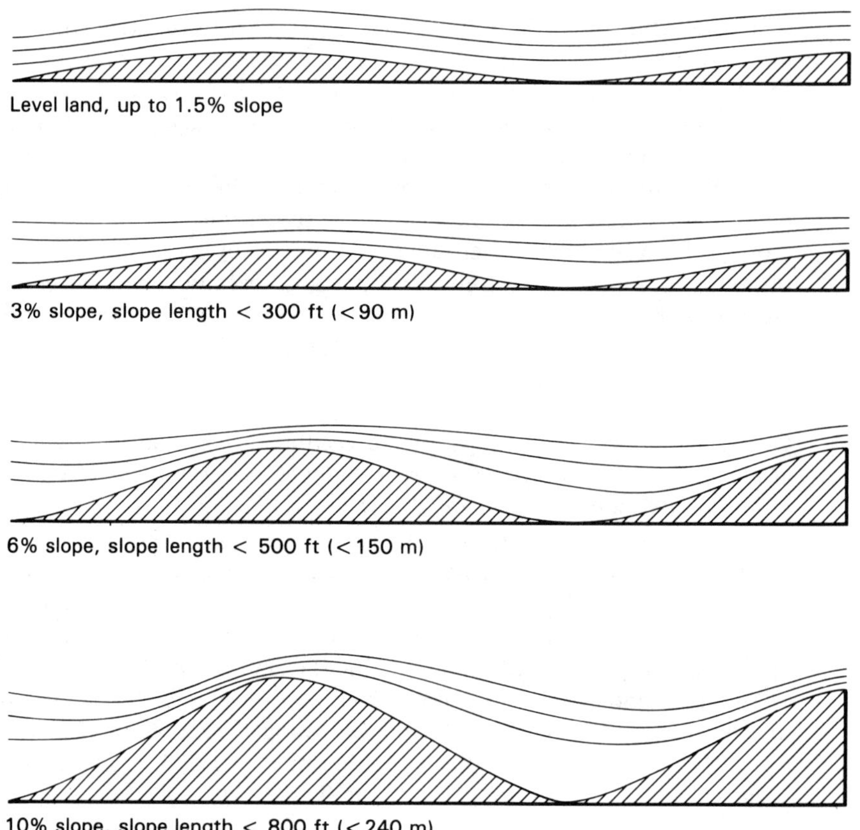

Figure 5-10 Lines of equal wind velocity over different land slopes. If the top line in each diagram represents 14 mi/hr (625 cm/s), this velocity is reached at approximately 12, 8, 4, and 2 in. (30.5, 18.3, 9.8, and 5.5 cm) above the knoll crest on the 1.5%, 3%, 6%, and 10% slopes, respectively. [Modified from the Journal of Soil and Water Conservation, Volume 19, p. 179–181, 1964 (Chepil et al.).]

soil erodibility. The more erodible the soil, the shorter the distance required to reach its load capacity. Distance needed to acquire maximum load varies from less than 180 ft (55 m) for a structureless fine sand to more than 5000 ft (1500 m) for a cloddy, medium-textured soil (Chepil and Woodruff, 1963). Many fields are not wide enough for the wind to pick up its maximum load.

5-6.6 Vegetative Cover

The most effective way to reduce wind erosion is to cover the soil with a protective mantle of growing plants or with a thick mulch of crop residue. Barriers of plant material raise ($D + Z_0$) farther from the surface and produce thick blankets of still air next to the soil.

The protection that plant cover provides is influenced by plant species (amount of vegetative cover and time of year when cover is provided), plant geometry and

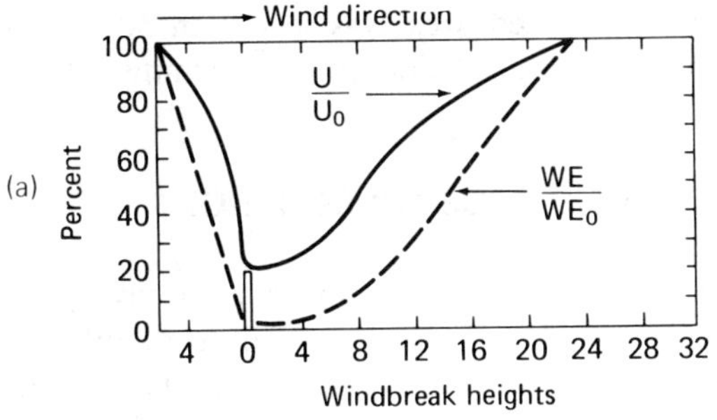

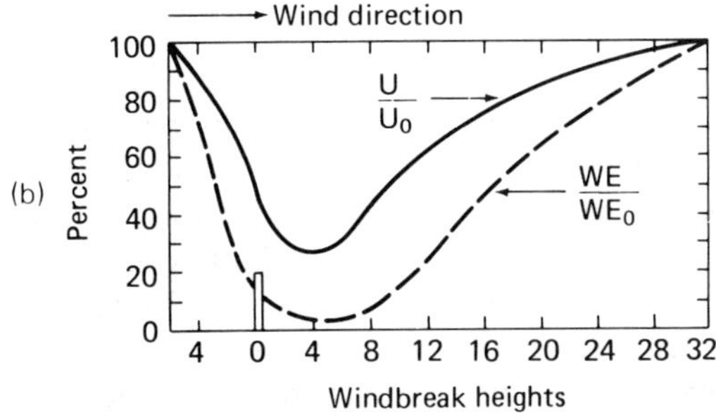

Figure 5-11 Ratio of sheltered to open field windspeed (U/U_0) and wind erosion (WE/WE_0) with all windspeeds above threshold velocity normal to (a) a 20% porous windbreak, and (b) a 40% porous windbreak. Wind speeds measured at 0.12H above the soil surface (where H = the height of the windbreak). (From Hagen, 1976.)

population, and row orientation. Crop residues left on the surface, especially if tall and dense, offer almost as much protection as growing plants.

A complete cover of growing plants offers maximum protection, but individual plants and rows of plants across the direction of the wind also reduce wind velocity and erosion. This is apparent where isolated weeds in fallow fields trap saltating grains and where soil piles up around wind barriers such as field shelterbelts.

Barriers are effective because air is a fluid. As air moves up to a porous barrier, part of it is pushed over or around the barrier. Air not deflected passes through the barrier at a fast rate (funneling effect), then immediately slows down as it spreads out to occupy all the space behind the barrier. Wind speed returns to normal only when the deflected air returns to its initial position in the windstream.

Bates (1924), using an artificial, porous barrier, found that wind velocity was reduced some eight times the barrier height (8*H*) to windward and 24 times the height (24*H*) to leeward. Greatest velocity reduction was about 5*H* to leeward, not immediately behind the barrier. He also found that wind swept around the ends of the barrier at increased velocities. More recent studies bear out these findings. Hagen (1976) determined relative wind speed and erosion for 20% and 40% porous windbreaks. His data are presented in Figure 5-11. They show that velocity and erosion were reduced from 6*H* windward to 24*H* leeward with the 20% porous windbreak and from 6*H* windward to 32*H* leeward with the 40% porous break.

Erosion in the protected area was less than 50% of that in the open from $2H$ windward to $16H$ leeward, and from $2H$ windward to $17H$ leeward, respectively.

5-7 PRINCIPLES OF WIND EROSION CONTROL

Wind erosion occurs whenever conditions are favorable for detachment and transportation of soil material by wind. Soil erodibility, surface roughness (ridging), climatic conditions (wind velocity and humidity), length of exposed surface, and vegetative cover influence how much erosion will take place. Little can be done to change the climate in an area, but it is usually possible to alter one or more of the other factors.

Many successful practices for reducing wind erosion have been developed by farmers based on their observations, and by research scientists as a result of their studies. These practices are not universally successful; some work well in one region, others are better in another. Regardless of the relative success of individual techniques, the aims or principles of soil drifting control are the same in all areas where wind erosion occurs. These are: to reduce wind velocity near ground level below the threshold velocity, to remove abrasive material from the windstream, and to reduce soil erodibility. Any practice that accomplishes one or more of these will reduce the severity of wind erosion.

SUMMARY

Wind erosion is a common phenomenon on most soils in dryland regions and on coarse-textured and high-organic-matter soils in humid areas. It damages land from which soil is removed and land on which sediment is deposited. Flying soil grains bury or abrade crops, damage buildings and equipment, and dust in the air is a health and safety hazard.

Soil moves in the wind in three general forms: the finest grains move in *suspension,* intermediate sizes in *saltation,* and coarsest erodible grains in *surface creep.* Finer and coarser sizes are difficult for even strong winds to dislodge, but intermediate-sized grains are relatively easy to move. Saltating particles start smaller and larger grains moving in suspension and in surface creep.

Wind velocity, turbulence, gustiness, and direction all affect the severity of erosion. Forces that start particles saltating include spin on soil grains, steep velocity gradient near the soil, and irregularities on soil grains and land surfaces. These lift or bounce susceptible particles a short distance vertically, where they are accelerated by the wind. When they drop back to the soil surface, they rebound higher and faster, or they knock other particles into motion.

Friction velocity represents the velocity gradient over the soil surface and is responsible for erosive power. Erosive force and detaching capacity of a wind are proportional to the square of the friction velocity; the carrying capacity is proportional to the cube of the friction velocity; and the amount of material eroded by wind from a unit area is proportional to the fifth power of the friction velocity.

Factors other than wind also affect wind erosion. Soil cloddiness, amount and nature of field ridging, amount of rainfall, topography (smooth or hummocky), length of erodible area in the direction of the wind, and amount, nature, and distribution of vegetative cover influence the amount of soil movement by wind.

There are three principal ways of reducing erosion: reduce the velocity of the wind close to the soil, remove abrasive material (saltating grains) from the windstream, and increase the soil's resistance to wind erosion.

QUESTIONS

1. Name and describe the three types of movement of soil particles in the wind.
2. Briefly describe the types of damage to soil, crops, and structures that can be caused by wind erosion.
3. List the characteristics of wind that influence the amount of soil that is eroded, and describe how each characteristic affects the erosion process.
4. What physical forces appear to be responsible for starting soil movement by wind?
5. Describe how each of the following soil properties affects the erodibility of soils: texture, structure, organic-matter content, lime content, and moisture content.
6. Describe each of the mechanisms by which vegetation reduces the amount of wind erosion.
7. What are the three principles of wind erosion control, and why is each effective?

REFERENCES

ARMBRUST, D. V., W. S. CHEPIL, and F. H. SIDDOWAY, 1964. Effects of ridges on erosion of soil by wind. *Soil Sci. Soc. Am. Proc.* 28:557–560

BAGNOLD, R. A., 1937. The transport of sand by wind. *Geog. J.* 89:409–438.

BAGNOLD, R. A., 1941 (1973 reprint). *The Physics of Blown Sand and Desert Dunes.* Chapman & Hall, London, 265 p.

BATES, C. G., 1924. *The Windbreak as a Farm Asset.* USDA Farm. Bull. 1405.

BISAL, F., and J. HSIEH, 1966. Influence of moisture on erodibility of soil by wind. *Soil Sci.* 102:143–146.

BISAL, F., and K. F. NIELSEN, 1962. Movement of soil particles in saltation. *Can. J. Soil Sci.* 42:81–86.

CHEPIL, W. S., 1945a. Dynamics of wind erosion: I. Nature of movement of soil by wind. *Soil Sci.* 60:305–320.

CHEPIL, W. S., 1945b. Dynamics of wind erosion: II. Initiation of soil movement. *Soil Sci.* 60:397–411.

CHEPIL, W. S., 1945c. Dynamics of wind erosion: III. The transport capacity of the wind. *Soil Sci.* 60:475–480.

CHEPIL, W. S., 1946. Dynamics of wind erosion: V. Cumulative intensity of soil drifting across eroding fields. *Soil Sci.* 61:257–263.

CHEPIL, W. S., 1950. Properties of soil which influence wind erosion: I. The governing principle of surface roughness. *Soil Sci.* 69:149–162.

CHEPIL, W. S., 1953. Factors that influence clod structure and erodibility of soil by wind: I. Soil texture. *Soil Sci.* 75:473–483.

CHEPIL. W. S., 1954. Factors that influence clod structure and erodibility of soil by wind: III. Calcium carbonate and decomposed organic matter. *Soil Sci.* 77:473–480.

CHEPIL, W. S., 1955. Factors that influence clod structure and erodibility of soil by wind: V. Organic matter at varying stages of decomposition. *Soil Sci.* 80:413–421.

CHEPIL, W. S., 1956. Influence of moisture on erodibility of soil by wind. *Soil Sci. Soc. Am. Proc.* 20:288–292.

CHEPIL, W. S., 1957. Dust bowl: Causes and effects. *J. Soil Water Cons.* 12:108–111.

CHEPIL, W. S., and R. A. MILNE, 1939. Comparative study of soil drifting in the field and in a wind tunnel. *Sci. Agric.* 19:249–257.

CHEPIL, W. S., and R. A. MILNE, 1941. Wind erosion of soil in relation to roughness of surface. *Soil Sci.* 52:417–431.

CHEPIL, W. S., F. H. SIDDOWAY, and D. V. ARMBRUST, 1964. Wind erodibility of knolly terrain. *J. Soil Water Cons.* 19:179–181.

CHEPIL, W. S., and N. P. WOODRUFF, 1963. The physics of wind erosion and its control. In *Advances in Agronomy,* Vol. 15. Academic Press, New York, p. 211–302.

DANIEL, H. A., 1936. The physical changes in soils of the southern high plains due to cropping and wind erosion and relation between sand plus silt over clay ratios in these soils. *J. Am. Soc. Agron.* 28:570–580.

FINNELL, H. H., 1951. *Depletion of High Plains Wheatlands.* USDA Circ. 871.

FREE, E. E., 1911. *The Movement of Soil Material by the Wind.* USDA Bur. Soils Bull. 68.

HAGEN, L. J., 1976. Windbreak design for optimum wind erosion control. *Proc., Symposium on Shelterbelts on the Great Plains,* Denver, Colorado, April 20–22, 1976.

HAGEN, L. J., and E. L. SKIDMORE, 1977. Wind erosion and visibility problems. *Trans. Am. Soc. Agr. Eng.* 20:898–903.

HAGEN, L. J., and N. P. WOODRUFF, 1973. Air pollution from duststorms in the Great Plains. *Atmospher. Environ.* 7:323–332.

HUSZAR, P. C., and S. L. PIPER, 1986. Estimating the off-site costs of wind erosion in New Mexico. *J. Soil Water Cons.* 41:414–416.

KING, F. H., 1894. *Destructive Effects of Winds on Sandy Soils.* Univ. Wis. Bull. 42.

LYLES, L., 1977. Wind erosion: Processes and effects on soil productivity. *Trans. Am. Soc. Agr. Eng.* 20:880–884.

LYLES, L. and J. TATARKO, 1986. Wind erosion effects on soil texture and organic matter. *J. Soil Water Cons.* 41:191–193.

MECH, S. J., and N. P. WOODRUFF, 1967. Wind erosion on irrigated lands. In *Irrigation of Agricultural Lands.* Monograph 11, American Society of Agronomy, Madison, Wis., p. 964–973.

MOSS, H. C., 1935. Some field and laboratory studies of soil drifting in Saskatchewan. *Sci. Agric.* 15:665–679

Stoekeler, J. H., 1962. *Shelterbelt Influence on Great Plains Environment and Crops.* USDA Prod. Res. Rep. 62.

U.S. Department of Agriculture, 1935. *Soil and Water Conservation Needs: A National Inventory.* USDA Publ. 971. Conservation Needs Inventory Committee of the U.S. Dept. Agric., 94 p.

Woodruff, N. P., 1954. *Shelterbelt and Surface Barrier Effects on Wind Velocities, Evaporation, House Heating, Snowdrifting.* Kans. Agr. Exp. Sta. Tech. Bull. 77.

Woodruff, N. P., D. W. Freyear, and L. Lyles, 1963. *Reducing Wind Velocity with Field Shelterbelts.* Kans. Agr. Exp. Sta. Tech. Bull. 131.

Woodruff, N. P., and F. H. Siddoway, 1965. A wind erosion equation. *Soil Sci. Soc. Am. Proc.* 29:602–608.

6

Predicting Soil Loss

The need to evaluate erosion losses and the effectiveness of control measures became apparent as soon as field workers started promoting conservation. U.S. Soil Conservation Service (SCS) research officers began to assess levels of erosion immediately and to study quantitatively the effects of physical characteristics and control measures on the erosion process.

Cause-and-effect relationships were worked out with individual practices and with each erosive factor. Eventually, soil loss prediction equations were devised for both water and wind erosion. Field technicians and others now have the means to predict soil loss under a wide variety of conditions. These equations are still being refined as new information becomes available, as farming practices change, and as new applications requiring erosion prediction develop.

6-1 TOLERABLE SOIL-LOSS

Tolerable soil loss was defined by Wischmeier and Smith (1978) as the maximum rate of soil erosion that will permit a high level of crop productivity to be sustained economically and indefinitely. The concept of soil loss tolerance (T values) was introduced by SCS research officers. They based their estimates on rates that would permit sufficient soil depth to remain for optimum crop growth, or that would leave enough fertility and organic matter for high crop yields, or that could be permitted and still not have gully formation. They assigned soil loss tolerances ranging from 2 to 6 tons/ac-yr (4 to 13 mt/ha-yr). This general range of tolerable losses was accepted by the SCS, but later it was agreed that 5 tons/ac-yr (11 mt/ha-yr) should be the maximum rate and that there were some soils so fragile that a rate of only 1 ton/ac-yr (2 mt/ha-yr) should be added. Thus the range of T values now used is 1 to 5 tons/ac-yr.

Four major factors affect the rate of erosion that can occur without permanent loss of soil productivity: thickness of soil, type of parent material, relative productivity of surface soil and subsoil, and amount of previous erosion. The thicker the soil (A + B horizons) and the greater the thickness of material permeable to plant roots, the faster erosion can occur without irreparable loss of productive capacity. Unconsolidated, fertile parent material such as glacial till or loess is more quickly converted into soil than is bedrock. Where surface soil is notably more fertile and productive than subsoil and parent material, loss of even small quantities of surface soil will seriously reduce productivity. A soil that has already suffered serious erosion cannot stand further losses as well as soils not previously damaged.

What do these loss rates signify? One ton of soil loss per acre is equal in weight to a uniform depth of 0.007 in. (0.18 mm) of soil from the acre. This loss seems insignificant, but if it continues for 143 years, an inch of soil will be lost; the 7-in. furrow slice will be lost in 1000 years.

No sound basis exists for tolerance soil loss values. In fact, there is considerable evidence that soil forms much slower than this. Soil does form fairly rapidly at the surface, but plants need deep soils to produce well, and subsurface layers develop slowly or very slowly, depending on the nature of the parent material.

Two studies in the U.S. Corn Belt indicate that A-horizon soil can develop fairly rapidly from B-horizon material or from raw parent material. In Iowa, 4 in. (10 cm) of surface soil, indistinguishable from normal topsoil in the area, developed on 24 in. (60 cm) of a subsoil fill in 100 to 125 years (Hallberg et al., 1978). Kohnke and Bertrand (1959) found in Indiana that 1 in. (2.5 cm) of soil developed at a 1-in. depth from glacial till in 58 years, but it took about 700 years for an inch of soil to develop if buried 24 in. (60 cm), and at 40 in. (1 m) it took over 1000 years.

Even though soil is eroded off the top, new soil to maintain soil depth must develop at the bottom of the profile. Thus, loss even at the 1 ton/ac (2.2 mt/ha) annual rate (cumulative rate of 1 in./143 yr) will not be fully replaced by the soil development rate found in Indiana until the soil depth is reduced to approximately 3 in. This makes one wonder if the "tolerable" losses mentioned above can really be tolerated.

There has been severe criticism recently of the accepted levels of tolerable loss (Johnson, 1987; Lal, 1985). This is based on a strong belief that soil is not rebuilt even under best conditions as fast as these rates require. There are many also who feel that other factors may sometimes restrict tolerable losses more than soil productivity damage alone.

Pierce et al. (1984) used the soil productivity index concept to develop a more quantitative soil loss tolerance. They mentioned two kinds of T values. One that measures the effect of erosion on physical properties that influence inherent productivity (T_1), and one that relates to other results of erosion that involve social goals (T_2). They did not mention the losses that result in fertility degradation, assuming perhaps that these losses can be made good by the use of fertilizers and by adopting other technological advances that will help to maintain or even increase crop yields in the short term.

Soils that are highly buffered against losses in productive capacity may need to be assigned tolerable loss values lower than the T_1 value because losses cause other problems. For example, more stringent restrictions may be needed to reduce pollution and sedimentation to acceptable levels in critical areas. Lower tolerable limits also may be necessary to prevent damage to crops by wind-driven soil (Hayes, 1965). Some crops are extremely sensitive; others are quite resistant to abrasion damage. Production of the more sensitive plants requires that soil losses be kept lower than the usual tolerable limits.

6-2 DEVELOPMENT OF A WATER-EROSION PREDICTION EQUATION

The first equations for predicting soil losses from water erosion were developed in the 1940s. Zingg (1940a, 1940b), Smith (1941), and Browning et al. (1947) developed equations for the midwestern United States that initially involved only slope steepness and length, then crops and special management practices were added, and finally, inherent soil erodibility was included. Musgrave (1947) reported the results of a workshop at which a new equation was developed that included a rainfall factor.

The staff of the USDA Agricultural Research Service made important contributions to the understanding of water erosion and particularly to the development of the soil-loss prediction equation. A rainfall-erosion index that accounts for a very large proportion of the soil-loss variation from storm to storm was defined (Wischmeier, 1959). A method for evaluating a cropping-management factor was also developed (Wischmeier, 1960).

6-3 WATER-EROSION PREDICTION EQUATION

Wischmeier and Smith (1965) proposed a method for estimating sheet and rill erosion losses from cultivated fields. This is now called the Universal Soil Loss Equation (USLE). The equation is

$$A = R \times K \times LS \times C \times P$$

where A = estimated average annual soil loss, tons/ac-yr
R = rainfall and runoff factor, 100s of ft-tons/ac-yr
K = soil-erodibility factor, soil loss per unit of rainfall-erosivity index from bare fallow on a 9% slope 72.6 ft (22.1 m) long, tons (of soil)/100 ft-tons (of rainfall)
LS = slope length and steepness factor, dimensionless
C = cover-management factor, dimensionless
P = supporting-practice factor, dimensionless

This equation predicts long-term average annual soil losses under specific conditions of climate, soil, topography, land use, and management practices

(Wischmeier, 1976). A represents losses by sheet and rill erosion but does not include soil eroded from gullies.

6-3.1 Rainfall Erosion Index (R)

Wischmeier (1959) found that total energy (E) and maximum 30-minute intensity (I_{30}) were the rainstorm characteristics most closely related to amount of erosion produced. Units for E are 100 ft-tons/ac (energy per acre); units for I_{30} are in./hr, but are converted to a dimensionless scale factor by dividing by 1 in./hr. EI_{30} values are calculated for each storm that exceeds 0.5 in. (13 mm) of rain from recording rain gauge charts. Individual e values for each uniform intensity period are obtained from the chart and Table 6-1. The E value for the storm equals $\Sigma\, e/100$. Maximum I_{30} value for the storm is also read from the charts. EI for a storm is the product of its E and I_{30} values. Energy values in Table 6-1 are based on the progressive increases in average drop size, velocity of fall, and kinetic energy that occur as rainfall intensity increases up to 3 in./hr (75 mm/h). Above this intensity drop size does not increase (Hudson, 1981, p. 68; McGregor and Mutchler, 1977).

The EI_{30} values for computed storms are summed over the years of record and divided by years to arrive at an average annual value, R (units are 100 ft-tons/ac-yr). EI_{30} is a statistical interaction that shows how energy of fall and maximum intensity combine to detach and transport soil particles. The factor for converting to metric equivalents (MJ/ha-yr) is 17.02 (Foster et al., 1981).

Average annual R values for the eastern two-thirds of the United States were

TABLE 6-1 KINETIC ENERGY, e, IN FT-TONS/AC, PER INCH OF PRECIPITATION AS INFLUENCED BY RAINFALL INTENSITY, I, IN IN./HR, BASED ON THE EQUATION $e = 916 + 331 \log_{10} I$

I (in./hr)	Rainfall intensity, I, (in./hr)									
	0.00	0.01	0.02	0.03	0.04	0.05	0.06	0.07	0.08	0.09
0	000	254	354	412	453	485	512	534	553	570
0.1	585	599	611	623	633	643	653	661	669	677
0.2	685	692	698	705	711	717	722	728	733	738
0.3	743	748	752	757	761	765	769	773	777	781
0.4	784	788	791	795	798	801	804	807	810	814
0.5	816	819	822	825	827	830	833	835	838	840
0.6	843	845	847	850	852	854	856	858	861	863
0.7	865	867	869	871	873	875	877	878	880	882
0.8	884	886	887	889	891	893	894	896	898	899
0.9	901	902	904	906	907	909	910	912	913	915
	0.0	0.1	0.2	0.3	0.4	0.5	0.6	0.7	0.8	0.9
1	916	930	942	954	964	974	984	992	1000	1008
2	1016	1023	1029	1036	1042	1048	1053	1059	1064	1069
3	1074[a]									

[a]All intensities greater than 3.0 in./hr also have e = 1074.

Source: Wischmeier and Smith, 1978.

calculated originally using data from 181 weather stations. Values were plotted and lines called iso-erodents were drawn through points of equal rainfall erosivity (Wischmeier, 1962). The map was later expanded to include the western states (Figure 6–1). For points between lines, R values must be interpolated. Interpolated values are not as accurate in the west as in the east because of irregular changes in rainfall associated with rapid changes in elevation. Renard et al. (1991) used data from many more locations and published more detailed iso-erodent maps for (1) 37 eastern states, (2) 8 mountain states, (3) Washington and Oregon, (4) California, and (5) Hawaii.

Continental U.S. values of R range from more than 700 in southeast Louisiana to less than 10 in the driest part of New Mexico and in many mountainous regions. In general, rainfall erosiveness in the United States is greater than it is in Europe, but less than it is in many tropical regions (Bergsma, 1981).

R values have been established for Africa (Arnoldus, 1977; Kalman, 1967; Masson, 1971; Masson and Kalms, 1971; and Roose, 1977), for Iraq (Hussein, 1986), for Zimbabwe (Elwell and Stocking, 1973), and for Australia (Rosewell, 1986).

Melting snow runoff affects erosion significantly in some areas, but there is little agreement on a method for taking it into account. Wischmeier and Smith (1978) suggested multiplying winter precipitation in inches of water by 1.5 and

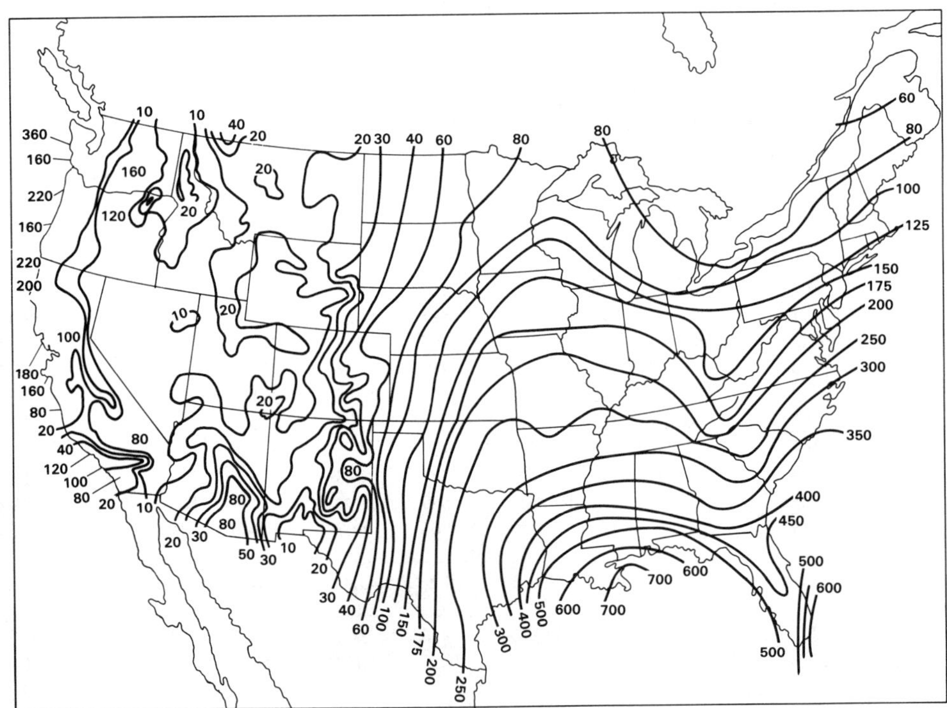

Figure 6–1 Rainfall erosion index (R) values in units of 100 ft-ton/ac-yr for the conterminous United States. (Modified from Renard et al., 1991.)

adding the product to the R value obtained in the conventional way. Renard et al. (1991) suggest changing SL factors for these situations.

Yearly distribution of erosive storms must be considered in assessing climatic erosiveness. Renard et al. (1991) delineated 119 zones in mainland United States with different yearly R distribution patterns. Figure 6–2 shows seasonally cumulative R patterns for three different zones.

6–3.2 Soil Erodibility Factor (K)

K values represent inherent erodibilities of soils. K is the rate of soil loss in tons per unit of R under standard conditions (9% slope, 72.6 ft or 22.1 m long, kept fallow by periodic tillage up and down the slope). Units of K are tons/100 ft-ton (tons of soil loss per unit of rainfall energy) (mt/MJ). $A = RK$ and has units of tons/ac-yr (mt/ha-yr). Numerical values of K in the metric system are 0.1317 times as large as those in the tons/ac system.

Several K values were obtained directly from measurements on soil conservation experiment stations. A few were calculated from erosion measurements on row-crop plots, corrected for vegetative cover. Many were determined by use of a rainfall simulator on small plots. Still others were estimated using a relationship between soil properties and soil erodibility developed by Wischmeier et al. (1971) (see Figure 6–3).

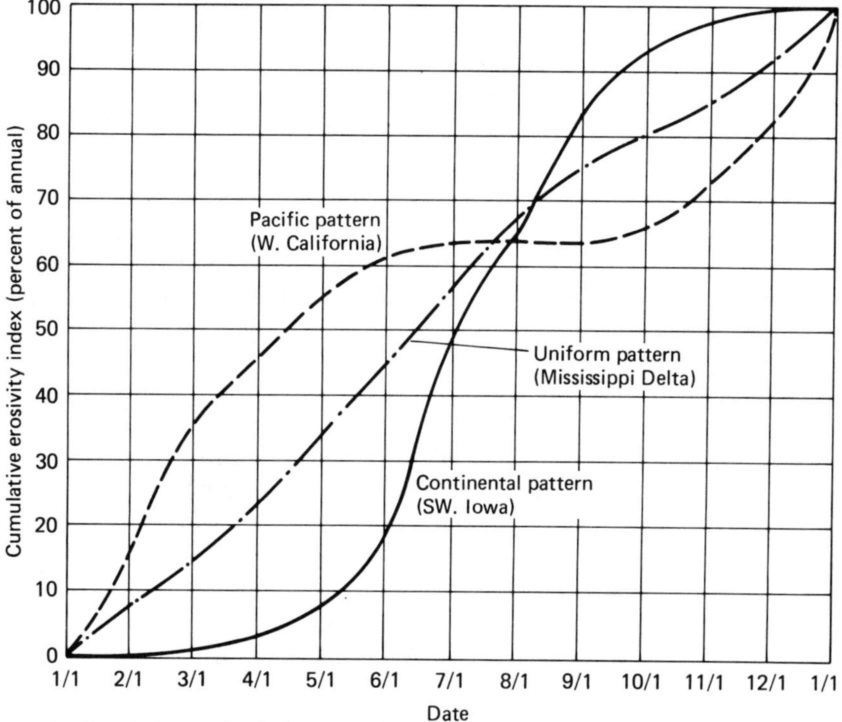

Figure 6–2 Cumulative erosion index curves for continental, Pacific, and uniform patterns of rainfall distribution. (Modified from Wischmeier and Smith, 1978.)

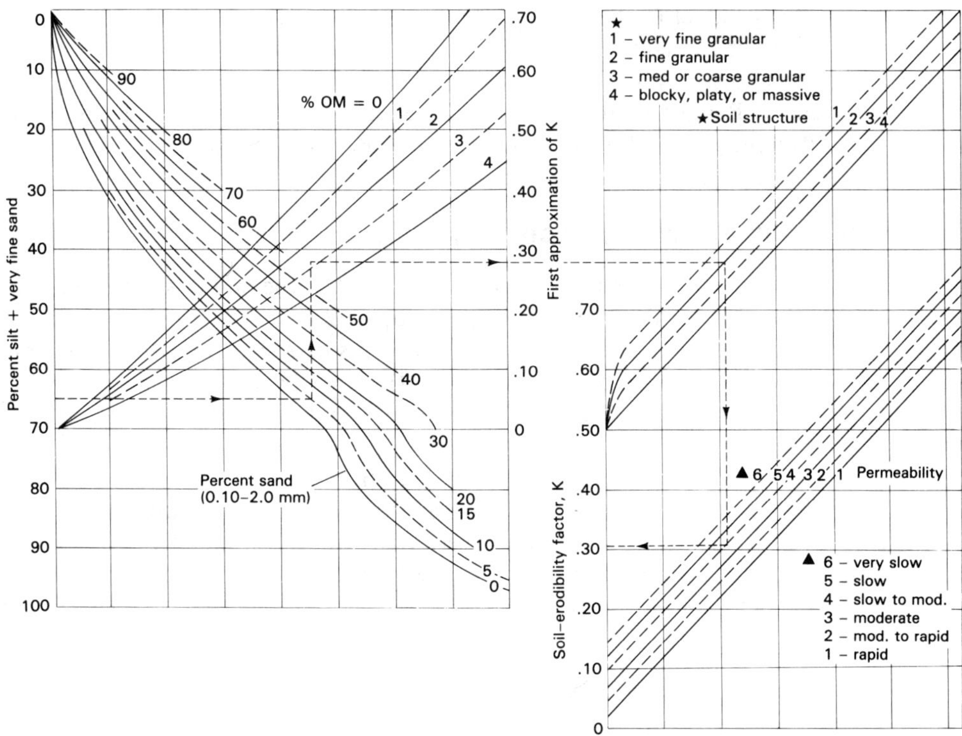

Figure 6–3 A nomograph to determine the soil-erodibility factor, *K*, from percent silt plus very fine sand (0.002 to 0.1 mm), percent sand (0.1 to 2.0 mm), percent organic matter, soil structure, and soil permeability. The dashed line shows how the nomograph is used to obtain a *K* value of 0.31 for a soil having 65% silt + very fine sand, 5% sand, 2.8% organic matter, fine granular structure, and slow to moderate permeability. This same sequence of properties must always be used to obtain *K* values from the nomograph. (From Wischmeier and Smith, 1978.)

Using measured and estimated *K* values as guides, the ARS/SCS have assigned additional *K* values to many other soils on the basis of known soil properties and observed erodibility. A few representative *K* values are presented in Table 6–2.

6–3.3 Slope Factor (*LS*)

Slope length is the horizontal distance downslope from the point where overland flow begins to where runoff enters a waterway or where deposition starts. Erosion is proportional to slope length raised to a power, *m*. Values of *m* range from 0.02 to >0.8 as slope steepness and rill/interrill sediment ratios increase.

The standard slope length used in determining *K* values is 72.6 ft (22.1 m). Thus

$$L = \left(\frac{\text{field slope length}}{72.6} \right)^m$$

TABLE 6-2 COMPUTED SOIL-ERODIBILITY (*K*) AND TOLERABLE SOIL-LOSS (*T*) VALUES FOR SOILS ON EROSION RESEARCH STATIONS

Soil type	Location	K[a] (tons/100 ft-ton)	T[b] (tons/ac)
Albia gravelly loam	Beemerville, NJ	0.03	–
Austin clay	Temple, TX	0.29	2
Bath flaggy silt loam with surface stones > 2 in. removed	Arnot, NY	0.05[c]	3
Boswell fine sandy loam	Tyler, TX	0.25	5
Cecil clay loam	Watkinsville, GA	0.26	4
Cecil sandy clay loam	Watkinsville, GA	0.36	3
Cecil sandy loam	Clemson, SC	0.28[c]	3
Cecil sandy loam	Watkinsville, GA	0.23	3
Dunkirk silt loam	Geneva, NY	0.69[c]	3
Fayette silt loam	LaCrosse, WI	0.38[c]	5
Freehold loamy sand	Marlboro, NJ	0.08	4
Hagerstown silty clay loam	University Park, PA	0.31[c]	4
Honeoye silt loam	Marcellus, NY	0.28[c]	3
Ida silt loam	Castana, IA	0.33	5
Keene silt loam	Zanesville, OH	0.48	4
Lodi loam	Blacksburg, VA	0.39	–
Mansic clay loam	Hays, KS	0.32	4
Marshall silt loam	Clarinda, IA	0.33	5
Mexico silt loam	McCredie, MO	0.28	3
Ontario loam	Geneva, NY	0.27[c]	–
Shelby loam	Bethany, MO	0.41	5
Tifton loamy sand	Tifton, GA	0.10	4
Zaneis fine sandy loam	Guthrie, OK	0.22	4

[a]Metric units in mt/MJ are 0.1317 times as large as these.

[b]Metric units in mt/ha are 2.24 times as large as these.

[c]Evaluated from continuous fallow. All others computed from row crop data.

Source: Modified from Wischmeier and Smith, 1978.

Renard et al. (1991) present m values for a variety of gradients and rill/interrill sediment ratios (Table 6–3).

Slope steepness is defined as the gradient expressed in units of vertical rise or fall per unit of horizontal distance (decimal fraction) or per 100 units of horizontal distance (percent). It is more convenient in the field to determine slope as the vertical fall per unit of distance along the land surface. Differences are negligible for gentle grades, but increase as slopes become steeper.

S in the LS factor is based on the percent slope as calculated by the land surface approach adjusted so that the standard 9% slope has a value of 1.0. S can be calculated from the equations

$$S = \begin{cases} 10.8s + 0.03 & s < 9\% \\ 16.8s - 0.50 & s = 9\% \text{ or more} \end{cases}$$

TABLE 6-3 SLOPE LENGTH EXPONENTS FOR A RANGE OF SLOPES AND RILL/INTERRILL EROSION CLASSES

	Rill/interrill ratio		
Percent slope (%)	Low (Pasture and range)	Moderate (Cultivated)	High (Excessively erodible)
0.5	0.04	0.08	0.16
1	0.08	0.15	0.26
2	0.14	0.24	0.39
3	0.18	0.31	0.47
4	0.22	0.36	0.53
5	0.25	0.40	0.57
6	0.28	0.43	0.60
8	0.32	0.48	0.65
10	0.35	0.52	0.68
12	0.37	0.55	0.71
14	0.40	0.57	0.72
16	0.41	0.59	0.74
18	0.42	0.60	0.75
20	0.44	0.61	0.76

Source: Modified from Renard et al., 1991.

where s is the vertical fall per unit (decimal fraction) along the land surface (McCool et al., 1987). Slope length and steepness are combined into a single LS factor which is

$$LS = \begin{cases} \left(\dfrac{\text{field slope length}}{72.6}\right)^{m} (10.8s + 0.03) & s < 9\% \\ \left(\dfrac{\text{field slope length}}{72.6}\right)^{m} (16.8s - 0.50) & s = 9\% \text{ or more} \end{cases}$$

Calculated LS values for various slopes and rill to interrill sediment ratios are shown in Tables 6–4A, 6–4B, 6–4C, and 6–4D. Slope lengths used in the development of the equations and Tables 6–4 were relatively short and uniform. Derived LS values work well for ordinary field conditions. Where slopes are very gentle, complex, or unusually long, values may not be accurate.

There is evidence that losses from slopes <3% are smaller than the USLE predicts (Murphree and Mutchler, 1981). This may be due to the cushioning effect of thick layers of surface water, rather than to an error in the LS factor. They suggested a change in R value as more appropriate than a change in LS values.

Shape of slope also affects average soil loss and relative loss from different segments of an irregular slope. Convex surfaces cause greater losses than uniform surfaces of the same average gradient; concave slopes cause smaller losses. Complex slopes (convex at the top and concave at the bottom) lose soil at slower rates than simple convex or uniform slopes, but faster than simple concave slopes. A method for predicting soil losses from irregular slopes is presented in Section 6–5.4.

TABLE 6-4A VALUES FOR TOPOGRAPHIC FACTOR (*LS*) FOR LOW-RATIO RILL TO INTERRILL EROSION, SUCH AS FOR RANGELAND

Slope (%)	Slope length (ft)											
	25	50	75	100	150	200	300	400	500	600	800	1000
0.5	0.08	0.08	0.08	0.09	0.09	0.09	0.09	0.09	0.09	0.09	0.09	0.09
1	0.13	0.13	0.14	0.14	0.15	0.15	0.15	0.16	0.16	0.16	0.17	0.17
2	0.21	0.23	0.25	0.26	0.27	0.28	0.30	0.31	0.32	0.33	0.34	0.35
3	0.29	0.33	0.36	0.38	0.40	0.43	0.46	0.48	0.50	0.52	0.55	0.57
4	0.36	0.43	0.46	0.50	0.54	0.58	0.63	0.67	0.70	0.74	0.78	0.82
5	0.44	0.52	0.57	0.62	0.68	0.73	0.81	0.87	0.92	0.97	1.0	1.1
6	0.50	0.61	0.68	0.74	0.83	0.90	1.0	1.1	1.2	1.2	1.3	1.4
8	0.64	0.79	0.90	0.99	1.1	1.2	1.4	1.5	1.6	1.7	1.9	2.0
10	0.81	1.0	1.2	1.3	1.5	1.7	1.9	2.1	2.3	2.5	2.7	2.9
12	1.0	1.3	1.5	1.7	2.0	2.2	2.6	2.8	3.1	3.3	3.7	4.0
14	1.2	1.6	1.8	2.1	2.4	2.7	3.2	3.6	3.9	4.2	4.7	5.2
16	1.4	1.8	2.2	2.5	2.9	3.3	3.9	4.4	4.8	5.2	5.8	6.4
18	1.6	2.1	2.5	2.8	3.4	3.8	4.6	5.2	5.7	6.1	6.9	7.6
20	1.7	2.4	2.8	3.2	3.8	4.4	5.2	6.0	6.5	7.1	8.1	8.9

Source: Modified from Renard et al., 1991.

TABLE 6-4B VALUES FOR TOPOGRAPHIC FACTOR (*LS*) FOR MODERATE-RATIO RILL TO INTERRILL EROSION, SUCH AS FOR ROW-CROPPED AGRICULTURAL AND OTHER MODERATELY CONSOLIDATED SOIL CONDITIONS WITH MODERATE COVER

Slope (%)	Slope length (ft)											
	25	50	75	100	150	200	300	400	500	600	800	1000
0.5	0.08	0.08	0.08	0.09	0.09	0.09	0.09	0.10	0.10	0.10	0.10	0.10
1	0.12	0.13	0.14	0.14	0.15	0.16	0.17	0.18	0.18	0.19	0.20	0.20
2	0.19	0.22	0.25	0.27	0.29	0.31	0.35	0.37	0.39	0.41	0.44	0.47
3	0.25	0.32	0.36	0.39	0.44	0.48	0.55	0.60	0.64	0.68	0.75	0.80
4	0.31	0.40	0.47	0.52	0.60	0.67	0.77	0.86	0.93	0.99	1.1	1.2
5	0.37	0.49	0.58	0.65	0.76	0.85	1.0	1.1	1.2	1.3	1.5	1.6
6	0.43	0.58	0.69	0.78	0.93	1.0	1.2	1.4	1.6	1.7	1.9	2.1
8	0.53	0.74	0.91	1.0	1.3	1.4	1.8	2.0	2.2	2.5	2.8	3.2
10	0.67	0.97	1.2	1.4	1.7	2.0	2.4	2.8	3.2	3.5	4.1	4.6
12	0.84	1.2	1.5	1.8	2.2	2.6	3.3	3.8	4.3	4.8	5.6	6.3
14	1.0	1.5	1.9	2.2	2.8	3.2	4.1	4.8	5.4	6.1	7.2	8.1
16	1.2	1.7	2.2	2.6	3.3	3.9	5.0	5.9	6.5	7.4	8.8	10.0
18	1.3	2.0	2.6	3.0	3.8	4.6	5.8	6.9	7.9	8.8	9.5	12.0
20	1.4	2.2	2.8	3.4	4.4	5.2	6.7	8.0	9.1	10.2	12.2	14.0

Source: Modified from Renard et al., 1991.

6-3.4 Cover-Management Factor (C)

Cover-management effects on erosion are complex and diverse. Type of crop, stage of growth, and crop and soil management are important. Some crops and crop sequences maintain good soil cover; others leave the land bare for extended periods.

TABLE 6-4C VALUES FOR TOPOGRAPHIC FACTOR (*LS*) FOR HIGH-RATIO RILL TO INTERRILL EROSION, SUCH AS FRESHLY PREPARED CONSTRUCTION AND SIMILAR HIGHLY DISTURBED SITES WITH LITTLE OR NO COVER

Slope (%)	Slope length (ft)											
	25	50	75	100	150	200	300	400	500	600	800	1000
0.5	0.07	0.08	0.08	0.09	0.09	0.10	0.10	0.11	0.11	0.12	0.12	0.13
1	0.10	0.13	0.14	0.15	0.17	0.18	0.20	0.22	0.23	0.24	0.26	0.27
2	0.16	0.21	0.25	0.28	0.33	0.37	0.43	0.48	0.52	0.56	0.63	0.69
3	0.21	0.30	0.36	0.41	0.50	0.57	0.69	0.80	0.88	0.96	1.1	1.2
4	0.26	0.38	0.47	0.55	0.68	0.79	0.98	1.1	1.3	1.4	1.6	1.9
5	0.31	0.46	0.58	0.68	0.86	1.0	1.3	1.5	1.7	1.9	2.2	2.6
6	0.36	0.54	0.69	0.82	1.0	1.2	1.6	1.9	2.2	2.4	2.9	3.3
8	0.45	0.70	0.91	1.1	1.4	1.7	2.2	2.7	3.1	3.5	4.2	4.9
10	0.57	0.91	1.2	1.5	1.9	2.3	3.1	3.8	4.4	5.0	6.0	7.0
12	0.71	1.2	1.5	1.9	2.5	3.1	4.1	5.0	5.8	6.7	8.2	9.6
14	0.85	1.4	1.9	2.3	3.1	3.8	5.1	6.3	7.4	8.4	10.4	12.2
16	0.98	1.6	2.2	2.7	3.7	4.6	6.2	7.6	8.9	10.3	12.7	15.0
18	1.1	1.9	2.5	3.2	4.3	5.3	7.2	8.9	11.0	12.1	15.0	17.7
20	1.2	2.1	2.9	3.6	4.8	6.0	8.2	10.2	12.1	13.9	17.4	20.6

Source: Modified from Renard et al., 1991.

TABLE 6-4D VALUES FOR TOPOGRAPHIC FACTOR (*LS*) FOR THAWING SOILS WHERE MOST EROSION IS CAUSED BY SURFACE FLOW

Slope (%)	Slope length (ft)											
	25	50	75	100	150	200	300	400	500	600	800	1000
0.5	0.05	0.07	0.09	0.10	0.12	0.14	0.17	0.20	0.22	0.24	0.28	0.31
1	0.08	0.11	0.14	0.16	0.20	0.23	0.28	0.32	0.36	0.40	0.46	0.51
2	0.14	0.20	0.25	0.29	0.35	0.41	0.50	0.58	0.64	0.71	0.82	0.91
3	0.21	0.29	0.36	0.42	0.51	0.59	0.72	0.83	0.92	1.0	1.2	1.3
4	0.27	0.38	0.47	0.54	0.66	0.77	0.94	1.1	1.2	1.3	1.5	1.7
5	0.33	0.47	0.58	0.67	0.82	0.94	1.2	1.3	1.5	1.6	1.9	2.1
6	0.40	0.56	0.69	0.79	0.97	1.1	1.4	1.6	1.8	2.0	2.2	2.5
8	0.52	0.74	0.91	1.0	1.3	1.5	1.8	2.1	2.3	2.6	3.0	3.3
10	0.62	0.88	1.1	1.2	1.5	1.8	2.2	2.5	2.8	3.1	3.5	4.0
12	0.70	0.98	1.2	1.4	1.7	2.0	2.4	2.8	3.1	3.4	3.9	4.4
14	0.76	1.1	1.3	1.5	1.9	2.2	2.6	3.0	3.4	3.7	4.3	4.8
16	0.82	1.2	1.4	1.6	2.0	2.3	2.9	3.3	3.7	4.0	4.7	5.2
18	0.88	1.2	1.5	1.8	2.2	2.5	3.1	3.5	3.9	4.3	5.0	5.6
20	0.94	1.3	1.6	1.9	2.3	2.7	3.2	3.8	4.2	4.6	5.3	5.9

Source: Modified from Renard et al., 1991.

Canopy density depends on planting method and on soil productivity. Tillage affects soil permeability and residue disposition. The cover-management factor (*C*) is the ratio between the amount of soil lost under specific crop-cover-management conditions and that lost when soil is fallow and cultivated regularly up and down the slope. Soil loss from a cropped field is usually much smaller than that from a continuously fallowed field.

The influence of management and plant growth change during the life of a crop. This must be assessed over time in order to calculate the crop's effect on erosion. Wischmeier and Smith (1978) described six growth stage periods for crops:

PERIOD F—*Rough fallow:* from inversion plowing to secondary tillage.

PERIOD SB—*Seedbed:* from secondary tillage for seedbed preparation until the crop has developed a 10-percent canopy cover.

PERIOD 1—*Establishment:* from the end of period SB until the crop has developed a 50-percent canopy cover (or 35-percent canopy cover for cotton).

PERIOD 2—*Development:* from the end of period 1 until canopy cover reaches 75 percent (60 percent for cotton).

PERIOD 3—*Maturing crop:* from the end of period 2 until crop harvest. This period may be subdivided on the basis of final percent canopy cover.

PERIOD 4—*Residue or stubble:* from harvest to plowing (or to new seeding if not plowed).

Continuous assessment of the cover-management factor is made possible in computer programs (e. g. RUSLE) that use models to evaluate changes in the effects of prior land use, canopy cover, surface cover, soil-surface roughness, and soil moisture on soil loss over the year. Either periodic or continuous assessments are translated into soil loss ratios that compare the amount of soil lost under specific cover-management regimes with that lost when the soil is fallow and cultivated up and down the slope.

Values for crop-stage periods were developed from analyses of thousands of plot-years of runoff and soil-loss data. These values encompass all factors of crop production that affect crop growth and erosion reduction.

Selected soil-loss ratios for several crops and sequences developed by Wischmeier and Smith (1978) are presented in Table 6–5. Line numbers in the table are from the original publication. Lines A and B compared to line 1 and the last line shows the beneficial effect of meadow in reducing erosion losses. A comparison of lines 9, 123, and 142 reveals the effects of different cultivated crops. The effect of residue cover is indicated in lines 1 and 3. The beneficial effect of reduced tillage is shown by the smaller values in lines 27 and 43 compared with those in line 1.

An estimate of C is obtained by summing the products of soil-loss ratio and percent of annual R for each growth stage period for a crop or cropping sequence. Specific steps in this procedure are described in Section 6–3.6. Many current computer solutions to USLE contain crop growth submodels that predict crop protection as the season progresses.

6–3.5 Supporting Practice Factor (P)

Special practices are frequently needed in addition to the protection provided by normal crop and soil management practices. Most common special practices for cropland are contour cultivation, contour strip cropping, and terracing. The P factor indicates the fractional amount of erosion that occurs when these special practices are used compared with what it would be without them.

TABLE 6-5 RATIO OF SOIL LOSS FROM CROPLAND TO CORRESPONDING LOSS FROM CONTINUOUS FALLOW

Line no.	Cover, crop sequence, and management	Spring residue lb	Cover after planting pct	Soil-loss ratio for cropstage period and canopy cover							
				F pct	SB pct	1 pct	2 pct	3:80 pct	3:90 pct	3:96 pct	4L pct
CORN IN MEADOWLESS ROTATION											
	Moldboard plow, conv. till										
1	Res. left, spring turnplow*	4500	–	31	55	48	38	–	–	20	23
3	Res. left, spring turnplow	2600	–	43	64	56	43	32	25	21	37
5	Res. left, fall turnplow	HP	–	44	65	53	38	–	–	20	–
9	Res. removed, spring turnplow	HP**	–	66	74	65	47	–	–	22	56
	Reduced tillage systems										
27	Notill, plant in crop residue	4500	80	–	5	5	5	–	–	5	15
43	Cons. tillage	4500	30	–	21	18	15	–	–	13	21
CORN IN SOD-BASED SYSTEMS											
	Moldboard plow, conv. till										
A*	1st year corn, spring plow	HP	–	8	22	19	17	–	–	10	14
B*	2nd year corn, spring plow	HP	–	22	44	38	32	–	–	18	20
SOYBEANS AFTER CORN											
123	Spring TP, RdL, conv. tillage	HP	–	33	60	52	38	–	20	17	38
SMALL GRAINS AFTER GRAIN CROPS											
129	Spring seeded, disked residues	4500	70	–	12	12	11	7	4	2	7
142	Fall seeded, conv. till, Rd left	HP	–	31	55	48	31	12	7	5	4
SMALL GRAINS AFTER SUMMER FALLOW											
146	Conv. tillage, after sm. grain	200	10	–	70	55	43	18	13	11	12
149	Cons. tillage, after sm. grain	1000	50	–	26	21	15	8	7	6	8
155	Cons. tillage, after row crop	1000	30	–	40	31	24	13	10	8	4
ESTABLISHED MEADOWS											
–	Grass and legume meadow	HP	–	–	–	–	–	–	–	–	0.4

*Calculated from information in Tables 5 and 5b of Wischmeier and Smith, 1978.

**HP = high productivity - 3- to 5-ton hay yields, 4500 lbs of spring residue.

Source: Modified from Wischmeier and Smith, 1978.

Contour Cultivation (P_c). Cultivating and planting on the contour, as opposed to farming up and downhill or parallel to field borders, is called contour cultivation. Ridges across the direction of runoff flow reduce erosion during low-to-moderate intensity rainstorms when gullying does not occur. Contouring is much less effective on gullied fields.

Wischmeier and Smith (1978) evaluated the effectiveness of contour cultivation from slope gradient. Renard et al. (1990) present a method that considers rainstorm intensity, size of contour ridges, and the degree that the ridges deviate from the strict contour in addition to slope gradient. A contouring subfactor (P_b) is derived from slope gradient and oriented ridge height (Table 6-6) and adjusted for expected storm erosivity to obtain an erosivity subfactor, P_r by means of Figure 6-4. The modified contour practice value (P_c) is obtained by using Figure 6-5 to adjust (P_r) for the row-grade variable (slope gradient along the rows/field slope gradient).

The determination of (P_c) can be illustrated by assuming a field with an 8-percent slope gradient, an average ridge height of 4 in. with an average slope gradient of 1 percent along the ridges, and an *EI* value of 80 for the anticipated maximum 10-yr storm (Note: 10-yr maximum storm erosivity values for 172 locations in the United States and Puerto Rico can be found in Table 18 of Wischmeier and Smith, 1978). A P_b value of 0.5 is read from Table 6-6 for 4-in. ridges on an 8-percent slope gradient. In Figure 6-4, projecting a line upward from the value of 80 on the *EI* scale to the curve for a P_b value of 0.5 and then horizontally to the Y axis leads to a value of 0.4 for P_r. The row grade/field slope ratio for this field is 1%/8% or 0.125. A line projected upward from 0.125 on the X-axis of the left-hand

TABLE 6-6 CONTOURING SUBFACTOR VALUES (Pb) FOR CONDITIONS WHERE TILLAGE MARKS ARE ORIENTED ALONG THE CONTOUR

Downhill slope %	Height of ridge or oriented roughness		
	Low (1–3″)	Moderate (3–5″)	Ridge system (>5″)
0.5	1.0	0.8	0.8
1	0.9	0.7	0.7
2	0.9	0.6	0.5
3	0.9	0.5	0.3
4	0.8	0.5	0.3
5	0.8	0.5	0.2
6	0.8	0.5	0.2
8	0.8	0.5	0.2
10	0.8	0.6	0.2
12	0.9	0.6	0.2
14	0.9	0.6	0.3
16	1.0	0.7	0.3
18		0.7	0.3
20		0.8	0.4
23		1.0	0.6
25			0.7
30			0.9

Source: Modified from Renard et al., 1991.

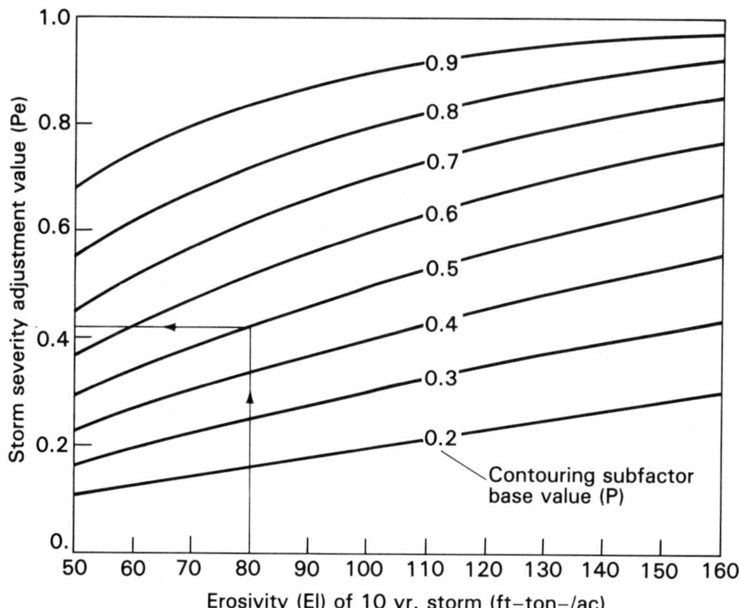

Figure 6–4 Effect of the 10-year storm erosivity on the contouring subfactor, P_b. The line with arrows on it illustrates how the graph is used for the example explained in the text. Source: Renard et al., 1991.

member of Figure 6–5 to the curve, then horizontally to the line for $P_r = 0.4$ in the right-hand member, and then downward to the X-axis gives a P_c value of about 0.6.

Contouring loses effectiveness on the lower parts of long slopes. Table 6–7 contains critical slope lengths for contouring on various slope gradients. The determination of P_c outlined in the preceding paragraph is based on the assumption that the slopes are no longer than the critical slope lengths. Additional measures may be needed to reduce soil losses on longer slopes.

Contour Strip Cropping (P_s). Contour strip cropping intersperses contour strips of sod in cultivated fields. The sod reduces erosion on the areas it occupies and traps sediment that moves from cultivated strips. The greater the proportion of sod, the more effective the system. P_s values are given in Table 6–7. The effectiveness of contour strip cropping is calculated by multiplying these P_s values by the P_c values discussed in the preceding paragraphs. Alternating different small grains and row crops without sod strips generally is not very effective (see column C in Table 6–7). Some benefit may be obtained on slope gradients $<3\%$ if the small grain strips are extra wide and include a winter cover seeding.

Terracing (P_t). Terraces combined with contour cultivation are very effective in reducing erosion. Terracing is effective because it reduces slope length and because it causes deposition of eroded soil within the field. Initially terracing was evaluated only on its reduction of slope length. Foster and Highfill (1983) suggested weighting terrace benefits (P_t) according to the effect terrace interval and channel grade have on deposition (see Table 6–8).

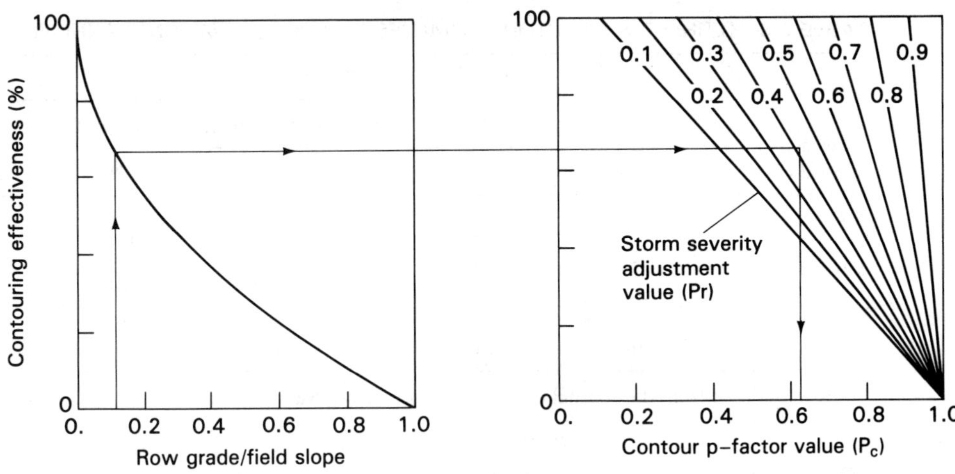

Figure 6–5 Adjustment to the contouring subfactor based on furrow grade on the left graph and determination of the contour factor-value (P_c) on the right graph. The line with the arrows illustrates how the graph is used for the example explained in the text. Source: Renard et al., 1990.

The final P value for a cropping system is obtained by calculating an appropriate value for P_c as outlined above and multiplying it by the proper value for P_t from Table 6–8. For example, assume that a 4% sloping field is contour cultivated and has underground-outlet terraces with distances from terrace ridge to the terrace channel below of 90 ft (27.5 m) and with 0.2% channel grade. A rotation of corn, oats, and two years of meadow is used, but strip cropping is not employed. The 10-yr EI value is 80, and the field has 4-in. ridges paralleling the terraces. Following the procedure already outlined for evaluating P_c, P_b = 0.5 (from Table 6–6), P_r =

TABLE 6–7 EROSION-CONTROL PRACTICE-FACTOR VALUES FOR STRIP CROPPING (P_s), RECOMMENDED SLOPE-LENGTH LIMITS FOR CONTOURING, AND MAXIMUM STRIP WIDTHS AND SLOPE-LENGTH LIMITS FOR CONTOUR STRIP CROPPING

	Contouring	Contour strip cropping				
	Maximum	P_s[a]			Maximum	Maximum
Land slope (%)	slope length (ft)	A	B	C	strip width (ft)	slope length (ft)
1–2	400	0.50	0.75	0.90	130	800
3–5	300	0.50	0.75	1.00	100	600
6–8	200	(these values are the same			100	400
9–12	120	for the steeper slope			80	240
13–16	80	gradients)			80	160
17–20	60				60	120
21–25	50				50	100

[a]A, for 4-yr rotation, row crop, small grain with meadow seeding, 2-yr meadow; B, for 4-yr rotation, 2-yr row crop, winter grain with meadow seeding, one-yr meadow; C, for alternate strips of row crop and small grain. The original publication lists a value of 1.0 (no credit) for small grain strips, but other sources suggest some reduction in soil loss, especially on slopes less than 3%.

Source: Modified from Wischmeier and Smith, 1978.

TABLE 6-8 TERRACE SUBFACTOR (P_t) VALUES FOR CONSERVATION PLANNING

Terrace interval (ft)	P_t subvalue				
	Closed outlets	Open outlets, with terrace grade of:			
		0.1–0.3%	0.4–0.7%	0.7–0.8%	>0.8%
<110	0.5	0.6	0.7	0.8	1.0
110–135	0.6	0.7	0.8	0.9	1.0
136–175	0.7	0.8	0.8	0.9	1.0
176–225	0.8	0.8	0.9	0.9	1.0
226–300	0.9	0.9	0.9	1.0	1.0
>300	1.0	1.0	1.0	1.0	1.0

Source: Modified from the Journal of Soil and Water Conservation, Volume 38, p. 48–51, 1983 (Foster and Highfill).

0.4 (from Figure 6–4), and the value of P_c is 0.6 (from Figure 6–5). P_t (from Table 6–8) is 0.6.

$$P = P_c \times P_t = 0.6 \times 0.6 = 0.36$$

Contouring and terracing reduce erosion in this field by 64% in addition to the slope-length reduction brought about by terracing. The effect of terraces on amount of sediment loss from fields is determined by using Table 6–9. The sediment yield factor for the example above is

$$P = P_c \times P_y = 0.6 \times 0.17 = 0.102$$

Only about 10% of the soil lost from the terrace interval will leave this field.

6-3.6 Predicting Soil Loss for a Particular Field

Factors set forth in the preceding sections are combined to predict soil loss. Calculation of the average soil loss from a field planted to continuous corn on a Marshall

TABLE 6-9 SEDIMENT DELIVERY SUBFACTOR (P_y) FOR TERRACING

Terrace channel grade (%)	Delivery subfactor, P_y
Closed outlet[a]	0.05
0.0 (level)	0.10
0.1	0.13
0.2	0.17
0.4	0.29
0.6	0.49
0.8	0.83
0.9	1.00
> 0.9[b]	1.00 or more

[a]Includes terraces with underground outlets.

[b]If net erosion occurs from terrace channel, P_y may exceed 1.00.

Source: From the Journal of Soil and Water Conservation, Volume 38, p. 48–51, 1983 (Foster and Highfill).

silt loam in southwestern Iowa will serve as an example. The field has a slope gradient of 8% and length of 500 ft (150 m), crop residue amounting to 4500 lb/acre remains on the field in the spring, the land is turn plowed in early April, and the seedbed is prepared subsequently by disking and harrowing. Planting and harvesting dates are May 15 and October 15, and no special erosion-control practices are employed.

Values for *R, K,* and *LS* are obtained from Figure 6–1, Table 6–2, and Table 6–4B, respectively. *C* is calculated in Table 6–10 and is equal to 0.37. *P* is 1.0 because no special practices are employed.

$$A = 175 \times 0.33 \times 2.2 \times 0.37 \times 1.0 = 47 \text{ tons/ac-yr}$$

This predicted soil loss is over nine times the tolerable rate for Marshall silt loam.

Several changes can be made to reduce the rate of soil loss. Minimum tillage can be used; contouring can be employed; terraces can be installed; or a crop rotation including meadow can be used. One low-cost combination that might be considered is minimum tillage and contouring. The *C* factor would drop to 0.15 (based on line 43 from Table 6–5, instead of line 1 as used in Table 6–10) and a *P* factor of 0.6 would be introduced for contouring (assuming a value equal to that obtained in the contouring example):

$$A = 175 \times 0.33 \times 2.2 \times 0.15 \times 0.6 = 11 \text{ tons/ac-yr}$$

This is still excessive for this one crop, and in addition, the field slope is too long for safe use of contouring. Strip cropping or terraces, or a year or more of meadow in rotation will be needed to bring the average erosion rate down below the tolerable limit.

An open terrace system with 100–ft terrace intervals and 0.2% channel grade would give an *LS* value of 1.0 (Table 6–4B), a P_c of 0.6 (Figures 6–4 and 6–5 and Table 6–6), and a P_t of 0.6 (Table 6–8). With this system in place,

$$A = 175 \times 0.33 \times 1.0 \times 0.15 \times (0.6 \times 0.6) = 3 \text{ tons/ac-yr}$$

Erosion predictions made with USLE for individual farms are anticipated long-term losses under normal conditions and average management. There are many

TABLE 6–10 CALCULATIONS FOR COVER-MANAGEMENT FACTOR (*C*) FOR THE CONTINUOUS CORN EXAMPLE CITED IN TEXT

Crop	Crop stage period	Crop stage dates	Curve values[a]	*EI* for crop period	Soil-loss ratio[b]	*C* value
			%	%	%	%
Corn in	F	Apr 1–Apr 21	3–7	4	31	1
meadowless	SB	Apr 21–May 31	7–18	11	55	6
rotation with	1	May 31–Jul 5	18–54	36	48	17
4500 lbs residue	2	Jul 5–Aug 8	54–69	15	38	6
remaining in the	3	Aug 8–Oct 15	69–97	28	20	6
spring	4L	Oct 15–Apr 1	97–3	6	23	1
				100		37

[a]Values taken from curve for southwest Iowa in Figure 6–2.

[b]From line 1, Table 6–5

farms that are managed in unconventional ways, so there will be cases where predicted losses will be larger or smaller than those actually taking place. Jackson (1988) studied a farm in Ohio that had been operated by the same Amish family in the same way for 150 years. Predicted soil loss was 15 tons/ac-yr (a loss equivalent to more than 15 in. of soil depth over the entire farm during that period). But the soils of the farm still matched the Wooster silt loam soil description as to horizon depth and other properties. Accordingly, actual erosion losses must have been near the rate of soil renewal.

6-3.7 Use of the Soil Loss Prediction Equation with Metric Units

In order to use the USLE where metric units are standard, it is necessary to convert some of the tables and figures presented above to metric equivalents. Foster et al. (1981) present mathematical transformations to metric units. They include a table for determining e values from metric measurements, a metric R-value map of the United States, and a metricized figure that may be used to determine K values from texture, organic matter, structure, and permeability information.

C values, which are dimensionless, can be obtained from tables in Wischmeier and Smith (1978) or from the computer programs mentioned in Section 6-10.

6-4 FIELD USE OF THE WATER-EROSION PREDICTION EQUATION

The water-erosion prediction equation was developed primarily to help field workers assess current erosion levels and plan control measures for cultivated farm fields. Several calculations need to be made for each field proposal developed.

To make the job easier and less time consuming, a special slide rule was developed that had fairly wide use. Later, SCS state staffs used computers to develop tables of data that permitted fieldmen to select values rather than calculate them, with great time savings. More recently, computer programs have been designed to solve the equation and develop resource material. One program currently being field tested on a massive scale is the Computer Assisted Management and Planning System (CAMPS). This software package was planned under SCS guidance. It is used in district offices to develop conservation plans and engineering designs for conservation measures, to compute soil loss, make soil interpretations, and track conservation progress. It is also used to manage workloads, develop public mailings, and prepare reports.

In October 1989, 2540 Soil Conservation District offices (80.5% of all districts) were using CAMPS. An additional 240 offices (11.9%) had computers but were not yet using CAMPS software. The program is being expanded into additional offices as rapidly as funds become available. Other computer programs and models are described in Section 6-10.

6-5 EXPANDED USE OF THE PREDICTION EQUATION

The USLE was designed to estimate sheet and rill erosion from cultivated fields in the United States east of the Rocky Mountains (Wischmeier and Smith, 1965). With modifications, it now has much wider geographic application and much broader use than predicting soil losses from farm fields. Still, care must be exercised to ensure that it is not being misused (Wischmeier, 1976). Examples of legitimate use of the USLE in new areas and for new purposes follow.

6-5.1 Regions Adjacent to the Original Thirty-Seven States

Snowmelt runoff and rain falling on thawing soils cause erosion losses larger than those predicted by the usual USLE *R* values. This is particularly a problem in the Palouse Region of the Pacific Northwest. Zuzel et al. (1982) reported that 12 of 14 runoff events they studied in northeastern Oregon were increased significantly by runoff caused by either snowmelt or by rain on thawing soils. Renard et al. (1991) developed an equation to calculate an equivalent *R* factor for such areas:

$$(R_{eq})_{wr} = -37.64 + 6.278 \text{ P}$$

where $(R_{eq})_{wr}$ = equivalent *R* factor for winter rilling

P = annual precipitation (in.)

Renard et al. (1991) also developed special *LS* data for thawing soils when most of the erosion is caused by surface flow. This information (Table 6-4D) should be used for regions where snowmelt is a serious factor in soil erosion.

R values have been calculated for the 11 western states and for Hawaii. Wischmeier and Smith (1978) provided initial values for these areas, but Renard et al. (1991) give more detailed information.

McGregor et al. (1980) have found that *R* values calculated from recent rainfall records in northern Mississippi are significantly higher than the ones presented by Wischmeier and Smith (1965, 1978). This fact is taken into account in local use of the equation.

The USLE predicts losses by sheet and rill erosion, but not from concentrated flow. Concentrated flow losses are usually much less than from the other two types, but they are important where they occur and should be included in soil-loss predictions. Foster and Lane (1983) measured sediment losses in accelerated runoff and estimates of these losses have been included in some computer models. The Chemicals, Runoff, and Erosion from Agricultural Management Systems (CREAMS) program was developed to predict the sediment load carried by gully flow as well as that carried in sheet and rill erosion (Knisel, 1980).

6-5.2 Regions with Limited Factor Value Data

Problems posed in expanding use of the USLE to new areas where basic data are available are usually fairly easy to solve. It is not so easy to develop a plan for use in countries lacking these data.

It is not essential to have all desirable information before starting to use the main concepts of the equation. Most countries have some data on at least some of the factors. In west Africa, for example, Roose (1977) studied the limited climatic data available and proposed that R values can be developed for west Africa from the average annual rainfall (H) in millimeters with an error of 5% or less from the equation

$$R = 0.85H$$

He made a first approximation of the relative rainfall erosivity in each country and developed an iso-erodent map of the area between the desert and the South Atlantic from Senegal to Chad.

Similarly, Hussein (1986) found weather records in Iraq insufficient to determine accurate EI_{30} values. Instead, he used the equation developed by Arnoldus (1977):

$$EI_{30} = 0.0302 \left(\frac{\sum_{i=1}^{n} p_i^2}{P} \right)^{1.93}$$

where EI_{30} is in metric units,

P = average annual rainfall, mm

p_i = average monthly rainfall, mm

n = number of rainy months

Values obtained ranged from <5 to >700 MJ/ha-yr. He prepared an iso-erodent map. He also obtained monthly contributions to annual EI_{30} values by using sums of squares of monthly rainfall. With these data as a first approximation, he predicted sheet and rill erosion with the USLE in northern Iraq.

Agricultural officers should also realize that only 23 soils in the United States were assigned K values on the basis of measured, long-time soil losses. A few K values are based on losses measured with rainfall simulators on plots; most have been assigned values obtained by use of the nomograph reproduced in Figure 6-3, using measured soil properties. Scientists in developing countries can do the same.

The equations relating slope length and gradient to soil loss have been extensively studied. They seem to apply in most parts of the world and should serve until local studies produce data to modify them.

C factor values are likely to be the most difficult to obtain. Values assigned to the various growth-stage periods in *Handbook 537* (Wischmeier and Smith, 1978) are based on percentage canopy cover. It should be possible to relate the protection of a wide variety of growing crops to these values, to assign growth-stage periods to local crops and crop production techniques, and to make good initial estimates of C values for local crops.

Most erosion-control practice-factor values initially have to be assigned with little or no local research substantiation. It seems likely, however, that the influence of contour cultivation, terraces, crop residue mulches, and other specific erosion-control practices will have the same or similar effects in other countries as in the United States.

6-5.3 Subsoil and Other Soil Material

K values used in the USLE are generally those for soils with surface soils intact or only partly removed by erosion. Predictions may be needed for construction sites or strip mine spoil banks where subsoil is exposed. Sediment losses from these sites can cause serious damage to properties below, and the effectiveness of suggested measures for erosion control need to be assessed. To do this with any assurance, *K* values that apply specifically to these soil conditions must be found. The nomograph shown in Figure 6-3 was developed by Wischmeier et al. (1971) to be used in these situations.

6-5.4 Nonuniform Fields

The USLE was designed for use on uniform fields. If soil, slope, or cover varies over a field, appropriate values for *K, LS,* and *C* can be determined, using Foster and Wischmeier's (1974) method. Table 6-11 gives the proportion of total erosion that is lost from each of two to five uniform length segments. A nonuniform slope is divided into from two to five sections in each of which soil, slope, and cover are reasonably uniform. An *LS* value for each segment is determined from Tables 6-4

TABLE 6-11 SOIL-LOSS FACTORS USED TO ESTIMATE SOIL LOSS ON A SEGMENT OF A UNIFORM SLOPE.

Number of segments in slope	Sequence number of segment	Fraction of soil loss from each segment (for *m* =)[a]								
		0.05	0.1	0.2	0.3	0.4	0.5	0.6	0.7	0.8
2	1	0.48	0.46	0.44	0.40	0.38	0.36	0.33	0.31	0.28
	2	0.52	0.54	0.56	0.60	0.62	0.64	0.67	0.69	0.72
3	1	0.32	0.30	0.26	0.24	0.22	0.19	0.17	0.15	0.13
	2	0.33	0.34	0.35	0.35	0.35	0.35	0.35	0.35	0.35
	3	0.35	0.36	0.39	0.41	0.43	0.46	0.48	0.50	0.52
4	1	0.23	0.22	0.19	0.17	0.14	0.12	0.11	0.10	0.08
	2	0.25	0.25	0.25	0.24	0.24	0.23	0.22	0.21	0.21
	3	0.26	0.26	0.27	0.28	0.29	0.30	0.30	0.30	0.31
	4	0.26	0.27	0.29	0.31	0.33	0.35	0.37	0.39	0.40
5	1	0.18	0.17	0.15	0.13	0.11	0.09	0.08	0.06	0.06
	2	0.20	0.19	0.19	0.18	0.17	0.16	0.15	0.15	0.14
	3	0.20	0.21	0.21	0.21	0.21	0.21	0.21	0.21	0.21
	4	0.21	0.21	0.22	0.23	0.24	0.25	0.26	0.26	0.27
	5	0.21	0.22	0.23	0.25	0.27	0.29	0.30	0.32	0.33

[a]Select *m* values for average slope from Table 6-3.

Source: Modified from Renard et al., 1991.

using field slope length and segment slope gradient. Each of these values is multiplied by an appropriate factor from Table 6–11 and by the K and C values for the segment. Values obtained for the different segments are summed for a corrected $K \times LS \times C$ value.

Assume that a cultivated, 500-ft (150-m) field (average slope = 4%) can be divided into three equal-length segments with 3, 7, and 2% gradients. LS values for each segment from Table 6–4B, using full slope length (500 ft) and individual segment gradients, are 0.64, 1.9, and 0.39. Select $m = 0.36$ from Table 6–3 (4% slope and moderate rill/interrill ratio). Using $m = 0.4$ (closest to 0.36) in Table 6–11, select soil-loss-factor values from the three-segment category (0.22, 0.35, and 0.43). Multiply these segment soil-loss-factor values by individual LS values (0.14, 0.66, and 0.17). The sum of these products (0.97) is the LS value for the total slope.

This same procedure can include soil variation in the field. If the soils in the three segments in the former example have K values of 0.48, 0.54, and 0.44 from the top down, the $K \times LS$ for the site can be calculated as follows:

Segment	LS value (Table 6–3B)	Proportional erosion (Table 6–11, $m = 0.4$)	Calculated LS value	K value	$K \times LS$
1	0.64	0.22	0.14	0.48	0.07
2	1.9	0.35	0.66	0.54	0.36
3	0.39	0.43	0.17	0.44	0.07
			0.97	$K \times LS =$	0.50

Moderate changes in cover coinciding with the segments also can be evaluated by adding a column for C to the table.

6–5.5 Cover Management (C) Values for Noncultivated Land

The USLE was designed for use on cultivated land. Keen interest developed in the use of the equation on native vegetation areas. Techniques have been developed for evaluating C for range and cutover forest areas (Dissmeyer and Foster, 1981; Singer et al., 1977; Wischmeier and Smith, 1978). Studies on erosion from native vegetation are used to check the accuracy of the values proposed. Dissmeyer and Foster (1981) used results from 39 research watersheds in forested areas to validate tables and figures that measured the influence of nine subfactors on erosion losses.

6–5.6 Use of the USLE for Pollution Prediction

The USLE was not designed to predict the sediment or chemical load that runoff waters carry beyond the boundaries of cultivated fields. Control officers in a variety of agencies have modified it for use in these ways and several computer programs have been developed to make these kinds of assessments. Chemicals, Runoff, and

Erosion from Agricultural Management Systems (CREAMS), Aerial Non-point Source Watershed Environmental Response Simulation (ANSWERS), and Agricultural Non-Point Source (AGNPS) are a few. Some care has been taken in developing these programs, but they were never envisaged when the USLE was being developed.

6-6 DEVELOPMENT OF THE WIND-EROSION PREDICTION EQUATION

Two main uses for an accurate wind-erosion prediction method are: assessing the erosion hazard in a particular field, and evaluating the protection offered by management alternatives. Attempts to use research results to predict wind erosion were made soon after information on the mechanics of wind erosion and the factors that influence the process began to accumulate.

Climate was the first factor shown to be quantitatively related to wind erosion. The amount of erosion was found to vary directly with the cube of the average March-April wind velocity and inversely with the previous year's rainfall (Zingg et al., 1952). Preliminary relationships between percent erodible aggregates, quantity of surface crop residue, soil ridge roughness, and amount of erosion taking place in a wind tunnel were developed as early as 1953. The original wind-tunnel equation was modified as new information developed and as new factors could be included. Much of the early work on wind-erosion prediction was done by W. S. Chepil, N. P. Woodruff, and A. W. Zingg. Woodruff and Siddoway (1965) published a prediction equation that had already undergone extensive field testing. It is still being refined at the ARS Wind Erosion Research Unit at Manhattan, Kansas, and elsewhere.

6-7 WIND-EROSION PREDICTION EQUATION

The wind-erosion prediction equation (WEQ) is

$$E = f(I', K', C', L', V)$$

where E = predicted soil loss, tons/ac-yr (mt/ha-yr)
I' = soil-erodibility factor, tons/ac-yr (mt/ha-yr)
K' = soil ridge roughness factor, dimensionless
C' = climatic factor, dimensionless
L' = width-of-field factor, ft
V = vegetative-cover factor, dimensionless

The WEQ, like the USLE, includes the major factors that determine the severity of erosion, but individual factors in the WEQ often interact. As a result, the equation involves more than simple multiplication of the various factors to obtain a product. WEQ-factor relationships require complex equations and complicated charts to find solutions.

6-7.1 Soil-Erodibility Factor (I')

Soil erodibility (I') is the potential annual soil loss from a wide, unsheltered, isolated field with a bare, smooth, noncrusted surface. Soil-erodibility values are based on wind-tunnel relative erodibilities and on soil losses measured in the vicinity of Garden City, Kansas, during 1954 to 1956, an excessively dry and windy period (Chepil, 1960). Conversion of relative erodibility to field loss must be considered an approximation at present because of difficulty of measuring soil losses. Scientists at the Wind Erosion Research Unit and elsewhere are currently using improved soil collecting devices to reevaluate field soil losses (Fryrear, 1986).

I values, obtained from Table 6-12, are modified for knolly topography. Figure 6-6 gives values for I_s. These are the relationships, in percent, of erodibilities of soils on particular slopes to their erodibilities on level land. I_s for a short 4% slope is about 195% on the crest of the knoll and about 160% on the upper windward slopes.

Wind-erosion prediction literature suggests that surface crusts reduce soil erosion and should be considered in estimating potential erosion. In practice, they are seldom evaluated in the prediction exercise because they are transitory. The soil-erodibility factor (I') usually is the product of soil erodibility (I) and knoll-steepness factor (I_s).

6-7.2 Soil-Ridge-Roughness Factor (K')

Surface roughness results from three elements: cloddiness of surface soil, I'; vegetative cover, V, to be discussed later; and ridges on the soil surface. The last is the element involved in the soil-ridge-roughness factor, K'.

TABLE 6-12 SOIL ERODIBILITY (I) VALUES IN TONS/AC-YR[a] FOR SOILS WITH VARIOUS PERCENTAGES OF NONERODIBLE CLODS (>0.84 mm diameter) AS DETERMINED BY STANDARD DRY SIEVING

Percentages (tens)	Percentages (units)									
	0	1	2	3	4	5	6	7	8	9
					tons/ac-yr					
0		310	250	220	195	180	170	160	150	140
10	134	131	128	125	121	117	113	109	106	102
20	98	95	92	90	88	86	83	81	79	76
30	74	72	71	69	67	65	63	62	60	58
40	56	54	52	51	50	48	47	45	43	41
50	38	36	33	31	29	27	26	24	23	22
60	21	20	19	18	17	16	16	15	14	13
70	12	11	10	8	7	6	4	3	3	2
80	2	—	—	—	—	—	—	—	—	—

[a]To convert tons/ac-yr to mt/ha-yr, multiply each value by 2.24.

Source: Reproduced from *Soil Science Society of America Proceedings,* Volume 29, p. 602-608, 1965 (Woodruff and Siddoway), by permission of the Soil Science Society of America.

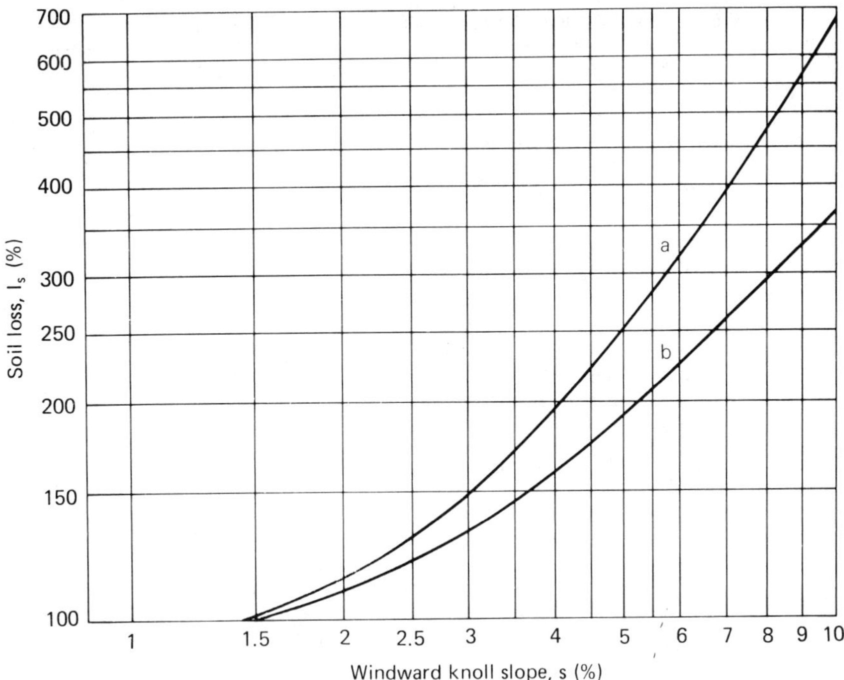

Figure 6–6 Potential soil loss, I_s, from the crest of knolls (a) and from the upper third of the windward side (b) of slopes <500 ft (150 m) long as percentages of I_s on level land. (Reproduced from *Soil Science Society of America Proceedings,* Volume 29, p. 602–608, 1965 [Woodruff and Siddoway], by permission of the Soil Science Society of America.)

K_r is the height of ridges composed of nonerodible, fine gravel with a height-spacing ratio of 1:4 that affect the erosiveness of the wind to the same extent particular field ridges do. For example, if 4-in. (10-cm) gravel ridges spaced 16 in. (40 cm) apart perpendicular to wind direction resist the wind as much as a particular field condition does, K_r for the field is 4 in.

Precise evaluation of K_r can be made only with a wind tunnel, but Skidmore (1983) developed a method for obtaining values from measured roughness in the field. This method is incorporated in Table 6–13. If measured field ridge height is 6 in. (15 cm) and ridge spacing is 30 in. (75 cm) in a downwind direction, K_r is 0.5 (the cell where the 30-in. spacing row and the 6-in. height column intersect).

6–7.3 Climatic Factor (C′)

Wind velocity affects erosion directly; precipitation and temperature affect it indirectly through their effects on surface soil moisture and plant growth.

Wind Velocity. The transporting capacity of wind is related to its velocity cubed. In developing the WEQ, Chepil et al. (1962) studied the effects of mean annual and mean monthly wind velocities. They suggested that the mean annual velocity be used where general propensity for wind erosion is the major concern.

TABLE 6-13 SOIL RIDGE-ROUGHNESS FACTOR (K_r) values

Ridge spacing (in.)	Ridge height (in.)											
	1	2	3	4	5	6	7	8	9	10	11	12
1	0.5	0.8										
2	0.5	0.6	0.8									
4	0.6	0.5	0.7	0.8								
6	0.7	0.5	0.6	0.8								
8	0.8	0.5	0.5	0.6	0.8							
10	0.8	0.6	0.5	0.6	0.8							
12	0.9	0.6	0.5	0.5	0.7	0.8						
14	0.9	0.6	0.5	0.5	0.6	0.8						
16	0.9	0.6	0.5	0.5	0.6	0.7	0.8					
18	0.9	0.7	0.5	0.5	0.5	0.6	0.8					
20	0.9	0.7	0.5	0.5	0.5	0.6	0.8					
22	0.9	0.7	0.6	0.5	0.5	0.6	0.7	0.8				
24	0.9	0.7	0.6	0.5	0.5	0.6	0.7	0.8				
26	0.9	0.8	0.6	0.5	0.5	0.5	0.6	0.8				
28	0.9	0.8	0.6	0.5	0.5	0.5	0.6	0.7	0.8			
30	0.9	0.8	0.6	0.5	0.5	0.5	0.6	0.7	0.8			
32	1.0	0.8	0.6	0.5	0.5	0.5	0.6	0.6	0.8			
34	1.0	0.8	0.6	0.5	0.5	0.5	0.5	0.6	0.7	0.8		
36	1.0	0.8	0.6	0.5	0.5	0.5	0.5	0.6	0.7	0.8		
38	1.0	0.8	0.6	0.6	0.5	0.5	0.5	0.6	0.7	0.8		
40	1.0	0.8	0.7	0.6	0.5	0.5	0.5	0.6	0.7	0.8		
42	1.0	0.9	0.7	0.6	0.5	0.5	0.5	0.6	0.6	0.7	0.8	
44	1.0	0.9	0.7	0.6	0.5	0.5	0.5	0.5	0.6	0.7	0.8	
46	1.0	0.9	0.7	0.6	0.5	0.5	0.5	0.5	0.6	0.7	0.8	
48	1.0	0.9	0.7	0.6	0.5	0.5	0.5	0.5	0.6	0.7	0.8	

Source: From the Journal of Soil and Water Conservation, Volume 38, p. 110–112, 1983 (Skidmore).

Moisture Content of Surface Soil. Soil moisture affects plant growth; plant material slows wind close to the ground. Soil moisture also influences soil aggregation. But it is not these effects that are evaluated by the moisture component of the climatic-erosiveness factor; it is the direct effect that atmospheric humidity and soil moisture have on soil cohesiveness and resistance to erosion. The more frequently soils are moistened by rain, and the longer they remain moist after each rain, the more difficult they are to dislodge. Chepil et al. (1962) assessed soil moisture by the P-E Index (Thornthwaite, 1931), as explained in Note 6–1.

NOTE 6–1
THORNTHWAITE'S HUMIDITY FACTOR

Thornthwaite (1931) suggested a complex rainfactor (P-E Index) to characterize atmospheric humidity:

$$P\text{-}E = 115 \sum_{i=1}^{12} \left(\frac{P}{T - 10} \right)_i^{10/9}$$

where P = monthly precipitation, in.
T = mean monthly temperature, °F

Thornthwaite used 28.4°F as his minimum mean monthly temperature, omitting recorded temperature data for colder months, [minimum ($T - 10$) value is 18.4]. This modification becomes important in higher latitudes where mean temperatures are considerably below freezing several months each year with consequent reductions in evaporation and with precipitation that falls nonerosively as snow. *P-E* is very small in dry regions; calculated *C* values would be excessively high there (as high as 1000 in some drier U.S. locations). To reduce these erroneously high values Chepil used 0.5 in. (13 mm) as a minimum monthly precipitation figure.

The climatic value used in the WEQ is $C = u^3/(P-E)^2$. The average value for C for Garden City, Kansas (where soil erodibility data to define I' were accumulated), is 2.9. The climatic-factor value (C') for any location, expressed as percent, should be the C value for that location divided by the C value for Garden City multiplied by 100:

$$C' = \frac{u^3}{(P-E)^2} \times \frac{100}{2.9} = 34.8 \times \frac{u^3}{(P-E)^2}$$

Chepil et al. (1962) developed a generalized climatic erosiveness map for the western half of the United States. Lyles (1983) calculated the C' factor values for many locations in the western states and in Alaska. Figure 6–7 contains a summary of C' values. More detailed C' value data were prepared for use by the Soil Conservation Service and other agencies.

Skidmore (1986) developed a new physically based, wind-erosion climatic factor:

$$CE = \rho \int_R^{\infty} \left[u^2 - \left(\frac{u_t - \gamma'}{\rho a^2} \right) \right]^{3/2} f(u)\, du$$

where ρ = air density
u = wind velocity at 33 ft (10 m)
u_t = threshold wind speed
γ' = soil cohesive resistance (proportional to relative surface soil water content – actual moisture content/moisture content at the permanent wilting point)
a = a constant (depending on the von Karman constant, height of wind speed measurement, and surface roughness parameter)
$f(u)$ = wind speed probability function

The *CE* factor is calculated from readily available climatic measurements—mean monthly wind speed, precipitation, and temperature—and from calculated solar and net radiation values. *CE* values are very similar whether soil relative moisture content (γ') is estimated using Budyko's Dryness Ratio or Thorthwaite's *P-E* Index.

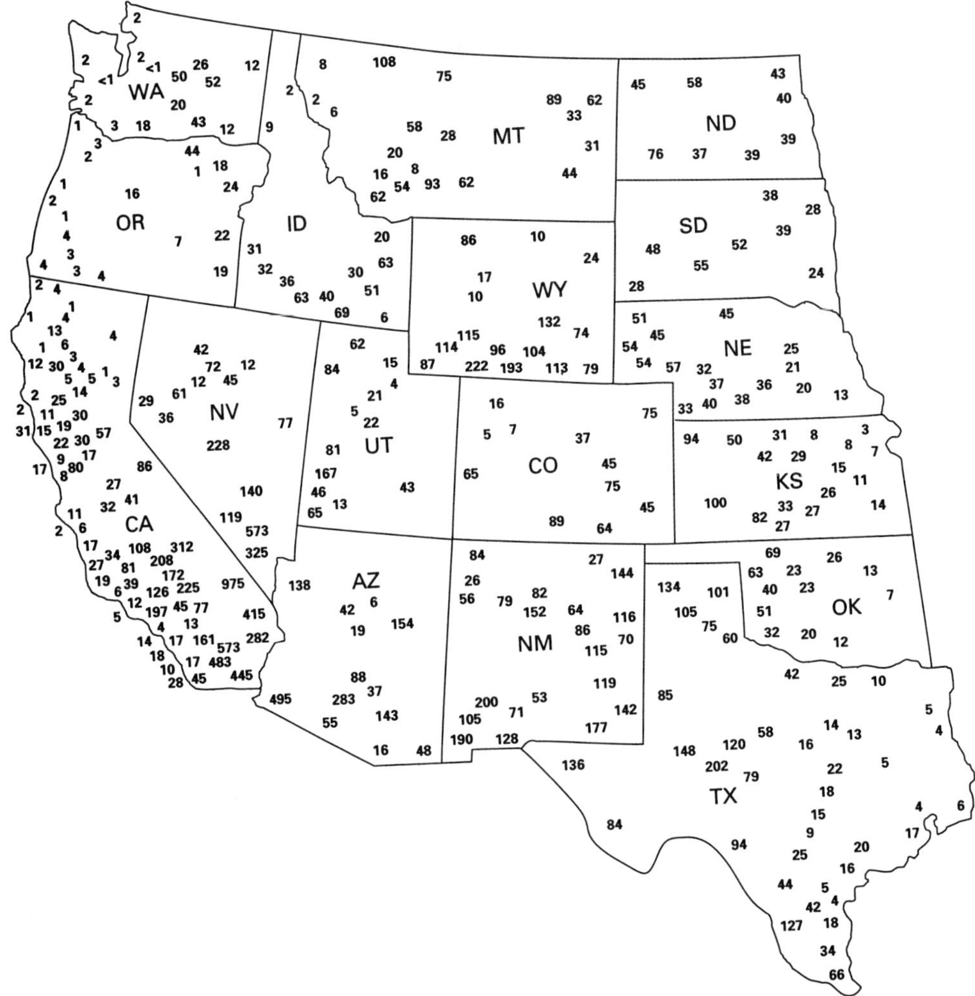

Figure 6-7 Wind-erosion climatic factor C' in percent of the value at Garden City, Kansas. [From the Journal of Soil and Water Conservation, Volume 38, p. 106–109, 1983 (Lyles).]

CE values can be used satisfactorily to solve the WEQ, and to predict seasonal or individual events. This method obviates the need to omit some weather data that make the values either excessively large or small.

Values for C' in the WEQ are dimensionless; accordingly, methods in addition to the one originally proposed can be used. For example, wind velocity and the humidity factor can be measured in metric units, using velocity in meters per second, precipitation in millimeters, and mean temperature in degrees Celsius. de Martonne's rain factor, $P/(T + 10)$, could be used.

$$C' = \frac{u^3}{\left(\dfrac{P}{T + 10}\right)^2}$$

The C value for Garden City, Kansas, by this method is 0.486, so C' in this method of characterization is

$$C' = \frac{100}{0.486} \times \frac{u^3}{\left(\frac{P}{T + 10}\right)^2} = 206 \frac{u^3}{\left(\frac{P}{T + 10}\right)^2}$$

This system gives C' values that approximate those of the original method closely enough for predictive purposes.

6-7.4 Width-of-Field Factor (L')

The width of a field (D_f) is the unsheltered distance in feet in the downwind direction. D_f would always be the same if all winds were from a prevailing direction. With variable winds, some travel longer, some shorter distances across a field.

The proportion of erosive forces that are parallel to, as opposed to forces perpendicular to, the prevailing wind direction is called the *preponderance factor.* A preponderance of 1.0 means that there is no prevailing wind direction; 2.0 means that there is a prevailing direction and twice as much erosive force is parallel to the prevailing direction as is perpendicular to it. Knowledge of prevailing wind direction and of preponderance is needed to calculate wind-erosion direction factors for individual locations or areas. These direction factors serve as multipliers for use on actual field lengths to give the median travel distance of the wind across a particular field. Note 6-2 describes the method used to determine wind-erosion direction factors.

NOTE 6-2
EQUIVALENT FIELD WIDTH

Skidmore (1987) expanded and improved the procedure developed by Skidmore and Woodruff (1968) to estimate the median travel distance, MTD (or D_f), across eroding fields. MTD is the distance for which half the erosive forces travel farther and half not as far as the prevailing wind across the field.

Wind-erosion roses for wind patterns of individual locations were obtained by using the equation of an ellipse in polar coordinates. The semi-major and semi-minor axes were varied to give preponderance values of 1.0 to 4.0. The axes were rotated to simulate prevailing wind direction ranging 0 to 90° from perpendicular to field orientation. Simulated length/width field dimensions were varied from I to 10. Wind-erosion-direction factors were calculated from the resulting data. Skidmore developed three tables of direction factors, one for each of three length/width ratios—2, 4, and 10—with a factor for each preponderance/orientation pair.

Preponderance values and direction of prevailing winds can be obtained from Skidmore (1987) or from individual Soil Conservation District offices. Wind-erosion direction factors for a variety of conditions are found in Tables 6–14. Finding MTD in April for a 1300- by 2600-ft (400- by 800-m) field (length/width ratio = 2) with an east-west bearing near Amarillo, Texas, will serve as an example. The preponderance at Amarillo is 1.4 and the prevailing wind direction is 203° (Skidmore and Woodruff, 1968). The prevailing wind has a deviation of 23° (203 − 180°). The wind-direction factor for this field is 1.27 (Table 6–14A). The MTD across the field will be 1651 ft (1300 × 1.27), or 503 m.

Any distance in a field that is sheltered by wind barriers (B) must be subtracted from the MTD. The sheltered distance for field hedges, tree shelterbelts, and similar barriers is 10 times the height of the barrier ($10B$). Thus the width of field factor (L') is the difference between (MTD) and sheltered distance ($10B$) or $L' = \text{MTD} - 10B$.

Calculation of the effect of L' on soil loss is complex. It depends on the amount of soil being carried in the wind. The nomogram in Figure 6–8 is used to assess the effect of L' on erosion loss by incorporating it along with soil-erodibility-soil-ridge-roughness-erosion estimates (E_2) and soil-erodibility-soil-ridge-roughness-climatic-erosion estimates (E_3) in the prediction equation.

6–7.5 Vegetative Factor (*V*)

The protection offered by vegetation depends on how much dry matter it contains, its texture, whether living or dead, standing or flat. The original work on vegetative protection involved flattened wheat straw. This condition is now the standard for

TABLE 6–14A WIND-EROSION DIRECTION FACTOR FOR RECTANGULAR FIELDS WITH LENGTH/WIDTH RATIO OF 2

Pre-	Angle of deviation (degrees)								
ponderance	0.00	11.25	22.50	33.75	45.00	56.25	67.50	78.75	90.00
1.0	1.42	1.42	1.42	1.42	1.42	1.42	1.42	1.42	1.42
1.2	1.30	1.31	1.35	1.40	1.42	1.43	1.44	1.46	1.46
1.4	1.20	1.21	1.27	1.36	1.42	1.44	1.48	1.52	1.55
1.6	1.14	1.15	1.22	1.32	1.42	1.46	1.53	1.62	1.66
1.8	1.10	1.11	1.18	1.29	1.42	1.47	1.58	1.72	1.80
2.0	1.07	1.09	1.16	1.28	1.42	1.47	1.62	1.82	1.96
2.2	1.05	1.07	1.14	1.27	1.42	1.48	1.65	1.94	2.00
2.4	1.04	1.06	1.13	1.26	1.42	1.49	1.68	1.97	2.00
2.6	1.03	1.05	1.12	1.26	1.42	1.49	1.70	1.99	2.00
2.8	1.02	1.04	1.12	1.25	1.42	1.50	1.72	2.00	2.00
3.0	1.02	1.04	1.12	1.25	1.42	1.50	1.73	2.00	2.00
3.2	1.01	1.04	1.12	1.25	1.42	1.50	1.74	2.00	2.00
3.4	1.01	1.04	1.12	1.25	1.42	1.50	1.74	2.01	2.00
3.6	1.01	1.04	1.12	1.25	1.42	1.50	1.75	2.01	2.00
3.8	1.01	1.04	1.11	1.25	1.42	1.50	1.76	2.02	2.00
4.0	1.01	1.04	1.11	1.25	1.42	1.51	1.76	2.02	2.00

Source: Modified from Soil Science Society of America Journal, Volume 51, p. 198–202, 1987 (Skidmore) by permission of the Soil Science Society ofAmerica.

TABLE 6-14B WIND-EROSION DIRECTION FACTOR FOR RECTANGULAR FIELDS WITH LENGTH/WIDTH RATIO OF 4

Pre-	Angle of deviation (degrees)								
ponderance	0.00	11.25	22.50	33.75	45.00	56.25	67.50	78.75	90.00
1.0	1.48	1.48	1.48	1.48	1.48	1.48	1.48	1.48	1.48
1.2	1.30	1.31	1.35	1.40	1.48	1.57	1.66	1.72	1.76
1.4	1.20	1.21	1.27	1.36	1.48	1.65	1.86	2.00	2.00
1.6	1.14	1.15	1.22	1.32	1.48	1.72	1.98	2.24	2.35
1.8	1.10	1.11	1.18	1.29	1.48	1.77	2.08	2.43	2.55
2.0	1.07	1.09	1.16	1.28	1.48	1.82	2.17	2.58	2.78
2.2	1.05	1.07	1.14	1.27	1.48	1.85	2.20	2.74	3.06
2.4	1.04	1.06	1.13	1.26	1.48	1.86	2.38	2.89	3.35
2.6	1.03	1.05	1.12	1.26	1.48	1.87	2.42	3.02	3.58
2.8	1.02	1.04	1.12	1.25	1.48	1.88	2.44	3.15	3.74
3.0	1.02	1.04	1.12	1.25	1.48	1.88	2.45	3.28	3.92
3.2	1.01	1.04	1.12	1.25	1.48	1.89	2.46	3.33	4.00
3.4	1.01	1.04	1.12	1.25	1.48	1.89	2.47	3.35	4.00
3.6	1.01	1.04	1.12	1.25	1.48	1.89	2.48	3.38	4.00
3.8	1.01	1.04	1.12	1.25	1.48	1.89	2.48	3.39	4.00
4.0	1.01	1.04	1.11	1.25	1.48	1.90	2.48	3.41	4.00

Source: Modified from Soil Science Society of America Journal, Volume 51, p. 198–202, 1987 (Skidmore) by permission of the Soil Science Society of America.

TABLE 6-14C WIND-EROSION DIRECTION FACTOR FOR RECTANGULAR FIELDS WITH LENGTH/WIDTH RATIO OF 10

Pre-	Angle of deviation (degrees)								
ponderance	0.00	11.25	22.50	33.75	45.00	56.25	67.50	78.75	90.00
1.0	1.48	1.48	1.48	1.48	1.48	1.48	1.48	1.48	1.48
1.2	1.30	1.31	1.35	1.40	1.48	1.57	1.66	1.72	1.76
1.4	1.20	1.21	1.27	1.36	1.48	1.65	1.86	1.99	2.00
1.6	1.14	1.15	1.22	1.32	1.48	1.72	1.98	2.33	2.55
1.8	1.10	1.11	1.18	1.30	1.48	1.77	2.10	2.76	3.08
2.0	1.07	1.09	1.16	1.28	1.48	1.82	2.26	3.18	3.73
2.2	1.05	1.07	1.14	1.27	1.48	1.85	2.34	3.61	4.47
2.4	1.04	1.06	1.13	1.26	1.48	1.86	2.61	4.01	5.22
2.6	1.03	1.05	1.12	1.26	1.48	1.87	2.70	4.38	5.93
2.8	1.02	1.04	1.12	1.25	1.48	1.88	2.77	4.73	6.61
3.0	1.02	1.04	1.12	1.25	1.48	1.88	2.82	5.03	7.28
3.2	1.01	1.04	1.12	1.25	1.48	1.89	2.74	5.20	7.79
3.4	1.01	1.04	1.12	1.25	1.48	1.89	2.86	5.31	8.17
3.6	1.01	1.04	1.12	1.25	1.48	1.89	2.88	5.39	8.54
3.8	1.01	1.04	1.12	1.25	1.48	1.89	2.90	5.46	8.91
4.0	1.01	1.04	1.11	1.25	1.48	1.90	2.91	5.51	9.27

Source: Modified from Soil Science Society of America Journal, Volume 51, p. 198–202, 1987 (Skidmore) by permission of the Soil Science Society ofAmerica.

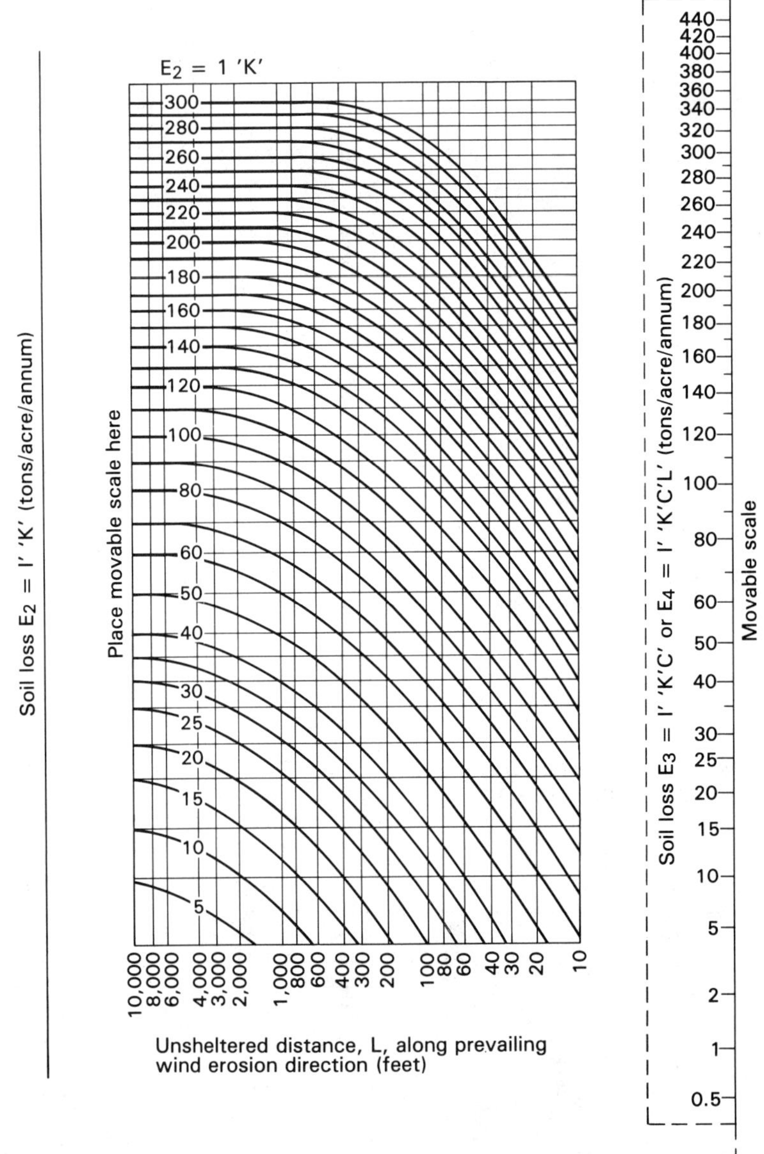

Figure 6-8 Nomogram to determine soil loss, $E_4 = f(I', K', C', L')$, from soil loss $E_2 = I \times K'$ and $E_3 = I' \times K' \times C'$ and the unsheltered distance L' across the field. In use, a copy of the movable scale is placed along the left side of the graph so that E_3 on the scale is aligned with E_2 on the graph. A line parallel to the curved lines is then followed to its intersection with the unsheltered distance line. The value of E_4 is located by following a horizontal line from the intersection back to the movable scale. For example, an E_3 value of 150 and an E_2 value of 120 combined with an unsheltered distance of 600 ft give an E_4 value of 130. [From *Soil Science Society of America Proceedings,* Volume 29, p. 602–608, 1965 (Woodruff and Siddoway), by permission of the Soil Science Society of America.]

determining V. Dry weights of growing crops or crop residues (R') are converted to equivalent quantities of flat wheat straw (V) by use of Figure 6–9. The effectiveness of vegetation (V) in reducing soil loss depends on the level of erosion. Figure 6–10 provides the means of relating erosion to V.

6–7.6 Assessing Vegetative Cover

The best way to estimate the amount of surface vegetation on a field is to hand pick, dry, and weigh the living plants or surface residue from a unit area. One square yard (or 1 m^2) is sufficient for small grains; 2 square yards is necessary for row crops. At least three separate samples should be taken for a reliable estimate of each location. Soil must be removed before weighing. Washing is much quicker than cleaning a dry sample. Results should be translated into lb/ac or kg/ha (Whitfield et al., 1962).

Hartwig and Laflen (1978) described a method where the total widths of the various pieces of residue touching one face of a meterstick is recorded. The stick is placed at random across the interrow area. Total length of contact per set is the percentage of residue cover. Sloneker and Moldenhauer (1977) described a method

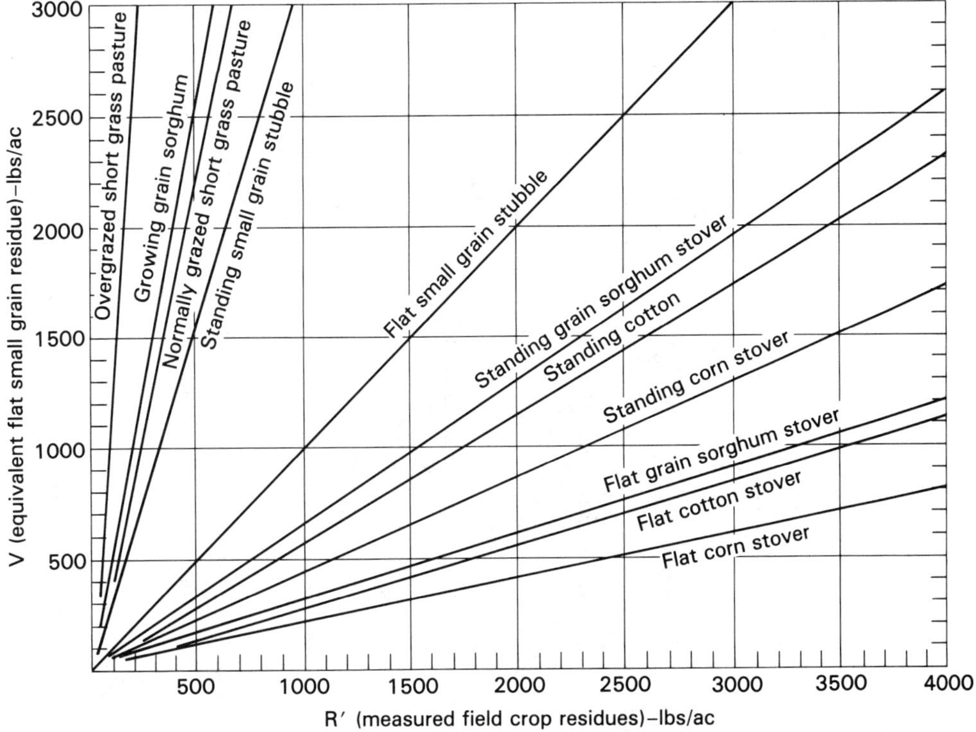

Figure 6–9 Curves to convert weights of living or dead crop material (R') into equivalent amounts of flattened wheat straw *(V)*. [Modified from Agronomy Journal, Volume 77, p. 703–707, 1985 (Armbrust and Lyles) by permission of the American Society of Agronomy; Journal of Range Management, Volume 33, p. 143–146, 1980 (Lyles and Allison); and Transactions of American Society of Agricultural Engineers, Volume 24, p. 405–408, 1981 (Lyles and Allison).]

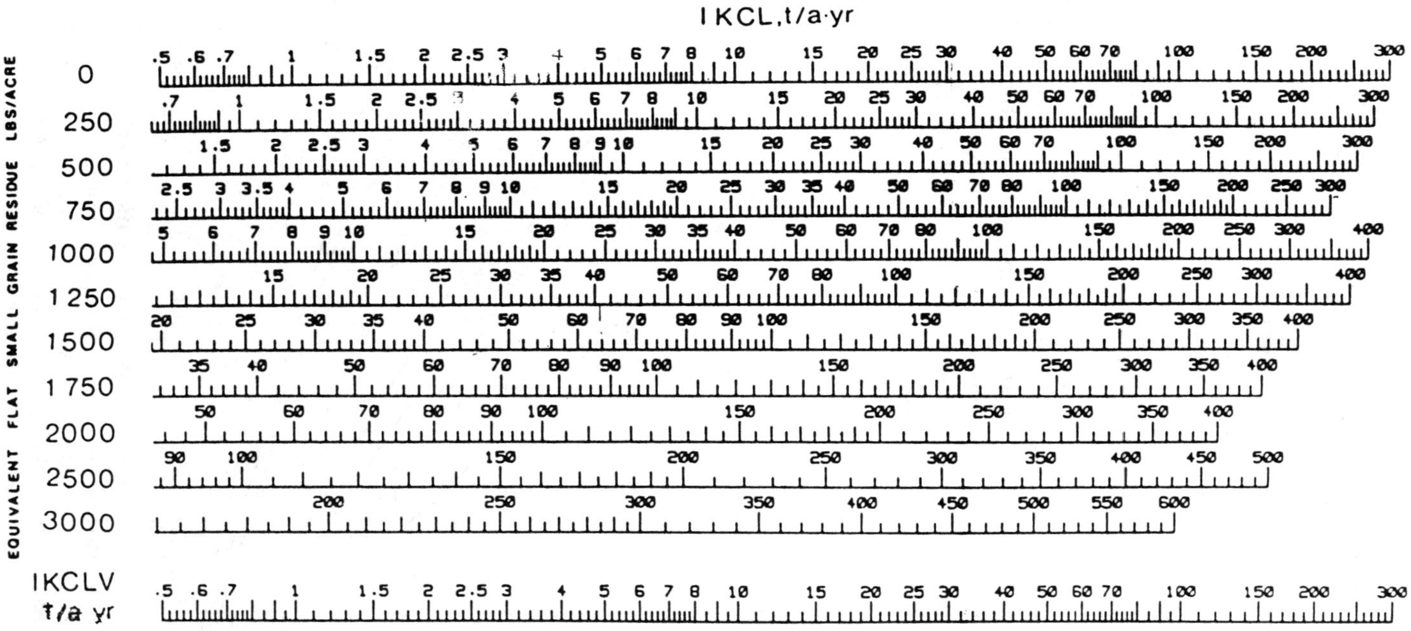

Figure 6–10 Revised wind erosion calculator scale for finding $E_5 = f(I', K', C', L', V)$ as a function of E_4 and designated values of equivalent flat small grain residue (V) in lb/ac. The E_5 value is determined by entering the graph on the left at the appropriate level of V and following it horizontally across to the value of E_4. A line vertically through the E_4 value will give the E_5 value in either the bottom or top scale. [From the Journal of Soil and Water Conservation, Volume 38, p. 110–112, 1983 (Skidmore).]

in which 50 beads were fastened at equal intervals along a string. The beaded string was stretched across the area to be evaluated. Each bead that touched a "significant" piece of residue was counted as 2% soil cover. At least six separate counts should be made and averaged in each field. These investigators found that fraction of surface cover can be translated into residue weight with the equations:

$$X = \begin{cases} -5278 \log (1 - Y) & \text{corn} \\ -15{,}519 \log (1 - Y) & \text{small grain} \\ -27{,}813 \log (1 - Y) & \text{soybeans} \end{cases}$$

where X = residues, lb/ac
Y = cover as a decimal fraction

6-7.7 Predicting Soil Loss for a Particular Field

A 2600- by 5200-ft (1/2- by 1-mi or 800- by 1600-m) field with long axis east-west on Ortello fine sandy loam in Ford County (Dodge City), Kansas, will serve as an example. The surface soil contains 25% nonerodible clods. Several knolls with short 3% slopes are in the field. A crop of grain sorghum was produced in 30-in. (75-cm) rows; 1150 lb/ac (1300 kg/ha) of tall standing stubble remains. The average ridge height is 6 in. (15 cm).

The predicted soil loss from the knolls in March is calculated as follows:

Step 1: $E_1 = I' = I \times I_s$.
I for 25% nonerodible clods is 86 tons/ac-yr (190 mt/ha-yr) (Table 6–12). The value for I_s on the knolls of a 3% slope is 148% (Figure 6–6).

$$E_1 = 86 \times \frac{148}{100} = 127 \text{ tons/ac-yr}$$

Step 2: $E_2 = E_1 \times K'$.
The soil-ridge-roughness condition (K_r) for $HR = 6$ and $IR = 30$ is 0.50 (Table 6–13).

$$E_2 = 127 \times 0.50 = 64 \text{ tons/ac-yr}$$

Step 3: $E_3 = E_2 \times C'$.
The C' value for Ford County is about 80 (Figure 6–7).

$$E_3 = 64 \times \frac{80}{100} = 51 \text{ tons/ac-yr}$$

Step 4: $E_4 = E_3 \times f(L')$.
The prevailing wind for March is due north (deviation = 0°). Preponderance is 2.4 (Skidmore and Woodruff, 1968). The wind-erosion direction factor from Table 6–14A is 1.04.

$$\text{MTD} = 2600 \times 1.04 = 2700 \text{ ft (825 m)}$$

Since no wind barrier was described, $L' = 2700$ ft. Following the directions given in the caption for Figure 6–8 for values of $E_2 = 64$, $E_3 = 51$, and $L' = 2700$ ft, we get $E_4 = 48$ tons/ac-yr.

Step 5: $E = E_4 \times f(V)$.

There is no growing crop, so R' is 1150 lb/ac. V from Figure 6–7 is about 750 lb/ac for $R' = 1150$ lb/ac of standing sorghum stubble. The value for E read from Figure 6–10 using $E_4 = 48$ tons/ac-yr and $V = 750$ lb/ac is 22 tons/ac-yr.

The tolerable loss for this soil has been set as 5 tons/ac-yr. How can the loss be reduced to the tolerable limit? About 750 lb/ac (850 kg/ha) of grain would be produced along with 1150 lb of stover. This is a low yield even for a dry area. Enough stover would be available (1950 lb/ac) to reduce erosion to the tolerable level if grain yield could be raised to 1300 lb/ac or above regularly. Another possibility would be to split the field in half and produce two crops in three years in a sorghum–fallow–wheat system. This would cut field width in half and so shorten L'. Great care would have to be taken to ensure that sufficient crop residues were produced and maintained on the soil for protection against wind erosion. See Chapter 10 for a discussion of conservation tillage.

6–8 FIELD USE OF THE WIND-EROSION PREDICTION EQUATION

The WEQ was developed primarily to help conservation technicians assess wind-erosion conditions and evaluate the changes in management needed to reduce an excessive erosion hazard. Solving the equation is time consuming. Needing to examine several options requires even more time. As a result, SCS specialists and others modified certain factor values and proposed calculation shortcuts.

6–8.1 Faster Methods for Assessing Some WEQ Factors

Establishment of Wind Erodibility Groups (WEGs) was a real timesaver. It allows the assessment of soils' I values without collecting, drying, and dry sieving samples. Nine groups were established, based on soil texture and lime carbonate content. The nine groups are described in Table 6–15. Note that WEG 1 has five different I values, depending on aggregate (sand) content.

Chepil, Zingg, and other staff in the Wind Erosion Research Unit collected and published a series of photographs that show the surface residue and ridge roughness condition of a range of field situations (Chepil and Woodruff, 1959). Each photo is labeled for residue weight and ridge roughness. These permit comparisons of field conditions with the photos, and quick evaluations of residue cover and ridge roughness. This replaces residue-sample collection, preparation, and weighing, and ridge height and spacing measurements, with a lot of laborsaving.

TABLE 6-15 WIND ERODIBILITY GROUP (WEG) CHARACTERISTICS

WEG	Predominant soil texture class of surface layer	Dry soil aggregates > 0.84 mm (%)	Wind erodibility index *I* (tons/ac-yr)[a]
1	Very fine sand, fine sand, or coarse sand	1	310
		2	250
		3	220
		5	180
		7	160
2	Loamy very fine sand, loamy fine sand, loamy sand, loamy coarse sand, or sapric organic soil materials	10	134
3	Very fine sandy loam, fine sandy loam, sandy loam, or coarse sandy loam	25	86
4	Clay, silty clay, noncalcareous clay loam, or silty clay loam with >35 percent clay content	25	86
4L	Calcareous loam and silt loam, or calcareous clay loam, and silty clay loam	25	86
5	Noncalcareous loam and silt loam with <20% clay content, or sandy clay loam, sandy clay, and hemic organic soil materials	40	56
6	Noncalcareous loam and silt loam with >20% clay content, or noncalcareous clay loam with <35% clay content	45	48
7	Silt, noncalcareous silty clay loam with <35% clay content, and fibric organic soil material	50	38
8	Soils not susceptible to wind erosion	>80	0

[a]To convert *I* values to mt/ha-yr, multiply each by 2.24.

Source: USDA Soil Conservation Service.

6-8.2 Methods of Accelerating Equation Solution

The first real timesaver was the development of the Fortran IV computer program WEROS (Fisher and Skidmore, 1970). This did not help field workers directly, but SCS central staff used it to prepare tables of erosion prediction values for individual areas such as soil conservation districts. Field workers could select values from these tables rather than calculate them. Field inspections were still required to determine WEG, ridge roughness, field width, and crop residue present, but the tables made most of the usual calculations unnecessary and permitted an analysis of the present situation and several alternatives to be made in a matter of minutes.

A second innovation was the wind erosion equation slide rule (Skidmore, 1983). This instrument also speeded the process of evaluating current conditions and alternate suggestions.

More recently, programs have been developed for personal computers that have increased the availability and adaptation of this new technology to conservation officers and others. The CAMPS computer program includes the wind erosion prediction equation and is now used in many soil conservation district offices.

6-8.3 Predicting Wind Erosion for Crop Periods

I', K', C', and V values in the WEQ are annual figures, but these values change with time. Bondy et al. (1980) studied changes in wind energy values over the year. They determined the portion of the wind energy that occurs each month and compiled a table in which cumulative monthly percentage of average annual wind energy is given for 76 weather stations in the 10 Great Plains states. Lyles (1983) developed similar information for the seven western states and Alaska. This was done so that estimates of erosion by periods could be made using the WEQ.

This method has several advantages. Changes with time in I', K', and V can now be cataloged, along with changes in C', so times during the crop year that show undue susceptibility to erosion can be pinpointed. If crop periods were employed in the WEQ, crop and residue values for these periods could be used in both the water and wind equations. Nearly all the computer programs that are mentioned in Section 6-10 analyze the erosion picture daily or over relatively short periods.

There are also disadvantages. Calculations for the crop-period method are more complex and take much longer than those for the original method. There are few experimental data to show specifically how the various factors, other than climate, change over time.

6-9 EXPANDED USE OF THE WIND-EROSION PREDICTION EQUATION

The WEQ was developed for use in the semiarid Great Plains region. Soil, climatic, and other data from this region were used to develop a practical and effective prediction tool. Scientists and technicians in other regions in the United States immediately became interested in the equation and started to use it.

6-9.1 Use on Cultivated Soil in Humid Regions in the United States

The WEQ has been used in many areas outside the Great Plains. The Wind Erosion Research Unit's portable wind tunnel was taken to some areas to check soils and results; in other areas the equation was used either without modification or with modifications based only on judgment of field situations.

A wind-tunnel study in northwestern Ohio showed soils there were more erodible than Great Plains soils with the same nonerodible clod composition. A new table relating the percent nonerodible clods to soil erodibility was set up for that area.

Carreker (1966) studied sandy soils of the coastal plains of southeastern United States and found a relationship between the percentage of coarse and very coarse sand (X) and soil erodibility.

$$I = 174 - 4.64X + 0.03X^2$$

Hayes (1965) compared I based on dry sieving results and on the WEG. He found that WEG values were not sufficiently accurate for the very sandy soils in New Jersey. WEG 1 was subdivided after this discovery. Hayes used the calculations method for determining K_r. He also pointed out the need to reduce wind-erosion losses to less than 5 tons/ac-yr to avoid damage to some crops.

In all of these studies, satisfactory estimates of the climatic factor could be obtained from research publications, or sufficient local data were available to evaluate climatic erosiveness. Reasonable estimates of erosion losses were generally obtained.

6-9.2 Use on Rangeland in Western United States

The Bureau of Land Mangement and other agencies and individuals are concerned about wind erosion on range- and pasturelands. Values for V can be obtained for these assessments by using relationships between range species and flattened wheat straw established by Hagen and Lyles (1988) and Lyles and Allison (1980). Values for other factors are obtained in the normal way.

6-9.3 Use of the WEG to Predict Air Pollution

Suspended dust is a serious air pollutant. It poses a threat to highway and air traffic and to human health. The WEQ evaluates soil movement of all kinds—surface creep, saltation, and suspension. Only suspended dust, which constitutes a very small fraction of the total amount of soil moved by wind, can be an important air pollutant.

Efforts have been made to modify WEQ to assess the amount of dust in the air under a variety of natural conditions. Wilson (1975) used I' values based on the WEG to predict dust emissions in New Mexico. He multiplied the E values he obtained by 0.003 to change eroding soil to suspended dust. The equation was useful in this survey, but great care must be exercised in using WEQ this way; results obtained must be viewed with caution.

6-9.4 Use of the Equation in Other Countries and Continents

Problems arise when the WEQ is used in areas very different from the ones for which it was developed. The relationship between percent nonerodible clods or WEGs and I is not universally constant, but the initial assumption that must be made in a new area is that the proposed relationship will hold. Values for K_r in new areas must be obtained by measurement using Table 6-13.

The equation's method of evaluating erosiveness of climate should give reasonable values in other areas with similar climatic conditions. A problem arises in very dry areas because the P-E value used to calculate C' becomes very small and makes C' very large. Using Budyko's Dryness Ratio might solve this problem (Skidmore, 1986). Lack of long-term weather records from which C' values can be obtained is likely to be another major problem. Climatic zones probably can be outlined and approximate relationships assigned on the basis of general knowledge. The major limitation resulting from a lack of wind and other weather records is relating the local climatic erosiveness to that at Garden City, Kansas, the standard on which the WEQ is based.

Wind records are also used to determine L' values. Where wind records are not sufficient to develop statistically valid prevailing directions and preponderances, the general direction of the prevailing winds during the major wind-erosion periods can be estimated at least as close as the nearest compass point (22.5°). Maximum travel distance (WL) along the prevailing wind direction can be estimated from field width (FW) and length (FL) and the declination angle (A) between the prevailing wind direction and side FW by the method suggested by Cole et al. (1983):

$$\mathrm{WL} = \begin{cases} \mathrm{FW} \sec A & \text{where FW Sec } A < \text{ or } = (\mathrm{FW}^2 + \mathrm{FL}^2)^{0.5} \\ \mathrm{FL} \csc A & \text{where FW Sec } A > (\mathrm{FW}^2 + \mathrm{FL}^2)^{0.5} \end{cases}$$

It should be recognized that WL is not the same as the average travel distance of wind along the prevailing direction. It will be the same for declination angles of 0° and 90° to FW, but average travel distance will decrease, slowly at first, then more rapidly as the declination angle separates from 0° or 90° until it is only half WL where WL equals $(\mathrm{FW}^2 + \mathrm{FL}^2)^{0.5}$, i.e. along the diagonal of the field. The sheltering effect of barriers should be the same worldwide.

Values for R' can be accurately obtained by picking, drying, and weighing the residues or growing crop, or they can be estimated by one of the line-transect methods or by photo interpretation. Surface residue should be translated into flat wheat straw by Figure 6–9. Unevaluated material will have to be translated to standard residue on the basis of its observed effectiveness in relation to small-grain or sorghum residue.

Predictions employing less precise techniques should be useful in assessing potential trouble and recommending needed control methods. Lack of some information required for accurate analyses is no excuse for disregarding the prediction equation altogether.

6–10 SLIDE RULES AND COMPUTER SOLUTIONS FOR PREDICTION CALCULATIONS

Special slide rules, mathematical models, and computer software have been developed to solve the erosion prediction equations easier and more quickly and to expand uses into broader fields. Two slide rules were designed. Both slide rules were widely used by SCS field officers; both have been replaced by computer software.

The complexity of the WEQ prompted development of WEROS, a Fortran IV mainframe computer solution (Fisher and Skidmore, 1970). Onstad and Foster (1975) developed the first of a variety of computer models based on the USLE.

The Erosion-Productivity Impact Calculator (EPIC) program was developed by ARS scientists to assess the long-time effect of soil erosion on soil productivity (Williams et al., 1983). Its primary initial function was to refine data for departmental reports to fulfill the 1977 Soil and Water Resources Conservation Act mandate for a periodic review of the condition of soil, water, and related resources on agricultural land and to make predictions on productivity losses by erosion and on management needed to control these losses. The model includes components of climate, runoff, erosion, soil moisture, soil chemistry, crop growth, crop and soil management, and economics. It computes erosion from a single point on the landscape; it does not consider sediment deposited in the field. It includes wind erosion prediction capability (Skidmore and Williams, 1991). Initially, it required a mainframe computer but now it is available for personal computers.

The Chemicals, Runoff, and Erosion from Agricultural Management Systems (CREAMS) program was developed by ARS scientists for use on small watersheds and has a component to assess nutrient losses on sediment and in runoff as well as simple runoff and soil loss (Knisel, 1980). It requires topographic input, information on soil erodibility, potential runoff, cover management, and climatic data. It requires a mainframe computer.

The Agricultural Non-point Source (AGNPS) pollution model was developed by ARS, SCS, the University of Minnesota, and the Minnesota Pollution Control Agency to estimate runoff water quality from agricultural watersheds ranging in size from 5 to 50,000 acres (Young et al., 1989a). It predicts runoff volume, peak rate of flow, eroded and delivered sediment, and nitrogen and phosphate, as well as oxygen required to decompose organic and inorganic chemicals that are added from feedlots, springs, wastewater treatment plants, etc. It can be run on an IBM-compatible personal computer. A user's guide is available (Young et al., 1989b).

A Revised Universal Soil Loss Equation (RUSLE) has been developed by ARS and other scientists (Renard et al., 1991). It is a computerized update of Wischmeier and Smith's 1978 *Agriculture Handbook*. The basic USLE has been retained, but nearly every factor is evaluated by new techniques, often using new data bases. The R factor has been expanded to cover mainland United States and Hawaii. Climatic data (monthly precipitation and temperature, frost-free period, and 15-day distribution of EI) are used to vary both K and C seasonally. The slope (LS) factor has been revised. The cover-management (C) factor has been expanded into a continuous function with four subfactors: prior land use, surface cover, crop canopy, and surface roughness. The conservation practice (P) factor has been expanded to include data for rangeland. The program can be used on microcomputers.

The Water Erosion Prediction Project (WEPP) program was initiated "to develop a new generation of water erosion prediction technology" for use by a wide range of user agencies involved "in soil and water conservation and environmental planning and assessment" (Foster and Lane, 1987). It includes a climate generator, a hydrology component, a plant growth simulator, and soils, irrigation, and erosion data banks. All factors vary with time, so each component is designed to incorporate time changes. It is process oriented and runs on personal computers. Three versions are planned: a Landscape Profile (Hillslope) Version, a Watershed Version, and a Grid Version. None can be used for areas with permanent gullies or stream channels. The Landscape Profile Version, like the USLE, will not predict sediment movement in concentrated flow. The Watershed and Grid Versions are specifically designed to estimate sediment flow in ephemeral gullies and in terrace channels and grassed waterways. A prelimary version of the technology was released in 1989. It will undergo testing and evaluation by a variety of user groups. At the same time, further research will continue to refine and improve the model prior to its final release in 1992.

Two new computer models are being developed to update and replace the WEQ (Hagen, 1991). An ARS team of scientists is coordinating this effort. The objective is to develop Wind Erosion Research Model (WERM) and Wind Erosion Prediction System (WEPS) programs. The new programs will be designed for use on croplands and on grass- and shrub-dominated rangeland. WERM will be a daily simulation model written in Fortran 77 for release in 1991. It will contain seven submodels: crop growth, plant material decomposition, soil, hydrology, tillage, weather, and erosion. These submodels will be reorganized, data bases will be expanded, and a user-friendly input/output section will be added to produce WEPS, which should be operational in 1993. It will be designed for use with personal computers.

SUMMARY

Erosion cannot be prevented, but it must be limited to tolerable rates. Methods for predicting erosion rates are needed for two main reasons: to ascertain the erosion hazard with present management, and to evaluate alternative methods of crop and soil management. Erosion-predicting equations have been developed for estimating soil losses by both water and wind.

The water-erosion prediction equation (USLE) was designed to predict soil movement by sheet and rill erosion in cultivated fields and has been widely and successfully used in the United States and in many other countries. It is

$$A = R \times K \times LS \times C \times P$$

where A is the expected average annual rate of erosion in tons/ac-yr based on factors for rainfall erosivity (R), soil erodibility (K), slope length and steepness (LS), cropping management (C), and special erosion-control practices (P). Techniques are available to calculate values for each factor from information obtained by field inspection and from tables, charts, and equations. The equation, or some modification of it, has been widely used by soil conservation technicians in working out effective alternative management practices for erosion control.

The USLE has been modified in ways that permit its use in predicting erosion losses in accelerated flow and in large gullies and along major stream channels. It has also been used to predict the amount of sediment removal from fields and the amount entering streams, and even the amount of chemical pollution that is caused by runoff water.

The wind-erosion prediction equation (WEQ), designed to evaluate the erosion hazard on cultivated lands in the Great Plains region of the United States, is now widely used by conservationists and others in many areas. It is

$$E = f(I', K', C', L', V)$$

where E is the expected average annual rate of erosion in tons/ac-yr as a function of soil erodibility (I'), soil-ridge roughness (K'), climatic erosiveness (C'), field length (L'), and vegetative cover (V). Techniques are provided for calculating values for each factor using information obtained by field examination along with tables, graphs, and equations.

The WEQ has been used successfully in the Great Plains each fall and winter to predict the likelihood and extent of wind erosion the following spring. It has also been employed to determine the current erosion hazard and to evaluate the effectiveness of alternative management and erosion-control programs. Considerable interest has developed in using the equation on highly erodible soils (sands and mucks) in humid regions.

Modifications of the equation have been introduced that have permitted its use in predicting erosion on perennially vegetated areas and in predicting airborne dust.

Many computer programs have been developed that speed up and broaden the use of the equations.

QUESTIONS

1. What needs prompted the development of the soil-loss prediction equations?
2. List the four major soil factors that affect the rate of erosion that can be tolerated, and point out why each factor is important.
3. What problems arise in applying the rainfall-erosivity index in a thinly populated developing country?
4. What is the water-erosion K factor? Describe three methods that have been used to establish specific K values in the United States.
5. Briefly describe the specific conditions for which the wind-erosion prediction equation was designed to estimate erosion losses accurately.
6. How does ridge roughness affect wind erosion? How was this effect evaluated initially?
7. (a) Describe a farm field and calculate the total erosion losses (water plus wind) predicted for it.

   (b) If the predicted losses exceed the tolerable amount, propose and justify control measures for reducing erosion.

REFERENCES

Armbrust, D. V., and L. Lyles, 1985. Equivalent wind-erosion protection from selected growing crops. *Agron. J.* 77:703–707.

Arnoldus, H. M. J., 1977. Methodology used to determine the maximum potential average annual soil loss due to sheet and rill erosion in Morocco. Annex IV in *Assessing Soil Degradation.* FAO Soils Bull. 34. FAO, Rome.

Beasley, D. B., and L. F. Huggins. 1982. *ANSWERS Users' Manual.* Publ. EPA-905-82-001. U.S. Environmental Protection Agency, Chicago., 54 p.

BEASLEY, D. B., E. J. MONKE, and L. F. HUGGINS. 1980. ANSWERS: A model for watershed planning. Trans. *Am. Soc. Agric. Eng.* 23:938–944.

BERGSMA, E., 1981. Indices of rain erosivity. *ITC J.* p. 460–484. International Institute for Aerial Survey and Earth Sciences, Enschede, The Netherlands.

BONDY, E. L., L. LYLES, and W. A. HAYES, 1980. Computing soil erosion by periods using wind energy distribution. *J. Soil Water Cons.* 35:173–176.

BROWNING, G. M., C. L. PARISH, and J. A. GLASS, 1947. A method for determining the use and limitation of rotation and conservation practices in the control of soil erosion in Iowa. *J. Am. Soc. Agron.* 39:65–73.

CARREKER, J. R., 1966. Wind erosion in the southeast. *J. Soil Water Cons.* 21:86–88.

CASTRO, C. D., and T. M. ZOBECK, 1986. Evaluation of the topographic factor in the universal soil loss equation on irregular slopes. *J. Soil Water Cons.* 41:113–116.

CHEPIL, W. S., 1960. Conversion of relative field erodibility to annual soil loss by wind. *Soil Sci. Soc. Am. Proc.* 24:143–145.

CHEPIL, W. S., F. H. SIDDOWAY, and D. V. ARMBRUST, 1962. Climatic factor for estimating wind erodibility of farm fields. *J. Soil Water Cons.* 17:162–165.

CHEPIL, W. S., and N. P. WOODRUFF, 1959. *Estimation of Wind Erodibility of Farm Fields.* USDA Prod. Res. Rep. 25.

COLE, G. W., L. LYLES, and L. J. HAGEN, 1983. A simulation model of daily wind erosion soil loss. *Trans. Am. Soc. Agric. Eng.* 26:1758–1765.

DISSMEYER, G. E., and G. R. FOSTER, 1981. Estimating the cover-management factor (*C*) in the universal soil loss equation for forest conditions. *J. Soil Water Cons.* 36:235–240.

ELWELL, H. A., and M. A. STOCKING, 1973. Rainfall parameters for soil loss estimation in a subtropical climate. *J. Agric. Eng. Res.* 18:169–177.

FISHER, P. S., and E. L. SKIDMORE, 1970. *WEROS: A Fortran IV Program to Solve the Wind Erosion Equation.* USDA, ARS, 41–174.

FOSTER, G. R., and R. E. HIGHFILL, 1983. Effect of terraces on soil loss: USLE *P* factor values for terraces. *J. Soil Water Cons.* 38:48–51.

FOSTER, G. R., and L. J. LANE, 1983. Erosion by concentrated flow in farm fields. In *Proc. Symp. to Honor D. B. Simons.* Colorado State Univ., Ft. Collins, Colo., June 28–30, 1983.

FOSTER G. R., and L. J. LANE, 1987. *(Compilers) User Requirements: USDA Water Erosion Prediction Project (WEPP).* NSERL Rep. 1. National Soil Erosion Research Laboratory, USDA-ARS, West Lafayette, Ind., 43 p.

FOSTER, G. R., D. K. MCCOOL, K. G. RENARD, and W. C. MOLDENHAUER, 1981. Conversion of the universal soil loss equation to SI units. *J. Soil Water Cons.* 36:355–359.

FOSTER, G. R., and W. H. WISCHMEIER, 1974. Evaluating irregular slopes for soil loss prediction. *Trans. Am. Soc. Agr. Eng.* 17:305–309.

FRYREAR, D. W., 1986. A field dust sampler. *J. Soil Water Cons.* 41:117–120.

HAGEN, L. J., 1991. Wind erosion prediction system: Concepts to meet user needs. *J. Soil Water Cons.* 46: (in press).

HAGEN, L. J., and L. LYLES, 1988. Estimating small grain equivalents of shrub-dominated rangelands for wind erosion control. *Trans. Am. Soc. Agric. Eng.* 31:769–775.

HALLBERG, G. R., N. C. WOLLENHAUPT, and G. A. MILLER, 1978. A century of soil development in soil derived from loess in Iowa. *Soil Sci. Soc. Am. J.* 42:339–343.

HARTWIG, R. O., and J. M. LAFLEN, 1978. A meterstick method for measuring crop residue cover. *J. Soil Water Cons.* 33:90–91.

HAYES, W. A., 1965. Wind erosion equation useful in designing northeastern crop protection. *J. Soil Water Cons.* 20:153–155.

HUDSON, N., 1981. *Soil Conservation.* 2nd ed. Cornell Univ. Press, Ithaca, N. Y., p. 324.

HUSSEIN, M. H., 1986. Rainfall erosivity in Iraq. *J. Soil Water Cons.* 41:336–338.

JACKSON, M., 1988. Amish agriculture and no-till: The hazards of applying the USLE to unusual farms. *J. Soil Water Cons.* 43:483–486.

JOHNSON, L. C., 1987. Soil loss tolerance: Fact or myth? *J. Soil Water Cons.* 42:155–160.

KALMAN, R., 1967. *Le Climatique de l'Erosion dans le Bassin duSEBOU (Maroc).* Project SEBOU, 32 p. (Quoted in ROOSE, 1977.)

KNISEL, W. J. (ED.) 1980. *CREAMS: A field scale model of Chemical, Runoff, and Erosion from Agricultural Management Systems.* Cons. Rep. 26. Science and Education Administration, USDA, Washington, D.C.

KOHNKE, H., and A. R. BERTRAND, 1959. *Soil Conservation.* McGraw-Hill, New York, 298 p.

LAL, R., 1985. Soil erosion in its relation to productivity in tropical soils. In *Soil Erosion and Conservation,* S. A. El Swaify, W. C. Moldenhauer, and A. Lo (eds.). Soil Conservation Society of America, Ankeny, Iowa.

LYLES, L., 1983. Erosive wind energy distribution and climatic factors for the west. *J. Soil Water Cons.* 38:106–109.

LYLES, L., and B. E. ALLISON, 1980. Range grasses and their small grain equivalents for wind erosion control. *J. Rge. Mgmt.* 33:143–146.

LYLES, L., and B. E. ALLISON, 1981. Equivalent wind-erosion protection from selected crop residues. *Trans. Am. Soc. Agr. Eng.* 24:405–408.

MASSON, J. M., 1971. *L'Erosion des Sols par l'Eau en Climat Méditerranéen. Méthode Expérimentale pour l'Étude des Quantités de Terre Érodée a l'Échelle du Champ.* Thèse Doct. Ing. Univ. Sciences et Techniques du Languedoc. CNRS NO. AO 5445, 213 p. (Quoted in ROOSE, 1977.)

MASSON, J. M., and J. M. KALMS, 1971. *Analyse et Synthèse des Facteurs de l'Érosion sur le Bassin Versant de la TET à VINCA.* Note 14/71. EDF/Univ. Montpellier, 90 p. (Quoted in ROOSE, 1977.)

MCCOOL, D. K., L. C. BROWN, G. R. FOSTER, C. K. MUTCHLER, and L. D. MEYER, 1987. Revised steepness factor for the Universal Soil Loss Equation. *Trans. Am. Soc. Agr. Eng.* 30:1387–1396.

MCGREGOR, K. C., and C. K. MUTCHLER, 1977. Status of the R factor in northern Mississippi. In *Soil Erosions Prediction and Control.* Soil Conservation Society of America, Ankeny, Iowa, p. 135–142.

MCGREGOR, K. C., C. K. MUTCHLER, and A. J. BOWIE, 1980. Annual *R* values in north Mississippi. *J. Soil Water Cons.* 35:81–84.

MEYER, L. D., and L. A. KRAMER, 1968. *Relation between Land-Slope and Soil Erosion.* Am. Soc. Agric. Eng. Pap. 68–749. (Abbreviated paper in *Agric. Eng.* 50:522–523.)

MURPHREE, C. E., and C. K. MUTCHLER, 1981. Verification of the slope factor in the universal soil loss equation for low slopes. *J. Soil Water Cons.* 36:300–302.

MUSGRAVE, G. W., 1947. The quantitative evaluation of factors in water erosion: A first approximation. *J. Soil Water Cons.* 2:133–138.

ONSTAD, C. A., and G. R. FOSTER, 1975. Erosion modelling on a watershed. *Trans. Am. Soc. Agr. Eng.* 18:288–292.

PIERCE, F. J., W. E. LARSON, and R. H. DOWDY, 1984. Soil loss tolerance: Maintenance of long-term soil productivity. *J. Soil Water Cons.* 39:136–138.

RENARD, K. G., G. R. FOSTER, and G. A. WEESIES (Coord.), 1991. *Predicting Soil Erosion by Water: A Guide to Conservation Planning with the Revised Universal Soil Loss Equation.* USDA Agric. Handbk. (in press).

ROOSE, E. J., 1977. Use of the universal soil loss equation to predict erosion in West Africa. In *Soil Erosion: Prediction and Control.* Soil Conservation Society of America, Ankeny, Iowa, p. 60–74.

ROSEWELL, C. J., 1986. Rainfall kinetic energy in eastern Australia. *J. Clim. Appl. Meteor.* (Cited in Renard et al. 1991).

SINGER, M. J., G. L. HUNTINGTON, and H. R. SKETCHLEY, 1977. Erosion prediction on California rangeland: Research developments and needs. In *Soil Erosion: Prediction and Control.* Soil Conservation Society of America, Ankeny, Iowa, p. 143–151.

SKIDMORE, E. L., 1983. Wind erosion calculator: Revision of residue table. *J. Soil Water Conserv.* 38:110–112.

SKIDMORE, E. L., 1986. Wind erosion climatic erosivity. *Clim. Change* 9:195–208.

SKIDMORE, E. L., 1987. Wind-erosion direction factors as influenced by field shape and wind preponderance. *Soil Sci. Soc. Am. J.* 51:198–202.

SKIDMORE, E. L., and J. R. WILLIAMS, 1991. Modified EPIC wind erosion model. In *Modeling Plant and Soil Systems,* J. Hanks and J. T. Ritchie (eds.). Agron, Monograph 31, American Society of Agronomy, Madison, Wis. (in press).

SKIDMORE, E. L., and N. P. WOODRUFF, 1968. *Wind Erosion Forces in the United States and Their Use in Predicting Soil Loss.* USDA Agric. Handbk. 346.

SLONEKER, L. L., and W. C. MOLDENHAUER, 1977. Measuring the amounts of crop residue remaining after tillage. *J. Soil Water Cons.* 32:231–236.

SMITH, D. D., 1941. Interpretation of soil conservation data for field use. *Agric. Eng.* 22:173–175.

THORNTHWAITE, C. W., 1931. Climates of North America according to a new classification. *Geograph. Rev.* 21:633–655.

WHITFIELD, C. J., J. J. BOND, E. BURNETT, W. S. CHEPIL, B. W. GREB, T. M. MCCALLA, J. S. ROBINS, F. H. SIDDOWAY, R. M. SMITH, and N. P. WOODRUFF, 1962. *A Standardized Procedure for Residue Sampling: A Committee Report.* USDA, ARS, 41–68.

WILLIAMS, J. R., K. G. RENARD, and P. T. DYKE, 1983. EPIC – A new method for assessing erosion's effect on soil productivity. *J. Soil Water Cons.* 38:381–383.

WILLIAMS, J. R., A. D. NICKS, and J. G. ARNOLD, 1985. Simulator for water resources in rural basins. *J. Hydraulic Eng.* 111:970–986.

WILSON, L., 1975. Application of the wind erosion equation in air pollution surveys. *J. Soil Water Cons.* 30:215–219.

WISCHMEIER, W. H., 1959. A rainfall-erosion index for a universal soil-loss equation. *Soil Sci. Soc. Am. Proc.* 23:246–249.

WISCHMEIER, W. H., 1960. Cropping-management factor evaluations for a universal soil-loss equation. *Soil Sci. Soc. Am. Proc.* 24:322–326.

WISCHMEIER, W. H., 1962. Rainfall erosion potential. *Agric. Eng.* 43:212–215.

WISCHMEIER, W. H., 1976. Use and misuse of the universal soil loss equation. *J. Soil Water Cons.* 31:5–9.

WISCHMEIER, W. H., C. B. JOHNSON, and B. V. CROSS, 1971. A soil erodibility nomograph for farmland and construction sites. *J. Soil Water Cons.* 26:189–193.

WISCHMEIER, W. H., and D. D. SMITH, 1965. *Predicting Rainfall-Erosion Losses from Cropland East of the Rocky Mountains.* USDA Agric. Handbk. 282.

WISCHMEIER, W. H., and D. D. SMITH, 1978. *Predicting Rainfall Erosion Losses: A Guide to Conservation Planning.* USDA Agric. Handbook 537.

WOODRUFF, N. P., and F. H. SIDDOWAY, 1965. A wind erosion equation. *Soil Sci. Soc. Am. Proc.* 29:602–608.

YOUNG, R. A., C. A. ONSTAD, D. D. BOSCH, and W. P. ANDERSON, 1989a. AGNPS: A nonpoint source pollution model for evaluating agricultural watersheds. *J. Soil Water Cons.* 44:168–173.

YOUNG, R. A., C. A. ONSTAD, D. D. BOSCH, and W. P. ANDERSON, 1989b. *AGNPS User's Guide, Version 3.50 – October 1989.* USDA-ARS, Morris, Minn.

ZINGG, A. W., 1940a. Degree and length of land slope as it affects soil loss in runoff. *Agric. Eng.* 21:59–64.

ZINGG, A. W., 1940b. An analysis of degree and length of slope data as applied to terracing. *Agric. Eng.* 21:99–101.

ZINGG, A. W., W. S. CHEPIL, and N. P. WOODRUFF, 1952. *Analysis of Wind Erosion Phenomena in Roosevelt and Currie Counties, New Mexico.* Region VI SCS Albuquerque, N. Mex. M-436.

ZUZEL, J. F., R. R. ALLMARAS, and R. GREENWALT, 1982. Runoff and soil erosion on frozen soils in northeastern Oregon. *J. Soil Water Cons.* 37:351–354.

7 Soil Surveys and Land Use Planning

The first soil survey was made in the United States in Michigan in 1899. The principal objective was to predict the probable success of a crop when planted on a soil where it never grew before. Another objective was to predict the response of a crop to irrigation.

Soil surveys made today are the principal means of transferring scientific agricultural information from one farm to another. This includes estimating yields of adapted crops, predicting erosion hazards, evaluating sites for wildlife, locating sand and gravel for construction, and identifying and conserving prime and unique agricultural lands for agricultural use.

7-1 SOIL SURVEYS

Land-grant universities and state and federal agricultural research stations were founded in the last half of the nineteenth century and grew vigorously. The research stations obtained results from field plots, but there was no assurance that the new ideas could be transferred successfully from experimental plots to farms and ranches. Could technology be transferred freely from soil to soil, or was there a link missing? There *was* a missing link—soil classification. Soil surveys were initiated in 1899, so technology could be transferred. The surveys have changed in many details since then, but their objective remains the same—to help resource managers make the most efficient use of soil and land. A soil surveyor at work is shown in Figure 7-1.

Soil surveys proved to be so valuable that they are being made now throughout the world. The United States now has more than 1000 soil surveyors currently mapping 13,000 or more discrete soil series. There are about 100,000 mapping units,

Figure 7-1 This soil surveyor is showing the farmer how he uses 10% HCl solution to detect the presence of calcium carbonate in soils and rocks. This information helps him classify the soil and make a map that will help natural resource managers make efficient long-term use of the land. (Courtesy USDA Soil Conservation Service.)

most of which are named for phases of soil series. Each series is divided into phases on the basis of slope, erosion, texture, or some other property significant to the use and management of the land.

7-1.1 Soil Surveys as Natural Resource Data

Soil surveys are used by many other people besides farmers and ranchers. The Council of State Governments (1977) sent questionnaires to 500 officials from all 50 state governments asking for the current level of use of natural resource data, including soil surveys. Results show that more than 50% of the states reported use of soil survey data.

No one type of resource data is used universally, but soil surveys and topographic maps were generally used by 11 of the 13 agencies. Even the two agencies that did not generally use soil surveys may find them useful in the future. The passage of Public Law 95-87, *Surface Mining Control and Reclamation Act* (U.S. Congress, 1977), made stockpiling of surface soil (topsoil) mandatory. This surface soil must be replaced after completion of mining operations to facilitate the reestablishment of protective vegetation. The information needed to remove and replace the surface soil is readily obtained from a soil survey map and report (see Chapter 11).

7-1.2 Soils and Agricultural Prosperity

The most prosperous farmers almost always farm the best soils. Olson (1977) presents evidence to support this statement in the environs of Syracuse, New York. He compared soil series, as mapped in standard soil surveys by the National Cooperative Soil Survey, with relative farm prosperity. The most prosperous farmers were farming Palmyra, Honeoye, and Lima soil series, all members of the Glossoboric Hapludalfs. (Consult a modern introductory soils textbook for information on the U.S. Soil Taxonomy.) The least prosperous farmers were farming Worth series (Typic Fragiorthods) and Empeyville series (Aquic Fragiorthods). Coarse texture, low fertility, fragipans, droughtiness, and cold temperatures limit productive agriculture on the latter soils.

7-1.3 Kinds of Soil Surveys

There are two general kinds of soil surveys—detailed and reconnaissance. A *detailed soil survey* is one where sufficient field work is done to observe all soil mapping units and to trace all soil boundaries throughout their length. A *reconnaissance soil survey* has only intermittent field observations. Much of the information is interpreted from aerial photos or other maps of the area.

The current detailed surveys being made in the United States for publication under the National Cooperative Soil Survey are known as *Standard Soil Surveys.* The maps and accompanying reports must meet certain standards to serve the needs of their users.

7-1.4 Soil Survey Reports

Soil surveys in the United States are made by the National Cooperative Soil Survey. Leadership is by the USDA-Soil Conservation Service and the respective land-grant university's Agricultural Experiment Station. In a few states, the cooperating agency is another organization. The respective federal agency is the cooperator on federal lands. Information obtained by the National Cooperative Soil Survey is published in soil survey reports, usually on a county basis. By 1989, soil survey reports had been published for about two-thirds of the 3097 counties in the 50 states and territories.

Soil survey reports in the United States consist of two parts, the text and the soil maps. The text tells how the survey was made, describes the county and the soils, tells how the soils are classified, and discusses their use, management, and conservation.

7-1.5 Base Maps

Base maps on which soil information is shown have experienced a genuine revolution. As late as the 1930s, some county soil maps were drawn on a base map made with a planetable for directions; distances were either paced or measured with an automobile tachometer. Topographic maps (made by the U.S. Geological Survey) were used when available. From about the 1930s to the 1950s, aerial photographs for most areas of the United States became available for use as base maps for soil surveys. These aerial photographs are updated periodically and continue to be the best base for drawing soil boundaries. The standard type is a black-and-white photograph with a matte (nonglossy) surface to facilitate marking soil boundaries and symbols in the field with a pencil.

Since the mid-1960s, infrared aerial photos have been used in some mapping. These color photos are superior to black-and-white photos where land use and vegetation are to be interpreted. Color photos are seldom used as soil survey base maps.

At about the same time as infrared photography became available, scanners (multispectral photographic systems) were developed. This technique permits the separation on the map of wetlands, dark soils, and well-drained soils but is useful only when the soil is bare of vegetation.

Thermal infrared sensors in aircraft can measure relative soil temperatures. Scanners are most useful at the time of day when the temperatures of well-drained soil, poorly drained soil, surface rock, and types of vegetation are expected to be in greatest contrast, usually at about 3 P.M.

For most of the world, Earth Resources Technology Satellites (Landsats 1 and 2) have photographed four-spectral-band data at 18-day intervals. Using Landsat maps at scales of 1:500,000 and 1:1,000,000, Klingebiel (1977) reports a technique for making a "good," "fair," and "poor" category map for food and fiber production in Mexico. This type of work has tremendous value for planning national development and identifying needs for more detailed soil surveys by conventional methods.

Although extremely useful as supporting and supplemental information, all air photo data require ground observations for full interpretation. Some reconnaissance-type soil surveys are made with minimal ground observations, but this diminishes the amount of information that can be mapped, and the accuracy is less than that of surveys made in the field.

7-1.6 Soil Maps

There are two kinds of soil maps in the Soil Survey Report:

1. *General soil map*—actually a Soil Association Map, made on a scale of 1:190,080. This map is especially useful in county-wide land use planning.
2. *Detailed soil map*—usually printed on a scale of 1:20,000 or 1:15,840 on an aerial photographic background.

7-1.7 Soil Map Units

The individual soil map units are almost all named as phases of soil series. The principal exceptions are areas covered with mine spoils, made land in and around cities and developments, rough broken land, and intermixed soil series too small in area to map separately.

A soil surveyor, with the aid of a mapping legend, draws boundaries on the map to separate the soil map units. The soil surveyor maps as nearly as possible the taxonomic units known as polypedons. The map symbol designates the type of polypedons plus the slope and erosion classes.

Polypedons are composed of adjacent pedons of the same soil series. One soil series is differentiated from another by properties inherent in the constituent *pedons* (Greek, *pedon* = ground is used to represent an individual unit of soil large enough to grow a representative plant). The soil pedons are typically about 1 m^2 in surface area and are characterized by the color, texture, structure, porosity (permeability), consistence of structural units (peds or clods), pH, concretions, clay coatings, organic matter, and root abundance of each horizon and the depth to bedrock or other root-restricting layer. Polypedon field characterizations also record the vegetation, surface drainage, slope class, erosion class, parent materials, stoniness, and land use (Soil Survey Staff, 1975).

The National Soil Survey Laboratory at Lincoln, Nebraska, determines scientific data on the 13,000 soil series mapped in the United States. Among the laboratory determinations on the soil series that are related to erosion predictions are: potential rooting depth for crop plants, permeability, air-filled porosity, organic carbon, extractable Ca and K, and coarse fragments (Grossman and Berdanier, 1982).

7-2 SOIL MAP UNIT INTERPRETATIONS

All mapping units in a modern soil survey report are interpreted for various uses in the text of the report. When the mapping units are used according to the limitations specified, the soils will remain productive, nonpolluting, and useful. Examples of soil map unit interpretations are included in the following sections.

7-2.1 Land Use Capability Groupings

The term "land" generally includes soil, mineral deposits, climate, water supply, location in relation to markets and transportation, vegetative cover, and improvements. However, in the definitions of the *land use capability groupings,* the word "soil" replaces "land" except in the name of each group and in the name of the subclass c indicating a limitation caused by climate.

There are eight *Land Use Capability Classes,* as shown in Figure 7-2, differentiated and described on the basis of *limitations* (hazards) that restrict intensity of use or require special treatment.

CLASS I: Soils that have few or no limitations for very intensive cultivation.

CLASS II: Soils that have moderate limitations that reduce the choice of adapted plants or that require moderate conservation practices.

CLASS III: Soils that have severe limitations that reduce the choice of plants, require intensive conservation practices, or both.

CLASS IV: Soils that have severe limitations that reduce the choice of plants, require very intensive management, or both.

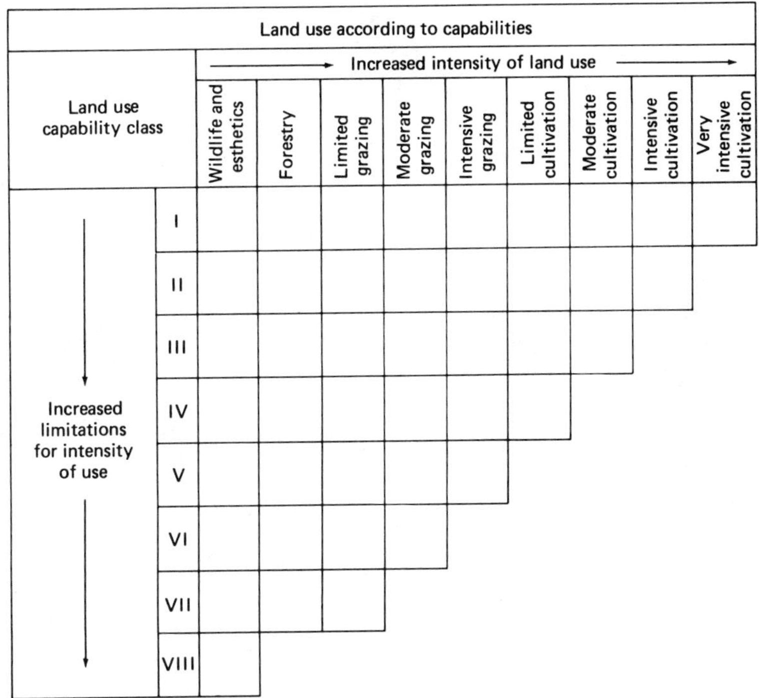

Figure 7–2 Land Use Capability Classes indicate the intensity of use for which soils are suited. Class I is suitable for any use, but other classes are restricted by various limitations and hazards. (Courtesy USDA Soil Conservation Service.)

CLASS V: Soils that are not likely to deteriorate but have other limitations, impractical to remove, that limit their use primarily to pasture grasses, range grasses, woodlands, wildlife, or esthetics.

CLASS VI: Soils that have severe limitations that make them generally unsuited to cultivation and limit their use primarily to pasture grasses, range grasses, woodlands, wildlife, or esthetics.

CLASS VII: Soils that have very severe limitations that make them unsuited to cultivation and that restrict their use primarily to pasture grasses, range grasses, woodlands, wildlife, or esthetics; an example is shown in Figure 7–3.

CLASS VIII: Soils and landforms that have limitations that preclude their use for commercial plants and restrict their use to wildlife, esthetics, recreation, and/or watersheds.

Land Use Capability Subclasses are groups within Land Use Capability Classes that designate the *dominant kind of limitation or hazard* restricting land use. The subclasses are designated by writing a lowercase letter following the Roman numeral that signifies the land capability class. The four subclasses are:

e: hazards of accelerated erosion and sedimentation.

w: hazards of excessive wetness.

Figure 7-3 Fairmont flaggy silty clay loam in Kentucky on 25% slopes. The soil is a Typic Hapludoll. It is in land use capability Class VII and subclass **e** (erosion limitation). Limited grazing is probably the most intensive use this soil can serve without excessive erosion. (Courtesy USDA Soil Conservation Service.)

- **s:** hazards of plant root restrictions, including excessive shallowness, extremely fine or coarse texture, stoniness, salinity, or sodicity.
- **c:** climatic hazards of excessive coldness or dryness for the normal growth of crop plants.

The relative abundance of these types of limitations in the United States is shown in Figure 7-4. Land Capability Class 1, by definition, has no hazards limiting its use and therefore has no subclass. Each of the other seven classes is divided into subclasses. Soil map units are classified into subclasses according to which one of the four types of hazards limits the use of the land to its designated capability class. When two subclasses limit land use equally, only one is used, priority being assigned in the sequence e, w, s, and c.

Land Use Capability Units are divisions of land use capability subclasses into smaller, more homogeneous groups of soil map units having similar use potential and management requirements. They have also been called "soil management groups." Capability units are established because subclasses are too broad and soil map units more specific than necessary for land management considerations. Therefore, soil map units with similar erosion hazards, degrees of wetness, stoniness, textural classes, and crop adaptations are grouped in the same land use capability unit.

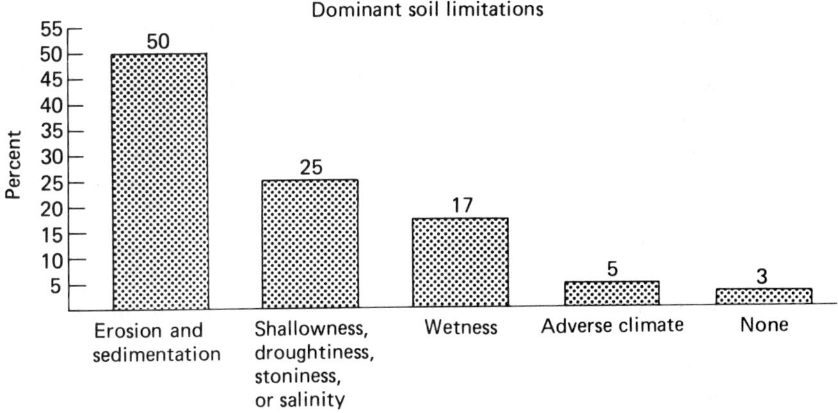

Figure 7–4 Dominant limitations (subclasses) that restrict the suitability of soils of the United States for more intensive use. Erosion and sedimentation limit the most intensive use of half of the soils of the nation. (From Soil Conservation Service, 1971.)

Capability units are identified by Arabic numbers added to the symbols for land use capability class and subclass. An example is IIIe-1. However, the land capability units are so variable throughout the 50 states that separate systems of designations and interpretations are established for individual counties.

Establishing economic vegetation on soils of land capability classes III to VI has been researched in Tennessee since 1983 and was ongoing in 1989. Adverse soils chosen for this research included soils that were poorly drained, droughty, eroded, steep, subject to flooding, or partly reclaimed coal mine spoils. Several different grass and tree species were used to find which species were best adapted to each adverse soil condition (Fribourg et al., 1989). Wide differences in productivity were identified. For example, bermudagrass yielded more than 12 times as much on the Collins soil series as it did on the reclaimed mine soil. American sycamore was found to yield less than loblolly pine on adverse soils, but the reverse was true on the more productive soils.

7–2.2 Predicting Crop Response

Soil survey reports published after 1965, and many published earlier, discuss general suitability of each soil map unit for the production of common farm crops, pasture, forage, and range grasses. Such discussions occur under "Descriptions of the Soils" and "Capability Groupings." In addition, under "Estimated Yields," all soil map units are rated for the average yields of their principal crops under two levels of management—average and high. Productivities for pasture-, range-, and woodland are included where appropriate. Field crop yields are indicated in bushels per acre, hay in tons per acre, and pasture in AUDs (animal unit days). AUDs are defined as the number of days that one cow or equivalent can be grazed on 1 acre (0.4 ha) without damage to the pasture. In semiarid range country, the soil map units with similar characteristics are grouped and used as a basis for delineating various range sites and their relative productivity.

7-2.3 Evaluating Rural Land

Soil map interpretations have been used in several states to evaluate rural land. For example, a study in Illinois compared the prices paid in 1509 rural land sales in 33 counties during 1966 to 1968 to soil productivity ratings of soil map units. The standard soil survey report and soil map can be used to evaluate rural land to help in equalization of taxes (Alexander et al., 1978).

Taxes on farm- and ranchland should be based on the productive potential of the soils and not on the management skill of the farmers and ranchers. Neither should taxes on rural property being farmed be based on its potential value for urban developments.

An economic analysis of yield potential and costs of production permits calculation of the potential agricultural value of each soil. Assessors equipped with these data and soil maps can calculate the potential crop income of a farm or ranch. The procedures and the crops considered vary from state to state, but the essential steps are:

1. Calculate the weighting factor to be assigned to each soil map unit.
2. Measure the area of each kind of soil in each land ownership.
3. Sum the products of area × weighting factor.
4. Adjust for buildings, location, and other factors.

Several states now use the above procedure to determine all or part of the assessed valuation for property taxes.

7-2.4 Upgrading Soil Test Recommendations

The soil testing laboratory can make more precise lime and fertilizer recommendations for all soil samples that are collected and labeled on the basis of a soil map unit. For example, in the Soil Survey of Green County, Illinois (Soil Conservation Service, 1974a) one soil series is named Clarksdale. With the words "Clarksdale Series" on the soil sample label, the soil testing laboratory can adjust the fertilizer and lime recommendations according to experimental data from Clarksdale and similar soil series.

The soil testing laboratory at Iowa State University, for example, requests the name of the soil series along with each soil sample so as to adjust the fertilizer recommendation based on known subsoil characteristics. Soil characteristics such as slope, depth of topsoil, and drainage can be supplied instead if the soil series is unknown.

7-2.5 Determining Need for Artificial Drainage

Soil surveys indicate soil series. One criterion for differentiating soil series is internal drainage. The natural internal drainage is classified as either excessively drained, somewhat excessively drained, well drained, moderately well drained, *somewhat poorly drained, poorly drained,* or *very poorly drained.* The last three soil drainage classes usually require some type of artificial drainage for optimum yields of most upland farm crops.

7-2.6 Evaluating Woodland and Windbreak Sites

Tree species adaptation and relative growth rates depend on many factors, including soil depth through which roots may grow without physical or chemical hindrance, available water-holding capacity of the soil, soil texture, organic matter, aeration, and depth to the water table. Information about all these factors can be interpreted from the soil map unit. Such information for each county in which forest trees grow naturally, as well as for semiarid areas where windbreaks and shelterbelts are common, can be found in each county soil survey report.

The Soil Survey Reports in humid regions have a section on "Woodland" that itemizes the soil map symbol, woodland group, potential productivity, seedling mortality, plant competition, equipment limitations, and preferred species for planting. The Soil Survey Reports of semiarid areas discuss the suitability of the various soils for windbreak plantings.

7-2.7 Selecting Sites for Wildlife Habitats

A table included in standard soil survey reports issued since 1965 rates all soil map units on suitability for "wildlife habitat elements," including grain and seed crops, grasses and legumes, wild herbaceous plants, hardwood trees and shrubs, coniferous trees, and wetland food and cover plants. Also, soil map units are rated for suitability to openland, woodland, and wetland wildlife.

7-2.8 Interpreting Engineering Uses

The most important soil characteristics for engineering uses are particle (grain) sizes, permeability to water, compressibility, shear strength, compaction, drainage, shrink-swell potential, plasticity, soil pH, depth to water table, depth to bedrock, and topography. Engineering test data are presented in tables in soil survey reports under the heading "Engineering Uses of the Soils." The interpretations are based on field testing, laboratory analyses, and estimations of soil properties.

The engineering test data can be used to predict the suitability of each soil map unit as a source of topsoil, sand, gravel, caliche, or road fill. They can also be used to evaluate the suitability of each soil map unit for constructing a sanitary landfill, a filter field for a septic tank, a sewage lagoon, a foundation for a house, a farm pond, a highway, or a playground. Other available information important to engineering uses of soils includes flooding hazard, relative wetness, erodibility, and stabilization of construction slopes with adapted vegetation.

7-3 MANAGING LAND

Land is used for many activities and purposes having a wide variety of soil requirements. Land managers can use soil survey information and interpretations to select soils and management best suited for particular uses.

7-3.1 Managing Agricultural Land

Farmers and ranchers need to be good land managers to make a profit without causing long-term soil deterioration. Soil survey reports provide information on which to base land-management decisions. They are useful for major decisions such as what land to purchase and what use to make of it. They are also useful for designing field layouts, planning conservation practices, and making general management decisions.

Selecting land for a particular enterprise is easier and more precise when soil survey information is used. For example, a rancher choosing land for a cattle ranch in the southern Great Plains would find that the Abilene soils shown in Figure 7-5 are known as Pachic Argiustolls to soil surveyors and deep hardland range soils to local ranchers. The native grasses are mid- and short-prairie grasses. Good grazing management is needed because overgrazing causes blue gramagrass and buffalograss to increase at the expense of the taller grasses. Forage production then declines from its normal 600 lb/ac to 90 lb/ac (700 down to 100 kg/ha) annually (Soil Conservation Service, 1974b).

Adapted varieties can be selected for farms on the basis of experiment station results when soil survey maps show that the soils are similar. Also, needs for artificial drainage or for erosion-control practices can be identified and serious damage avoided. The general likelihood of needing lime and fertilizer may also be indicated in a soil survey report, but soil samples from the actual field should be tested when specific fertility recommendations are needed.

7-3.2 Mechanization in Developing Countries

Developing countries want to move rapidly from hand-hoe cultivation to animal-power cultivation to cultivation by tractors. These transitions sometimes succeed and sometimes fail. One reason for the failure of animal-powered farming in humid Africa is trypanosomiasis (African sleeping sickness) carried by several species of tsetse fly (*Glossina*). In humid Africa, many governments want to lead their farmers from the use of the village-made hoes directly into the use of the most sophisticated tractors.

Rapid mechanization is feasible on some soils. For example, nearly level and fertile Vertisols occur in Ethiopia and Sudan (eastern Africa) and in Ghana and Nigeria (western Africa). Tractors are the most suitable farm power on Vertisols because animals cannot pull plows and other implements through such fine-textured soils.

By contrast, the ferruginous soils of Ghana in western Africa are so steep and

Figure 7-5 A soil profile of the Abilene series (Pachic Argiustoll) in the 25-in. (640-mm) precipitation belt in Texas. This soil supports a good growth of nutritious range grasses. The root zone is about 3 ft (nearly a meter) deep to the whitish calcium carbonate zone at the bottom of the photo. (*Note:* the arrow is at 1 m.) (Courtesy Texas Agricultural Experiment Station.)

irregular in topography, so low in fertility, and so high in plinthite (ironstone, laterite) that they cannot be cultivated with a tractor.

7-3.3 Delineating Nutritional Problem Areas

As early as 1878, President Welch of the Agricultural College at Ames, Iowa (now Iowa State University of Science and Technology) suggested that there should be a national study of soils in relation to animal and human nutrition. The Annual Report for 1898 of the USDA-Bureau of Animal Industry contained a section on the relationship between a bone disease of animals and the forage from pastures on the "noncalcareous" soils of the Gulf Coastal Plains. Later it was discovered that the soils were acid and low in calcium and phosphorus. The bone disease became known as osteomalacia. Extreme cases were reported in the 1930s in some northern states where animals ate only native prairie grasses and overwintered on prairie hay. Soils likely to supply only small amounts of phosphorus can be identified on soil maps and checked by nutrient tests. Phosphorus percentages in most forages can be increased by a soil application of phosphorus fertilizer or by liming acid soils. The phosphorus fertilizer will also increase forage production and reduce erosion on soils low in available phosphorus.

Forage plants growing on soils that are poorly drained, both on Histosols (peats and mucks) and on wet mineral soils, may contain concentrations of copper and molybdenum that are toxic to cattle and sheep (Kubota, 1975). These soils are readily identifiable on soil maps.

Some nutritional problems such as those mentioned relate to specific areas that can be mapped. People in most developed nations obtain food from a wide area and many soils. A balanced diet is therefore likely to contain adequate nutrients.

7-3.4 Cleansing the Environment

Pollution of the environment is a serious threat to human life. Pollutants discarded in oceans and other bodies of water may not degrade; water may preserve them. Soil is the only biodegrading medium for rational disposal of many kinds of polluting wastes (Chapter 17).

Soils vary in the kinds of pollutants each can absorb and the efficiency with which each is degraded. Soils that are ideal for use as septic tank drain fields are usually not ideal for sewage lagoons or sanitary landfills. Even different types of landfills require different soil characteristics. Table 7-1 rates seven soil series in Kansas as "good," "fair," or "poor" for use as a disposal site for each of these kinds of polluting wastes. Similar tables can be found in other modern soil survey reports.

In general, a septic tank drain field requires a soil that is well drained, sandy-loam to loam textured, as deep as possible to a water table or a water-restricting layer, nearly level, pH 6.5 to 8.5, high in cation-exchange capacity, high in organic matter, and free from coarse fragments. In contrast, the ideal soil for a sewage lagoon is fine-textured, poorly drained with no possibility of contaminating the surface or ground waters, structureless (puddled), level, any pH, low in organic matter, and free from coarse fragments. Soils for use as sanitary landfills should

TABLE 7-1 RELATIVE RATINGS AND THE REASONS FOR THE RATINGS OF SELECTED SOIL SERIES IN KANSAS FOR USE IN WASTE DISPOSAL

	Relative ratings				
			Sanitary landfill		
Soil series	Septic tank drainfield	Sewage lagoon	Trench type	Area type	Reason(s) for ratings
Carwile	Poor	Good	Poor	Fair	Slow internal drainage
Goshen	Fair	Fair	Fair	Fair	Occasional flooding, rapid permeability
Grable	Fair	Fair	Fair	Fair	Rapid permeability, water table
Likes	Good	Poor	Poor	Poor	Rapid permeability, sandy
Lula	Fair	Fair	Poor	Good	Hard bedrock at 40 to 60 in. (1 to 1.5 m)
McLain	Poor	Good	Fair	Fair	Fine-textured, slow permeability, occasional flooding
Riverton	Fair	Fair	Fair	Fair	Rapid permeability, coarse fragments

Source: Olson, 1974; Soil Survey Staff, 1975.

have properties intermediate between those ideal for drain fields and those ideal for sewage lagoons. However, since a trench-type landfill requires more soil manipulation under varying moisture conditions, its soil should be deep, medium-textured, and high in organic matter, and have stable structure.

7-3.5 Planning and Development

Soil survey reports and soil maps have been used in almost every conceivable type of land resource planning, zoning, and general development. The largest project is that for the entire 201-county watershed of the Tennessee Valley, comprising parts of seven states.

7-4 LAND USE PLANNING

Land use planning is often perceived as having four objectives: (1) to protect current land use, (2) to guide future developments, (3) to reduce present and future conflicts, and (4) to avoid pollution (Gold et al., 1989). An area of stratified sandy glacial deposits will serve as an example of the use of soil survey maps to plan land use and avoid pollution. Sandy deposits are natural locations for rainwater to recharge aquifers. For this reason, they should be avoided when locating a landfill, a storage lagoon for manure, a salt-storage pile for deicing roads, or a drain field for a septic tank. Neither should such deep sandy deposits be fertilized heavily with nitrogen fertilizer, animal manures, or sewage sludges.

These stratified drift deposits must be identified and located accurately to avoid their misuse. This can be done with proper use of soil survey maps or U.S. Geological Survey maps. Fortunately, these two kinds of maps are in agreement about 85% of the time. Both kinds of maps must be used because neither kind is available for all areas where such deep sand deposits exist. Geological maps are available for 5 to 10% of the U.S. and soil survey maps for about 66%.

7-4.1 Land Use in the United States

Major uses of nonfederal rural land in the United States are listed in Table 7-2: cropland, 28%; pastureland, 9%; rangeland, 27%; forestland, 26%; and other nonfederal rural land, 10%.

TABLE 7-2 USE OF NONFEDERAL RURAL LAND IN THE UNITED STATES IN 1982

Land use	Acres (millions)	Hectares (millions)	Percent of total
Cropland	421.4	170.7	28
Pastureland	133.3	54.0	9
Rangeland	405.9	164.4	27
Forestland	393.8	159.5	26
Subtotal	1,354.4	548.5	90
Other nonfederal rural lands	143.2	58.0	10
Grand total	1,497.6	606.6	100

Source: National Research Council, 1986, p. 7.

7-4.2 *T* Factor, Land Use, Erosion, and Sedimentation

Each soil map unit has a *T* factor that designates the rate of erosion it can tolerate without permanent loss of soil productivity. Map unit characteristics that influence this *T* factor are depth of the solum (A + B horizons), type of parent material, relative productivity, and previous erosion. Use and management of the soil map unit determine the actual erosion rate (Chapter 6).

There is little doubt that a well-managed full growth of forest provides maximum protection against soil erosion and sediment loss. Next in rank of soil protection is a thick cover of grass, and least protective is bare soil. But how much does erosion increase when a forest is logged, burned, cleared and cropped, or when a pasture is plowed and cropped? Table 7-3 contains answers to these and related questions. The erosion data in Table 7-3 are averages for the entire United States and must be used only for generalized comparisons of erosion or sedimentation rates. Nationwide reductions in total erosion and sedimentation could be achieved if only Class I land were used for the most intensive cropping and all other Land Use Capability classes were used within their designated limitations. Human needs dictate that most land must be used as intensively as its limitations permit, and the country needs to reserve its best agricultural land for agricultural purposes. A new national concern for prime and unique agricultural lands recognizes this concept.

It can be concluded from Table 7-3 that (1) both water and wind erosion are most severe on cropland; (2) grazed forestland has more than three times as much erosion as nongrazed; and (3) water erosion on pastureland and rangeland are equal.

7-4.3 Prime and Unique Agricultural Lands

There has been increasing concern that the best lands for agricultural use were being irreversibly converted for such purposes as residential and business sites as shown in Figure 7-6. This concern has led to efforts to define and identify prime and unique agricultural lands. The following definitions come from a paper by Johnson (1975) delivered to a conference called to discuss these issues in Washington, D.C.

TABLE 7-3 AVERAGE ANNUAL SHEET, RILL, AND WIND EROSION

	Sheet and rill erosion		Wind erosion	
Land use	tons/ac-yr	mt/ha-yr	tons/ac-yr	mt/ha-yr
Cropland				
All	4.4	9.86	3.0	6.72
Cultivated	4.8	10.75	3.3	7.39
Pastureland	1.4	3.14	0.0	0.00
Rangeland	1.4	3.14	1.5	3.36
Forestland				
Grazed	2.3	5.15	0.1	0.22
Not grazed	0.7	1.57	0.0	0.00

Source: National Research Council, 1986, p.8.

Figure 7-6 Most of the soil under this subdivision in Maryland would be classified in Land Use Capability Class I and would be considered "prime agricultural land." Building costs were less than elsewhere because the area is nearly level and adequately drained. Who should determine whether it should be used for housing or reserved for agriculture? (Courtesy USDA Soil Conservation Service.)

Prime farmland is land that has the best combination of physical and chemical characteristics for producing food, feed, forage, fiber, and oilseed crops. The land could be cropland, pastureland, rangeland, forestland, or other land, but not urban built-up land or water. It has the soil quality, growing season, and moisture supply needed to economically produce sustained high yields of crops when treated and managed according to modern farming methods.

Prime agricultural lands are characterized by these eight parameters:

1. Adequate natural rainfall or adequate good quality irrigation water to meet normal needs 7 out of 10 years.
2. Mean annual summer soil temperatures warmer than 59°F (15°C) at a depth of 20 in. (50 cm).
3. Lack of excessive moisture: (a) flooding no more often than once in two years, and (b) water table below rooting zone.
4. Soil not excessively acid or basic (pH between 5.5 and 8.6), not saline nor sodic.
5. Permeability at least 0.38 in./hr (1.0 cm/h) in the upper 20 in. (50 cm) of soil.
6. Gravel, cobbles, or stones not excessive enough to interfere with power machinery.

7. Soil deep enough to any root restricting layer to permit adequate moisture storage for crop plants.
8. Soil not excessively erodible. The universal soil loss equation K-factor multiplied by slope percentage is 5 or less.

Unique farmland is land other than prime farmland that is used for the production of specific high-value food and fiber crops. It has the special combination of soil quality, location, growing season, and moisture supply needed to economically produce sustained high quality and/or high yields of a specific crop when treated and managed according to modern farming methods (Johnson, 1975).

Unique agricultural lands include cranberry bogs, citrus orchards, and rice fields, as examples. Three criteria characterize such lands:

1. Adequate soil moisture from whatever source
2. Soil temperatures high enough and a growing season long enough to produce a satisfactory harvest of the selected crop
3. A location that has the favorable attributes needed, such as nearness to market, good air drainage, the proper aspect (direction of slope), favorable relative humidity, and suitable soil temperature

7-4.4 Soil Surveys for Planning and Zoning

Examples of specific uses of soil survey information for planning and zoning will be briefed for a city, two counties, and for "critical areas" in general.

Soil surveys were used in establishing subdivision regulations in Canfield, Ohio, as early as 1966. Canfield is a town in northeastern Ohio under 5000 in population. Based on those properties relevant to construction, public health, and erosion and sedimentation hazard, all soil series in Canfield were placed in one of five groups as follows (Soil Conservation Service, 1967):

I: Favorable soils (well drained, 2 to 12% slopes)
II: Steep soils (12 to 50% slopes)
III: Seasonally wet soils (0 to 6% slopes)
IV: Permanently wet soils with high shrink-swell potential (0 to 6% slopes)
V: Restricted soils (flood hazard, nearly level)

Each of the first four soil groups had specific mandatory foundation construction specifications, whereas group V soils were not to be used for buildings without very costly flood control structures approved in advance.

Black Hawk County in north-central Iowa is a prosperous agricultural and industrial area with a population of 133,000 persons. Before zoning, pressures were tremendous to use prime agricultural lands for housing developments. Prime agricultural land was defined as any land that would produce 6900 lb/ac (7735 kg/ha) or more of corn. Based on this criterion, 68% of the county was rated as "prime."

After a soil survey of Black Hawk County was completed in 1973, a public hearing was held on a proposed county order to zone the county. One very controversial section of the order prohibited the use of prime agricultural lands for residential developments. The county board of supervisors passed the order and land developers moved to the surrounding counties. Within a year, however, the adjoining counties started passing similar orders (Vincent, 1977).

Walworth County, Wisconsin, using a 1966 soil survey as fundamental resource information, passed a sanitary code in 1968 and a shoreland and subdivision zoning order in 1971. Orders such as this help prevent disasters such as that shown in Figure 7–7.

Critical areas are those that either possess unique economic, recreational, historic, or cultural values to the nation, or that pose environmental hazards. Examples of national concern include floodplains, virgin redwood forests, Indian burial grounds, lakeshores, ocean beaches, groundwater recharge areas, unique wilderness areas, waterfowl flyways, prime agricultural land, and historic trails. Soil surveys are as important for delineating critical areas as in preparing and enforcing city and county zoning ordinances and orders.

7–4.5 Environmental Impact Statements

Projects involving major soil disturbances such as starting a new housing development, building a new highway, opening a surface mine for coal, or siting a power

Figure 7–7 A zoning order based on soil maps would have prevented this house from being located on this area of Linside soil series. The soil is a Fluvaquentic Eutrochrept—the prefix "Fluv-" indicates the flooding hazard. (Courtesy H. C. Porter, Virginia Agricultural Experiment Station, Virginia Polytechnic Institute and State University.)

plant must have prior approval based on an environmental impact statement submitted to the U.S. Council on Environmental Quality. By 1977, 22 states had passed laws requiring that an environmental impact statement also be filed with the designated state agency.

The essentials of an environmental impact statement include an inventory of air quality, water quality, aquatic life, terrestrial wildlife, people, jobs, transportation, and endangered plant and animal life. Another part of the report consists of predictions of the changes and disturbances that will be caused by the proposed activity. Soil considerations are usually crucial in environmental impact statements because of the wind and water erosion and sedimentation that result from land disturbance.

Teams set up to research and write an environmental impact statement should consist of subject-matter specialists trained in the various environmental areas involved. For example, a forester should be a member of a study team in a forested or potentially forested area, an urban planner in an urban or potentially urban area, and a dairy specialist where dairies exist or are being considered. Because several specialties are involved, the average environmental impact team consists of 15 to 20 members. Any such team needs to have engineers, scientists, and planners concerned with soil, water, vegetation, and wildlife in addition to those dealing with construction of the proposed development. The team should be under the direction of an administrator who will assure that all pertinent factors are considered on their merits without bias.

SUMMARY

Soil surveys started in the United States in 1899 and are now used throughout the world. The first surveys in an area are sometimes reconnaissance type, but most others are detailed. Most map units on detailed soil surveys are named as phases of soil series. The surveys are published, usually on a county basis, as a bound volume containing explanatory text and the soil maps on a photographic base.

Land Use Capability Classes, Subclasses, and possibly Units are interpreted from the soil map units. The objective is to place all map units into larger management groups and thereby facilitate maximum intensity of use without excessive erosion and sedimentation.

Each soil map unit can be interpreted for crop adaptations and predicted yields, land value, drainage needs, woodland sites, wildlife habitats, recreational sites, engineering qualities for construction, and other purposes. Soil surveys provide a sound basis for land management for farms and ranches, for mechanizing cultivation in developing countries, for identifying areas of nutritional deficiencies and toxicities for animals and people, for proper disposal of wastes, and for general land development.

Soil survey reports (texts and maps) are valuable as a scientific basis for land use planning. The concepts of *prime* and *unique* agricultural lands were developed to preserve productive soil for essential food, feed, and fiber crops. Such areas are delimited only with the help of a soil survey. Town and county planning and zoning agencies are now using soil surveys as a physical basis for their ordinances and orders.

Various construction projects that result in major soil disturbances now require environmental impact statements. Soil factors are important considerations in the preparation of environmental impact statements.

QUESTIONS

1. What are the principal purposes of a soil survey?
2. Soil surveys are one kind of natural resource data. What are the other principal kinds? Compare the relative use of soil surveys by natural resource and transportation agencies in relation to other kinds of natural resource data.
3. Describe the contents of any recent soil survey report.
4. Select two contrasting soil map unit interpretations and explain their significance to natural resource experts in these respective subjects.
5. Explain the use of soil surveys as a scientific basis for rational planning and zoning.

REFERENCES

ALEXANDER, J. D., S. G. CARMER, and J. B. FEHRENBACHER, 1978. Usefulness of detailed and general soil maps for rural land equalization. In *Agronomy Abstracts.* American Society of Agronomy, Madison, Wis., p. 165.

BEESON, K. C., and G. MATRONE, 1976. *The Soil Factor in Nutrition: Animal and Human.* Marcel Dekker, New York, 152 p.

CONSTANTINESCO, I., 1976. *Soil Conservation for Developing Countries.* Soils Bull. 30. FAO, Rome.

COUNCIL OF STATE GOVERNMENTS, 1977. *General Description of Council of State Governments' Natural Resources Data Study.* Preliminary report, mimeographed, unnumbered. Lexington, Ky., 6 p.

FRIBOURG, H. A., G. R. WELLS, H. CALONNE, E. DUJARDIN, D. D. TYLER, J. T. AMMONS, R. M. EVANS, A. HOUSTON, M. C. SMITH, M. E. TIMPSON, and G. G. PERCELL, 1989. Forage and tree production on marginal soils in Tennessee. *J. Prod. Agric.* 2:262–268.

GOLD, A. J., T. SAIPING, P. V. AUGUST, and W. R. WRIGHT, 1989. Using soil surveys to delineate stratified drift deposits for groundwater protection. *J. Soil Water Conserv.* 44:232–234.

GRAVEEL, J. G., H. A. FRIBOURG, J. R. OVERTON, F. F. BELL, and W. L. SANDERS, 1989. Response of corn to soil variation in west Tennessee, 1957–1980. *J. Prod. Agric.* 2:300–305.

GROSSMAN, R. B., and C. R. BERDANIER, 1982. Erosion tolerance for cropland: Application of the soil survey data base. In *Determinants of Soil Loss Tolerance* Spec. Publ. 45, p. 113–130. American Society of Agronomy and Soil Science Society of America, Madison, Wis.

JOHNSON, W. M., 1975. Classification and mapping of prime and unique farmlands. In *Recommendations on Prime Lands.* Prepared at the Seminar on Retention of Prime Lands, July 16-17, USDA, p. 189-198.

KLINGEBIEL, A. A., 1977. Soil survey methodology-Use of landsat for determining soil potential. In *Soil Resource Inventories.* Proceedings of a workshop held at Cornell University, Ithaca, N.Y., April 4-7, p. 101-105.

KUBOTA, J., 1975. The poisoned cattle of Willow Creek. *Soil Cons.* 40(9):18-21.

MEGAHAN, W. F., 1972. Logging, erosion, sedimentation: Are they dirty words? *J. For.* 70:403-407.

NATIONAL RESEARCH COUNCIL, 1986. *Soil Conservation: Assessing the National Resources Inventory,* Vol. 1. National Academy Press, Washington, D.C., 114 p. Data source: USDA Soil Conservation Service, *1982 National Resources Inventory.*

OLSON, G. W., 1974. *Using Soils of Kansas for Waste Disposal.* Univ. Kans., Bull. 208.

OLSON, G. W., 1977. *Using Soils as Ecological Resources.* Inf. Bull. 6, Biological Sciences, Agronomy 1, Cornell Univ., Ithaca, N.Y., 15 p.

SCHNEPH, M. (ed.), 1977. *Land Use: Tough Choices in Today's World.* Soil Conservation Society of America, Ankeny, Iowa, 454 p.

SOIL CONSERVATION SERVICE, 1967. *Subdivision Regulations for Canfield, Ohio,* p. 20-35.

SOIL CONSERVATION SERVICE, 1971. *Two Thirds of Our Land: A National Inventory.* Program Aid 984. USDA, Washington, D.C.

SOIL CONSERVATION SERVICE, 1974a. *Soil Survey of Green County, Illinois.* In cooperation with the Ill. Agr. Expt. Sta.

SOIL CONSERVATION SERVICE, 1974b. *Soil Survey of Cottle County, Texas.* In cooperation with the Tex. Agr. Expt. Sta.

SOIL SURVEY STAFF, 1975. *Soil Taxonomy: A Basic System of Soil Classification for Making and Interpreting Soil Surveys.* USDA Agric. Handbook 436.

U.S. CONGRESS, 1977. *Surface Mining Control and Reclamation Act of 1977.* Public Law 95-87, Washington, D.C.

VINCENT, G., 1977. Land use control by law. *Successful Farming,* Oct., p. A6.

WHETZEL, J., and C. HOGELIN, 1977. Revegetation in the Rockies. *Soil Cons.* 43(5):4-5.

8

Cropping Systems

The natural protection offered by trees, grasses, and other plants is lost when land is converted to cropland. Cropping systems, that is, the crops grown and the techniques used to grow them, need to be chosen to provide adequate protection for the land. The usual result of a poor cropping system is accelerated soil loss that reduces soil productivity and increases environmental pollution.

Many cropping systems leave much of the soil surface exposed during part of the year. The impact of water or wind on the soil at such times can cause high rates of erosion and serious damage. The damage in many fields could be greatly reduced by adjusting the cropping systems to minimize exposure of the soil to the most erosive wind- and rainstorms. Cropping systems should be designed to protect both present and future productivity by providing adequate vegetative cover to control erosion.

8-1 PLANT COVER

The first requirement for a crop is that it be adapted to the environment where it is to be grown. Tropical fruits need warm, frost-free climates. Warm-season crops such as corn and soybeans can evade cold winters if summer moisture is available, whereas earlier maturing crops such as small grains are grown where the summers are dry or the growing season is short. Every crop has its own limited range of climatic adaptation.

Soil factors are also important for producing plant growth. A wet, puddled soil is good for paddy rice but bad for most other crops. Blueberries, strawberries, and other iron-loving crops do best in acid soils, but most other crops produce maximum growth in the slightly acid to nearly neutral range.

Poor crop growth can be a disaster to the soil and the environment as well as to the grower. Poor growth exposes the soil to erosion by raindrop splash, runoff, and wind. The eroded soil is deposited elsewhere, often burying plants, filling reservoirs, eutrophying streams, and causing other damage to the environment.

8-1.1 Amount of Plant Cover Needed

The amount of plant cover needed to protect a soil depends on the erodibility of the soil and the intensity of erosive forces. Loose soil on steep slopes needs permanent vegetation to intercept raindrops and to limit the amount and velocity of runoff. Vegetation may be needed to deflect high wind velocities even if the land is immune to water erosion. Usually, the need for cover is much greater at some seasons than at others. The soil-loss equations discussed in Chapter 6 provide a means of estimating the adequacy of the cover produced by various cropping systems in particular situations.

8-1.2 Types of Crops

Many kinds of crops are grown in the world. Only a few can be included here, so this discussion will be limited to groups or types of crops that cover large areas of land. The full meaning of crops includes any plants or parts of plants grown for agricultural production. Most crops are considered within the collective domains of agronomy, horticulture, and forestry. Usually, some kind of management or culture is needed to encourage crop growth so that a good yield can be harvested. The harvest may come after a few weeks or months, or it may be delayed for years. Annual crops must be planted every year, but certain perennial crops may be planted once and harvested many times.

For discussion purposes, crops will be divided into row crops, small-grain crops, cultivated forage crops, and tree crops. Some characteristics of each group will be considered in this section; management factors will be discussed in later sections.

Row Crops. Many crops have traditionally been planted in rows about 40 in. (1 m) apart so that they can be cultivated. Often these are a farmer's most profitable crops and therefore the ones that receive the most attention. Corn, cotton, potatoes, sorghum, soybeans, sugar beets, sugarcane, and sunflowers are examples of field crops that are usually grown in rows. Truck crops such as most vegetables and small fruits are also grown in rows. The rows facilitate tillage to control weeds, spraying or dusting of pesticides, application of supplemental fertilizer as side-dressing after the crop is established, and finally the harvesting of the crop.

Row crops frequently create problems for soil conservationists. An unprotected area between the rows, as shown in Figure 8-1, may be exposed to several erosive rainstorms. Cultivation keeps the soil loose and erodible. Rills form easily where the rows guide water down a slope. More sheet, rill, and gully erosion occur

Figure 8–1 The soil between these young soybean rows was puddled by raindrops and crusted when it dried. (Courtesy F. R. Troeh.)

under row crops than under close-growing crops in a similar environment. The frequency of growing row crops in a rotation is often limited by the erosion hazard.

Small Grains. Rice, wheat, barley, oats, and rye are known as small grains or cereal crops. These crops are widely adapted and are used to produce bread, cereals, and other foods for people and animals. Rice is the main staple of many areas with warm climates and will grow in wet conditions that exclude most other crops. Rye, wheat, barley, and oats are often the only cash crops grown where cool climates cause short growing seasons and in warmer areas with dry summers because they produce most of their growth during cool seasons. Summer fallow helps to extend their range into still drier climates. In more humid areas, the small grains may be grown in rotation with row crops and forage crops.

Small grains are usually drilled in rows about 6 to 10 in. (15 to 25 cm) apart or else broadcast. Their fast early growth and relatively close plant spacing provide much better erosion control than row crops but not as good as that of most forage crops.

Forage Crops. Crops grown to be fed to livestock as pasture or hay are known as forage or fodder crops. Many grasses and legumes are included either singly or in combination. Some are annuals, some are biennials, and some are perennials. Some are native plants, some are introduced from other parts of the world, and some have been improved by intensive plant breeding.

Forage crops are maintained as permanent cover on areas that are not cultivated because of the soil, climate, or some other reason. They are grown elsewhere as part of the crop rotation. They may occupy the land for only a few months in some fields, for a year in others, and for several years in succession in still others.

Forage crops are grown with close spacing between plants except in areas too dry to support dense vegetation. Maximum cover is attained by planting crops that grow rapidly, by planting the forage crop along with a companion crop, or by maintaining established stands for a long time.

Forage crops are often considered to be "soil-building crops." This concept is true in some ways but false in others. Improved soil fertility is often inferred because many forage crops are legumes, and nitrogen-fixing *Rhizobium* bacteria grow on their roots. Crops such as alfalfa or sweetclover have been used extensively to replenish the nitrogen supply of the soil before growing a corn or wheat crop. A large tonnage of plant material should be disked or plowed into the soil when a positive fertilizer effect is desired. Leaving only roots and stubble results in little or no net addition of nitrogen to the soil and causes a significant removal of all other nutrients. As shown in Table 8-1, forage crops remove larger amounts of many nutrients than most other crops remove. This soil-depleting effect can be reduced by feeding the forage to livestock and returning manure to the land.

The close spacing of forage plants coupled with the improved soil structure and permeability they produce provide good protection against erosion. Forage crops are therefore regarded as soil conserving and are useful where the erosion hazard is too great for other crops.

TABLE 8-1 NUTRIENTS CONTAINED IN TYPICAL YIELDS OF VARIOUS CROPS

	Yield (tons/ac)	Nutrients (lb/ac)					
		N	P	K	Ca	Mg	S
Forage crops							
Alfalfa hay	4	192	20	157	117	25	23
Lespedeza hay	4	168	15	75	80	15	[a]
Red clover hay	2.5	95	10	82	57	19	7
Sweetclover hay	5	260	23	178	125	23	41
Timothy hay	2	44	6	64	14	7	5
Row crops							
Corn grain	4	112	22	23	1	8	9
Peanuts	1	60	9	11	2	4	5
Potatoes	9	72	9	86	2	5	4
Soybeans	1	120	12	30	5	6	5
Sugar beets	20	104	16	100	16	12	4
Small grains							
Barley	1.5	57	12	15	2	4	5
Oats	1.5	54	14	12	2	5	6
Rice	1.5	38	8	10	2	4	2
Rye	1	40	7	9	2	2	3
Wheat	1.5	63	12	13	1	4	6

[a]Data not available.

Source: Calculated from percentage compositions in F. B. Morrison, *Feeds and Feeding,* 1956, Morrison Publishing Co., Ithaca, N.Y.

Tree Crops. Trees are grown for many purposes ranging from wood and paper products to Christmas trees and other ornamental uses, to fruit products, to helping restore the fertility of tropical soils. Some trees are grown in pure stands, some are mixed with other species of trees, and some grow along with a wide variety of shrubs, grasses, and herbaceous plants.

Tree crops are suited to a wide range of environments. Apple trees grow where the soil freezes in the winter, oranges and other citrus fruit sensitive to frost are grown in warmer climates, and coconuts require tropical conditions. Trees grow in some of the warmest and wettest climates on earth and prevail far into the cold climates but give way to smaller plants in drier climates.

Trees combined with undergrowth and a litter layer provide strong protection against erosion. Raindrops seldom strike the soil surface because they are gently absorbed by the litter layer after having been intercepted several times by the leaves, branches, and undergrowth. The protected soil surface retains a porous structure and the infiltration rate is much faster than it would be if a crust could form. Increased infiltration reduces the runoff volume. Runoff velocity is slowed as the water trickles through the litter layer. Most soil loss from such settings is either by solution erosion in the percolating water or by sudden, rare, intense rains that produce enough concentrated runoff to wash away the cover and cut a gully. Even then, areas outside the main flow of runoff may be undamaged.

Not all trees provide as much protection as outlined in the preceding paragraph. Exposed soil in a clean-cultivated orchard, for example, is subject to erosion. Raindrop impact can be damaging even under the trees because drops falling off tree branches are often large. Erosion control requires cover to intercept these drops again nearer the soil surface.

8-1.3 Plant Population and Row Spacing

A bluegrass pasture normally has millions of plants per acre, while a few hundred trees may cover a nearby acre. Most other plant populations fall somewhere between these extremes. The number of plants is, of course, likely to be inversely related to their size.

Increasing the population of plants per acre can improve both crop yields and erosion control. Newer varieties of some crops have been developed to be grown at higher populations than were formerly common. For example, top corn yields are likely to require 20,000 to 28,000 plants per acre (50,000 to 70,000 per hectare) instead of the old standard of about 12,000 plants per acre (30,000 per hectare). The older varieties do not produce well at the higher densities because crowding causes many barren stalks and reduces grain production.

Increased plant population in row crops is achieved by either narrower rows or closer spacing in the row or both. Although spacing plants equally in all directions minimizes crowding and maximizes protection against erosion, cultivation and harvesting practices often require that certain crops be grown in rows.

Field crops such as corn, cotton, potatoes, sorghum, soybeans, and sugar beets were planted in rows 40 in. (1 m) apart so that a horse could walk between the rows for cultivation. The 40-in. spacing survived in many places long after tractors replaced horses. Narrower rows of 20- or 30-in. (50- or 75-cm) spacing have increased in popularity in recent years where tractors have become the rule and herbicides have eliminated much of the cultivation. Some variable spacings are used with wider intervals for the wheel tracks than for other rows.

Narrow rows are often elected because they usually increase crop yields. The plants are better spaced to absorb sunlight, and the more complete crop canopy keeps the soil cooler so that less water is lost by evaporation. Erosion control is also improved. Crops in 20-in. (50-cm) row spacing, for example, grow together and cover the space between the rows at an earlier date than those planted in 40-in. (1-m) rows. Fewer raindrops are able to strike the bare soil and cause erosion where the rows are narrow, more water infiltrates because the soil surface is less likely to crust, and less water accumulates in any one place to become erosive runoff. Mannering and Johnson (1969) found that infiltration was increased by 24% and soil loss was reduced by 35% where soybeans were grown in narrow rows (20 in.) rather than wide rows (40 in.).

8-1.4 Soil Fertility and Fertilizers

Dramatic reductions in erosion and sedimentation can often be achieved through proper fertilization. Well-fertilized crops grow more vigorously and protect the soil much more effectively than weak ones. Fertilizers are therefore as important for conserving soil as they are for increasing yield.

A good soil fertility program combined with the best crop varieties and close plant spacing can reduce soil loss to less than half as much as would occur under the same crop with low fertility and wide row spacing (Whitaker et al., 1961). Higher fertility produces a better stand and larger plants at all stages of growth including the critical early period when the soil is most exposed to erosion.

The proper amount and timing of fertilizer applications depend on soil, crop, and weather. The fertility status of the soil may be estimated if one knows the nature of the soil and its cropping and fertilizer history. Rather than rely on such an estimate, however, it is usually better to test the soil at least once every four years. The cost of such tests is easily regained through more accurate fertilization. Excess fertilizer is expensive and can contribute to water pollution; too little fertilizer results in reduced yield.

Each crop has its own fertility needs and its own pattern of response as the availability of essential nutrients varies. A few examples will illustrate this point. Legumes such as beans, peas, and clovers normally do not need nitrogen fertilizer because they obtain nitrogen from their symbiotic relationship with *Rhizobium* bacteria. They do need adequate supplies of all other nutrients, and many legumes, especially those used as forage crops, need enough lime to keep the soil pH near neutral. Most nonlegume crops, on the other hand, respond dramatically to nitrogen. Large amounts of nitrogen fertilizer are used for members of the grass family such as corn, small grains, and the forage grasses.

The tonnage produced and the part of the plant harvested influence the fertilizer needs of both the current crop and the next crop to be grown. As was shown in Table 8-1, a crop of 5 tons of sweetclover hay removes much larger quantities of nutrients than a 1.5-ton crop of barley or oats. The large hay crop demands a good supply of nutrients. Also, the next crop may require extra amounts of potassium fertilizer because of the large amount of K^+ removed in the hay.

Weather influences fertilizer use in several ways, including the choice of crop, the rate of crop growth, the loss of nutrients by leaching and erosion, the availability of nutrients that remain in the soil, and the ability of the soil to support a truck loaded with fertilizer. Even an adapted crop may suffer if the weather is cooler than usual in the spring or warmer than usual in the summer.

Weather cool enough to retard growth is often wet enough for poor drainage to further limit growth on wet soils or for leaching to deplete the supply of available nutrients in drier soils. Intermittent wetness leads to the loss of much available nitrogen by denitrification. Warm, dry weather also can limit nitrogen availability as capillary movement and evaporation at the soil surface combine to concentrate nitrates in a surface crust where there is very little root activity. A good rain can wash this nitrogen back down into the root zone and cause the crop to turn green again.

Wet conditions can seriously hamper potassium absorption by plants. The absorption process requires energy because potassium is usually more concentrated inside the root than in the soil solution. Excessive wetness reduces aeration and slows the oxidation processes that provide energy for nutrient absorption and root growth. Extra potassium is therefore needed in wet years and in poorly drained soils.

8-1.5 Seasonal Changes in Plant Cover

Seasonal variations occur in both the amount of plant cover produced by a crop and in the amount of protection the soil needs against erosive forces. A storm that causes disastrous erosion when there is little plant cover on the ground might cause very little damage later in the season when plants are larger and offer more protection.

The most hazardous periods occur when the soil is exposed by tillage for the planting of a new crop and during the early growth stages while the plants are too small to adequately protect the soil, as shown in Figure 8-2. The erosion hazard diminishes as the percentage of bare ground remaining between plants decreases. Such changes are considered as components of the cropping factors in the soil-loss equations discussed in Chapter 6.

Seasonal changes are most significant where annual crops are grown because the soil often has little cover during a cold or a dry season between crops. Some soils suffer excessive erosion, for example, when the land is plowed after harvest in the fall and left exposed until a spring crop is planted. The exposure time is even longer where a year of summer fallow is used. A period of bare soil may sometimes help control weeds, insects, and plant diseases, but it greatly increases the erosion hazard. Usually, there are cropping and tillage alternatives that provide cover most of the time in the form of either plant residues or growing plants. Tillage practices that leave plant residues on the surface can also help conserve moisture for the next crop, as discussed in Chapter 9.

Perennial crops also have seasonal changes that should not be overlooked. The cover in a hay field is greatly reduced for a time after the hay is cut. Even a pasture

Figure 8-2 The erosion hazard is greatest while plants are small and diminishes as the growing plants cover the soil more completely. (Courtesy F. R. Troeh.)

may be grazed heavily enough to permit storms to cause erosion. Overgrazing is especially serious when it occurs along with trampling damage during a wet season or while the vegetation has stopped growing because of drought or cold weather.

8-2 MANAGING MONOCULTURES

Cropping systems in which the same crop is grown on the same land year after year are known as monocultures. The advantages and disadvantages of monocultures and crop rotations have been long debated without either system being eliminated. Each system is important in its own time and place. Monocultures will be discussed in this section and crop rotations in Section 8-3.

A monoculture permits a farmer to specialize in a crop and to manage the land for the benefit of that crop. Usually, the chosen crop is highly profitable because it is very well suited to the soil and climate. Sometimes the land on a farm justifies two or more monocultures rather than a rotation. For example, a farmer in a humid region might grow a row crop continuously on level land, hay on sloping land, and pasture or trees on steep land. Another farmer in a drier climate might use large areas for rangeland, grow wheat on the most productive nonirrigated land, have an orchard on permeable sloping irrigated land, and perhaps use a crop rotation on the flatter irrigated terraces. Wet bottomland might be used for pasture. Each crop is grown where it fits best rather than trying to grow them all in a rotation.

8-2.1 Annual Cash Crops

Arguments against monocultures usually center on the effects of growing annual crops such as wheat, corn, or cotton year after year on the same land. Farmers often grow these crops on as much land as possible as a source of cash income. Monocultures put the most profitable crops on the best land every year rather than alternating them with other crops.

It was long assumed that certain monocultures such as continuous corn would ruin land. Indeed, yields from such systems soon dropped to low levels when they were tried without fertilizers. But later it was found that well-fertilized continuous corn could produce high yields, though probably not as high as that grown in rotation (Crookston and Kurle, 1989). The yield results satisfied some people, but others argued that the soil structure was deteriorating and the rate of erosion was excessive. The argument continues even now, partly because each side has situations that illustrate its point and partly because some people worry more than others about erosion and soil structure.

Corn as a monoculture is now considered acceptable on certain soils, but other soils are damaged by such treatment. The damage is either excessive soil erosion and sedimentation on rolling land or breakdown of soil structure and poor drainage on level land. Users of monocultures and other intensive-use cropping systems should be alert to such problems. Sometimes an intensive rotation is worse than a monoculture. For example, Van Doren, et al. (1984) found erosion from a corn–soybeans rotation to be 45% more than that from continuous corn. They concluded that soybeans predisposed the soil to water erosion.

Several things can be done to reduce the detrimental effects that may occur with intensive cropping systems. First, such systems should be limited to suitable soils. The next thing is to plant in narrow rows and provide all the lime, fertilizer, improved drainage, and other factors the crop needs to grow well. Then, enough crop residues should be left on the surface for protection against erosion while there is no crop growing and to return as much organic matter to the soil as possible.

8–2.2 Forage Crop Monocultures

Close-growing perennial grasses and legumes are often used for hay or pasture on land that is too steep for row crops and small grains. These forage crops are often combinations of grasses and legumes, so they are not strictly monocultures. However, since the same crop remains on the land year after year, it is convenient to group these mixed forages with the true monocultures.

Good management of land in forage crops can increase profit and reduce soil loss at the same time. Three main factors are involved—soil fertility practices, good grazing or harvesting management, and occasional reseeding where feasible and needed. Some pastures in humid regions also need to be clipped (mowed) once or twice a year to keep weeds, trees, and brush from invading the pasture.

Fertilizer and lime can be used not only to increase forage production but also to help control the composition of mixed forages. Liming to near neutral pH combined with adequate phosphorus, potassium, and any other deficient nutrients will help maintain legumes in the stand. Nitrogen applications favor the grasses and are often omitted where the grasses might crowd out the legumes.

Managing the livestock in a pasture and the haying equipment in a hay field are the most important means of controlling erosion on these lands. Enough plant growth should be left on the land to protect the soil and to maintain vigorous plants. The plants should be allowed to reseed periodically, especially on land that is never tilled. Late fall and early spring grazing should be avoided or limited to avoid weakening the plants.

Systems of rotation grazing usually result in more forage production and better utilization than uncontrolled grazing. Large pastures may be managed like rangeland as discussed in Chapter 13. Smaller, more intensively managed pastures are sometimes subdivided into daily pastures by means of a movable electric fence. The livestock are concentrated in a small pasture so they eat all the forage in one day. This system causes livestock to eat forage that they would leave untouched if they had more room to roam. Rotation grazing thereby achieves the rapid and complete utilization and long regrowth period that are normally characteristic of a hay field.

Much land in forage crops is too shallow, stony, rough, wet, or otherwise limited to be tilled. Some land, however, is used to produce hay or pasture because of steep slope, dry climate, or some other reason that will permit occasional tillage. It is sometimes worthwhile to till such land and reseed it to improve the forage composition. Often the legume component is increased by reseeding, and the dominant grasses may be replaced with more desirable species. A small-grain companion crop may be grown with the new seeding. Erosion is limited because the sod from the previous forage crop helps hold the soil until the new crop becomes established. The fast-growing grain crop also helps control erosion, and the harvested grain helps defray the costs. Alternatively, a range or pasture may be renovated without plowing. A herbicide or perhaps shallow tillage with a disk may be used to kill part or all of the old vegetation before reseeding.

8-2.3 Tree Crops

Forest management is discussed in Chapter 13, but crops such as orchards and Christmas trees are included here. These crops provide income and erosion control in many places where other crops are less desirable. The scale of tree-crop enterprises ranges from a backyard tree or two to large orchards covering many acres. Some enterprises consist entirely of tree crops, whereas others use them only in odd corners, on steep slopes, or in other problem areas. Tree crops are versatile and could be useful to many people that do not presently grow them.

Tree crops occupy land for years at a time. The harvest usually extends over a period of years either as an annual fruit harvest or by selective tree cutting. The crop may be extended indefinitely by planting new trees when old ones are removed.

Properly managed tree crops provide excellent erosion control even on steep land. Usually a grass or legume cover crop is needed between the trees. The needs of the cover crop must be considered when applying lime, fertilizer, and irrigation water. A hay crop is sometimes removed from between the trees before the fruit is harvested. The cover crop helps protect the soil from erosion and from the traffic that passes through the orchard. The drastic amount of erosion that can occur where there is no cover crop shows in some orchards where each tree stands on an island of soil surrounded by eroded areas.

Some crop rotations in the tropics use trees as soil-improving crops in the slash-and-burn system of shifting cultivation (Section 20–2). This makes agriculture possible in places where soil fertility is difficult to maintain. The trees improve both the soil structure (through the effects of their root systems) and the soil fertility (through their ashes after they are burnt) that deteriorate under annual crops (Chapter 20). The system works where there is enough land so that one to three years of annual crops can be rotated with 10 to 20 years of forest. Unfortunately, the forest period is getting too short in many areas because of increased population pressure. Fertilizers help maintain the soil fertility but do little for the soil's physical condition.

8–3 CROP ROTATIONS

Two or more crops alternating on the same land constitute a crop rotation. A rotation may control erosion, plant diseases, and other problems on land where a monoculture of the most profitable crop might be disastrous. The soil-conserving crops not only protect the soil while they are growing but also have a carryover effect that reduces erosion while the next crop is growing. The soil loss from a field of cotton, for example, might be only half as much following a forage crop as it would be if the cotton followed cotton. Rotations can also break insect and disease cycles and control persistent weeds resulting from monocultures.

A crop rotation often provides more continuous cover than is possible when the same annual crop is grown year after year. For example, growing a warm-season row crop two years in succession often leaves the soil without any crop during the winter. However, a cool-season forage crop might be grown to conserve and improve the soil during that time if the winter is not too severe. Some forage crops are plowed under as green manure before planting a row crop; others are left for one or more years of hay or pasture in the rotation.

Crop rotations necessarily differ from one part of the world to another in response to climatic conditions, crops grown, kind of soil, and the kind and severity of erosion problems. The crops and management suited to tropical areas with wet–dry seasons, for example, differ from those adapted to the warm–cold seasons of temperate regions. But both of these climates have a season when the soil may be unprotected because the weather is unfavorable to the primary crops of the area. Rotations that provide cover during these dry or cold seasons help control erosion.

8–3.1 Planning a Rotation

The sequence of crops in many rotations is fixed and repetitive and can be projected as many years into the future as desired. Such rotations are designed to produce nearly constant amounts of each crop each year as a basis for planning and managing crop production. Planning such a rotation begins by dividing the land into as many parts as there are years in the rotation. A four-year rotation, for example, requires four fields or groups of fields of fairly equal productive capacity.

As an example of a fixed rotation, consider a farmer using a corn–

corn–oats–meadow rotation (CCOM). Six fields on this farm are to be rotated. These fields contain 54, 48, 45, 18, 18, and 15 acres, respectively. The three small fields are equivalent to one field of 51 acres, so the rotation can be applied on the basis of four fields containing 54, 48, 45, and 51 acres. Each field can be assigned to a specific crop each year, as shown in Table 8–2. With this arrangement, there are always two fields in corn, one in oats, and one in meadow.

A farmer using a three-year rotation on the example farm could match each small field with one of the larger fields to form three pairs totaling 69, 66, and 63 acres, respectively; or two 99-acre field groups could be formed for a two-year rotation.

If two or more rotations are used on the same farm, each should have its own set of fields with balanced productive capacities. The total production of the farm is automatically balanced when the individual rotations are balanced.

Fixed rotations allow productivity and erosion control to be adjusted to the capability and needs of the land, but such scheduling is not always possible. Variable weather, for example, may require that plans be adjusted sometimes. Rotations can still be beneficial under variable conditions, but their effects and benefits are less predictable than those of fixed rotations.

8–3.2 Companion Crops

A small-grain crop and a forage crop are often planted together as companion crops. The small-grain crop grows rapidly and is harvested within a few months. The forage crop is often alfalfa or a clover and/or a perennial pasture grass. It becomes well established about the time the small grain is harvested. The forage crop is used for hay or pasture for one or more years (and/or for green manure as discussed in Section 8–3.4).

The small-grain member of companion crops has sometimes been called a "nurse crop." This erroneously implies that the tiny grass and legume plants need protection from the elements. Actually, the forage crop planted alone becomes established more rapidly and often produces a better stand. Companion crops compete for water, plant nutrients, and sunlight, causing the forage crop seedlings to develop slowly. It is usually wise to plant less small-grain seed per acre when there is a companion crop than would be used for maximum grain yield.

Fertilizer can be used to help control the growth of companion crops. Nitrogen

TABLE 8–2 FIELD PLAN FOR A CORN–CORN–OATS–MEADOW CROP ROTATION

	Years				
	1	2	3	4	5[a]
Field 1	C	C	O	M	C
Field 2	C	O	M	C	C
Field 3	O	M	C	C	O
Field 4	M	C	C	O	M

[a]The fifth year is the same as the first. Succeeding years are repetitions of the second and later years.

would favor the grain crop and should be used sparingly. Most other fertilizer elements and lime should be applied at rates determined by soil tests to encourage growth of the forage crop. Grass-type forages can be fertilized with nitrogen after the grain crop has been harvested.

Companion crops help control soil erosion and sedimentation. The small grain starts fast and provides reasonable protection within a short time. It covers the soil during the establishment period for the forage crop. Harvesting the small grain leaves both its residue and the growing forage crop to protect the soil. Later, the close-growing forage crop provides excellent protection, and its soil-conserving effects carry over into the succeeding row crop.

8-3.3 Cover Crops

Cover crops protect the soil by filling gaps in either time or space when the other crops would leave the ground bare. Cover crops in rotations are grown during cold or dry seasons unfavorable to the cash crops. Cover crops in orchards are grown between and beneath the trees. Some of them are harvested, but their main purpose is erosion control. Dry climates limit their use because they use soil water that is needed for the next crop.

Hardy plants are needed to stand the cold or dry conditions when cover crops are grown in rotations. They are either slow-starting plants that can be seeded with the preceding crop or fast-growing plants that can become established rapidly after the previous crop is harvested. Several small-seeded legumes such as sweetclover, red clover, crimson clover, and vetch are examples of slow-starting cover crops. Fast-growing types include Austrian winter peas, rye, oats, and ryegrass. Timing is critical to allow the fast-growing types to grow enough between harvest and the cold or dry weather so they will protect the soil.

The fertilizer needs of cover crops must be considered along with those of the other crops. Otherwise, yield decreases may occur, especially if a non-legume is used without adding nitrogen (Wagger, 1989). However, a legume cover crop may supply significant amounts of nitrogen for a succeeding crop, especially if it is worked into the soil as a green manure (Frye and Blevins, 1989). Cover crops are also good for soil structure because active microbes produce exudates that stabilize soil aggregates.

Herbicides are sometimes used to kill or stop the growth of cover crops so that a no-till crop can be planted. Such a system gives maximum erosion protection for growing row crops.

Perennial forage crops such as alfalfa and/or grasses are often used as cover crops in orchards and vineyards. A mixture including one or more grass species produces the thickest stand and provides the best erosion control. Legumes in the mixture help to reduce the nitrogen requirement of the crops.

A vigorous cover crop is desirable for erosion control in an orchard or vineyard but it may interfere with harvesting the fruit. Two alternatives are available: the forage crop may be harvested and removed or it may be beaten down into a mat before the fruit is harvested.

8-3.4 Green Manure

Plowing or disking a growth of forage into the soil as green manure benefits a soil's organic-matter content, structure, and permeability. Either the growth produced by a cover crop or the last growth of a forage crop may be used in this manner. The more growth there is the better, except that young succulent growth is best because it contains a higher concentration of plant nutrients and decomposes faster than older material.

Green manure easily adds more tons of organic matter per acre to the soil than would likely be added in manure or other organic materials spread on the soil. The fresh organic matter decomposes readily and the soil microbes multiply. This microbial activity produces cementing agents that have a strong positive effect on soil structure. Soil permeability and aeration are often increased by new root channels, by tillage channels held open by the plant residues, and by improved soil structure.

Green manure crops are often followed by impressive crop yields attained with little or no fertilizer. Part of this effect can be attributed to the nitrogen fixed when a legume is used for green manure. But the effect also occurs with nonlegume green manures and with nutrients other than nitrogen. The release of nutrients from the decomposition of the green manure is the key to this enhanced fertility. Nutrients that are normally released slowly from the soil can often be made available fairly rapidly by decomposition. The green manure crop thus serves to accumulate available nutrients for release to the next crop.

8-3.5 Crop Residue Utilization

Crop residues are much too valuable to be ignored. Sometimes they are used to feed livestock either by allowing them to graze in the field or by hauling the straw, stalks, or other residues to the livestock. Another type of utilization is sought by research aimed at making plastic or an energy source such as alcohol from the residues. But to a soil conservationist, crop residue utilization means using the residues either as mulch to protect the soil or as raw material for soil organic matter. Using the residues to protect the soil is important enough to claim first priority. Enough residues should be left to control erosion and maintain satisfactory soil physical conditions.

The soil protection afforded by crop residues is roughly proportional to the percentage of the soil surface that they cover. Residues that have been plowed under no longer provide soil cover. Leaving residues on the soil surface is an easy way to conserve soil and water.

Different crops produce different kinds and amounts of residues. The stubble and straw from a small-grain crop usually provide adequate protection if they are simply left in place; neither wind nor rain is able to exert much erosive power on the soil surface. The coarser residues left from a corn crop may need to be beaten down or chopped into smaller pieces to cover the soil between the rows.

Any tillage performed on the residues will affect their value as a mulch. Plowing will cover most of the residues and leave little or no soil protection. Disking covers about half of the residues but still leaves considerable protection. Chisel-type implements often leave about 80% of the residues on the surface. The practice of leaving significant amounts of residues on the surface during periods between harvest and planting, as shown in Figure 8-3, is known as *stubble mulching.*

Negative feelings toward stubble mulching and other crop-residue utilization practices arise when residues plug tillage implements. Many older implements plugged easily, but newer machines have cutters and large open frameworks so they can work through the residues. The old practice of burning stubble or other crop residues has been mostly eliminated by using these machines and adding fertilizers that help decompose residues.

Plant residues mixed with soil decompose at rates depending on the nature of the residues, the supply of available nutrients (especially nitrogen), and the soil temperature, moisture, and aeration. Half or more of the residues will decompose during the first few months if conditions favor microbial activity. The remainder is more resistant and decomposes more slowly. The last remaining organic material is resistant enough to be considered humus. Humus is finely divided and plant parts are no longer identifiable. Probably less than 20% of the original residue weight remains, and most of that is microbial residues. The time required to convert residues into humus ranges from a few months in a well-drained tropical soil to many years in a cold climate or centuries in a swamp or bog.

Soil humus decomposes much more slowly than fresh plant residues, but it does decompose and release plant nutrients. Humus decomposition needs to be offset by new humus formed from residues to maintain the organic-matter content of the soil. The microbes that carry out decomposition produce exudates that help hold soil aggregates together and stabilize soil structure. Decomposing organic

Figure 8-3 Stubble mulching protects the soil with both crop residues and clods. (Courtesy Washington State University.)

materials thus contribute to both soil fertility and to a desirable soil physical condition. Organic materials that are not in the process of decomposing contribute relatively little to soil fertility and soil structure but may increase permeability and reduce erosion and sedimentation.

Decomposition is often slowed by an inadequate supply of nitrogen. Many crop residues such as straw, stalks, and leaves are high in carbon but low in nitrogen. Microbes decomposing these residues use nitrogen from the soil. A deficiency of available nitrogen at this time slows both decomposition and plant growth. Under such conditions, crops respond dramatically to nitrogen fertilizer. Enough fertilizer should be applied to meet the needs of both the microbes and the crop.

Crop residues provide shade that keeps a mulched soil cooler than a bare soil. The temperature difference on a hot day can reach 10 to 20°C (18 to 36°F) at a depth of 1 cm, although average differences are only 2 or 3°C (3 to 5°F). The cooling effect of the mulch is beneficial in tropical climates and during hot summers. It is detrimental, however, in the spring when a wet soil needs to dry out and warm up before it can be tilled and a crop planted. Mulching in temperate regions is therefore most desirable on well-drained soils. Fortunately, the well-drained soils usually coincide with the sloping areas that most need mulching for erosion control.

8-4 MULTIPLE CROPPING

Multiple cropping, also called *sequential cropping* (two or more crops a year in sequence) or *intercropping* (two or more crops on the same field at the same time), is related to crop rotations in that the same land is used to produce more than one crop.

Sequential cropping is like a crop rotation all in one year. Crop rotations involving companion crops and monocultures such as orchards with a cover crop are closely related to intercropping. The difference is that intercropping overlaps the main growth phases of two or more harvestable crops. The crops involved include a variety of annual crops and tropical tree crops. At least one crop is planted in wide enough rows for another crop to be grown in between. An example of a schedule used in some experiments in Peru is shown in Figure 8-4.

Multiple cropping is most common in the humid tropics. Many such areas have small holdings that are intensively used, mostly to produce food for families and local markets (Roy and Braun, 1983). Multiple cropping produces a more varied and nutritious diet than monocultures or ordinary crop rotations would provide. Multiple cropping is similarly used in gardens anywhere in the world, and some

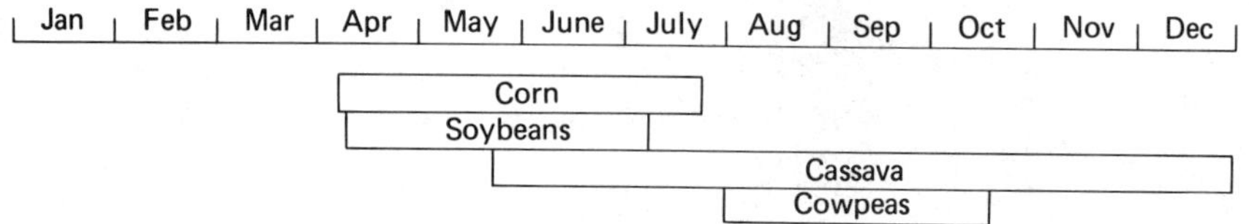

Figure 8-4 A multiple cropping schedule used in some fertility and row-spacing experiments in Peru. (After Soil Science Department, North Carolina State University, 1974.)

studies have shown potential for combinations such as wheat and peas (Murray and Swensen, 1985) or corn or sorghum with oats or rye (Helsel and Wedin, 1981) in temperate regions.

Many tropical crops are intercropped in various combinations. Multiple benefits are obtained, for example, by growing bananas among coffee trees. The banana plants quickly grow above the coffee trees and produce an abundance of leaves that protect the coffee from sun and wind, cover the soil, and control erosion (Constantinesco, 1976).

Figure 8-5 shows intercropped upland rice and banana plants. The annual rice crop provides soil cover while the banana plants are young. The combination is said to protect against insects by confusing them as they try to locate their host plant by smell.

One objective of multiple cropping is to increase the total production from the land. Work done with intercrops in Costa Rica and El Salvador showed yields of individual crops ranging from 30 to 107% of monoculture yields (Table 8-3). The intercropping systems were considerably more profitable than the monocultures, as the additional crops more than offset the reduced production of individual crops. Fertilizers improved yields and profits from both multiple crops and monocultures.

Soil conservation is an important bonus from multiple cropping. Two or more crops grown together cover the ground better and/or longer than a single crop. More raindrops are intercepted, runoff is slowed, and erosion is markedly reduced. Erosion data are scarce, but the difference is often obvious without measurement, especially in comparison to a row crop monoculture.

Figure 8-5 Bananas and rice being intercropped in The Gambia, West Africa. (Courtesy Roy L. Donahue.)

TABLE 8-3 RELATIVE YIELDS OF INTERCROPPED SHORT-STATURED CROPS EXPRESSED AS PERCENTAGES OF MONOCULTURE YIELDS

Crop	Fertility level		
	Low	Medium	High
	Percent of monoculture yield		
Rice (January planting)	32	38	46
Rice (May planting)	44	30	29
Beans (bush-type)	87	91	78
Beans (climbing-type)	56	64	78
Soybeans (Jan. planting)	107	70	84
Soybeans (May planting)	54	52	50
Sweet potatoes	93	92	86

Source: Soil Science Department, North Carolina State University 1974.

8-5 STRIP CROPPING

Strip cropping divides a field into long narrow parcels that cross the path of the erosive force of water or wind. The strips with more vegetative cover slow runoff, reduce wind velocity, and catch soil eroded from the more exposed strips. Thus the average soil loss may be reduced to as little as one-fourth of what it would be without the strips (see Section 6–3.5).

Some applications of strip cropping have permanent vegetation in designated protective strips and use the remaining area for either a crop rotation or a monoculture. More often, the protective vegetation is one of the crops in a rotation that shifts annually from one strip to the next. Such systems combine the favorable effects of crop rotations with contour tillage (Section 9–7), and often include the use of cover crops, green manures, and crop residues. Such a combination of practices is very effective for reducing erosion and sedimentation.

Strip cropping is an inexpensive means of reducing erosion and is usually very effective. Nevertheless, it is used less now than it once was. The decline resulted partly from many farmers changing from crop rotations to monocultures and using larger implements. Other factors limiting its use are the susceptibility of the long exposed borders to disease and insect attacks and to the desiccating effect of hot dry winds in semiarid climates.

8-5.1 Contour Strip Cropping

Contour strip cropping is one of the most effective means of controlling water erosion while growing crops in a rotation. It works well where the slopes are long and smooth, as shown in Figure 8–6. Variable slope gradients and rolling topography make it less practical to use contour practices of any kind.

One of the most important design factors of contour strip cropping is the width of the strips. Row crop strips must be limited in width to avoid excessive runoff and erosion. Forage crop strips must be at least wide enough to afford adequate protection and capacity to filter sediment from the runoff water. Recom-

Figure 8-6 Contour strip cropping divides the slope length into short segments to control erosion. (Courtesy F. R. Troeh.)

mended strip-width limits are given in Table 8–4. Rainfall intensity influences the maximum slope length that can be protected in this manner. These limits assume a deep soil of average erodibility where the relief (elevation difference) is about 15 ft (4.5 m) where the rainfall factor (as shown in Figure 6–1) is 250, or 25 ft (8 m) where the rainfall factor is 150. The relief may be measured with a surveying instrument, or it may be calculated if the slope length and gradient are known. For example, a 5% slope 300 ft long equals 15 ft of relief. Terraces may be used to divide the slopes into segments where the relief is excessive.

The strip widths chosen for a field should be exact multiples of the width of the row crop equipment to be used. Thus a farmer planting, cultivating, and harvesting six 30-in. (75-cm) rows at a time would use a multiple of 15 ft (4.5 m) for strip widths. On a 5% slope, for example, the forage strips would be 30 ft (9 m) wide with 90 ft (27 m) of row crop. These widths would fit a five-year rotation including three years of row crop, one year of small grain, and one year of hay. Each year in the rotation is assigned a 30-ft (9-m) strip and the three years of row crop together total 90 ft (27 m). The small-grain strip would be included in the layout as shown in Figure 8–7 but is omitted from the calculations because its soil loss will be near the average of that for the other crops.

Contour strip cropping on slopes up to 2 or 3% may not always include forage

TABLE 8-4 RECOMMENDED LIMITS FOR STRIP WIDTHS FOR CONTOUR STRIP CROPPING

	Forage crop strip minimum width		Row crop strip maximum width	
Slope (%)	ft	m	ft	m
2	25	8	120	36
5	30	9	100	30
8	40	12	90	27
12	50	15	80	24
18	80	24	50	15

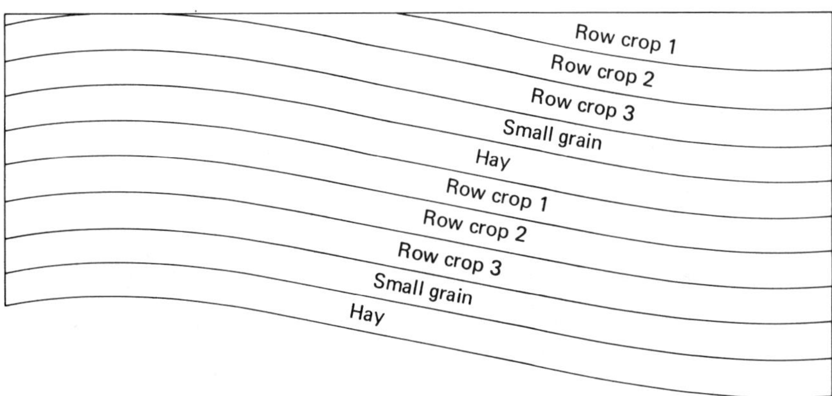

Figure 8–7 A contour strip cropping layout for a five-year rotation.

strips. Instead, the small-grain strip may be relied upon to provide the needed protection. Such strips should be about three times as wide as a hay strip would need to be and should include a winter-cover green-manure crop.

The row crop may be left out of a strip cropping system on very steep slopes. Strips of small grain may then be grown in rotation with a forage crop. The small-grain strips can be about as wide as row crop strips on a slope only half as steep.

Contour strips necessarily deviate from the exact contour where slopes are variable, but the slope along a strip boundary should usually be less than 2%. Small deviations are acceptable if the flow of water along the rows is slow enough to be nonerosive, and if the flow is toward a swale rather than a ridge. An accumulation of water on a ridge would flow down the side of the ridge and probably cause a gully. Such flow can be avoided by making the contour strips slightly straighter than the true contour lines. This effect will usually result if an initial guideline is laid out along a contour line near the top of the slope. Strip boundaries are kept parallel to the initial guideline as long as the deviations from contour lines are small. Small filler areas of permanent vegetation can be used to avoid excessive deviations, as shown in Figure 8–8.

Grassed waterways are needed where too much water accumulates in the swales of contour-stripped fields. The waterways catch silt and raise the elevations of the swales rather than allowing gullies to form.

Contour strip cropping slows the velocity, although it may have little effect on the amount of runoff from a field. Slower velocity causes soil lost from the row crop strips to be caught in the forage strips and grassed waterways. However, the effectiveness declines as water accumulates on the lower part of a long slope and becomes too much for the forage strips to control. Slopes longer than a few hundred feet often need a diversion terrace to remove excess water from the middle of the field (see the relief criteria in the forepart of this section).

Contour strip cropping usually increases the number of point rows and odd corners in a field. Point rows occur where the strips meet field boundaries at angles such as those around the edges of the field and at the waterway in Figure 8–8. Point rows reduce operational efficiency—more turning is required and small irregular areas may not be cropped.

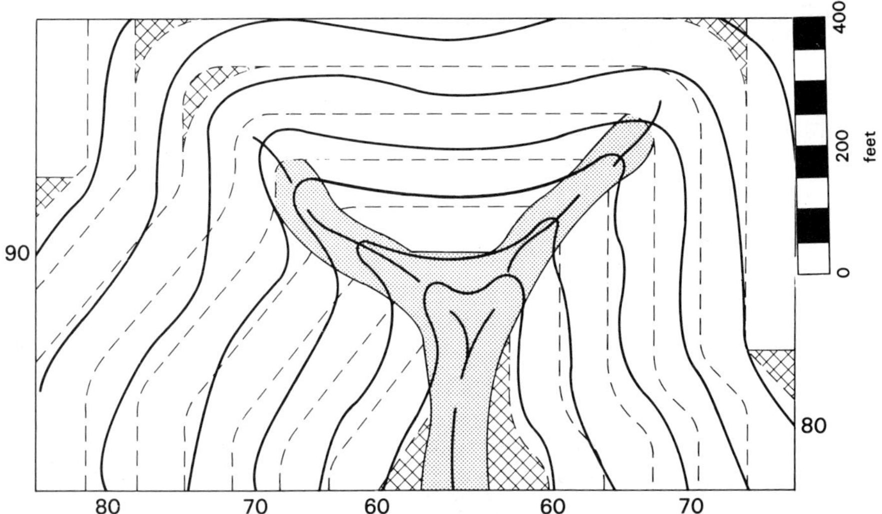

Figure 8–8 A contour strip cropping design for a small field. The solid lines are contour lines with elevations shown in feet above an arbitrary base level. The dashed lines are strip boundaries. The filler areas are crosshatched. The stippled area is grassed waterway.

Odd-shaped areas like the upper corners in Figure 8–8 may be planted to permanent vegetation or, since these are relatively flat, they can be planted to the same crop as the adjoining strips. Another possibility is to relocate the field boundaries to better match strip boundaries and thus minimize point rows and odd corners. The reverse has already been done on the right side of Figure 8–8, where strip boundaries parallel field boundaries that nearly follow contour lines.

The vegetation in filler areas may be harvested as hay along with an adjoining strip. Another good alternative is to manage filler areas and odd corners for wildlife purposes. Appropriate grass, shrub, and tree plantings can provide both food and cover for animals and birds. Some such areas are used as sites for bee colonies or for growing Christmas trees. Any of these uses are preferable to annual crops in such locations. Crops are seldom profitable on small irregular areas and do not provide the erosion control that results from permanent vegetation.

8–5.2 Buffer Strip Cropping

Buffer strip cropping is designed to work on rolling topography with irregular slope gradients that make contour strip cropping impractical. It lengthens the filler areas into continuous buffer strips that separate the crop strips. The crop strips are uniform in width, but the buffer strips are variable to allow for slope irregularities. The buffer strips are positioned to include any rocky areas or other problem spots that occur in the field, as shown in Figure 8–9.

Buffer strips are planted to permanent vegetation to slow the runoff and to catch sediment eroded from the next higher crop strips. Perennial forage crops that can be used for hay or pasture are often grown on buffer strips. Areas of trees and shrubs may also be included. "Alley cropping" as discussed in Section 13–4 is an example of this type of use in which lines of leguminous trees and shrubs are planted

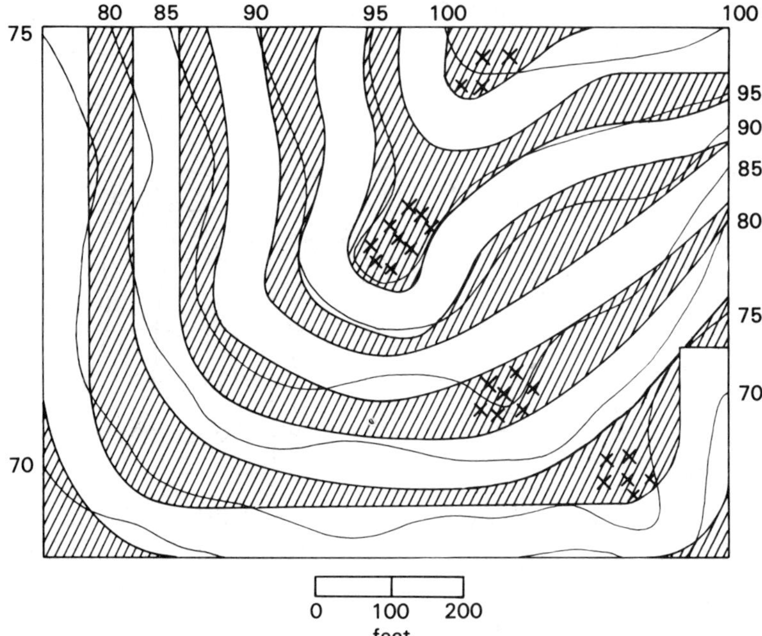

Figure 8-9 A buffer strip cropping design on a contour map. Elevations are shown in feet above an arbitrary base level. The X's represent uncroppable rocky areas.

on the contour in tropical countries. The effectiveness of buffer strips for reducing erosion depends on the nature of the protective vegetation, the crop and buffer strip widths, and the topography, soil, and climate of the area. The *P* factor for contour strip cropping can be used in calculating soil loss (Chapter 6) where the crop and buffer strip widths meet the requirements of Table 8-4.

8-5.3 Field Strip Cropping

Field strip cropping is sometimes used on land that is too rolling even for buffer strip cropping. It consists of straight rectangular strips of uniform width laid out parallel to one side of a field. These strips cross the general slope of the area but do not follow contour lines. The system is managed like contour strip cropping but is less effective where the deviations from the contour are too large. Grassed waterways are usually needed in low areas because water flows along the sloping rows and accumulates in the swales.

8-5.4 Wind Strip Cropping

Strip cropping designed to control wind erosion crosses the path of the prevailing winds rather than following the contour. Wind strip cropping is laid out in straight lines like field strip cropping, but the crops are different. Wind strip cropping is used in semiarid areas such as the Great Plains of the United States and the Prairies of Canada.

The soil-conserving vegetation in wind strip cropping needs to be dense enough to catch saltating sand particles and prevent them from jumping again. The protective strips need to be wide enough to keep saltating particles from jumping completely across a strip. Several feet would suffice, but cropping considerations make widths of 150 to 250 ft (50 to 80 m) more practical. Because crops shift yearly from one strip to the next, each strip should be wide enough to be cropped conveniently. The chosen width is normally a multiple of the width of equipment used in farming operations. The maximum width is limited by the increased saltation resulting from avalanching where exposed areas are too wide.

Close-growing vegetation such as bluegrass can stop saltation even when the grass is only a few centimeters tall. Bunchgrasses, however, are common in climates where wind erosion is most likely to be a problem. The open areas between clumps of grass need to be protected by vegetation that is at least as tall as the width of the open areas. The taller vegetation gives a windbreak effect in addition to its ability to catch and hold saltating sand particles.

Wind strip cropping is often used with a wheat–fallow rotation. The wheat strips control saltation quite effectively after the wheat is 4 to 6 in. (10 to 15 cm) tall. The wheat stubble continues to protect the soil after the wheat is harvested and can even provide some protection during the fallow year if it is left on the surface as a stubble mulch.

Strips that catch soil particles in the summer can also catch drifting snow during winter. Holding snow on the fields contributes to the soil moisture supply and increases productivity.

8–5.5 Barrier Strips

Narrow strips consisting of a few rows of small grains, grasses, or other crops can provide significant protection from wind erosion. These barrier strips must be spaced fairly close together to compensate for their narrowness. Even so, they occupy much less land than the protective strips in wind strip cropping.

Fryrear (1963) found that two rows of either sudangrass or grain sorghum made effective barriers for Texas conditions because they grew when protection was most needed. He recommended a 23-ft (7-m) spacing for sudangrass strips or 13 ft (4 m) for grain sorghum to protect against winds up to 40 mi/hr (65 km/h). The highest-cut stubble afforded winter protection even after harvest.

Hagen et al. (1972) also recommended two-row barrier strips on the basis of their work in Kansas. Single-row barriers used the land most efficiently but sometimes broke and failed when wind speeds exceeded 30 mi/hr (50 km/h). They found that winter wheat barriers 4 in. (10 cm) tall were 20% effective for trapping soil particles from a 30 mi/hr wind. Sudangrass barriers 1 ft (30 cm) tall were 60% effective under the same conditions. They calculated that a two-row rye barrier 8 in. (20 cm) tall could protect a strip about 100 ft (32 m) wide against a 30-mi/hr wind.

8-5.6 Border Strips

A strip of grass or other close-growing vegetation helps keep soil from being carried into streams and ponds, living areas, or other sites that need protection. Border strips may be used to control movement of soil by wind after the manner of wind strip cropping, or they may be designed to restrict water transport. Their main purpose is often to control air and water pollution; reducing erosion may be secondary.

Lush grass growing between a field and a body of water is very effective for catching sediment and reducing eutrophication (Chapter 17). The grass filters soil particles from the runoff water and absorbs dissolved nutrients from the water. The low nutrient content in the purified water limits the growth of algae and other plants in ponds and streams. The water, nutrients, and fertile soil caught in the border strip help produce a lush growth that catches even more sediment and nutrients.

The dimensions of border strips vary with the situation but should usually be at least as wide as strips serving a similar purpose in fields. Most strips controlling water purity should be at least 30 ft (10 m) wide and need to be wider where the water flow is large or where the slope gradient exceeds 1 or 2%. Wind-erosion control usually requires wider borders to keep the air clean—often 150 to 300 ft (50 to 100 m) across, with exact dimensions depending on topography and wind direction and velocity. These areas are often large enough to be used for pasture or hay production.

8-6 EVALUATING CROPPING SYSTEMS

A satisfactory cropping system must meet several standards. Economics, erosion control, pest control, physical and chemical effects on the soil, and environmental concerns are all important. Evaluation of all these factors is seldom more than a reasonable estimate based on extrapolation of long-term trends.

Economic considerations require a desirable cropping system that produces a profit for the user. Adequate crop yields must be attainable on a long-term basis. Some economic aspects of soil conservation are discussed in Chapter 18, but much of the economics of cropping systems is beyond the scope of this book.

8-6.1 Cropping Systems and Soil Loss

The soil-loss prediction equations discussed in Chapter 6 are useful for selecting appropriate cropping systems. Several possibilities can be analyzed and their results predicted before a choice is made. The more intensive cropping systems usually give larger profits but are likely to result in larger soil losses. Continuous row crops and other intensive cropping systems are therefore commonly preferred where conditions are favorable but should be avoided where they would cause excessive erosion.

Erosion naturally varies according to soil and topographic conditions. A decision must therefore be made regarding which cropping systems are suitable for specific conditions. The most erodible part of the field (not just the average) needs to be checked before the system can be rated as satisfactory. The hazards of averaging can be illustrated by an example wherein the annual soil loss from a 40-acre (16-ha) field averages 2 tons/ac (4.5 mt/ha) from most of the field, but 40 tons from 1 acre (90 mt/ha from 0.4 hectare). The field average is 3 tons/ac (7 mt/ha) and is less than the specified tolerable rate for most soils. The system nevertheless would rapidly ruin the 1 acre of highly erodible land and should not be used there.

Adjusting land use and cropping systems to the most erodible land is usually impractical. Rather, these calculations help identify problem areas that need different treatment than the rest of the field. A cropping system suited to the 39 good acres in the example could be used if field boundaries were changed to place the erodible acre in an adjoining pasture or woodland.

Changing field boundaries solves some problems but does not work where the erodible land is surrounded by land suitable for intensive use. Terracing can help where the erosion hazard results from a steep slope. Another approach is to use a dual-cropping system. For example, if the best land is suitable for continuous row crops, the part needing protection might have a rotation of row crops, small grain, and hay. The grain and hay crops must be handled separately, but row crop will cover the entire field about half of the years. Such systems permit different parts of the field to be used in accordance with their potential and their need for protection as indicated by the soil-loss prediction equations.

8-6.2 Maintaining Soil Productive Potential

Maintaining the productive potential of soil over the long term is a fundamental purpose of soil conservation. Evaluation of the productive potential, however, is difficult. Crop yields depend on weather and management as well as soil potential. New crop varieties coupled with improved management and increased use of fertilizer have often produced larger yields even while the soil was becoming shallower and harder to work. Thus the crop yields can be increasing while the productive potential is decreasing.

Some items that influence productive potential are much easier to measure than the potential itself. Soil depth is one such item. Not only is the total soil thickness significant, but also the thickness of the A horizon is likely to influence soil productivity. Yield differences also depend on the nature of the subsoil—subsoil that is too dense or otherwise unsuitable for root development increases the importance of topsoil thickness.

Another negative effect of erosion on soil productivity occurs through reduced soil fertility. Erosion has sometimes been called "the great robber" because small mineral and organic particles are carried away along with their associated fertility, while the less fertile coarse particles are left behind. The largest differences occur when fertilizers are left on the soil surface and are eroded away with the soil. Additional fertilizer to compensate for the nutrient losses may maintain nearly equal yields, but the costs are considerable. The profit from crops grown on eroding land therefore declines even if the yield is held constant by fertilization.

The removal of fine particles by erosion makes many soils gradually become more sandy, gravelly, or stony. The increased percentage of coarse material makes these soils more droughty and lowers the productive potential of many of them.

8-6.3 Maintaining Soil Structure

Tillage, erosion, and reduced organic-matter content weaken the structure of intensively cropped soils. Destruction of soil structure into a puddled condition is favorable for paddy rice production but is undesirable for other crops.

Significance of Soil Structure. As soil structure weakens, the soil tilth becomes poorer, the likelihood of crusting increases, and the soil permeability decreases. Soil *tilth* refers to how easily the soil can be tilled and cropped. Tilth is most important in soils high in clay because clay soils with poor tilth form hard clods when they dry, especially if they are tilled when wet. Poor tilth increases the power required to till the soil and sometimes increases the number of tillage operations required to prepare a seedbed.

Stable structure within the various soil horizons is important for maintaining permeability in all but the very coarse-textured soils. Permeability depends on pore space between the soil peds. New pores are formed as roots and other living things force their way through the soil. Shrinking and swelling caused by moisture and temperature changes help form new aggregates and soil peds. But tillage breaks aggregates and peds and blocks pores if the soil structure is weak. Permeability then declines, aeration and pore space are reduced, and the soil becomes less favorable for root growth.

Crusts form where raindrops beat on the soil surface and break down its structure. Loose particles from broken soil aggregates plug soil pores and often reduce the water infiltration rate to a fraction of its initial value. Runoff, erosion, sedimentation, and pollution increase. After the rain, the surface hardens into a crust that may markedly reduce the stand of a crop because it is too strong for seedlings to break through. Crust formation and reduced seedling emergence are the most readily observed symptoms of weak soil structure.

NOTE 8-1
MEASURING STRUCTURAL STABILITY

Several methods are used to evaluate the structural stability of soils. The two outlined here involve little equipment and can be used to compare differences resulting from contrasting treatments such as cropland versus pastureland or fields versus fencerows.

The percentage of water-stable aggregates can be determined by placing a weighed soil sample on a sieve with 0.01-in. (0.25-mm) openings. The sieve is then dipped 50 times (or some other standard number) in a container of water. The material remaining on the sieve is dried, weighed, and corrected for sand content to calculate the percentage of water-stable aggregates.

The structural stability of soil clods can be compared by dripping water onto them from a buret as shown in Figure 8-10. The volume of water required to wash the soil through the screen and into the beaker is an indication of structural stability.

Strength of Soil Structure. The terms *weak, moderate,* and *strong* are often used to indicate the distinctness of soil structure, although it is difficult to measure the strength quantitatively. Aggregate stability is a related property that can be evaluated as described in Note 8-1. Such procedures can be used to measure changes produced by different cropping systems and management practices. The soil in one field might be compared with that from a nearby field or with the less disturbed soil in a fencerow. Such comparisons often reveal large differences in aggregate stability accompanied by observable differences in porosity and crusting, as shown in Figure 8-11.

Effect of Crops on Soil Structure. The fine fibrous root system produced by a dense growth of grass helps produce stable aggregates in soil. Deep taproots such as those of alfalfa help open channels in the lower soil horizons. These improvements in soil structure are important reasons why an alfalfa-grass mixture is widely regarded as a soil-improving crop. Most forage crops have similar effects but to different degrees.

Row crops such as sugar beets, cotton, corn, and beans usually weaken the soil structure and contribute to erosion and sedimentation. Narrow rows and high yields cause these crops to cover the soil faster and permit their root systems to penetrate more uniformly through the entire soil volume, thus reducing but not eliminating the soil deterioration. Each combination of soil, cropping system, and management

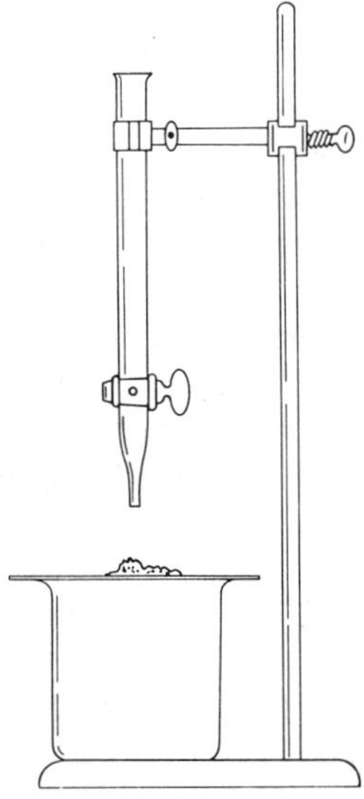

Figure 8-10 The volume of water required to wash a soil sample though a screen is an indication of structural stability.

Figure 8–11 Soil structure differences resulting from a corn-wheat-hay rotation (a) and two years of corn-soybeans (b). (Courtesy Maryland Agricultural Experiment Station.)

practices has an equilibrium of structural stability and of many other properties as well. As time passes, the soil shifts toward its equilibrium. The rate of change is roughly proportional to the difference between the present condition and the equilibrium condition.

Small-grain crops produce more cover and generally stronger soil structure than row crops but less cover and weaker structure than forage crops. Tree crops are much like row crops in their effect on soil structure unless there is a litter layer or a cover crop or other vegetation between the trees.

Most crops can be related to one or another of the groups already discussed. A good first approximation is that the effect of a crop on soil structure is closely related to how thoroughly its roots permeate the soil. The effect of companion crops on soil structure is often more favorable than that of either crop grown by itself. The effect of a crop rotation is an integration of the effects of all crops in the rotation. Some properties such as soil-aggregate stability change fast enough to exhibit noticeable differences from one crop to another during a rotation.

Weakened soil structure is sometimes a reason to modify an intensive cropping system. Low permeability resulting from weak soil structure causes runoff and erosion problems on slopes and wetness and sedimentation problems on flat lands. The remedy is usually to shift toward a system that includes more close-growing vegetation.

8–6.4 Environmental Effects of Cropping Systems

Most cropping systems accelerate erosion by wind and water. Eroded soil contaminates air with dust particles and water with sediment. The sheer mass of the eroded soil and the chemical and biological entities carried with it are significant. For example, soil carries plant nutrients that contribute to eutrophication (Chapter 17).

The early emphasis of the soil conservation program was to protect land from excessive soil loss. Environmental concerns have made water and air pollution strong additional reasons to control erosion. Pollution caused by soil erosion extends far beyond the eroding area, making it a public as well as a private concern. Several states have responded by passing laws requiring the use of soil-conserving practices under certain conditions, as discussed in Chapter 19.

Environmental considerations cause some cropping system changes that protect air and water rather than soil. Border strips of close-growing vegetation to keep sediment out of streams and ponds are a good example of adjustments that reduce water pollution.

Most soil-conserving practices benefit both the land where erosion is reduced and the environment where the eroded soil would have gone. Cropping practices such as rotations, cover crops, and strip cropping reduce air and water pollution as well as protecting soil productivity. Mechanical practices such as terraces and conservation tillage also protect both soil productivity and the environment. Recognizing the environmental values of such practices increases the incentive to apply them.

Reducing erosion and its polluting effects to minimal values would be relatively simple if land were not needed for growing crops. However, the world's population needs to be fed, clothed, and housed. Cropping systems therefore need to be carefully designed to meet needs without causing excessive erosion and pollution.

SUMMARY

Native vegetation normally provides enough cover to control erosion, but most cropping systems leave the soil surface exposed periodically. Poor crop growth can allow disastrous erosion to ruin the land and pollute both air and water. Properly adapted crops and well-planned cropping systems limit erosion to acceptable rates.

Most crops can be classified into four groups. Row crops usually produce the most profit and the most exposure to erosion. Small-grain crops give more protection because the plants grow fast and close together. Forage crops produce still thicker cover and provide excellent erosion control. Tree crops with undergrowth and a litter layer on the soil surface almost eliminate erosion.

Practices that increase crop yields usually reduce soil erosion. Crops in narrower rows cover the soil sooner and protect it better. High soil fertility also increases both yield and soil cover.

Monocultures permit farmers to specialize and grow each crop where it is best suited. Fertilizers and lime may make it possible to maintain yields under continuous cash crops, but the soil structure may deteriorate and erosion, sedimentation, and pollution increase. Land that is too steep for row crops and grain crops may be used for hay, pasture, or tree crops.

Crop rotations often provide more continuous soil cover than monocultures and help control erosion, plant diseases, and insects. Companion crops and cover crops help to keep the soil covered almost continuously; some crops offer carryover effects that reduce erosion while the next crop is growing. Crop residues can be used for soil cover when no crop is growing.

Multiple cropping is used in many gardens and in tropical areas to increase variety and total amount of production. Its contributions to soil conservation are a bonus.

Contour strip cropping is effective for controlling water erosion; buffer strip cropping and field strip cropping are useful where the land includes small uncroppable areas or the topography is rolling. Wind strip cropping is laid out across the prevailing wind to catch saltating particles. Barrier strips consisting of one, two, or a few rows of tall, close-growing crops are also effective for reducing wind erosion if the exposed area between them is not too wide. Border strips are single strips of close-growing vegetation used to reduce pollution by keeping soil particles out of air and water.

The soil-loss prediction equations are useful for selecting appropriate cropping systems and for identifying areas that need special treatment. Appropriate cropping systems maintain adequate soil depth, fertility, and water-holding capacity to conserve the productive potential of the soil. Stable soil structure is needed to resist crusting and maintain adequate permeability. Forage crops usually have favorable effects on soil structure, whereas most row crops cause soil structure to deteriorate. The effect of any crop on soil structure is related to how thoroughly its roots penetrate the soil.

Cropping systems need to protect the environment as well as the soil. Pollution resulting from soil erosion contaminates air and water far beyond the eroding area. Well-designed cropping systems produce food and fiber for the world's population without causing excessive erosion and pollution.

QUESTIONS

1. How can a forage crop be both a "soil-building crop" and a "soil-depleting crop"?
2. What effects do rows and row spacings have on soil and water conservation?
3. Why do many farmers grow crops as monocultures rather than using crop rotations?
4. Under what conditions would the use of a companion crop for the establishment of a forage crop increase erosion? When would it reduce erosion?
5. Why do many farmers prefer to plow crop residues under rather than leave them on the soil surface?
6. Explain the differences between crop rotations, sequential cropping, and intercropping.
7. List five different types of strip cropping and distinguish them from one another.
8. How can the use of fertilizer: **(a)** reduce water pollution? **(b)** increase water pollution?

REFERENCES

ALLEN, J. R., and R. K. OBURA, 1983. Yield of corn, cowpea, and soybean under different intercropping systems. *Agron. J.* 75:1005–1009.

BLACK, A. L., and F. H. SIDDOWAY, 1976. Dryland cropping sequences within a tall wheatgrass barrier system. *J. Soil Water Cons.* 31:101–105.

CONSTANTINESCO, I., 1976. *Soil Conservation for Developing Countries.* Soils Bull. 30. FAO, Rome, 92 p.

CROOKSTON, R. K., and J. E. KURLE, 1989. Corn residue effect on the yield of corn and soybean grown in rotation. *Agron. J.* 82:229–232.

DAO, T. H., and H. T. NGUYEN, 1989. Growth response of cultivars to conservation tillage in a continuous wheat cropping system. *Agron. J.* 81:923–929.

FOX, R. H., and W. P. PIEKIELEK, 1988. Fertilizer N equivalence of alfalfa, birdsfoot trefoil, and red clover for succeeding corn crops. *J. Prod. Agric.* 1:313–317.

FRYE, W. W., and R. L. BLEVINS, 1989. Economically sustainable crop production with legume cover crops and conservation tillage. *J. Soil Water Cons.* 44:57–60.

FRYREAR, D. W., 1963. Annual crops as wind barriers. *Trans. Am. Soc. Agr. Eng.* 6:340–342, 352.

HAGEN, L. J., E. L. SKIDMORE, and J. D. DICKERSON, 1972. Designing narrow strip barrier systems to control wind erosion. *J. Soil Water Cons.* 27:269–272.

HELSEL, Z. R., and W. F. WEDIN, 1981. Harvested dry matter from single and double-cropping systems. *Agron. J.* 73:895–900.

MANNERING, J. V., and C. B. JOHNSON, 1969. Effect of crop row spacing on erosion and infiltration. *Agron. J.* 61:902–905.

MURRAY, G. A., and J. B. SWENSEN, 1985. Seed yield of Austrian winter field peas intercropped with winter cereals. *Agron. J.* 77:913–916.

PAGE, B. E., 1985. Trees, trees, and more trees. *J. Soil Water Cons.* 40:414–416.

PAPENDICK, R. I., P. A. SANCHEZ, and G. B. TRIPLETT (eds.), 1976. *Multiple Cropping.* Spec. Publ. 27. American Society of Agronomy, Crop Science Society of America, and Soil Science Society of America, Madison, Wis., 378 p.

ROY, R. N., and H. BRAUN, 1983. Fertilizer use under multiple cropping systems—an overview. In *Fertilizer Use under Multiple Cropping Systems.* FAO Fert. Plant Nutr. Bull. 5, p. 9–23.

SKIDMORE, E. L., J. B. LAYTON, D. V. ARMBRUST, and M. L. HOOKER, 1986. Soil physical properties as influenced by cropping and residue management. *Soil Sci. Soc. Am. J.* 50:415–419.

SOIL SCIENCE DEPARTMENT, North Carolina State University, 1974. *Agronomic-Economic Research on Tropical Soils.* Annual Report for 1974, Raleigh, N.C., 230 p.

VAN DOREN, D. M., JR., W. C. MOLDENHAUER, and G. B. TRIPLETT, JR., 1984. Influence of long-term tillage and crop rotation on water erosion. *Soil Sci. Soc. Am. J.* 48:636–640.

WAGGER, M. G., 1989. Cover crop management and nitrogen rate in relation to growth and yield of no-till corn. *Agron. J.* 81:533–538.

WHITAKER, F. D., V. C. JAMISON, and J. F. THORNTON, 1961. Runoff and erosion losses from Mexico silt loam in relation to fertilization and other management practices. *Soil Sci. Soc. Am. Proc.* 25:401–403.

9 Tillage Practices for Conservation

Dense perennial vegetative cover provides the best erosion control known. Where annual crops are raised every effort must be made to ensure that living crops and crop residues provide as much protection as possible (Moldenhauer et al., 1983). Some tillage practices can help to control erosion by reducing the destruction of crop residues, and in other ways.

9-1 OBJECTIVES OF TILLAGE

Three major objectives of cultivation are: to prepare seed and root beds, to control weeds, and to establish surface soil conditions that favor water infiltration and erosion control.

9-1.1 Preparation of Seed and Root Bed

Surface soil condition should favor effective seed placement, germination, and early emergence and should permit unrestricted plant growth and development. Cultivation to ensure these conditions ranges from simply stirring with the planter or grain drill to conducting many operations with a variety of implements.

9-1.2 Control of Weeds

Weeds compete with crop plants for moisture, nutrients, space, and light. Tillage buries weed seeds and kills seedling and mature weeds. Chemical herbicides control many but not all weeds, and some tillage is usually needed to control resistant weeds so they will not reduce crop yields.

Tillage in excess of that needed to control weeds does not benefit crops on most friable medium- and coarse-textured soils. On these soils, weed control by scraping the soil surface or by applying chemicals is generally as effective as tillage. Crop growth does benefit from more tillage than needed for weed control on some soils that have low permeability and low organic-matter content.

9-1.3 Soil and Water Conservation

Tillage that stirred the soil after every rain to form a dry soil mulch was recommended for moisture conservation in the early years of this century. Field tests failed to show increased moisture storage or improved crop growth. The smooth, dry surface also increased susceptibility to wind erosion, so the practice lost favor.

Cultivation to break up a crusted soil surface and to produce a rough, cloddy soil condition increases infiltration and reduces erosion but the effect is usually short-lived because rain and wind soon smooth the surface.

Crop residues on the soil surface reduce both water and wind erosion. Accordingly, tillage that leaves straw and stubble on the soil surface instead of turning it under has much to recommend it.

9-2 TYPES OF TILLAGE IMPLEMENTS

Hand tools and power equipment generally perform the same tasks, but power equipment works faster and often is used to stir or mix the soil deeper and to bury more vegetative cover and plant residues. Hoes such as those shown in Figure 9-1 are used to "plow" the land, to prepare a seedbed, to open the furrow or hole for seed placement, to weed the growing crops, and even to harvest some crops. These

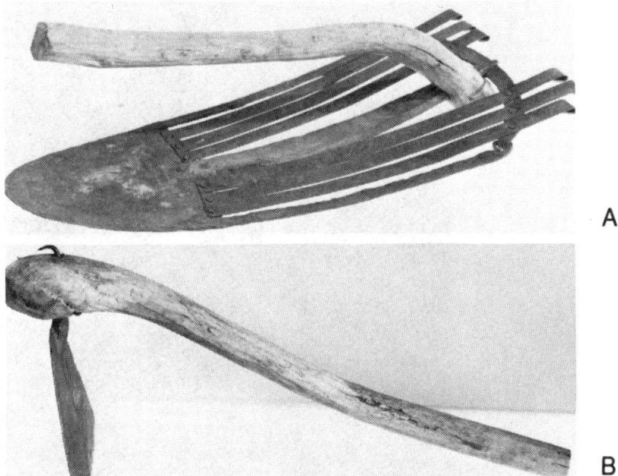

Figure 9-1 Hoes are the traditional tillage tools where hand labor is used for agriculture. The large hoe (a) is used to "plow" the land. Its blade is approximately 12 in. (30 cm) wide by 24 to 30 in. (60 to 75 cm) long. The small hoe (b) is a general-purpose tool called a lalanya. It is used to control weeds, rebuild ridges, and harvest crops. The blade is roughly triangular with a cutting edge about 6 in. (15 cm) wide. (Courtesy J. A. Hobbs.)

hoes are locally made in developing countries and are effective agricultural tools where capital is scarce and labor is plentiful and cheap. Agricultural machinery company brochures are replete with descriptive names for specific tillage implements but there are relatively few distinctly different tillage tools.

9-2.1 Plows

The original animal-drawn plow was a sharpened spike drawn through the soil. It did not invert the soil and killed few weeds. In Europe, its soil-penetrating part was modified and a soil-turning part, originally of wood, was added. It became the *moldboard plow.* Later the wooden moldboard was changed to iron, and then to steel to enhance its ability to turn the furrows cleanly and use less power (see Figure 9-2). Plowing requires considerably more power than most other types of tillage. Plows invert the furrow and actually lift and move all soil in the plow layer. The soil is left rough and cloddy, but not ridged. *Disk plows* with very large sloping disks were developed for use on stony land and on soils that did not scour cleanly off moldboards.

A *lister plow* loosens and moves soil into ridges on each side of the working unit. It uses either small back-to-back moldboards or disks to excavate the furrow and build the ridges. Soil under the ridges is buried but not cultivated.

9-2.2 Disk Cultivators

Implements with a number of saucer-shaped metal components mounted on axles are called disks. Two sets (gangs) of disks are usually connected and faced in

Figure 9-2 A roll-over (two-way) moldboard plow. The plow share or cutting edge, the curved moldboard, and the landside are clearly visible on the units in the air. Also visible is the cutting, inverting, and crumbling action on the soil. The "two-way" feature makes it possible to turn all furrows in one direction, an excellent feature in a soil conservation program. (Courtesy Massey Ferguson, Inc., Des Moines, Iowa.)

opposite directions to each other to eliminate sidedraft. The angle between the axles and the line of travel is adjustable; in operation the axles are turned so that the disks cut and move the soil. A *tandem disk* (Figure 9-3) has two gangs of disks mounted in front and two behind. The first set turns the soil out from the center and the following set moves it back.

A *one-way-disk plow* consists of a series of large disks 20 in. (50 cm) or more in diameter, all saucered in the same direction. It replaced the moldboard plow as the primary tillage tool on vast areas of the Great Plains. It requires considerably less power than the plow and it covers land more quickly.

An *offset disk,* shown in Figure 9-4, has disks mounted in tandem, single gangs that move soil in opposite directions. Disks are larger than those on one-ways.

9-2.3 Tine Cultivators

Some primary and much secondary tillage is performed by implements with points or blades mounted on a frame or on curved shanks fastened on the frame. The simplest is the *drag harrow,* which has rectangular individual frames carrying fixed spikes about 8 in. (20 cm) long that break clods and smooth the soil surface. Individual frames are mounted in series across the direction of travel so that units

Figure 9-3 A tandem disk. The front disks turn the furrows out from the center, the rear disks toward the center. Such implements produce a relatively smooth surface and cover part of the crop residues. This unit is equipped with a "floating" central small disk that cuts the ridge left by the front disk gangs. (Courtesy Deere and Co., Moline, Illinois.)

Figure 9-4 An offset disk. This heavy-framed, large implement has replaced the moldboard plow and disk plow as an initial tillage tool on many farms. (Courtesy Hutchinson/Wil-Rich Manufacturing Co., Wahpeton, North Dakota.)

many feet wide can be pulled across a field in a single pass. The implement is less commonly used today, and almost never used in dryland regions.

A *chisel plow* is a ripping implement that can be used with narrow points (2 in. or 5 cm), wider points (3 in. or 7.5 cm), or blades up to 12 in. (30 cm wide). The implement has several tiers of shanks on the frame, as shown in Figure 9-5. It usually penetrates 8 to 12 in. (20 to 30 cm) deep when narrow points are used. Wider blades are set to overlap 2 to 4 in. (5 to 10 cm) and to penetrate to the depth needed to cut weed roots. A rugged, *heavy-duty chisel,* shown in Figure 9-6, is used for soil ripping and is designed to penetrate 12 to 16 in. (30 to 40 cm) deep. A subsoiler, designed to penetrate 24 in. (60 cm) or more, is still more rugged.

Sweep and blade cultivators have individual blades wider than 20 in. (50 cm); some are more than 6 ft (2 m) wide. Most have V-shaped blades mounted on very rugged shanks at the point of the V (see Figure 9-7); some are equipped with straight blades with shanks at each end. Several of these cultivators can be mounted behind a single tractor.

Figure 9-5 A chisel plow equipped with narrow points. This particular model combines a bank of heavy-duty chisels and a row of regular chisel points. Shanks are mounted on the frame so that there is easy flow of bunched residue through the machine. (Courtesy Hutchinson/Wil-Rich Manufacturing Co., Wahpeton, North Dakota.)

Figure 9-6 A heavy-duty chisel. The very heavy shanks and narrow points are mounted on a V-shaped frame so that the center shank is ahead of those on each side. (Courtesy Allis-Chalmers Corporation, Milwaukee, Wisconsin.)

Figure 9-7 A Noble (patent) blade implement with rugged construction and large clearance between adjacent shanks and between blades and frame. This model has nine 6-ft (1.8-m) "V" blades for a total working width of 49.5 ft (15 m). The frame is flexible so that each blade will conform to the land surface and work at a uniform depth. [Courtesy Cereal Implements (Vicon), Portage la Prairie, Manitoba.]

9-2.4 Miscellaneous Cultivators

A *rotary tillage machine* has a series of knives or blades mounted on a shaft set transverse to the direction of travel. It is powered by its own engine or by a power take off from the tractor. The shaft and blades rotate at a high speed.

The *rotary hoe* has a multitude of curved-spoke, rimless wheels about 4 in. (10 cm) apart, mounted on an axle transverse to the direction of travel. The spokes penetrate easily into the soil but as they are pulled out, they lift or throw the soil, crop residues, and small weeds. A *treader,* really a rotary hoe pulled backwards, has spokes curved so that they press the surface and force residues and the surface soil into the soil. The spokes leave the soil cleanly without disturbance. Figure 9-8 shows the spoke shapes of rotary hoes and treaders. The axle of a *skew treader* is mounted at an angle rather than perpendicular to the direction of forward movement. Two treaders can be hooked up in tandem with a long chain or bar on one side and a short one on the other.

The *rod weeder* has a backward-rotating bar or rod that runs below the ground surface. It cuts off and twists weeds and firms the soil. It cannot be used successfully in soils that contain stones or large pebbles, or in previously unstirred soil. The rod weeder can be made to penetrate uncultivated land if the bar is equipped with cultivator points or teeth (Miller rod).

9-3 TILLAGE, CROP RESIDUE, AND SOIL PROPERTIES

Tillage influences soil and water conservation by its effects on surface crop residues, surface soil roughness, both cloddiness and ridging, and on soil infiltration rate and permeability. Tillage generally buries at least part of a former crop's residue. Moldboard and disk plows which invert the furrow, and rotary tillers which mix the cultivated layers, bury or cover nearly all crop residue. A lister covers nearly all crop

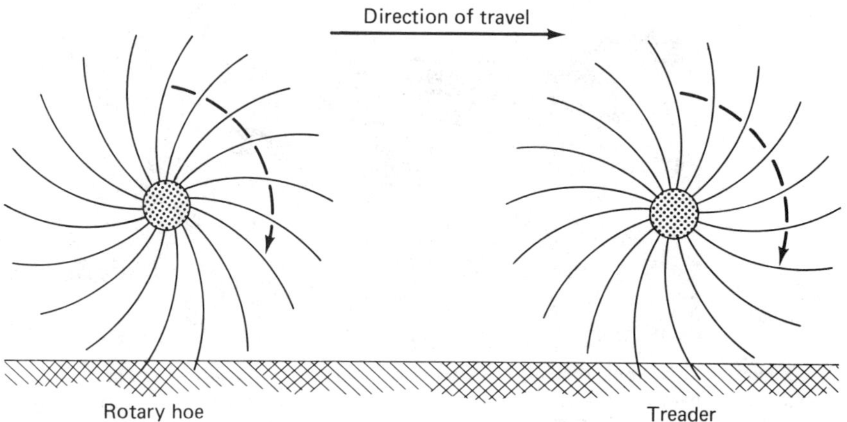

Figure 9-8 Diagram of spike tines of the rotary hoe and treader. The angle of entry into and exit from the soil determines whether the curved tines lift the soil or press it down.

residue even though it inverts only half of the surface soil. Implements that cultivate below the surface leave 75 to 90% of the residue on top; the wider sweeps and blades leave 85 to 90%. Other implements bury intermediate amounts of residue as indicated in Table 9–1.

Plows leave the soil surface cloddy and rough. Listers prepare a very ridged surface. Rotary tillers make the surface smooth, loose, and fluffy unless they are used when the soil is moist. Disk implements leave the soil smoother and less cloddy than the plow. Chisels, especially when worked deep, leave the surface cloddy and rough. Tine implements with smaller blades usually leave the surface somewhat cloddy and rough, but wide-blade cultivators leave a smoother and less cloddy surface.

Effects of tillage on residue cover, cloddiness, and ridging depends on speed and depth of operation as well as on type of implement (Woodruff and Chepil, 1958). Higher speeds make larger ridges, but bury more trash, loosen stubble from the soil, and break down aggregates and clods more completely. A speed of about 2 mi/hr (3 km/h) produces the most cloddy surface but produces little ridging except with the lister. The best compromise speed for a cloddy, ridged surface appears to be about 4 mi/hr (6 km/h). Deeper tillage (6 in. or 15 cm or more), regardless of implement used in seedbed preparation, produces more nonerodible clods of greater stability than shallower tillage (2 to 4 in. or 5 to 10 cm).

The greater the angle of attack (angle between a horizontal line through the

TABLE 9–1 EFFECT OF A SINGLE OPERATION WITH VARIOUS TILLAGE IMPLEMENTS ON CROP RESIDUE LEFT ON THE SOIL SURFACE

Implement	Proportion of original residue remaining on surface (%)
Moldboard plow (5 to 7 in. deep)	10
Moldboard plow (8 in. or deeper)	0
Chisel (twisted points)	50
Chisel (straight points)	75
Tandem disk (regular blades)	50
Tandem disk (large blades)	30
One-way disk (24 to 25 in. blades)	50
Chisel	75
Field cultivator (16 to 18 in. sweeps)	80
Skew treader	90
Blades (36 in. or wider)	90
Sweeps (24 to 36 in.)	85
Rodweeder (plain)	90
Rodweeder (with small shovels or sweeps)	85
Harrow	90
Fertilizer applicator (injection)	90
No-till slot planter	90
Row crop planter	80
Furrow drill	80
Conventional grain drill (disk openers)	90

Source: Modified from the Journal of Agronomic Education, Volume 15, p. 23-26, 1986 (Thien) by permission of the American Society of Agronomy.

axis of an individual disk and the direction of machine travel) the more residue will be buried, the finer the clods will be, and the smaller will be the ridges. The angle of attack seems to be less important during the second and subsequent operations.

Tillage operations that leave more crop residue on the soil surface maintain higher infiltration rates. Plowed land initially has a very high infiltration rate and permeability but these decline rapidly because of little protective cover.

9-4 FLAT VERSUS RIDGED TILLAGE AND PLANTING

Farmers use systems of seedbed preparation and planting that experience indicate are best for their local conditions. Often the land is prepared flat and is seeded with no attempt to ridge the soil (small grains—usually, row crops—sometimes).

More commonly row crops are grown in ridged fields. The crop may be seeded in the bottom of a furrow between two ridges. Mechanical cultivation breaks down the initial ridges and builds new ones over the crop rows, burying seedling weeds in the crop row and cutting off weeds between the rows. It also mounds soil around the base of the plants and is conducive to the growth and development of adventitious (brace) roots.

Ridges are generally used when row crop land is prepared, seeded, and cultivated by hand. The land is ridged and seeds are planted on top of the ridges. Postplanting cultivation controls weeds and rebuilds the ridges as rain washes them down.

A relatively new form of seedbed has been developed for use in some mechanized, humid, or irrigated regions. Flat beds wide enough to accommodate two crop rows are constructed above the general soil level, and are separated by deep furrows that provide better surface drainage and early season aeration than regular flat planting. Specially designed implements are needed to build these beds. Growing crops must be cultivated very carefully to ensure that the beds are maintained as long as necessary. Furrows are used for irrigation on some land, but alternate-row irrigation is less effective on slowly permeable soils than every-row irrigation.

9-5 CONSERVATION TILLAGE

Conservation tillage is defined as "any tillage or planting system in which at least 30% of the soil surface is covered by plant residue after planting to reduce erosion by water; or, where soil erosion by wind is the primary concern, at least 1000 pounds per acre of flat small grain residue equivalent are on the surface during the critical erosion period" (Schertz, 1988). Farmers need to make certain that enough residues are left on the land so that after their tillage activities are completed these requirements are met (Skidmore et al., 1979).

Crop residues can be used for other things such as livestock feed, energy production, raw material for building products, and so on. Too many people forget their role in maintaining soil fertility and tilth. The farmer must ensure that sufficient residue for productivity maintenance and erosion control is available before any diversion is allowed to other uses.

Conservation tillage reduces soil or water losses by leaving crop residues on or above the surface and/or by making the surface porous, cloddy, rough, or ridged. A variety of names has been applied to individual tillage systems that provide for this kind of erosion protection.

9-5.1 Stubble Mulch Tillage

The aim of *stubble mulch tillage* is to keep crop residue on the surface to protect both crops and soils from damage by water and wind erosion. Crop residue must be handled carefully from harvest through planting time. Straw choppers and spreaders on combines, especially on modern, wide combines, are essential. Combine-harvesters can now be equipped with "air reels" so that heads of small grains, sorghum, and similar crops can be harvested with a minimum of stalks. This leaves a taller standing stubble for soil protection and smaller amounts of straw behind the combine to interfere with subsequent tillage.

In 1938, Duley and Russell initiated a tillage concept that purposely retained crop residues on the soil surface for erosion control (Allen and Fenster, 1986). Their original tillage tool had two 22-in. (55-cm) sweeps mounted on a modified 42-in. (105-cm) corn cultivator frame. The method was tested, recommended, and used to some extent in almost all climatic regions in the world where commercial agriculture is practiced. Although stubble mulch tillage caught on first in the drier areas for control of wind erosion, research workers, conservation specialists, and practicing farmers have adapted it to water-erosion control in more humid regions.

Implements for Stubble Mulch Tillage. No single cultivation implement meets all the needs of stubble mulch tillage; none works equally well under all conditions to retain surface cover, or to produce cloddiness and roughness. Tools with the right features for the local soil conditions must be selected (Allen and Fenster, 1986). Undercutting tools such as sweep and blade machines and rod weeders are highly recommended, but other implements are also used.

Disk concavity affects the amount of residue buried, efficiency of weed kill, and cloddiness and roughness produced. The "lift" of a blade affects the amount of clod disintegration and the size of ridges left by tillage. Shape of chisel points affects ridging and cloddiness produced. Implements should be adjustable for depth of cultivation, tilt of working surface, and in disk implements, angle of attack.

Vertical distance between the implement frame and the soil surface must be at least 18 in. (45 cm), and horizontal distance between adjacent shanks must be sufficient to allow bunched residue to slide through and clear the machine. Narrow-bladed instruments need several banks of shanks, one behind the other, with tines offset so that crop residue can pass through. Rolling coulters are needed in front of each shank, especially when working through fresh, heavy residues.

Planting equipment had to be modified to work through heavy residue. Some no-till row crop planters now do a good job of seeding through trash (Figure 9-9). Grain drills changed more slowly. Heavy disk and shoe drills (Figure 9-10) have been developed that will work through limited amounts of residue. An example of a

Figure 9–9 A no-till row crop planter. The planter is equipped to open the furrow, push crop residue to the side, fertilize, and apply herbicides. This type of implement will work equally well in untilled wheat stubble or in clean-tilled land. (Courtesy Fleischer Manufacturing, Inc., Columbus, Nebraska.)

no-till grain drill is shown in Figure 9–11. It will operate satisfactorily through heavy residue.

Significantly more crop residue can now be left on the surface because of improvements in tillage tools and planters and development of more effective herbicides. Eco-fallow, an essentially till-less method of growing crops in dryland areas, is being used successfully and is strongly recommended.

Choosing Implements. Stubble mulch tillage has to be flexible. In some cases all possible residue must be kept on the surface; in others part of the residue must be purposely incorporated. The amount of flattened wheat straw needed to control wind erosion on soils is shown in Figure 9–12. Standing wheat stubble is about twice as effective as an equal weight of flattened stubble. Sorghum stover is about half as effective for controlling wind erosion as wheat straw is. Larger quantities of residues will increase moisture storage and subsequent yields (see Chapter 14).

The proper choice of tillage implements to handle crop residues for optimum erosion control and crop production requires a knowledge of the quantity of residues needed (Figure 9–12), the amount of residue available (Section 6–7.6), and the proportion of residue incorporated by each tillage implement (Table 9–1).

If 3000 lb/ac (3300 kg/ha) of standing stubble and straw are left on a silt loam soil (WEG 6) after wheat harvest (July 1) in a region with a C' value of 100, and if three tillage operations usually are needed to control weeds and prepare a seedbed for the next wheat crop, what implement or combination of implements in Table 9–1 could be used to prepare the land for seeding and still leave the amount of residue needed on the field after planting? What is needed to control soil drifting? Figure

Figure 9-10 A heavy double-disk grain drill designed to seed small grain through reasonable quantities of crop residue. It can be purchased with a variety of furrow openers. (Courtesy Deere and Co., Moline, Illinois.)

9-3 indicates about 1350 lb/ac. The furrow drill reduces cover to 80%; field cultivators, blade machines, and rod weeders leave 80 to 90%; a tandem disk leaves

Figure 9-11 A no-till grain drill with rugged, high-clearance furrow openers and a combined air seeder/fertilizer applicator. This unit is 39 feet (12 m) wide and is capable of seeding through dense residues on untilled small grain or row crop fields. An herbivcide application attachment is available. (Courtesy Flexi-coil Industries Ltd., Saskatoon, Saskatchewan, Canada. Photograph was provided by Alberta Farm Machinery Research Centre, Lethbridge, Alberta, Canada.)

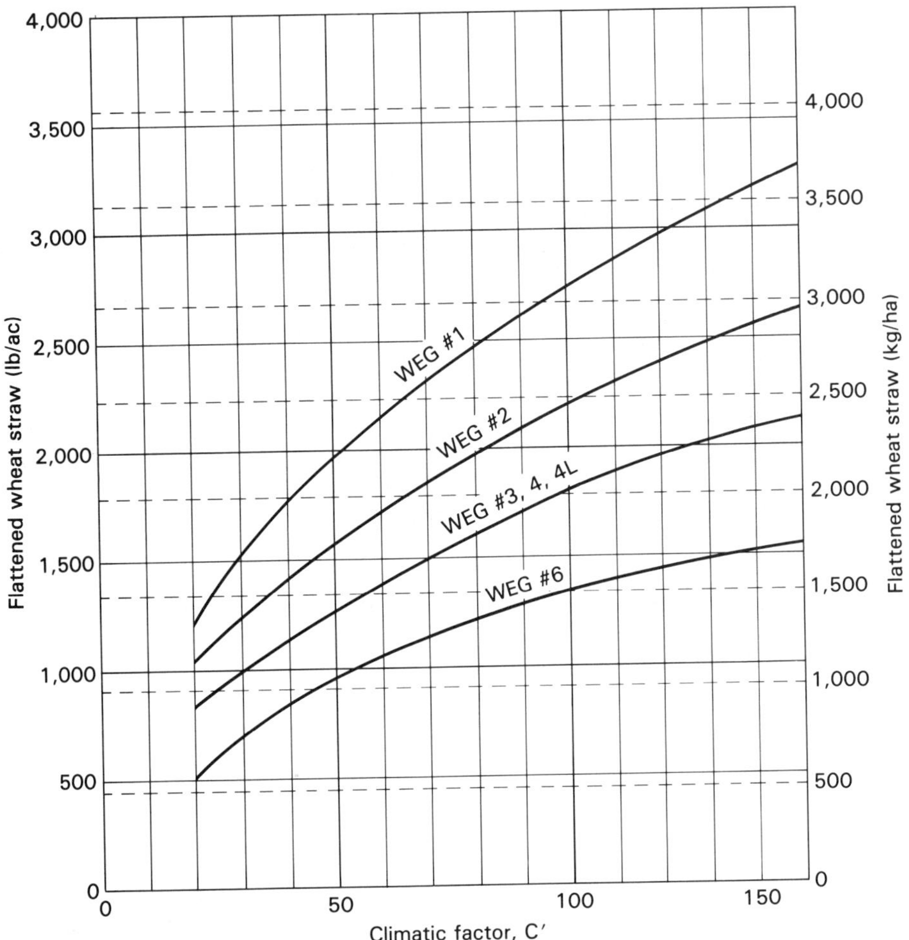

Figure 9–12 Graph showing the relationship between soil erodibility (WEG), climatic factor C' (Chapter 6), and the amount of flattened wheat stubble needed to keep soil loss by wind erosion below 5 tons/ac-yr (11 mt/ha-yr). [Modified from Crop Residue Management Systems, p. 17–33, 1978, published by the American Society of Agronomy (Skidmore and Siddoway) by permission of the American Society of Agronomy.]

50%. If a furrow drill, tandem disk, large blade implement, and field cultivator are used, the amount of residue remaining after planting will be

$$3000 \times 0.8 \times 0.5 \times 0.9 \times 0.8 = 864 \text{ lb/ac}$$

This is not enough, so the tandem disk should be replaced with an implement that leaves 80% or more of the residue. Thien (1986) has developed a computer program that solves this sort of tillage selection problem.

Field Experience with Stubble Mulch Tillage. The first experience a farmer had with stubble mulch tillage in pre-herbicide days was nearly always bad. Tillage tools plugged up with straw; weed control was often inadequate; planting, particularly with disk-type grain drills, was not always successful; and crop yields were often reduced. Zingg and Whitfield (1957) reviewed the results of much of the early research with this practice in the western half of the United States. They found that this practice was better adapted to semiarid regions. With better planting and cultivating equipment, and with herbicides available, much improvement has been made in dryland areas and in adapting it to more humid conditions. Still problems exist.

Causes of Lowered Crop Yields. Poorer crop growth appears to be caused by reduced available nitrogen supply, less satisfactory weed control and seedbed quality, and lower soil temperature.

The top 36 in. (90 cm) of soil under stubble mulch tillage contains less nitrate nitrogen than similar depths under plowed land. Applications of extra nitrogen fertilizer have not always brought yields up to those on plowed plots. Dryland crop yields are not always reduced by lower available nitrogen content because the soil may contain enough nitrogen to produce the amount of crop that the soil moisture is capable of supporting.

Weeds cut off but not buried by tillage may survive unless dry conditions desiccate them. The more humid the area, the greater is the chance of rain shortly after cultivation, and the greater is the chance for weed survival.

Implements other than disks and sweep machines rake up abundant residues. If trapped residue accumulates, it lifts the implement off the surface. Weeds are not controlled and a poor seedbed results. Poor planter operation in heavy residues causes poor stands with many skips and misses.

Surface mulch insulates the soil from temperature changes. Soil stays warm longer in the fall; warming is delayed in the spring and the mulched plots are 2 to 4°F (1 to 2°C) cooler than unmulched plots at 2 to 3 in. (5 to 7 cm) below the surface. Soil temperature below 85°F (30°C) reduces early corn growth and subsequent yields. Above 90°F (32°C) lowered temperatures are beneficial (van Wijk et al., 1959; Larson et al., 1960; Allamaras et al., 1964). Studies in the central Great Plains show that soil temperature in stubble-mulched land in the early spring is as much as 7°F (4°C) lower than that in soil without mulch cover. Temperatures cooler than 50°F (10°C) were noted in mulched plots as long as 40 days after wheat regrowth started. Field and growth chamber studies show that spring regrowth of wheat is seriously reduced by temperatures below 50°F lasting for as short a period as 18 days.

Some scientists warned that insects and crop diseases might be a problem where residues are not buried, but to date there is little evidence of this in the winter wheat or corn belt areas. Some insects have been more troublesome on mulch tilled land in spring wheat areas.

Current Use and Future of Stubble Mulch Tillage. New, more effective herbicides, and cultivation equipment and drills designed to work effectively through large amounts of residues have overcome several of the more important factors that contributed to low performance and yields initially. It is now possible to leave as much as 3000 lb/ac (3300 kg/ha) of stubble and residue on the soil surface and to produce excellent yields regularly. The practice spread from those who first made it work and is now used extensively for small grain and row crop production where moisture limits crop growth and where danger of wind erosion is high (Figure 9-13). Many fields that farmers claim to have prepared by stubble mulching do not end up at planting time with enough straw to qualify. Improvements in techniques are needed on many farms.

9-5.2 Minimum and No Tillage

Scientists and some farmers in the summer-fallow area of the United States used 2,4-D, a selective herbicide, as a way to reduce tillage costs in the summer fallow operation in the late 1940s. This chemical kills most broad-leaved weeds, but most grass-family crops and weeds are immune. The use of this chemical could not replace tillage.

Soon after, concern developed over soil deterioration because of declining soil organic-matter content, soil structure degeneration, and increasing subsoil compaction. Concerned farmers and scientists devised ways to reduce tillage operations, especially for row crop production. The main reductions were made in the preplant period. No chemical herbicides were involved at the outset.

Reduced Preplant Tillage. Reduced tillage systems dispensed with moldboard plowing or with one or more subsequent cultivations. Crops were produced successfully where land was prepared and seeded in one or two passes across the field if weeds were controlled. Methods were given a variety of names, among them *plow-plant* and *wheel-track-plant.* A once-over tillage and planting system was called *till-plant.* For the most part farmers developed their own equipment often pulling several implements in tandem behind a single tractor. A commercial till-plant machine was manufactured for a brief period at that time. Less traffic caused less soil compaction. The looser condition between the rows permitted more

Figure 9-13 Undercutting wheat stubble with a four-blade implement (22.5 ft or 6.9 m wide) leaves abundant stubble standing on the soil surface.

rapid infiltration, so less water ran off and erosion was reduced. Satisfactory crop stands were obtained, and yields approximated those from conventional tillage. Weeds were often less of a problem in the plow-plant and wheel-track-plant systems, but in the till-plant system weeds became a severe problem before wide-spectrum herbicides were available.

The partial success of till-plant systems emphasized that there are two zones in a row crop field: the seed zone in the row area, and the moisture storage zone between the rows. Better infiltration and less runoff and erosion occur when the latter zone is left loose, but some packing of the seed zone is usually necessary to get uniform planting and good seed-soil contact.

While results with corn and soybeans were satisfactory with these techniques, sorghum, a crop that requires a warmer seedbed and therefore a later planting date, did not do as well. Weed stands often were dense and hard to control. Plow-plant and till-plant systems were seldom successful with sorghum.

Despite some success, these techniques never became really popular until effective chemical herbicides were developed. Many farmers were reluctant to use these techniques because planting rate was reduced to the speed of preparing the seedbed. Farmers with large acreages to seed to row crops want to plant rapidly.

Reduced Pre- and Postplanting Tillage. Additional incentive to reduce tillage came in the early 1970s with the drastic increase in price of tractor fuel and the possibility of severely curtailed supplies for agriculture. Increasing numbers of farmers reduced cultivation or omitted it entirely (Figure 9–14). Weed control in the *no-till* systems is accomplished wholly with chemicals. No-till systems provide some

Figure 9–14 Row crops can be seeded in untilled soil with a no-till planter. This machine is adapted to plant on former crop ridges in order to maintain a ridged condition for erosion control. Attachments are available for this and other makes and models to apply either dry or liquid herbicides in addition to dry fertilizer. (Courtesy Fleischer Manufacturing Co., Columbus, Nebraska.)

gains, some losses. The major benefits are lower fuel and machinery costs, considerably less soil compaction, and better runoff and erosion control. An intangible benefit is the farm operator has more time to think, plan, and supervise farm operations.

The major disadvantages of no-tillage is that not all weeds are controlled even when chemicals are used. Chemicals restrict cropping choices and may damage crops. Herbicide results are not precisely predictable. Soil properties such as soil reaction, organic-matter content, clay content, and drainage characteristics, the amount of crop residue on the soil surface, and the climate all affect the activity and longevity of the chemicals. Options for fertilizer placement are seriously reduced with no-tillage, but this is not as serious as was originally feared. Plants can absorb even immobile phosphorus satisfactorily from surface-applied fertilizer if the residue cover keeps the surface soil moist and if roots are not pruned by postplanting cultivation. Other types of reduced tillage do not restrict fertilizer placement as severely as no-tillage.

Cost and Energy Requirements of Reduced Tillage. Less tillage can save considerably on repair and maintenance costs and cuts fuel bills in half (Unger et al., 1977). This does not guarantee less farming expense because the cost of buying and applying chemicals can be high. Overall costs have been reduced by judicious selection of the most effective and economical combinations of tillage and chemical treatments.

Reduced Tillage and Soil Compaction. Reduced tillage systems in which plowing is eliminated can be expected to produce less soil compaction in the plowsole zone. During the first several years the top 6 in. (15 cm) of soil is often denser under reduced tillage than it is when plowed regularly; this is especially true in no-till systems (Hammel, 1989). Permeability and infiltration rates are likely to be slower in no-till system soil (Lindstrom et al., 1984). Some studies show that surface soil becomes less dense as no-till systems continue but most show continued high density. Increased surface residues reduce surface sealing and so may maintain or improve infiltration rate.

Reduced Tillage and Runoff and Erosion Losses. Reduced tillage generally reduces runoff and erosion. No-till has variable effects on runoff, but usually reduces erosion losses. Burwell and Kramer (1983) report that conservation tillage reduced runoff and soil losses to 85% and 42%, respectively, of those experienced on conventionally tilled plots. A Mississippi study showed that conventional tillage caused significantly more erosion than no-till in all cropping systems (Table 9–2).

Whitaker et al. (1973) found when Mexico silt loam (a clay pan soil) was cropped no-till that runoff and erosion increased significantly and that crop yields decreased significantly (Table 9–3). The mechanical treatment was apparently better because tillage broke a pronounced crust on this soil and permitted better infiltration of rainwater.

Investigations of the way reduced tillage affects wind erosion have been conducted both in the drylands of the Great Plains and on sandy soils in more humid

TABLE 9-2 EFFECT OF TILLAGE SYSTEM ON RUNOFF AND SOIL LOSS AT BILOXI, MISSISSIPPI, 1970, 1971, AND 1972

Tillage and crop system	Runoff (%)	Soil loss (tons/ac-yr)
No-till, soybean-wheat double crop	23	0.8
No-till, corn after soybeans	33	2.3
No-till, soybeans after corn	24[a]	0.6[a]
No-till, continuous soybeans	23	1.1
Conventional tillage, continuous soybeans	29	7.8

[a]Only two-year average results.

Source: From Transactions of the American Society of Agricultural Engineers, Volume 18, p. 918–920, 1975 (McGregor et al.).

regions. Black and Power (1965) found that chemically fallowed soil had a higher percentage of nonerodible clods in the surface soil and more surface crop residues than even stubble mulched fallow soil. Potential erodibility of the chemical fallow soil is therefore even lower than that of stubble mulched land.

The no-till method of seedbed preparation was compared to conventional tillage including moldboard plowing on sandy soils in northwestern Ohio. The no-till technique left 2 to 3 tons/ac (4 to 7 mt/ha) of corn residue on the soil surface, while the surface with conventional tillage was nearly bare. The conventionally treated area lost 130 tons/ac (291 mt/ha) of soil during one severe windstorm, whereas the no-till area lost only 2 tons/ac (4 mt/ha). Corn yields over the two years of the study averaged 68 bu/ac (4265 kg/ha) on the conventionally treated land and 93 bu/ac (5833 kg/ha) on the no-till area (Schmidt and Triplett, 1967).

Adapting Reduced Tillage Systems to Soils. Experience with reduced tillage shows that soils respond differently to various chemical-tillage combinations. For example, a seedbed preparation system was developed for sorghum in a wheat–sorghum–fallow sequence on the silt loam soils in a 21- to 26-in. rainfall area in western Kansas. Two specific tillage operations and one (or two) herbicide treatment(s) controlled wind erosion and increased yields above those obtained with conventional tillage. This system did not work on sandy soils in the area, or on hardland soils in slightly drier areas farther west.

Galloway et al. (1977) grouped the soils of Indiana on the basis of topographic

TABLE 9-3 EFFECT OF CHEMICAL AND MECHANICAL WEED CONTROL ON RUNOFF, SOIL EROSION, AND CORN YIELD ON MEXICO SILT LOAM AT THE MIDWEST CLAYPAN EXPERIMENT FARM NEAR MCCREDIE, MISSOURI, FOUR-YEAR AVERAGE, 1966–1969

Treatment	Precipitation (in.)	Runoff		Erosion (tons/ac-yr)	Corn yield (bu/ac)
		in.	%		
Chemical	40	9.5	23.7	10.5	105
Mechanical	40	8.7	21.8	6.7	113

Source: Modified from the Journal of Soil and Water Conservation, Volume 28, p. 174–176, 1973 (Whitaker et al.).

position, drainage, color, texture, permeability, and slope, and evaluated the usefulness of various forms of tillage deeper than 6 in. (15 cm) (plowing and chiseling) versus less than 6 in. (disking, till-plant, ridge-plant, and no-till) on individual soils. They rated reduced, shallow tillage poor on muck soils. Reduced tillage, especially no-till, rated high on sloping, well-drained, permeable, coarse- and medium-textured soils. Moldboard plowing, as an initial tillage technique, rated best on poorly drained, slowly permeable soils with less than 4% organic matter and was quite satisfactory on somewhat poorly drained, permeable soils with 2 to 4% organic matter.

It takes time and effort to find the best system of reduced tillage for a particular soil, but the possibilities of reduced costs, and improved erosion control, make the extra effort worthwhile.

Current Use and Future of Conservation Tillage. Conservation tillage is based in part on a reduction in the number of operations used in preparing a seedbed and on a change of tillage implements—moldboard plows downgraded, undercutting implements emphasized. Since SCS first reported on "minimum tillage" in 1963 the acreage has been steadily increasing and the technology is reportedly being adopted more quickly than any other soil and crop management innovation in U.S. agricultural history. A 1975 USDA assessment predicted that some form of conservation tillage would be used on 95% of cropland by 2010. Schertz (1988) suggests that between 63 and 82% of cropland will be conservation tilled by 2010. This level of use would greatly reduce soil loss on steeper lands and in dry, windy areas, with consequent reductions in rate of soil degradation and of pollution contributed by agriculture.

Some question the accuracy of these statistics and of the prediction. They claim that implement use may have changed that much, but that many fields cultivated with disks and undercutting tools have far too little crop residue remaining on the soil surface during the late seedbed preparation period to reduce soil losses appreciably (Dickey et al., 1987). A survey in Nebraska showed that 55% of the farmers considered they were using conservation tillage. Field inspections showed that less then 5% of fields had 30% of surface cover immediately after planting.

Because farmers are concerned with tillage costs and efficiencies and with soil losses, interest in and use of conservation tillage will increase. It is a demanding technique requiring greater and more sophisticated managerial ability than conventional methods. Extension and conservation personnel will have to plan and execute outstanding promotional and guidance programs to ensure the benefits of increased use.

9-6 DEEP TILLAGE

Many U.S. experiment stations conducted studies that compared the effects of different depths of plowing, subsoiling, and dynamiting on crop growth and yield. The results of early work showed that plowing deeper than 7 to 8 in. (18 to 20 cm) had no merit on soils without root inhibiting zones near plow depth. Soils containing pans at or below normal plowing depth that seriously restrict root penetration sometimes are benefited by plowing 12 to 20 in. (30 to 50 cm) (Fehrenbacher et al., 1958).

9-6.1 Deep Chiseling and Subsoiling

Deep chiseling is the practice of opening the soil 12 to 16 in. (30 to 40 cm) deep with a heavy-duty chisel or chisel plow that penetrates and rips the soil without inverting the ripped layer (Figure 9-15). *Subsoiling* involves ripping the soil 20 in. (50 cm) or more without inversion. Power requirements for deep chiseling and subsoiling are high. Chiseling the soil every 22 in. (55 cm) to a depth of 16 in. (40 cm), or subsoiling 22 to 24 in. (55 to 60 cm) deep every 44 in. (110 cm) takes more power than plowing 6 in. (15 cm) deep.

Water moves readily into chisel cracks and slots as long as they remain open at the soil surface. When slots are covered over or filled, water infiltration is limited by the small pores at the surface. Subsurface cracks that are not connected to the surface can drain excess water from saturated soil, but they cannot help water infiltrate. Even tillage slots that are filled artificially with crop residues (*vertical mulching*) do not increase infiltration after the surface of the slots is covered by tillage or natural forces. Deep chiseling usually has no direct effect on the control of runoff and erosion except immediately after the tillage operation, and on soils with swelling clays where the chisel marks may reopen as soil shrinkage cracks in dry weather (White, 1986).

Most investigations show little or no yield response to this practice. Where pans are found at plow depth or slightly below, chiseling between old crop rows as an initial step in seedbed preparation increases infiltration and reduces runoff and erosion (Moldenhauer et al., 1983). Shattering such pans allows roots to penetrate

Figure 9-15 Deep-chiseling a field leaves clods on the surface and deep chisel marks in the soil. (Courtesy Allis-Chalmers Corporation, Milwaukee, Wisconsin.)

better into the subsoil also. Campbell et al. (1974) found that chiseling to a depth of 15 in. (38 cm) loosened Norfolk sandy loam and Varina sandy loam (Ultisols) enough to improve root penetration. The larger root systems collected enough extra moisture to permit the growing crop to evade damage during short drought periods, but did not increase crop yields in years of adequate and timely rainfall or in years of long droughts.

9-6.2 Deep Plowing

The methods of deep tillage mentioned in Section 9-6.1 involve stirring the soil or cracking it open. Deep plowing involves inversion of the cultivated layer by very large disk plows [disks up to 3 ft (1 m) or more in diameter] or with large moldboard plows. Some of the latter can turn a furrow slice 6 ft (2 m) deep.

Deep plowing has been employed successfully where a productive soil has been buried by unproductive erosion sediments or where an infertile or a highly erodible surface layer is underlain by more productive or less erodible material. This was first used successfully in California where deep layers of mixed and rocky material from eroding hilly land were deposited on productive bottomland soils. There the layer of sediment was turned under and the old topsoil returned to the surface. The soil had to have a high productive capacity initially in order to make this practice economical. Large areas of bottomland covered by relatively sterile, sandy, flood deposits also have been restored to something like their original productivity by deep plowing.

Deep plowing has also been successful in the southern Great Plains of the United States where highly erodible sandy surface layers of soil overlie finer-textured subsoils. Thousands of acres of sandy, highly erodible soils were deep-plowed in Kansas, Oklahoma, and Texas in the late 1940s and especially in the 1950s. Results of studies showed that *appropriate* soils were made less erodible and more productive. Clay and organic matter contents of surface soils were increased; soil cloddiness was improved. Soil erodibility was reduced and crop yields increased. After five to six years, clay and organic matter had returned to near pre-deep plowing levels, nonerodible aggregates were halfway back to pre-plowing quantities, and erodibility had increased dramatically. Crop yields also were lowered quickly. These degradations occurred even where subsequent wind erosion was not a factor.

The following precautions should be taken in deep plowing a sandy soil:

1. Plow only soils that contain less than 10% clay in the surface, and more than 20% in the subsoil within 12 to 16 in. of the surface. Do not deep plow soils that have more than 40% clay in the subsoil.
2. Plow deep enough to turn up at least 1 in. of finer-textured subsoil for each 2 in. of sandy surface soil present.
3. Plow in large, solid blocks to minimize the proportion of the area of the deeply ridged, plowed land that will be covered by sand drifting in from nonplowed areas.
4. Fields with small areas of soils that have less than 20% clay in the subsoil can

be deep-plowed if the extent of the sandy subsoil phase is less than 10% of the field area.

5. Furrows must be turned completely over so that the subsoil is on top rather than mixed with the topsoil. Moldboard plows invert best with minimal mixing; if a disk plow is used, the disks must have a diameter at least twice the expected depth of plowing.
6. Supplementary erosion-control practices and other good management techniques must be employed to prevent subsequent damage to the deep-plowed sandy land.

9-7 CONTOUR CULTIVATION

Contour cultivation (or *contouring*) is tillage and planting of crops along contour lines rather than up and down hill or parallel to field boundaries. It is used in humid and moist subhumid regions mainly to reduce soil erosion. It is used in semiarid and drier portions of subhumid regions primarily to increase soil moisture by reducing runoff losses. Its soil conservation features are discussed in the following pages; its moisture conservation potential is discussed in Chapter 14.

Contour cultivation is an ancient practice. In countries with a long history of cultivation, it is rare to find sloping cultivated lands in a good state of productivity that have not been contour cultivated. In the United States contouring was used first in the southeast. Very few farmers employed the practice until the 1940s. Adoption has been slow and resistance to acceptance is still very strong, even though contouring is an inexpensive practice to initiate.

Contour ridges produced by tillage, planting, and crop rows such as those in Figure 9-16, form barriers that slow or stop downhill water movement. Effective-

Figure 9-16 Contour cultivation on 1 to 3% slopes in Kansas. The ridges reduce soil erosion by acting as barriers to the flow of water. (Courtesy USDA Soil Conservation Service.)

ness of ridges in trapping water and reducing soil loss decreases as slope gradient increases. Larger ridges are more effective than small ones. Lister ridges are most effective. Where contoured lister furrows are blocked (dammed) at intervals along their length, forming basins, rain is held where it falls and runoff and soil loss are further reduced. This practice is rather common in parts of Africa and Asia, where it is called tie-ridging but is seldom used where agriculture is mechanized because the ties make the land too rough to be comfortably cultivated.

9-7.1 Contour Cultivation, Erosion, and Crop Yields

A summary of results from early contour studies from various state and federal sources, compiled and mimeographed for the Soil Conservation Service by J. H. Stallings, showed 25 to 76% reductions in water erosion resulting from contour cultivation compared to farming up and down hill. Smith (1946) quotes experimental results that showed contouring reduced soil erosion losses by 40 to 80%. A study near Ottawa, Canada, on Rideau clay soil showed that contour cultivation of land in corn reduced erosion from 7.8 to 2.6 tons/ac-yr (17.5 to 5.8 mt/ha-yr) (Ripley et al., 1961).

Two points should be kept in mind when viewing contouring results from small plots: Rows in plots are short and have little row grade to carry water to a low spot, whereas contoured fields usually have some row gradient and water does move behind the ridges. Farmers usually farm parallel to a field boundary rather than directly up and down hill. Thus farm field erosion is likely to be less severe and the erosion reduction a farmer can achieve by changing to contour cultivation is usually less than that obtained in experimental plots.

Studies show that farming across the slope increases crop yields. There were only seven sets of comparisons, out of over 600, compiled by Stallings, where the contour-treated land failed to outyield noncontoured land. Average corn yields increased about 10%, average wheat yields about 29%, soybeans 11%, and sorghum about 28%. Reasons for these increases include more available moisture, a less eroded, more productive soil, less washing out of seeds, and less burying of seedlings.

9-7.2 Drawbacks of Contour Cultivation

With all contouring's potential benefit, much land is still farmed parallel to the fenceline. The most common reasons given for continuing to "farm with the fence" is that working a field on the contour is inconvenient, causes many short rows and extra turning, and increases labor and machinery time and cost. These objections become stronger as farm equipment gets bigger. But contouring produces longer rows as well as shorter ones and tractors are known to operate more efficiently on the level. Costs in time and inconvenience of contouring may well be more than offset by reduced fuel costs and the benefits of erosion control and higher yields.

9–7.3 When and Where to Use Contour Cultivation

Contouring is most efficient on gentle and short slopes. Intense rainstorms on steeper slopes cause water to accumulate behind the ridges until it breaks over, rushes downhill, and forms rills and gullies. Erosion becomes progressively more severe on longer slopes until more erosion actually occurs in the gullies on the contoured land than in the rills between crop rows on noncontoured land. Limits on slope gradient and length therefore have been set beyond which contouring alone is not recommended.

Slope-length data for successful contouring were presented in Table 6–7. These are average values and can change with soil characteristics (length can be greater on more permeable soils), with type of crop grown (longer for more protective crops, such as small grains), and with the area's rainfall characteristics (longer with less intense storms). Experience with no-till and other reduced tillage systems that leave the soil surface well protected with crop residue show that field lengths far in excess of those given in Table 6–7 can be used safely, but extra residue must protect the soil every year if field lengths exceed these limits. Terracing (Chapter 10) is the only convenient way to reduce long slope lengths to the limits indicated.

9–7.4 Farming a Contoured Field

Wherever possible, upper and lower field boundaries should be changed to follow the contour. Natural drainageways should be prepared to handle extra water that will be guided onto them by tillage marks and crop rows. Waterways that are to serve as access roadways for implements will need to be extra-wide as regular travel up and down the center of a waterway damages the grass cover.

Water flowing onto the field from higher land should be intercepted by a diversion built along the upper field boundary and carried away from the field. A new waterway may be needed or an existing one widened and reshaped to accommodate the diverted water.

A few fields have simple, uniform slopes that make it possible to farm the whole field parallel to a single guideline, but most fields have complex slopes, and several guidelines are needed to lay out a contouring plan as shown in Figure 9–17. Best guidelines are terrace ridges, but if a field is to be contour-cultivated without terraces, the guidelines must be laid out and marked permanently. It is seldom advisable to have these guidelines exactly on the contour. They need a slight grade so tillage marks and crop rows will direct water toward waterways. Grades between 0.1 and 2% can be used on permeable soils and between 0.2 and 0.6% on less permeable ones (Carter and Carreker, 1969; Harris and Watson, 1971).

The top guideline ordinarily is laid out about one terrace interval below the upper side of the field. Other guidelines are established wherever needed to keep row gradients within permissible limits. Guidelines should be laid out by engineers or conservation workers who have the necessary equipment and experience. This service is free to all Conservation District cooperators (Chapter 19).

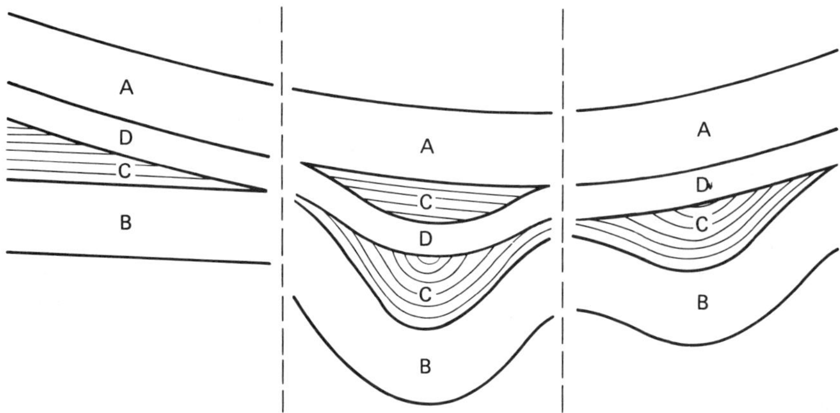

Figure 9–17 Diagram showing techniques for cultivating nonuniform-width contour strips for most efficient field management and erosion control. The areas are planted in the sequence ABCD as explained in Note 9–1. D is the turn-row strip. (Courtesy USDA Soil Conservation Service.)

The farmer should mark the guidelines by plowing a furrow or by other suitable means before the layout crew leaves the field. Permanent stakes must be set in fencerows or elsewhere to mark the ends of guidelines that do not coincide with terraces.

All cultivating and planting operations are started along a guideline. Slopes remain the same along all tillage marks or plant rows where the guidelines are parallel but change with distance above or below nonparallel lines. Two situations arise:

1. The distance between an adjacent pair of guidelines is greater (the land is flatter) in the center of the field than at the edges. In this case, successive rows parallel to and below a guideline carry water toward the field edges along progressively steeper gradients. Rows above and parallel to a guideline move water toward the field center.
2. The width between guidelines is narrower (the land is steeper) in the center and rows above a guideline direct water toward the field boundaries; those below a guideline direct water toward the center.

All cultivation and planting operations should be performed so that each furrow leads excess water to the sides of fields or to other vegetated areas established to carry the water safely to the foot of the slope. Such rigid water control is seldom practical because of the inconvenience of farming many areas of short (point) rows, so systems are developed that keep the number of furrows that lead water away from field borders and other vegetated areas to a practical minimum, but which also keep the number of point rows within bounds (Note 9–1).

NOTE 9-1
FARMING CONTOURED FIELDS

Fieldwork between parallel contour guidelines is commonly performed halfway up and halfway down from adjacent guidelines. It is advisable to work the areas between adjacent nonparallel guidelines (on irregular slopes) in the following sequence:

1. Cultivate or plant full-length rows about halfway down at the narrowest width from the upper guideline (area A in Figure 9-17).
2. Cultivate or plant the same number of rounds up from the lower guidelines, leaving an unworked strip wide enough to turn at the narrowest point (area B).
3. Fill the intervening spaces with short rows (area C) according to field conditions as shown in Figure 9-17, leaving a uniform turn-row strip wide enough for the equipment used across the entire field length (area D). Usually the area of short rows is below the turn-row strip. Field work here is done so that the ridges and plant rows grade down toward the field edges or to a waterway. Short rows should be worked out both above and below the turn-row strip where there are more short rows in C than full-length rows in B.
4. Cultivate or plant the turn-row area (area D). This area can be seeded to the crop planted in the field, to another annual crop, or to a perennial grass or grass-legume mixture.

It is especially important to follow these instructions when planting a contoured field to row crops; the sequence is less critical when planting small grains. Water will flow toward the center of the field in some strips in area A of each section of Figure 9-17. Maximum permissible slope lengths have therefore been established and terraces are recommended to help control runoff where the slopes are too long.

9-7.5 Contour Furrows for Range- and Pastureland

Overgrazed or otherwise depleted rangeland may suffer from erosion. Contour furrows and pits have been recommended as ways of reducing runoff, increasing plant growth, and reducing erosion. Contour furrows are not likely to be effective on sandy or rocky soils, on claypan areas, or on steep slopes. Best results are obtained if the range includes grass species that spread by rhizomes or by stolons. Bunchgrasses that spread by seed or by tillering only are slow to respond.

Design and Construction of Range Furrows. Rangeland furrows should be laid out on the exact contour for best results. Key contour lines are laid out as on cropland, about one terrace interval apart. The furrowing implement is worked halfway up and halfway down from the contour guidelines, with the odd-shaped lands filled in afterward.

Furrows are most commonly constructed with small shovels mounted on tractor tool bars. Sturdy equipment is needed to withstand the heavy pull through the sod and the fast speed required to scatter the turned sod. The tool bar should be capable of fast lift so that furrows can be stopped short of rills, gullies, and roadways. Furrows may be from 3 to 12 in. (7.5 to 30 cm) wide and from 3 to 6 in. (7.5 to 15 cm) deep. Furrows that expose subsoil may reduce or prevent improvement and spread of vegetation. Furrows should be broken at intervals by lifting the shovels out of the ground in order to reduce the danger of water concentrating at breakover sites where the furrows are not on the exact contour.

Range Pitting. Range pitting involves working the soil surface with specially prepared, large disk implements that have alternate disks removed. The remaining disks are either mounted eccentrically or have one-third of the circumference cut away so that each disk bites into the soil only part of the time. Range pitting, less expensive than furrowing, is less effective. Contour lines to guide the pitting operation should be laid out in the usual way at about normal terrace intervals.

9-8 EMERGENCY TILLAGE FOR WIND-EROSION CONTROL

Wind erosion starts in some fields in spite of precautions taken to reduce the erosion hazard. Some soils are naturally very erodible, but the predominant factor that sets the stage for soil drifting is the lack of adequate vegetative cover. Drought, winter killing, insect depredations, and diseases affect the amount of top growth produced and the protective cover on the land. Whatever the cause of poor cover, strong winds striking bare soil can cause drifting. Once movement starts, it usually spreads across the field, pasture, or range, and may also spread to neighboring areas. Emergency tillage is used to stabilize the drifting soil as quickly as possible and to prevent the spread of erosion.

The Soil Conservation Service reports that about 6 million ac (2.4 million ha) receive emergency tillage each year in the 10 Great Plains states. This figure should decline as tillage methods to leave surface residues are used more effectively, but there will always be some land in a vulnerable state.

9-8.1 Emergency Wind-Erosion Control

There are two general methods of emergency soil-drifting control. One is to spread straw, manure, and other vegetative mulches, asphalt and similar sprays, even very coarse sand and fine gravel. The second method is to roughen the surface of the soil by tillage to reduce wind velocity at the soil surface and to trap flying soil particles.

Mulching. There is seldom enough vegetative mulching material available for large agricultural fields. The nonvegetative organic mulches and the coarse aggregates are too expensive for widespread agricultural use.

Emergency Tillage. Implements that have been used in emergencies to control soil drifting include rotary hoes, disks, cultivators, chisels, listers, sweep and blade machines, and rod weeders. The main requirement for emergency control on fallow or other bare fields is to roughen the soil surface rapidly over a large area (Figure 9-18).

9-8.2 Controlling Active Soil Drifting

A strip of soil is roughened across the direction of the wind starting at the windward side of the field. The implement is then moved downwind to where soil is being picked up again by the wind and another pass is made parallel to the first. Successive passes are made across the field at intervals narrow enough to trap all saltating soil grains in the roughened soil. The space between tilled strips should be narrower than the immediate need if wind velocity is likely to increase.

Spacing the passes across the field rather than tilling the whole field accomplishes three things: It speeds up the emergency operation, permitting a much

Figure 9-18 Emergency tillage to control soil drifting in a wheat field in Kansas. A chisel with wide spacing was used to produce ridges and furrows across the path of the wind where the cover provided by the wheat crop was inadequate. A large part of the crop was not damaged by the chisel operation. (Courtesy USDA Soil Conservation Service.)

greater area to be controlled; it reduces the cost of the operation; and it leaves uncultivated strips that can be tilled in a second emergency action if the clods turned up by the first tillage break down under the wind.

9-8.3 Emergency Tillage and Crop Damage

Emergency tillage destroys some plants if there is a crop on the land. A speedy decision therefore has to be made when erosion starts on a cropped field: shall emergency tillage be performed, or shall erosion be permitted to continue in the hope that soil movement will stop before much damage is done? Knowing how much a crop is damaged by tillage is helpful in making this decision.

A study near Dodge City in southwestern Kansas compared the effects of emergency tillage on wheat yields. The yields of wheat after summer fallow and of wheat after wheat are shown in Table 9-4. Yield decreases closely parallel the area damaged by tillage on wheat after wheat. Fallow wheat crop damage was proportionately much less than the area of crop damaged by tillage. As wind erosion was never allowed to occur on the experimental field, this trial measured only the damage done by the tillage operations; it did not measure the benefits brought about by erosion control.

Lyles and Tatarko (1982) studied the effect of emergency tillage on yields of fallow winter wheat on a sandy loam and on a silty clay soil over the period 1977-1981. Tillage was accomplished with chisels 2-in. (5-cm) wide. Point spacings ranged from 60 in. (152 cm) to complete coverage. Tillage was performed in mid-March each year. Yields were reduced significantly only one year (1980) and on only one site (the sandy loam soil). In all other years and at both sites wheat yields were not significantly reduced by any tillage operation. Wind erosion was not a problem in any of the five years so the study measured the damage done by the tillage, but did not measure any benefits that might have evolved from controlling soil drifting.

The results of both studies indicate that emergency tillage rarely causes excessive damage to crops. Even when plants are uprooted, those remaining grow well and should compensate for tillage damage in a severe soil drifting period.

TABLE 9-4 EFFECT OF EMERGENCY TILLAGE ON WHEAT YIELDS IN SOUTHWESTERN KANSAS

	Wheat after summer fallow		Wheat after wheat	
Treatment	Yield (bu/ac)	Reduction (bu/ac)	Yield (bu/ac)	Reduction (bu/ac)
No emergency tillage	25.8	–	18.6	–
List every 20 ft	24.5	1.3	15.6	3.0
List every 10 ft	21.6	4.2	14.2	4.5
Chisel every 3 ft	24.3	1.5	14.6	4.0

Source: 1959 Annual Report of Southwest Kansas Experimental Field, Minneola, Kansas.

9-8.4 Implement Operation

Woodruff et al. (1957) studied the effect of speed and depth of tillage, spacing of points on a variable-spacing machine such as a chisel, and the type of points (narrow, heavy-duty, and shovels) on the effectiveness of the operation and on power requirements. Results can be summarized as follows:

1. Speeds in excess of 4 mi/hr (6 km/h) give the most effective immediate results on compact soils. A larger area can be covered more quickly and at lower costs with these high speeds. Slightly slower speeds, $2^{1}/_{4}$ to 4 mi/hr (3.5 to 6 km/h), are better for longer-term effectiveness.
2. Close spacing (27 in. or 70 cm) of chisel points is more effective for erosion control. Chisel spacings of 3 to 5 ft (1.0 to 1.5 m) may permit control with less crop damage if soil drifting is not too intense.
3. Narrow-pointed implements work best for compacted soils, and shovel points are best for looser, medium-textured soils. Very loose soils, such as sands and loamy sands, usually cannot be prevented from drifting by tillage except by deep listing. Even listing works only for brief periods.

SUMMARY

There are three generally accepted objectives of tillage: to prepare a seed and root bed, to control weeds, and to prepare the soil to absorb water and resist erosion. Many tillage implements are used in soil management and crop production. Some of these make the soil more erodible under certain conditions; some generally reduce erodibility. The tools that reduce erosion the most are those that increase soil cloddiness, produce surface roughness, and leave crop residue on the soil surface. Planting through a trashy surface and leaving the soil in a ridged condition reduce erosion.

Conservation tillage is a term that is applied to a variety of systems that leave the soil surface trashy, cloddy, and ridged. Water and wind erosion are reduced by tillage systems that leave more crop residue on the soil surface and make the soil more permeable. Two good examples of conservation tillage are stubble mulch tillage and reduced tillage.

Stubble mulch tillage is a method of farming with undercutting implements and associated equipment so that crop residue remains on the soil surface at seeding time to control erosion until the new crop provides its own protection. Stubble mulch tillage has been widely accepted in dryland regions but not generally adopted in humid areas.

Reduced tillage dispenses with some or all of the preplant and postplant tillage operations. Tillage operations, first omitted to reduce soil damage by implement traffic, are now omitted mainly to reduce operating costs. Systems of reduced tillage generally require the use of chemical weed control.

Tillage deeper than 7 in. (18 cm) has seldom proved beneficial or economical. Powerful modern tractors and huge implements have provided the potential for very deep tillage. *Deep chiseling* or *subsoiling* may help where there is a subsoil condition that interferes with root penetration or with nutrient or moisture uptake, especially in years when the rainfall is insufficient for normal crop growth and development. *Deep plowing* has been used to bury infertile surface material and bring up productive soil from below.

Contour cultivation reduces erosion on gentle slopes. Contouring combined with terraces has wide adaptability and great potential for erosion control. Contouring used on cropland and contour furrows on rangeland help conserve water and soil.

Emergency tillage with a chisel implement reduces active wind erosion by bringing clods to the surface and forming ridges that trap the drifting soil. The implement must be pulled across the direction of the wind in passes close enough together to trap all abrasive material. Emergency tillage can be used both on fallowed land and on land in crop.

QUESTIONS

1. Is any tillage implement (for example, the plow) really indispensable now? Explain.
2. Under what specific conditions would a one-way-disk plow be a useful instrument on a dryland farm?
3. What can a subsistence farmer in western Africa do to conserve soil while growing grain sorghum, when little if any crop residue remains on the land at the beginning of the rains when seedbed preparation starts? (What the farmer has not removed for his own use is harvested by nomadic cattle herds or by termites.)
4. State the soil conditions that would be necessary for deep tillage with a 26-in. (65-cm) subsoiler to be a profitable practice.
5. Diagram the proper layout of contour guidelines on a real or hypothetical field and describe how to prepare the seedbed and plant a row crop on the field.
6. Tell what kind of implement is best and how it should be used for emergency tillage to control wind erosion.

REFERENCES

Allamaras, R. R., S. C. Gupta, J. L. Pikul, and C. E. Johnson, 1979. Tillage and plant residue management for water erosion control on agricultural land in eastern Oregon. *J. Soil Water Cons.* 34:85–90.

Allamaras, R. R., W. C. Burrows, and W. E. Larson, 1964. Early growth of corn as affected by soil temperature. *Soil Sci. Soc. Am. Proc.* 28:271–275.

Allen, R. R., and C. R. Fenster, 1986. Stubble mulch equipment for soil and water conservation in the Great Plains. *J. Soil Water Cons.* 41:11–16.

BLACK, A. L., and J. F. POWER, 1965. Effect of chemical and mulch fallow methods on moisture storage, wheat yields, and soil erodibility. *Soil Sci. Soc. Am. Proc.* 29:465–468.

BURWELL, R. E., and L. A. KRAMER, 1983. Long-term annual runoff and soil loss from conventional and conservation tillage of corn. *J. Soil Water Cons.* 38:315–319.

CAMPBELL, R. B., T. A. MATHENY, P. G. HUNT, and S. C. GUPTA, 1979. Crop residue requirement for water erosion control in six southeastern states. *J. Soil Water Cons.* 34:83–85.

CAMPBELL, R. B., D. C. REICOSKY, and C. W. DOTY, 1974. Physical properties and tillage of Paleudults in the southeastern Coastal Plains. *J. Soil Water Cons.* 29:220–224.

CARTER, C. E., and J. R. CARREKER, 1969. Controlling water erosion with graded rows. *Trans. Am. Soc. Agric. Eng.* 12:677–680.

DICKEY, E. C., P. J. JASA, B. J. DOLESH, L. A. BROWN, and S. K. ROCKWELL, 1987. Conservation tillage: Perceived and actual use. *J. Soil Water Cons.* 42:431–434.

FEHRENBACHER, J. B., J. P. VAVRA, and A. L. LANG, 1958. Deep tillage and deep fertilization experiments on a claypan soil. *Soil Sci. Soc. Am. Proc.* 22:553–557.

GALLOWAY, H. M., D. R. GRIFFITH, and J. V. MANNERING, 1977. *Adaptability of Various Tillage-Planting Systems to Indiana Soils.* Purdue Univ. Coop. Ext. Serv. Bull. A.V. 210.

HAMMEL, J. E., 1989. Long-term tillage and crop rotation effects on bulk density and soil impedance in northern Idaho. *Soil Sci. Soc. Am. J.* 53:1515–1519.

HARRIS, W. S., and W. S. WATSON, JR., 1971. Graded rows for the control of rill erosion. *Trans. Am. Soc. Agric. Eng.* 14:577–581.

LARSON, W. E., 1979. Crop residues: Energy production or erosion control? *J. Soil Water Cons.* 34:74–76.

LARSON, W. E., W. C. BURROWS, and W. O. WILLIS, 1960. Soil temperature, soil moisture, and corn growth as influenced by mulches of crop residue. *Trans. 7th Int. Cong. Soil Sci.,* Madison, Wis., Vol. 1, p. 629–637.

LINDSTROM, M. J., S. C. GUPTA, C. A. ONSTAD, W. E. LARSON, and R. F. HOLT, 1979. Tillage and crop residue effects on soil erosion in the Corn Belt. *J. Soil Water Cons.* 34:80–82.

LINDSTROM, M. J., W. B. VOORHEES, and C. A. ONSTAD, 1984. Tillage systems and residue-cover effects on infiltration in northwestern Corn Belt soils. *J. Soil Water Cons.* 39:64–68.

LYLES, L., and J. TATARKO, 1982. Emergency tillage to control wind erosion. *J. Soil Water Cons.* 37:344–347.

MANNERING, J. V., and C. R. FENSTER, 1983. What is conservation tillage? *J. Soil Water Cons.* 38:141–143.

MCGREGOR, K. C., J. D. GREER, and G. E. GURLEY, 1975. Erosion control with no-till cropping practice. *Trans. Am. Soc. Agric. Eng.* 18:918–920.

MOLDENHAUER, W. C., G. W. LANGDALE, W. FRYE, D. K. MCCOOL, R. I. PAPENDICK, D. E. SMYKA, and D. W. FRYREAR, 1983. Conservation tillage for erosion control. *J. Soil Water Cons.* 38:144–151.

RIPLEY, P. O., W. KABBFLEISCH, S. J. BOURGET, and D. J. COOPER, 1961. *Soil Erosion by Water.* Can. Dept. Agric. Publ. 1083.

SCHERTZ, D. L., 1988. Conservation tillage: An analysis of acreage projections in the United States. *J. Soil Water Cons.* 43:256–258.

SCHMIDT, B. L., and G. B. TRIPLETT, JR., 1967. Controlling wind erosion. *Ohio Rep. Res. Devel.* 52:35–37.

Skidmore, E. L., M. Kumar, and W. E. Larson, 1979. Crop residue management for wind erosion control in the Great Plains. *J. Soil Water Cons.* 34:90–94.

Skidmore, E. L., and F. H. Siddoway, 1978. Crop residue requirements to control wind erosion. In *Crop Residue Management Systems.* American Society of Agronomy, Madison, Wis., p. 17–33.

Smith, D. D., 1946. The effect of contour planting on crop yield and erosion losses in Missouri. *J. Am. Soc. Agron.* 38: 810–819.

Thien, S. J., 1986. Residue management: A computer program about conservation tillage decisions. *J. Agron. Educ.* 15:23–26.

Unger, P. W., A. F. Wiese, and D. R. Allen, 1977. Conservation tillage in the southern plains. *J. Soil Water Cons.* 32:43–48.

Van Wijk, W. R., W. E. Larson, and W. C. Burrows, 1959. Soil temperature and the early growth of corn from mulched and unmulched soil. *Soil Sci. Soc. Am. Proc.* 23:428–434.

Whitaker, F. D., H. G. Heinemann, and W. H. Wischmeier, 1973. Chemical weed controls affect runoff, erosion, and corn yields. *J. Soil Water Cons.* 28:174–176.

White, E. M., 1986. Longevity and effect of tillage-formed soil surface cracks on water infiltration. *J. Soil Water Cons.* 41:344–347.

Woodruff, N. P., and W. S. Chepil, 1958. Influence of one-way-disk and subsurface-sweep tillage on factors affecting wind erosion. *Trans. Am. Soc. Agric. Eng.* 1:81–85.

Woodruff, N. P., W. S. Chepil, and R. D. Lynch, 1957. *Emergency Chiselling to Control Wind Erosion.* Kans. Ag. Exp. Sta. Tech. Bull. 90.

Zingg, A. W., and C. J. Whitfield, 1957. *Stubble Mulch Farming in the Western States.* USDA Tech. Bull. 1166.

10

Conservation Structures

The effects of crops, cropping systems, and tillage on the control of erosion were pointed out in the preceding two chapters. Nothing else need be done to control water and wind erosion where these practices work successfully; where they are not sufficient one or more special conservation structures may be needed. These include terraces, diversions, terrace outlets, waterway and gully control devices, streambank protectors, dams, and artificial wind barriers.

10-1 TERRACES AND DIVERSIONS

Terraces have been used in many parts of the world to reduce erosion from cultivated soils. *Bench terraces,* the oldest type, were built where the supply of good, level, agricultural land was limited and population pressure forced cultivation up steep slopes.

The first terraces used in the United States were narrow and steep-sided and could not be cultivated with conventional farm implements. Water frequently overtopped them during intense storms; weeds were a real problem.

Priestly H. Mangum of Wake Forest, North Carolina, designed the first really "farmable" terrace in 1885. It was wide enough to be cultivated, seeded, and harvested with ordinary machinery. The *"Mangum"* or *broad-based,* combination ridge and channel terrace is now widely used.

A *graded terrace* has a graded channel that collects runoff and slowly leads it to a vegetated area or specially prepared outlet. A *level terrace,* discussed in Chapter 14, is built with a level channel. Accumulated water is held behind the ridge until it is absorbed by the soil.

Terraces cannot be used effectively on sandy areas, on stony land, or on shallow soils (over bedrock or fine-textured, impermeable subsoils). They are not practical on fields with complex topography and become too expensive for mechanized agriculture on slopes in excess of 8 to 12%.

10–1.1 Bench Terraces

Early bench terraces were constructed by carrying soil from the uphill side of a strip to the lower side so that a level step or bench was formed. The nearly vertical back slopes below the terraces were stabilized by vegetation or by neatly fitted stonework.

Even more labor was required where erosion had left only a shallow, stony soil. Stones were gathered and carefully fitted into walls across the slope. Soil was then basket-carried from where it had been deposited in the valley back up the hill and was placed behind the stone wall.

Some early bench terraces are still being used successfully as shown in Figure 10–1. Bench terraces are still being built where rapidly increasing population and a dwindling food supply force cultivation of ever-steeper slopes. The high cost of this kind of terrace prevents its use in commercial agriculture except in some cases for irrigation.

10–1.2 Graded Terraces

Graded terraces such as the one shown in Figure 10–2 intercept runoff and carry it to

Figure 10–1 Bench terraces on a steep mountain slope in the Punjab, India. (Courtesy Dr. G. S. Sekhon.)

a protected outlet. In some cases runoff is not reduced, but erosion is invariably less because of shortened slope length, slowed runoff velocity, and trapped sediments. Terraces may empty onto pastures or wooded areas, or into natural waterways. Specially shaped waterways of the type described in Chapter 12 often must be prepared.

Terraces are most effective when supported by contouring, but many farmers farm parallel to the field boundaries even on terraced land. Noncontour cultivation is easier with large equipment, but noncontour use always causes more rapid terrace deterioration.

Advantages and Disadvantages. Graded terraces shorten effective slope length, which reduces amount and velocity of runoff. Soil erosion, particularly rill and gully formation, is reduced and soil productivity maintained. Seeds, seedlings, and growing plants are less damaged by runoff water.

Terraces roughen otherwise smooth fields and *increase land slope*. Vertical fall from one terrace to the next is increased by the height of the ridge crest above the channel bottom; horizontal distance over which water moves is reduced by the length of the front slope from the ridge to the channel. On 4% sloping land, the average slope from terrace crest to the center of the terrace channel immediately below is increased to over 5%.

Sometimes sections of the channel stay wet, causing delays in cultivation, planting, and harvesting, and reducing crop yields. Terrace construction seriously reduces the productive capacity of channel areas on shallow soils and on soils with less productive or impermeable subsoils (Phillips and Kamprath, 1973).

Figure 10-2 A graded terrace carrying excess water from the terrace interval to a grassed waterway. (Courtesy USDA Soil Conservation Service.)

10-1.3 Steep-Backslope Terraces

The steep-backslope (grass-backed) terrace was developed to permit parallel-bordered strips to be cultivated safely on relatively steep land. They have relatively flat front slopes and narrow, steeply sloping (2:1 or steeper) backslopes. A newly constructed steep-backslope terrace is shown in Figure 10-3.

Advantages and Disadvantages of Steep-Backslope Terraces. The major advantage of steep-backslope terraces is that they are easy to farm (no point rows). They reduce the gradient between terraces by the amount of excavation below the terrace. The field gradient becomes even lower as terraces are farmed and soil washes into the terrace channel. This type of terrace can therefore be used on land too steep to farm with broad-based terraces (Wittmus, 1973).

The major disadvantage is steep untillable backslopes, which reduce cultivated area and confine all up- and down-field-equipment movement to field edges. Steep slopes can contribute to accidents. Insects and other pests increase on uncultivated steep slopes; rodents burrow through the ridges, opening channels for ponded water to escape.

10-1.4 Terrace Design

Terraces are usually designed to handle the runoff from a ten-year frequency storm (American Society of Agricultural Engineers, 1989). SCS national standards call for a minimum of 8 ft^2 (0.75 m^2) of channel cross section on slopes less than 5%, 7 ft^2 (0.65 m^2) on 5 to 8% slopes, and 6 ft^2 (0.55 m^2) on slopes steeper than 8%. Channels must be 12 to 18 in. (30 to 45 cm) deep and sometimes considerably deeper. Steep-

Figure 10-3 A newly constructed steep-backed terrace in Iowa. This terrace is straight and parallel to the fence line. The near end of the channel is blocked and the water drains through a vertical white pipe at the bottom of the channel into an underground pipeline. (Courtesy F. R. Troeh.)

backed terraces usually have larger cross sections and deeper channels. Larger channel capacity must be provided where field operations angle across terraces rather than running parallel to them.

The front slopes of steep-backslope terraces and both slopes of broad-based terraces must be wide enough to accommodate the equipment that will be used in the field, generally not less than 15 ft (4.5 m). The flatter the slopes, the easier they are to farm but the more expensive they are to build. Front and back slopes steeper than 10:1 should not be cropped; ones steeper than 4:1 must be seeded to perennial vegetation.

Terrace channel gradients should be sufficient to drain off water and prevent overtopping, but not great enough to cause channel erosion. Maximum permissible gradient is about 0.4% for most soils to avoid serious erosion of unprotected channels. Steeper gradients should be protected by perennial grasses. The minimum gradient to move water along the channel without ponding in microdepressions is about 0.1% on permeable soils and about 0.2% on less permeable ones. Systems with parallel terraces require variable-channel gradients which call for cuts and fills during construction. They are more convenient to farm but more expensive to build.

Terraces should not be longer than 2000 ft (600 m) because of the danger of water buildup and overtopping in intense storms, nor longer than 1200 ft (375 m) on already gullied land. Where the distance to be protected is greater, terraces need to be split with an outlet provided for each segment.

The interval between terraces must make the land farmable as well as control erosion. More permeable soils, less intense rainfall, more erosion-resisting crops, and more surface residue permit wider terrace spacing. Terrace spacing is commonly defined in terms of the vertical interval *(VI)*. The U.S. Soil Conservation Service calculates *VI* with the following equation:

$$VI = xS + y$$

where x = a rainfall factor
S = slope, percent
y = a soil and cropping factor

Where VI is expressed in feet, x has values of 0.4 to 0.8 (0.12 to 0.24 metric); y values are 1.0 to 4.0 (0.3 to 1.2 metric). Distribution of x values in the United States is shown in Figure 10–4. If a soil is very erodible and row crop is produced with conventional tillage y has a value of 1.0; 4.0 is used for an erosion-resisting soil combined with no-till production (a minimum of 1.5 tons of residue/ac after planting). The higher values of y should not be used to calculate intervals unless residue and cropping conditions will be met every year. In northeastern United States ($x = 0.7$), the vertical interval on a 7% slope for a permeable soil (K about 0.3) producing a row crop with conventional tillage ($y = 2.0$) is

$$VI = (0.7 \times 7) + 2.0 = 6.9 \text{ ft } (2.1 \text{ m})$$

Other empirical formulas for determining vertical interval have been worked out in other countries (Hudson, 1981; Bensalem, 1977). Most of these give VI values similar to ones derived from the SCS equation. The Israeli equation gives larger values for lower gradients.

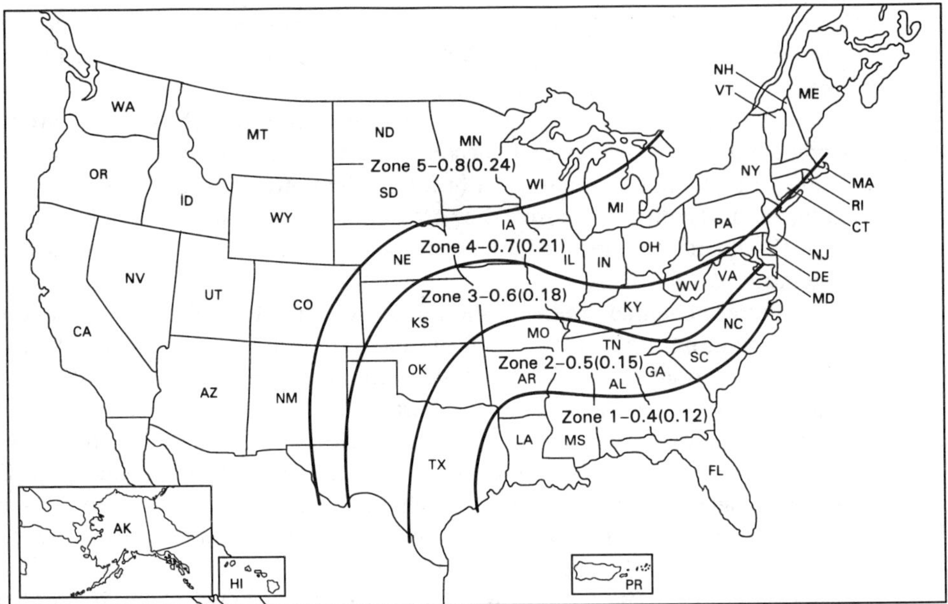

Figure 10-4 Distribution of the rainfall factor χ for the vertical-interval equation in mainland United States. Figures in parentheses are values of χ when metric units are used. (Modified from ASAE Standards, Standard S268.3, 1989, American Society of Agricultural Engineers.)

The horizontal interval *(HI)* between terraces can be calculated by means of the formula

$$HI = (xS + y) \times 100/S$$

$$= \frac{VI}{S} \times 100$$

For the former example, the horizontal interval is

$$HI = \frac{6.9}{7} \times 100 = 98.6 \text{ ft } (30.1 \text{ m})$$

HI is actually the *horizontal* interval, not the distance between terraces measured *across the surface* of the land, but the two measurements are similar for gradients commonly encountered in fields to be terraced. For example, the distance across the land surface between terrace lines is 98.8 ft rather than the 98.6 ft calculated from the equations for the 7% slope mentioned previously. Calculated spacings should be adjusted to the nearest multiple of the width of the cultivation and planting equipment to be used on the terraced area.

Calculated terrace spacings are often too narrow for convenient farming with modern large-scale agricultural implements. Where wider spacings are used, other measures may have to be employed to bring predicted soil loss down to tolerable levels. The SCS does not recommend intervals narrower than 100 ft (30 m). The horizontal interval on hand-cultivated land can be considerably narrower than on mechanized farms.

Terrace Layout. Laying out a terrace system involves choosing appropriate sites for the terraces, selecting suitable channel gradients, and "shooting" the terrace lines. Some terrace systems are designed on a 50- to 100-ft (15- to 30 m) topographic survey grid. The following technique is effective, quicker, and cheaper.

The conservation technician evaluates the water regime of the field from observations, soil surveys, and other information and selects waterway locations (natural draws or sites for new construction). Locations for needed vegetated waterways should be selected, staked, shaped, and seeded, and tile lines to remove runoff, if they are to be used, should be located and laid before terraces are constructed. When waterways and terraces are designed and constructed at the same time, terrace outflow must be kept off the waterways by berms (earth ridges) until waterways are vegetated and can handle the runoff safely.

The high point in the field is located first, and the average gradient of the top sector of the slope (to a point about 100 to 150 ft downhill) (30 to 45 m) is ascertained with an engineering level. The recommended *VI* is calculated and the point where the terrace should enter the waterway is determined (*VI* downhill from high point). The terrace channel center is staked back from the waterway using an appropriate gradient, increasing the gradient for the first 50 ft (15 m) to about 0.4% and adding 6 in. (15 cm) of extra drop to account for the depth to the center of the finished waterway. Stakes should be placed about every 100 ft (30 m) along the proposed channel except where relatively sharp curves or gullies are encountered (stakes 30 to 50 ft apart) (9 to 15 m). After the line is completed, it should be viewed, and very crooked portions restaked. Adjustments should be kept to a minimum; otherwise, too-deep cuts and fills will be necessary during construction. Second and subsequent terraces are staked by calculating new *VI*s for each and repeating the procedure.

Parallel Terraces. Farmers' greatest objection to terraces can be overcome by building them parallel to each other and designing them either straight or gently curving as well.

Parallel terraces cost more and generally require deeper soils than regular ones do because of the extra cutting and filling required.

A guide terrace with calculated gradient is staked out in an appropriate place about midslope. Other terraces, parallel to the guide, are laid out above and below at correct intervals. Two or more guide terraces may be needed in some fields with complex slopes.

Preliminary land smoothing may be required before parallel terraces are built. Where swales or gullies cross terrace lines, grassed waterways or underground outlets should be provided.

The modern trend in the U.S. Corn Belt is toward parallel terraces, built straight across the landscape wherever possible, and to tile outlets. Long-radius curves are made where the topography will not permit straight terraces.

Construction. The field to be terraced should be cleared of trash, dead furrows filled, and small ridges leveled before construction is started. Soil productivity of the terrace channels is improved if topsoil is removed, stockpiled, and later spread over the terrace channel as construction is completed. (This increases construction costs so much that it is seldom done.) Conventional terraces can be built with bulldozers, motor patrol graders, carryall scrapers, elevating-grader terracers, moldboard plows, disk tillers with 24-in. (60-cm) or larger disks, and with hand tools and baskets, headpans, or other carrying devices. Contractors using large-scale, earth-moving equipment build most of the terraces in countries with a commercial agriculture, where labor is expensive. Bulldozers are probably most economical for moving soil short distances; graders do a better job of smoothing and packing the terrace (see Figure 10-5). Carryall scrapers are needed for terraces involving much cutting and filling.

Publications available from state extension services and from the Soil Conservation Service describe the building and maintenance of terraces. Blakely et al. (1957) describe methods for building terraces with farm implements, but these implements are not adapted for building steep-backslope terraces. Figure 10-6 shows a terrace being built by hand in a developing country.

After the terraces are built, the gradients of the completed channels and the height of the settled ridge top above the channel need to be checked to ensure that they meet specifications. High spots in the channels and low spots in the terrace ridges must be corrected before heavy rains fall. Terrace ridge tops must be level, particularly across swales or gully areas.

Terrace ridges wear down and channels fill with sediment as land is farmed, so maintenance procedures must be undertaken on a regular basis if the system is to remain effective. Blakely et al. (1957) described cultivation techniques with ordinary farm equipment that can be used to maintain terraces. Powell (1989) and the American Society of Agricultural Engineers (1989) also give terrace maintenance hints. In general, tillage should move soil uphill between terraces and from the terrace channel to the ridge on the front slopes.

10-1.5 Farming Terraced Fields

Seedbed preparation, planting, cultivating, and harvesting operations should be conducted parallel to terraces to minimize water and soil movement between terraces and to reduce tillage damage to the terrace ridges. Operations parallel to a terrace get a little more off contour as distance from the terrace increases, causing tillage marks and rows to have a gradient. Water may run down toward the terrace outlet, which is desirable if it is not too swift, or it may run back toward the upper end of the terrace, which is not desirable. Proper placement of the short rows assures that all water flows toward the waterway or the lower end of the terrace channel. Figure 10-7 is a guide to planning cultivation patterns on terraced land. A plan for field operations is given in Note 10-1.

A

B

Figure 10–5 Large equipment constructing a terrace in Kansas. (a) A bulldozer pushing up a terrace ridge. (b) A motor patrol grader smoothing and packing the terrace. (Courtesy USDA-Soil Conservation Service.)

Figure 10–6 Farmers in central India building terraces with village-made hand hoes and head baskets. The state ministries of agriculture lay out and supervise the construction. (Courtesy Roy L. Donahue.)

NOTE 10–1
FARMING TERRACED LAND

The plan proposed in Note 9–1 for farming contoured fields may be followed between terraces, or terrace intervals can be farmed so that furrows always guide water to the waterway or to the terrace channels. Where the terrace interval is narrowing, long rows or furrows *parallel to the upper terrace ridge* will all carry excess water toward the waterway, as in the upper example in Figure 10–7. The short section-B rows also will guide the water toward the waterway, but will release it into the terrace channel. Where the terrace interval is widening, all furrows *parallel to the lower terrace* will carry excess water toward the waterway, as in the middle example of Figure 10–7. The lower example illustrates a complex situation where the terrace interval is wide at both ends and narrow in the middle. The long rows will carry water all the way to the waterway if they are parallel to the upper terrace (as the interval gets narrower) and to the lower terrace (as the interval widens). The short rows should be parallel to the long rows in their section of the field so they will guide water to the waterway or to the terrace channel.

Terrace intervals can be farmed in the field by working the (A)-area long rows first, then filling in the (B)-area short rows. The front slopes of the terrace ridges (C) are used for turn areas and are worked

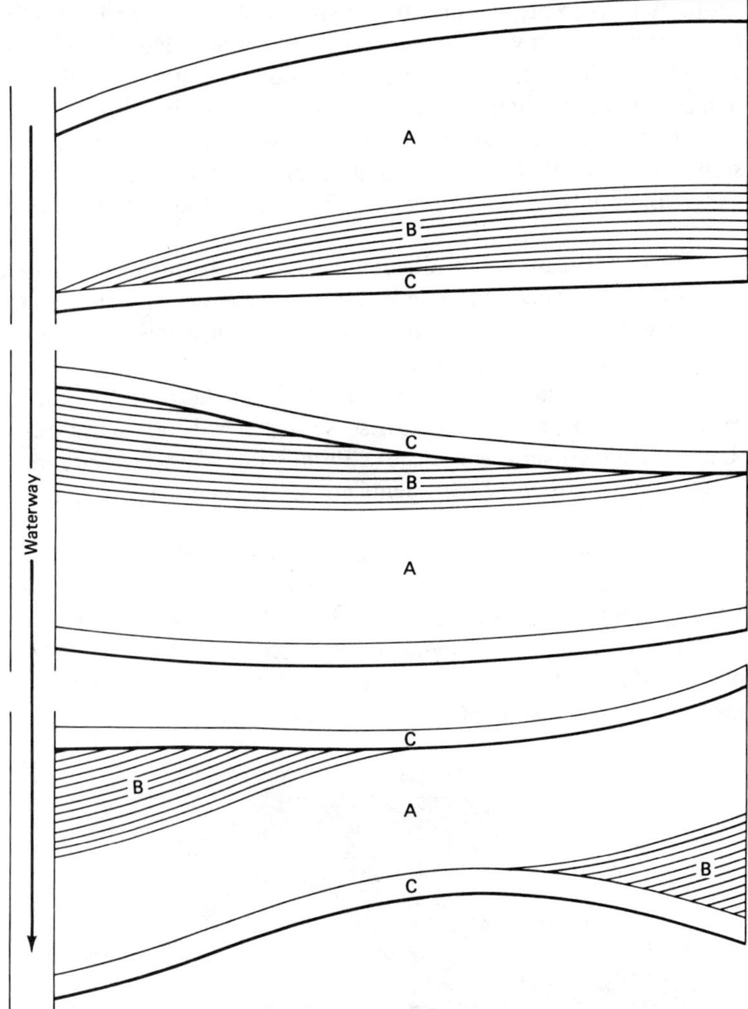

Figure 10-7 Guide to planning cultivation patterns on terraced land. In the diagram the heavy lines represent terrace ridges and the lighter lines terrace channels. Unshaded sections represent long-row areas; shaded sections are short-row areas to be worked parallel to the shading lines.

last. Drilled crops are often harvested as if there were no terraces, but with row crops the last rows planted (C) are harvested before the short rows (B).

10-1.6 Diversions

A diversion, a ditch or channel with an accompanying ridge on the downhill side, is designed to intercept runoff water and carry it away at a nonerosive velocity. Diversions are usually constructed at the top or the foot of steep slopes or on property lines to protect productive soil from erosion or inundation. They are used to carry water away from the heads of gullies, roads (Figure 10–8), and around farmsteads. They also direct water to ponds, to water-spreading sites, and to special planting areas. In many erosion-control plans, a diversion is the first structure that intercepts runoff. It must be well sited and carefully laid out and constructed. Many states have laws that control activities that change the flow path and the volume of water; these laws must be kept in mind when designing diversions.

Specifications. A diversion designed to protect a cultivated area should have sufficient capacity to handle a 10-year-frequency storm. Diversions for protection of houses, farmsteads, or expensive engineering works will need capacity to control up to 50-year storms.

Diversions are usually vegetated. They need to permit more rapid water movement than graded terraces, so sediment will not settle out, but not so rapid that channel erosion will occur. Permissible flow velocity depends in part on vegetative cover density. Gradients are often as high as 0.5% and sometimes as high as 0.8%.

Diversions commonly have flat bottoms 3 to 20 ft (1 to 6 m) wide and straight front and back slopes (trapezoidal shape). The sides often have slopes of about 4:1, although they may range from 2:1 to 6:1. Channel depth ranges from 15 to 40 in. (38 to 100 cm). Actual size depends on the volume of water to be handled. Diversions, particularly those with steep side slopes, are difficult to construct with farm implements, so the work is generally done by conservation contractors.

Figure 10–8 A diversion ditch in Nigeria designed to carry water from a highway ditch safely away from the right-of-way. Spreading the water on naturally vegetated sites dissipates its energy. (Courtesy J. A. Hobbs.)

10-2 TERRACE OUTLETS AND WATERWAY AND GULLY CONTROL STRUCTURES

A protected waterway is needed wherever runoff is discharged from terraces or diversions. Usually, vegetated waterways such as those described in Chapter 12 are the cheapest effective man-made structures. There are conditions that reduce the effectiveness of vegetation so much that special structures are necessary to control erosion in waterways and gullies. Underground outlets are used in some of these situations.

10-2.1 Underground Outlets

Tile lines serve as underground outlets to take runoff water from low points in terrace or diversion channels or from behind other forms of earthen embankments and carry it through a pipeline to a safe discharge point. Underground outlets are used when the possible waterway sites are too steep for nonerosive water movement, the rate of peak runoff must be reduced for flood control, or the cost of installing a system of underground pipe is less than that of forming the grassed waterway and taking the area out of crop production. Underground outlets are not new, but they were not widely used until the concept of detention storage in the collecting system was introduced in the early 1960s.

There are four major parts to an underground water outlet system. The *tile-inlet tube (riser),* made of plastic, metal, or concrete, rises from a pipeline below the soil and has holes or slots at intervals above the ground level. An *orifice plate,* positioned between the base of the inlet tube and the horizontal conducting pipe, regulates the rate of downward water movement and prevents water pressure from building up in the pipe and flooding lower-lying terrace channels. The *conducting pipe,* also of plastic, metal, or concrete, carries water from one or more inlet tubes down to the final outlet. The system *outlet* is usually located in a natural waterway with enough protection to handle the runoff water without excessive erosion.

Advantages and Disadvantages. A major advantage of an underground outlet is that soil loss from the field is reduced because sediment settles out in the stored-water area and the water carries only suspended material to the final outlet. Low sections in terrace channels in the vicinity of former gullies tend to fill up with the sediment washed down from the land above the terrace, leveling the field. Peak runoff rates from terrace systems or diversions are reduced because of the incorporated detention storage. Where outlets replace grassed waterways, more land is available for cultivated crop production. High land values make this an increasingly important advantage.

Underground outlets are costly to install and the design and construction are much more critical than for a simple grassed waterway. Crops in the detention areas may be damaged by ponding during and after excessive storms or if the riser inlet holes or the orifice plate become plugged with trash. The system and lower-lying fields can be damaged if excess rainfall overtops the ridges.

Specifications. Underground outlets are usually required to store rain from a 10-year-frequency storm and dispose of the accumulated runoff in less than 48 hours. The actual size of the tile-inlet holes, orifice plates, conducting pipe, and outlet must be designed to meet these criteria. The slope of the conduit pipe influences speed of discharge and must be considered.

The tile-inlet riser should be approximately 3 to 4 in. (7.5 to 10 cm) higher than the adjacent terrace or diversion ridge and should be equipped with a removable cap to prevent entry of debris and to permit cleaning the orifice plate. The terrace or diversion ridge must be level in the vicinity of the major storage area to minimize the chance of overtopping. Figure 10–9 shows a terrace system in Kansas with tile inlets.

Developing an appropriate design is a complicated procedure, beyond the scope of this book. Beasley et al. (1984) describe methods for use in arriving at satisfactory design criteria. Farmers can obtain planning assistance from Soil Conservation Service technicians.

Construction. Construction of an underground outlet system is similar to the installation of tile drain lines (Chapter 15). The conduit pipe, with inlets for the surface risers are laid in a trench with a proper grade, and the trench is filled and compacted all the way to the surface. The diversion or the terraces are then constructed compacting the ridges well, especially over the trench area. The conduit is exposed again in the center of each channel area, and each riser with its orifice plate is installed. The soil is again packed in place and the system is ready for use.

Figure 10–9 A terrace system in Kansas with tile inlets. Water drains through the black riser pipes in the terrace channels. This area received 9 in. (230 mm) of rain in 3 hours the day before the photo was taken. (Courtesy USDA Soil Conservation Service.)

10-2.2 Artificial Mulch for Waterways

Artificial mulches are often used to control water erosion on newly formed waterways and other areas while a vegetative cover is being established. Burlap was one of the first materials used for this purpose but is too costly now. Several types of mulch mats consisting of shredded wood, paper, or plastic strips held in wide-mesh, fine-string envelopes 6 ft (2 m) or more wide by 50 ft (15 m) or more long are now available commercially. Envelopes are staked side by side over the shaped, seeded, and smoothed surface (Figure 10–10).

The mulch intercepts the erosive forces of raindrops and of running water, thus reducing erosion until the seeding produces its own protective cover. These mulches maintain their integrity for two to six months, depending on construction material and climate. Water from outside the protected area may need to be diverted by means of a berm. One consisting of a furrow turned onto the mulch nets serves double duty—diverting foreign water and preventing wind from getting under the nets and ripping or blowing them away.

Asphalt, latex, and other synthetic mulches are used to control both water and wind erosion in road cuts, ditches, and on other construction sites until vegetation can be established (Armbrust and Lyles, 1975). They have so far proven too costly for use on agricultural fields. A fast-growing companion crop or a preliminary cover

Figure 10–10 A fibrous protective mulch placed over a shaped streambank in Virginia. The mulch will control erosion until the seeded vegetation is established. (Courtesy USDA Soil Conservation Service.)

crop that either freezes or is killed before the permanent cover is planted is more cost effective (Chapters 11 and 12).

10-2.3 Broken Rock for Gully Control

Stone and broken rock have long been used for reducing erosion in waterways and gullies. Riprap, which is a loose covering of stone on the soil surface, has been widely employed for this purpose. The stones used to be sorted and placed by hand, but are now more likely to be dumped over the surface and smoothed by machine. More rock is required this way, but the amount of labor is markedly reduced.

The surface needs to be smooth before rock is applied, so that water cannot flow below the stones. The thickness of the protective stone layers is dictated by the nature of the site and the velocity of the runoff water. Material used ranges from coarse sand or fine gravel next to the soil, increasing in size by layers to stones too large for the stream to move on the top.

Rock Barriers. A barrier or a series of barriers is often needed to reduce water's erosive power in steeply sloping waterways and in many gullies. Piles of rocks can serve to accomplish this end, but a range of sizes must be used with surface rocks too large and carefully laid to be moved by the runoff water. Wire netting can serve as a fence to prevent the breakdown of a rock dam, or it may be used to form a basket (gabion). The netting is laid all the way across the channel and loose stones are placed on its upstream half. The remaining netting is folded over the rocks and is wired to the edge of the netting on the ground. These rock barriers are flexible enough to maintain contact with the soil even if the ground settles under them. A stepped condition develops where several barriers are installed in a waterway or gully. Erosion is reduced on the flatter slopes between barriers, and vegetation has a chance to grow there (Chapter 12).

10-2.4 Brush, Log, or Timber Barriers

Temporary wooden structures have been used to slow runoff and trap sediment in waterways and gullies where labor was more plentiful than money. Wood and other natural materials are still recommended and used regularly in many developing countries (Kunkle and Harcharik, 1977).

Brush and Log Barriers. Posts driven vertically into the soil at 3-ft (1-m) intervals in two parallel rows about 18 in. (45 cm) apart across the waterway or gully bed are used to anchor brush barriers in place. Loose branches, small trees, or logs are packed tightly between the rows of posts, making sure that the bottom members make firm contact along the sides and bottom surface. Ends of the brush piles should be dug into the channel walls and soil packed tightly around them. Logs must be dug into the bottom as well as the sides of the channel. Materials are wedged and piled tightly between the upright posts and held in place by crosspieces spiked or wired to the posts. The barrier must be impermeable enough to prevent water jetting through and undermining the structure. A large flat notch should be left in the middle of the barrier so that overflow water will be guided onto an apron and not wash away the banks (Heede, 1976).

Timber Barriers. Large-dimension lumber or timber, or a series of thick posts driven closely together, can be used. Posts are driven vertically into the soil to support the barrier, or the timber itself may be driven vertically over half its length into the ground and reinforced with horizontal members. A rectangular notch must be used as a spillway. Larger or thicker pieces of wood and treated or termite-resistant timbers last longer.

10–2.5 Brick Barriers

Brick barriers can be used to stop gully erosion. Fired construction bricks (expensive), and sand–cement or soil–cement blocks can be used. Sun-dried clay bricks (easily weathered) and laterite blocks cut from soil and desiccated are available in many developing countries.

A poured concrete or layered rock foundation is necessary for any barrier built with bricks or blocks. The ends of the barrier must penetrate the gully wall and be sealed with tightly packed soil material (not topsoil) between the barrier ends and the excavated gully walls. Water must not be permitted to seep around the ends.

A straight wall of bricks and mortar is relatively weak; it must be buttressed on the downstream side for strength. Walls that arch upstream are also strong. This design passes water force from the center to the outer ends of the wall where it butts into the soil. The gully wall where the barrier impinges must have very strong compression resistance.

All barriers must have a notch or low area in the top center large enough to permit passage of the largest expected flood. The gully floor immediately below the notch must be protected so that the falling water cannot erode the gully surface and undercut the barrier. Loose stones are suitable for protection if they are large enough to resist movement by floodwater. Smaller stones must be anchored in some way on the gully floor.

10–2.6 Drop Structures and Chutes

Barriers discussed previously are built to control erosion until vegetation can be established. Sometimes permanent structures are needed.

Drop Structures. Drop structures are small dams used to stabilize steep waterways and other channels, to level waterways so they need not be planted to perennial vegetation, to serve as outlets for highway culverts and ditches, and to trap sediment. They can handle large volumes of runoff water and are effective where falls are less than 8 ft (2.5 m).

A drop structure can be built of timber, sand–cement blocks, rubble masonry, poured concrete, or corrugated metal. Figure 10–11 shows the main structural features. The main wall is across the gully or channel. Cutoff walls extend into the banks of the channel to anchor the structure and ensure that water will not cut

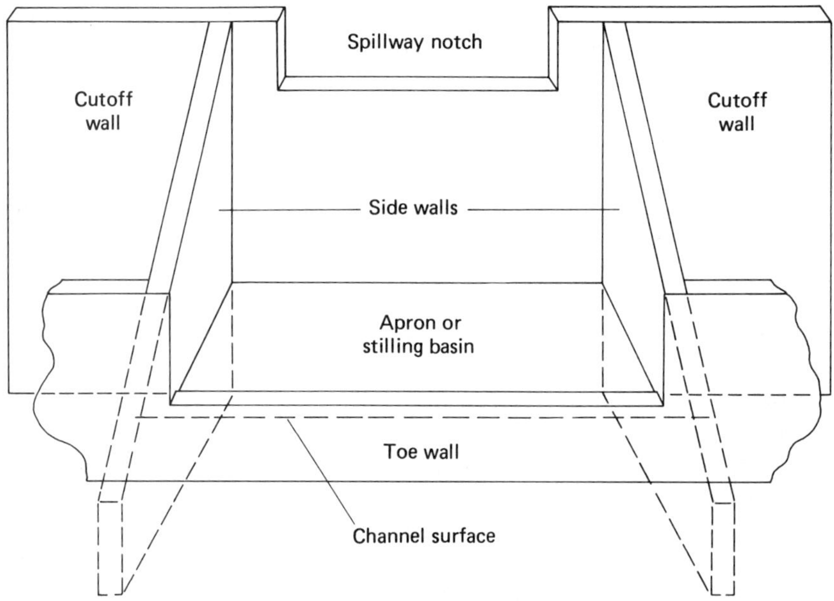

Figure 10–11 Diagram of a concrete drop structure. The side walls join the toe wall and extend sideways as indicated by the solid lines if the waterway below the structure is parallel to the toe wall. Where the waterway below the structure is perpendicular to the toe wall, the side walls extend down the waterway as indicated by the dashed lines.

around it. The main wall has a notch or a box inlet (for larger volumes of runoff) that serves as a spillway. A horizontal apron or stilling basin is provided below the spillway to absorb the energy of the falling water. The apron front is reinforced and stabilized by a toe wall that projects into the soil parallel to the main wall. Side walls extend from the main wall to the end of the apron or beyond. Structures with long main walls may need one or more buttress supports between the side walls on the downstream face.

Failure of drop structures usually results from water washing soil away at the structure–soil interfaces, so the cutoff walls and the toe wall must be long enough to protect against water undercutting the apron. Soil material must be packed very tightly against these elements to prevent water damage. The notch size required can be calculated from the weir formulas in Figure 16–7. A box inlet can be used where the channel is too narrow to allow a large enough straight notch to handle the expected runoff. Flow rate into a box inlet can be predicted from the combined length of the sides and end(s) of the open box and the depth of water flowing over the lip.

Chutes. Chute spillways collect runoff water at one elevation and carry it down a slope to a lower elevation (Figure 10–12). Chutes for short slopes and for small amounts of runoff (1 to 3 ft^3/sec or 0.03 to 0.09 m^3/s) may be built without forms by excavating the desired shapes in the surface of the ground. Mixed concrete is poured onto the prepared surface and smoothed in place. Wire mesh reinforcing is required in areas where large temperature variations are expected.

Figure 10–12 A concrete chute designed to carry runoff water safely down a slope to a road ditch at the bottom. (Courtesy F. R. Troeh.)

Flat slab limestone and other rocks were used to form chute spillways in the early days of conservation work. Rocks were placed on the channel and the joints were filled with a sand–cement mortar. These structures were reasonably satisfactory, but they frequently cracked at the stone edges and deteriorated with time, especially where freezing and thawing occurred. Their main advantages are that less cement is needed and the chute surface is usually rough enough to reduce flow velocities.

The shapes of the inlet and outlet sections of chutes are important. Water attains very high velocities on the smooth surfaces, and energy-dissipating structures must be provided. These usually consist of a boxlike device that holds a pool of water and overflows at ground level. Boxes partly filled with stones too large to be moved by the water velocities expected serve well.

Formed sidewalls and cutoff walls are needed where larger amounts of water must be carried or where the drop is more than 6 ft (2 m). Formed wing walls may be required to channel runoff into the chute.

10–3 EARTHEN DAMS

Earthen dams are used in conservation to trap sediment, to stabilize drainage ways and reduce erosion, to store excess water temporarily to reduce flood damage, and to store water for livestock, irrigation, household, or municipal use. Dams for water storage are discussed in Chapter 14. Earthen dams are divided into three classes on the basis of the severity of the damage that present or possible expanded future development might suffer if the dam failed and the impounded water rushed downstream.

Class A dams are located in strictly rural or agricultural areas. Failure will cause water to inundate farm fields and may do damage to local (township or county) roads. Farm buildings, but not homes, may lie in the path of the floodwaters.

Class B dams are located in predominantly rural and agricultural areas. Failure may cause damage to isolated homes, as well as to farm buildings, main (state and federal) highways, branch railroad lines, and public utilities.

Class C dams are located where failure would cause serious damage to homes, industrial and commercial buildings, utilities, main highways, and main railroad lines.

Most dams constructed for individual farmers are Class A dams. Most dams built in the SCS small watershed program also belong to Class A, but some are Class B, and a few near urban centers are Class C structures.

10-3.1 Soil-Saving Dams (Sediment-Storage Dams)

A soil-saving dam is designed to intercept and trap waterborne sediments. It has a notch or box as a principal spillway that passes the water off slowly so that most sediment will settle out. Sufficient freeboard must be provided so that floodwater will never overtop the dam.

10-3.2 Grade-Stabilization Dams

Grade-stabilization dams are used to prevent gullies from eating back into fields (Figure 10-13), to stabilize or raise gully channel floors, or to drop water from

Figure 10-13 A class B dam constructed to stop erosion in a gully and to provide a waterfront for recreation. (Courtesy USDA Soil Conservation Service.)

terraces, waterways, or diversions to stream channels at lower elevations. The size and cost of the structure or set of structures required increases rapidly as a gully grows, so speedy response to gully stabilization needs is important. Gullies generally flow on fairly flat gradients because the nonvegetated surfaces and deep, narrow channels are conducive to high flow velocities or reduced slope gradients or both (Manning's formula, Note 4–2, can be used to evaluate these effects). Low slope gradients cause many gullies to become deeper as they eat back into landscapes.

The most effective way to stop a gully is to place the dam at the site of the overfall. Some dams are placed downstream because the site at the gully head is not suitable. Several small dams should be placed in a long gully rather than one large one. Need for land shaping above a dam should be considered. High vertical walls should be pushed in, shaped, fertilized, and revegetated, especially where further sloughing is expected. The water pool will fill with sediment in time.

10–3.3 Flood Control Dams

Flood control in the United States comes under the jurisdiction of two government agencies. The U.S. Army Corps of Engineers is responsible for flood control along the main rivers. USDA Soil Conservation Service is responsible for flood control on small watersheds in the upper reaches of rivers and streams. The Watershed Law (1947) provided for watershed districts to be set up under state laws. Federal funds are funneled through these districts to design and build flood control structures. Most of the small flood control dams in the United States have been designed, constructed, and paid for under the watershed program.

Most small flood control dams serve two main purposes: flood control and grade stabilization. They also trap sediment. Sediment storage is designed into each flood storage reservoir to provide a life expectancy of about 50 years.

Flood control dams are built with capacity to store temporarily the runoff from a 10- to 50-year storm. Floodwater passes from the storage pool through the principal spillway, usually a pipe through the dam, for several days. Excess runoff from unusually intense storms passes immediately over an emergency spillway—usually a grassed waterway.

Some flood control dams in arid regions seldom contain any water but have large capacities to control flash floods. Figure 10–14 shows one of several structures built to protect Las Cruces, New Mexico. These structures impound large volumes of runoff water and release it at a controlled rate. They have handled all runoff since they were built with no flood damage to the city.

10–3.4 Design and Construction of Dams

A wide variety of detailed technical information is needed to select a suitable site, plan, justify, and build an earthen dam. It should be undertaken only by well-qualified and experienced people (Beasley et al., 1984). District conservationists in the U.S. Soil Conservation Service may plan small stock water dams, but plans for larger dams must be developed by the SCS State Engineer. Dams are defined as "larger" if the product of the height of the dam crest above the spillway floor (ft)

Figure 10–14 Flood-control dam protecting Las Cruces, New Mexico. This is one of several similar structures built to impound runoff water from heavy rainstorms in the hills above the city. This structure is about a half mile (1 km) long and has a road along the top. (Courtesy F. R. Troeh.)

times the dam capacity (ac-ft) exceeds 500, or more simply if the watershed area is greater than 25 to 100 acres (10 to 40 ha), depending on rainfall.

10–4 STREAMBANK EROSION-CONTROL STRUCTURES

Bank erosion in perennial streams is often severe. Not only is soil lost, but new channels meander across fields on alluvial plains. In severe cases banks may erode inland at a rate of 175 to 250 ft/yr (50 to 75 m/yr).

Vegetative and mechanical means of protecting streambanks have been developed. Vegetative control measures are discussed in Chapter 12. The nonvegetative techniques can be divided into those that divert the faster-flowing water away from the bank and those that protect the erodible bank with mechanical covers.

In the United States it is necessary to obtain a permit before the direction or volume of flow in a perennial stream can be changed. The permit will usually be issued if inspection by representatives of the U.S. Army Corps of Engineers (and of the state water resources protection agency, where necessary) shows that the planned work will not damage land across the channel or downstream.

10–4.1 Current Deflectors

Two main types of *dikes* are used to divert faster-flowing water away from eroding stream banks: regular dikes and vane dikes. Regular dikes consist of loose stone or rock piles that extend above the stream surface and are built out into the water at a slight angle downstream. They may extend 3 ft (1 m) or so above the low-flow water level or may go to full bank height. They are usually shorter in height farther from the bank. The stones and rock pieces used must not move in flood currents. Dikes can also be made of poles driven vertically into the streambed. These are probably the most reliable stream bank protectors, but they are expensive. *Vane dikes* have no bank contact. They are placed far enough upstream to deflect the current away from the bank needing protection.

10-4.2 Bank Protectors

Mechanical covers to protect eroding streambanks include toe protectors, hard-points, and revetments.

Toe Protectors. The toe of a streambank is the part where the gradient of the relatively steeply sloping bank changes abruptly near the water line. Toe protectors cover the toe and part of the more steeply sloping bank with stones, rocks, or other protective material (Figure 10-15). The material can be either hand placed or dumped and spread by machine. Hand placing saves material but requires much more labor. Usually, the toe is protected intermittently at the more seriously eroding sites along the bank. The distance between areas of protection depends on the severity of the erosion hazard.

Hardpoints. Hardpoint protection usually consists of stones or rocks dropped over the edge of the bank onto the toe of the slope. No attempt is made to place or spread the pieces. In general the height of the protection up the bank slope is limited, but the protected spots along the bank are closer together than in toe protection.

Figure 10-15 A toe protector to stabilize a streambank. The rock covers the bank from the low water level to the height of normal flood stage. (Courtesy Kansas City District, Corps of Engineers, U.S. Army, Kansas City, Missouri.)

Revetments. A revetment is a retaining wall or facing consisting of protective material placed over and anchored to the soil. One of the longest-lasting types of revetments, shown in Figure 10–16, is a vertical stone wall shielding the land from the stream.

A windrow revetment is a pile of stone and rock placed on the surface of the soil at the upper edge of the bank, as shown in Figure 10–17. As the bank erodes, the rock drops down and lodges near the toe, thus forming a line of protection along the bank. A windrow revetment contains from 1.5 to 5 tons of rock per linear foot (4 to 15 mt/m) of bank.

Used automobile tires can serve as a revetment, as can old flattened car bodies. Individual members must be fastened together securely and the entire assembly anchored firmly to the ground.

A fence consisting of a double row of posts driven vertically into the ground, cabled together, and filled with protective material such as stones, tires, or logs can be used as a temporary measure. Riprap of graded gravel and stones can also be used. Broken concrete from old highways or building foundations can serve effectively if slabs are laid flat on the sloping area needing protection. Gabions of smaller stones also may be used.

10–4.3 Floodways

Floodways are used to protect valuable property (urban usually) from flooding and erosion damage. These range in size and complexity depending on the nature of the hazard and the value of the property. The city of Winnipeg in western Canada has suffered irregularly from flooding caused by rapid snowmelt and ice jams in the

Figure 10–16 Rock wall revetment protecting a cultivated field from floods of the Urubamba River near Machu Picchu, Peru. (Courtesy F. R. Troeh.)

Figure 10–17 A windrow revetment. The stones are piled in a windrow near the edge of the streambank. As the stream erodes the bank, the stones fall and protect the toe of the slope from further erosion. (Courtesy Kansas City District, Corps of Engineers, U.S. Army, Kansas City, Missouri.)

Assiniboine River and the Red River of the North. A floodway, built after the very severe 1950 flood, consists of a very wide shallow channel with broad, low levees on each side. It starts at the Red River some distance south of the built-up area, intercepts excessive water flow, carries it to the east and north, and dumps it back into the river about 15 mi (25 km) north of the city. No serious flooding has occurred in the city since the structure was completed.

10–5 WIND EROSION-CONTROL STRUCTURES

Soils that are extremely susceptible to wind erosion should be returned to perennial vegetation, with special protection provided while the vegetation is being established, or they should be protected permanently by vegetative barriers. Occasionally, an overwhelming need for food requires that highly erodible soils be used indefinitely for cultivated crop production. These areas must be specially protected. Artificial wind barriers may be used in establishing perennial cover or for protecting the cultivated soil. The barriers control wind erosion for a combined windward–leeward distance of about ten times their height. For most effective protection the barrier must be placed perpendicular to the direction of the erosive winds.

10–5.1 Woven Mat Barriers

Mats of woven plant materials are erected as barriers to erosive winds in many areas where land scarcity forces the use of erodible soils. Grasses, reeds, and crop stalks are sometimes woven into mats which are later erected at sites where they are needed. In other cases the barriers are constructed at the site and cannot be moved without being dismantled.

Figure 10–18 shows barriers of reeds used to protect tomatoes along the Mediterranean Sea about 40 mi (65 km) west of Algiers. The principal barriers run perpendicular to the seacoast at intervals of about 35 to 50 ft (10 to 15 m). The secondary barriers, perpendicular to the primary ones, are spaced about 30 in. (0.75 cm) apart between tomato rows. These barriers control soil movement and also reduce desiccation damage from the hot, dry winds.

10-5.2 Snow Fence and Other Wooden Barriers

Temporary fences are used in parts of the United States and in other countries to stop snow from drifting onto highways, airport runways, and other critical areas. A fence consists of slats of wood about 0.25 in. (0.75 cm) thick, 1.5 in. (4 cm) wide, and 48 in. (122 cm) long fastened together by wire so that the slats are spaced about 1 in. (2.5 cm) apart (approximate porosity 40%). The fencing is usually mounted on steel posts driven into the ground and can be dismantled, stored, and used again. This commercially available fencing is often used where temporary soil protection is needed, such as stabilizing active sand dunes or recently denuded, erosive land (Figure 5–4).

Taller barriers made of vertically mounted boards can also be used, but they are very expensive and are suitable only for high-value crops or in critical situations where an attempt is being made to revegetate eroding sites. A more permanent solution, use of field shelterbelts, is discussed in Chapter 12.

Figure 10–18 Woven-reed wind barriers in Algeria. The primary barriers are about 6 ft (2 m) tall, the secondary ones about 30 to 40 in. (75 cm to 1 m) tall. (Courtesy Mrs. A. W. Zingg.)

10-5.3 Dune-Leveling Devices

Crests of dunes often have to be reduced in height before the dunes can be stabilized. Modern earth-moving equipment can perform this task and may be the cheapest way to do the job where labor is expensive. Wind deflectors and barriers have been used to increase wind velocity and sweep the sharp crests off the active dunes. Snow fencing can be stretched along the dune crests so that the wind blows under as well as over the barrier. As the crest is cut off, the fence is lowered progressively. When the crest is reduced enough, the barrier is lowered to the surface to protect it from erosion while vegetation is established.

Sand-filled burlap sacks were used in the fight against encroaching dunes in the Great Plains and around the Great Lakes. Accelerated wind whipping between adjacent sacks swept away the exposed sand and the sacks gradually settled down without attention by the farmers, except for occasional straightening. Some means of reducing wind velocity must be provided after dune crests are lowered to prevent soil drifting while vegetation is being established on the flattened dunes.

SUMMARY

Crop and soil management practices do not always provide enough erosion control on cultivated land. Runoff and soil loss from native vegetation also may be excessive. Special conservation structures are needed to reduce these losses to tolerable levels.

Bench terraces are a very old means of controlling runoff and erosion and are still widely used in areas with large populations and limited areas of arable land. Graded terraces are used in areas with commercial agriculture where machinery is available and labor costs are high. A graded terrace consists of a channel with a ridge on the downhill side. The channel slopes gently toward a protected outlet. Graded terraces reduce erosion because they shorten slope lengths, reduce runoff volume and velocity, and trap sediment. Parallel and steep back-slope terraces are modifications that make farming terraced fields easier. Terraces need maintenance to retain adequate channel capacity and must be repaired when storms cause major damage.

Diversions direct runoff water away from gullies, around cultivated fields, and to ponds and storage reservoirs. The diversion channel is usually a high-capacity grassed waterway and is seldom cropped.

Diversions and graded terraces must have protected outlets into which the accumulated runoff water is released. Grassed waterways are common outlets, but underground pipe outlets are becoming more popular because they release land for cultivated crop production.

Erosion sometimes occurs in the beds of vegetated waterways as well as in gullies on cultivated fields and on grass- and timberlands. Structures needed to control this erosion may be either temporary or long-term. Temporary structures are often used to control erosion in waterways and gullies while perennial vegetation or other permanent control is being established. Temporary structures include artificial mulch in shaped and seeded waterways and barriers in channels. Artificial mulch may consist of burlap or specially prepared cloth, paper, plastic, or shredded wood mats staked to the soil. Barriers may be made of rock, wood (natural or dressed), or brick. They must make firm and intimate contact with both floor and walls of the waterway or gully so that water cannot wash under or around the structure.

Concrete drop structures and chutes are permanent control devices used where it seems impractical to control erosion by vegetative means. Simple concrete chutes may be used for relatively small water volume and short water drops, but reinforced concrete is needed where the volume is large or the drop great. The most critical parts of drop structures and chutes are the inlets, outlets, and the aprons onto which the water falls and from which it flows onto the soil at a lower level.

Several types of storage dams are used in soil and water conservation activities. Dams may be built to trap sediments, to stabilize gullies or channel grades, or to store runoff temporarily to reduce flooding, soil loss, and sedimentation.

Current deflectors and bank protectors have been used with varying degrees of success in attempts to control streambank erosion. No attempt to deflect current can be undertaken in the United States without first obtaining permission from the U.S. Army Crops of Engineers or the state water control agency or both.

Wind-erosion control structures are used to stabilize erodible soils that either must be or have been cropped. Woven mat barriers and snow fences have been used successfully to reduce wind velocities at ground level. Dune-leveling devices have been used to smooth dune topography to make it easier to establish vegetation.

QUESTIONS

1. What are the differences in purpose and in structure of graded terraces and diversions?
2. Describe the important elements involved in the construction of simple barriers in waterways and gullies. Why is each important?
3. What are the major differences in specifications for dams built to **(a)** trap sediment? **(b)** stabilize a gully that is cutting back into a field? **(c)** store floodwater? Explain why these differences exist.
4. Describe the major conditions that dictate which technique (such as toe protectors, windrow revetments, tire revetments, or protective fence) will be chosen for reducing stream-bank erosion. Explain why each of these conditions is important in making the correct choice.
5. Under what conditions would you expect to find artificial wind barriers used in a country with a highly developed commercial agriculture?

REFERENCES

American Society of Agricultural Engineers, 1989. *ASAE Standards: Design, Layout, Construction, and Maintenance of Terrace Systems.* Publ. S.268.3. American Society of Agricultural Engineers, St. Joseph, Mich., p. 500–504.

Armbrust, D. V., and L. Lyles, 1975. Soil stabilizers to control wind erosion. In *Soil Conditioners.* Spec. Publ. 7. Soil Science Society of America, Madison, Wis., p.77–82.

Beasley, R. P., J. M. Gregory, and T. R. McCarty, 1984. *Erosion and Sediment Pollution Control,* 2nd ed. Iowa State Univ. Press, Ames, Iowa, 354 p.

Bensalem, B., 1977. Examples of soil and water conservation practices in North African countries, Algeria, Morocco, and Tunisia. In *Soil Conservation and Management in Developing Countries.* Soils Bull. 33, Paper 10. FAO, Rome, p.151–160.

Blakely, B. D., J. J. Coyle, and J. G. Steele, 1957. Erosion on cultivated land. In *Soil,* Yearbook of Agriculture. USDA, Washington, D.C., p. 290–307.

Heede, B. H., 1976. *Gully Development and Control.* USDA For. Serv. Res. Paper RM-169.

Hudson, N., 1981. *Soil Conservation.* 2nd ed. Cornell Univ. Press, Ithaca, N.Y., 324 p.

Kunkle, S. H., and D. A. Harcharik, 1977. Conservation of upland wildlands for downstream agriculture. In *Soil Conservation and Management in Developing Countries.* Soils Bull. 33, Paper 9. FAO, Rome, p.133–149.

Phillips, J. A., and E. J. Kamprath, 1973. Soil fertility problems associated with land forming in the Coastal Plains. *J. Soil Water Cons.* 28:69–73.

Powell, G. M., 1989. *Maintaining Terraces.* Kans. State Univ. Coop. Ext. Serv. C709.

Wittmus, H., 1973. Construction requirements and cost analysis of grassed backslope terrace systems. *Trans. Am. Soc. Agric. Eng.* 16:970–972.

11

Vegetating Mining and Construction Sites

Areas drastically disturbed by mining are an environmental menace because they are a source of large quantities of sediment; some are strongly acid with toxic heavy metals. Iron and coal tailings often contain iron pyrite which can cause soil conditions too acid for plant growth. Acid mine waters may contain toxic quantities of copper, iron, aluminum, and manganese. In addition, the mine spoils may contain toxic heavy metals such as cadmium, copper, lead, and zinc. Most mine spoils have steep, unstable slopes; many are compact; some are excessively stony; some are deficient in silt and clay and have very low water-holding capacities; most are low in fertility. In arid regions, mine spoils are too dry and may be too saline or sodic for satisfactory vegetation establishment. Some mine spoils have been reclaimed and revegetated, but a large proportion were mined before land reclamation was mandated and remain as the mining operation left them—bare, scarred by gullies, useless, and unsightly.

Soils drastically disturbed by construction activities are often difficult to revegetate because the soil material has been compacted so much by heavy machinery that plant roots cannot penetrate it. Land slopes are generally steeper than before construction was started. The texture of the exposed material on some sites may not permit storage and release of adequate amounts of water. Essential plant nutrients may not be present in the new surface material in available form or in balanced proportions. Nitrogen is invariably deficient; phosphorus is generally in short supply. The sites may be too wet because of a naturally high water table or because of an inflow of water. Despite these problems, considerable success has been attained in vegetating soil along highways, around buildings, on airfields, and along pipelines. The task of revegetation is generally expensive per unit area of land, but the cost is small compared to the total cost of the project.

11-1 SURFACE MINING

At present, surface mines such as that shown in Figure 11-1 produce slightly more than half of the U.S. coal output. In addition, 90% of all copper ore, 94% of iron ore, and all of the phosphate ore are mined by surface techniques. Surface mining is expected to develop faster than shaft mining in the future. For each unit of mineral produced, surface mining disturbs more than ten times as much land as shaft mining.

11-2 SURFACE MINING LEGISLATION

On August 3, 1977, the U.S. Congress passed Public Law 95-87 to "establish a nationwide program to protect society and the environment from the adverse effects of surface coal mining operations." Special provisions were added to protect "prime farmland." This law specifies that the respective states must establish their own laws on the subject. The state laws were to mandate equal or greater environmental integrity.

Provisions of the federal law protecting prime farmland include these mandates for surface coal mining operators:

Figure 11-1 A small-scale surface (strip) coal mine in Pennsylvania. The soil materials are drastically disturbed and may be difficult to revegetate. (Courtesy EPA-DOCUMERICA.)

1. Demonstrate the "technological capability to restore such mined areas . . . to equivalent or higher levels of yield."
2. Remove and replace the key individual soil horizons separately and construct a root zone as deep and as good as in the premined soil. Exceptions may be granted upon proof that another technique will produce equal or higher crop yields.
3. Post a performance bond that will be released only after "soil productivity has returned to equivalent levels of yield as nonmined land of the same soil type in the surrounding area under equivalent management. . . ." Crops used to test whether the mined land has been restored to "equivalent levels of yield" include wheat, rye, barley, and grain sorghum. Corn is a more "demanding" crop because of its late-in-the-season water requirement. Soil tests are used for determining lime and fertilizer requirements of test crops but cannot be used alone for release of performance bonds. (Research in Illinois indicated that at the same soil test level, twice as much P fertilizer was required for corn on mine spoils as for undisturbed soils.) (Dunker et al., 1988)
4. Start the restoration process within 10 years after surface mining operations have ceased. (Plotkin, 1987, U.S. Congress, 1977)

Technical assistance in reclamation is provided by the USDA–Soil Conservation Service under long-term agreements. Cost-sharing with the landowner is permitted up to 80% of the cost of such reclamation for a maximum of 120 acres (48 ha) for each cooperator.

11–3 AREAS DISTURBED BY MINING AND AREAS RECLAIMED

The Soil Conservation Service estimates that 69% of the spoils on abandoned mines in need of reclamation in the United States are located in Appalachia, 29% in the midwest, and 2% in the far west. Before the enactment of Public Law 95–87, there were 31 state laws mandating reclamation of both active and abandoned mine spoils. All states had started reclaiming mine spoils by July 1978, including those from 1.1 million acres (450,000 ha) of abandoned mines.

About 3.63 million acres (1.74 million hectares) in the United States were drastically disturbed by the various mining activities indicated in Figure 11–2. This represents 0.16% of the total land area of the 50 states. It does not include areas disturbed by oil and gas exploration. During the same period, 43% of all areas disturbed by mining were reclaimed. However, the area reclaimed in 1971 was equal to 80% of the land disturbed by mining in any one year. A vivid portrayal of the state-by-state location of areas drastically disturbed by both surface and shaft coal mining is presented in Figure 11–3. Surface (strip) coal mining increased faster than shaft mining in the 1970s, and total coal use doubled from 1975 to 1985.

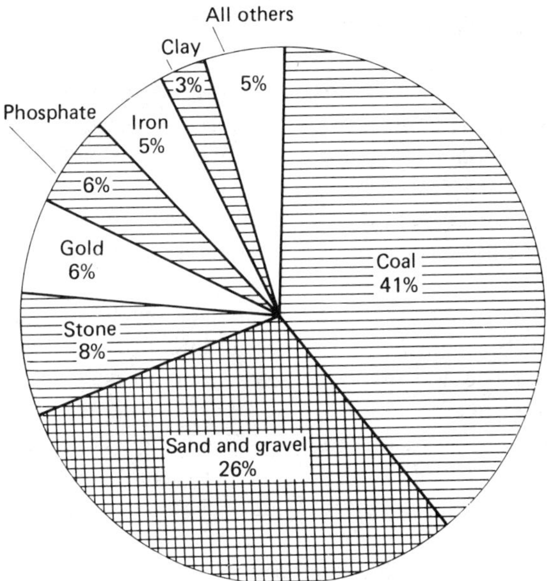

Figure 11-2 Land area disturbed by mining for various materials as percentages of the total mining disturbance in the United States. Coal plus sand and gravel account for two-thirds of the land disturbed by mining in the United States. (Courtesy EPA-DOCUMERICA.)

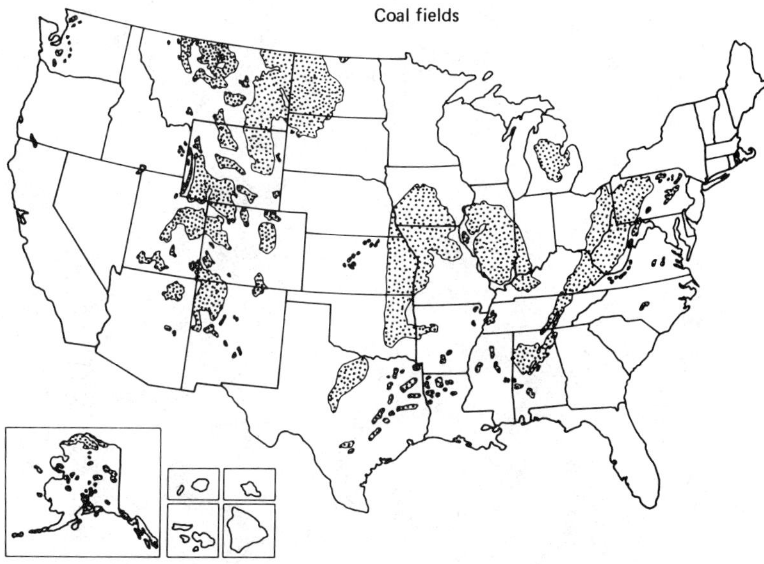

Figure 11-3 Disturbance of land by coal mining is a national problem. At least 28 of the 50 states have significant coal fields and 15 states have reported erosion, sedimentation, and toxic drainage as major problems. (From U.S. Department of Agriculture, 1974.)

11-4 ESTABLISHING VEGETATION ON MINE SPOILS

In this discussion, the reclamation of mine spoils includes revegetation of mine dump sites and the control of acid waters and toxic materials such as heavy metals. Temporary mechanical techniques to retain mine spoils at the site include the use of sediment basins, terraces, berms, or diversion dams. Steep slopes must be graded, as shown in Figure 11-4, and the topsoil must be replaced after mining activities have ceased. The final step is the establishment of either perennial vegetation or cultivated crops.

Many mine spoils are so compacted by heavy machinery that plant roots cannot grow through them. The measurement of bulk density and the use of a cone penetrometer provide two parameters used to determine relative soil compaction (Thompson et al., 1987).

Soil drastically disturbed by surface mining can be restored for successful crop production. Figure 11-5 shows an experiment established in Illinois in an area of Muscatine silt loam (an Aquic Argiudoll) to compare corn yield on (1) undisturbed soil, (2) topography regraded after mining but not topsoiled, and (3) topography regraded after mining and surfaced with 10 in. (25 cm) of topsoil. Comparative

Figure 11-4 The "highwall" labeled A in this mine in Montana resulted from strip mining before Montana law mandated highwall reduction and elimination of impoundments. The area labeled B was mined later and reduced to a 1:3 (33%) gradient to meet state and federal requirements. (Courtesy USDI Bureau of Mines.)

Figure 11-5 This cornfield in Illinois was regraded for corn production after surface mining of coal. The area on the right was covered with 10 in. (25 cm) of topsoil that the area on the left did not receive. (Courtesy Alten F. Grandt, Peabody Coal Co.)

yields of corn for the four-year period 1975–1978 were (personal communication from Alton F. Grandt):

	Yield of corn	
	lb/ac	kg/ha
Undisturbed Muscatine soil	7557	8472
Soil disturbed by mining		
With topsoil	6465	7248
Without topsoil	4246	4760

11-4.1 Techniques for Establishing Vegetation

Materials that can produce extreme acidity or extreme alkalinity or excessive soluble salts should be identified before mining begins. These adverse materials can be located by laboratory testing of core samples. All such materials should be kept separate during excavation and buried below plant root depth before the final grading of the surface.

Final reclamation of mine spoils consists of establishing perennial vegetation, cultivated crops, ponds, or lakes over the entire area. Sometimes temporary vegetation is used to stabilize the surface until perennial vegetation can be established to hold the soil against water and wind erosion. Management techniques for improving the productive capability of disturbed soil include topsoiling, liming (if acid), fertilizing, applying manure or sewage sludge, and mulching.

Topsoiling means to apply a productive surface soil to the final soil grade. Lime and fertilizers are usually applied on the basis of a soil test before planting vegetation. Each soil sample should represent a smaller area on mine spoils than on cropland because of the greater variability of the spoils. Czapowskyj (1973) reported the following variabilities in spoils from Kentucky, Indiana, and Pennsylvania:

N = <0.1 to 0.2%	pH = 2.2 to 7.3
P = 6.6 to 64.2 ppm	Ca = 1.0 to 17.5 me/100 g spoil
K = <0.1 to 0.8 me/100 g spoil	Mg = 0.3 to 4.8 me/100 g spoil

A unique problem in many mine spoils of humid regions and in a few in arid regions is the presence of pyrite (FeS_2). Pyrite oxidizes to sulfuric acid when exposed to the atmosphere (Note 11–1) and may kill all vegetation. The acid is produced by bacterial action, and the process stops when the conditions become so acid that neither the bacteria nor any other living thing can tolerate it (a pH between 2 and 3). The acidity can be neutralized with lime, but the neutralization may last for only a few months until more sulfuric acid is formed. The best solution is to bury the spoils that contain pyrite; an expensive alternative is to apply lime whenever a soil test indicates a need for it, and to use acid-tolerant vegetation as described in Section 11–4.2.

NOTE 11–1
OXIDATION OF PYRITE

Pyrite (FeS_2) is a pale brass-yellow mineral known as "fool's gold" that commonly exists as impurities in coal deposits. Upon exposure to moist air, pyrite oxidizes to ferrous sulfate and sulfuric acid. This reaction is represented as follows:

$$2\ FeS_2 + 7\ O_2 + 2\ H_2O \rightarrow 2\ FeSO_4 + 2\ H_2SO_4$$

A second reaction takes place when the *ferrous* sulfate is oxidized to *ferric* sulfate:

$$4\ FeSO_4 + O_2 + 2\ H_2SO_4 \rightarrow 2\ Fe_2(SO_4)_3 + 2\ H_2O$$

The ferric sulfate then hydrolyzes to form colloidal ferric hydroxide (called "yellow-boy" by miners) and sulfuric acid:

$$Fe_2(SO_4)_3 + 6\ H_2O \rightarrow 2\ Fe(OH)_3 + 3\ H_2SO_4$$

Mine spoils are ideal sites for heavy applications of manure and sewage sludge. Nearly all spoils are low in organic matter, droughty, and low in available plant nutrients. Furthermore, few mine spoil sites are used for food crops that might become contaminated with pathogens or toxic heavy metals from sewage sludge.

Numerous trials have shown that sewage sludge and wastewaters can be used to help revegetate acid mine spoils. An example from Ohio is shown in Figure 11-6. Another example occurred where digested sewage sludge from Chicago was applied on extremely variable coal mine spoils in Fulton County, Illinois. Rates as high as

Plot A

Plot B

Plot C

Figure 11-6 A revegetation experiment on acid (pH 2.3) mine spoils in Ohio. The spoils were high in pyrite, and no vegetation grew without special treatment. A sparse stand of rye grew in Plot A, where 4.5 tons/ac (10 mt/ha) of lime had raised the pH to 3.3 and 900 lb/ac (1000 kg/ha) of 6-24-12 fertilizer was applied. A normal stand of rye was produced in Plot B, where 90 tons/ac (200 mt/ha) of lime raised the pH to 5.8 and 900 lb/ac (1000 kg/ha) of 6-24-12 was added. The best growth was obtained from Plot C, where 300 tons/ac (660) mt/ha of sewage sludge (air-dry weight) raised the pH to 5.8 and improved the fertility without any lime or mineral fertilizer beinging added. (From Sutton and Vimmerstedt, 1973; photos courtesy Paul Sutton.)

446 tons/ac (1000 mt/ha) (dry basis) were sprayed as a slurry. All application rates hastened the establishment of annual and perennial vegetation. Runoff was trapped by a levee built around the perimeter of the mine spoils.

Variable rates of municipal sewage sludge and wastewaters were applied to coal strip-mine spoils in Pennsylvania before seeding or planting perennial vegetation. Most species of grasses, legumes, and trees grew better on the areas treated with sewage sludge. However, do toxic trace metals concentrate in vegetation and animals? This subject was researched by Alberici et al. (1989), in Pennsylvania. Sewage sludge at the rate of 60 tons/ac (134 mt/ha) was applied on tall fescue, orchardgrass, and birdsfoot trefoil. The results were:

1. Cr was the only metal higher in vegetation in the sludge-amended site than recommended by the Council for Agricultural Science and Technology.
2. Zn, Co, Ni, and Cu concentrations were higher in birdsfoot trefoil than in other plant species.
3. Pb and Cd concentrations were higher in birdsfoot trefoil and orchardgrass than in other species.
4. Cu, Zn, Co, and Ni in vole (a mouse-like animal) tissues were not higher in sludge-treated areas. However, Cr concentrations in vole kidney and bone and Pb in vole liver and bone were significantly higher in sludge-treated areas.

Surface mulching with organic wastes reduces splash erosion, surface puddling, and sealing of the soil. Mulches are usually applied immediately after seeding or planting, but they also may be applied earlier to protect the bare soil until the proper season for seeding or planting. The most common organic mulches are wood chips, wood fibers, grain straws, and hay. Amounts vary, but the materials should have a packed thickness of 1 to 2.5 in. (3 to 6 cm) over all disturbed soil surfaces.

11-4.2 Vegetating Mine Spoils in Humid Regions

Several soil-plant management principles must be applied to assure success in establishing vegetation on mine spoils in humid regions:

1. Spoil materials are extremely variable; a soil test for pH and plant nutrients is essential.
2. Either acid-tolerant vegetation must be used or heavy applications of lime or organic wastes must be applied where the soil pH is low. Both practices must be applied where the pH is below 3.5.
3. Forage legumes will not grow well if the pH is below 4.5.
4. A vegetative cover is crucial. Sometimes a fast-starting cereal grain and a slower-to-establish perennial are seeded together as companion crops. Or, the cereal may be grown alone and its residues used as a mulch for seeding perennial vegetation.
5. Various forage grasses and legumes, trees for lumber or pulp, and shrubs,

vines, and brambles have different adaptations. The type and species of vegetation must be chosen to fit the climate and the soil conditions.

Grasses. Many common grasses have been tested on mine spoils with widely varying results. The results depend greatly on the pH of the spoil, as shown in Figure 11-7. Only deertongue, Korean lovegrass, weeping lovegrass, and switchgrass are recommended in humid regions of the United States where the spoil pH is less than 4.0 (Soil Conservation Service, 1978). Reed canarygrass, sand lovegrass, and tall fescue are suited to a pH between 4.0 and 5.5. Chinese silvergrass, coastal panicgrass, orchardgrass, and perennial ryegrass do well on spoils with pH above 5.5. All grasses grew better at the higher pH values even if they survived at a lower pH.

Cold hardiness must also be considered in selecting a grass species. The three

Figure 11-7 Selection of an adapted grass species is imperative for vegetating acid mine spoils. The upper photo shows that at pH 4.0, weeping lovegrass was the best of the five species shown (but it must be limited to warm climates because frost may kill it) and switchgrass was second. The lower photo shows that all five grasses grew satisfactorily on this spoil at pH 4.5. (Courtesy USDA Forest Service.)

lovegrasses are cold-sensitive grasses that are restricted to warm climates; orchardgrass is adapted to cooler climates such as northern United States. The remaining seven grasses recommended on spoil materials are adapted throughout the humid part of the United States.

Legumes. Legumes are desirable on mine spoils because of their ability to fix atmospheric nitrogen. Many legumes were tested on acid mine spoils, but only seven gave good results, and none below pH 4.0. Birdsfoot trefoil, crownvetch, flatpea, and sericea lespedeza survived at pH 4.0 to 5.5; alfalfa and alsike clover did not do well in southern United States (Soil Conservation Service, 1978). Legumes may not fix appreciable quantities of N at a pH below 5.5. Legumes are usually seeded with adapted grasses to increase the chances of a successful stand.

Trees. Trees may be used to vegetate mine sites, but usually grass is seeded between the tree seedlings to protect the soil until the trees provide enough canopy and litter to do so. Only two tree species tested, black locust (a legume) and European black alder, tolerated a pH less than 4.0. Black alder grows well even at pH 3.0. Black locust grew well from spoil pH less than 4.0 to above 8.0. American sycamore, eastern cottonwood, green ash, loblolly pine, northern red oak, Norway spruce, red maple, red pine, Scotch pine, silver maple, sweetgum, Virginia pine, and white pine were established on many sites with pH 4.0 to 5.5. Shortleaf pine such as that shown in Figure 11-8, and hybrid poplar can be used only when the pH is above

Figure 11-8 Trees can be used to stabilize mine spoil with pH ranging from less than 4.0 to more than 8.0. This shortleaf pine planting on mine spoil in Kentucky is adapted to pH above 5.0. (Courtesy USDA Soil Conservation Service.)

5.5 (Soil Conservation Service, 1978; Ashby et al., 1985; Davidson and Vogel, 1983). Loblolly pine, shortleaf pine, and Virginia pine are adapted primarily to a warm climate such as that of the southern United States.

11-4.3 Vegetating Mine Spoils in Arid and Semiarid Regions

Surface mining in arid and semiarid regions of the United States is expected to increase in the future, mainly because 90% of the low-sulfur coal is located there. Increased mining will be accompanied by a need for vegetating the area of mine spoils produced. Federal mining laws now require the topography to be smoothed and surface soil replaced; however, there are still many difficulties in establishing vegetation under arid conditions (Monsen and Richardson, 1984):

1. Fewer plant species are adapted, and their density and productivity will always be much less than in humid areas because too little water is available during the growing season.
2. Time of seeding or planting is more critical because of seasonality of available moisture.
3. Soils often contain toxic quantities of total soluble salts or boron. Some soils contain excessive molybdenum and selenium that are taken in by plants and are toxic to livestock.
4. Some soils contain excessive sodium that causes a high pH and a dispersed physical condition unfavorable for plant growth.
5. As a general rule, the amount of precipitation is less and its variability is greater from month to month, season to season, and year to year.
6. Some mine spoils are too sandy, too stony, too salty, or too dry to support any plant growth.

Plants tolerant of drought, sodium, bicarbonates, alkalinity, and/or boron are generally also tolerant of total soluble salts. A list of plants moderately or highly tolerant of total soluble salts is given in Table 11-1. All of these plants have been used successfully to vegetate mine spoils in arid and semiarid regions. Ayers and Westcot (1976) have ranked several grasses according to their comparative resistance to total soluble salts as follows: wheatgrasses > barley > fescue > bermudagrass > perennial ryegrass. Selected drought-tolerant trees and shrubs are listed in Chapter 12.

The productivity of the surface soil on the final grade after mining can be increased by deep chiseling, tillage to a depth of about an inch (2 to 3 cm), adding gypsum if the exchangeable sodium is excessive, and applying nitrogen and phosphorus fertilizers according to a soil test. Native vegetation can be used successfully to revegetate some sites. Exotic species such as crested wheatgrass, intermediate wheatgrass, Russian wildrye, smooth bromegrass, sweet clover, and alfalfa are used extensively to establish stands by seeding. Sometimes wheat, oats, or barley can be grown on areas that are level enough to be harvested with a combine (Power et al.,

TABLE 11-1 RELATIVE SALT TOLERANCE OF PLANTS USED FOR VEGETATING MINE SPOILS IN ARID AND SEMIARID REGIONS[a]

Moderate (4–8 mmhos/cm)	High (8–12 mmhos/cm)
Alfalfa[b]	Alkali sacaton
Birdsfoot trefoil	Alkaligrass
Bromegrasses	Barley
Hardinggrass	Bermudagrass[b]
Oats	Fescue grasses[b]
Orchardgrass	Fourwing saltbush
Reed canarygrass[b]	Perennial ryegrass
Rye, cereal	Saltgrass[b]
Sorghums	Sweetclovers
Wheat	Switchgrass[b]
	Wheatgrass
	Pubescent
	Crested
	Slender
	Tall
	Wildryegrass
	Beardless
	Russian

[a]Relative salt content is measured by electrical conductivity in millimhos per centimeter at 25°C on a saturated soil extract.

[b]Salt-tolerant but not very drought-resistant.

Source: Bernstein, 1964, Environmental Protection Agency, 1975.

1978). A successful seeding of grain sorghum in Wyoming is shown in Figure 11-9. The sorghum residue helped stabilize the spoils until perennial vegetation was established.

Five techniques have been used to increase the chances of success in establishing vegetation in arid and semiarid regions:

1. Chisel to break up compacted mine spoils.
2. Replace topsoil and apply soil amendments and fertilizer as indicated by soil tests.
3. Prepare a seedbed on the mine spoils similar to that prepared for seeding a cultivated crop. Drill or broadcast the seed just before the onset of the normal rainy season.
4. Apply a suitable organic mulch after seeding.
5. Consider the practice a success if a stand of vegetation is established on an average of once in four attempts. The odds can be improved by irrigating for a period of about two months or until the seeded vegetation has become well established.

Figure 11-9 This grain sorghum was seeded on raw coal mine spoil in Wyoming and grew as tall as 2 ft (60 cm) even though no irrigation water was applied. The average annual precipitation at the site is 14 in. (350 mm). (Courtesy USDI Bureau of Mines.)

11-5 CONSTRUCTION ACTIVITY AND THE ENVIRONMENT

Each year an estimated 1.5 million acres (600,000 ha) of land surface is drastically disturbed by construction of new urban areas, roads, and highways. Other construction activities that disturb soil include pipeline burial, communication establishment, pond and lake development, and dredging and other water developments. These disturbances cause serious erosion on 0.5 million acres (200,000 ha) (Larson et al., 1981).

Construction activities destroy much of the vegetative cover and disturb the soil. Exposure to beating raindrops together with compaction of the soil surface reduces soil infiltration and increases runoff and erosion, as shown in Figure 11-10. Subsoil covers or becomes mixed with topsoil in some construction areas, thus increasing the clay content of the new topsoil and reducing its fertility and productivity. Compacting fill sites and excavated areas with heavy earth-moving equipment and packers may add to the soundness and safety of the structure being built, but it also reduces the infiltration rate of the soil and makes it a very unsuitable medium for establishing plant growth. The slope of the land is often increased by land forming that accompanies construction activity, again increasing the tendency for runoff and erosion. In many situations, surface waters concentrated in new watercourses cause gully erosion as shown in Figure 11-11. Even after the exposed area

Figure 11–10 This construction site is an example of gross negligence. Erosion was measured and reported to be about 27,000 cubic yards per mile (13,000 m3/km) of roadbed. The weather when the picture was taken was too cold to establish perennial vegetation, but annual vegetation plus mulch could have controlled most of the erosion and sedimentation. (Courtesy USDA Soil Conservation Service.)

has been shaped and reseeded, runoff from the impervious structural surfaces may cause additional erosion.

The U.S. Geological Survey made a study of sediment yield from highway construction sites in Scott Run Basin near Washington, D.C. Although they occupied only 11% of the land area, highway construction activities were the source of 85% of the total sediment eroded and transported. Soil sediment yield each year from highway construction activity was 75 tons/ac (168 mt/ha) under conditions of normal rainfall (Cywin and Hendricks, 1969). This was 10 times as much as from cultivated land, 200 times as much as from grassland, and 2000 times as much as from forestland.

Construction sites should be stabilized by water-control structures and temporary cover while work is in progress. Terraces and diversion ditches that lead into a debris basin as in Figure 11–12 can retain most or all soil sediments originating on the site.

11-6 VEGETATING CONSTRUCTION SITES

Reseeding grasses and legumes and planting seedling trees and shrubs on a prepared site are relatively straightforward and simple tasks. But preparing the site for

Figure 11-11 The vegetation held the soil in place here until a highway was built. Diverted runoff water cut this gully through the trees and shrubs. Drop structures (Chapter 10) are now needed along with vegetation to stabilize the soil. (Courtesy USDA Forest Service.)

seeding and protecting it until the planted vegetation can provide protection is complicated and requires that adapted techniques be chosen for different areas and sites.

11-6.1 General Site Preparation and Planting Technology

In general, topsoil from the site should be removed and stockpiled during the early stages of construction. Steep exposed banks may have to be formed into benchlike terraces to prevent excess water from washing out the seeds and seedlings and causing excessive erosion. Hard soil surfaces must be scarified, and heavily compacted areas must be loosened by ripping with a chisel device or similar implement (Chapter 9). On extremely steep slopes, it may be necessary to loosen the soil with hand tools. The topsoil should be spread over the surface of the exposed areas after construction is complete. Replacing topsoil is most important when the exposed material is unduly sandy, stony, or clayey, or contains toxic materials. Soil samples should be taken from the top 6 in. (15 cm) of the exposed areas and tested for lime requirement and available N, available P, and exchangeable K. The necessary lime and fertilizer applications for the site should be applied and worked into the soil.

The plant material for construction sites should be selected with great care, usually with professional guidance. Single species or complex mixtures may be

Figure 11–12 A debris basin is often the only way to retain sediment from soil erosion on the site during construction activities. Sediment from this project in West Virginia would pollute stream waters if the basin were not used. (Courtesy USDA Soil Conservation Service.)

needed to satisfy local conditions. Steeply sloping land should be seeded as soon after construction as possible. On less erodible sites, it may be possible to wait for the best time of year. Even on gentle slopes, it often pays to cover the surface with a mulch or to seed a temporary cover to hold the soil until it is time to seed the perennial crop. Some steep slopes may be spray-seeded with a mixture of seed, fertilizer, and mulching material, using a blower designed for this purpose, as shown in Figure 11–13. Seedling trees should be set out after all other seeding and mulching is complete.

11–6.2 Specific Site Preparation and Planting Technology

Establishing vegetation is site specific. Soil amelioration, selection of plant species, time of seeding or planting, kind and rate of fertilizer and lime applications, and maintenance are technical factors unique in combination to each construction site. For this reason, techniques will be presented that were used for establishing vegetation on specific construction sites in Alaska, California, Colorado, Mississippi, Montana, New Mexico, and Virginia (Environmental Protection Agency, 1975).

Alaska. Vegetating soils disturbed in the process of laying the 800-mile (1300-km) Alaska oil pipeline (1974–1977) were hampered by inadequate research.

Figure 11-13 The final slope for this roadcut has been chiseled; now cellulose mulch plus seed and fertilizer in a slurry are being blown on the cut surface. This technique of revegetating disturbed sites has proved successful and economic in humid but not arid regions. In arid regions the seed must be drilled and then mulched. (Courtesy USDA Soil Conservation Service.)

In 1978, a 4800-mile (7700-km) gas pipeline was approved for construction in the same tundra environment. The area is humid even though the average annual precipitation is only 10 in. (250 mm). Soils are fine textured and belong mostly to the extensive Great Group of Cryaquepts. There are about 100 freeze-free days per year. Permafrost (permanently frozen layer) is common. Maintaining a continuous surface cover of some type of organic or inorganic insulating material is essential to prevent the ice lenses from melting and the surface soil from collapsing. The ecosystem (soil and vegetation) is so fragile that if a person walked across the landscape 10 to 20 times in the same path, that path would be visible for 25 years or more. The tracks made by a Caterpillar tractor pulling a cargo sled across the soil surface in 1945 appeared to be freshly made in 1978.

The following forage seeding is recommended for drilling or broadcasting on disturbed soils in central Alaska:

Seeding mixture	Variety (cultivar)
Fescue	Arctared
Creeping foxtail	Garrison
Kentucky bluegrass	Nugget, Merion
White Dutch or alsike clover	Use local source of seed
Bering hairgrass	Collect local seed of native species

Figure 11-14 shows three grasses growing in the Alaskan environment. Woody plants adapted to wet soil in Alaska are bog rosemary and wintergreen. Woody

Figure 11–14 A grass experiment in central Alaska not far from the Alaska oil pipeline. The grasses are fescue, arctared variety (left); Bering hairgrass (center); and Kentucky bluegrass, Nugget variety (right). The fescue and bluegrass were equally as vigorous as the hairgrass but were more palatable to herbivorous animals. (Courtesy W. W. Mitchell, Agricultural Experiment Station, University of Alaska.)

plants adapted to drier sites in central Alaska include dwarf caragana (peashrub), creeping juniper, cinquefoil, and Indian snowberry.

California. Research efforts to vegetate two contrasting construction sites in California will be described briefly, one in a subhumid mountainous area and one in the Mohave Desert.

The first site was a roadway cut slope near Lake Tahoe in the Sierra Nevada Mountains. The average annual precipitation at the site is 31.5 in. (800 mm), received mostly in the winter. The soil is classified as a Meeks very stony loamy coarse sand in the Entic Cryumbrepts. It was successfully vegetated with these techniques:

1. A loose rock breast wall was built and willow cuttings were buried in it.
2. Bundles of woody brush (wattles) were buried across the slope on contour lines with a 3-ft (1-m) vertical interval.
3. Orchardgrass, big bluegrass, crested wheatgrass, pubescent wheatgrass, intermediate wheatgrass, and cicer milkvetch were seeded.
4. Big sagebrush, penstemon, squawcarpet, pinemat manzanita, and bitterbrush were planted.

The second research effort described here attempted to establish vegetation along the right-of-way of the second Los Angeles Aqueduct in the Mohave Desert.

The mean annual precipitation is 7.9 in. (200 mm). The soil is Arizo gravelly loamy sand, a member of the Typic Torripsamments. The vegetation used consisted of five native shrubs. Treatments included spot seeding versus transplanting, and watering with 2 liters of water per planting site at seeding or transplanting versus not watering (Graves et al., 1978). The survival percentages after two years showed that 2 liters of water did not improve survival. The survival rates were 56% for seedings of fourwing saltbush, 6% for desert saltbush, 8% for scalebroom, and none for white bursage and creosotebush. Transplanting improved the survival rate of white bursage to 44%, desert saltbush to 25%, and creosotebush to 12%, but did not help the fourwing saltbush and scalebroom.

Colorado. Cut-and-fill slopes on an 8-mile (13-km) section of Interstate 70 west of Denver were successfully vegetated by seeding a mixture of grasses, white clover, and ponderosa pine. The area receives an average annual precipitation of 17.7 in. (450 mm). The soils are gravelly loams with the predominant soil, the Stecum series, classified in the Typic Cryorthents. Four years after seeding, the vegetation was dominated by crested wheatgrass, which constituted 75 to 80% of the soil cover. Intermediate wheatgrass and smooth bromegrass made up most of the remaining 20 to 25%.

Mississippi. Annual precipitation in Mississippi averages 57 in. (1450 mm). Research on vegetating highway and other construction slopes was conducted there for soils classified in the Great Groups of Fragiudalfs and Paleudults. These soils are low in essential elements, have rolling topography, erode readily and produce much sediment, and are difficult to vegetate. Forage species combinations recommended statewide include:

Bahiagrass and sericea lespedeza

Bermudagrass, annual lespedeza, and *Lespedeza vergata*

Weeping lovegrass and sericea lespedeza, bahiagrass, vetch, and crownvetch

Montana. Two techniques of establishing shrubs on construction slopes in Montana are reported by Hodder (1970). In areas receiving about 10 in. (250 mm) of annual precipitation, seeds of shrubs such as caragana were planted in a greenhouse in plastic tubes about 2.5 in. (6 cm) in diameter and 2 ft (60 cm) long. The tubes were filled with fine soil in the bottom and coarse soil on top. After the plants were well established in the tubes, they were planted on construction sites in holes made by a power-driven auger. Survival was satisfactory.

The second technique of planting shrubs on construction sites in arid areas consisted of the following. A pit about 10 in. (25 cm) in diameter and about 4 in. (10 cm) deep was dug for each shrub. The shrub was planted in the center of the pit on a mound of soil about 2 in. (5 cm) high. A clear plastic film with a slit for the shrub stem was laid over the entire pit, as shown in Figure 11-15. Moisture condensed on the bottom side of the plastic, soaked into the soil around the plant roots, and supplied adequate moisture for growth.

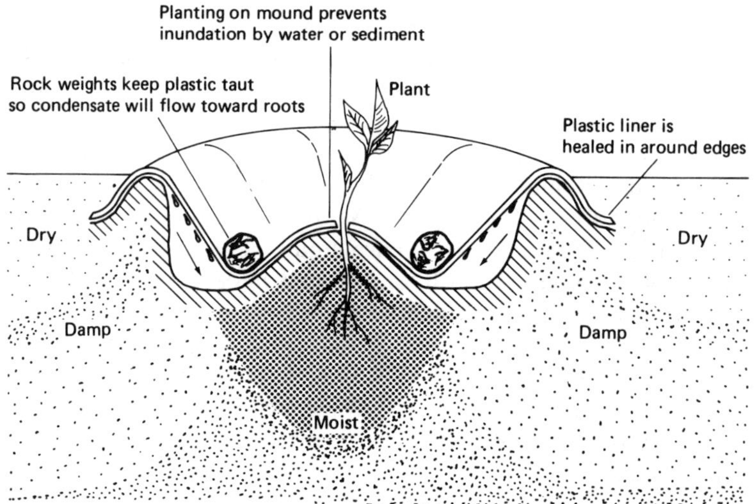

Figure 11–15 A plastic sheet can be used to concentrate soil moisture for establishing shrubs in arid regions. (Courtesy Richard L. Hodder, Montana State University.)

New Mexico. The successful establishment of roadside vegetation in southwestern New Mexico is representative of other southern desert areas in western United States, including parts of Texas, Arizona, California, Nevada, and Utah. Mean annual precipitation on the demonstration site is 10 in. (250 mm), half of which is normally received during summer. The soil is fine textured and classified in the Great Group of Haplargids. The usually intense summer rainfall adds to the difficulty of soil stabilization. The relationship between soil textural class and the adaptability of six grasses in this arid region is shown in Figure 11–16. This figure indicates that on a sand soil, black gramagrass is best; on a loam soil, crested wheatgrass and sideoats gramagrass are both well adapted; and on a clay soil, western wheatgrass grows best (Currier, 1971). Other plants adapted to the southern desert include alkali sacaton, Lehmann lovegrass, blue gramagrass, and fourwing saltbush. Irrigation is usually necessary in establishing all vegetation.

Virginia. Precipitation in the Piedmont Plateau on the vegetated site described here averages 41 in. (1050 mm) a year. Soils belong to the Cecil and Appling soil series, members of the Typic Hapludults. Usually lime, nitrogen, and phosphorus are necessary to assure the establishment of adapted vegetation on construction slopes; only by a soil test, however, can the needed rates be determined. The recommended grasses and legumes are:

Perennial grasses: tall fescue, redtop, and weeping lovegrass

Annual grasses: rye, wheat, annual ryegrass, and German millet

Legumes: crownvetch and sericea lespedeza

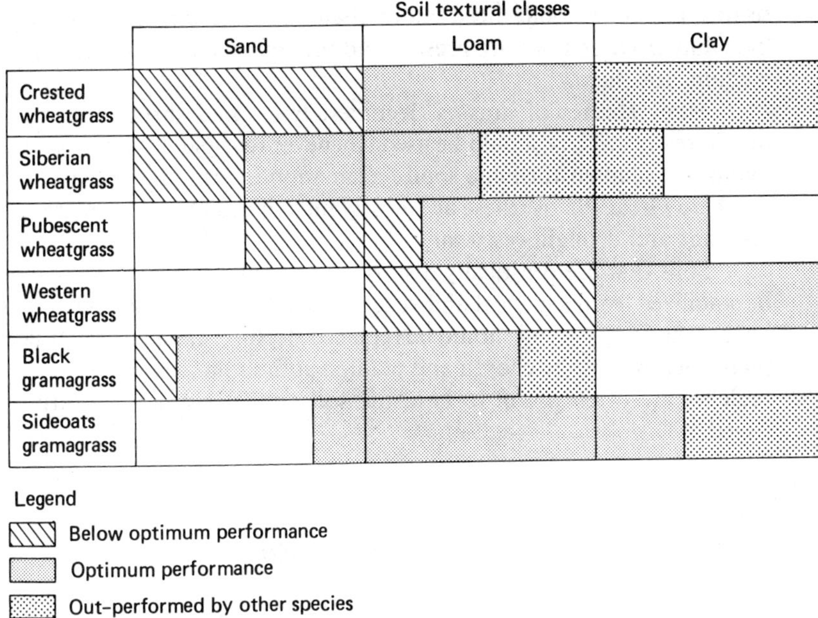

Figure 11–16 Relative adaptability of six grass species to sand, loam, and clay soils in southern desert areas of western United States. (Courtesy U.S. Forest Service, Region 3, Albuquerque, New Mexico.)

SUMMARY

Mine spoils are refuse mainly from surface mining. Spoils consist of rock and soil materials in all degrees of coarseness and fineness. Some contain heavy metals in toxic concentrations and pyrite that oxidizes to toxic sulfuric acid. Some spoils and highwalls are steeper than the stable angle of repose for that material; this causes slumping and destruction of established vegetation.

Mining is necessary to obtain essential minerals. The spoils must be smoothed and vegetated to avoid serious environmental damage. Of all land disturbed by mining in the United States, 41% has been mined for coal, 26% for sand and gravel, and 33% for all other materials. About 40% of the 4.3 million acres (1.74 million hectares) in the United States disturbed by mining has been reclaimed. Reclamation is now taking place at a much faster rate. The U.S. Surface Mining Law 95–87 of 1977 aids the states in enforcing environmentally acceptable reclamation standards for mine spoils. A performance bond on all coal mined is paid by coal companies into a reclamation fund in the Department of Interior. This fee is refunded when the minesoil has been stabilized. Technical assistance in reclamation is provided by the Soil Conservation Service.

Almost all mine spoils are deficient in nitrogen and phosphorus, and some require lime to enhance plant growth. Mulching is also generally helpful. Legumes seeded on mine spoils need more than the normally recommended *Rhizobium* inoculum because none are present and the spoil environment is not an ideal growth medium for them.

Many species of grasses, legumes, trees, and shrubs tolerate acid spoils in humid regions. They should be used whenever feasible. Usually, a different group of plants are adapted for mine spoil reclamation in arid and semiarid regions. For the northern Great Plains, these are mostly introduced cool-season grasses that are salt-resistant and drought-resistant.

Soils that are drastically disturbed by road and highway construction need to be stabilized by mechanical and vegetative techniques. Compacted materials need to be loosened and topsoil should be replaced, fertilized, and limed as needed. Adapted plant species must be chosen and planted at the right season. Companion crops and mulches are often useful to hold the soil until perennial vegetation can be established.

QUESTIONS

1. Explain why mine spoil reclamation is difficult and sometimes almost impossible.
2. What are the mandates of Public Law 95–87 on surface mining legislation?
3. What is pyrite? Why is it environmentally undesirable? What can be done about it?
4. Name two grass and four tree species that can be used to reclaim mine spoils with a pH of 4.0 to 5.5.
5. Discuss the principal differences encountered in reclaiming mine spoils in arid versus humid regions.
6. What principles are important for establishing and maintaining vegetation on all construction sites?

REFERENCES

ALBERICI, T. M., W. E. SOPPER, G. L. STORM, and R. H. VAHNER, 1989. Trace metals in soil, vegetation, and voles from mine land treated with sewage sludge. *J. Env. Qual.* 18: 115–120.

ALDON, E. F., 1978. Reclamation of coal-mined land in the southwest. *J. Soil Water Cons.* 33(2):75–79.

ASHBY, W. C., W. G. VOGEL, and N. F. ROGERS, 1985. *Black Locust in the Reclamation Equation.* Northeastern For. Exp. Sta., Gen. Tech. Rep. NE–105, USDA Forest Service.

AYERS, R. S., and D. W. WESTCOT, 1976. *Water Quality for Agriculture.* Irrig.-Drain. Paper 29. FAO, Rome.

BARKER, R. E., R. E. RIES, and P. E. NYREN, 1977. Forage species establishment and productivity on mined land. *N. Dak. Farm Res.* 34(6):8–12.

BENNETT, O. L., E. L. MATHIAS, W. H. ARMIGER, and J. N. JONES, JR., 1978. Plant materials and their requirements for growth in humid regions. In *Reclamation of Drastically Disturbed Lands.* American Society of Agronomy, Madison, Wis., p. 285–306.

BERG, W. A., 1975. Revegetation of land disturbed by surface mining in Colorado. In *K. W. Mohan (ed.), Practices and Problems of Land Reclamation in Western North America,* Univ. of North Dakota Press, Grand Forks, N. Dak. p. 78–89.

BERNSTEIN, L., 1964. *Salt Tolerance of Plants.* USDA Inf. Bull. 283, p. 10–12.

CARROLL, J., 1978. New federal agency tackles surface mining problems. *J. Soil Water Cons.* 33:77–79.

CURRIER, W. F., 1971. Basic principles of seeding critical areas. In *Proc., Critical Area Stabilization Workshop.* Rep. 7. New Mexico Inter-Agency Range Committee, Albuquerque, N. Mex., p. 106–111.

CYWIN, A., and E. L. HENDRICKS, 1969. An overview of USDI's role in sediment control. *Proc., National Conference on Sediment Control.* U.S. Department of Housing and Urban Development, Washington, D.C.

CZAPOWSKYJ, M. M., 1973. Establishing forest on surface-mined land as related to fertility and fertilization. *Forest Fertilization Symposium Proceedings.* USDA Forest Service, General Tech. Rep. NE-3, p. 132–139.

DAVIDSON, W. H., and W. VOGEL, 1983. Hybrid poplar for reclamation. *Proc., Better Reclamation with Trees,* June 2–3, Terra Haute, Ind. Dept. of Forestry, Purdue University, West Lafayette, Ind.

DUNKER, R. E., ET AL., 1988. *Prime Farmland Reclamation Research in Illinois.* Paper presented at the National Association of State Land Reclamationists annual meetings, Sept. 13–15, La Salle, Ill.

ENVIRONMENTAL PROTECTION AGENCY, 1975. *Methods of Quickly Vegetating Soils of Low Productivity, Construction Activities.* Publ. EPA-440/9–75–006, p. 149–166.

GENERAL ACCOUNTING OFFICE, 1974. *Report to Congress: Modernization of the 1872 Mining Law Needed to Encourage Domestic Mineral Production, Protect the Environment, and Improve Public Land Management.* Rep. B-118678, p. 7.

GRAVES, W. L., B. L. KAY, and W. A. WILLIAMS, 1978. Revegetation of disturbed sites in the Mohave Desert with native shrubs. Calif. Agric. 32:4–5.

HODDER, R. L., 1970. *Roadside Dry-Land Planting Research in Montana.* Montana State Univ., Bozeman, Mont.

LARSON, W. E., L. M. WALSH, B. A. STEWART, and D. B. BOELTER (eds.), 1981. *Soil and Water Resources: Research Priorities for the Nation.* Soil Science Society of America, Madison, Wis. p. 173–184.

MONSEN, S. B. and B. Z. RICHARDSON, 1984. Seeding shrubs with herbs on a semiarid mine site with and without topsoil. In *Proc., Symp. on the Biology of Atriplex and Related Chenopods;* Ogden, Utah. Int.-172. Intermountain For. Range Expt. Sta. USDA Forest Service.

PAONE, J., P. STRUTHERS, and W. JOHNSON, 1978. Extent of disturbed lands and major reclamation problems in the United States. In *Reclamation of Drastically Disturbed Lands.* American Society of Agronomy, Madison, Wis., p. 11–22.

PARIZEK, R. R., 1987. Use of waste products to reclaim stripmined lands. In *Innovative Approaches to Mined Land Reclamation,* C. L. Carlson and J. H. Swisher (eds.). Southern Illinois Univ. Press, Carbondale and Edwardsville, Ill. p. 223–281.

PLOTKIN, S. E., 1987. The Office of Technology Assessment's review of prime farmland reclamation under the 1977 Surface Mining Control and Reclamation Act. In *Innovative*

Approaches to Mined Land Reclamation, C. L. Carlson and J. H. Swisher (eds.). Southern Illinois Univ. Press, Carbondale and Edwardsville, Ill., p. 31–58.

POWER, J. F., R. E. RIES, and F. M. SANDOVAL, 1978. Reclamation of coal-mined land in the Great Plains. *J. Soil Water Cons.* 33:69–74.

ROBINSON, J., 1987. Unresolved issues in the reclamation of western mined lands. In *Innovative Approaches to Mined Land Reclamation,* C. L. Carlson and J. H. Swisher (eds.). Southern Illinois Univ. Press, Carbondale and Edwardsville, Ill., p. 59–70.

SOIL CONSERVATION SERVICE, 1978. *Plant Performance on Surface Coal Mine Spoil in Eastern United States.* Publ. SCS-TP-155, p. 76.

SOPPER, W. E. and E. M. SEAKER, 1983. *A Guideline for Revegetation of Mined Land in the Eastern United States Using Municipal Sludge.* The Pennsylvania State University, School of Forest Resources and Institute for Research on Land and Water Resources, University Park, Pa.

SUTTON, P., and J. P. VIMMERSTEDT, 1973. *Treat Stripmine Spoils with Sewage Sludge.* Ohio Rep. 58:121–123. Ohio Agricultural Research and Development Center, Wooster, Ohio.

THAMES, J. L. (ed.), 1977. *Reclamation and Use of Disturbed Land in the Southwest.* Univ. of Arizona Press, Tucson, p. 362.

THOMPSON, P. J., I. J. JANSEN, and C. L. HOOKS, 1987. Penetrometer resistance and bulk density as parameters for predicting root system performance in mine soils. *Soil Sci. Soc. Am. J.* 51:1288–1293.

U.S. CONGRESS, 1977. *Surface Mining Control and Reclamation Act of 1977.* Public Law 95–87, Washington, D.C.

U.S. DEPARTMENT OF AGRICULTURE, 1974. *Our Land and Water Resources,* May, p. 14.

VERMA, T. R., and J. L. THAMES, 1975. Rehabilitation of land disturbed by surface mining coal in Arizona. *J. Soil Water Cons.* 30:129–131.

12

Vegetating Other Areas of High Erosion Hazard

The actions of water and wind are so concentrated in certain areas that they cause intense erosion hazards. These areas are usually small, but they are the source of large quantities of sediment. This eroded soil is more concentrated than that from other areas and therefore more likely to cause serious sedimentation problems.

Soil particles in transport augment the erosion process by making air and water more abrasive. Wind has to be strong enough to break off large pieces of plants or structures before the airflow can do much damage, but wind carrying soil particles causes damage at much lower velocities. The sandblast effect can erode the stems of plants and wear away fenceposts as well as take the paint off buildings and machines. Soil particles in streams of water also serve as gouging tools that help the stream erode its banks and wear away its bed even where it flows on solid rock.

Concentrated erosion commonly leads to concentrated pollution problems as well. The soil particles in transit produce muddy water and dusty air. When deposited, they fill ponds and lakes by their sheer bulk and contribute plant nutrients that cause unwanted algae to grow in the water (Chapter 17). Floods and wind both deposit thick layers of sediment on land where it can smother plants, cover productive soil, and damage structures and machines. Concentrated erosion, abrasion, and deposition problems are best controlled at the source by protecting the areas of high erosion hazard. This chapter deals particularly with waterways and areas subject to wind erosion.

12–1 WATERWAYS

Runoff water concentrates in waterways that may or may not be stable against erosion. Unstable waterways produce gullies and eroding streambanks that often call for drastic measures to prevent severe damage. Protective action may be needed to slow down runoff from the fields above a waterway as well as in the immediate area. Cropping systems, tillage methods, and structures that hold more of the water in the fields are discussed in Chapters 8, 9, and 10. This section deals with measures applicable to the area of a waterway or the banks of a pond.

12-1.1 Gully Control

Gullies are distinguished from rills by size—the gullies are too large to be crossed and smoothed by normal farming operations. Gullies grow toward the source of runoff water by the eroding action of water falling into them and are deepened by the abrasive action of sediment in the water flowing through them. Some gullies, such as the one shown in Figure 12-1, grow extremely large. Gully control is expensive and becomes even more so when the gully is allowed to grow larger and more complex.

The following procedures are useful for controlling erosion and healing a gully:

1. Diverting water from the head of the gully. This is usually done by constructing a diversion terrace above the head of the gully and diverting the water into a dense forest, a luxuriant pasture, or a constructed vegetated waterway. The diversion terrace should be removed after vegetation in the gully is well

Figure 12-1 Part of a gully near Lumpkin, Georgia, that was neglected and continued to grow for over 100 years until it became several miles long and 50 to 200 ft (15 to 60 m) deep and affected an area of about 100,000 acres (40,000 ha). (Courtesy USDA Soil Conservation Service.)

established. Sometimes the establishment of a terrace system on a field above the gully is more desirable than construction of a single diversion terrace.

2. Grading the head and both sides of the gully to a slope no steeper than the angle of repose for the particular soil. The stable angle is commonly between a 2:1 (26.5° or 50%) and a 3:1 (18.5° or 33%) slope.
3. Building temporary dams across the gully, starting at the head. Any trash or debris in the gully should be removed before dams are built. Each dam of a series constructed down the gully should have the top of the spillway on the same level as (or so the slope is no steeper than 0.5% to) the toe of the dam above it (like stair steps). Temporary check dams can be made of loose rock, lumber, logs, or brush laid between posts (Chapter 10). It is very important to extend the bottom and sides of all dams about 6 in. (15 cm) into undisturbed soil, leave the center low for water to flow over, and to construct an apron on the downhill side of the dam to reduce the velocity of the overflow water and thereby reduce the hazard of water undercutting the dam. The gully may be gradually filled by building new check dams at higher elevations when sediment has filled the space behind the old check dams.
4. Establishing adapted perennial vegetation using some combination of grasses, legumes, trees, and shrubs. The selection of species, varieties, and cultivars is determined by climate, soils, and personal desire of the decision maker.
5. Fencing the entire area around gullies in pasture or range to exclude domestic animals until the vegetation has become established. Fencing is also necessary when trees and shrubs are grazed (browsed) by herbivorous wild animals such as deer.

The five-step control of gullies may be modified on large watersheds [more than 50 acres (20 ha)] by building permanent check dams in the gullies. The materials may be concrete or rock masonry. Sometimes loose rock dams are superior because hydrostatic pressure is not as great behind them, nor do freezing and thawing and the burrowing of wild animals disrupt them as much as concrete or rock masonry dams. Regardless of the type of dam constructed, perennial vegetation should be established around it to deal with the shifting of erosive forces over time. Rigid dams in a dynamic environment are usually not as long-lasting as adapted perennial vegetation.

Some gullies may be controlled by constructing a drop inlet at the head, sloping the banks, installing flumes as shown in Figure 12–2, or converting the eroding gully into a noneroding grassed waterway.

12–1.2 Establishing Vegetated Waterways

Vegetated waterways are natural or constructed channels that have been shaped to transport water at a nonerosive velocity from fields, diversions, terraces, and road ditches. Waterways often must be established on sites that have been seriously damaged by erosion and may suffer from compaction and low soil fertility. Essential steps in establishing waterways include the following:

a

b

Figure 12–2 (a) A large active gully in Alabama. (b) The gully was healed by grading and installing a flume with a drop structure at each end. (Courtesy USDA Soil Conservation Service.)

1. Divert all surface and subsurface flow of water by a diversion terrace or berm before establishing the waterway.
2. Design the size, shape, length, and gradient of the waterway according to the area of watershed, type of vegetation to be used, and maximum 10-year, 24-hour runoff or perhaps 25-year, 24-hour runoff.
3. Construct the waterway and establish erosion-resisting vegetation before constructing terraces or other water-concentrating facilities, as shown in Figure 12–3.
4. The cross section of the waterway may be V-shaped, parabolic, or trapezoidal, as shown in Figure 12–4. If a spring causes continuous wetness in the waterway and stones are readily available, parabolic and open V-shaped waterways should be lined with stone for greater erosion control, as shown in Figure 12–5. An alternative is to place a drain tile line beneath the waterway as described in Chapter 15.

Establishing and maintaining vegetation in the waterway channel requires the application of engineering and agronomic principles and practices. The ability to determine relative soil erodibility is important. The waterway must be designed with a suitable channel gradient and a large enough cross section to carry the runoff water at a nonerosive velocity. Agronomic factors include plant selection, seedbed preparation, soil testing to diagnose lime and fertilizer needs, time and rate of seeding or planting, the use of an appropriate mulch to hasten plant establishment, and proper maintenance of vegetation. Figure 12–6 shows a well-designed and vegetated waterway. Table 12–1 indicates maximum permissible water velocities for

Figure 12–3 This V-shaped grassed waterway in North Carolina was vegetated with tall fescue in preparation for terracing the field. It provides a safe channel to guide runoff water to a permanent stream. (Courtesy USDA Soil Conservation Service.)

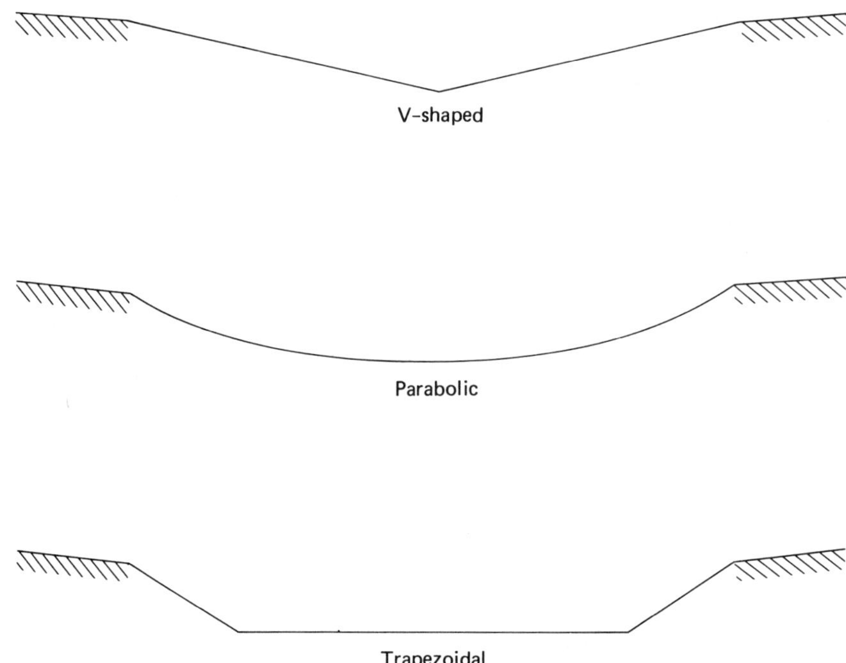

Figure 12–4 Cross sections of most grassed waterways are V-shaped, parabolic, or trapezoidal.

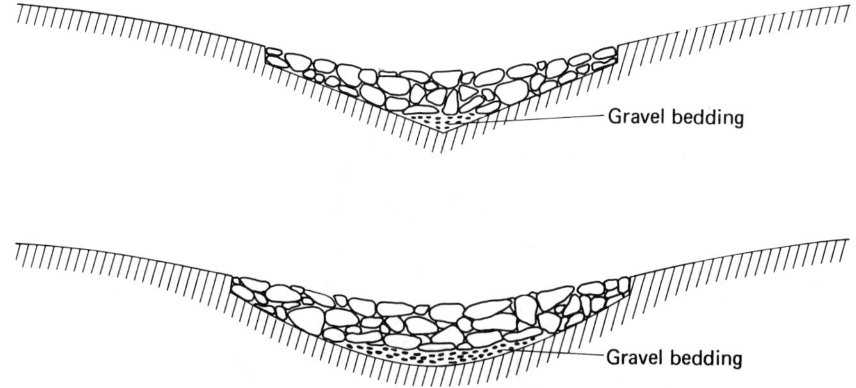

Figure 12–5 Waterways constructed where there is prolonged wetness may need to be drained with a tile line (Chapter 15) or lined with stone, as indicated here, for greater erosion resistance. Stone linings work well with either the V-shape (a) or the parabolic shape (b). (Courtesy USDA Soil Conservation Service.)

specified conditions. Probable velocities for different slope, depth, and surface conditions can be estimated using Manning's formula (Note 4–2).

Following is a brief description of eight grasses used extensively in the areas of their adaptation for vegetating waterways:

Bermudagrass is ideal for use in vegetating constructed waterways in southern,

Figure 12–6 A well-designed and vegetated waterway with a concrete drop outlet to reduce erosion and sedimentation and a tile drain to reduce the time the channel stays wet (note outlet into structure). (Courtesy USDA Soil Conservation Service.)

central, and southwestern United States. It is a tough, vigorous, sod-forming, perennial grass that tolerates both wet and dry soils, as well as acid and alkaline soils. Bermudagrass grows best on fertile fine-textured soils. It propagates by aboveground stolons, belowground rhizomes, and by seed.

Italian ryegrass is a cool-season annual bunchgrass that is adapted to the Pacific Coast states west of the Cascade Mountains and as a winter-season grass in the south. It has a special function on disturbed soils as a rapidly established grass that will stabilize erosion and sedimentation until the proper season for establishing perennial vegetation.

Kentucky bluegrass is a cool-season, sod-forming, long-lived perennial that spreads by underground rhizomes. It grows throughout the humid and irrigated regions of the United States except in the lower part of the Gulf Coast states. It can survive at a soil pH of 6.0 but grows best in the limestone regions where the pH may approach 8.0.

Reed canarygrass is noted for its ability to grow on poorly drained soils and even in standing water. It will grow throughout the United States on acid soils (pH 5.0) and on alkaline soils (pH 8.0). Although a cool-season bunchgrass, when growing in wet soils, it forms a sodlike surface mass of erosion-resisting adventitious roots.

Redtop is a cool-season perennial grass that grows well in northern humid areas on poorly drained soils as acid as pH 4.0. It reproduces by underground rhizomes and tolerates low soil fertility.

Smooth bromegrass is a widely used, cool-season, sod-forming perennial grass that grows best in soils of very high fertility. It is used in soil erosion and sediment

TABLE 12-1 PERMISSIBLE (NONEROSIVE) WATER VELOCITIES ON EROSION-RESISTANT AND EROSION-PRONE SOILS IN CONSTRUCTED WATERWAY CHANNELS SEEDED TO VARIOUS RECOMMENDED GRASSES AND LEGUMES

Grass or legume	Slope range (%)	Permissible water velocity on: Erosion-resistant soils ft/sec	Erosion-resistant soils m/s	Easily eroded soils ft/sec	Easily eroded soils m/s
Bermudagrass	0–5	8	2.4	6	1.8
	5–10	7	2.1	5	1.5
	>10	6	1.8	4	1.2
Bahiagrass, Buffalograss, Kentucky bluegrass, Smooth bromegrass, Blue gramagrass, Tall fescue	0–5	7	2.1	5	1.5
	5–10	6	1.8	4	1.2
	>10	5	1.5	3	0.9
Grass mixtures, Reed canarygrass	0–5	5	1.5	4	1.2
	5–10	4	1.2	3	0.9
Sericea lespedeza, Weeping lovegrass, Yellow bluestem, Redtop, Alfalfa, Red fescue, Common lespedeza, Sudangrass	0–5	3.5	1.1	2.5	0.8

Source: Adapted from U.S. Department of Agriculture, Soil Conservation Service.

control plantings. Two distinct types are identified: northern, adapted to western Canada and the northern Great Plains, and southern, adapted to the Corn Belt and the central Great Plains.

Tall fescue is a vigorous-growing, cool-season, perennial bunchgrass that forms a sodlike cover when seeded heavily. It grows in humid and irrigated areas of the United States except on the lower Gulf Coast. Tall fescue will grow satisfactorily on soils of low fertility. It does better on fine-textured than on coarse-textured soils. Its pH tolerance extends to as low as 5.0 and as high as 8.0.

Western wheatgrass is a cool-season, sod-forming, perennial grass that grows from Wisconsin south to Texas and west to the Pacific Ocean. It is drought resistant and tolerates high soil alkalinity and high sodium.

All of these grasses need to be managed carefully to maintain vigorous stands in vegetated waterways. They should be mowed and fertilized regularly. Both animal and vehicular traffic should be kept off them when they are wet enough to be damaged.

12-1.3 Pond Bank Stabilization

Sometimes a gully is controlled by building an earthen dam across the lower end. The pond thus formed may be cheaper than an excavated or embankment pond of the same volume, but it is likely to have steep banks. Most small farm ponds, however, are formed by excavation in a location where the watershed is large enough to provide the amount of water needed. Water control is important because fluctuating water levels make it difficult to maintain vegetation on the banks.

The proper number of acres of watershed to furnish a specific amount of runoff water for the proper depth and surface area of a pond can be obtained from the regional engineering handbooks of the USDA-Soil Conservation Service.

Specific techniques for establishing adapted vegetation on critical areas around newly constructed ponds, such as that shown in Figure 12-7, are similar to those for stabilizing gullies (Section 12-1.1) and for vegetating construction sites (Chapter 11). However, one special practice may be needed on pond banks subject to wave action caused by high winds. Until the vegetation is well established on such sites, wave energy may be dissipated by floating logs anchored near the shore or by bales of straw anchored in the shallow water.

Figure 12-7 The banks are being stabilized with adapted vegetation around this well-constructed pond in Minnesota. It is a part of the West Willow Creek Watershed project and is designed to store 200 acre-ft (250,000 m³) of water from a 2000-acre (800-ha) drainage area. (Courtesy USDA Soil Conservation Service.)

12-1.4 Streambank Stabilization

Streambank erosion is a major problem. Landowners who can control gullies, stabilize pond banks, and establish effective vegetated waterways often believe that streambank erosion cannot be prevented because it is a form of natural geologic erosion. Whether perceived as geologic or anthropic, streambank erosion cannot be stopped but can be controlled. Work on navigable streams in the United States is the responsibility of the Army Corps of Engineers. Hydraulic engineers and agronomists with the Soil Conservation Service have a mandate from the U.S. Congress to assist landowners in applying streambank erosion control and other conservation activities to smaller streams. The Soil Conservation Service estimates that there are 300,000 mi (480,000 km) of streambanks in the United States that yield 500 million tons (450 million metric tons) of sediment each year.

The following practices help to control streambank erosion:

1. Clearing the stream channel of all trees, shrubs, brush, stumps, and debris drifts.
2. Fencing the critical areas to exclude all livestock until the control measures are firmly established.
3. Establishing one or more of the following mechanical or combination mechanical-vegetative devices according to size of watershed, 10-year maximum flow, and available materials.
   - **(a)** With a planning grant from the Virginia Division of Soil and Water Conservation, Kohnke and Boller (1989) supervised the construction of a wooden crib embedded into an eroding stream bank. Stones were used to stabilize the structure and live plant cuttings (branches) were buried into the bank with the ends exposed. Plants whose branches grew successfully included willow (any species), cottonwood, river birch, sycamore, red maple, and forsythia. All branches were 5 to 10 ft (1.5 to 3 m) long. The branches took root and stabilized the eroding bank (Figure 12–8).
   - **(b)** Mechanical structures such as dikes, toe and hardpoint protectors, revetments, and riprap (Chapter 10) are used if vegetation alone will not provide enough protection. Riprap is illustrated in Figure 12–9.

12-2 WINDBREAKS AND SHELTERBELTS

Windbreaks and shelterbelts are groups of trees and shrubs planted at right angles to the prevailing winds for the purpose of moderating the winds, reducing wind erosion, trapping dust and snow, reducing evaporation, increasing relative humidity, ameliorating the environment for livestock and wildlife, reducing fuel costs in heating and cooling a home, and enhancing the environment for people. *Windbreaks* are small groups of trees and shrubs planted to protect livestock and people. *Shelterbelts* are extensive groups of trees and shrubs planted primarily to protect fields from erosive winds. Windbreaks and shelterbelts can be seen in Figure 12–10.

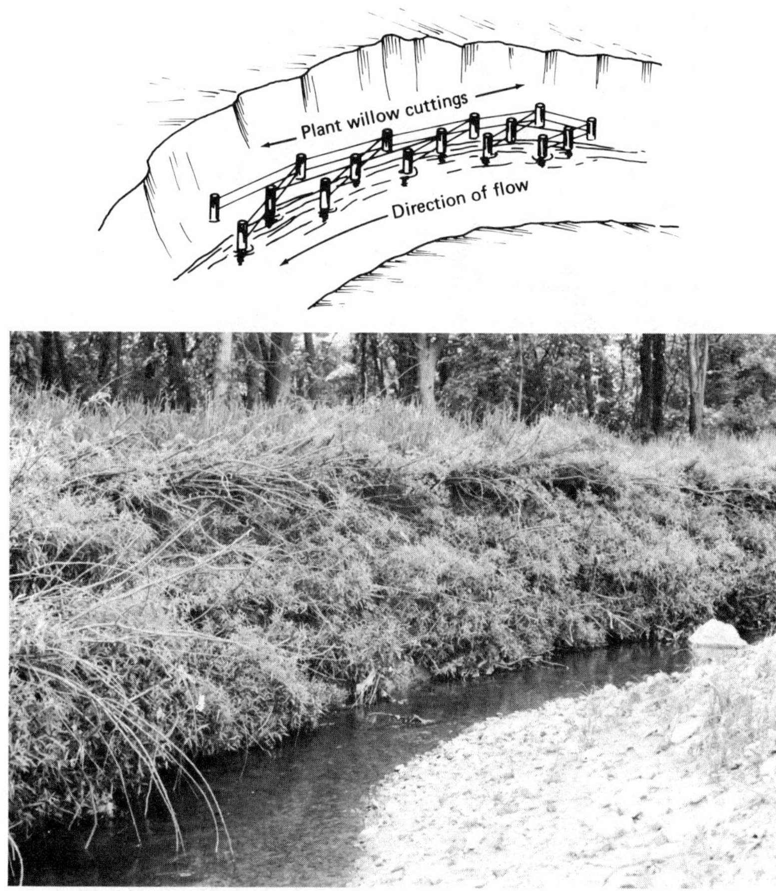

Figure 12–8 Planted woody cuttings have stabilized this eroding streambank in Virginia. The shrubs next to the water are forsythia; trees are willow and cottonwood. (Courtesy Northern Virginia Soil and Water Conservation District.)

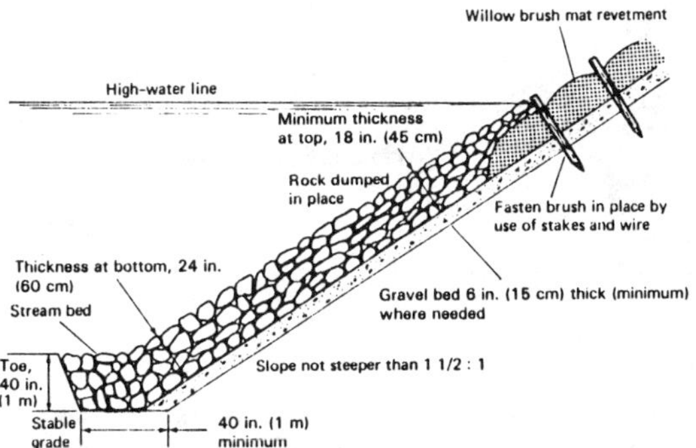

Figure 12–9 Riprap stabilizes a streambank with stones too large for the stream to move. The stones are underlain by gravel so neither soil nor gravel can be washed away. The upper bank is protected by willows. (Courtesy USDA Soil Conservation Service.)

Figure 12–10 Windbreaks around homes and farmsteads ameliorate the weather for people and livestock, and shelterbelts along field borders protect crops against wind erosion in North Dakota (a) and on the High Plains of Texas (b). (Courtesy USDA Soil Conservation Service.)

12-2.1 Wind Erosion

Wind erosion is often very severe in the Great Plains of the United States and Canada and in the USSR (Kort, 1988; Mattis, 1988). Windbreaks and shelterbelts have been used extensively for wind erosion control.

12-2.2 Windbreak and Shelterbelt Effectiveness

Windbreaks reduce winter fuel bills, protect cattle and other livestock, and reduce wind erosion. They also provide food and habitat for wildlife. During the early days of the promotion of windbreaks, the Lake States Forest Experiment Station conducted an experiment at Holdrege, Nebraska, on the home fuel saved by the proper establishment of a windbreak. Two identical homes were selected, one with a windbreak and one without. The home with a windbreak used about 23% less fuel.

Windbreaks and shelterbelts are desirable and almost necessary for economical production of range livestock in northern states. The University of Montana researched this relationship and reported that during a mild winter, tree-protected cattle gained 35 lb (16 kg) more and during a severe winter lost 10 lb (4.5 kg) less than cattle without protection from a windbreak or shelterbelt (USDA-Forest Service).

A windbreak or shelterbelt that is well designed and properly oriented will reduce wind speed to less than half of that in the open, as shown in Figure 12-11. Windbreak effectiveness extends as far leeward as 15 or 20 times the height of the windbreak and windward for about twice its height. Dense windbreaks give the most reduction in wind velocity near the windbreak, but more open ones are effective for a greater distance downwind. The most effective windbreaks have porosities of about 50%. Any reduction in wind speed is important in decreasing wind erosion because the amount of soil eroded is proportional to the fifth power of the wind speed (Chapter 5). Thus the amount of wind erosion is approximately halved when the wind velocity is reduced to 87% of what it would have been without the windbreak.

12-2.3 Trees and Shrubs for Windbreaks

Suitable trees and shrubs for windbreak and shelterbelt plantings adapted to conditions in the northern Great Plains are listed in Table 12-2 and those for the southern Great Plains in Table 12-3. Selection of the most appropriate species depends partly on the number of rows to be included in the windbreak. Traditional windbreaks have had seven rows, with the tallest trees flanked by shorter trees and shrubs. One row of trees should be evergreens for winter protection.

The seven-row windbreak effectively diverts the wind upward but it occupies a lot of land area. This may be justified if the trees chosen can be marketed for wood products when they mature. Otherwise, a smaller windbreak with fewer rows may be preferred. The most effective wind diversion with three-, five-, and seven-row

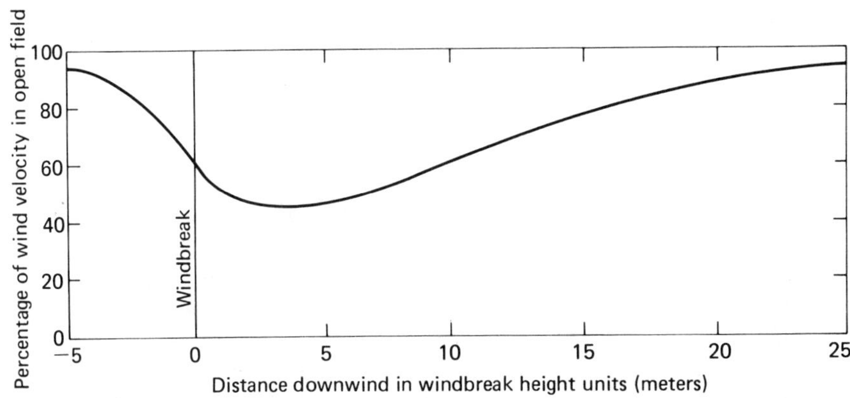

Figure 12–11 Wind velocities about 16 in. (40 cm) above ground level in the vicinity of a windbreak as percentages of what they would be without the windbreak. The curve represents average results of data from several sources. Many data vary ±10% from the curve depending on width, height, and porosity of the windbreak, wind velocity, and topographic features.

windbreaks occurs with the tallest trees in the second, fourth, or fifth row downwind, respectively. The most efficient use of land for windbreaks is achieved with single-row windbreaks. These are usually composed of evergreens so they will provide both summer and winter protection, and they must have branches near the ground so the wind cannot blow under them.

Tree spacing is also important and should be proportioned to the ultimate size of the trees. The mature windbreak should still be open enough to permit some air movement through the windbreak, but there must be no major gaps. Missing trees should be replaced promptly because wind speeds through a gap are likely to be

TABLE 12-2 TREE AND SHRUB SPECIES ADAPTED FOR PLANTING WINDBREAKS AND SHELTERBELTS IN THE NORTHERN GREAT PLAINS

Trees	Shrubs
Austrian pine	American plum
Black Hills spruce	Amur maple
Bur oak	Arnold hawthorn
Colorado blue spruce	Buffaloberry
Cottonwood	Caragana (Siberian peashrub)
Eastern red cedar	Common chokecherry
Green ash	Cotoneaster
Hackberry	Hanson hedgerose
Robusta poplar	Late lilac
Rocky Mountain juniper	Nanking cherry
Siberian crabapple	Redosier dogwood
Scotch pine	Saskatoon serviceberry
White spruce	Silverberry
White willow	Skunk bush sumac
	Tartarian honeysuckle
	Western sandcherry

Source: Soil Conservation Service, 1984a, 1984b.

TABLE 12-3 TREE AND SHRUB SPECIES ADAPTED FOR PLANTING WINDBREAKS AND SHELTERBELTS IN THE SOUTHERN GREAT PLAINS

Trees	Shrubs
Crack willow	American plum
Desert willow	Buckthorn
Eastern redcedar	Caragana (Siberian peashrub)
Hackberry	Chickasaw plum
Honeylocust (thornless)	Cotoneaster
Kentucky coffeetree	Lilac
Mulberry	Redbud
One-seed juniper	
Osage-orange	
Pecan	
Russian olive	
Shortleaf pine	
Sycamore	

Source: USDA–Forest Service.

about 120% of what they would be without the windbreak. Also, windbreaks should end in sheltered or vegetated areas because wind velocities reach about 120% of normal around the ends. Windbreaks should be fenced to keep livestock from eating the vegetation needed to form a good barrier near the ground.

12-2.4 Prairie States Forestry Project

The U.S. Congress authorized the establishment of the Prairie States Forestry Project in 1934 following the drought and dust-storm years of the early 1930s. During the years from 1935 to 1942, 218 million trees and shrubs were planted on 31,000 farms and ranches to establish 20,000 mi (32,000 km) of windbreaks and shelterbelts in the ten Great Plains states from Texas to the Canadian border.

Farmers and ranchers in the Great Plains were pleased to have the new plantings of trees and shrubs because it seemed a sign of government concern during the crisis years of drought and economic depression. Since then, however, farms and ranches have been bought by people from other regions. To operate more efficiently in "normal years," farms have become larger, tractors and equipment larger and more powerful, and large center-pivot irrigation systems are being used in many areas.

12-2.5 Recent Trends

Many farmers, most economists, and some technical agriculturists claim that soil management systems such as strip cropping, stubble mulching, minimum tillage, and clod tillage eliminate the need for windbreaks and shelterbelts. Many existing tree belts are being destroyed, mostly by newcomers to the Great Plains. They refuse to believe that wind erosion and dust storms are hard facts of life in the area.

Many conservationists, however, believe that the new soil management practices are necessary and, furthermore, that plantings of trees and shrubs as windbreaks should be increased tenfold. So, while some windbreaks and shelterbelts in the Great Plains are being destroyed, new ones are being planted. The Forest Service and the Soil Conservation Service offer assistance in establishing trees and shrubs. Recent soil survey reports list the tree and shrub species recommended for planting as windbreaks and shelterbelts on each soil map unit. Cost sharing for planting trees in the Great Plains is available through the Agricultural Stabilization and Conservation Service. Twenty-three plant materials centers operated throughout the United States by the USDA–Soil Conservation Service are constantly searching for and testing new plants for use as windbreaks and shelterbelts in arid and semiarid regions and for water erosion control in humid regions.

12–2.6 Irrigation and Windbreaks

Thousands of windbreaks and shelterbelts have been removed because they interfered with the establishment of large center-pivot irrigation systems. These systems are carried by wheels traveling in concentric circles as described in Chapter 16. The tracks for the wheels must be smooth and nothing should obstruct the moving irrigation pipe; hence, no shelterbelts. However, windbreaks are needed to calm the winds to assure even application of irrigation water.

An example of a compromise solution to the irrigation-windbreak dilemma is presented in Figure 12–12. Four of the usual 133-acre (54-ha) irrigation circles can be

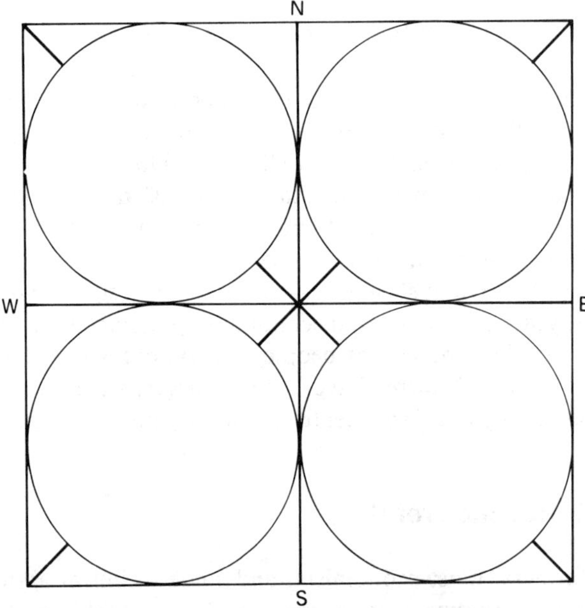

Figure 12–12 A section of land in the United States (1 square mile, 640 acres, or 259 ha) has room for four standard center-pivot irrigation systems. Each circle irrigates about 133 acres (54 ha) of land. Shelterbelts can be planted around the outside and across the middle of the section and, if necessary, along the diagonals. Such shelterbelts reduce wind velocities near the tree lines and improve the distribution of the irrigation water.

arranged in one section (a square mile containing 640 acres or 259 ha) of land and still have a windbreak located every 1/2 mi (0.8 km). The nine odd-shaped areas outside the circles can also be planted to trees or they may be seeded to grass or nonirrigated crops. Such an arrangement will adequately protect the land within about 500 ft (150 m) downwind and 100 ft (30 m) upwind from the windbreaks if the trees are 50 ft (15 m) tall.

12-3 SAND DUNES

Conditions are conducive to the formation of sand dunes on about 3.58 billion acres (1.45 billion hectares), or 11% of the total world land area. Most sand dunes occur in areas of Psamments astride the Tropics of Cancer and Capricorn (23 1/2° north and south latitude, respectively). In the United States, sand dunes occur on many sandy soils in windy areas adjacent to the Atlantic Ocean, the Gulf of Mexico, the Pacific Ocean, and around the Great Lakes. Sand dunes also occur on sandy areas in the interior, such as in Idaho and Nebraska.

Stabilization techniques vary widely, but the principles include reducing wind velocity and establishing a vegetative cover. Dunes in dry climates need irrigation and mechanical obstructions such as a lath "snow" fence to reduce wind velocity and the abrasive action of moving sand while vegetation is becoming established. A surface covering of brush, hay, gravel, clay, oil, or emulsified asphalt can also be used on critical areas. All plants selected should be resistant to damage by grazing and browsing animals. Salt-tolerant plants must be used to vegetate dunes next to salt water.

The first mechanical structure or vegetation established must be on the windward side to reduce wind velocity and thus decrease the amount of moving sand. The entire dune can then be vegetated in stages. Stabilization is more effective and of longer duration when bands of adapted herbaceous plants are planted at right angles to the prevailing winds on the windward side, then a band of shrubs, and finally, a band of trees.

12-3.1 Stabilizing Coastal Dunes

Sand dunes are very active along the coastlines of the Pacific and Atlantic Oceans and the Gulf of Mexico. Shifting sands can be stabilized by planting adapted salt-tolerant vegetation, starting at the high waterline of the ocean. Recommended plants to establish first along the Atlantic Coast from Maine to North Carolina are American beachgrass, European beachgrass, and Volga wildrye. From North Carolina southward to Florida and westward along the Gulf of Mexico, sea oats and sea panicgrass are favored along with broomsedge bluestem and trailing wildbean. On the Texas Gulf Coast, sand dunes have been partially controlled by seacoast bluestem, weeping lovegrass, and veldtgrass. On the Pacific Coast, tall fescue, red fescue, hairy vetch, and beachpea have been used successfully.

Grass should be planted rather than seeded for stabilizing dunes because strong winds along the coasts blow the seed away and sandblast young seedlings. A complete fertilizer should be broadcast over the plantings as soon as growth starts in the spring. Brush is sometimes laid over the plantings to prevent them from blowing out in critical areas.

Adapted shrubs and trees should be interplanted among the grasses to further stabilize the sand. Along the northern part of the Atlantic Coast, native shrubs recommended for planting are beach plum and bayberry. Tree species used successfully include Scotch pine, mugho pine, Austrian pine, and pitch pine. Trees used successfully from North Carolina to Texas to interplant among herbaceous plants include sand pine, Virginia pine, loblolly pine, sweetgum, and several local species of willows. On the Pacific Coast, Scotchbroom (a shrub), Monterey pine, and shore pine are planted among the grasses to further stabilize sand dunes.

12-3.2 Stabilizing Inland Dunes

Sand dunes in the interior of the United States have been stabilized by two contrasting techniques, one without irrigation water and one using irrigation. The nonirrigation system of stabilization consists of first establishing drought-resistant annual plants such as grain sorghum, sudangrass, or rye. Adapted grasses such as sand bluestem, side-oats grama, Indiangrass, switchgrass, and Canada wildrye are seeded in the residues of the annual plants just prior to the next rainy season. When irrigation water is available, the sand dunes can be leveled to slope gradients less than 5%, fertilized according to soil test, and planted to alfalfa, wheat, corn, Irish potatoes, or other adapted field or forage crop.

12-3.3 Stabilizing Great Lakes Dunes

The Great Lakes region has more than 530,000 acres (215,000 ha) of sand dunes. Some of the early practical but scholarly work on sand-dune stabilization was done around the Great Lakes by Michigan State University (Sanford, 1916). It was confirmed by field tests that the proper place to start control was on the windward side of dunes. A typical planting of vegetation to stabilize sand dunes consisted of several rows each of:

1. European beachgrass, American beachgrass, and/or Volga wildryegrass at the windward edge of the shifting sands.
2. Beach pea, wild lupine, sandgrass, wildryegrass, or a combination of these herbaceous plants.
3. Wild rose, ground hemlock, wax myrtle (bayberry), sweetgale, wild red cherry, Virginia creeper, redosier dogwood, snowberry, or a combination of these shrubs.
4. Willow cuttings from any local willow species.
5. A mixture of adapted fast-growing hardwoods and slower-growing conifers. Recommended hardwoods include cottonwood, white poplar, trembling aspen, white birch, red oak, sassafras, silver maple, and black locust. Approved conifers include jack pine, Scotch pine, white spruce, hemlock, and white cedar.

12-3.4 Managing Stabilized Dunes

Good management is essential to prevent deterioration after sand dunes have been stabilized by perennial vegetation. Sand may start blowing again when the vegetation is destroyed along recreation trails of off-road vehicles. Even a foot path may be enough to destroy the protective vegetation. Overgrazing is a common cause of damage; some vegetation is destroyed by fire. Homesites or commercial buildings located on stabilized sand dunes can easily kill enough vegetation to permit the sands to become mobile again.

Persons managing stabilized sand dunes must be alert to all of the preceding hazards. Prompt action must be taken whenever the vegetation is damaged and the soil exposed to the wind. Traffic should be diverted from such areas and steps taken to revegetate them as soon as possible. Mechanical wind barriers may be used either temporarily or permanently in critical areas.

12-4 Disturbed Alpine Sites

Disturbed alpine sites that require rehabilitation include areas overgrazed by sheep, trails for hiking and recreation vehicles, road construction, pipelines and powerlines, reservoir construction, and mining and mineral exploration. The growing season in alpine regions is usually about 60 days, winds are strong, and precipitation comes mostly as snow. Soils are usually thin, rocky, and infertile. Native vegetation is sparse, of few species, and reseeding usually takes three to five years. Common native species are best for seeding in alpine Colorado; these include tufted hairgrass, alpine bluegrass, alpine timothy, spike trisetum, slender wheatgrass, and sedges (Brown and Johnson, 1981).

SUMMARY

Soils in areas of high erosion hazard such as waterways and sites subject to wind erosion need to be stabilized by vegetation. On some sites, the vegetation must be accompanied by mechanical structures. Almost every barren area can be successfully vegetated by using proper agronomic and engineering practices. Good management is needed to maintain the vegetation after it is established.

Gullies are controlled by diverting water from them, grading the banks to stable slopes, building temporary dams, and establishing vegetation. Vegetated waterways can prevent the formation of gullies if they are properly maintained. Pond banks and streambanks need protection from waves and running water.

Windbreaks are established primarily to enhance the ecological environment for people and domestic livestock. Shelterbelts are established for the purpose of reducing wind velocity and wind erosion on cropland. Massive efforts have been expended to establish shelterbelts and windbreaks in the Great Plains where wind erosion and dust storms are a threat during every season of low rainfall.

Sand dunes occur around ocean and lake shorelines and inland in arid and sandy regions. They can be stabilized with vegetation, but several years may be required to establish vegetation on them. Careful management is essential even after the dunes have been stabilized.

QUESTIONS

1. Explain how to control a gully.
2. Why shouldn't waterway channels be allowed to stay wet all the time? How can they be drained?
3. Name three techniques for controlling erosion along streambanks.
4. What are the recent trends in the use of windbreaks and shelterbelts?
5. Explain how to stabilize sand dunes.

REFERENCES

BROWN, R. W., and R. S. JOHNSON, 1981. Reclaiming disturbed alpine lands. *West. Wildlands,* 7(3):38–42.

ENVIRONMENTAL PROTECTION AGENCY, 1975. *Methods of Quickly Vegetating Soils of Low Productivity, Construction Activities.* Publ. EPA-440/9-75-006, p. 467.

ENVIRONMENTAL PROTECTION AGENCY, U.S. ARMY CORPS OF ENGINEERS, and USDA, 1977. *Process Design Manual for Land Treatment of Municipal Wastewater.* Publ. EPA 625/1-77-008 and COE EM 1110-1-501, Oct.

KOHNKE, R. E., and A. K. BOLLER, 1989. Soil bioengineering for streambank protection. *J. Soil Water Cons.* 44:286–287.

KORT, J., 1988. Benefits of windbreaks to field and forage crops. In *Agric. Ecosyst. Environ.* 22/23:165–190.

MATTIS, G., 1988. Scientific achievements in agricultural afforestation in the USSR. In *PFRA Shelterbelt Centre.* Proc. 40th Annual Meeting Great Plains Agricultural Council, Forestry Committee, Regina, Saskatchewan, Canada, p. 98–108.

SANFORD, F. H., 1916. *Michigan's Shifting Sands: Their Control and Better Utilization.* Mich. Agr. Exp. Sta. Spec. Bull. 79, p. 31.

SOIL CONSERVATION SERVICE, 1984a. *Farmstead and Feedlot Windbreak.* Tech. Guide Notice ND-39, North Dakota. Standards and Specifications, Section IV, 380-1.

SOIL CONSERVATION SERVICE, 1984b. *Field Windbreaks.* Tech. Guide Notice ND-39, North Dakota. Standards and Specifications, Section IV, 392-1.

U. S. DEPARTMENT OF COMMERCE, 1987. *Comparative Climatic Data for the United States through 1986.* National Oceanic and Atmospheric Administration, National Climatic Data Center, Federal Bldg., Ashville, N.C.

WRIGHT, D. L., H. D. PERRY, and R. E. BLASER, 1978. Persistent low-maintenance vegetation for erosion control and aesthetics in highway corridors. In *Reclamation of Drastically Disturbed Lands.* American Society of Agronomy, Madison, Wis., p. 553–583.

13

Pastureland, Rangeland, and Forestland Management

There are no better soil stabilizers than luxuriant pasture grasses and legumes, range grasses, and forest trees and shrubs. Close-growing perennial vegetation cushions the impact of raindrops on soil and thereby decreases soil dispersion and sheet erosion. The velocity of surface water flow is reduced by contact with plant stems and residues. The result is clean water flowing slowly along the soil surface, more and faster infiltration of water into deep soil horizons, and less soil erosion and sediment. Vegetation also stabilizes soil against wind erosion by the "holding" action of plant roots and by decreasing wind velocity at the soil–atmosphere interface.

An example of the effectiveness of vegetation in increasing infiltration of rainfall, and thereby decreasing runoff and erosion, is reported by Hart (1974) as shown in Figure 13–1. Soils used for pastures and meadows permit more rapid infiltration than soils used for clean-tilled crops. Heavy grazing in pastures and bare areas in cropland reduced the infiltration rates.

In humid areas, soils subject to wind erosion, such as sand dunes along the shores of the Great Lakes and most oceans, are relatively easy to stabilize. Salt-resistant perennial vegetation can be established even near an ocean. Wind erosion in arid and semiarid areas is much more difficult to control because there is seldom enough water to support close-growing vegetation.

13–1 PASTURELAND, RANGELAND, AND FORESTLAND

Pastureland usually refers to an intensively managed humid area that supports forage such as improved grasses or a mixture of grasses and legumes. Pastureland is usually plowed and fertilized every few years. Pastures in arid and semiarid areas are often irrigated.

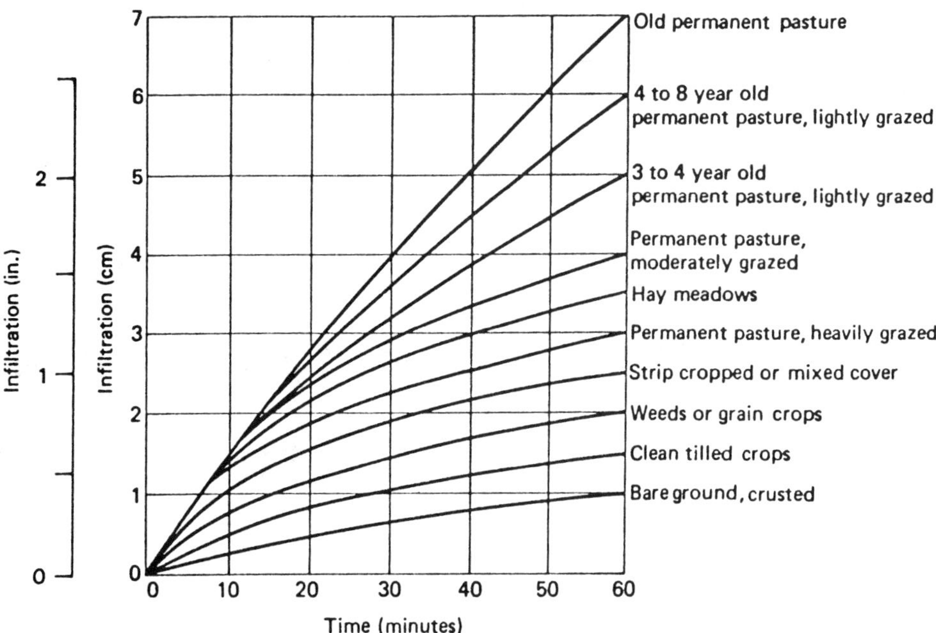

Figure 13-1 Increasing intensity of use reduces the rate of water infiltration into soil. (Courtesy USDA Agricultural Research Service.)

Rangeland refers to unplowed areas where native grasses, forbs, shrubs, and trees are used for forage. Some ranges may be fertilized and reseeded to native or exotic grasses; they are seldom plowed.

Forestland is an area of growing trees or of soil capable of supporting trees. A tree is any woody plant at least 15 ft (4.5 m) high supported by a single stem. Table 13-1 shows the area of pastureland, rangeland, and forestland in the United States.

The general distribution of pastureland, rangeland, and forestland can be inferred from the map of native vegetation of the conterminous 48 states shown in Figure 13-2. Most of the pastures are in areas that originally grew either forests or tall grasses. Present rangeland for domestic livestock includes most of the areas shown as shortgrass, mesquitegrass, sagebrush, creosote bush, and arid woodland. A large percentage of the forests of southeastern United States is also used as

TABLE 13-1 PASTURELAND, RANGELAND, AND FORESTLAND IN THE 50 UNITED STATES

Land use	Total area	
	million acres	million ha
Pastureland	133.3	53.9
Rangeland	405.9	164.3
Forestland	393.8	159.4
Total pasture-, range-, & forestland	933.0	377.6

Source: National Research Council, 1986a.

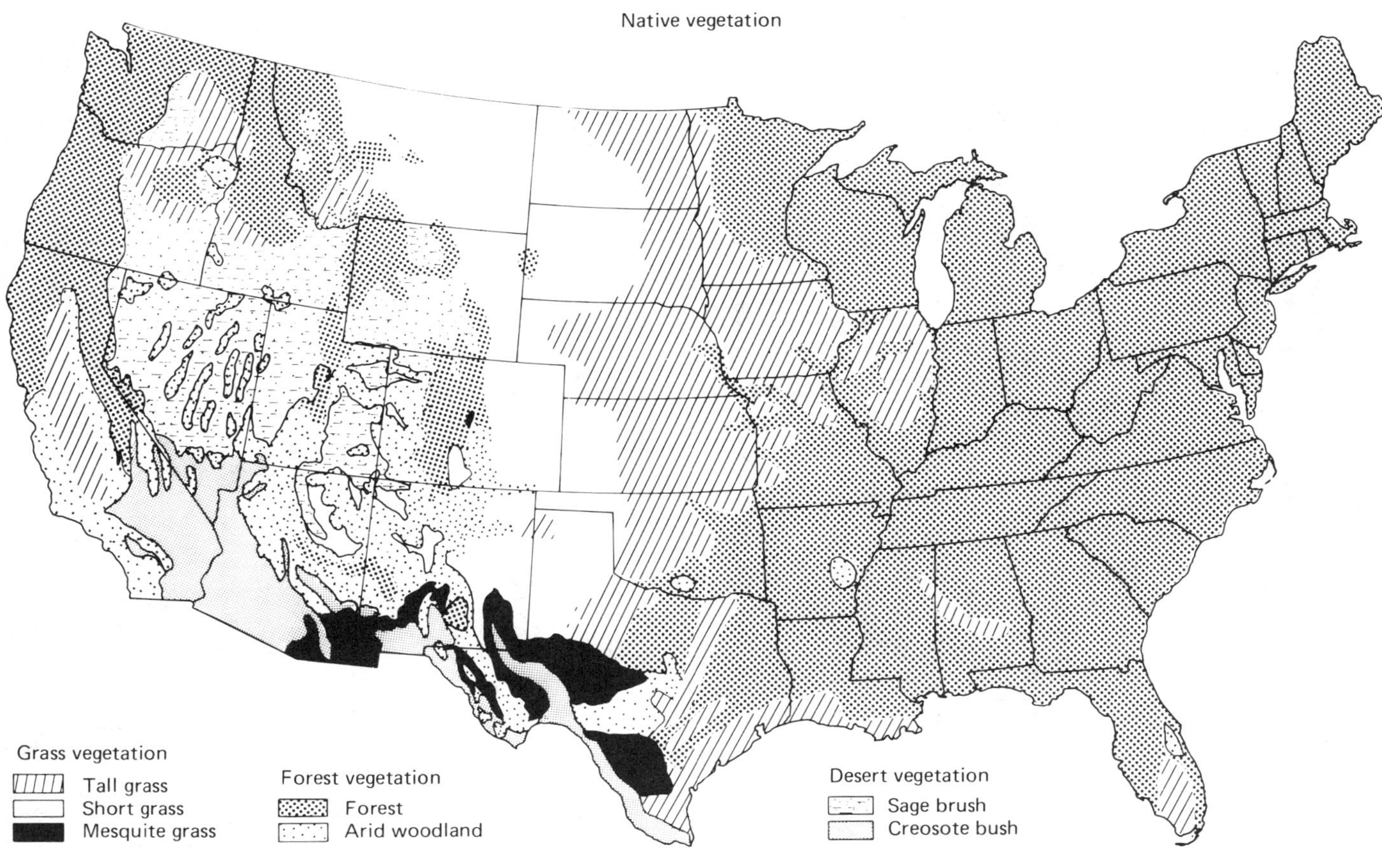

Figure 13-2 Native vegetation in the conterminous 48 states. (Courtesy Raphael Zon, USDA Forest Service, and H. L. Shantz, USDA.)

rangeland. Most forestlands occupy parts of the areas identified in the map as forest vegetation. Tree growth is the most efficient way known for converting carbon dioxide into carbohydrate and oxygen.

The U.S. Department of Agriculture estimates that it will take up to 45 million acres (18 million hectares) of new forest trees to absorb and store the carbon dioxide produced by fossil fuel. It is claimed that only in this way can global warming and the greenhouse effect be controlled (Dudeck, 1988).

13-2 PASTURELAND MANAGEMENT

The approach of the pasture manager should be agronomic; that is, the manager uses pasture species suited to the soil and climate of the area. Lime and fertilizers are applied according to soil test recommendations that are correlated with field plot responses. Tillage operations are used when needed to improve the quality of the pasture. All of these activities are coordinated with the livestock specialist for the ultimate benefit of the livestock producer. On the average, pastures in the United States are well managed for erosion control. Soil erosion by water averages 1.4 tons/ac (3 mt/ha) annually, and erosion by wind is near zero. About 9% of U.S. pastures are irrigated.

13-2.1 Fertility Management of Pastures

Soil tests can identify needs for fertilizers and soil amendments. Fertilizers cannot be utilized efficiently by plants when the soil is too acid or toxins are present in lethal quantities. On acid soils, the application of lime will reduce acidity, lower the exchangeable aluminum, and make soil phosphorus more readily available. Excessive sodium and alkalinity may be corrected with gypsum.

Nitrogen is the nutrient most likely to limit the growth of pasture grasses. However, excessive applications cause luxury consumption and lead to a large increase in top growth but not in root growth. High rates of nitrogen fertilizers favor grasses in a legume-grass mixture and decrease atmospheric nitrogen fixation by legume *Rhizobium*. Even moderate rates of nitrogen fertilizer on sandy soil may move into the water table and increase the nitrate (NO_3) level above 10 ppm, the threshold for potable water (Owens, 1989).

Phosphorus is often the second most critical nutrient in pasture production and, indirectly, in controlling soil erosion. Phosphorus fertilizer is most efficiently applied before or at the time of seeding. As much as a three-year supply of phosphorus can often be applied at this time because very little will leach from the soil. Topdressing a pasture with phosphorus fertilizer is less efficient because the phosphorus moves downward very slowly.

Potassium is required on many pastures, especially in humid regions and on sandy soils in semiarid areas. Plants will absorb more potassium than they need (luxury consumption) when it is applied in surplus. Low available soil magnesium or surplus plant absorption of K^+ or NH_4^+ may cause a decrease in plant uptake of magnesium. When forages contain less than 0.20% magnesium (Mg) and cattle blood serum is less than 1.5 mg/100 ml, grass tetany (hypomagnesemia) usually results. This nutritional disease is often fatal to cattle.

Animal manures and sewage sludges are effective fertilizers on pastures. The amounts and the times of application, however, must be reasonable to comply with pasture plant requirements as well as to ensure environmental integrity (Chapter 17).

13-2.2 Grazing Management of Pastures

Grazing management is one of the most neglected pasture practices. The principal management systems are: (1) continuous, (2) rotational, and (3) deferred grazing.

Continuous grazing means placing livestock on a pasture and allowing them to graze there until the end of the grazing season. When the stocking rate is moderate, this system is suitable for such grass species as bermudagrass, Kentucky bluegrass, pangolagrass, perennial ryegrass, and tall fescue. There is a tendency, however, to graze the pasture with the same stocking rate throughout the grazing season, with the result that it is underused during the spring flush of growth and overgrazed during dry weather and dormant periods. Consequently, pasture productivity may decrease and soil erosion and sediment yield may take place if the land is sloping.

Rotational grazing means placing fences so that livestock can graze only part of the pasture at a time. This grazing system is best adapted to grasses such as bromegrass and intermediate wheatgrass. Such grasses should not be grazed closer to the ground than about 4 in. (10 cm). This system has the potential of producing more total pasturage per unit of land by permitting the seeding of each subdivision to grasses or grass mixtures with different seasons of growth. For example, tall fescue, a cool-season grass, might be seeded in one pasture subdivision and grazed early in the spring. Another subdivision could be seeded to bermudagrass, which produces most abundantly in midsummer.

Some pastures are rotated on a daily basis by means of movable electric fences. Daily pastures with many animals in a small area cause the livestock to utilize the vegetation more completely rather than choosing only the most succulent growth. This technique reduces the bloat hazard of grazing legumes such as alfalfa.

Deferred grazing means delaying the grazing period either to permit the most desirable grass species to become more vigorous or produce seed or both, or until a freeze has stopped growth of leaves and stems. Such "frosted pasturage" is often ideal when other forage is scarce or expensive. Deferred grazing and rotational grazing work well in combination. The livestock can graze in one pasture while another is being deferred. Different pastures can be deferred each year in a rotation sequence that maintains productive vegetation in all of them.

13-2.3 Pasture Renovation

Most perennial pastures deteriorate at times because of overgrazing, soil compaction, drought, insects, diseases, a decrease in percentage of legumes, or a depletion of one or more essential plant nutrients. On sloping pastures, such deterioration is usually accompanied by soil erosion and sediment transport that pollutes surface waters. The solution is pasture renovation.

Pastures should be renovated when their productivity declines to between 50 and 75% of their potential. A small-grain crop is sometimes grown before reseeding pasture if the soil is suitable, but pasture is reseeded immediately where the erosion hazard is high. Either way, a suitable seedbed must be prepared, preferably with crop residues left as a protective mulch.

Renovation of a pasture is usually accomplished by chiseling or disking on the contour, sometimes applying herbicides to kill existing vegetation, adding lime and fertilizers as indicated by soil tests, then reseeding with the pasture mixture recommended for that specific soil series and season. Livestock must be kept off the renovated pasture until the new vegetation is well established.

A newer technique of pasture renovation to reduce soil erosion includes heavy grazing of the existing forage followed by the use of a contact herbicide and then seeding the pasture mixture directly into the dead sod. A modification of this system uses a special implement that ties the dead sod down to mineral soil in bands about 4 in. (10 cm) wide in which the seeds are planted. In the southern United States, cool-season legumes such as crimson clover may be seeded into a warm-season grass pasture. In the northern United States, legumes such as white clover, alfalfa, birdsfoot trefoil, and crownvetch can be seeded in this manner.

13-3 RANGELAND MANAGEMENT

Rangeland is soil on which the native vegetation is predominantly grasses, grasslike plants, forbs, or shrubs suitable for grazing or browsing. This includes natural grasslands, savannas, shrublands, open woodlands, deserts, tundra, mountain (alpine) vegetation, coastal marshes, and wet meadows (Wright and Siddoway, 1982).

The range manager should take an ecological approach; that is, use mostly native plants, and control kinds and numbers of livestock to encourage the growth of the most desirable forage species. The control of soil erosion and sedimentation is of immediate concern to the range manager because water and wind erosion reduce the forage produced for the range livestock. Sedimentation cannot be ignored because it reduces the storage capacity of watering ponds after each heavy rain. Since the range manager usually cannot directly control erosion, the best recourse is to prevent it by limiting the rate of stocking. A five-year study was made on Oklahoma and Texas rangelands versus croplands to compare runoff and erosion sediment yield. Whereas runoff was greater on cropland by only 12% (1.5 in./yr = 38 mm/yr), erosion on croplands was 295% more than on rangelands (Smith et al., 1983).

On privately owned rangelands in the United States, wind erosion is estimated to average 1.5 tons/ac-yr (3.4 mt/ha-yr) and water erosion about 1.4 tons/ac-yr (3.1 mt/ha-yr) (National Research Council, 1986b). The beneficial effects of proper grazing management can be seen in Figure 13-3.

13-3.1 Grazing Management of Rangelands

Although rangelands include much of the open pine and hardwood lands of humid regions, the principal areas are in the arid and semiarid regions. Rangelands in these

Figure 13-3 Highly productive bluestem grasses on alkaline soils in Texas rangeland managed by the U.S. Forest Service (right) and deteriorated private rangeland (left) where a sparse growth of buffalograss has replaced the bluestems in this 32-in. (800-mm) precipitation zone. (Courtesy USDA Soil Conservation Service.)

drier regions include tall grass prairies, short grass plains, and semidesert areas supporting sparse bunchgrasses, forbs (broadleaved, herbaceous plants), and woody shrubs.

The following range management practices increase the amount and efficiency of use of range forage as well as protect the soil against wind and water erosion, as shown in Figure 13-4.

1. Seeding of improved grass cultivars.
2. Delaying spring grazing until the grasses have a good start and the soil is dry enough to avoid trampling damage.
3. Grazing the range simultaneously with cattle and sheep.
4. Adjusting the rate of stocking to the season of growth of grass and to precipitation.
5. Leaving about 50% of all range forage for reserve and residue. In the words of the best ranchers, "graze half and leave half."
6. Integrating range grazing with the grazing of irrigated pastures.
7. Practicing rotational and deferred grazing. This usually requires building more cross fences, establishing more water facilities as in Figure 13-5, and adding more salt boxes.
8. Moving salt periodically to undergrazed areas away from the water so that cattle will graze the range as uniformly as possible. Cattle need both salt and water, but not together. Beef cattle can walk a mile or more for a drink, and need only one drink every second day.

a

b

Figure 13–4 Stocking rates must be adjusted to the season of growth of the grass and to the precipitation, as shown by these semiarid rangelands in California. (a) Overgrazed rangeland with benchlike slumping caused by cattle trails and weakened grasses. (b) Well-managed rangeland with abundant grass and stable soils. (Courtesy Agricultural Experiment Station, University of California.)

Figure 13-5 Good grazing management includes establishment of enough fences and water facilities to permit rotational and deferred grazing. A cowboy noticed wild iris growing here and realized it meant wetness. This small pond dug with a bulldozer provides livestock water throughout the grazing season. (Courtesy U.S. Department of Agriculture.)

9. Clearing brush from ranges to encourage the growth of desirable forage grasses.

Proper grazing management will keep wind and water erosion to acceptable levels (*T*-values) except in areas where conditions are too severe for treatment to be feasible. Such an area is the Sonoran Basin, a desert area in southern California, western Arizona, and southern Nevada. Mean annual precipitation is 2 to 4 in. (50 to 100 mm). Although water erosion is negligible, wind erosion is severe (National Research Council, 1986c).

13-3.2 Burning Bluestem Ranges

In the Great Plains, annual burning of the little bluestem and big bluestem range increases the quality of forage for livestock. Reasons cited in favor of burning include weed control, insect control, earlier growth, more total growth, and improved forage quality. Opponents of range burning claim it increases air pollution and soil erosion and is poor aesthetically.

Hyde and Owensby (1970) cite results of range burning in the 30-in. (760-mm) annual precipitation belt in Kansas for a 20-year period. They concluded that burning a bluestem range at the same time the bluestem grasses start to grow, usually about May 1, results in the greatest gain of yearling beef cattle, 104 lb/ac (117 kg/ha) versus 94 lb/ac (105 kg/ha) for the unburned range. This is true despite the fact that the unburned range produced the most total forage. Damage to the environment from range burning must be weighed against the 10 lb/ac additional gain in beef each year. The conflict can be solved only by further research that measures aesthetics, air pollution, and soil erosion against range condition and beef production.

13-4 FORESTLAND MANAGEMENT

Chlorophyll in green plants has the capability to use energy from the sun, carbon dioxide from the air, and water to make glucose and liberate molecular oxygen. A simplified equation of this reaction follows:

$$\underset{\substack{\text{carbon}\\ \text{dioxide}}}{6\ CO_2} + \underset{\text{water}}{12\ H_2O} \xrightarrow[\substack{\text{chlorophyll in}\\ \text{chloroplasts}}]{\text{light}} \underset{\substack{\text{glucose}\\ \text{(fixed}\\ \text{organic}\\ \text{carbon)}}}{C_6H_{12}O_6} + \underset{\substack{\text{molecular}\\ \text{oxygen}}}{6\ O_2} + \underset{\text{water}}{6\ H_2O}$$

Trees fix more organic carbon and release more molecular oxygen than other plants to neutralize the "greenhouse effect" (Mellor and Jensen, 1986).

Agroforestry techniques such as "alley cropping" have recently become popular, especially in tropical countries. This is a practice of planting leguminous trees and shrubs on sloping lands in widely spaced rows on the contour and growing cultivated crops between them. Leaves and small branches are pruned periodically and used as a surface mulch and fertilizer. The rows of trees and shrubs catch enough eroding soil to establish a terrace (Eylands and Yamoah, 1989; Kang and Onafeko, 1989; Shannon et al., 1989; Raintree, 1982).

Forests grow mostly in humid regions; however, the term "forestlands" includes many semiarid areas. The definition of forestland requires only 10% of the area to be occupied by trees. Total area in the United States so classified is 393.8 million acres (159.5 million hectares) distributed as shown in Figure 13-6.

13-4.1 Forests and Watersheds

Well-managed forests are unsurpassed as a vegetative cover for watersheds. Leaves, branches, and the leafy organic layer on the forest floor break the velocity of falling raindrops. Rain may slowly infiltrate layers or be held by the spongy leaf litter and fine roots. Some water moves down branches and trunks and infiltrates into the soil along root channels. The net result is that a properly managed forest has more infiltration and less runoff, erosion, and sedimentation than it would have as cropland. Furthermore, slow, deep seepage gives rise to many springs and to a three- to five-day delay in flood crests.

Figure 13–6 Commercial forestland in the conterminous United States. (Courtesy USDA Forest Service.)

Forest trees are excellent protectors of the watershed but only after a uniform cover of at least 2 in. (5 cm) of surface leaves or needles has accumulated and remains throughout the year, as shown in Figure 13–7. A new pine plantation on severely eroded and eroding soils in northern Mississippi, for example, effectively controlled erosion and sediment yield only after a period of about four to five years (Ursic and Dendy, 1963).

The selection of forest tree species that are adapted to the soil is important in reforestation, whether done primarily to grow commercial forests or to reduce soil-erosion sediments. Guidance is given by several agencies, but the reports and maps of the National Cooperative Soil Survey are the most site specific. The soil interpretations for woodland use are based on 22,000 plots of trees planted or managed on representative soil series throughout the United States where climate and soils favor tree growth.

13–4.2 Harvesting Methods and Erosion Potentials

Harvesting forest trees always makes the soil less productive. Heavy logging machinery compacts the soil, thus increasing its bulk density and soil strength, decreasing water infiltration and decreasing growth of the next generation of trees by 5 to 15%. Furthermore, from 5 to 10% of the forest area must be dedicated to haul roads, thereby decreasing the area of tree growth and causing erosion on the bare sloping soils.

Figure 13–7 This 10-year-old slash pine plantation in Oklahoma was established on abandoned, eroded cropland. These trees and their thick needle layer have been fully protecting the area against erosion and sedimentation for at least five years. (Courtesy USDA Soil Conservation Service.)

Skid trails lay bare up to 10% of the forest tract being logged. Such trails can cause serious erosion, soil compaction, and loss of soil productivity. The burning of slash following logging also has a detrimental effect on soil productivity for the succeeding forest crop. Hot slash fires cause soil hydrophobicity (resistance to wetting), resulting in less infiltration and more runoff and erosion. Light slash burns remove the slash cover, exposing the darker soil surface, which absorbs more rays of the sun. Tree seedlings may thereby be killed by heat. The resulting ash may be a beneficial fertilizer if not in excess. Large amounts of ash from slash fire could increase surface soil pH so high as to cause phosphorus tie-up and reduced availability of Fe, Mn, Cu, and Zn (Froehlich, 1988; Megahan, 1988; Ballard, 1988).

Research studies by the Southeastern Watershed Research Laboratory at Tifton, Georgia, have shown that streamside trees are good filters of sediment and nutrients that could contaminate surface waters. Trees filtered out and there was deposited an average of 19.4 tons of sediment per acre per year (43.5 mt/ha-yr). The streamside trees also absorbed substantial amounts of N, P, K, and Mg (Lawrance and Leonard, 1988). Care should be taken to preserve these benefits when harvesting trees near a stream.

The amounts of bare soil and sediment produced by a variety of pine timber harvesting methods were compared in eastern Texas. The traditional method is to clear cut, kill hardwoods by knocking them down with a bulldozer while piling slash and burning it, and replant pine. For comparison, clearcutting was followed by a large, sharp chopper-roller. The chopper exposed about one-fourth as much bare soil and resulted in less than one-tenth as much sediment yield as the bulldozer (DeHaven, 1983).

There are four principal methods of harvesting trees: selection, shelterwood, seed tree, and clearcutting. Each method has its own advantages and effects on erosion potential as follows.

Selection. The selection method consists of removing individual trees or small groups of trees as they mature. The result is a stand of trees with all ages intermixed. It is adapted to tree species that will reproduce satisfactorily under severe competition for soil moisture, nutrients, and light. Less tolerant tree species need larger openings in the forest canopy to favor their reproduction. The only significant erosion potential resulting from the selection method of harvest is that caused by traffic to remove the trees.

Shelterwood. The shelterwood system removes all mature trees in a series of harvests several years apart. Heavy-seeded species such as oaks usually reproduce well under the partial shade resulting from this system. The resulting forest stands are nearly even-aged, yet there is always an overstory to shelter the site. Very little erosion and sedimentation result from the shelterwood method.

Seed Tree. The seed-tree method leaves only enough trees to bear seed for natural regeneration. The seed trees may be harvested after a new even-aged forest is established. It is applicable to trees such as the southern pines (loblolly, longleaf, shortleaf, and slash) having light seed that can be borne by the wind. The potential for soil erosion and sediment pollution is great for a few years after harvest.

Clearcutting. Clearcutting removes all the trees from the logged area. The purpose is to clear the area to establish a new even-aged stand of a valuable fast-growing species that will not reproduce satisfactorily in the shade of other trees. It is often used for Douglas-fir in the Pacific Northwest, for certain species of pine, and for black cherry in the Allegheny Mountains. The clearcut area may consist of patches, strips, or an entire watershed. It has the advantage of permitting efficient use of high-lead, skyline, balloon, or helicopter logging systems. Clearcutting is strongly opposed by many environmentalists because it causes a severe erosion hazard.

13-4.3 Log Transport Systems and Soil Disturbance

The principal log transport systems include logging by tractor, highlead cable, skyline cable, balloon cable, and helicopter as shown in Figure 13-8. In general, the systems that cause the least soil disturbance are the most expensive.

Tractor Logging. Tractor logging is the most popular system of moving logs to the log yard for loading. Forests on slopes of less than about 30% are usually logged by tractors; on slopes of more than 30% and on very fragile soils, the skyline, balloon, and helicopter systems of transport are less injurious to the environment.

Tractor logging is substantially less expensive than other log transport systems. Soil disturbance, however, is greater than for any other log transport system because the tractors and the logs they drag make erodible skid trails across the forest floor.

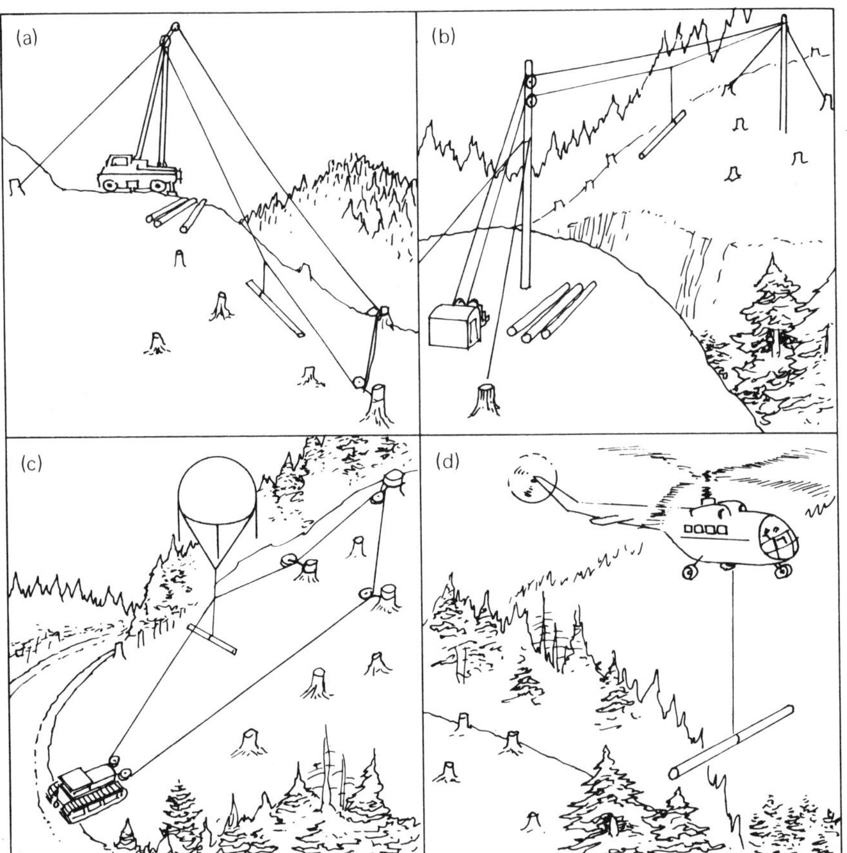

Figure 13-8 The principal log transport systems used to remove logs from a forest being harvested are (a) high-lead cable, (b) skyline cable, (c) balloon cable, (d) helicopter, and (not shown) tractor logging.

In northwestern United States, the return to normal bulk density of soil on skidtrails made by tractor logging was studied by Froehlich et al. (1985). The 2-in. (5-cm) depth of skid trails on granitic soil was the only soil layer whose bulk density returned to normal in 23 years. At all other depths on granitic soil and at all depths on volcanic soil, the bulk density remained higher than normal. Such soil layers restrict plant root growth.

High-Lead Cable. The high-lead system of logging uses a mobile spar and yarder with mounted engine and winches to drag logs toward a loading yard. Only the front ends of the logs are lifted to clear obstacles or to reduce soil disturbance. The logs make skid trails as they are moved to the yarding area. Each skid trail could be the beginning of a gully.

Skyline Cable. As early as 1915, skyline cable logging was tried as a method adaptable to remote areas, steep slopes, and unstable soils where road building creates excessive erosion from landslides and exposed cuts and fills. When operated skillfully, skyline cable logging does not produce skid trails because the entire log is lifted in transport. Erosion is therefore minimal.

Balloon Cable. This system uses a balloon to lift and transport logs. It is well adapted to steep slopes (up to 90%) and shallow or fragile soils, where only helicopter logging or skyline logging may compete. The system is also adapted to selective logging where the minimum harvest is about 1000 ft^3/ac (70 m^3/ha).

Balloon logging causes soil disturbance only at the yarding areas, from which trucks haul the logs to the mill. Yarding areas can be as far as 3000 ft (900 m) apart, but they must be downhill from the logged areas and therefore may be a hazard to streams. Balloon logging is more expensive than all other logging systems except helicopter logging.

Helicopter Logging. Logging by large helicopter so minimizes erosion that it is the apparent answer to the fondest dreams of concerned environmentalists. Logging by helicopter requires fewer access roads (and therefore results in minimized sediment pollution of streams) and is the most versatile system of moving logs from where they are cut to a yarding area for truck loading and hauling, but it costs more per cubic foot of lumber. A weakness in the helicopter system is the need to enter the forest on the ground to replant, thin trees, and take out the commercial thinning (poles) and for fire control.

Typical soil disturbance caused by each of the log transport systems, except helicopter, in the northwestern United States is presented in Table 13-2. Tractor logging causes more bare soil and more soil compaction than any other log transport system. Logging by balloon causes the least soil disturbance. Balloon logging causes 83% less bare soil and 94% less compacted soil than tractor logging. Soil disturbance by the helicopter system would be about the same as that for balloon logging.

13-4.4 Grazing Forestlands

About half of all forestlands are grazed by domestic livestock. The percentage varies from 41% in the northeastern to 83% in the western United States. Forest range as a

TABLE 13-2 EFFECTS OF LOG TRANSPORT SYSTEMS ON SOIL DISTURBANCE

	Soil disturbance[a] (%)	
Log transport system	Logged watershed with bare soil	Logged watershed with compacted soil
Tractor	35.1	26.4
High-lead	14.8	9.1
Skyline cable	12.1	3.4
Balloon cable	6.0	1.7

[a]Compacted soil averaged about 40 to 50% higher in bulk density than uncompacted soil. Actual values of the 0-2 in. (0-5 cm) depth of the latter were between 0.6 and 0.7 g/cm^3.

Source: Rice, et al. (1972).

percentage of all land is depicted by states and regions in Figure 13-9. The results of livestock grazing farm woodlands are nearly always detrimental to tree reproduction and growth. Animals trample and compact the soil (especially fine-textured soil), injure shallow roots, and browse on tree seedlings and sprouts.

Grazing of nonfarm forestlands is usually not as destructive as grazing of farm woodlands because of fewer cattle per unit area of forest, more coarse-textured and stony soils, less soil compaction by trampling, and more conifers that are not browsed as much as hardwoods. In addition, the pinelands of the southern and western states include many open forests with areas of forage grasses. The grasses, forbs, and hardwood seedlings and sprouts make fair-to-good forage during the months of April through July. Supplemental forage can be supplied by establishing improved pasture on all fire lanes and forest roads. When livestock graze these fire lanes, forest roads, and the forestlands in general, they reduce the fire hazard by removing vegetation that is flammable when dry.

Grazing of forestlands always increases the hazard of water erosion. Table 13-3 indicates that the average grazed forest in the United States erodes at the rate of 2.3 tons/ac-yr (5.2 mt/ha-yr). Forests not grazed erode at less than one-third of this rate. Wind erosion in forests is negligible.

13-4.5 Fertilizing Forestlands

The use of chemical fertilizers on forests has been increasing along with the value of forest products. The present fertilizer used on forest is mostly nitrogen; its use is centered on the Douglas-fir region of the Pacific Northwest and in the southern pine region. In addition, young stands of commercial redwood in northern California and the western hemlock-sitka spruce forest type along the coasts of Alaska,

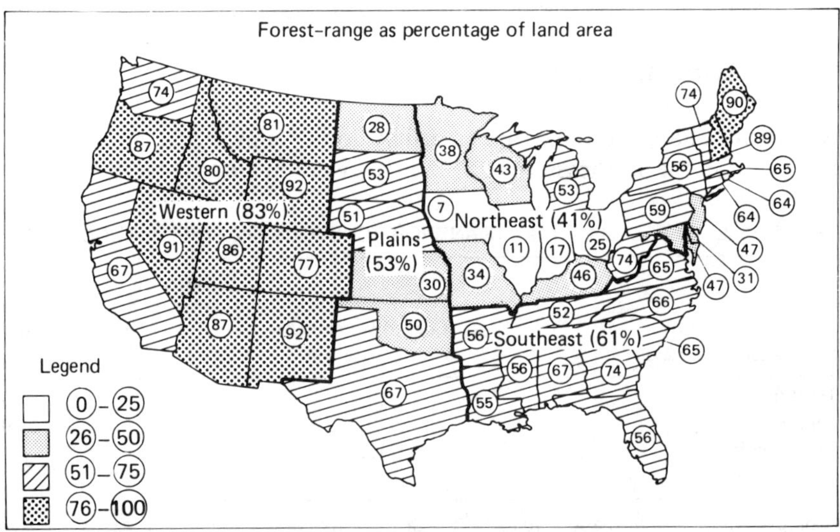

Figure 13-9 Forestland grazed by domestic livestock as a percentage of the total land area by states and regions in the United States. (From U.S. Department of Agriculture, 1974.)

TABLE 13-3 EROSION BY WATER AND WIND ON GRAZED AND NOT GRAZED FORESTLANDS IN THE UNITED STATES

	Water erosion		Wind erosion	
Forest management land use	tons/ac-yr	mt/ha-yr	tons/ac-yr	mt/ha-yr
Grazed	2.3	5.2	0.1	0.2
Not grazed	0.7	1.6	0.0	0.0

Source: National Research Council, 1986a.

Washington, and Oregon are judged to have a potential for responding economically to the application of fertilizer.

Douglas-fir has responded to nitrogen fertilization with about 30% faster growth during a five- to seven-year period; trees as old as 300 years have shown growth acceleration.

Southern pines on well-drained soils respond well to fertilization. Nitrogen alone is expected to enhance their growth by about 5% a year. A second area of present and predicted future response is in the flatwoods coastal plains where both nitrogen and phosphorus give increased growth of pines.

Helicopters are preferred for use in fertilizing forests. They are environmentally safer than fixed-wing aircraft because they can fly slower, spread fertilizer more accurately on the land intended, and avoid streams and lakes.

Guidelines for environmentally safe application of fertilizers to forests include the following (Environmental Protection Agency, 1973):

1. Fertilize only when a soil test indicates that benefits are expected to be economical.
2. Fertilize at rates that do not exceed the adsorption capacity of the soil and the uptake capability of timber stands.
3. Frequent fertilization at low rates is environmentally safer than infrequent application at high rates.
4. Do not fertilize water courses; leave buffer strips between streams and fertilized areas.
5. Apply fertilizers when wind drift is minimal.
6. Avoid fertilization just prior to periods of anticipated heavy rainfall.
7. Coarse-pelleted fertilizers are environmentally safer than fine pellets or dusts; liquid fertilizers have the greatest fugitive loss potential and the greatest water-pollution hazard.

Besides the use of fertilizers, two other fertility techniques have been researched: growing legumes within the forest and the use of a symbiotic fungus. Fifty-two understory legumes were sown on forest sites in the lower Coastal Plains of Virginia, North Carolina, and South Carolina, and the Piedmont of Virginia and North Carolina. The objective was to find legumes that would fix atmospheric nitrogen (N_2) to enrich the soils and enhance the growth of accompanied forest trees. The eight perennial legumes that were established successfully were: tick-clover, false indigo, bicolor lespedeza, sericea lespedeza, Thunberg lespedeza, virgata lespedeza, birdsfoot trefoil, and big trefoil. Sericea lespedeza grew the best (Jorgensen and Craig, 1983).

A symbiotic mycorrhizal fungus, *Pisolithus tinctorius,* has been used successfully to inoculate trees and shrubs in the nursery. Woody plants so inoculated have greater survivability when planted in adverse environments such as dry soils, low-nutrient soils, and mine spoils. Common plants benefited by mycorrhizae include pines, birches, beeches, hemlock, oaks, and spruces (Figure 13–10). Plants inoculated with mycorrhizae may have a survival and growth rate in excess of 20% over those not inoculated (Cordell et al., 1987).

SUMMARY

Pasture, range, and forest should be managed to obtain continuous high productivity combined with minimum soil erosion and polluting sediment. Pastures usually

Figure 13–10 Loblolly pine seedlings one year old. (a) Only naturally occurring mycorrhizal fungus present. (b) Ectomycorrhizal fungus, *Pisolithus tinctorius,* has been added. (Courtesy USDA Forest Service.)

are in humid regions or are irrigated, are seeded to improved grass plus legume cultivars, and are limed (if acid) and fertilized. Ranges normally are in semiarid and arid regions or are a secondary use of land such as open forest in humid or semiarid regions. Native species are used for grazing, although some exotic species have been used to reseed the range. Forests, by definition, must have 10% of the area covered by trees, and a tree is a woody plant at least 15 ft (4.5 m) high.

There are many erosion-resisting pasture grasses, pasture legumes, and range grasses, and each one has its own area of adaptation. Nitrogen fertilizer makes grasses more productive but may cause them to crowd out legumes. Pastures should be renovated when their productivity declines to 50 to 75% of its potential. Rotational and deferred grazing are good management techniques to improve pasture and range productivity.

Forest cover usually keeps erosion to very low levels except when roads are built and trees are logged. Trees are harvested by the selection, shelterwood, seed-tree, or clearcutting methods. Log removal is by tractor, high-lead cable, skyline cable, balloon cable, or helicopter. About half of all forest land is grazed by livestock; the percentage is highest in the south and west where there are open areas with grass vegetation in the forest. Forest fertilization is increasing now along with the value of forest products.

QUESTIONS

1. Define: pastureland, rangeland, forestland. Compare and contrast wind and water erosion potentials on pasturelands, rangelands, and forestlands.
2. What is meant by "fertility management" of a pasture?
3. Why is grazing management the key to successful range management?
4. Describe a timber harvesting method and a log transport system that minimize soil erosion and sediment yield. Why aren't these two methods used universally?

REFERENCES

ANDERSON, D. A., and W. A. SMITH, 1970. *Forest and Forestry.* Interstate Printers and Publishers, Danville, Ill., p. 357

ARCHIE, S., and D. M. BAUMGARTNER, undated. *Clearcutting in the Douglas-Fir Region of the Pacific Northwest.* Washington Woodland Council, p. 17.

BALLARD, T. M., 1988. Soil degradation associated with forest site preparation. In *Degradation of Forested Land: Forest Soils at Risk.* Proc. of 10th B.C. Soil Science Workshop, Feb. 1986. Land Mgmt. Rep., 56, Dec., p. 74–81. Ministry of Forests, British Columbia, Canada.

BEASLEY, R. S., E. L. MILLER, and E. R. LAWSON, 1987. *Chemical Properties of Soil and Streams in Natural and Disturbed Forest Ecosystems in the Ouachita Mountains.* Publ. 132, Arkansas Water Resources Center, Univ. of Arkansas, Fayetteville, Ark., p. 93.

CORDELL, C. E., M. E. FARLEY, J. E. OWEN, and D. H. MARX, 1987. A beneficial fungus for mine land reclamation. In *Innovative Approaches to Mined Land Reclamation.* C. L. Carlson, and J. H. Swisher, (eds.), Southern Illinois Univ. Press, Carbondale and Edwardsville, Ill., p. 499–524.

DEHAVEN, M. G., 1983. *Assessment of Stormflow and Water Quality from Undisturbed and Site Prepared Forest Land in East Texas.* Tech. Rep. 122. Texas Water Resources Institute, Texas A&M Univ., College Station, Tex., 125 p.

DUDECK, D., 1988. Cited in news item: Trees seen as answer to global warming. *J. Soil Water Cons.* 43:474.

DUFFY, P., 1977. *Fertilization to Accelerate Loblolly Pine Foliage Growth for Erosion Control.* USDA For. Serv. Res. Note SO-230.

DYRNESS, C. T., 1972. *Soil Surface Conditions Following Balloon Logging.* USDA For. Serv. Res. Note PNW-182, 7 p.

ENVIRONMENTAL PROTECTION AGENCY, 1973. *Process, Procedures, and Methods to Control Pollution from Silvicultural Activities.* Publ. EPA 430/9-73-010, 91 p.

EYLANDS, V. J. and C. F. YAMOAH, 1989. Nutrient cycling in a Sesbania alleycropping system. In *Agronomy Abstracts.* Annual meetings of American Society of Agronomy, Crop Science Society of America, and Soil Science Society of America, Las Vegas, Nev., p. 53.

FOOD AND AGRICULTURE ORGANIZATION, 1976. *Conservation in Arid and Semiarid Zones.* Conservation Guide 3. FAO, Rome, 125 p.

FOOD AND AGRICULTURE ORGANIZATION, 1978. *Special Readings in Conservation.* Conservation Guide 4, FAO, Rome, 101 p.

FROEHLICH, H. A., D. W. R. MILES, and R. W. ROBERTS, 1985. Soil bulk density recovery on compacted skid trails in central Idaho. *Soil Sci. Soc. Am. J.* 49:1015–1017.

FROEHLICH, H. A., 1988. Causes and effects of soil degradation due to timber harvesting. In *Degradation of Forested Land: Forest Soils at Risk.* Proc. 10th B.C. Soil Science Workshop, Feb. 1986. Land Management Rep. 56, Dec., p. 3–12. Ministry of Forests, British Columbia, Canada.

GROMAN, W. A., 1972. *Forest Fertilization: A State-of-the-Art Review and Description of Environmental Effects.* Publ. EPA-R2-72-016, Environmental Protection Agency, 57 p.

HART, R. H., 1974. Crop selection and management. In *Factors Involved in Land Application of Agricultural and Municipal Wastes.* USDA, Beltsville, Md., p. 178–200.

HYDE, R. M., and C. E. OWENSBY, 1970. *Burning Bluestem Range.* Publ. L-277. Kansas State Univ., Manhattan, Kans.

JORGENSEN, J. R., and J. R. CRAIG, 1983. *Legumes in Forestry: Results of Adaptability Trials in the Southeast.* Southeast. For. Exp. Stn. Res. Pap. SE-237.

KANG, B. T., and O. ONAFEKO, 1989. Spacial chemical soil variability in alley cropped plots. In *Agronomy Abstracts.* Annual meetings of American Society of Agronomy, Crop Science Society of America, and Soil Science Society of America, Las Vegas, Nev., p. 55.

LAWRANCE, R., and R. A. LEONARD, 1988. Streamflow nutrient dynamics on coastal plain watershed. *J. Environ. Qual.* 17:734–740.

MCCLURKIN, D. C., 1970. Site rehabilitation under planted red cedar and pine. In *Tree Growth and Forest Soils.* Proc. 3rd North American Forest Soils Conf., North Carolina State Univiversity, Raleigh, N.C., p. 339–345.

MCEVOY, T., 1989. Common sense erosion control. *Am. For.,* 95(5&6):32–34, 66–67.

McNuit, R. B., et al., 1972. *Soil Survey of Chilton County, Alabama.* USDA Soil Conservation Service and USDA Forest Service, in cooperation with the Ala. Agr. Exp. Sta. and Ala. Dept. of Agriculture and Industries, 82 p. and 47 soil maps.

McVickar, M. H., 1974. *Approved Practices in Pasture Management.* Interstate Publishers, Danville, Ill., 400 p.

Megahan, W. F., 1988. Roads and forest site productivity. In *Degradation of Forested Land: Forest Soils at Risk.* Proc. of the 10th B.C. Soil Science Workshop, Feb. 1986. Land Management Rep. 56, Dec., p. 54–65. Ministry of Forests, British Columbia, Canada.

Mellor, R. S., and R. G. Jensen, 1986. Photosynthesis: Nature's big green machine. *Sci. Agric.* 4(1):14–19.

National Research Council, 1986a. *Soil Conservation: Assessing the National Resources Inventory.* Vol. 1, p. 7. Data are for 1982.

National Research Council, 1986b. *Soil Conservation: Assessing the National Resources Inventory.* Vol. 2, p. 163–203.

National Research Council, 1986c. *Soil Conservation: Assessing the National Resources Inventory.* Vol. 2, p. 175–177.

Owens, L. B., 1989. Pastures need help for clean bill of health. *Agr. Res.* 37(9):13.

Patric, J. H., 1973. *Deforestation Effects on Soil Moisture, Stream flow, and Water Balance in the Central Appalachians.* For. Serv. Res. Paper NE-259. USDA, Upper Darby, Pa.

Raintree, J. B., 1982. *A Methodology for Diagnosis and Design of Agroforestry Land Management Systems.* International Council for Research in Agroforestry, Nairobi, Kenya.

Rice, R. M., J. S. Rothacher, and W. F. Megahan, 1972. *Erosional Consequences of Timber Harvest: An Appraisal.* Proc. Symp. on Watershed in Transition, Ft. Collins, Colo., June 19–22, p. 321–329.

Rogerson, T. L., 1985. *Hydrologic Responses to Silvicultural Practices in Pine-Hardwood Stands in the Ouachita Mountains.* Proc. 5th Central Hardwood Forest Conf., Urbana-Champaign, Ill., Apr. 15–17, p. 209–214.

Sander, I. L., 1977. *Oaks in the North Central States.* USDA For. Serv., Gen. Tech. Rep. NC-37, 35 p.

Shannon, D. A., K. N. Kabaluapa, and M. L. Mpoy, 1989. Alley cropping: A promising technology for the savanna of Zaire. In *Agronomy Abstracts.* Annual meetings of American Society of Agronomy, Crop Science Society of America, and Soil Science Society of America, Las Vegas, Nev., p. 59.

Smith, S. J., R. G. Menzel, E. D. Rhoades, J. R. Williams, and H. V. Eck, 1983. Nutrient and sediment discharge from southern plains grasslands. *J. Range Mgmt.* 36:435–439.

Swanston, D. N., 1974. *Slope Stability Problems Associated with Timber Harvest in Mountainous Regions of the Western United States.* USDA For. Serv. Gen. Tech. Rep. PNW 21.

Tennessee Valley Authority, 1962. *Reforestation and Erosion Control Influences Upon the Hydrology of the Pine Tree Branch Watershed, 1941 to 1961.* TVA Div. of Water Control Planning, unnumbered.

Ursic, S. J., and F. E. Dendy, 1963. *Sediment Yields from Small Watersheds under Various Land Uses and Forest Covers.* USDA Misc. Pub. 970.

U.S. Department of Agriculture, 1974. *Land Use Planning assistance available through the United States Department of Agriculture.* U.S. Dept. Agr., Washington, D.C., 52 p.

U.S. Department of Agriculture, 1976. *Agricultural Statistics.* U.S. Dept. Agr., Washington, D.C., 613 p.

USDA—Agricultural Research Service, 1976. *Improved Vegetation and Management Practices for Range.* USDA Publ. ARS-NRP 20110, USDA Prog., 22–677, 45 p.

USDA Forest Service, 1972. *The Nation's Range Resources: A Forest-Range Environmental Study.* USDA For. Res. Rep. 19.

USDA Forest Service, 1973. *The Outlook for Timber in the United States.* USDA Publ. FRR-20, 367 p.

Weber, F. R., 1977. *Reforestation in Arid Lands.* Action/Peace Corps, Washington, D.C., and VITA (Volunteers in Technical Assistance), Mt. Rainier, Md., 248 p.

Wright, J. R., and F. H. Siddoway, 1982. Determinants of Soil Loss Tolerance for Rangelands. In *Spec. Publ. 45.* American Society of Agronomy and Soil Science Society of America, Madison, Wis., p. 67–74.

14

Water Conservation

Average annual precipitation ranges from almost zero in the deserts of Africa and central Asia to over 650 in. (16,500 mm) at one location in Hawaii. Precipitation fluctuates widely from year to year at all locations.

People can survive under all but the most extreme ecological conditions, and can readily adjust to minor changes in rainfall. An extended dry period is serious any time it occurs when rains are expected; major problems arise when rainfall is considerably below normal for two or more years.

We always hope that some new weapon, some panacea, will be discovered that will easily and cheaply increase moisture for crop growth. Any number of exotic avenues have been examined—weather modification, chemicals that will make soils more permeable to water, those that might reduce evaporation and/or transpiration, and many more. We have learned that the old methods, or modifications of them, work best—proper and timely tillage, effective and efficient use of crop residues, selection of adapted and high yielding crop varieties planted on time and at proper rates, land forming, and most important of all—control of weeds and volunteer plants at every stage. These are the tools we have; they work; we must use our ingenuity to perfect their effectiveness still further.

Crop damage from dry weather during the growing season can be reduced by irrigation or by conserving as much of the rain received as possible. Irrigation is discussed in Chapter 16; water conservation is the subject of this chapter.

14-1 WHAT IS DROUGHT?

The terms *dryland* and *drought* are associated but are not synonymous. A dryland area is one in which the major factor limiting plant growth is shortage of water. A specific average annual rainfall cannot serve to distinguish between drylands and humid areas because other factors such as rainfall distribution and reliability, humidity, temperature, rate of evaporation, and soil characteristics all determine whether a given amount of rainfall will be sufficient for, or will limit, plant growth. Droughts of varying severity and duration are common in drylands but also occur in more humid areas.

14-1.1 Definition of Drought

Attempts have been made to define drought in terms of precipitation, but temperature and wind also affect plant needs for water. The evapotranspiration concepts of Penman (1948) and Thornthwaite (1948) provide a sound basis for describing sufficiency or deficiency of rainfall in an area for normal or average conditions, but not for specific periods.

Climatic conditions alone cannot define drought either. Soil properties and crop and soil management practices influence water uptake by plants. Crops may survive a dry period without serious damage if the soil initially contains an abundance of stored water within the root zone.

In terms of crop production, drought is a period in which lack of water reduces growth and final yield of the staple crops of a region. In terms of wheat production, drought is relatively common in the Great Plains but is rare in the U.S. Corn Belt. Drought occurs more frequently in the Corn Belt if it is assessed in terms of corn growth.

There are two types of drought: atmospheric drought caused by some combination of low humidity, high temperature, and high wind velocity; and soil drought, caused by low soil moisture, the result of low precipitation, low soil permeability, and/or low soil storage capacity. Both types cause plant stress. Severity and duration of the stress determine the amount of plant damage. Plant stress develops as a dry period continues—first on soils with limited stored water, but eventually on all soils. Short periods of stress reduce plant growth; extended stress increases the damage and eventually kills plants.

14-1.2 Effect of Drought on Plants, Animals, and People

A plant's ability to survive dry conditions depends on the severity of the drought and on plant characteristics. Some plants are in a race with drought. The annuals that have very short growing periods (desert ephemerals) *escape* drought by germinating, growing, and producing flowers and seeds in a very brief life span, usually maturing if there is enough moisture to germinate the seed. Some plants *evade* drought by having large absorbing root systems, low transpiration rates, or having mechanisms for reducing leaf area or closing stomata. A third group *endures* drought by means of massive water-storage organs (cacti) or by shedding leaves and becoming dormant (mesquite).

Crops for agriculture must come from the drought-evading group. The drought escapers have too limited production; the drought endurers grow too slowly. Actually, a cultivated crop's ability to survive drought is less important than its ability to produce some grain or forage even under drought stress. Cereal grains are preeminent dryland crops despite their relatively rapid collapse under severe drought stress (Barnes, 1938).

People also suffer when drought kills plants and animals. They could migrate, but distance to less droughty areas often is excessive; fear of the unknown and attachment to home makes flight unwelcome.

Inhabitants of most large, developed countries can survive a drought because food and finances from outside the drought area can be made available. In many developing countries with dense populations and poor transport systems, there is no quick way for people to seek or get outside help. Massive famines have occurred regularly in the developing world, as for example in the Sahel region of western and central Africa in the 1970s, and in Ethiopia and the Sudan in east Africa in the 1980s.

14-2 COMBATING DROUGHT

Combating drought is one of the primary objectives of successful dryland farming and may be important in more humid areas. Every effort must be made to conserve rainfall, store it in the soil, and use it wisely.

Crops need to be adapted to the area. Many experiment stations show that the best-adapted varieties commonly outyield poorer ones by 35 to 75% or more (Walters, 1989). Yet the best and poorest use nearly equal amounts of water. Farming and ranching success is not assured even by efficient water use. Several successive drought years may reduce current production and income below that necessary to meet even minimum living requirements and farm expenses. Dryland farmers must accumulate reserves during favorable years.

Livestock owners face additional difficulties. Water supplies often are deficient in dry periods. Deeper wells may solve this problem, or additional ponds and dugouts that store runoff water and snowmelt may help. Reserve feed is more difficult and often more expensive to accumulate and store, especially in hotter areas. A cereal crop can be planted on a fallowed field specifically for animal forage in the higher latitudes of temperate regions where summer fallow is common. Then if forage is not needed, the crop can be harvested for grain.

Four to seven consecutive years of drought occurred in parts of the Great Plains and Canadian Prairies during the 1930s and 1950s. In these areas the best livestock venture is one that can be cut back quickly when a drought occurs and can be built up speedily when more normal weather returns.

14-3 WHAT HAPPENS TO RAINFALL?

Estimates of water used (transpired) by a wheat crop at Akron, Colorado, range from about 17% of the 16.5-in. (419-mm) annual precipitation based on Briggs and Shantz (1914) data to about 40% based on evapotranspiration studies. What happens to the rest of the rainfall? Why isn't more used by the crop? Answers to these questions will suggest ways to improve conservation and wise use of the rain that falls both in dryland and in humid areas.

Precipitation *(P)* is "lost" because it is intercepted *(I)*, runs off *(R)*, evaporates *(E)*, is transpired by weeds or volunteer plants *(T)*, or percolates below root depth *(D)*. The amount of water available for use by the crop or for storage in the soil *(A)* may be expressed as

$$A = P - (I \pm R + E + T + D)$$

14-3.1 Interception

Vegetation intercepts and holds some rain during each storm. This evaporates into the air without ever touching the ground. It has little effect on water availability for crop use because the energy used to evaporate free water from the surface of plants is not available to evaporate water from the soil.

14-3.2 Runoff

Some of the rain that penetrates the vegetative canopy runs off the land instead of soaking into the soil. Runoff from individual sites ranges from zero on highly permeable, vegetated, and level soils to over 75% of the rain on impermeable, poorly vegetated, steeply sloping sites. Runoff from watersheds (including both surface runoff and subsurface flow) in the continental United States ranges from 57% in the Middle Branch of the Westfield River watershed in Massachusetts to 2.4% for the Smoky Hill River watershed in Kansas. Runoff is affected by rainfall intensity, soil properties, soil configuration, and vegetative cover.

Coarse-textured and well-aggregated soils have high infiltration rates; fine-textured, poorly aggregated soils have low infiltration and high runoff rates. Infiltration rates are usually higher at the beginning of a storm, when soils are dry, but drop off quickly as soils become wet.

Increasing slope gradient increases the amount and velocity of runoff; surface soil depressions hold water and permit local water, and even runoff from other areas, to be absorbed. Vegetation, both living plants and dead crop residues, reduces the number of raindrops that hit the soil directly, reducing soil crusting and keeping infiltration rates high.

14-3.3 Evaporation

A saturated soil loses water by evaporation as fast as a free water surface. When surface soil is dry, evaporation is reduced to the rate that water vapor moves upward through the dry layer. Losses often exceed 50% of the annual rainfall. Hot areas have greater evaporation losses than cold areas. Dark-colored soils absorb more heat than light soils, so they are hotter and lose more water by evaporation. South- and west-facing slopes in the northern hemisphere are warmer and have higher evaporation rates than north- and east-facing slopes. Drylands with low relative humidities and high wind velocities lose a larger proportion of rainfall by evaporation than do humid regions. Living and dead vegetation reduces evaporation by insulating against heat and deflecting wind away from the soil.

14-3.4 Transpiration

Transpiration by a crop cannot be measured or predicted accurately, but estimates range from about 2.7 in. (69 mm) to produce a crop of dryland wheat to 16.5 in. (420 mm) for the growth of corn in a humid region. Transpiration by crop plants is not really a "loss" of water, because it is being used to grow the crop. Transpiration by weeds or volunteer grains is a loss wherever it occurs: on fallowed fields, on land being prepared for immediate seeding, or in fields producing a crop. These losses are more completely under the control of the farmer than almost any other type of moisture loss.

14-3.5 Deep Percolation

Water that percolates below plant roots is lost to those plants. Some plant roots can penetrate as deep as 30 ft (9 m), but usual root penetration is no more than 50 to 60 in. (125 to 150 cm) for annual spring-seeded cereals, 60 to 70 in. (150 to 180 cm) for winter cereals, and 100 in. (250 cm) or so for some fibrous-rooted perennial grasses. The limited rainfall in dryland areas seldom penetrates below root depth in medium- and fine-textured soils, even when the land is summer fallowed; in humid regions, considerable water is lost for plant growth by deep percolation.

14-3.6 Storage

Rainfall not lost by one of the foregoing processes is used by crops or is stored in the soil. Stored water is the key to plant survival in dryland areas. It is the cushion that helps to level the excesses and deficiencies of rainfall. Rains rarely occur daily, so between rains plants must use stored water. The more arid the region, the longer the duration of these dry periods and the longer plants have to depend on stored water. Water-conservation activities, water-storage techniques, and efficient use of stored water all help to maintain adequate stored water supplies.

Three of the five avenues of moisture loss—runoff, evaporation, and transpiration by weeds—cause water losses that can be significantly reduced. Water loss by deep percolation is important in many humid areas and on very coarse-textured soils in dryland regions. Water conservation must include management methods that (1) decrease runoff, (2) reduce evaporation, (3) reduce deep percolation, and (4) prevent unnecessary loss from storage.

14-4 DECREASING RUNOFF LOSSES

Runoff losses can be reduced but not prevented. Contour cultivation, level terraces, and water-spreading devices help hold rain water on the soil and give it time to infiltrate. Leaving crop residue on the surface rather than burying it, application of mulches, and the use of soil-conserving cropping systems increase infiltration and reduce runoff by maintaining or increasing soil permeability.

Runoff is a loss to upland farmers, but people downstream may benefit from it. Impounded water may be used for irrigation. Where upland farmers use water conservation practices, inflow into storage reservoirs will be reduced. This is already posing problems in some irrigated areas east of the Rocky Mountains in the United States.

14-4.1 Contour Cultivation

Contour cultivation, as shown in Figure 14-1, produces miniature furrows and ridges across the slope that trap rainwater and give it more time to infiltrate. More water is conserved by contouring on gentle than on steep slopes; channel capacity decreases as the slopes become steeper. Large ridges, such as those produced by a lister, trap more water than the small ridges thrown up by a disk, chisel implement, or cultivator.

Tillage furrows are seldom exactly on the contour so some water moves to low spots. A *damming* or *basin lister* was developed to prevent movement in lister furrows. This implement reduced lateral water movement, but the dams made tractor travel so rough and uncomfortable that few mechanized farmers use the machine. With larger tractors, and especially with larger, wider tires, there is renewed interest in this practice in the southern Great Plains (Harris and Krishna, 1984). A similar system called tie ridging has been successful in countries where hand tillage is used.

A study on Rideau clay soil showed that contour cultivation of a corn field reduced runoff from 1.51 to 0.63 in. (38 to 16 mm) or from 8.7 to 3.6% of seasonal rainfall (Ripley et al., 1961). A classic study on a 0.5% slope at Spur, Texas, showed that farming cotton up and down the slope permitted 2.75 in. (70 mm) of runoff compared to 1.95 in. (50 mm) from contour-cultivated land. Water loss was reduced from 13.7% of the annual rainfall to 9.7% (Fisher and Burnett, 1953).

Figure 14-1 Contour cultivation on broad, gentle slopes in the central Great Plains in a crop system of alternate wheat and fallow. (Courtesy USDA Soil Conservation Service.)

Some of the "saved" water invariably is stored in the soil; crop yields are higher on contoured plots. At Spur, Texas, lint cotton yields were 25% higher on contoured plots (146 to 117 lb/ac or 167 to 131 kg/ha).

14-4.2 Terracing

Graded terraces do not conserve water. Terraces that are designed to conserve runoff must hold the water on the soil surface until it soaks in; the channel must be level to be effective. There are two major types of level terraces: level ridge-type terraces and conservation-bench terraces.

Level Ridge-Type Terraces. These are combination ridge and channel structures similar in appearance to the broad-based terraces described in Chapter 10 except that the channels are level. Runoff water ponds in the channels as shown in Figure 14-2. They help to reduce water erosion and they improve water conservation.

Level terraces were built on the experiment stations at Spur, Texas, and Goodwell, Oklahoma, in 1926. A few terraces had partly closed ends and periodic blocks along the channel so that water could not escape. This design allowed excessive rain to run off, but held all the water from less intense storms reducing runoff losses and improving water-conservation efficiency. At Spur, terraces supported by contour cultivation increased lint cotton yield 42 lb/ac (40 kg/ha), a 29% increase, over contouring alone.

Level terraces are designed for ten-year-frequency storms. Channel capacity is generally larger than for graded terraces on comparable slopes. Terrace spacing is determined with the vertical and horizontal interval equations used for regular terraces (Chapter 10). Under no circumstances should the horizontal spacing exceed 400 ft (125 m).

Figure 14-2 A level-terraced field with water ponded in the terrace channels after a heavy rain. (Courtesy USDA Soil Conservation Service).

Level terraces should be constructed only on deep, permeable soils that have large water-storage capacities. Land slope should be gentle, not exceeding 5%. Terrace length may be up to 3000 ft (950 m); it can be even longer if the terrace channel is blocked at intervals. This not only enhances water storage, it guards against excessive damage if the structure is overtopped in intense storms. Excess runoff must be discharged safely. Outlets may be natural waterways, grassed areas, shaped and vegetated waterways, or underground conduits.

Three general designs of level ridge-type terraces are shown in Figure 14–3. Normal ridge-and-channel terraces can be used anywhere that conditions suit level terraces. Steep-backslope terraces can be used only on deep loess or other permeable soils and must be provided with outlets. They can be used on slopes up to 20%, but the structures on steep slopes are so massive and close together that construction costs are very high. Flat-channel terraces can be used where regular level terraces are suited, with two additional requirements: all soil exposed in the cut area must be permeable, and the slope must not exceed 4%. Fields should have quite uniform slopes; largest permissible slope variation along each terrace site is one-fifth of the average slope for that particular terrace. The smaller the slope variation, the easier it is to design and build the terrace system. The width of the flat channel is 100 ft (30 m) on a 0.5% slope with a ridge height of 20 in. (0.5 m); narrower channels are used on steeper slopes.

Conservation-Bench (Zingg) Terraces. Zingg and Hauser (1959) described an experimental system consisting of a series of level benches separated from each other by unleveled, runoff-contributing areas (Figure 14–4). A set was built on a land slope of 1 to 1.8% at the A.R.S. Field Station at Bushland, Texas, where the proportion of contributing area to leveled area was 2:1. Benches occupied 13-acres

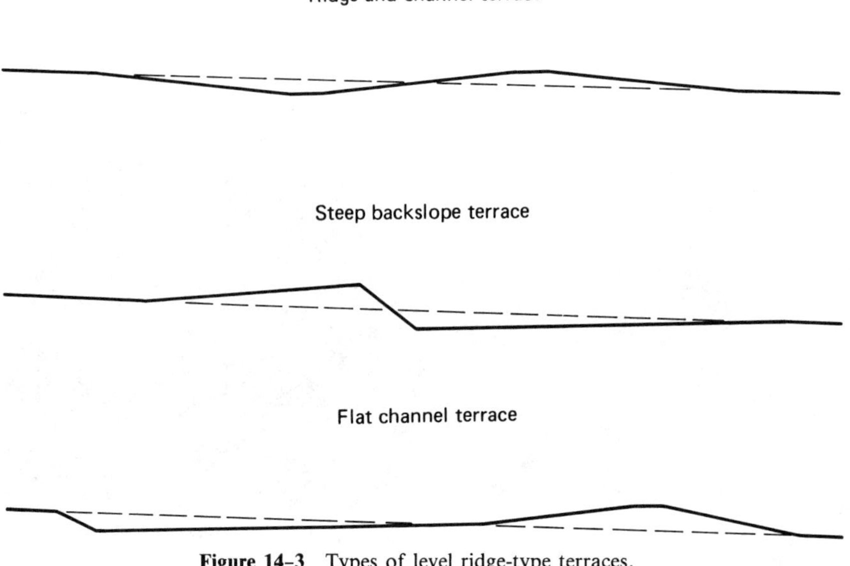

Figure 14–3 Types of level ridge-type terraces.

Figure 14-4 Diagram of a conservation (Zingg) terrace.

(5.25-ha) in a 40-acre (16-ha) field. They varied in length from 1100 to 1400 ft (335 to 425 m) and in width from 80 to 145 ft (24 to 44 m). Maximum cut-and-fill depth was about 12 in. (30 cm). Each bench was provided with a lip on the downhill side to prevent trapped water from flowing off the front of the benched area. Four other sets were constructed in Colorado, Kansas, South Dakota, and Texas. Contributing area to benched area ranged from 1:1 to 3:1. Contributing areas were used for cropping systems common in the area, including summer fallow. The benched areas were seeded each year to an adapted crop, often grain sorghum, that can tolerate standing water for short periods.

Under conditions favorable for runoff production, water losses were markedly reduced and yields on leveled areas were nearly doubled (Black, 1968; Cox, 1968; Hauser, 1968; Mickelson, 1968). These terraces were not totally successful. Crop yields on the excavated sections of the benches were lower than on the built-up areas, but this changed over time with good management. Water ponding in more humid regions and in wetter-than-normal years in drier areas caused occasional crop damage.

Conservation-bench terraces have not been built on many production farms. A farmer in Kansas started to replace regular level terraces with conservation benches in 1969; the system was completed within 10 years. The lips on the downhill side of his benches have outlets so that excessive collected water can be released, but he claims that no runoff water leaves his farm. Crop yields on the benches are as high each year as yields on untreated land that is fallowed every second year. It is strange that his neighbors have not taken up this practice.

14-4.3 Water Spreading

Methods of concentrating runoff and trapping it in prepared sites is an ancient art in sections of the Negev and Sinai Deserts. This area is too dry for normal crop production. These early catchment structures and channels, often covered with flat stone flakes, diverted runoff from winter rainstorms down hillsides and onto prepared, permeable sites in the valleys. The valley sites were crisscrossed with stone fences that trapped soil and water so that each unit of soil was moistened to capacity to considerable depths. The moistened sites were then used to produce the food needed by the relatively large population.

Runoff concentration was also accomplished by constructing individual microwatersheds, each delivering runoff toward its center where a single fruit tree or a small patch of vegetables or vine crops was located. Contributing land, as much as 20 to 25 times the area of the cultivated site, was compacted and kept free of vegetation (Medina, 1976). Israeli farmers use this technique to grow crops in areas that receive less than 8 in. (200 mm) of annual rainfall.

The "syrup pan" system of water spreading was developed in the southern

Great Plains. Runoff from a 1200-acre (485-ha), sloping, native grassland area at Spur, Texas, was diverted back and forth across a 120-acre (50-ha) cultivated field, as shown in Figure 14–5. The water flow was controlled by a series of 13 diversions 30 to 40 in. (75 to 100 cm) high with vertical intervals of about 18 in. (45 cm). This system added an average of 4 in. (100 mm) of water to the cultivated field, equivalent to a 20% increase in rainfall. Systems were established on other research stations, but the practice has not spread to private farms.

Lagoon leveling has been studied. A lagoon (pothole, slough, or swale) is a small depression that collects runoff water from the surrounding land and remains wet or ponded for extended periods. Lagoons in pastures serve as temporary water holes, but in cultivated fields the wet spots are a nuisance and rarely produce a good crop.

Lagoon water can be spread more widely by moving soil from above normal water level to the center of the depression. Water is absorbed more quickly when spread over more surface. This improves both farming convenience and crop yields.

Several lagoons were leveled at Akron, Colorado. One 2-acre (0.8-ha) lagoon was leveled to 4 acres (1.6 ha) by backsloping the lagoon walls to a 5% slope and using the excavated material to fill the center of the depressed area. Maximum cuts were about 24 in. (60 cm); maximum fills were 20 in. (50 cm). Cost of leveling was considerably less than the price of productive land. Annual forage yields are as good as, or superior to, those on unleveled upland sites. The lagoons are no longer a hindrance to field operations (Mickelson and Greb, 1970). This practice has not been widely accepted either.

Polyethylene film and similar impermeable materials have been used to waterproof soils and cause 100% runoff to catchment sites. The extra water makes crop production possible every year on half the land instead of alternating fallow and crop every other year on all the land. The cost of the film and its short life in windy climates make the practice uneconomical.

Mehdizadeh et al. (1978) sprayed microwatersheds in Iran with an imperme-

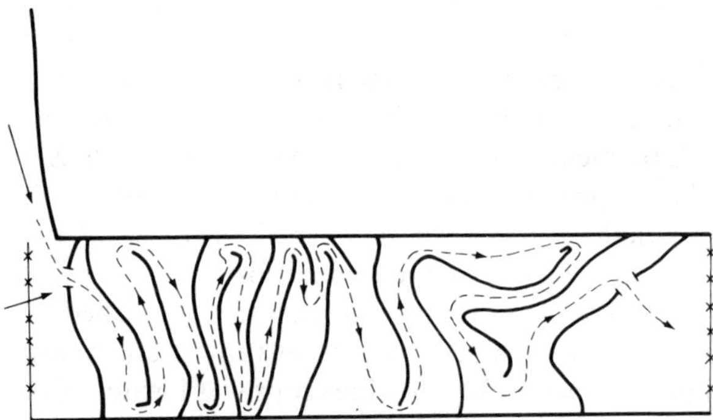

Figure 14–5 Syrup-pan water-spreading system at Spur, Texas. The water entering the system from the left is passed from side to side of the spreading area by diversions until it soaks in or exits on the right. (Courtesy Texas Agricultural Experiment Station.)

able asphalt formulation and used the runoff to supplement rainfall for tree production. The contributing area was 1.5 times the cultivated area. During five years the collecting areas received 19.2 in. (487 mm) of extra runoff, or 35% of the total rainfall. This is an attractive alternative to providing irrigation water for tree growth.

Recharging underground aquifers by spreading runoff water on soil is an important practice where water is available and where the surface conditions and the underlying geological formations are suitable. The usefulness of this practice and some of the available techniques are discussed in Chapter 16.

14-4.4 Use of Chemical Wetting Agents

Chemical wetting agents (surfactants) were first suggested for increasing water infiltration into dryland soils in the early 1950s. Several materials were developed and tested, but none was practical on normal dryland soils. More recently, wetting agents have been recommended as additives for use in sprinkler irrigation systems. Farmers use some of these materials, but there is no proof that they increase water intake rates on normal irrigated soils. Letey (1975) demonstrated that surfactants increase infiltration rate in water-repellant soils in California, but he does not recommend their use on normal soils (Note 14-1).

NOTE 14-1
EFFECT OF SURFACTANTS ON INFILTRATION

The major force moving water into and through soils during rainfall is capillary attraction. Capillary attraction is equal to twice the product of the surface tension of water and the cosine of the wetting angle, divided by the radius of curvature ($2y \times \cos \theta / r$). A surfactant (wetting agent) reduces both surface tension of water and the wetting angle between water and the solid it contacts. Effective wetting agents decrease surface tension in laboratory systems by over 50%. If the capillary attraction is to be increased (to increase infiltration), the wetting angle must be decreased enough so that the cosine of the angle is increased more than the surface tension is decreased. The wetting angle between normal soil and water is generally 10° or less ($\cos 10° = 0.985$). It is impossible therefore to decrease this angle enough to increase $\cos \theta$ by 50%. Thus it is theoretically impossible for wetting agents to increase infiltration in normal soils.

Nonwetting soils have wetting angles much greater than those for normal soils; the angle may exceed 90°. The cosine of an angle greater than 90° has a negative value; these soils are truly water repelling. Capillary force will be greater and infiltration will be increased if this angle can be reduced sufficiently by surfactant addition.

14-4.5 Use of Surface Crop Residues

The most practical way to maintain high infiltration rates (to reduce runoff) and to trap snow that might otherwise blow off the fields is to keep vegetation and vegetative residues on the land. Stubble is most useful for trapping snow when it is standing tall, not flattened. Single and double rows of tall wheatgrass spaced 40 to 60 ft (12 to 18 m) apart are especially effective in trapping snow. Extra moisture from trapped snow increases crop yields. Net returns from these increases were estimated at $5.00 to $14.00/ac depending on region (Snyder et al., 1980).

Use of chemical herbicide or of undercutting implements leaves more stubble standing. Three ways to get the greatest possible moisture conservation benefits from vegetation are:

1. Use crop rotations, cropping systems, and crop management practices that keep the soil well covered for as long as possible each year.
2. Leave as much of the crop residue on the soil surface as practical, particularly between crops.
3. Apply mulches to fields that would otherwise be bare and unprotected.

14-4.6 Improving Soil Structure

Runoff is inversely related to the infiltration rate and permeability of the soil. Soil texture and structure determine the rate of water movement into and through soil. Changing soil texture is impractical, but soil structure can be altered by management practices including use of sod crops, crop and animal residues and mulches, reduced tillage, and addition of chemical soil conditioners.

Cropping Systems and Soil Structure. The crops raised and the practices used in their culture affect soil structure. In drylands, where moisture conservation is most important, there are few adapted crops and few cropping systems that are practical. Sod crops are impractical in cultivated cropping sequences because of the difficulties of getting stands and the slow rate of establishment.

Crop and Animal Residues and Organic Mulches. Crop residues incorporated into the soil contribute part of the beneficial effect of crops on soil structure. Leaving residues on or adding an organic mulch to the soil surface helps maintain a better and more stable structure. Annual applications up to 25 tons/ac (55 mt/ha) of manure or sewage sludge improve soil structure and increase soil productivity if the supplement contains no harmful chemicals. Applications to dryland soils often upset soil moisture relations and may reduce crop yields temporarily.

Tillage. The immediate effect of tillage on soil permeability is often beneficial. A recently plowed field is much more permeable than firm, unplowed land. Postplanting cultivation of fine-textured, low-organic-matter soils improves permeability and reduces runoff temporarily. The long-term effect of tillage usually is reduced permeability. The more tillage a soil receives, the denser it becomes, the lower its infiltration rate, and the slower its permeability.

Chemical Conditioners. Chemicals have been added to soils to improve soil structure and permeability and to reduce runoff. Sodic soils have deflocculated clay and poor structure. If the exchangeable sodium in these soils is replaced by calcium (by application of gypsum), the colloid will flocculate and desirable structure will regenerate, improving soil permeability.

Several synthetic organic chemicals have been promoted as soil conditioners. Hydrolyzed polyacrylonitrile (HPAN), was developed and promoted under the trade name Krilium by Monsanto Chemical Company in 1950. Several research articles on Krilium and other synthetic soil conditioners appeared in the June 1952 issue of *Soil Science.* Since that time, claims for many other materials with soil-conditioning properties have been made. Some materials improve soil structure or increase aggregate stability, but all have been economically impractical. Duley (1956) reported that applications of 0.5 to 2 tons of HPAN/ac (1.1 to 4.4 mt/ha) increased the size of aggregates and also increased infiltration rate. He also showed that applications of 2.5 tons of straw/ac (5.6 mt/ha) had about twice as much effect on infiltration as HPAN. The chemical then sold for $1.00 to $1.60 per pound.

14–4.7 Water-Storage Structures

Methods for reducing runoff losses described so far all involve water storage in the soil. Aboveground storage in ponds, lakes, and reservoirs to meet irrigation, livestock, industrial, or human needs is also common.

Farm Ponds and Dugouts. Trapping surface runoff behind small earthen dams is a common way to provide water for livestock in areas where suitable well water is scarce or unavailable, or where additional watering sites are needed to ensure better use of pasture or range. Stock water dams are usually sited on small watercourses that drain 25- to 100-acre (10- to 40-ha) grassed watersheds. They are relatively simple structures with a grassed spillway at one end about 3 feet (1 m) lower than the crest of the dam (Figure 14–6). Dugouts may be used to store water on more level land, especially in higher latitudes where snow accumulates over winter and melts during a short spring thaw. Dugouts should be large and deep to hold enough water for the entire summer season (Figure 14–7).

Sites for both dams and dugouts must be selected carefully. Bottoms and sides of reservoirs and the dam embankment must be impermeable to retain stored water. Construction material for dams is obtained from the site of the reservoir. This minimizes hauling distance and makes the reservoir deeper—a factor that reduces the proportion of stored water lost by evaporation.

If impermeable soil is not available at the site, bentonite, a swelling clay, may be purchased and spread over the floor of the reservoir at a rate of 1 to 3 lb/ft^2 (5 to 15 kg/m^2) and mixed with the top 6 in. (15 cm) of soil. This adds materially to the cost of the structure. The bed of the reservoir and the dam itself should be

Figure 14-6 A farm pond in Kansas that combines catfish production with water storage for irrigation. (Courtesy USDA Soil Conservation Service.)

thoroughly compacted during construction using a sheepsfoot packer or herding cattle or other animals in the basin to help seal the surface.

An alternative is to place plastic film, butyl rubber, or a thin asphalt layer over the entire reservoir bed. The film or layer must be applied very carefully to ensure complete coverage with no breaks, and the film must be protected with 6 in. (15 cm) or more of fine (not cloddy or stony) soil. It is absolutely essential that a site so treated be fenced to exclude livestock.

Small dams and dugouts can be constructed by individual farmers, but many will want to have the work done by a competent conservation contractor with large earth-moving equipment. Construction specifications for both dams and dugouts

Figure 14-7 A dugout excavated in glacial till to impound water for livestock. A pump is located in the far corner. (Courtesy Canada-Manitoba Soil Survey.)

should be obtained from the Soil Conservation Service or from a competent engineering consultant.

Ponds should be fenced to prevent bank trampling and to reduce eutrophication. A pipe should be installed to carry water to a trough or tank below the dam. Dugouts must also be fenced to keep livestock away from the steeply sloping sides. Animals may be permitted access to the water by way of the ramp used by the earth-moving equipment during construction, but it is better to keep them out and pump water to a tank above the dugout. A reservoir providing water for home use must be fenced and animals should be kept out of the entire watershed to reduce the possibility of pollution.

Municipal Water Supply Reservoirs. Many small- to medium-sized dams have been built to trap streamflow (runoff) for use in municipal water systems. More reservoirs will be required as population increases.

Large Irrigation-Water Reservoirs. Flow in the major rivers of most countries is seasonally greater than the needs of downstream users. Where irrigation water can be used effectively, seasonal surpluses can be stored for use during the growing season. Many reservoirs such as the one shown in Figure 14–8 have been built in the western half of the United States and in dryland areas of other countries. Since more surplus water flows in the rivers and streams of humid areas than in most

Figure 14–8 Lovewell Dam and Reservoir in north central Kansas was built by the Bureau of Reclamation as an irrigation storage reservoir. The irrigation-water discharge outlet and canal are in the foreground beside the spillway. Water was being discharged from the spillway when the picture was taken. (Courtesy USDA Soil Conservation Service.)

dryland rivers, storage for use in the short dry periods in humid regions may be a reasonable project of the future. It is essential to recognize that water stored behind dams inundates valley land, often the best and most productive land in the area. Agricultural gains from use of this stored water must be measured against production losses from the inundated soils.

14-5 REDUCING EVAPORATION LOSSES

The quantity of water lost from soils by evaporation may exceed 70% of the annual precipitation in dryland regions. In subhumid areas, the evaporation loss probably amounts to 30 to 50%. Reducing this loss, especially in drylands, would significantly increase the water supply for crop production.

The earliest recommended method for reducing evaporation from soil was to use a *dust mulch.* This practice has been discredited because it did not increase available moisture in the dryland regions, and it produced an extremely erodible soil surface. Using vegetative mulches and other mulching materials, and forcing water to percolate deeper, are the methods presently used to reduce evaporation from soil.

14-5.1 Vegetative Mulches

Mulches of crop residue, forest litter, sawdust, and wood chips greatly reduce evaporation by reducing soil temperature and wind velocity near the soil. A German investigator first demonstrated the effects of mulches on evaporation. In a one-month study with constantly moist soil he found that evaporation was reduced 89.2%, from 2.26 in. (5.739 cm) from bare soil to 0.24 in. (0.621 cm) from a soil mulched with 2 in. (5 cm) of fir needles (Eser, 1884).

More recent studies show that early losses from unmulched, moistened soils are much more rapid than from mulched soils; over time, losses from the mulched plots overtake those from unmulched land if additional moisture is not supplied. Mulches reduce water loss most in years or in regions in which rain wets the soil frequently (Brun et al. 1986).

14-5.2 Other Mulches

Nonvegetative mulches also reduce evaporation loss. Stones and gravel on surface soil increase infiltration and reduce water loss. Fairbourn and Gardner (1975) coated natural soil aggregates with water-repellent materials and applied the treated aggregates as mulches with reasonable success. Tar-paper caps placed on ridges between sorghum rows increased yields from 38 to 240% in western Kansas. Yield increases were credited to three effects of the mulch:

1. Evaporation was reduced because a smaller surface area was exposed to sun and wind.
2. Rainfall was concentrated onto smaller areas so it percolated deeper into the soil and was less subject to evaporative forces.

3. The cover maintained faster water absorption by preventing raindrops from compacting a large part of the soil surface.

In another study, corn was grown to maturity on plots covered with black plastic film which prevented evaporation but also stopped rainfall from entering the soil. Corn on the plastic-covered plot, with only the water in the soil at seeding time, produced a yield nearly as high as the adjacent unmulched plot that received normal rainfall supplemented by several irrigations (121 compared to 129 bu/ac or 75.9 to 80.9 q/ha) (Shaw, 1959).

In an Arizona study, asphalt sprayed on the soil immediately after cotton and sorghum seeding held more moisture in the seed zone and improved germination and early growth. Good results were obtained on some soils, but the surface had to be smooth to economize on the asphalt used. If soil shrinkage occurred, the film cracked and was useless.

Black polyethylene film has been used in irrigated areas and in humid parts of the United States to produce high-value vegetable crops. Vegetable-yield increases resulted from weed control, and from raised soil temperature which promoted increased early growth, as well as from reduced evaporation.

14–5.3 Forcing Deeper Water Penetration

Water close to the soil surface is more subject to evaporation than water deeper in the profile, so deeper percolation should save water. The Kansas study using tar-paper caps (Section 14–5.2) caused deeper percolation because runoff water was concentrated on a smaller area of soil. Fairbourn and Gardner (1974) used this technique at Akron, Colorado. The soil surface was formed into beds 6.6 ft (2 m) wide. Each bed had two 29.5-in. (75-cm) sloping (3:1) contributing areas leading down from each side onto a 20-in. (50-cm) flat collecting area. The flat area had a 6-in. (15-cm) deep vertically-mulched slot running down the middle with two rows of sorghum 6 in. on each side. The slopes were treated with hydrophobic material to further reduce water penetration on the sloping shoulders. Check dams were constructed at intervals across the flat furrows to prevent water movement in the furrow. The treated plots saved 41% more rainfall and produced from 37 to 150% more sorghum grain than did regular flat-planted, unmulched land.

14–5.4 Reducing Losses from Reservoirs

Much of the runoff water caught in reservoirs is lost by evaporation. Annual evaporation from open water surfaces in agricultural regions ranges from about 13.8 in. (350 mm) in north central Canada (54°N latitude) to over 78 in. (2000 mm) in northern Nigeria (13°N). Hot desert areas suffer even larger losses. Evaporation rates are directly related to temperature and wind velocity, and inversely related to relative humidity. Losses from small reservoirs often exceed livestock and household use.

Methods for reducing evaporation losses from reservoirs are constantly being sought. For example, a field shelterbelt planted around a reservoir site reduces evaporation losses by reducing wind velocity over the water. Trees beautify the site and make a useful recreational area and wildlife sanctuary. They also may trap snow for reservoir recharge. Trees should be at least 100 ft (30 m) from the water to reduce transpiration losses from the reservoir.

Materials such as hexadecanol and other long-chain fatty alcohols form monomolecular films on water surfaces, reducing evaporation about 20%. Gentle winds blow the films toward the water's edge and leave the water surface less protected. They are not very practical because they are biodegradable and lose effectiveness with time. Nicholaichuk (1978) described rafts made of inexpensive, lightweight concrete that are as effective as monomolecular films and much more durable.

14-6 REDUCING DEEP PERCOLATION LOSSES

Deep percolation losses are of little significance in nonirrigated dryland areas because the limited rainfall can usually be trapped in the root zone, except possibly in sands. Percolation losses do occur in humid and irrigated areas.

Deep percolation is a common avenue of water loss in humid regions, but this loss does not seriously reduce the amount of water available to plants unless the soil has a low water-holding capacity. Most deep medium- and fine-textured soils hold 6 to 10 in. (150 to 300 mm) of available water before water moves below plant roots. This is usually sufficient to last the crop through a short dry period. Sandy soils lose large amounts of water through percolation because some of them hold less than 2 in. (50 mm) of available water in the root zone. Reducing deep percolation losses in sands could increase water available to crops and might increase crop yields.

Erickson et al. (1968) demonstrated that horizontal asphalt barriers 22 to 24 in. (55 to 60 cm) below the soil surface in Bridgman fine sand (unclassified) and Grayling loamy sand (Typic Udipsamment) appreciably increased the water available to plants. Vegetable crop yields were increased by 35 to 40% on the fine sand, but only small increases occurred on the loamy sand soil. A trial in Taiwan on a sandy soil showed paddy rice yields were increased 10- to 14-fold with barriers placed at depths of 8 to 24 in. (20 to 60 cm). Material costs have increased greatly since 1968, but there are situations where the technique may still be usefully employed (Erickson, 1972).

Somani and Sharma (1985) compacted subsurface layers of sandy soils to reduce seepage losses with some benefit in a dryland area of India. This practice is not likely to be practical in commercial agriculture unless it is mechanized. Not all sands can be compacted to reduce percolation rate.

A chemical that absorbs water might prove useful for holding more water in sandy soils. A copolymer of starch and acrylonitrile named "super slurper" was reported to absorb up to 1400 times its weight of water. Preliminary reports indicated that additions increased the water-holding capacity of sandy soils, but were not economically feasible.

Deep percolation leaches nutrients and makes soils more acid. Controlled runoff (without serious erosion) in humid regions actually may be less damaging than deep percolation, particularly where fertilizers and lime are expensive and hard to obtain. In many tropical areas with monsoon rainfall, water conservation is important mainly at the beginning and the end of the rains. In the heart of the rainy season, good water management should emphasize controlled surface drainage rather than surface detention and infiltration.

14-7 STORING WATER IN SOIL

Soils in humid regions are usually wet to field capacity beyond rooting depth at least once each year. Water stored over winter in North America's Corn Belt soils makes high corn and soybean yields possible even though rainfall is not sufficient to meet crop short-term needs during periods in July and August. It can be equally beneficial in sections of the intermountain valleys and the Pacific Northwest. Winter storage would be important in dryland areas also but it is limited by meager precipitation. Crop production under these conditions may not be possible every year, even when all practical water-conservation measures are used.

Water can be stored in the soil during a growing season if plant growth is prevented. This water will supplement rainfall in the next growing season. This practice of storing water in the soil during one crop-growing season for use by a crop planted the next season is called *summer fallow*. This must be distinguished from the *fallow* under several years of forest or grass regrowth used for soil recuperation in shifting cultivation.

Summer fallow has been used in various parts of the world for several centuries, including extensive use in England during and after the Roman occupation. It was first used in North America in the early 1850s by the Selkirk settlers in the area north of Winnipeg, Canada, but it was not widely used in dryland regions until the 1880s, shortly after the Great Plains area of the United States was first settled. The area of summer fallowed land west of the Mississippi River in the United States averages a little less than 35 million acres (15 million ha). Summer fallow is also common in western Canada, over vast areas of the USSR, in Australia, and in many of the wheat-growing areas in southern South America. Recent studies in a semiarid area in southern Africa show that fallow also improves water use efficiency and increases crop yields there (Jones and Sinclair, 1989).

14-7.1 Objectives of Summer Fallow

The major objective of summer fallowing is to store water in the soil for subsequent crop use. Weed control, release of extra nitrogen for the use of a succeeding crop, and spreading the workload of seedbed preparation over a longer period may be reasons for using summer fallow in some areas.

14-7.2 Efficiency of Water Storage by Fallow

A large number of federally supported agricultural research stations and several state stations studied moisture storage in fallow-crop and continuous-crop systems from the early 1900s until the late 1940s. The average amount of rainfall stored during a 15- to 19-month fallow period ranged from 1.5 in. (38 mm) (6%) at Dalhart, Texas, to 6.17 in. (157 mm) (24.6%) at Sheridan, Wyoming, in the summer rainfall area. Over the same period moisture stored between harvest and planting in continuous-crop systems ranged from 0.76 in. (19 mm) (10%) at Dalhart to 3.88 in. (99 mm) (40%) at Sheridan (Mathews and Army, 1960). Fallow storage efficiency at Swift Current in western Canada was nearly 27% (Doughty et al., 1949). These results explain why summer fallow is used less commonly in hot drylands. More recent studies quoted by Smika and Unger (1986) show increasing efficiency of water storage with improved cultivation methods (Table 14–1).

Water-storage efficiency of summer fallow in the winter rainfall area of the United States is usually greater than in the Plains area. More than 60% of the precipitation is stored during the early winter period when temperature is low and precipitation relatively abundant. Gains during the dry summer season are very small; there is often a net loss of soil moisture during the summer.

Soil permeability also affects the efficiency of water storage in fallowed land. Sandy soils are permeable and absorb rainfall readily. Percolating water goes deeper into a sandy soil than it does into a finer-textured soil and is less likely to be lost by evaporation. Sandier soils store rainfall more efficiently only if they have sufficient storage capacity to hold the percolating water in the root zone. The best soils for

TABLE 14–1 EFFECT OF IMPROVED TECHNOLOGY ON WATER STORAGE AND WHEAT YIELDS ON SUMMER FALLOW IN THE CENTRAL GREAT PLAINS

		Fallow water storage			Wheat yield	
Years	Tillage during fallow[a]	Inches	mm	Percent of precipitation	bu/ac	q/ha
1916–1930	Maximum tillage; plow, harrow (dust mulch)	4.0	100	19	15.9	10.7
1931–1945	Conventional tillage; shallow disk, rod weeder	4.6	116	24	17.2	11.5
1946–1960	Improved conventional tillage; began stubble mulch in 1957	5.4	137	27	25.7	17.2
1961–1975	Stubble mulch; began minimum tillage with herbicides in 1969	6.2	157	33	32.1	21.5
1976–1990	Projected estimate; minimum tillage; began no tillage in 1983	7.2	183	40	40.0	26.8

[a]Based on 14-month fallow period, mid-July to second mid-September.

From Advances in Soil Science, Volume 5, p. 111–138, 1986 (Smika and Unger) by permission of Springer-Verlag, New York, and the authors.

efficient water storage are those with sandy surface layers overlying medium-textured subsoils.

14–7.3 Cultivating Fallow Land

Efficient storage of moisture in fallowed land depends on successful weed control and on maintaining crop residues on the soil surface. Weeds must be killed by undercutting implements or by chemicals, but tillage should not be performed more often than necessary to control weeds. Extra tillage dissipates moisture, costs money, buries residues, and does not increase crop yields.

Frequency of fallow in a cropping system should be governed by soil moisture and by climatic conditions at the time. A dryland soil should be fallowed when its moisture content just before seeding is insufficient to assure a reasonable yield. Medium- and fine-textured soils in dryland regions are generally fallowed once in two to four years. Government restrictions on crop production in the United States have forced farmers to cut back on cash-crop area, which in dryland areas has meant more land is summer fallowed. More land is being fallowed than necessary in many areas.

14–7.4 Crop Response to Summer Fallow

Crop yields on summer fallow in dryland areas are higher than yields on land that produces a crop each year. The more favorable the condition for extra moisture storage by fallowing, the larger are the increases in yields. Average wheat yield increases up to the early 1950s ranged from a low 0.2 bu/ac (13 kg/ha) (4.4%) at Big Spring, Texas, to 10.7 bu/ac (7.2 q/ha) (120%) at Colby, Kansas, in the Great Plains, to 30.2 bu/ac (20.3 q/ha) (153%) at Moscow, Idaho, in the winter rainfall area of the intermountain valleys.

Other adapted crops respond to summer fallow about the same as wheat does. Percent yield increases of oats and barley are as great as those of wheat in the northern Great Plains. Percent yield increases of sorghum are as great as, or greater than, those of wheat in the southern Plains. Corn is not well adapted to most dryland areas; its response to fallow is small and erratic. Yield increases indicate, as does water-storage efficiency, that summer fallow is most useful in dryland areas with cool temperatures where evaporation losses during storage are relatively small.

14–7.5 Summer Fallow and Saline Seeps

Opportunity for water losses from fallowed soils by deep percolation increases as efficiency of moisture storage increases. Stored water may move downward in the soil beyond the reach of crop roots and be lost for crop production. It carries dissolved salts from the soil causing loss of plant nutrients. These percolating waters may resurface farther down the slope and provide plants there with extra water and nutrients. The salts in excess of those used by plants are left in the soil and in time may produce *saline seeps*. Considerable areas of saline seeps are developing in the northern Great Plains.

One obvious method of reducing the magnitude of saline seeps is to restrict fallowing to areas where the water that can be saved in the soil will not exceed the amount that can be stored in the root zone. This would mean a shift from alternate fallow and crop to less frequent fallow or to continuous cropping when water losses are reduced.

14-8 EFFICIENT USE OF STORED SOIL WATER

Water storage in soils is not an efficient process, but water that is stored is extremely important to a subsequent crop. It must be husbanded carefully if it is to serve the crop and the farmer well.

There are several ways to reduce unnecessary loss of stored soil water: (1) plant crops only when there is enough water for a reasonable chance of successful production, (2) grow efficient crops, (3) plant and cultivate with timeliness and precision, (4) plant at the proper seeding rate, (5) control weeds and volunteer crop plants, and (6) use windbreaks to reduce transpiration.

14-8.1 Predicting Successful Crop Production

Water stored in a soil will be wasted if a planted crop fails to mature. A technique for predicting cropping success can help reduce unnecessary water loss. Hallsted and Mathews (1936), Thomson (1947), and Fisher and Burnett (1953) developed relationships between soil moisture at seeding time and yield of winter wheat, spring wheat, and cotton, respectively. Each expressed available moisture in terms of depth of wet soil and pointed out how a knowledge of depth of wet soil at seeding time could be used to estimate the likelihood of successful crop production.

A crop should not be planted when chances for successful growth are low, as when 12 in. (30 cm) or less of moist soil is available. Rather, the land should be set aside and kept free of weeds so that additional water can be stored for growing a crop at the next planting season. Hallsted and Mathews also recommended that soil moisture content be used to make the decision on whether to abandon a winter wheat crop. Early abandonment (April) permits the saving of some soil moisture for the next crop.

Wise postponement of planting and judicious use of abandonment permit farmers to obtain the advantages of summer fallow in many places without specifically setting aside large areas of land for this purpose every year. It gives them more flexibility. This technique has never been widely used by U.S. or Canadian farmers because of government controls on planting area or on marketing.

14-8.2 Growing Efficient Crops

Crop plants use 15 to 30% of the rainfall each year. Water-requirement studies show that the transpiration ratio (pounds of water transpired per pound of dry matter produced) averages 298 for sorghum, 368 for corn, 481 for wheat, and over 1000 for some grasses (Briggs and Shantz, 1914). This suggests that sorghum and corn should produce more drymatter than wheat on a specified amount of water (though not necessarily more harvestable grain). In fact, they use almost identical amounts of water in dry areas such as the Great Plains; they use all that is available. Crops should be selected for dryland areas on the basis of performance, not on transpiration ratio.

In less arid areas, selecting crop varieties on the number of days required to reach maturity permits partial control of the amount of soil water that is used and how much remains in the soil at harvest time. It also determines the time that will be available for water recharge between harvest and the next seeding.

Farmers in many developing countries use mixtures of varieties and even of species, seeding drought-tolerant and water-loving types together, so that the chance of crop failure is reduced in drier years without losing productive potential in more humid periods. In commercial agriculture such mixtures are not used.

14–8.3 Timeliness of Operations

There is an optimum time for most crop production operations—controlling weeds, planting crops, etc. Delayed cultivation or spraying to control weeds means moisture loss. In the case of seeding winter wheat, too early means the crop grows too luxuriantly and uses excess stored water in the fall; if too late, the crop grows slowly and may fail to establish properly before winter. In humid regions, it is usually possible to plant within a few days of the optimum date; in drier areas, planting often must wait for a "planting" rain to replenish surface soil moisture to ensure germination and early growth. There may be only one "planting" rain or none close to the optimum planting date.

Land must be ready for planting—weed free and in good shape to receive seed—when seeding time arrives. When the rain comes you wait for the surface to dry off and begin seeding without wasting time or moisture. If the soil needs cultivating when the rain is received, moisture will be lost by tillage and the soil may become too dry for planting. You lose the moisture and the chance to plant, and must wait for another rain.

Because of the uncertainty of rainfall at planting time, there is pressure to plant winter wheat when a good rain comes two or three weeks before the optimum date. Some of the detrimental effects of early planting can be counteracted by judicious pasturing in the fall and early spring. Pastured wheat does not deplete the moisture reserves as much as the unpastured crop does. It still protects the soil from wind erosion and often yields more than an unpastured crop.

Timeliness is also important in tropical areas with wet-dry seasons. Delayed planting at the end of the monsoon may allow too much water to be lost from the soil by evaporation and leave too little for the crop.

14–8.4 Rate of Seeding

The amount of water available for crop production dictates the number of plants that can be supported. Population density must be restricted where moisture is limited, or all plants will suffer moisture stress.

Corn, soybeans, and other crops that do not tiller must be planted at the population dictated by the climate, soil fertility, and other factors. Widely spaced corn plants (low populations) may produce bigger ears under favorable conditions, or more than one ear per plant in some varieties, but yield per acre will not reach the potential for that set of ecological conditions. Wheat, other small grains, and sorghum often counteract low seeding rates by tillering profusely under favorable conditions. Thus wheat yield may not be greatly different whether seeded at rates of 30 or 75 lb/ac (35 or 85 kg/ha) because the thin crop will tiller to fill the space. But if too much seed is used, the plants compete for water and space so that no individual plant grows well; in extreme cases, water is insufficient to bring the crop to maturity. A thinner stand under the same low-moisture regime may survive and produce a harvestable crop.

Studies were conducted in the drylands of North America to find out if planting row crops in widely spaced rows would reduce water use enough to increase the growth of wheat the following year. Moisture use was reduced by this technique and yields of the succeeding wheat crops were increased. The yields of the widely spaced row crops, however, were reduced by wide spacing, and the total production per unit area (row crop plus wheat) was always less on the widely spaced plots. For example, at Colby, Kansas, wheat yields averaged 3.9 bu/ac (2.6 q/ha) more on the 80-in. (2-m) row-spaced corn land than on the 40-in. spacing, but the corn in wide rows yielded 5.1 bu/ac (3.4 q/ha) less. Use of widely spaced corn did not ensure against wheat failure either. Only once in 31 years was grain harvested on the 80-in. row area when no crop was harvested on the 40-in. row plot (Kuska and Mathews, 1956).

14-8.5 Controlling Weeds and Volunteer Plants

All plants absorb and transpire water. Weeds and other unwanted plants use moisture from seedbeds, from summer fallow, and from cropped fields. One Russian thistle plant uses about as much water as three sorghum plants, and two wild sunflowers use as much as five corn plants. Widely spaced Russian thistle plants (100 ft^2 or 9 m^2 per plant) in western Canada used nearly 500,000 lb water/ac (560,000 kg/ha). This is enough to produce 8 bu/ac (4 to 4.5 q/ha) of wheat.

Weed and volunteer plant growth must be prevented if maximum conservation of available water is to be achieved and maximum crop yields obtained. Transpiration by weeds and volunteer crop plants often is the largest single cause of stored water loss. It is especially costly under dryland conditions, where every drop of water is precious. Control of this loss is almost completely in the hands of the farmer.

14-8.6 Windbreaks and Field Shelterbelts

Barriers perpendicular to the wind reduce wind velocity and affect air temperature near the ground. Potential transpiration close to the barrier is reduced. Reductions in transpiration of 10% or more are obtained for as far as 15 to 20 times the height of the barrier to leeward. Greatest reductions are at night, with the maximum, about

30%, being found at a point twice the windbreak height to leeward. Greatest reduction at midday, about 20%, is attained about eight times the windbreak height to leeward (Woodruff et al., 1959).

Changes in transpiration are sufficient at times to prevent desiccation of plants in the shelter of the windbreaks and to reduce the effect of drought on yield. Unfortunately, reductions in crop transpiration are offset in part by use of water by the trees, reducing crop yields next to the windbreak unless the tree roots are severely pruned (see Chapter 13).

14-8.7 Antitranspirants

Long-chain fatty alcohols and some long-chain fatty acids are known to reduce transpiration by plants. Wilting of transplanted tree seedlings and other plants has been reduced by spraying leaves with octadecanol and hexadecanol. Trials with field crops also show reduced transpiration, but plant growth is reduced also. Similar applications to soils rather than to plants have no significant effect on water use (Peters and Roberts, 1963).

Fuehring (1973) reported reductions in water use and significant increases in crop growth from small applications of phenylmercuric acetate (PMA), atrazine, and Folicote to sorghum just before the boot stage. Brengle (1968) showed that although PMA reduced water use when applied to spring wheat at heading or flowering, plant growth also was reduced. Interest in antitranspirants remains high, and other materials will be found that decrease transpiration without decreasing yield, but it seems unlikely that any will prove economically useful.

SUMMARY

Dry periods of varying length cause problems for crops, livestock, and people all over the world. Problems are most severe in areas with the driest climates. Without irrigation, the only way to meet the challenge of dry weather and drought is to conserve and use wisely the water that is received. Good water management prevents damage from nearly all water shortages in humid regions; the use of all practical conservation measures prevents damage and hardship in only the least severe droughts in arid areas.

Water from precipitation is lost by plant interception, runoff, evaporation, transpiration, and deep percolation. The largest losses in humid areas are from runoff and deep percolation. Evaporation and unnecessary transpiration are most serious in dryland regions.

The principal ways to reduce runoff are to increase the soil's infiltration rate, to hold water on the soil surface longer so that it may infiltrate, and to trap runoff in dugouts, ponds, and reservoirs.

Evaporation losses are hard to control. Some reduction results from the use of crop residues and other mulches. Soil bedding designed to concentrate water in the crop row area has increased yields, but the technique is too complicated and too costly for common field use. Use of chemical monolayer and other surface evaporation barriers on reservoirs are not economically feasible.

Crops in dryland areas generally use all the water that is available each year, so crop selection and population density have little effect on water use. Control of weeds and volunteer crop plants reduces unnecessary transpiration loss. Windbreaks have some effect over a limited area. Antitranspirants have not reduced water loss economically in the field.

Summer fallow is often a useful practice where sufficient water cannot be stored for profitable annual crop production. Efficiency of fallow storage was originally low but has been increased dramatically by better weed-control and residue-management practices. Fallow is used successfully for wheat and other small grains and for sorghum production. Increased moisture-storage efficiency is the cause of some saline seeps in the northern Great Plains.

The precious water that has been stored in the soil must be guarded zealously. Great care must be taken to grow the right crops in the right way so that water is used efficiently and crops are grown successfully.

QUESTIONS

1. Describe the five avenues by which precipitation is lost from soils and the factors that influence each.
2. Describe the water-control structures needed in dryland areas.
3. What are the principal mechanisms by which surface crop residue increases the amount of soil water available for crop use in dryland areas? What is the relative effectiveness of each mechanism?
4. List the approaches that have been used to reduce water losses from soils and explain how each one works.
5. How efficient is moisture storage by summer fallowing? Where is summer fallow recommended for regular use?

REFERENCES

BARNES, S., 1938. *Soil Moisture and Crop Production under Dry Land Conditions in Western Canada.* Can. Dept. Agric. Publ. 595. Ottawa, Canada.

BLACK, A. L., 1968. Conservation bench terraces in Montana. *Trans. Am. Soc. Agric. Eng.* 11:393–395.

BRENGLE, K. G., 1968. Effect of phenylmercuric acetate on growth and water use by spring wheat. *Agron. J.* 60:246–247.

BRIGGS, L. J., and H. L. SHANTZ, 1914. Relative water requirements of plants. *J. Agric. Res.* 3:1–63.

BRUN, L. J., J. W. ERZ, J. K. LARSEN, and C. FANNING, 1986. Springtime evaporation from bare and stubble-covered soil. *J. Soil Water Cons.* 41:120–122.

Cox, M. B., 1968. Conservation bench terraces in Kansas. *Trans. Am. Soc. Agric. Eng.* 11:387–388.

Doughty, J. L., W. J. Staple, J. J. Lehane, F. G. Warder, and F. Bisal, 1949. *Soil Moisture, Wind Erosion, and Fertility on some Canadian Prairie Soils.* Can. Dept. Agric. Publ. 819 (Tech. Bull. 71). Ottawa, Canada.

Duley, F. L., 1956. The effect of a synthetic soil conditioner (HPAN) on intake, runoff, and erosion. *Soil Sci. Soc. Am. Proc.* 20:420–422.

Erickson, A. E., 1972. Improving the water properties of sand soil. In *Optimizing the Soil Physical Environment Toward Greater Crop Yields,* D. Hillel (ed.). Academic Press, New York, p. 35–41.

Erickson, A. E., C. M. Hansen, and A. J. M. Smucker, 1968. The influence of subsurface asphalt barriers on the water properties and the productivity of sand soils. *Trans. 9th Int. Cong. Soil Sci.,* Adelaide, Australia, Vol. 1, p. 331–337.

Eser, C., 1884. Investigations on the influence of the physical and chemical properties of the soil on the evaporation potential. *Forsch. Geb. Agric. Phys.* 7:1–124.

Fairbourn, M. L., and H. R. Gardner, 1974. Field use of microwatershed with vertical mulch. *Agron. J.* 66:741–744.

Fairbourn, M. L., H. R. Gardner, 1975. Water-repellant soil clods and pellets as mulch. *Agron. J.* 67:377–380.

Fisher, C. E., and E. Burnett, 1953. *Conservation and Utilization of Soil Moisture.* Tex. Agr. Exp. Sta. Bull. 767. College Station, Tex.

Fuehring, H. D., 1973. Effect of antitranspirants on yield of grain sorghum under limited irrigation. *Agron. J.* 65:348–351.

Hallsted, A. L., and O. R. Mathews, 1936. *Soil Moisture and Winter Wheat with Suggestions on Abandonment.* Kans. Agr. Exp. Sta. Bull. 273. Manhattan, Kans.

Harris, B. L., and J. H. Krishna, 1989. Furrow diking to conserve moisture. *J. Soil Water Cons.* 44:271–273.

Hauser. V. L., 1968. Conservation bench terraces in Texas. *Trans. Am. Soc. Agric. Eng.* 11:385–386, 392.

Jones, M. J., and J. Sinclair, 1989. Effects of bare fallowing, previous crop and time of ploughing on soil moisture conservation in Botswana. *Trop. Agric.* 66:54–60.

Kuska, J. B., and O. R. Mathews, 1956. *Dryland Crop-Rotations and Tillage Experiments at the Colby (Kansas) Branch Experiment Station.* USDA Circ. 979.

Letey, J., 1975. The use of nonionic surfactants on soils. In *Soil Conditioners.* Spec. Publ. 7. Soil Science Society of America, Madison, Wis. p. 145–154.

Mathews, O. R., and T. J. Army, 1960. Moisture storage on fallowed wheatland in the Great Plains. *Soil Sci. Soc. Am. Proc.* 24:414–418.

Medina, J., 1976. Harvesting surface runoff and ephemeral streamflow in arid zones. In *Conservation in Arid and Semi-Arid Zones.* Conservation Guide 3. FAO, Rome, p. 61–73.

Mehdizadeh, P., A. Kowsar, E. Vaziri, and L. Boersma, 1978. Water harvesting for afforestation: I. Efficiency and life span of asphalt cover. *Soil Sci. Soc. Am. J.* 42:644–649.

Mickelson, R. H., 1968. Conservation bench terraces in eastern Colorado. *Trans. Am. Soc. Agric. Eng.* 11:389–392.

Mickelson, R. H., and B. W. Greb, 1970. Lagoon levelling to permit annual cropping in semiarid areas. *J. Soil Water Cons.* 25:13–16.

Nicholaichuk, W., 1978. Evaporation control on farm-size reservoirs. *J. Soil Water Cons.* 33:185–188.

PENMAN, H. L., 1948. Natural evaporation from open water, bare soil, and grass. *Proc. Roy. Soc., Ser. A* 193:120–145.

PETERS, D. B., and W. J. ROBERTS, 1963. Use of octa-hexadecanol as a transpiration suppressant. *Agron. J.* 55:79.

RIPLEY, P. O., W. KABBFLEISCH, S. J. BOURGET, and D. J. COOPER, 1961. *Soil Erosion by Water.* Can. Dept. Agric. Publ. 1083.

SHAW, R. H., 1959. Water use from plastic-covered and uncovered corn plots. *Agron. J.* 51:172–173.

SMIKA, D. E., and P. W. UNGER, 1986. Effect of surface residues on soil water storage. In *Advances in Soil Science,* B. A. Stewart (ed.). Springer-Verlag, New York, 5:111–138.

SNYDER, J. R., M. D. SKOLD, and W. W. WILLIS, 1980. Economics of snow management for agriculture in the Great Plains. *J. Soil Water Cons.* 35: 21–24.

SOMANI, L. L., and S. P. SHARMA, 1985. Improving moisture conservation and nutrient utilization by wheat through subsurface compaction of a sandy soil. *Trans. Indian Soc. Desert Tech.* 10:82–87.

SWAN, J. B., J. A. STARICKA, M. J. SHAFFER, W. H. PAULSON, and A. E. PETERSON, 1990. Corn yield response to water stress, heat units, and management: Model development and calibration. *Soil Sci. Soc. Am. J.* 54:209–216.

THOMSON, L. B., 1947. *Progress Report 1937–47,* Dominion Exp. Sta., Swift Current, Saskatchewan. Canada Department of Agriculture, Ottawa.

THORNTHWAITE, C. W., 1948. An approach toward a rational classification of climate. *Geog. Rev.* 38:55–94.

WALTERS, T., 1989. *1989 Kansas Sorghum Performance Tests, Grain and Forage.* Kans. Agric. Exp. Sta. Rep. Prog. 321. Manhattan, Kans.

WOODRUFF, N. P., R. A. READ, and W. S. CHEPIL, 1959. *Influence of a Field Windbreak on Summer Wind Movement and Air Temperature.* Kans. Agric. Exp. Sta. Tech. Bull. 100. Manhattan, Kans.

ZHAI, R., R. G. KACHANOSKI, and R. P. VORONEY, 1990. Tillage effects on the spatial and temporal variations of soil water. *Soil Sci. Soc. Am. J.* 54:186–192.

ZINGG, A. W., and V. L. HAUSER, 1959. Terrace benching to save potential runoff for semiarid land. *Agron. J.* 51:289–292.

ZUZEL, J. F., J. L. PIKUL, JR., and P. E. RASMUSSEN, 1990. Tillage and fertilizer effects on water infiltration. *Soil Sci. Soc. Am. J.* 54:205–208.

15

Drainage of Cropland

The terms "poorly drained" and "well drained" tell whether crop growth is or is not limited by excess water. Well-drained soils have no excess water limitations, and moderately well-drained soils have only minor ones. Somewhat poorly drained soils can be cropped but have high water tables long enough to cause problems and delays in planting, tillage, or other practices. Poorly drained soils usually cannot be cropped without artificial drainage, and very poorly drained soils are saturated with water most of the time.

Artificial drainage is appropriate in some places but inappropriate elsewhere. Some soils are already well drained, and the wet conditions of others may benefit the most appropriate use of the land. Wetlands in the United States are protected under the "swampbuster" provisions of the 1985 Food Security Act so they will be used mostly for wildlife and recreation rather than cropland or pasture. And some drained land becomes so alkaline from sodic conditions (Chapter 16) or so acid from the oxidation of sulfides (Chapter 11) that nothing will grow on it. Artificial drainage should be provided only where soil conditions are suitable and the land use will benefit.

15-1 OCCURRENCE OF WETLANDS

Water accumulates in low places even in arid regions. Wetness occurs wherever the water supply by precipitation, overland flow, and seepage into an area exceeds the water loss by outward flow, seepage, and evapotranspiration. For example, the valley of the Dead Sea and Death Valley both accumulate salt water at their lowest points because the water has no other place to go. The water level rises until there is enough wet area for all incoming water to escape by evapotranspiration. Salt is left behind when the water evaporates.

Seep spots occur in many footslopes and hillsides where water flows above impermeable strata. The water may infiltrate on a nearby level hilltop in a humid region, or it may enter the soil and rock layers in hills or mountains, pass through several kilometers of rock, and reach the surface again in an arid valley. Such water can be under enough pressure in its aquifer to produce an artesian well (Figure 15–1). The water flow through aquifers varies from slight seepage to voluminous springs. At the largest springs in the world, near Thousand Springs, Idaho, water flows from basalt cliffs in such volume that Idaho Power Company uses it to produce electricity (Figure 15–2). Much of this water is believed to have entered the basalt layers 120 miles (200 km) away where Big Lost River, Little Lost River, and some smaller streams disappear into openings in the rock.

Not surprisingly, wetlands are more abundant in humid regions than in arid ones. Zwerman (1969) estimated that one-fourth of the cropland in New York state needs drainage. The situation is similar in many other humid areas. Any broad flat area underlain by a layer with low permeability can have wet soil when precipitation exceeds evapotranspiration. Some areas are wet for only part of the year and may have a water deficit at other times. The limitations imposed by wetness depend on how wet, how long, and when. Many crops are unaffected by wetness during winter; wetness in spring may delay planting, and wetness in fall often interferes with harvest.

15-2 CHARACTERISTICS OF WET SOILS

Poorly and very poorly drained soils produce sedges, reeds, and other water-loving vegetation. The vegetation usually contrasts with that on better drained soils even during dry seasons. Crops grown on such soils may be markedly better or poorer than on nearby soils whether or not artificial drainage is provided. Several distinctive soil characteristics result from wetness. Features that help identify wet areas

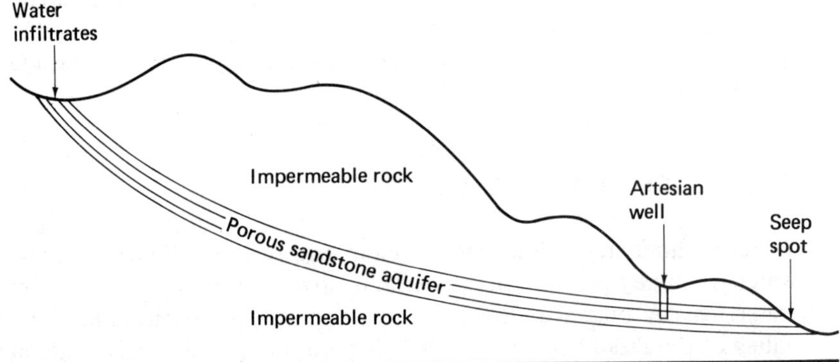

Figure 15–1 A cross section of a landscape showing an aquifer carrying water to an artesian well and a seepage spot.

a

b

Figure 15-2 Electric power is produced from the springs emerging from the canyon wall near Thousand Springs, Idaho. (a) The springs as they once appeared. (b) The power plant. (Courtesy S. Z. Thayer.)

include the vegetation and the soil color patterns, organic-matter content, clay type and amount, and soil pH and related chemical factors.

15-2.1 Colors of Wet Soils

A wet soil has characteristic colors and color patterns that persist even during dry periods. Most poorly and very poorly drained soils have relatively thick dark (often black) surface colors because of high organic-matter contents. The subsoil colors are normally grayer and duller than those common in drier soils, although rust mottles occur in soil horizons that sometimes receive oxygen. Mottles show how much the water table fluctuates. The bluish-gray color of the permanently wet part causes it to be called "blue clay" (even though its texture ranges from sand to clay). White colors result from salt accumulations on the surface of arid-region soils where water moves upward from a water table.

15-2.2 Organic Matter in Wet Soils

Soil organic-matter contents increase progressively from the driest to the wettest soils of an area. The driest soils usually have the least plant growth to produce organic matter and lose organic matter by erosion and oxidation. The wet soils accumulate organic matter, not only because they receive organic matter eroded from dry soils above them, but also because decomposition is slowed and organic matter preserved by oxygen deficiencies.

High organic-matter contents contribute to high fertility and favorable soil structure in many wet soils. However, drainage improves the aeration and causes the organic-matter content to decline gradually, so the fertility and structural conditions move toward the norms for cropped soils of the area.

Organic-matter losses are most serious in peat and muck soils. Losses by wind erosion and oxidation cause many of these organic soils to subside (shrink) at rates of 1 to 2 in. (2 to 5 cm) per year when they are drained and cropped. Organic soils disappear in a few decades or, at most, a few centuries of cropping. These soils are highly productive while they last, but they cannot be cropped without being gradually lost. The rate of loss can be minimized by keeping the water table as high as possible at all times and saturating the soil when there are no crops.

15-2.3 Clay in Wet Soils

Erosion and weathering give many wet soils more clay than their drier neighbors. Weathering progresses faster and forms more clay where the soil stays moist. Erosion takes fine particles from sloping soils and deposits them on flat areas, making the sloping soils coarser and the flat soils finer textured. Erosional sorting is most effective in materials that contain a wide range of particle sizes (are well graded). It has little effect on a well-sorted material such as many loess deposits.

Wetness also influences the type of clay in mature soils. Most soils of warm climates are dominated by kaolinite and oxide clays formed as advanced weathering removes silica. However, the wet soils retain their silica and enough bases to form montmorillonitic clay instead. The montmorillonite clay contributes to higher cation-exchange capacities and fertility in areas where the drier soils have very low fertility.

15-2.4 Reducing Conditions in Wet Soils

A few wet soils have a moving water table that carries dissolved oxygen. Most, however, have stagnant water in their saturated zones. Decomposable organic matter uses up the oxygen, produces reducing conditions, and slows microbial activity in such zones. Some microbes reduce nitrates to N_2, N_2O, or NO gases where oxygen is deficient. Others reduce ferric iron to ferrous iron and thus produce bluish-gray colors. Rust mottles are formed where air enters and oxidizes the ferrous iron back to the ferric state.

Certain wet soil and rock materials, especially those associated with coal deposits, contain iron pyrite (FeS_2, or "fool's gold"). Like most sulfides, pyrite has very low solubility and causes no problem in a wet soil, even where it is present in the nodular concretions known as "cat-clay." However, drainage ruins such a soil because the sulfide is oxidized to sulfate:

$$2\ FeS_2 + 7\ O_2 + 2\ H_2O \xrightarrow[\text{bacteria}]{\text{sulfur}} 2\ FeSO_4 + 2\ H_2SO_4$$

Sulfuric acid formed by this and subsequent reactions (see Note 11-1) acidifies the soil to a pH between 2 and 3. The reaction stops when nothing will grow, not even the sulfur bacteria.

Neutralization of sulfuric acid produced by oxidation of sulfides requires so much lime that it is usually better to avoid draining such soils. Material containing sulfides is sometimes drained however, when someone fails to recognize cat-clay (a costly oversight) or when coal mine spoil is left in a heap (an old practice that is now illegal in most states). Acidity from coal mine spoil is especially objectionable because it endangers nearby bodies of water (see Chapter 11).

15-2.5 Alkalinity in Wet Soils

Low-lying soils in arid regions may have excess water in their subsoils at least part of the year. These soils accumulate soluble salts when water moves upward from a saturated zone. Such salts commonly include carbonates that cause alkaline reactions. The amount of water is important and depends greatly on the depth of the saturated zone as well as the nature of the soil material. Types of soils influenced by water tables are shown in Figure 15-3. The water table may be regional, but in many places it is a temporary perched water table or even a saturated zone with only a few yards (meters) of lateral continuity.

A layer of soil just above the water table, known as the capillary fringe, is saturated with water by capillary rise. The capillary fringe may be 6 or 8 in. (15 or 20 cm) thick where the soil pores are small but is thinner where larger pores are present. The soil to a height of 12 to 16 in. (30 to 40 cm) above the water table is usually

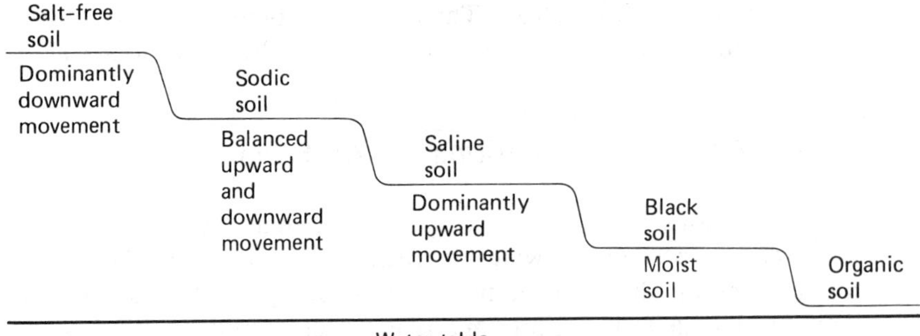

Figure 15–3 Soils developing in uniform material above a water table in an arid region.

poorly aerated and preserves enough organic matter to be black. Salts do not accumulate here because they diffuse back down through the moist soil.

Soils with white salt crusts occur where water moves upward to a dry surface. The water table usually occurs at a depth of 20 to 40 in. (50 to 100 cm), depending on the size of the soil pores. The white crust disappears when the soil is wet but reappears as the soil dries. These soils, known as saline soils, develop high osmotic concentrations when dry. Lowering the water table makes them less suitable for plant growth unless they are leached to reduce their salt contents. This process, known as soil reclamation, is discussed in Chapter 16.

Sodic soils form where upward and downward movement of water are nearly balanced. Their salt contents are not high, but Na^+ constitutes more than 15% of their exchangeable cations. This condition develops where the climate is arid and the water table is at a depth of 3 to 5 ft (100 to 150 cm). The sodium component increases because its salts are highly soluble and easily carried back to the surface. Other factors, such as the salt content of the water table and the sodium content and rate of weathering of the parent material, also influence the formation of sodic soils. A sodic condition causes dispersed clay, shrinkage and cracking when dry, and very low permeability when wet. High sodium concentrations accompanied by carbonate anions cause the soil pH to rise above 8.5. The organic-matter contents are normally low, and what little there is dissolves at the high pH and moves with the soil water. Sodic soils are called "black alkali" because a thin black organic coating forms as water evaporates at the soil surface. Water seeping from a sodic soil into a drainage ditch or other outlet appears brown and oily with dissolved organic matter. Little or nothing grows on such soils, and they are very difficult to reclaim (Chapter 16).

Saline, sodic, and salt-free soils are often intermixed on alluvial bottomlands that have spots and lenses of gravel, sand, silt, and clay. The variations in texture cause variations in capillary rise that produce the soil differences. Salt-free soils occur, for example, where a gravel lens interrupts the capillary rise.

15–3 LIMITATIONS RESULTING FROM WETNESS

The original land survey maps for some of the flatter parts of the U.S. Corn Belt labeled whole counties as "unfit for agricultural use" because of poorly drained soils. Rolling land where excess water could escape was considered best. Erosion on the hills and drainage on the flats have since reversed the ratings. The flat land now produces higher yields than the hills.

The surveyors undoubtedly realized the physical problems of wet soils—especially the lack of support for animals and vehicles and the stickiness of soils with high clay contents. Mosquitoes and flies also would have caught their attention. These factors are still important along with other physical and chemical limitations.

15-3.1 Physical Limitations of Wet Soils

Wetness has a strong influence on soil strength. Water weakens the bonds between clay particles and makes it easier for them to shift under a load. A wet clay soil becomes very weak, especially for supporting a load concentrated on a small area.

Sand behaves quite differently from clay, as a sandy beach will illustrate. Dry sand is easily blown into dunes and has little strength to support moving objects. Moistening the sand increases its strength. Sand castles with vertical walls can be built with moist sand because the water films bind the particles together. Vehicles travel easily on the moist sand several feet inland from the waterline but are likely to get stuck if they stray into the dry sand above or the wet sand below the waterline. Neither the dry sand nor the saturated sand has air-water interfaces to produce the surface tension that holds sand particles in place. Also, water provides buoyancy that makes it easier to move particles. Upward-flowing water can add enough buoyancy to separate the sand particles and make the sand into quicksand.

Most soils contain enough clay to provide binding strength to support a load when dry, but neither clay nor sand provides much strength under saturated conditions. Also, thick films of water make clay particles sticky, causing soil to adhere to feet, wheels, and other objects.

Traffic across a wet soil causes soil damage like that shown in Figure 15-4. Soil compacted by feet or wheels is often converted into a puddled mass that dries to a smooth, hard surface and later resists penetration by plant roots. Animal and vehicular traffic should therefore be kept away from wet soils for the sake of both soil and traffic.

Wetness often delays tilling and planting for several days. The more clay the soil contains, the longer the delay. Soil wetness in temperate climates causes low soil temperatures in the spring (Note 15-1). Seed planted too early will rot and not germinate. Even a few wet spots in a field create a problem. The farmer must either wait for them to dry before working the field or work around them and come back later.

NOTE 15-1
EFFECT OF WETNESS ON SOIL TEMPERATURE

Wetness lowers the temperature of soil in two ways—by evaporation and by the heat capacity of the water. Each gram of water evaporating at 20°C absorbs 585 cal of heat (539 cal at 100°C). More water evaporates and therefore more heat is withdrawn from a wet soil than from a dry one. Cooling by evaporation remains significant until the soil surface becomes dry.

The heat capacity of water does not actually cool the soil, but it does increase the amount of heat required to warm the soil. The heat capacity of water is 1.0 cal/g, whereas that of dry soil is about 0.2 cal/g. A comparison of a dry soil and a wet soil will illustrate the effect of heat capacity:

	Soil near wilting point	Saturated soil
Percent H_2O by weight	20%	60%
Heat capacity per gram of solid:		
From solids	0.2 cal	0.2 cal
From water	0.2 cal	0.6 cal
Total heat capacity	0.4 cal	0.8 cal

Heat applied to the saturated soil in this example would raise its temperature only half as fast as it would that of the dry soil, even without allowing for evaporation.

The actual temperature difference between wet and dry soils is limited by the tendency of cool soil to absorb more heat and lose less than warm soil. Wesseling (1974) cites data for temperature differences of 2 to 4°C (3.5 to 7°F) between drained and undrained sandy soils and from 0.5 to 1°C (1 to 2°F) in clay soils. The drained clay soils retained more water and showed less difference than the sandy soils.

The importance of differences in soil temperature was demonstrated by Walker (1969). He found that 1°C difference in temperature could make as much as 50% difference in initial growth rates of early-planted corn.

A rain that produces runoff often makes ponds in low spots even after a crop has been planted. Sometimes the crop is drowned and the wet spot becomes a weed patch unless it is replanted. Heavy rain may cause another problem when a crop has been planted but not yet germinated. The pounding raindrops may puddle the surface and form a crust that dries so hard it prevents seedlings from emerging.

15-3.2 Chemical Effects of Wetness

Most chemical effects of wetness are caused by oxygen deficiencies resulting from poor aeration. Plant roots need oxygen for respiration to provide energy for growth, nutrient absorption, and other life processes. Small amounts of oxygen may be obtained from water as in solution culture, but this source requires frequent replenishment. Rice and some other water-loving plants absorb oxygen above the

Figure 15-4 Cattle trampled this pasture when it was wet, killed about half of the grass, and produced a rough surface. (Courtesy F. R. Troeh.)

water level and transport it inside the plant to the roots. But most plants rely on oxygen absorbed from soil air. Their roots will not grow into saturated soil or even into soil that has isolated pockets of air in its larger pores. There must be enough interchange with the atmosphere to replenish the oxygen supply in the soil and exhaust carbon dioxide.

Researchers have shown that root growth of a wide variety of plants needs minimum oxygen diffusion rates between 5 and 25 $\times$ 10^{-8} g of O_2/cm^2 per minute. Patt, et al. (1966) reported that citrus trees need 8 to 10% of aeration porosity by volume in the 10- to 30-in. (25- to 75-cm) layer to produce an adequate root density. The effective depth of many soils is limited by poor aeration rather than by soil strength.

Certain plant nutrient deficiencies can be attributed to soil wetness. Two of these will be discussed here—potassium and nitrogen. Several others could be added, especially if the effects of pH changes produced by draining wet soils, as discussed in Section 15-2, were considered.

Potassium absorption by plant roots is slowed by poor aeration. Plants normally use energy from root respiration to absorb potassium and make it much more concentrated inside the roots than in the soil water. Potassium is said to be physiologically unavailable when a deficiency is caused by a shortage of oxygen.

Nitrogen deficiencies are most likely to occur in soils that are alternately saturated and unsaturated for a few days at a time, like the soil shown in Figure 15-5. Nitrifying bacteria convert ammonium ions to nitrates during the periods when oxygen is available. Other microbes reduce the nitrates to gaseous N_2, N_2O,

Figure 15–5 This corn is pale green as a result of nitrogen deficiency caused by denitrification in this intermittently wet area. The cracked and curled soil surface is a result of ponding. (Courtesy F. R. Troeh.)

and NO during the saturated periods. This denitrification process can use up large quantities of available nitrogen.

Another chemical problem results where metal pipelines cross both wet and dry soils. Redox potential differences cause an electrolytic action that ionizes metal, creating pits in the pipe that may become holes in one-fourth to one-half of its normal life expectancy. Saline soils make the problem worse because dissolved salts increase the electrical conductivity of the water.

15–4 WATER REMOVED BY DRAINAGE

Soil water is commonly classified as unavailable, available, and gravitational, according to how tightly it is held in the soil. Drainage systems remove only gravitational water, and not even all of that. The line between available and gravitational water is called field capacity and is commonly taken to be $^1/_3$ bar (0.33 atm or 0.34 kg/cm^2). This line is gradational and varies from values as low as $^1/_{10}$ bar for very sandy soils to as high as $^1/_2$ bar for clay soils. These fractional changes in soil moisture tension near field capacity influence the amount of available water as much as variations of several bars near the wilting point, as shown by the soil moisture retention curve in Figure 15–6.

Field capacity is defined as the amount of water retained by the soil when downward movement into dry soil below nearly ceases. The time required varies from about a day for sandy soils to three or four days for soils with low per-

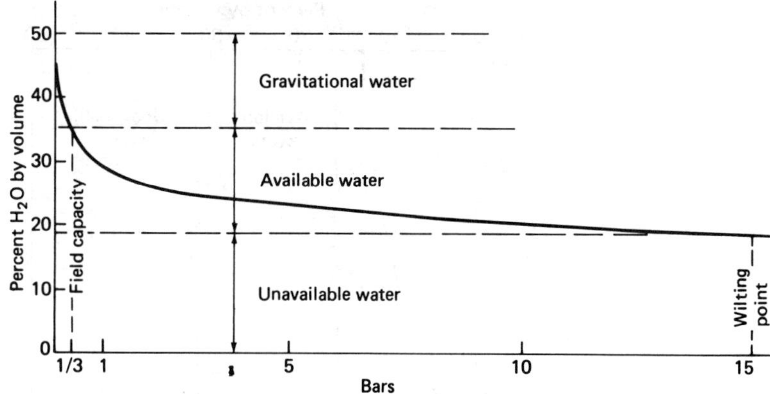

Figure 15-6 A soil-moisture-retention curve showing water relationships in a representative loamy soil with 50% pore space.

meability. The dry soil below is important because the soil-moisture tension of a loamy soil exerts as much force on the water as about 10 ft (3 m) of gravitational head. Sandy soils exert 3 to 6 ft (1 or 2 m) of tension and clay soils as much as 16 ft (5 m).

Soils with water tables obviously do not have dry soil below to exert soil-moisture tension. A subsurface drainage system functions by gravitational force and would theoretically have to lower the water table to a depth of 11 ft (3.4 m) to produce a tension of 1/3 bar at the soil surface. Few drains are placed that deep, so less tension is created and more available water is left in the soil. Figure 15-7 shows the amount of air space resulting from a drain at a depth of 7 ft (2 m) in a soil like that of Figure 15-6.

15-5 SURFACE VERSUS SUBSURFACE DRAINAGE

Areas that need artificial surface drainage are either nearly level or depressional. The excess water to be removed by surface drains has not had enough time to infiltrate. Most of it comes from precipitation on either the wetland or nearby higher areas.

Subsurface drainage is used where there is a high water table. The water may have come from precipitation on the land, surface flow, seepage from nearby land, or from seeping a long distance through an aquifer. Irrigation water also contributes to the need for subsurface drainage in irrigated areas. Whatever the source, excess water is already in the soil and must be removed from below.

15-6 METHODS OF REMOVING WATER

Ditches are often used for surface drainage and tile for subsurface drainage, but there are exceptions. Ditches can be used for subsurface drainage and tile lines can

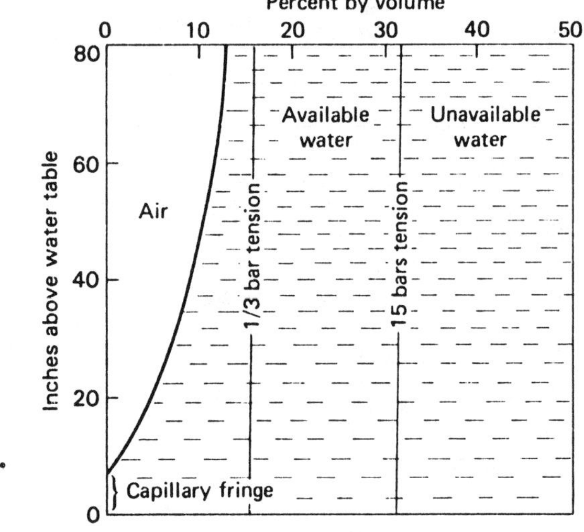

Figure 15-7 Air and water held by a soil like that of Figure 15-6 above a water table at 7 ft (2 m).

have surface inlets. Several other drainage methods also are available, including land smoothing, wells, bedding systems, and mole drains. Drainage methods are chosen according to the amount of water to be removed, soil characteristics, cost and convenience factors, availability of equipment and materials, and personal preferences.

15-6.1 Land Smoothing

Filling low places in a field is called land smoothing or, in irrigated areas, land leveling. Leveling improves both the irrigation and the drainage of irrigated land. Actually, the "leveled" land usually has a gentle slope that is as uniform as possible. Elimination of high and low areas in a field is costly, but leveling makes it possible to greatly improve the uniformity of water application by surface irrigation.

Land smoothing for drainage purposes can improve both surface and subsurface drainage. Eliminating depressions lets water flow across the area without being trapped. Subsurface drainage is also improved by more uniform infiltration and because the soil surface of the former low area is higher above the water table.

Land smoothing a field like that shown in Figure 15-8 may be the only drainage practice needed, or it may be used to make a ditch or tile drainage system function better. An important advantage of land smoothing is that it usually requires no maintenance.

15-6.2 Drainage Ditches

Cato discussed Roman methods of farm drainage by ditches as an established practice in 200 B.C. (King, 1931). The Egyptians, Babylonians, and perhaps others practiced drainage centuries before Cato's time. Ditches offer high capacity for

Figure 15-8 Land smoothing to allow water to escape would have saved the crop in this depression in an Iowa cornfield. (Courtesy F. R. Troeh.)

either surface or subsurface drainage, even where there is little slope. Installation costs are usually less than those for a covered drain installed at the same depth. Ditches often require more maintenance than covered drains to remove sediment and unwanted vegetation that inhibit the water flow, but it is easy to see when maintenance is needed. Ditches such as that shown in Figure 15-9 are often used for main drains and as outlets for tile and other covered drains. The principal disadvantage of ditches is that their channels and banks occupy land that could be cropped if a covered drain were used. In addition, ditches can be hazardous obstacles to the

Figure 15-9 This 20-ft (6-m) deep ditch in Idaho serves as an overflow for irrigation water if the canal above gets too full, as an interceptor for seepage water, and as an outlet for drainage systems in the valley. (Courtesy F. R. Troeh.)

movement of people, animals, and machines. Ditches are often placed along field boundaries to minimize these disadvantages.

Variations in ditch gradient are much less serious than variable gradients in covered drains. Ditches are therefore preferred for the initial drainage of unstable land that may settle unevenly. Covered drains may be installed after settling has ceased. Many ditches are nearly flat because there is little elevation difference between the wet land and the outlet. The steepest gradient used should produce a nonerosive velocity of no more than 0.06 to 0.24 ft/sec (0.2 to 0.8 m/s), depending on the erodibility of the soil.

Ditches are usually widely spaced—hundreds of yards (meters) apart where possible—to minimize the obstacle problem and the amount of land removed from crop production. Ditches for surface drainage should be designed to carry the maximum anticipated flow when filled to no more than 80% of their depth. Their capacities can be calculated by Manning's formula, as explained in Note 4-2.

Ditches for subsurface drainage usually are deeper and farther apart than tile drains would be placed. Ditches 6 to 10 ft (2 to 3 m) deep provide adequate drainage in many soils even though they are spaced 300 to 650 ft (100 to 200 m) or more apart. Soils that need more drainage may have tile lines that empty into ditches 1/4 mile (400 m) or more apart. These ditches, too, need to be several feet deep to serve as outlets for the tile.

Steep ditch banks minimize the amount of soil to be moved and the land area occupied, but a safety margin should be allowed, and maintenance requirements need to be considered. Donnan and Schwab (1974) indicate that common side slopes in clay soils range from 0.5:1 (1 ft horizontal to 2 ft vertical) to 1.5:1 and that coarser-textured soils need side slopes between 1:1 and 2:1, or 3:1 for some very sandy soils. Cleaning by dragline requires side slopes no steeper than 1:1, grazing by livestock requires slopes of 2:1 or flatter, and banks to be mowed or crossed by machinery should be no steeper than 3:1 (Soil Conservation Service, 1973).

Vegetation as shown in Figure 15-10 is both beneficial and harmful to drainage ditches. Vegetation helps stabilize ditchbanks against slumping and erosion and may be of value to wildlife. Water lilies, cattails, and other water plants, however, slow the flow, raise the water level, and reduce the effectiveness of the drain. After all, the effectiveness of subsurface drainage depends on the water level rather than the ditch depth.

15-6.3 Tile Drainage

Tile lines are commonly used when a drainage system must extend into the interior of a field. They are especially common for subsurface drainage, but some have surface inlets to drain depressions or low areas above terraces. This last use has developed in recent years as a means of making terraces as straight and parallel to one another as possible (Chapter 10) and to eliminate the grassed waterways used previously.

Tile drainage has been practiced for hundreds of years. "Horseshoe tile" were invented in France about the fourteenth or fifteenth century, then forgotten and reinvented in England in the seventeenth or eighteenth century (King, 1931). They

Figure 15-10 Vegetation stabilizes the banks of this drainage ditch, but the vegetation growing in the water slows the flow and raises the water level. (Courtesy F. R. Troeh.)

were made by hand from baked clay with a U-shaped cross section and were placed with the open side down in the bottom of a trench, sometimes with a flat clay pallet beneath them. The practice of tiling was brought to the United States from Scotland in 1835 (Wooten and Jones, 1955). A tile-making machine was invented in England in 1841, but tile continued to be placed in hand-dug trenches until a steam-powered trenching machine was marketed about 1883. Tile are now placed by wheel-type or bucket-ladder-type trenching machines, most of which can dig as deep as 6 ft (1.8 m). Cuts deeper than 6 ft require special large trenchers, backhoes, or draglines and are considerably more expensive.

Tile drainage permits normal equipment and livestock traffic across the field. A good system should function for hundreds of years with little maintenance (some sewer tile thousands of years old are still serviceable). The biggest disadvantage is cost—unless, of course, something prevents tile drainage from working. Conditions that limit the use of tile include shallow soil, excessive stoniness, and soils with hydraulic conductivities below 0.2 to 0.4 in./hr (0.5 to 1 cm/h).

Types of Tile. Three types of tile are now in common use—clay, concrete, and plastic. All three types have round cross sections. Clay tile are the traditional type, made by forming moist clay into pipes 1 ft (30 cm) long and baking them until they are dry and hard. They are available with inside diameters ranging from 4 to 12 in. (10 to 30 cm). The walls are usually between 0.5 and 0.6 in. (12 to 15 mm) thick. Clay tile are brittle and will deteriorate if subjected to freezing and thawing but are otherwise very durable.

Concrete tile are similar to clay tile except that they are usually 2 or 3 ft (60 or 90 cm) long and are available in larger sizes up to 3 ft (90 cm) in diameter. Concrete tile resist freezing and thawing and are therefore better than clay tile for lines that are above the frost line. Concrete is subject to attack by acids, so it should not be used in extremely acid soils.

The newest type of tile is made of either PVC or polyethylene plastic and began to be marketed in the 1960s. It is thin-walled and corrugated to give it strength and flexibility. As shown in Figure 15–11, it comes in rolls 200 to 300 ft (60 to 90 m) long and has slots for water to enter. Diameters range from 3 to 10 in. (7.5 to 25 cm). Plastic resists damage by both freezing and acids, but there have been reports of rodents chewing holes in it. It is less rigid than clay or concrete and relies more on proper packing of soil around it for support to keep it from collapsing. The long lengths and easy joining of plastic tile eliminate the misalignment problems that can occur with clay or concrete.

Several types of pipe, including steel, aluminum, rigid plastic, and fiber, are used where strength or rigidity are needed in a drainage system. Most of these are not true tile because they have no holes for water to enter. A 20-ft (6-m) length of corrugated steel is commonly used at the outlet of a tile line. Rigid pipe also may be needed where a tile line passes under a road, through a very deep cut with heavy overburden, or through soils that may shrink and settle unevenly.

Depth and Spacing of Tile Lines. Hand-dug tile lines were often placed at depths of 20 to 24 in. (50 to 60 cm) and were spaced only 15 or 20 ft (5 or 6 m) apart in some fields. Most lines are now placed at depths of 3 to 5 ft (90 to 150 cm) in humid regions and about 6 or 7 ft (2 m) in arid regions. Many tiling contractors charge extra for placing tile deeper than 4 ft (120 cm). Deeper placement protects against frost, heavy vehicles, and plant roots and permits wider spacings between

Figure 15–11 The newest type of tile is made of corrugated plastic, comes in rolls, and has holes for water to enter. (Courtesy F. R. Troeh.)

lines. The 2-m depth for arid regions prevents capillary rise from carrying salts to the soil surface. Tile lines are now commonly placed between 30 and 120 ft (10 to 40 m) apart depending on the soil and the depth of placement.

Soil permeability is a factor in determining the depth and spacing of tile lines. Less permeable soils need closer-spaced, shallower lines to remove the water within a reasonable time. The horizontal permeability is most important because drainage water moves horizontally more than vertically. Basak (1972) found horizontal hydraulic conductivity to be 1.0 to 1.6 times as high as in the vertical direction. Variation in the properties of soil horizons also should be considered. Going deeper into a less permeable horizon may not affect water removal, but reaching a more permeable layer may be very beneficial.

Maintaining suitable slope gradients for water flow in tile lines is more important than constant depth. Donnan and Schwab (1974) suggest a minimum gradient of 0.1% for 4-in. (10-cm) drain lines and 0.05% for 6-in. (15-cm) lines. Larger tile lines also should have gradients of at least 0.05% (Beauchamp, 1955). Line gradients steeper than 1% require that tile joints be wrapped with durable material such as tar-impregnated paper and packed tightly with soil to keep the tile properly aligned. Or, sewer tile with sealed joints can be used on steeper grades that do not need drainage. Breathers (vents) to allow air entrance are sometimes needed at the top of a slope, and relief wells at the bottom to prevent pressure buildup and facilitate water flow.

Laying Tile. Tiling is greatly facilitated by trenching machines. Some machines made a wide trench so that a worker could ride inside a trailing shield and place the tile by hand. Other workers used tiling hooks as shown in Figure 15–12.

Figure 15–12 Concrete tile being placed with tiling hooks behind a trenching machine. (Courtesy W. H. Lathrop.)

New machines provide a tile chute that guides tile from an aboveground loading point down into place in the trench. Nearly all flexible plastic tile is placed automatically as shown in Figure 15–13. Such machines lay tile at rates up to about 130 ft (40 m) per minute (Fouss, 1971).

Topographic surveys are needed for planning tile depths and gradients. The trenching machine is usually controlled by either a guideline or a laser beam. The guideline method involves setting stakes to hold a line at a specified height above the level of the tile line. The machine operator then keeps a pointer on the machine at the level of the guideline.

The laser method is an example of new technology applied to an old problem. The laser beam is aimed parallel to the desired grade line in place of the staked guideline. A photo sensor on the tiling machine detects the laser beam and signals controls that keep the machine on grade. The laser unit can control the depth for distances up to 1700 ft (500 m) with a vertical accuracy of 1 cm (Agricultural Research Service, 1967).

Plastic tile has holes for water to enter, but clay and concrete tile allow water entrance only at the joints. Spacings of 1/8 in. (2 or 3 mm) are recommended for most soils. Larger openings, such as those resulting from changes in direction, should be covered to keep soil from entering the tile.

The soil or other material next to the tile needs to be permeable to water, stable enough to stay out of the tile, and shaped to support the tile on all sides. Subsoil

Figure 15–13 Flexible plastic tile being installed by a tiling machine. (Courtesy USDA Soil Conservation Service.)

often does not meet these requirements. Some surface soils with stable granular structure will serve for *blinding* (surrounding and covering) the tile. Coarse sand and gravel mixtures also can be used for blinding.

15-6.4 Other Closed Drains

Closed drains are those that are covered and concealed. These include tile drains, box drains, rock drains, and mole drains.

Box drains consist of boards made into a box with triangular or rectangular cross section and buried in a trench. They have a short life expectancy unless treated with a wood preservative to prevent rotting. They and rock drains were usually homemade and only used to drain very small areas. They were most common in pioneer times. Rock drains are constructed by placing several layers of rocks in the bottom of a trench and covering them with soil. The capacity is low and becomes even lower if soil fills the space between the rocks.

Mole drains are drawn rather than laid. A torpedo-shaped "mole" hooked behind a long shank is pulled through the soil to create an unlined channel about 4 in. (10 cm) in diameter. Mole drains are commonly made at depths of 20 to 30 in. (50 to 75 cm) and spaced 10 to 15 ft (3 to 5 m) apart. The close spacing and the fracturing produced by the shank help make mole drains effective. Any open slots left by the shank should be tilled shut as soon as possible to keep soil from falling into the mole channel.

Mole drains are relatively inexpensive and can be made quickly when the soil is dry on top and moist below. They should be drawn more slowly in wet soil because a vacuum can cause the channel to close behind the mole. Sandy soils are generally too unstable for mole drains, but properly installed moles in clay subsoils probably will last from 3 to 15 years; those in organic soils may last three to five years. Sometimes a new set of mole drains is drawn when an old set becomes ineffective. Mole drains are best suited for temporary drainage of an area where the need may disappear (as for removing excess salts from a saline soil) or where a more permanent drainage system will be installed later (as for draining an organic soil that will settle unevenly at first).

15-6.5 Bedding Systems

Bedding systems are sometimes used for surface drainage on land with slope gradients less than 1%. These systems are the most common type of surface drainage in Europe. They are used where slow permeability and moderate soil depth prevent the use of most other types of drainage. The crops are often pasture or hay, although some row crops and truck crops are grown on bedded land.

Bedding is also called crowning because the areas between drains are usually graded into a raised convex shape. The beds can be formed by always plowing in the same direction, but it is much faster to use earth-moving equipment. Shallow grassed waterways about 20 in. (0.5 m) deep with about 8:1 side slopes are located between the crowned areas. Row crops may be grown on the crowned areas but not in the waterways. The rows run parallel to the waterways. The crowned areas are usually about 65 ft (20 m) wide, their exact width being a multiple of the width of the equipment used to crop them.

15-6.6 Vertical Drainage

Both pumped wells and dry wells are used for drainage. Pumped wells are relatively expensive to install and operate, but they can tap a deep gravel layer and thus reduce the water table to lower levels than other drainage methods. The pumped water may be useful for irrigation or livestock. Pumped wells also may be used to remove water from aquifers and thus reduce their contribution to water tables and springs.

Dry wells, otherwise known as drainage wells or vertical drains, act as wells in reverse. Either surface or subsurface water is permitted to run into the well and down to an adsorbing layer below. Most states have public health laws restricting or prohibiting the use of dry wells because this simple solution to a drainage problem entails significant hazards. One, the possibility that sediment may plug the pores in the adsorbing layer, can be reduced by filtering the water before it enters the well. Another peril is the pollution potential from surface water entering an aquifer.

15-7 RANDOM, REGULAR, AND INTERCEPTOR DRAINS

The topography of the area, source of excess water, and pattern of wetness are important factors in determining whether the design of a drainage system will be random, regular, or interceptor.

Random drains are used in rolling topography with small wet areas. The drains follow the lowest connecting areas from one wet area to the next. Either ditch or tile drainage may be used, but the layout depends on the locations of wet spots.

Regular drainage systems consist of several parallel ditches or tile lines draining broad flat areas. A variety of patterns are possible, including two basic ones known as parallel and herringbone, as shown in Figure 15-14. Laterals may enter the main drain from one or both sides in either system. The herringbone pattern allows both the laterals and the main line to flow down the general slope of an area rather than directly across it.

Interceptor drains are placed between the source of excess water and the area needing drainage. The drain must be deep enough to intercept the main flow of water. The water being intercepted in humid regions comes from natural precipitation, whereas in arid regions it may come from an irrigation canal.

15-8 DESIGN FACTORS FOR DRAINAGE SYSTEMS

The first consideration in the design of a drainage system is what land should be drained. Areas that will benefit and other areas that might be harmed by removal of water should be identified and mapped. Soil maps, topographic maps, geologic maps, and hydrologic maps are all useful for planning drainage systems.

A soil survey helps identify both problems and potentials. It locates wet soils

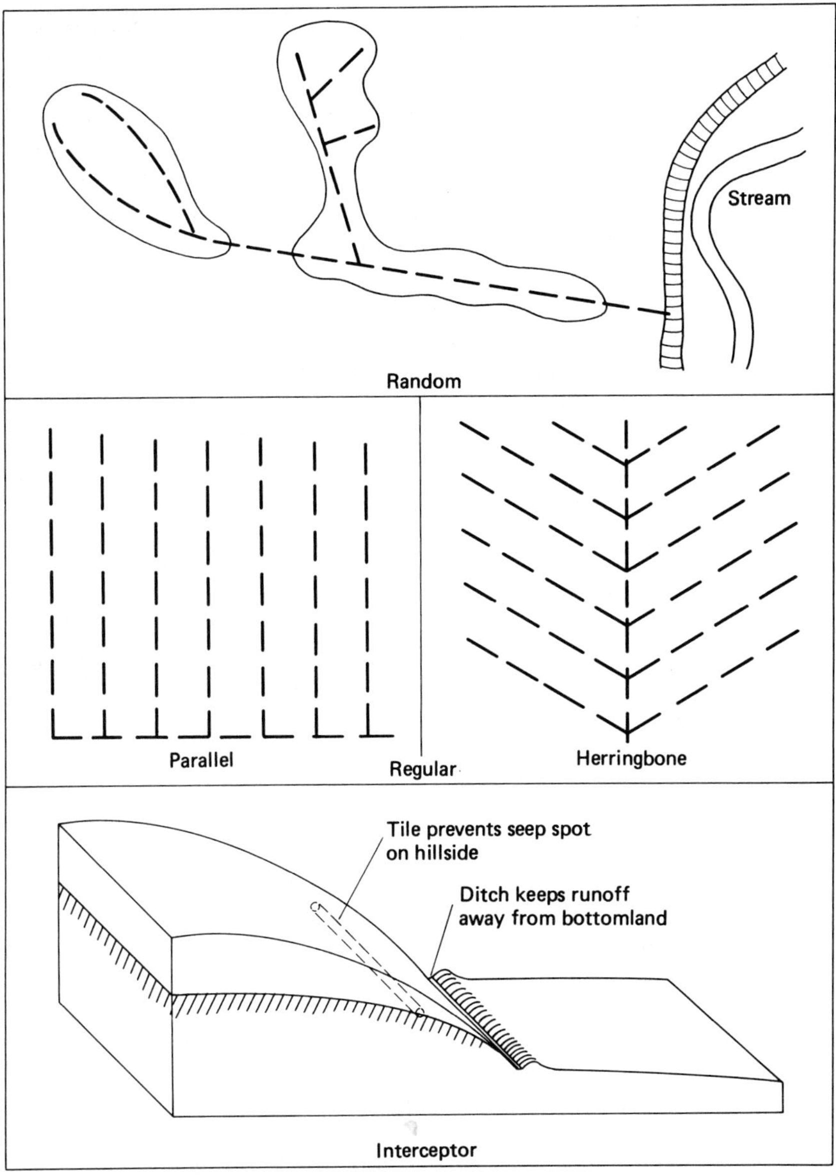

Figure 15–14 Random, regular, and interceptor drainage systems each have their own distinctive layout patterns.

and identifies soils high in clay, organic matter, and/or sodium. Soils shallow to bedrock or other impermeable layers are shown on soil maps. Soil surveys also show which soils are permeable enough to drain easily and which ones are already adequately drained for their intended use.

Precise topographic information is needed for drainage design. Elevations of the outlet and of high and low points throughout the system must be known. Often a full topographic survey is worthwhile. Some elevations may need to be measured even if a topograpic map is already available.

Geologic maps tell what underlies the soil to a greater depth than soil maps. Permeable layers that can carry water either in or out of the area are identified, and the nature and locations of impermeable rock layers are revealed.

Hydrologic maps show the source of the water, its direction of movement, and the depth of the water table at various points. They help identify places where an interceptor drain can be used instead of placing several drainage lines across the field.

All of these types of maps plus field observations may be necessary for a complex project, but many simpler projects are designed from one or two maps plus some field observations. Aerial photographs are often very helpful. For example, a sandy strip that carried water into the corner of an orchard in Idaho was much easier to see on an aerial photograph than on the ground.

15-8.1 Choosing the Type of System

Decisions regarding drainage systems are based on the information sources discussed in the preceding paragraphs and the preferences of the persons involved. Some choices become obvious as information is gathered. The Idaho orchard mentioned in the last paragraph should be drained by an interceptor system. Rolling land with several wet spots needs a random system, whereas a large uniformly wet area calls for regularly spaced parallel drains.

Surface drainage works where water stays on the land surface long enough to be gathered and carried away. Subsurface drainage is required when the water enters the soil rapidly or from beneath. Sometimes the best system is a combination of surface and subsurface drainage.

The decision to use ditches, tile lines, wells, or some other method to remove excess water is strongly influenced by economics and convenience factors; preferences and customs are also factors. Tile lines are advantageous in fields where ditches would be in the way. Ditches, on the other hand, are often used for main outlets where the large tile required to carry the water would be too expensive. The special adaptations of other types of systems were explained in Section 15-6.

15-8.2 Layout of a Drainage System

The outlet is a critical part of a drainage system and is a natural beginning point for a design. Its location and elevation are significant to the placement of ditches and tile lines. Also, the outlet must have adequate capacity to handle the water and be legally accessible for that purpose.

Figure 15-15 shows three different kinds of drainage systems on a farm in a humid region. Water from all three systems drains into a main ditch that belongs to and is managed by a drainage company. The smaller ditches and the tile lines belong to the farm owner. The bottomland in the southwest corner of Figure 15-15 is surrounded by ditches on all sides. The main ditch is about 8 ft (2.5 m) deep across this bottomland, and the two farm ditches have gradients of about 0.1%, so the

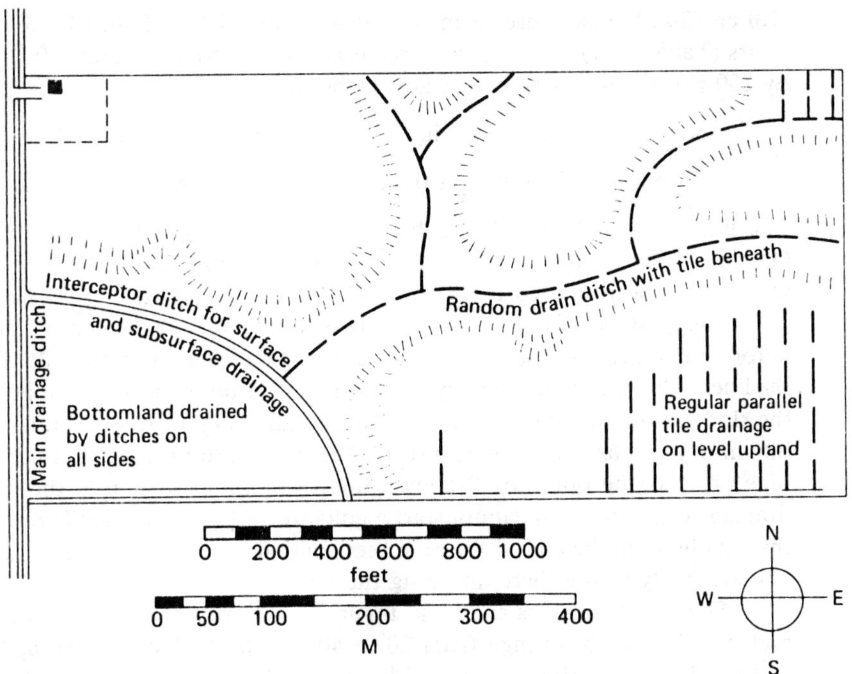

Figure 15–15 This 80-acre (32-ha) area has drainage ditches surrounding a bottomland, a random system of ditches with tile beneath following natural drainageways, and a regular parallel tile drainage system on a level upland. The single branch tile line near bottom center of the map allows air to enter the line at the top of a slope.

water flows at nonerosive velocities into the main ditch. All three ditches have side slopes of 1.5:1. This bottomland soil is sufficiently permeable that these three ditches provide adequate drainage, especially since both surface and subsurface water from the upland are intercepted by one of the ditches. The ditch capacities could have been calculated by Manning's formula as explained in Note 4–2, but this was unnecessary because of their large surplus capacity. If it had been needed, additional surface drainage for the bottomland could have been provided by a few field ditches or a bedding system, and subsurface drainage could have been supplemented by tile lines.

The level upland in the southeast corner of Figure 15–15 is drained by a parallel tile system. The most important design factors for a regular system such as this are the depth, spacing, gradient, and size of the tile lines. These are approximately 4 ft (1.2 m) deep at the main line and as shallow as 3 ft (0.9 m) at the upper ends of the laterals. A spacing of 80 ft (25 m) between lines was chosen for this moderately permeable soil. The laterals are 4-in. (10-cm) clay tile placed on a controlled 0.2% gradient. The upper end of each lateral is closed to keep out soil and burrowing animals.

Most drainage laterals have more than adequate capacity, but the size of main line required must be calculated. For the system shown in Figure 15–15, the *drainage coefficient* (the depth of water to be removed in 24 hours) is taken as 0.4 in./24 hr

(1.0 cm/24 h). Elsewhere, it might range from 0.1 to 1.5 in. (0.3 to 4 cm) per 24 hours (Table 15–1). The drained area is equivalent to a rectangle 500 by 830 ft (150 by 250 m), so the amount of water to be removed is

$$500 \text{ ft} \times 830 \text{ ft} \times 0.4 \text{ in./24 hr} \times 1 \text{ ft/12 in.} = 13{,}833 \text{ ft}^3\text{/24 hr}$$

$$\text{or } 150 \text{ m} \times 250 \text{ m} \times 1.0 \text{ cm/24 h} \times 1 \text{ m/100 cm} = 375 \text{ m}^3\text{/24 h}$$

The main line in Figure 15–15 has a slope gradient of 0.1% and needs a 6–in. (15–cm) tile to transport this quantity of water (Table 15–2). An 8–in. (20–cm) tile would have been needed if the line had had surface inlets.

The gradient of the main line increases to about 1% for the last 300 ft (100 m) before it empties into the ditch and could cause a vacuum that would draw soil into the lines. This problem can be overcome (1) by installing a surface inlet at the top of the slope so air can enter the line, or (2) by allowing air to enter through a branch line in dry soil as shown in Figure 15–15. A 20-ft (6-m) length of corrugated steel pipe protects the outlet of the main line by spilling water into the middle of the drainage ditch so that it cannot start a gully by undercutting tile. Three rods inserted through holes in the end of the pipe keep animals out. Animals that crawl into a tile line are likely to die there and plug the line.

The random drains shown in Figure 15–15 are a combination of field ditches and tile. The ditches range from 20 to 40 in. (0.5 to 1 m) in depth, have bottom widths of 0 to 7 ft (0 to 2 m), and have side slopes between 3:1 and 4:1. They are crossable with farm machinery and have a cover of smooth bromegrass to control erosion. Other sod-forming grasses such as Kentucky bluegrass, tall fescue, bermudagrass, and dallisgrass can be used in their appropriate climatic zones. Reed canarygrass is used in cool climates and bahiagrass in warm climates where tough sods are needed to resist gully formation. Switchgrass has become important for field ditches because it resists the triazine herbicides that have killed other grasses in many waterways.

Tile lines located under one side of the field ditches provide subsurface drainage to dry the waterway after a rain. These are mostly 4–in. (10–cm) tile, but 6–in. (15–cm) tile is used for the lower part of the main line. Locating them at the side of the ditch area reduces the likelihood of surface water eroding holes down to the tile. The upper ends of the lines are closed and the lower end is protected by a

TABLE 15–1 DRAINAGE COEFFICIENTS FOR SUBSURFACE TILE DRAINAGE[a]

	Field crops		Truck crops	
	in./24 hr	cm/24 hr	in./24 hr	cm/24 hr
Arid regions (irrigated)	0.12–0.25	0.3–0.6	0.25–0.50	0.6–1.2
Humid regions				
Mineral soils	0.25–0.50	0.6–1.2	0.50–0.75	1.2–1.8
Organic soils	0.50–0.75	1.2–1.8	0.75–1.60	1.8–4.0

[a]The values should be doubled or a known amount added where surface drainage is also carried by the tile.

Source: Based on Soil Conservation Service, 1973, and Donnan and Schwab, 1974.

TABLE 15-2 FLOW VELOCITIES[a] AND CARRYING CAPACITIES[b] OF WELL-ALIGNED CLAY OR CONCRETE TILE[c]

Tile diameter	Tile gradient 0.05%	0.1%	0.2%	0.5%	1.0%
4-in. (10-cm) tile:					
Velocity of flow					
ft/sec	[d]	0.82	1.18	1.83	2.59
m/s		0.25	0.36	0.56	0.79
Capacity					
ft^3/24 hr		6,030	8,500	13,450	19,020
m^3/24 h	—	171	241	381	539
5-in. (12.5-cm) tile:					
Velocity of flow					
ft/sec	0.69	0.95	1.35	2.13	3.02
m/s	0.21	0.29	0.41	0.65	0.92
Capacity					
ft^3/24 hr	7,730	10,900	15,420	24,420	34,510
m^3/24 h	219	309	437	692	978
6-in. (15-cm) tile:					
Velocity of flow					
ft/sec	0.75	1.08	1.54	2.43	3.41
m/s	0.23	0.33	0.47	0.74	1.04
Capacity					
ft^3/24 hr	12,560	17,750	25,090	39,520	56,100
m^3/24 h	356	503	711	1,120	1,590
8-in. (20-cm) tile:					
Velocity of flow					
ft/sec	0.92	1.31	1.84	2.92	4.13
m/s	0.28	0.40	0.56	0.89	1.26
Capacity					
ft^3/24 hr	27,030	38,110	53,990	85,400	120,680
m^3/24 h	766	1,080	1,530	2,420	3,420
10-in. (25-cm) tile:					
Velocity of flow					
ft/sec	1.08	1.51	2.13	3.41	4.79
m/s	0.33	0.46	0.65	1.04	1.46
Capacity					
ft^3/24 hr	49,050	69,160	98,100	154,910	219,140
m^3/24 h	1,390	1,960	2,780	4,390	6,210
12-in. (30-cm) tile:					
Velocity of flow					
ft/sec	1.21	1.71	2.43	3.84	5.41
m/s	0.37	0.52	0.74	1.17	1.65
Capacity					
ft^3/24 hr	79,750	112,570	159,150	251,950	356,400
m^3/24 h	2,260	3,190	4,510	7,140	10,100

[a]Velocity based on Manning's formula with slope as a decimal and tile radius in feed ($V = 86\ R^{2/3}S^{1/2}$) or meters ($V = 58.5\ R^{2/3}S^{1/2}$).

[b]Capacity $= \pi r^2 \times$ velocity $\times$ time

[c]The corresponding velocities and capacities for corrugated plastic drain tubing are about two-thirds as large.

[d]Four-in. tile is not recommended on 0.05% slope.

steel pipe like the one already described for the regular tile drain. The three short lines in the northeast corner of Figure 15–15 form a regular drainage system that outlets through the random tile line.

15-8.3 Installing a Drainage System

The installation of a drainage system begins at the outlet and moves upward so that the water can escape without ponding. In fact, some systems have been installed without surveying by watching how fast the water flowed away while the ditch or trench was being dug. Surveying is strongly recommended, though, so the system can be planned and the installation optimized.

Junctions involve special techniques in both ditch and tile systems. A branch ditch is often given a short length of steeper gradient near the junction so that its water level will be slightly above that of the larger ditch. This prevents water from flowing up the branch ditch and depositing sediment.

Many lines have been installed by "chipping tile" (breaking out pieces to make them fit), but the use of manufactured junction tile is recommended for a faster installation and a tighter fit that will keep soil from entering. Special tile are available for branches, corners, and size changes. These and the pipe needed for the outlet and for road crossings should be on hand when the job begins.

Installing surface inlets to tile lines involves special techniques. Inlets need to be located in low points on the land surface, although the low point can be moved some by land smoothing. Many surface inlets are installed in fencelines or enclosed in a small area to protect them from machinery. Others are tall conspicuous standpipes with holes or slots that control water entrance. Some inlets are flat so traffic can cross them and are covered by gratings. These tend to catch trash that needs to be removed frequently. Another variation, the "blind inlet," consists of a pit filled with gravel or small stones.

Any type of inlet should have openings small enough to keep out animals and trash. Surface inlets should enter a branch line about 15 ft (5 m) long rather than going directly into a main tile line. The main line will then function even if the inlet line is plugged.

Occasionally, one wants to drain an area that is too wet to enter with drainage equipment. Dynamite has been used successfully for the initial drainage of some areas with cohesive soils. This method is not satisfactory for gravel or loose dry soils. Bennett (1947) suggested that charges be placed about 20 to 30 in. (50 to 75 cm) apart and 30 in. (75 cm) deep. A few trial charges should be used to determine the optimum placement and size of charge.

15-8.4 Maintenance of Drainage Systems

Drainage ditches need to be kept free of excess vegetation and debris. Many ditches, especially the flatter ones, accumulate sediment that must be removed once every few years. Regular maintenance is essential to keep ditches functioning properly.

Grass growing on ditch banks is usually desirable for erosion control, but reeds and cattails in the water slow the flow, raise the water level, and make the ditch less effective. Mowing, burning, use of herbicides, and hand removal are all used to limit the amount of growth in ditches, but none gives a permanent remedy.

Tile lines also need maintenance, although less frequently than ditches. A tile outlet covered by debris or by high water in an outlet ditch may cause sediment to be deposited in the line and thus reduce its capacity. Pressure may build up in the line and cause water to flow outward and wash out a hole. Tile falling into such holes cause misalignments that allow soil to enter and block the line. Similar problems result when a heavy load crushes one or more tile.

Problem spots in tile lines produce wet spots and/or holes in the field. Either of these conditions should be remedied promptly by digging a hole to expose the tile so that the damage can be repaired. Excessive delay permits more soil to be washed into the line; sections of the line can become so blocked by sediment that they have to be dug up, cleaned, and relaid.

15-8.5 Inadequate Drainage Systems

Sometimes a drainage system becomes inadequate. Perhaps the soil has lost permeability, or a new cropping system may be planned. More lines may then be needed to make the system function adequately again. The procedure for a ditch system may be as simple as digging new ditches between the existing ditches.

A need for additional tile lines may be noticed when the area midway between lines stays wet too long after a rain. Unfortunately, the exact location of the existing tile lines may not be obvious. If available, a map of the original system can be very helpful. Sometimes the lines can be seen faintly on an aerial photo or located by watching for tile chips or different-colored soil in the field. The fastest-drying soil and the earliest-maturing crops also help identify the approximate locations of tile lines. Precise locations can be determined with a probe and suitable plans made for enlarging the system.

SUMMARY

Wetlands occur in arid as well as in humid climates and are identified by black, rust, bluish-gray, and white colors. They usually have higher organic-matter contents and often have more montmorillonitic clay than neighboring soils. Reducing conditions influence their chemical behavior. Wet soils containing sulfides can become strongly acid when drained, and those with excess sodium salts can become highly alkaline.

The limitations resulting from wetness depend on how wet the land is, when the wetness occurs, and how long it stays wet. Clay soils become sticky and too weak to support heavy loads when wet. Sandy soils are strongest when moist but not wet. Traffic can puddle wet soil so it will harden when it dries. Wet soil delays planting because of coldness as well as wetness. Lack of oxygen prevents root growth of most plants and results in denitrification and reduced availability of potassium.

Either surface or subsurface water can be removed by open ditches, tile, or various other methods. Land smoothing and bedding systems are means of surface drainage. Mole drains are the least expensive and shortest-lived means of subsurface drainage. Both pumped wells and dry wells are sometimes used for drainage.

Ditches offer high capacity and are less expensive than tile, but they occupy significant land areas and are inconvenient to have in fields. Tile lines cost more, especially in large sizes, but require less maintenance than ditches and do not restrict traffic. Tile are available in clay, concrete, and plastic and are usually placed at depths between 3 and 5 ft (90 to 150 cm) in humid regions or about 6 or 7 ft (2 m) in arid regions.

Drainage systems are designed in random, regular, or interceptor patterns. The outlet is a very important feature of a drainage system and is the beginning point for installation. A drainage coefficient must be assumed in calculating how much capacity is needed before minimum tile or ditch sizes and gradients can be determined. After a drainage system is installed, it needs proper maintenance to keep it functioning properly.

QUESTIONS

1. Explain how well-drained, somewhat poorly drained, and poorly drained soils are identified in the field.
2. What causes some wet soils to become strongly acid when drained and others to become highly alkaline?
3. What factors determine whether a drainage system should be surface or subsurface, ditch or tile, and random or regular?
4. Describe a circumstance where an interceptor drain would be useful and explain how it would be installed.
5. How does land smoothing improve drainage?
6. What special precautions are needed for locating and installing a tile drainage outlet?

REFERENCES

AGRICULTURAL RESEARCH SERVICE, 1967. Laser beam controls pipe depth. *Agr. Res.*, Apr., p. 8–9.

BASAK, P., 1972. Soil structure and its effects on hydraulic conductivity. *Soil Sci.* 114:417–422.

BEAUCHAMP, K. H., 1955. Tile drainage—Its installation and upkeep. In *Water,* Yearbook of Agriculture, USDA, Washington, D.C. p. 508–520.

BENNETT, H. H., 1947. *Elements of Soil Conservation.* McGraw-Hill, New York, 406 p.

DANE, J. H., and S. HRUSKA, 1983. In-situ determination of soil hydraulic properties during drainage. *Soil Sci. Soc. Am. J.* 47:619–624.

DONNAN, W. W., and G. O. SCHWAB, 1974. Current drainage methods in the U.S.A. In *Drainage for Agriculture.* Agronomy Monograph 17. American Society of Agronomy, Madison, Wis., p. 93–114.

FAUSEY, N. R., and G. O. SCHWAB, 1969. Soil moisture content, tilth, and soybean *(Glycine max.)* response with surface and subsurface drainage. *Agron. J.* 61:554–557.

FOUSS, J. L. 1971. Tomorrow's drainage systems today. *Crops Soils* 23(7): 12–14.

HOPMANS, J. W., and J. H. DANE, 1986. Temperature dependence of soil hydraulic properties. *Soil Sci. Soc. Am. J.* 50:4–9.

KING, J. A., 1931. *Tile Drainage.* Mason City Brick and Tile Co., Mason City, Iowa, 108 p.

PATT, J., D. CARMELI, and I. SAFRIR, 1966. Influence of soil physical condition on productivity of citrus trees. *Soil Sci.* 102:82–84.

SOIL CONSERVATION SERVICE, 1973. *Drainage of Agricultural Land.* Water Information Center, Inc., Port Washington, N.Y. p. 430.

SPOOR, G., P. B. LEEDS-HARRISON, and R. J. GODWIN, 1982. Some fundamental aspects of the formation, stability, and failure of mole drainage channels. *J. Soil Sci.* 33:411–425.

VOORHEES, W. B., D. A. FARRELL, and W. E. LARSON, 1975. Soil strength and aeration effects on root elongation. *Soil Sci. Soc. Am. Proc.* 39:948–953.

WALKER, J. M., 1969. One degree increments in soil temperatures affect maize seedling behavior. *Soil Sci. Soc. Am. Proc.* 33:729–736.

WESSELING, J., 1974. Crop growth and wet soils. In *Drainage for Agriculture.* Agronomy Monograph 17. American Society of Agronomy, Madison, Wis., p. 7–90.

WOOTEN, H. H., and L. A. JONES, 1955. The history of our drainage enterprises. In *Water,* Yearbook of Agriculture. USDA, Washington, D.C., p. 478–491.

ZWERMAN, P. J., 1969. *Land Smoothing and Surface Drainage.* Cornell Ext. Bull. 1214. Cornell Univ., Ithaca, N.Y.

16

Irrigation and Reclamation

Irrigation and reclamation are powerful means of increasing land productivity. Adding irrigation water can overcome drought limitations and improve both the quality and the quantity of crop production. Reclamation increases land productivity through the irrigation, drainage, salt removal, or other amelioration of soils so that better crops can be grown on them. Both irrigation and reclamation help supply the food and fiber needs of the world's growing population.

Irrigation and reclamation are obviously significant in arid regions (Note 16–1). Most land reclamation occurs in arid or semiarid conditions, but supplemental irrigation to meet special or occasional needs is used in subhumid and even humid climates.

NOTE 16–1
ARID CLIMATES AND ARID REGIONS

An arid climate is defined in *Soil* (the 1957 Yearbook of Agriculture, p. 752) as "a very dry climate like that of desert or semidesert regions where there is only enough water for widely spaced desert plants." Arid regions are defined as "areas where the potential water losses by evaporation and transpiration are greater than the amount of water supplied by precipitation." Arid regions encompass the areas of arid climates plus large additional areas of semiarid climates.

The maximum precipitation for arid climates and arid regions depends on temperature and, to some extent, on the season when most of the precipitation occurs. The upper limit of precipitation for arid climates is about 10 in. (250 mm) per year in cool regions and about 20 in. (500 mm) per year in the tropics. Arid region limits are two to three times as much as those for arid climates.

The precipitation in arid climates is seasonal and erratic as well as limited in amount. Plants must either grow during short periods of favorable moisture or rely on irrigation.

Some wet soils occur even in arid climates. These regions include hilly or mountainous areas with humid conditions at their higher elevations. Water flows or seeps down to the lower elevations and saturates the soil in some low areas. Even the limited precipitation within an arid area generates runoff and seepage that cause local wet spots. These wet spots can often be used as sources of water for household or livestock needs. Some of the larger ones can be developed for irrigation water sources.

Every continent has some irrigation, but Asia has about three times as much as all other continents combined. China is in first place with about 188 million acres (76 million ha) of irrigated land followed by India with 69 million acres (28 million ha) (Table 16–1).

TABLE 16–1 IRRIGATED LAND IN THE MAJOR IRRIGATING COUNTRIES OF THE WORLD (DATA MOSTLY FOR THE YEARS 1968 TO 1971)

Country	Irrigated area: Millions of acres	Irrigated area: Millions of hectares	Cultivated area: Millions of acres	Cultivated area: Millions of hectares	Percentage of cultivated land irrigated
1. China	188	76	272	110	69
2. India	69	28	408	165	17
3. United States	39	16	475	192	8
4. Pakistan	30	12	47	19	64
5. USSR	27	11	576	233	5
6. Indonesia	17	6.8	45	18.0	38
7. Iran	13	5.3	41	16.7	32
8. Mexico	10	4.2	59	23.8	17
9. Iraq	9	3.7	25	10.2	36
10. Egypt	7	2.9	7	2.9	100
11. Japan	6.9	2.8	13.6	5.5	51
12. Italy	5.9	2.4	30.6	12.4	19
13. Spain	5.9	2.4	50.9	20.6	12
14. Thailand	4.4	1.8	28.2	11.4	16
15. Argentina	4.0	1.6	64.2	26.0	6
16. Turkey	3.7	1.5	67.7	27.4	5
17. Australia	3.7	1.5	110.2	44.6	3
18. Chile	2.7	1.1	11.4	4.6	24
19. Peru	2.7	1.1	7.4	3.0	37
20. Bulgaria	2.5	1.0	11.1	4.5	22
Total	504	204	3600	1457	14

Source: Economic Research Service, 1974.

16-1 EFFECTS OF IRRIGATION

Irrigation changes low-priced grazing land into expensive cropland. New crops can be grown and much risk taken out of growing the usual crops, even in humid regions. Farming systems, including field arrangements, crops, fertilization, and field operations are adjusted to work with the irrigation system. Costs and returns both increase, and good management is needed to take advantage of the opportunities while avoiding the pitfalls. The change requires many more workers to manage the land.

16-1.1 Increased Production with Irrigation

Arid-region food production can be multiplied several fold if irrigation water is available for land reclamation. Low-intensity grazing land becomes diversified high-producing cropland.

Irrigation in humid regions may not change the crop to be grown, but it increases production by increasing yields. Humid region soils may lose water by runoff and deep percolation, but there are often droughty periods as well. The available water-holding capacity of the soil helps determine whether irrigation is needed. A deep loamy soil able to store 10 or 12 in. (25 or 30 cm) of available water can support a crop through a much longer dry period than a shallow or sandy soil storing only 4 in. (10 cm).

A reliable water supply increases yields so much that 30 to 40% of world agricultural production comes from the 14% of cropland that is irrigated (Booher, 1974). Adequate water often improves the crop quality as well as increasing the quantity. Drought causes quality problems in various growth factors and in fruit production.

In addition to overcoming drought, sprinkler irrigation systems have been used to protect sensitive fruit crops from frost damage. The heat released by freezing water holds the temperature near 0°C rather than letting it drop low enough to freeze plant tissue.

16-1.2 Hazards of Irrigation

Some notable hazards occur along with the benefits associated with irrigation and reclamation. One is the economic risk from high irrigation costs. Another is productivity loss caused by excess salts accumulating from improper use of water, as shown in Figure 16-1. Some such soils can be reclaimed, as discussed later in this chapter, but the effort is not always economical.

Erosion hazards often increase with irrigation. Irrigation often forms rills; the cumulative effects of many such irrigations can be ruinous. Deposition of sediment can also be so damaging that continued irrigation becomes impractical. A well-designed program of soil and water conservation may reduce erosion to tolerable rates, but they are usually still faster than the natural rate.

The hazards associated with irrigation have led some observers to suggest that all irrigation systems are temporary. Some irrigation systems have never produced a

Figure 16-1 Excess salts prevent crop growth in this spot in a California barley field. Similar bare spots can result from sodic conditions or from boron toxicity. (Courtesy U.S. Department of Agriculture.)

marketable crop, most often because of sodic soils. Others have failed after some decades of use, most commonly because of erosion and sedimentation problems. Even so, some irrigation systems have endured, and it is unfair to suggest that the failure of some means that all will fail.

Gulhati and Smith (1967) enumerate many examples of long-lasting irrigation systems. Egyptians have been practicing basin irrigation for more than 5000 years. Iranians are still using 2500-year-old *kanat* (tunnels) to supply irrigation water, as shown in Figure 16-2. Japanese paddy fields have been irrigated for more than 2500 years. Other ancient irrigation works occur in India, Pakistan, China, Peru, Central America, southwestern United States, and elsewhere. Some of these have been abandoned, but many are still in use. Some have been resurrected when modern surveyors discovered that their new survey followed the precise course of a long-lost, sediment-filled canal.

16-2 SELECTING LAND FOR IRRIGATION

Several factors must be favorable for irrigation to be practical. Soil factors will be considered in this section and water in the next. Other important factors such as climate, suitable crops, roads, and markets will be assumed to be favorable.

Important soil factors that can make the land unprofitable to irrigate include depth, texture, slope, and salt content. These factors may already be known if the land has been cropped before, either with or without irrigation. A preliminary evaluation of uncropped land can be made visually—smooth topography and good

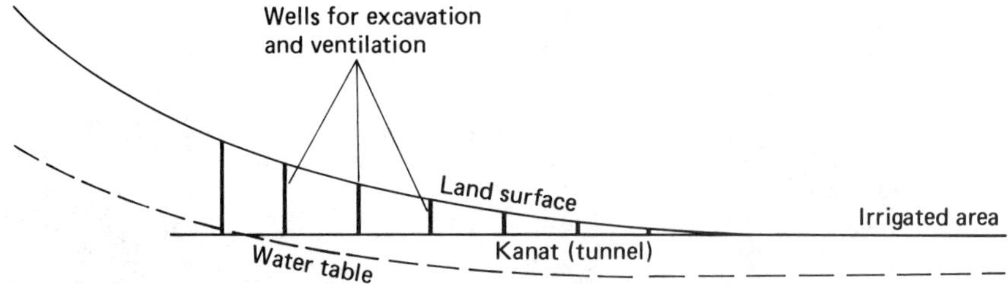

Figure 16–2 Kanat are used in several Asian and African countries to tap the water table under higher land and carry it out onto the lower land.

vegetative cover usually indicate good soil. Soil maps and topographic maps are very helpful for evaluating land.

The minimum depth of soil for irrigation varies with other soil properties, the crop, and the irrigator. Any soil less than 5 ft (150 cm) deep may reduce yields, and less than 3 ft (100 cm) is often considered a limiting factor. Nevertheless, some irrigated soils are only 1 ft (30 cm) deep to hard bedrock. Such shallow soils require frequent irrigation because they cannot store much water. Deep tillage is out of the question, and the topography must be left unchanged because little or no land leveling can be done on these shallow soils. Erosion control is vital to retain what little soil there is.

Loamy soil textures throughout the solum are generally desirable, although sandy loams may be preferred for ease of tillage, faster infiltration rate, and easy harvesting of root crops. Very sandy soils have low water-holding and nutrient-storage capacities and are easily eroded by surface irrigation. Wind erosion becomes a serious factor with fine sand. Clay soils often have slow infiltration rates, water-logging, and stickiness. A clay subsoil can cause waterlogging even if the surface soil is favorable. Nearly pure silt, as found in some loess or alluvial deposits, is the easiest texture of all to erode by running water. Stony conditions cause tillage difficulties and reduce the water-holding capacity of the soil.

The ideal slope gradient for surface irrigation is about 0.5%. Surface irrigation is difficult on slopes flatter than 0.2% because the water stream required to irrigate them becomes too deep. Such problems can be solved by using basin, trickle, or sprinkler irrigation or by "leveling" the field into segments that have enough slope for the water to flow. Steep or irregular slopes cause more serious problems. Trickle, sprinkler, or contour irrigation offer only limited solutions. Large elevation differences make uniform water application more difficult no matter what method is used. Variable soils and slow infiltration rates are common complications.

Erosion is a potential problem wherever surface irrigation is practiced on slopes. In the United States, the usual maximum slope for surface irrigation varies from 3% in the Gulf Coastal Plain to 6% in the central Great Plains to 20% for pasture and hay in Colorado, to 35% with good cover in the Pacific Northwest (Maletic and Hutchings, 1967). Irregularities in slope gradient and direction make irrigation more difficult than uniform slopes.

Salt content may be easy to overlook, yet it may make the soil barren, as shown in Figure 16–1. Salt problems vary from minor and easily remedied to severe and not worth reclaiming. Excess salts, high percentages of sodium, and boron concentrations are serious hazards to plant growth.

16-3 WATER FOR IRRIGATION

The water supply for irrigation is usually more limiting than the area of suitable soil. Most of the available water in arid regions is already in use. Humid regions have more water, but their water supplies also tend to run low when they are most needed. Inadequate supplies of water result in competition among irrigators, would-be irrigators, and other users such as cities and factories. Furthermore, streams and lakes need to have water left in them for fish, wildlife, recreational, and navigational uses.

16-3.1 Water Rights

Water use has both economic and legal aspects. The simplest way to allocate water is to sell it to the highest bidder. However, the interaction between water and land values requires a more complex analysis—often the water is not for sale apart from the land. Laws regulating the use of water also influence its economic value.

Two legal doctrines known as *riparian rights* and *prior appropriations* underlie water rights in the United States. The riparian rights doctrine is based on old English law and allows the owners of land along a stream or lake to use the water (Busby, 1955). Riparian rights are used in the eastern part of the United States (Wisconsin, Iowa, Missouri, Arkansas, Louisiana, and all states east of these states). Nobody actually owns the water, but it can be used for domestic needs, including household, livestock, garden, and lawn, regardless of the effect on stream flow. Other uses are allowed if they do not diminish downstream flow or if they are within the land owners' reasonable share of the water remaining after all domestic needs are satisfied. Irrigation has a low priority for water use under riparian rights.

The prior appropriations doctrine is based on beneficial use of water and is used in western United States (Minnesota and all states farther west, except that California, Oklahoma, North Dakota, and South Dakota use a combination of riparian rights and prior appropriations). A potential user must apply to the state for a permit to divert and use a certain amount of water from a certain place (Busby, 1955). The permit is granted if the water has not been granted to someone already. The land does not have to be adjacent to the water source. A license is granted after "beneficial use" has been established. This license is renewable as long as the beneficial use is uninterrupted; it is treated as real property that can be bought and sold. Prior appropriations gives higher priority to irrigation and other nondomestic water use than riparian rights gives them.

Other laws can modify the riparian rights and prior appropriations doctrines. Municipalities and some organizations can obtain water by condemnation proceedings in some states. In some places, 20 years of use establishes a legal right to continue.

Many recent laws designed to maintain water quality place limitations on the sewage, chemicals, and other pollutants that can be emptied into streams or lakes. Also, water used for cooling a power or manufacturing plant must not be warm enough to damage aquatic life when it is returned to the stream.

16-3.2 Surface Water

Water from streams and lakes is used for irrigation on both small and large scales. Irrigation began thousands of years ago with simple diversions of stream water onto nearby bottomland. Large diversions are distributed to many users by canal and ditch systems.

Bottomland is usually irrigated first because water diverted a short distance upstream can reach the land by gravity flow. Higher land requires either a long canal to carry water diverted far upstream, a high dam, or a means of lifting the water. Many lifting devices have been used, including water wheels, Archimedean screws, and pumps. Pumps were once powered by people or animals but in developed countries are now driven by engines or electric motors. The ancient methods are still common in developing countries.

Irrigation by diversions is limited by low stream flow during dry seasons. An upstream reservoir can make the water supply more reliable. Such reservoirs are often placed on a small tributary rather than across the main stream. A diversion from the main stream can be used to fill the reservoir without overloading it with all the floodwaters and sediment carried by the main stream.

16-3.3 Harvesting Rainwater

Land surfaces are sometimes treated to decrease infiltration and make more runoff water available for irrigation and other uses. The runoff can be stored in a reservoir to supply water for households, livestock, gardens, small fields, and wildlife. Rainwater harvest has been practiced for thousands of years and can be used where average annual rainfall is as low as 2 to 3 in. (50 to 75 mm).

Ditches were used in ancient times to harvest rainwater from hillsides or gentle slopes where the soil permeability was slow. Newer practices include decreasing soil permeability by treatment with sodium salts or using water-repellent compounds such as asphalt, paraffin, or silicone to resist infiltration. Some projects produce runoff with large sheets of plastic covered by a layer of gravel.

Harvested rainwater may be guided directly to a field or garden and distributed through some form of irrigation system. A simple water-spreading system can be very helpful in an arid climate if the soil is deep enough to store additional water.

Storage reservoirs are needed when collected water is to be saved for later use. Evaporation can be a problem because the air is usually very dry in such areas. A deep reservoir with minimum surface area helps reduce evaporation. Still less evaporation occurs from an oversize reservoir filled with stones, gravel, and sand as shown in Figure 16-3. The sand also filters the water and thus improves its quality. A well is used to remove water from such reservoirs.

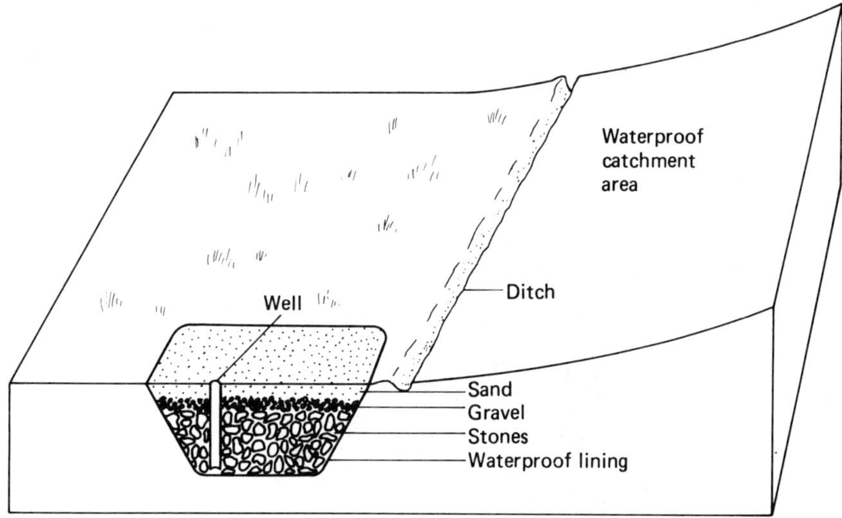

Figure 16–3 A landscape cross section showing a catchment area and storage basin for harvesting rainwater.

16–3.4 Underground Water

Far more fresh water is stored underground than aboveground. Thomas and Peterson (1967) estimate that there is enough underground water to cover the land surface to a depth of about 100 ft (30 m). Much of this water is held in tiny pores or occurs at great depth. Also, much of it occurs in humid regions where it may not be needed. Still, there is much underground water that could be used for irrigation, as shown in Figure 16–4.

Good supplies of groundwater depend on porous rock layers that hold water loosely and have surface connections so they can be recharged. Most gravel and sand layers in valleys are good sources; sandstone, limestone, and some basalt flows are potential sources. Most other rocks are too dense to supply water at a significant rate.

Groundwater has several advantages over surface water:

1. The underground water reservoir minimizes supply fluctuations from wet to dry periods.
2. The water quality is relatively constant and favorable in most places.
3. A well may make long conveyor systems and the attendant rights-of-way unnecessary.
4. Groundwater may be used to irrigate land that has no riparian rights to surface water (but the prior appropriations doctrine often applies to both groundwater and surface water).

Long-term groundwater use must be based on recharge rates rather than on the amount present. Pumping may lower the water table until the well can no longer

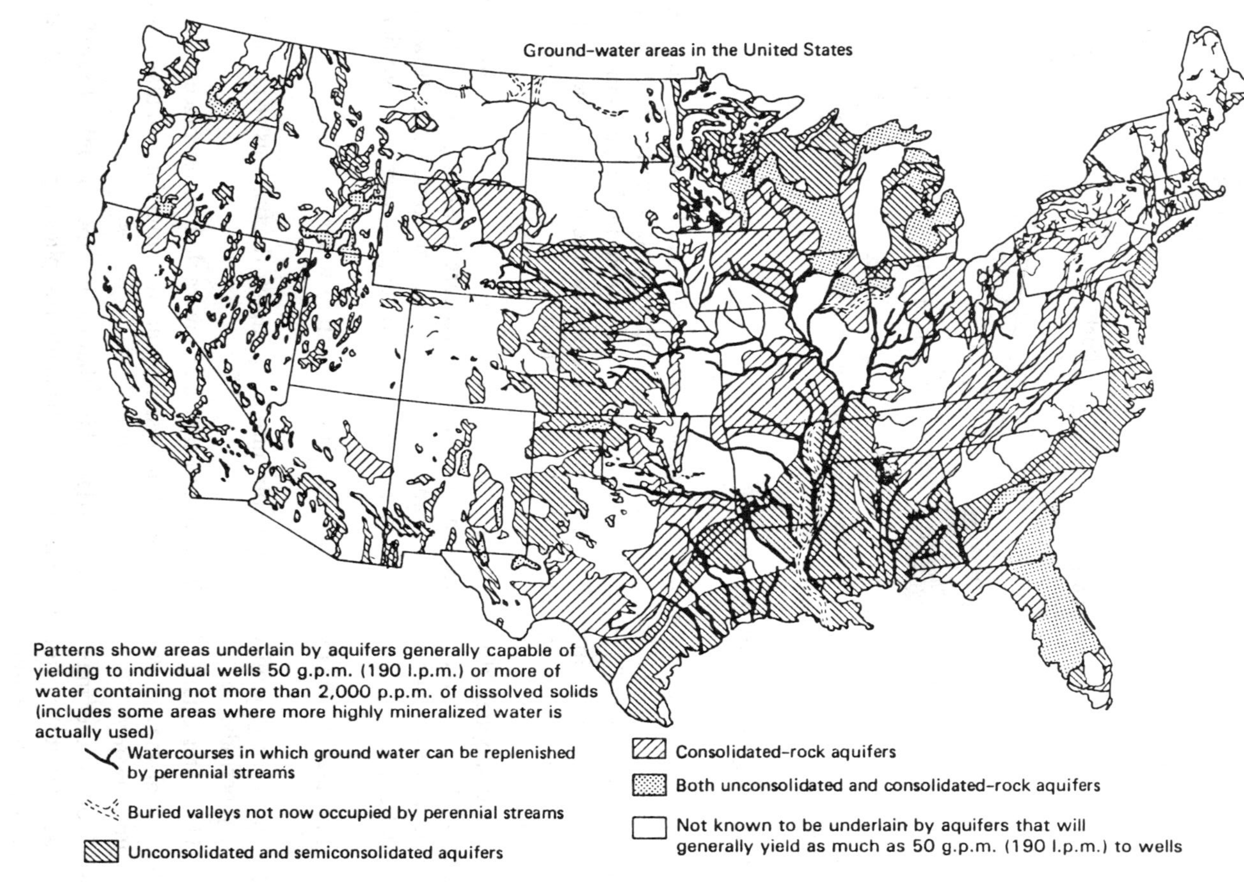

Figure 16-4 Areas in the United States where groundwater aquifers will supply individual wells with 50 gal/min (190 liters/min) or more of water containing less than 2000 ppm dissolved solids. (From Thomas, 1955.)

supply adequate water. Wells that are then drilled deeper and pumped again are essentially mining water. Some wells in southwestern United States are now pumping from depths of 1000 ft (300 m). Such pumping cannot long continue; "fossil water" that took many centuries to accumulate has disappeared in a few decades.

Since recharge rates limit the long-term use of wells, some projects have arranged to recharge an aquifer artificially. This may be possible if the aquifer connects to a higher area where there is a surplus of water. The technique normally involves spreading the water over an area of porous soils that overlie part of the aquifer.

Sometimes there are two water tables under the same land – a shallow perched water table and a deeper permanent water table, as shown in Figure 16–5. The perched water table is not a reliable water supply; it will usually disappear during dry seasons. Another factor shown in Figure 16–5 is the difference between permanent water tables in humid and arid regions. Water percolates through humid region soils down to a water table in the substratum. Water accumulates until the water table is high enough for water to flow toward an escape point such as a stream or a spring. In an arid region, evaporation and plant growth use all of the available water so that water rarely reaches the substratum. Water tables in arid regions originate from streams or low-lying wet soils. Consequently, the water table slopes away from these water sources.

Underground water is most often obtained from wells, but other possibilities should not be overlooked. Some springs are large enough and reliable enough to be used for irrigation. Other good water sources occur where the water table is exposed in gravel pits, rock quarries, or other excavations.

16–3.5 Icebergs

Glacial ice contains about three-fourths of the world supply of fresh water. Some glacial ice melts before it reaches the ocean, but much of it breaks off and floats

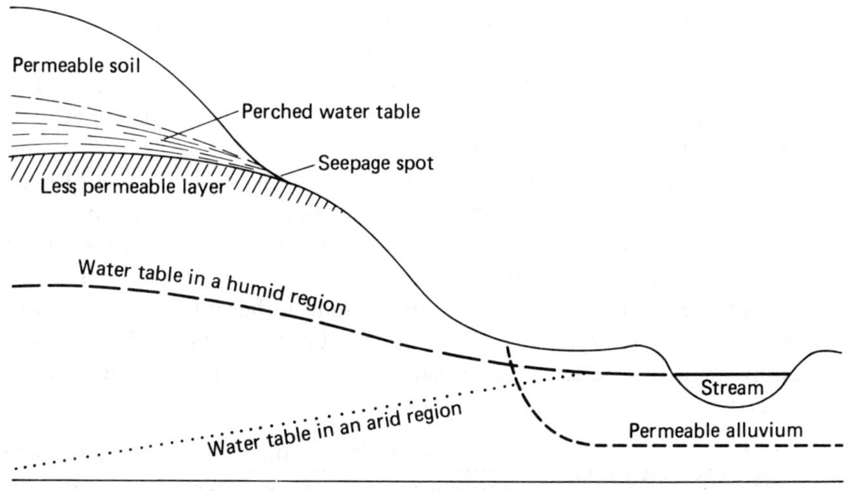

Figure 16–5 Representative forms of a perched water table and permanent water tables in humid and arid regions.

away as icebergs. Many icebergs are huge—miles across and hundreds of feet thick. They melt and break apart as they float in the ocean.

The idea of using icebergs as sources of fresh water for desert lands was explored in a conference at Ames, Iowa, in 1977. The water is good, but technical and economic problems of navigating the icebergs, containing the meltwater, and distributing the water are still unsolved.

16-3.6 Desalinized Water

Oceans contain 97% of the water on earth, but it is too salty for most uses (its salt content is about 3.5%, mostly NaCl). Ocean water can be desalinized by such techniques as distillation, electric membrane processes, and ion-exchange resins. These methods are useful for modest needs such as supplying water for a ship at sea or even for city water supplies, but all are too expensive for irrigation purposes. Furthermore, transportation and lifting costs could be prohibitive if the water were to be used anywhere except at low elevations near a coast.

16-3.7 Water Quality

Water falling as rain or snow is nearly pure H_2O. The initial runoff into a nearby stream is still relatively pure unless it picks up a sediment load. Water that seeps through soil and rock layers, however, dissolves various materials. Water is classified as medium hard if it contains more than 50 parts per million (ppm) calcium and magnesium salts, and hard if it contains more than 100 ppm because such water requires much soap for cleaning purposes. These limits are far below the acceptable amount of salt for irrigation water.

Streams pick up more and more seepage water and dissolved salts as they flow into flatter areas and lower elevations. The salt content increases more rapidly in arid regions than in humid regions because the dilution factor is smaller. In addition, the water in arid regions is likely to have been diverted, used for irrigation, and returned to the stream several times. Each cycle returns less water and more salt to the stream. The highest concentrations occur in arid regions in the lower parts of long small rivers. Arid soils contain leachable salts, and long small streams permit several leaching cycles to occur with little dilution.

Four factors should be considered for predicting the effect of irrigation water on soils and crops: (1) total salt concentration, (2) the proportion of Na^+ to Ca^{++} and Mg^{++} ions, (3) toxic ions, and (4) solid matter such as weed seeds and sediment.

High salt concentrations make it difficult for plants to absorb water. The plants therefore need a high moisture content in the soil. Additional water is needed to leach the salts from the soil, or it may become saline. The traditional leaching requirement has been based on salt concentrations in the irrigation and drainage waters:

$$\text{leaching water} = \frac{\text{salt conc. in irrigation water}}{\text{salt conc. in drainage water}} \times \begin{array}{c}\text{amount of}\\ \text{irrigation water}\end{array}$$

The salt concentration in drainage water is often taken as that which would cause a

50% decrease in yield in uniformly saline soil. Some researchers have maintained that a smaller amount of leaching water will suffice if salts are allowed to precipitate outside the root zone with trickle irrigation or in the lower part of the root zone with surface irrigation (Agricultural Research Service, 1974).

Electrical conductivity in mmhos/cm has been widely used to evaluate salt concentration because it is easily, quickly, and reliably measured with a conductivity meter. Other measures of concentration can be estimated by these approximations:

$$1 \text{ mmho/cm} \cong 640 \text{ ppm} = 0.064\% \cong 10 \text{ meq/liter} = 0.01\ N$$

Water quality classes for salt concentration as used by the U.S. Department of Agriculture are shown on the horizontal scale in Figure 16–6. The sodium hazard of irrigation water is evaluated by the sodium adsorption ratio (SAR) shown as the vertical scale in Figure 16–6. The SAR value is calculated as

$$\text{SAR} = \frac{\text{Na}^+}{\sqrt{(\text{Ca}^{++} + \text{Mg}^{++})/2}}$$

where the ion concentrations are expressed in milliequivalents per liter. High SAR values are hazardous because such water tends to increase the exchangeable sodium percentages (ESP) and produce saline-sodic and sodic soils. High proportions of bicarbonate ions in the water increase the tendency to produce sodic soils because HCO_3^- reacts with Ca^{++} and Mg^{++} and precipitates $CaCO_3$ and $MgCO_3$. Precipitation of Ca^{++} and Mg^{++} increases the SAR and ESP values.

Borate ions are the most common toxic ions in irrigation water. Boron concentrations as low as 1 ppm may injure apples, cherries, grapes, and several other fruit and nut crops. Boron-tolerant crops such as alfalfa, asparagus, and date palms tolerate up to 3 or 4 ppm of boron. Chlorides and some other ions may reach high enough concentrations to be detrimental to plant growth but seldom kill the plants. Several ions, however, can be toxic to animals without injuring plant growth. These include ions of arsenic, fluorine, lithium, nitrogen, selenium, and several heavy metals.

Solid matter in irrigation water can cause a variety of problems or, occasionally, be helpful. Sediment can block irrigation furrows and smother young plants, or it can plug soil pores and thus reduce permeability. Plugging some pores might be good for a very porous soil, but it is detrimental to most soils. Sediment may also carry pesticides and other chemicals from the area where they were applied to other crop areas or bodies of water where they are not wanted. Soil conservation is the best solution to sediment problems.

Weed seeds are another detrimental form of solid matter. Weeds line many irrigation reservoirs and ditch systems that therefore serve as conveyors distributing weed seeds to fields.

16–4 DISTRIBUTING WATER

Canals and ditches are used to distribute water for surface and subsurface irrigation; pipelines are needed for sprinkler and trickle irrigation. Canal systems are operated

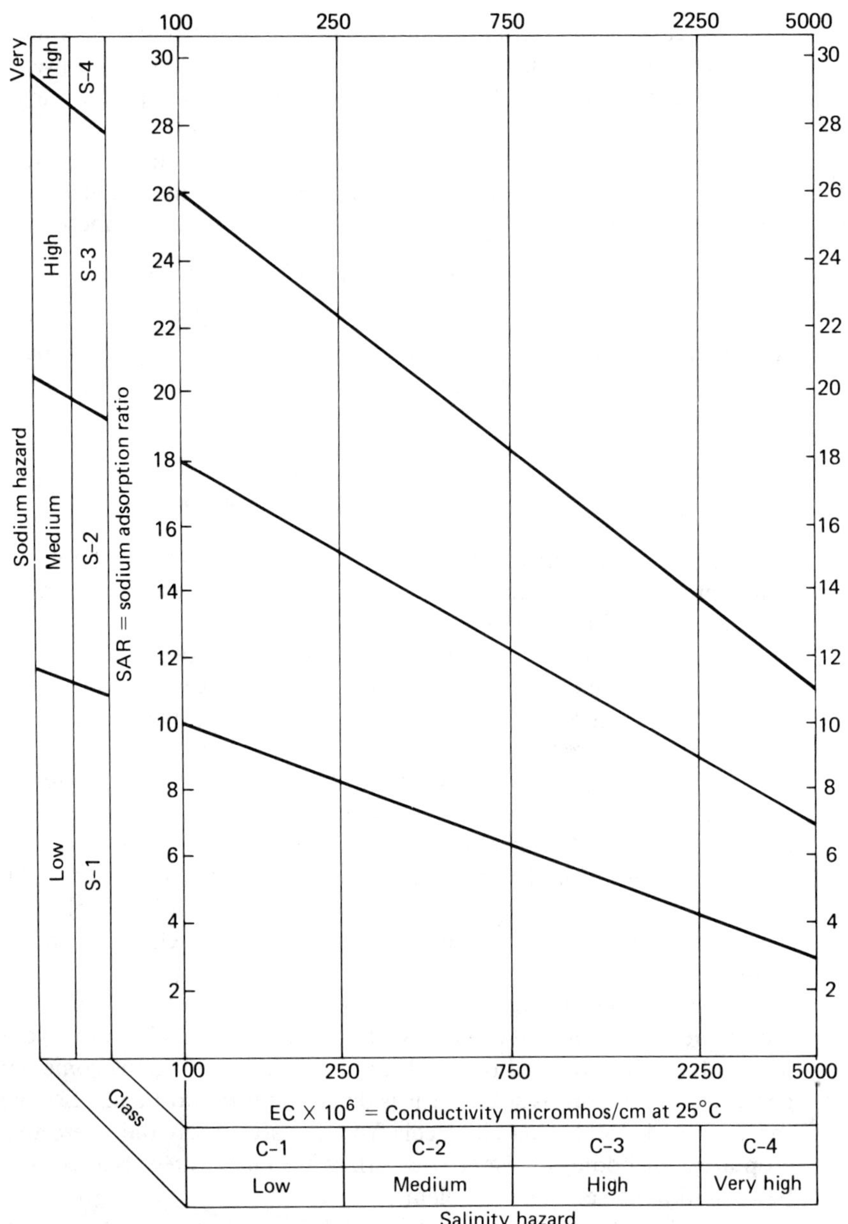

Figure 16-6 USDA classes of salinity and sodium hazard for irrigation water. (Source: *Diagnosis and Improvement of Saline and Alkali Soils,* USDA Agr. Handbook 60, 1954.)

by irrigation districts, companies, or cooperatives that sell water to individual farmers. Sometimes a government agency such as the U.S. Bureau of Reclamation builds the reservoirs, diversions, canals, and main ditches to deliver the water to users.

Canals flow on a flatter gradient than the rivers from which they were diverted. Thus they gradually reach a position on the side of the valley and higher than the river. They may have to cross permeable alluvial fans, go around or through hills, and cross the valleys of tributary streams. Canals need clay or concrete lining where large water losses on the alluvial fans produce seepage spots below the canal. Upland drainage and reduced grazing are needed to stabilize some hillsides where landslides and hillside sediment may obstruct the canal. Often the canal must cross tributary streams in a flume, or through a large pipeline. Valleys are expensive to cross even if the streams are dry during the irrigation season.

Water from a canal is often subdivided three or four times on its way to the fields. First, a main ditch or lateral leaves the canal and flows down the divide between two tributary streams. Smaller ditches that serve a few farms branch from the lateral. Even after the water reaches the individual users, it may be divided into still more parts to irrigate individual fields and parts of fields.

16-4.1 Measuring Water Flow

Each division point requires a metering device to control the flow of water. These may be adjustable metal gates that partially cover a submerged opening, or an adjustable opening for the water to spill over. A device to measure how much water is being delivered may be included. Weirs are the most common measuring devices; they are relatively inexpensive and a good installation has an accuracy of ±2%. Three styles of weirs are shown in Figure 16–7.

Rectangular weirs are simple to build, but the flow constriction below the notch requires extra arithmetic to calculate the water flow. The Cipoletti weir has a trapezoidal shape with 1:4 side slopes that offset the constriction tendency and simplify the calculations. Triangular weirs have a wide range of capacity with good percentage accuracy at small flows as well as large, but they require a large head loss between the water levels above and below the weir.

Weirs need a pool on their upstream side so that the water will not approach them fast enough to increase the flow. The head should be measured in the pool at least four times as far from the notch as the head (depth) of water flowing over the notch. Undersize or sediment-filled pools increase the discharge by as much as 10 or 15%. Weir notches need a sharp edge to cut the water cleanly and a free fall below the notch so that the water escape is unrestricted.

Parshall flumes (lower part of Figure 16–7) are often used where the land is too flat to allow the head loss required for free flow over a weir. Parshall flumes speed the water flow down a narrow passage and then shoot it back up nearly as high as the inflow. A good installation should measure water flow with an accuracy of ±3%, but a faulty one might be ±10% (Robinson and Humphreys, 1967). Excessive flow that submerges the drop and rise characteristics of a Parshall flume may reduce delivery by 25% or more.

The delivery equation for Parshall flumes given in Figure 16–7 is only approximate. Robinson and Humphreys (1967) list values of coefficients and exponents that vary by about ±3% from those given. They also describe a flume with trapezoidal

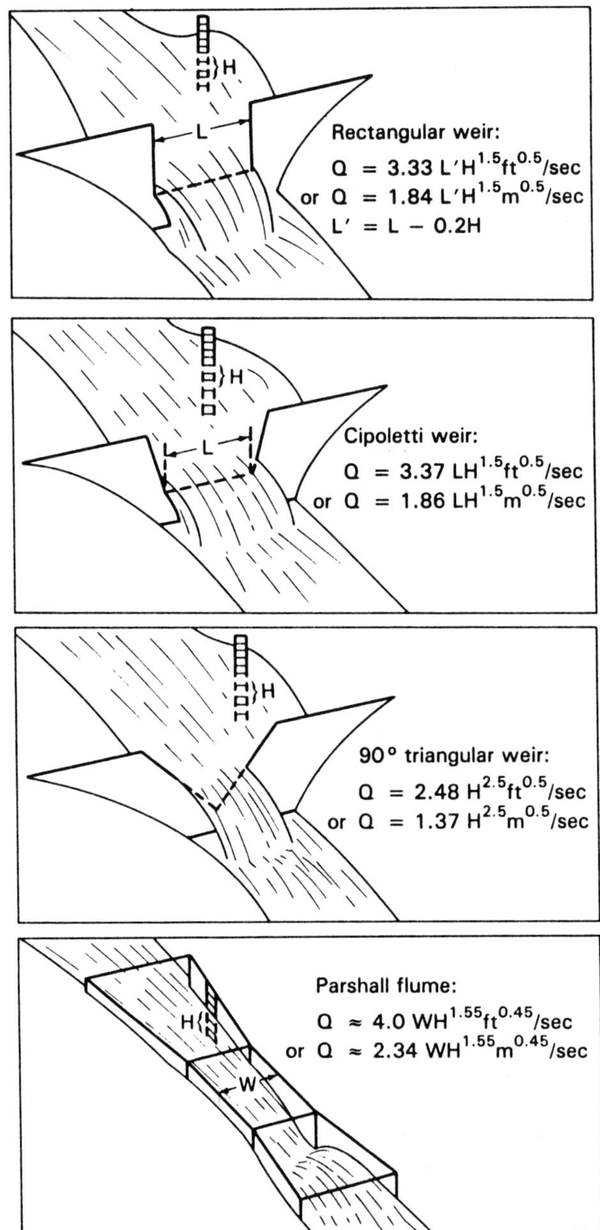

Figure 16–7 Water-measuring devices and equations for calculating their flow. The $ft^{0.5}$ or $m^{0.5}$ in the equations completes the cubic form of the units. The constants must be adjusted if units other than feet or meters are used.

cross section instead of vertical walls. Several other devices, such as submerged orifices and current meters, can also measure water, but these are less common than weirs and flumes.

Figure 16–8 A series of drop structures protecting a ditch in Idaho. (Courtesy USDA Soil Conservation Service.)

16–4.2 Water-Control Structures

Canals are usually placed on a constant nonerosive grade that requires few structures other than outlets to laterals. An emergency spillway is sometimes needed because cost factors require that the canal be built with little spare capacity; a heavy rain or damage to a ditch could require rapid diversion of a large volume of water.

Laterals and smaller ditches often flow down slopes steep enough to require erosion control. Concrete-lined ditches are one solution. Drop structures such as the one diagrammed in Figure 10–11 are another way to keep a ditch from eroding. Often, they are placed like stairsteps with the apron of each drop structure level with the notch of the one below it, as in Figure 16–8. Large drop structures are usually made of poured concrete; smaller ones may be poured or made of concrete blocks with their cores filled with concrete.

Check structures are used to raise the flow of water in a ditch for irrigating the field next to it. A drop structure with boards in its notch can serve as a check. A simple check structure consists of the main wall and notch of the drop structure but without the apron and side walls.

A division box such as that shown in Figure 16–9 controls the direction of water flow. Boards dropped in slots close one channel while another is opened. Division boxes take various forms to fit ditch patterns and topography. Some are made of wood, but those made from poured concrete or concrete blocks are more durable. Special concrete blocks are cast with slots to hold the control boards.

16–4.3 Distributing Water from Ditches

When water finally reaches the field to be irrigated, it must somehow be taken out of the ditch and applied to the land. Usually, the water has been flowing below ground level and must be raised by blocking the ditch. Boards may be placed in a check for

Figure 16–9 A division box for diverting water in any of three directions. (Courtesy F. R. Troeh.)

this purpose, or a temporary blockage such as a sod dam or a canvas dam (a canvas sheet attached to a pole) may be used. The canvas lies in the ditch upstream from the pole and is held there by water pressure. A sod dam is made of pieces of sod taken from the ditchbank with a shovel.

Turnouts (notches through the ditch bank) are the simplest way to turn water onto the field, but other methods offer better control. Siphon tubes as shown in Figure 16–10 are a popular means of irrigating. They come in several sizes and their flow can be adjusted by raising or lowering the outlet end. One type has water traps on each end to hold its prime when the ditch is dry. Spiles (tubes permanently installed at ground level through the ditch bank) are another means of removing water from ditches. Spiles usually have adjustable outlets to control their flow.

16–4.4 Irrigation Pipelines

Metal pipelines are required to sustain the pressure of most sprinkler irrigation systems. The main lines are often buried for permanent systems but portable for temporary installations. Either type uses portable branch lines that attach to risers on the main lines.

Metal pipe is expensive whether it is made of steel for maximum strength or of a lightweight metal such as aluminum for portability. Systems are therefore designed to use minimum sizes and amounts of metal pipe. Irrigation engineers use flow-rate tables to calculate required pipe sizes and friction losses for a particular system.

A pipeline that carries water from a high point across a low area to another high point is called an inverted siphon. Fills or flumes can serve the same purpose but are barriers to traffic and occupy land area that can be cropped if buried pipelines are used. Concrete pipe is the least expensive type generally available that meets the strength and durability requirements. Ordinary concrete pipe can with-

Figure 16-10 Siphon tubes conducting water from an irrigation ditch in Idaho. (Courtesy F. R. Troeh.)

stand pressure heads up to 15 or 20 ft (5 or 6 m) of water. Higher heads require the use of reinforced concrete, steel, or other high-pressure pipe.

Carrying capacities of inverted siphons and other concrete pipelines can be calculated using the average slope from the inlet to the outlet and the data in Table 15-2. An intervening low area has no effect on carrying capacity unless air is trapped in the pipeline. Air entrapment is avoided by having only one low point in the line.

Pipelines need to be installed below frost depth to avoid damage by freezing. Most of them need concrete structures at each end for erosion protection. Some pipelines are built into a division box at one or both ends. Properly installed pipelines should last for many decades and nearly eliminate water losses by seepage and evaporation.

16-5 IRRIGATION METHODS

Irrigation methods can be divided into four main types—surface, subsurface, sprinkler, and trickle irrigation—and many subtypes. Surface irrigation is the oldest type and still constitutes about three-fourths of all irrigation. Subsurface irrigation is limited in its adaptation. Sprinkler irrigation can be used in any climate, is the most popular method in humid regions, and is still expanding in use. Trickle irrigation, the newest type, makes the most efficient use of water.

16-5.1 Surface Irrigation

Surface irrigation includes both furrow and flood types as distinguished by whether the water flows in distinct lines or if it floods the entire surface.

Furrow Irrigation. Furrow irrigation uses the ridges formed by cultivation to guide water across fields of row crops. The rows can be fed with siphon tubes or with spiles or in groups from ditch turnouts. A serious erosion hazard occurs because the water flows where cultivation has loosened the soil. The maximum nonerosive stream flow can be estimated from the equation

$$Q\text{ max} = \frac{9.5\text{ gallons/min}}{\text{percent slope}} \quad\text{or}\quad \frac{36\text{ liters/min}}{\text{percent slope}}$$

The factor should be decreased if the soil is known to be more erodible than average. This equation should not be used for slopes of less than 0.3% because the furrow capacity will limit the flow.

Irrigating furrows without eroding them is difficult on slope gradients steeper than 2%. Large streams would erode the soil and small streams will flow only a short distance. Contour furrows overcome this problem because they are placed on a gradient of about 0.5% across the main slope. Extra care must be taken to be sure that water does not cross from one furrow to the next. The lower furrow could overtop and begin a chain reaction that would produce a gully.

Uniform irrigation requires that irrigation furrows be no longer than the distance that water will flow in one-fourth of the irrigation period. For example, irrigation water should reach the lower end of the rows in two hours out of an eight-hour irrigation period. The maximum length of irrigation rows therefore depends on soil infiltration rate and erodibility, slope, and the amount (depth) of water to be applied. Table 16-2 contains estimates of appropriate row lengths for various conditions.

Furrow irrigation according to the principles outlined in the preceding paragraphs can achieve about 60% efficiency in water use. The other 40% is lost by evaporation, deep percolation in the upper ends of the rows and in the most permeable soil, and in wastewater from the lower end of the rows. Wastewater loss can be lessened by reducing the size of the irrigation streams when they approach the lower end of the rows. The extra water can then be used elsewhere, perhaps on a pasture that needs a short irrigation period. Transferring part of the water helps conserve both water and soil.

Principles similar to those outlined for furrow irrigation apply to other forms of row irrigation. Small furrows known as corrugations are used for noncultivated grain and forage crops. Such vegetation protects the soil better than row crops, but corrugations are too small to carry large streams of water. The row lengths are therefore similar to those for furrow irrigation.

Flood Irrigation. The three main types of flood irrigation are basin irrigation, border irrigation, and wild flooding. Basin irrigation is a simple method and is probably the oldest method of all. It was practiced in Egypt more than 5000 years ago (Gulhati and Smith, 1967) and is still used for long-term flooding of paddy rice or for shorter periods for many other crops.

Basin irrigation requires a narrow ridge between 6 and 20 in. (15 to 50 cm) high on all sides of each area to be flooded. The entire basin should be as level as possible—certainly within a range of 2 to 4 in. (5 to 10 cm). Basins range in size from

TABLE 16-2 SUGGESTED MAXIMUM LENGTHS IN FEET (M) OF CULTIVATED FURROWS FOR DIFFERENT SOILS, SLOPES, AND DEPTHS OF WATER IN IN. (CM) TO BE APPLIED

Furrow slope (%)	Clays				Loams				Sands			
	Average depth of water applied (in.)											
	3	6	9	12	2	4	6	8	2	3	4	5
	maximum furrow length in feet											
0.05	1000	1300	1300	1300	400	880	1300	1300	200	300	500	620
0.1	1100	1440	1540	1640	590	1100	1440	1540	300	400	620	720
0.2	1200	1540	1740	2030	720	1200	1540	1740	400	620	820	980
0.3	1300	1640	2030	2620	920	1300	1640	1970	500	720	920	1300
0.5	1300	1640	1840	2460	920	1200	1540	1740	400	620	820	980
1.0	920	1300	1640	1970	820	980	1200	1540	300	500	720	820
1.5	820	1100	1410	1640	720	920	1100	1300	260	400	620	720
2.0	720	880	1100	1300	590	820	980	1100	200	300	500	620

Furrow slope (%)	Clays				Loams				Sands			
	Average depth of water applied (cm)											
	7.5	15	22.5	30	5	10	15	20	5	7.5	10	12.5
	maximum furrow length in meters											
0.05	300	400	400	400	120	270	400	400	60	90	150	190
0.1	340	440	470	500	180	340	440	470	90	120	190	220
0.2	370	470	530	620	220	370	470	530	120	190	250	300
0.3	400	500	620	800	280	400	500	600	150	220	280	400
0.5	400	500	560	750	280	370	470	530	120	190	250	300
1.0	280	400	500	600	250	300	370	470	90	150	220	250
1.5	250	340	430	500	220	280	340	400	80	120	190	220
2.0	220	270	340	400	180	250	300	340	60	90	150	190

Source: Booher, 1974. Courtesy Food and Agriculture Organization of the United Nations.

those designed to irrigate individual trees or small areas of vegetable crops to rice paddies occupying several acres. Their maximum size may be limited by elevation changes, by the area that the available water supply can cover uniformly, or by cropping factors.

A ditch or other water supply must be available for each basin. Water is turned in until the desired depth is reached, then cut back to hold a constant depth of about 4 in. (10 cm) for paddy rice or shut off completely for other crops. The water in the basin is allowed to infiltrate completely, except that some may be drained onto a lower basin after a specified time on a few low-permeability soils.

Border irrigation can be described as elongated basins with a gentle slope in the long direction. Water supplied at the upper end flows down the length of the border as though it were a very wide furrow, as shown in Figure 16–11. Borders range from 10 to 100 ft (3 to 30 m) wide and must be level across their width so that the water will spread uniformly across them. Their lengths are about the same as those of furrows on similar soils and slope gradients (Table 16–2).

Border irrigation can be used on slope gradients between 0.2 and 2% for

Figure 16–11 Border irrigation in California. (Courtesy F. R. Troeh.)

cultivated crops, up to 4 or 5% for small grain or hay crops, and up to about 8% for pastures. Extensive land leveling is often required because the topography must be smoother than for furrow irrigation. Land leveling costs are offset by the low labor requirement for turning water into a few borders rather than into many furrows or corrugations.

The slope range of border irrigation is increased by the use of irrigation terraces. The length of the terrace surface may either slope like a border or be level like a basin.

Wild flooding is used on uneven topography to irrigate pasture or hay and sometimes small grains. The pastures may have slope gradients as steep as 10 or 15%. Water floods across the land from ditches on the ridges. The irrigator uses a shovel to make small furrows and ridges to guide water to any areas that would otherwise remain dry. Water that accumulates in swales may be redistributed with short spreader ditches.

Wild flooding is inefficient in use of water and labor, but it irrigates land that cannot be managed by other methods of surface irrigation. The soil may be too shallow or stony to have its surface smoothed by land leveling, and it may not be used intensively enough to justify a large investment.

16–5.2 Subsurface Irrigation

Subsurface irrigation, also called subirrigation, is essentially a controlled drainage system. Ditches are usually used, but some systems use tile lines. Water is removed during wet seasons and added during dry seasons so that the water table is always at a controlled depth. That depth might be as little as 1 ft (30 cm) for shallow-rooted vegetation in a coarse sandy soil or as great as 4 ft (120 cm) in some loamy soils. The surface soil should be dry, but most of the root zone should be moist. The field can even be cultivated and irrigated at the same time (Stanley et al., 1981).

Relatively little land is subirrigated because the required conditions are very stringent. The land surface must be quite smooth and have a slope gradient of less than 0.5%. The subsoil must be highly permeable, but it must have a shallow water table or be underlain by an impermeable layer that permits a perched water table to be maintained. Both the soil and the irrigation water must be low in salts to avoid forming saline and sodic soils. Suitable conditions for subsurface irrigation most often occur on glacial outwash plains, terraces, or deltas in humid or subhumid areas. Where it works, it can be highly advantageous.

16-5.3 Sprinkler Irrigation

Sprinkler irrigation is much newer than surface irrigation because the necessary pipes, pumps, and power supply were not available long ago. Advantages such as portability, adaptability to a wide range of soil and topographic conditions with little or no land smoothing, and good control of water application have made sprinkler irrigation popular. Efficient water application may save energy, reduce leaching of nitrates and other nutrients, and help avoid erosion. Disadvantages include high equipment and operating costs, moving lines in muddy conditions, salt damage to some plants if poor-quality water is used, and disease problems with some plants.

Most field sprinklers use a rotating sprinkler head such as the one shown in Figure 16-12. Although the sprinklers may be fixed in permanent locations for limited areas of high-value crops, they are usually mounted on either moving or portable lines.

Figure 16-12 A sprinkler at the top of a riser on a portable line in a potato field. Water strikes the protruding arm and makes it work back and forth against a spring. This action rotates the sprinkler and helps distribute the water. (Courtesy F. R. Troeh.)

Portable Lines. Hand-moved sprinkler lines are conventional in many areas. They are used on a regular schedule throughout the growing season in arid climates, but in humid climates they are often kept in storage except during periods of drought.

Irrigation once every 7 to 10 days with applications of 3 to 4 in. (7 to 10 cm) of water each time is common. The application rate should be slow enough to avoid runoff. Sprinklers are available to apply water at rates between 0.1 to 0.2 in./hr (3 to 5 mm/h), but faster rates are usually more efficient. Rates that result in irrigation sets of 8 or 12 hours are convenient for work schedules.

The number of irrigation lines needed depends on the size of the field, the irrigation period and frequency, and the area irrigated by each line. A field 1/4 mile (400 m) square (40 acres or 16 ha) might be irrigated from a main line across the middle of the field as shown in Figure 16–13. Each lateral line could have 21 sprinkler pipes, each 30 ft (9 m) long, plus a 15-ft (4.5-m) coupling to the main line. Outlets every 30 ft along the main line would irrigate an area 1/8 mile by 30 ft (0.45 acre or 0.18 ha) at any one time. Complete irrigation of the 40 acres requires 88 sets (1/2 mile ÷ 30 ft). An irrigation period of 8 hours (three per day) and a frequency of once every 10 days would result in 30 irrigation periods. Such a system requires three lines (88 ÷ 30). Four lines may be used so that the soil can dry and one line be moved while the other three lines are operating.

The system described above and illustrated in Figure 16–13 is designated as a 30- by 30-ft system because it uses 30-ft pipe lengths and 30 ft between lines. Other systems may use pipe lengths from 20 to 40 ft and line spacings from 30 to 60 ft.

Irrigation pipes have quick-coupling devices on each end permitting them to be uncoupled, carried to the next position, and reconnected. A sprinkler is attached to

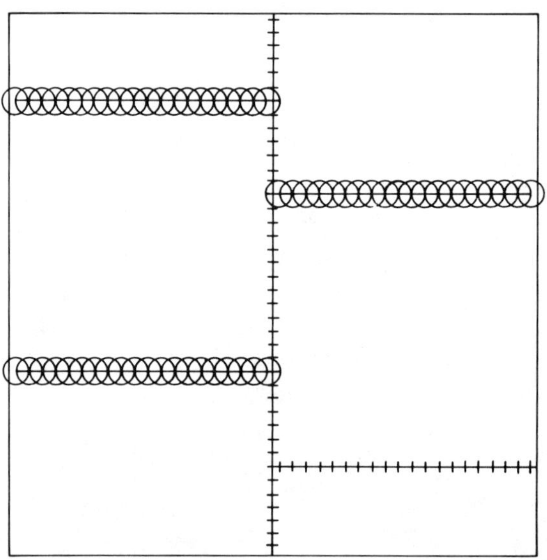

Figure 16–13 A hand-moved sprinkler irrigation system for a field 1/4 mile (400 m) square using four lines with three operating at any one time. The lines are spaced around the field so that the moving distance is only from one position to the next.

the reinforced area near the coupling. Most sprinklers spray past the next sprinkler position for complete coverage. Sprinkler irrigation is usually about 75% efficient in use of water—the other 25% is lost by evaporation and by deep percolation where the water application is heavier than average. Excess wind distorts the pattern and reduces efficiency.

Rolling Lines. One way to make sprinkler lines easier to move is to mount them on wheels. Some lines run through the hubs of large wheels. Other systems use small wheels on each side of the line. Some rolling lines have long flexible supply lines so that they can be motor-driven to roll during the irrigation period. Others are detached, moved, and reconnected much like a hand-moved line.

Center-Pivot Systems. Center-pivot irrigation systems are the most convenient and the most expensive movable systems. Either a well or a buried main line supplies water to the pivot point. The sprinkler line is supported at about 100-ft (30-m) intervals by two-wheeled, motor-driven towers that carry it at a height of about 7 to 10 ft (2 or 3 m), as shown in Figure 16–14. Either hydraulic or electric power moves the towers in concentric circles at a rate proportional to their distance from the pivot point. The number and size of sprinklers vary along the line to equalize the water applied.

The most common size of center-pivot system is a line 1/4 mile (400 m) long that irrigates a 125-acre (50-ha) circle in a 160-acre (64-ha) square. Water spraying beyond the end of the line will cover a few more acres. The corners may or may not be irrigated. Some lines have an extension that irrigates the corners but trails behind when it is not needed. Another method uses a very large sprinkler known as a "big gun" at the end of the line to irrigate the corners.

Figure 16–14 A center-pivot irrigation line in Texas. (Courtesy F. R. Troeh.)

The use of center-pivot systems has increased rapidly in recent years, especially in the Great Plains and the southwestern parts of the United States. Their high installation cost is offset by the convenience and labor savings of their automated operation.

16-5.4 Trickle Irrigation

Trickle irrigation, also called drip irrigation, supplies water to individual plants through small plastic lines. It is the newest method and the only one efficient enough to deliver 90% of the irrigation water to the plant root zone. Water is supplied either continuously or so frequently that the root zone is constantly moist.

Trickle irrigation is especially suitable for watering trees or other large plants. Much of its use has been in orchards and vineyards but it has also been used to irrigate many row crops including various vegetables and fruits. Its advantages are greatest where areas between plants can be left dry. It has no advantage for close-growing vegetation such as lawns, pastures, or small grain crops.

An Israeli engineer named Symcha Blass developed the idea of trickle irrigation in the 1930s (Shoji, 1977), but practical systems had to wait until plastic tubing was available. Trickle irrigation in the United States increased from 100 acres (40 ha) in 1960 to over 125,000 acres (50,000 ha) in 1976 out of a worldwide total of about 160,000 ha. California has nearly half of the trickle irrigation in the United States, some of it in avocado orchards with slopes up to 50 or 60%. Erosion is not a problem because there is no runoff.

A bonus with trickle irrigation is its ability to use water with a higher salt content than any other method—up to about 2500 mg/liter. The constant flow of water from the trickle emitter toward the outer edges of the plant root zone carries the salt along with it. Salt concentrations become very high in the dry areas between plants but not in the active root zone.

Trickle irrigation saves water, functions well in all but the extremes of coarse- and fine-textured soils, works on almost any topography without causing erosion, and requires little labor after it has been installed. The main problems are high equipment costs and plugging of the lines by sediment, salt encrustation, or algae.

Trickle irrigation normally includes a control box that filters the water, regulates its pressure, and adds fertilizers and herbicides. Chlorine may be added to eliminate algal growth. Trickle irrigation normally uses 5 to 15 $lb/in.^2$ (0.4 to 1 kg/cm^2) of water pressure (Shoji, 1977) as compared to 15 to 120 $lb/in.^2$ (1 to 8 kg/cm^2) for sprinkler irrigation. Some trickle controls increase the pressure periodically to flush the lines and reduce clogging.

Trickle irrigation lines have multiple branches at three or four stages to provide the many outlets required. The last stage is a flexible plastic lateral line 0.5 to 1.25 in. (12 to 32 mm) in diameter that lies either on or just below the soil surface and applies the water either through small holes in the line or through emitter nozzles. Emitter nozzles provide more constant flow and reduce plugging by leading the water through a long spiral path that slows the flow and permits a larger emission hole to be used.

16-6 IRRIGATION FREQUENCY

Trickle irrigation and subsurface irrigation may be either continuous or quite frequent, but the other methods normally have several days between irrigations. Longer intervals result in more extensive root systems, but the surface should not be allowed to dry out enough to curtail transpiration (Proffitt, et al., 1985). The usual solution is to irrigate when about half of the available soil water has been used by the growing crop. Enough water is then applied to refill the soil profile (putting on much less would leave a dry zone that could become a root barrier). Each water application should therefore apply about half of the soil's available water-holding capacity. The proper interval between irrigations can be calculated by dividing the amount of water to be applied by the daily consumptive use of water. The result may be as short as a few days or as long as two or three weeks.

16-7 LAND RECLAMATION

Reclamation in its broad sense means modifying land to make it suitable for cropping. Vegetating mine spoils and construction sites (Chapter 11), drainage of wet lands (Chapter 15), and irrigation of arid lands are all reclamation processes. One more type, the reclamation of saline and sodic soils, is considered in this section.

The formation of saline and sodic soils by water moving upward from a water table was discussed in Section 15-2.5. Saline soils form where upward water movement is dominant; sodic soils form where upward and downward water movements are nearly balanced. Saline and sodic soils can be defined as follows:

> *Saline soils* have electrical conductivities of saturation extracts higher than 4 mmhos/cm (or higher than 2 mmhos/cm if certain salt-sensitive crops are grown). This is measured by saturating a soil sample with water, extracting the water by vacuum, and measuring the conductivity. They contain less than 15% exchangeable Na^+.
>
> *Sodic soils* have more than 15% of their cation-exchange capacity occupied by exchangeable Na^+. They are low in total salt content and electrical conductivity.
>
> *Saline-sodic soils* have electrical conductivities higher than 4 mmhos/cm and have more than 15% exchangeable Na^+.

The only important difference between saline-sodic and saline soils is that leaching changes saline-sodic soils into sodic soils.

Both saline and saline-sodic conditions are called white alkali because the soluble salts form a white deposit on dry soil. The soluble salts make it more difficult for plant roots to absorb water. Plants vary widely in salt tolerance (see Table 16-3). Electrical conductivity of 4 mmhos/cm represents an arbitrary division point that sometimes needs to be lowered or raised according to the kind of crop

TABLE 16-3 SALT TOLERANCE OF CROPS DURING THEIR RAPID GROWTH PERIOD IN TERMS OF ELECTRICAL CONDUCTIVITIES OF SATURATED SOIL EXTRACTS

	Conductivity in mmhos/cm at 25°C causing yield reductions of:		
	10%	25%	50%
Forage crops			
Bermudagrass	13	16	18
Tall wheatgrass	11	15	18
Crested wheatgrass	6	11	18
Tall fescue	7	10	15
Perennial ryegrass	8	10	13
Bird's-foot trefoil	6	8	10
Beardless wildrye	4	7	11
Alfalfa	3	5	8
Orchardgrass	2	4	8
Alsike clover, red clover	2	3	4
Field crops			
Barley	12	16	18
Sugar beets, cotton	10	12	16
Wheat, safflower	7	10	14
Sorghum	6	9	12
Soybeans	6	7	9
Corn, paddy rice	5	6	7
Flax	3	4	6
Field beans	1	2	3
Vegetable crops			
Beets	8	10	12
Spinach	6	7	8
Tomatoes, broccoli	4	6	8
Cabbage	2	4	7
Potatoes, corn, sweet potatoes	2	4	6
Lettuce, bell pepper	2	3	5
Onions	2	3	4
Carrots	1	3	4
Beans	1	2	3

Source: Bernstein, 1964.

being grown. The stage of growth is also important—plants are more sensitive to salinity during the germination and seedling stages than they are later.

Very few soils are as unproductive and as difficult to reclaim as sodic soils. The high Na^+ percentage causes the soil colloids to disperse and the pH to rise above 8.5 (often to about 10) when the Na^+ is not masked by a high salt concentration. The permeability of very sandy soils drops to less than 0.1 in./hr (1 or 2 mm/h) and that of silty or clayey soils becomes negligible. A smooth, crusted, barren surface forms that is so slippery when wet that sodic soils are commonly called "slick spots." The organic-matter content of sodic soils is usually less than 1%, and what organic matter there is becomes soluble at the high pH. Soil water carries some of it to the soil surface where it forms a thin black covering that is the basis for the common name “black alkali.” Dissolved organic matter gives a brown, oily appearance to drainage water seeping from sodic soils.

16–7.1 Reclaiming Saline Soils

Suitable irrigation water, appropriate means of application, and good drainage are required for reclaiming saline soils. Large quantities of water are needed with low enough salt content to leach salts from the soil until the salinity is low enough for the desired purpose. Flood irrigation is usually best because the entire soil surface needs to be covered, often for two, three, or more days. Methods such as furrow and trickle irrigation reclaim part of the soil at the expense of the rest by moving salt to the drier parts.

Salt-tolerant vegetation helps reclaim saline soils, especially those that are fine textured. Plant roots help keep the soil permeable and the top growth helps control erosion. The plant growth must also tolerate enough leaching water to remove the excess salts. This is often a water depth between 0.5 and 1.5 times the soil depth.

A good drainage system is required to remove the leaching water and keep the water table from rising while a saline soil is being reclaimed. Intermittent leaching is sometimes used to give more time for drainage and to reduce the leaching water requirement. Allowing one- or two-day “dry” intervals permits about 70% as much leaching water to dissolve the same amount of salts.

Reclamation is futile unless the land is well managed afterward. The water table should be kept low enough to prevent the soil from becoming saline again, and enough irrigation water should be applied for drainage to remove the salts contained in the water. Section 16–3.7 explains how to calculate the amount of drainage water needed.

16–7.2 Reclaiming Saline-Sodic Soils

Saline-sodic soils need a soil amendment to replace Na^+ prior to the leaching process described for saline soils. The amount of amendment can be calculated as in Note 16–2 when the required chemical data are available. The gypsum requirement may also be measured directly by mixing a soil sample with a saturated solution of $CaSO_4$ and determining how much Ca^{++} is adsorbed by the soil. The gypsum in this test reacts with both the exchangeable Na^+ and the Na_2CO_3 because Ca^{++} is adsorbed more strongly than Na^+, and insoluble $CaCO_3$ precipitates.

NOTE 16–2
SOIL-AMENDMENT CALCULATIONS

Problem

A saline-sodic soil contains 9 meq of exchangeable Na^+/100 g plus 0.5% soluble Na_2CO_3 by weight. Calculate the amounts of gypsum, sulfur, or calcium chloride needed to amend the soil to a depth of 20 in. (50 cm).

Solution

1. The weight of soil can be calculated by assuming an average bulk density of 1.3 g/cm³ (81.12 lb/ft³):

$$1 \text{ ac} \times 20 \text{ in.} = 43{,}560 \text{ ft}^2 \times {}^{20}\!/_{12} \text{ ft} \times 81.12 \text{ lb/ft}^3$$

$$= 5{,}889{,}312 \text{ lb} = 2945 \text{ tons}$$

or

$$1 \text{ ha} = 10^4 \text{ m}^2 = 10^8 \text{ cm}^2$$

$$10^8 \text{ cm}^2 \times 50 \text{ cm} \times 1.3 \text{ g/cm}^3 = 6.5 \times 10^9 \text{ g} = 6500 \text{ mt}$$

2. Each 100 g of soil contains:
   (a) 9 meq × 23 mg/meq = 207 mg = 0.207 g of exch Na^+
   (b) 0.005 × 100 g × (46/106) = 0.217 g of soluble Na^+
   (0.5%) (wt of $2Na/Na_2CO_3$) 0.424 g of Na/100 g of soil

3. Each acre of soil 20 in. deep (hectare 50 cm deep) contains:

$$2945 \text{ tons} \times 0.424 \text{ g Na/100 g of soil} = 12.5 \text{ tons of Na/ac}$$

or

$$6.5 \times 10^9 \text{ g} \times 0.424 \text{ g Na/100 g} = 2.76 \times 10^7 \text{ g of Na/ha}$$

$$= 27.6 \text{ mt of Na/ha}$$

4. The required amounts of each amendment can be calculated from the equivalent weights of each material divided by that of Na:

(a)	$CaSO_4 \cdot 2H_2O$	12.5 tons	×	86/23	=	46.7 tons/ac
	(172/2 = 86)	27.6 mt	×	86/23	=	103 mt/ha
(b)	S	12.5 tons	×	16/23	=	8.7 tons/ac
	(32/2 = 16)	27.6 mt	×	16/23	=	19 mt/ha
(c)	$CaCl_2$	12.5 tons	×	55.5/23	=	30.2 tons/ac
	(111/2 = 55.5)	27.6 mt	×	55.5/23	=	67 mt/ha

Step 2 shows that about half of the soil amendment this soil needs is to replace exchangeable Na^+ and the other half for the soluble Na_2CO_3. Actually, some Na^+ would remain because the process is not 100% efficient, but any of these amendment applications should reduce the sodium content to a safe level.

Gypsum is often the cheapest amendment for saline-sodic soils, but a large amount is required and the process is slow. Gypsum may be added to the irrigation water, but an acre-foot of irrigation water will dissolve only about 2 tons (1,000,000 liters or 10 ha-cm of water will dissolve 1.4 mt) of gypsum. Mixing the gypsum into the soil helps, but reclamation still takes months or years.

The low equivalent weight of sulfur minimizes the amount required for sodium replacement. However, sulfur has its own limitations. Soil bacteria need months or years to oxidize the sulfur to sulfuric acid. The H^+ of the acid will react with soil lime to release Ca^{++}, which in turn exchanges for soil-adsorbed Na^+. Only then is the Na^+ ready for leaching. Lime is common in saline-sodic soils, but its presence should be verified rather than assumed.

Calcium chloride is a highly soluble, fast-acting soil amendment that can be spread on a saline-sodic soil or added to the irrigation water. Reclamation then proceeds in the same manner and at the same rate as if it were a saline soil. The main problem is high cost.

The amount of soil amendment needed to reclaim a saline-sodic soil may be greatly reduced if salty irrigation water is available. The soil would become sodic if leached with pure water, but salty water can be used as a preliminary treatment. Water containing mostly calcium salts is best, but even seawater has been used. After partial reclamation, the reduced amendment requirement can be applied and nonsaline water used to finish reclaiming the soil.

16-7.3 Reclaiming Sodic Soils

Sodic soils are difficult to reclaim because their slow permeability prevents water from carrying amendments into the soil. Mechanical mixing can help get the amendment into the soil and open up some passages for water percolation. Unfortunately, deep plowing may not provide enough mixing and any other method is usually quite expensive. However, sodic soils often occur as small spots mixed with more productive soils. Some such spots have been improved by mixing the soil with a backhoe. Many sodic soils have layers containing gypsum and lime concentrations underlying the solum. Mixing incorporates these free soil amendments into the soil.

Sodic soils are low in soluble salts and therefore require less soil amendment than saline-sodic soils. The soil in Note 16-2 would have required only half as much amendment if it had been sodic instead of saline-sodic. However, the reclamation process is very slow, and few plants will grow on them until some reclamation has been achieved. Even weeds should be encouraged because their roots open channels that improve soil permeability. Permitting the soil to dry and crack open occasionally is also helpful (sodic soils shrink and swell more than other soils of similar clay content).

Salty water is much better than pure water for the initial stages of sodic soil reclamation because salts help flocculate the soil colloids and increase the soil permeability, often by one or two orders of magnitude. Calcium ions in the water are especially helpful because they replace exchangeable Na^+.

16-8 CONSERVATION IRRIGATION

An irrigator can either waste or conserve large amounts of soil and water. Attitude is important because the easiest way to irrigate is often not the best way, and the best methods are often costly. One interaction is usually favorable—irrigation methods that conserve water also conserve soil.

The method of irrigation influences how much soil and water are wasted. Careful management of surface irrigation can achieve about 60% efficiency in water use; typical sprinkler irrigation systems are about 75% efficient; and trickle irrigation is about 90% efficient.

Subsurface, sprinkler, and trickle irrigation should not produce any runoff and therefore should not cause erosion. In fact, the increased vegetative cover may reduce both wind and water erosion. Sprinkler and trickle irrigation are sometimes used on steep slopes that need both vegetative and mechanical erosion-control practices. These needs would exist if the land were cropped without irrigation.

Surface irrigation can be a significant cause of erosion because large amounts of water flow across the land. The worst case results when preirrigation is used to store water in the soil before a crop is planted. Residues from the previous crop can reduce the hazards of preirrigation. Irrigation frequency is also important, especially where row crops are cultivated between irrigations. Most of the erosion occurs during the first hour of irrigation while the soil is still loose. A few long irrigations therefore erode less soil than an equal amount of water applied in several shorter irrigations.

Long furrows, corrugations, and borders are convenient because it takes fewer rows and less work to cover the same area. But long rows require large, erosive streams of water and make it more difficult to irrigate uniformly. Rows that are too long therefore waste both soil and water. One solution to long-row problems is to place portable gated pipe such as that shown in Figure 16-15 across the middle of the rows. The lower half of the field is irrigated first, then the pipe is removed and the upper half is irrigated. Tillage, planting, and harvesting operations run the full length of the rows.

Figure 16-15 Gated pipe being used in Iowa for furrow irrigation. Each opening in the pipe has an adjustable gate to control the water flow. (Courtesy USDA Soil Conservation Service.)

Variations in soil permeability and slope gradient both cause nonuniform applications that waste water. Soil erosion may also result on the steeper parts. Variable soil permeability usually cannot be corrected, but variable slope may be smoothed by land leveling. Major land leveling requires staking the field on a grid pattern, surveying the elevations of the stakes, and preparing a plan that balances the cuts and fills. Cuts and fills are then marked on the stakes, and large earth-moving equipment levels the land to the prescribed uniform slope gradient. Carryalls such as those used for building roads are used for major leveling. Lighter smoothing work is done with a land plane such as that shown in Figure 16–16.

Miller, et al. (1987) found that the size of the maximum nonerosive irrigation stream increased considerably when crop residues were present, especially those grown in place. They combined the use of residues with a "surge-flow" irrigation technique to obtain maximum uniformity of water application in furrows. In surge flow, they alternately ran water in a furrow for 20 minutes, then turned it off for 20 minutes. These surges carried water to the ends of the furrows nearly as fast as continuous flow. Continuous flow was used after the furrows were wet full length.

Ditch erosion is another irrigation hazard. Farm ditches placed on an ideal gradient of about 0.15% seldom erode much (larger ditches need to be flatter). But ditches that must go down a steeper slope can easily cause erosion. Drop structures, concrete-lined ditches, and irrigation pipelines are all used to avoid ditch erosion. Lined ditches and pipelines are also good ways to minimize seepage losses.

SUMMARY

Irrigation is practiced on every continent, but about three-fourths of the world's irrigation is in Asia. Irrigation causes changes in both crop and soil management.

Figure 16–16 A land plane is used to smooth land surfaces for more uniform surface irrigation. (Courtesy F. R. Troeh.)

Average worldwide yields with irrigation are over twice as high as rainfed yields; crop quality may be improved as well. However, irrigation costs are high and erosion and sedimentation may result.

Soil suitable for irrigation must have satisfactory depth, texture, structure, and topography. Maximum slope gradients vary from 3% to over 35%, depending on soil, climate, crop, and type of irrigation system. Water rights are an important issue for irrigators and are based on either riparian rights or prior appropriations. Water for irrigation comes from surface water diverted from streams, harvested rainwater, and underground water. Water quality depends on salt content, sodium adsorption ratio, toxic ions, and solid matter such as sediment and weed seeds. Salts in either the soil or the water can produce saline and sodic soils.

Water for small projects is distributed by ditches or pipelines. Large projects require canal systems that branch into laterals and ditches for individual users. Weirs and flumes measure water flow, and drop structures, checks, and division boxes are used to control it. Water flow in ditches is blocked by checks, canvas dams, or sod dams and delivered to fields through turnouts, siphon tubes, or spiles. Pipelines are used for sprinkler irrigation and for problem spots in ditch systems.

Irrigation includes surface, subsurface, sprinkler, and trickle methods. Surface methods include furrows, corrugations, basins, borders, and wild flooding. Subsurface irrigation is limited to specific conditions where a controlled drainage system can be used. Most sprinkler irrigation uses portable lines, rolling lines, or center-pivot systems. Trickle irrigation is the newest method and is the most efficient for watering individual plants. It can use water containing more salt than the other methods.

Land reclamation includes drainage of wet lands, irrigation of arid lands, and correction of saline and sodic conditions. Salinity can be leached from a soil, but sodium replacement requires a soil amendment such as gypsum or sulfur.

Sprinkler irrigation usually applies water more uniformly than surface methods and trickle irrigation supplies the water directly to the plant root zone for maximum efficiency. Erosion from surface irrigation is reduced by limiting lengths of irrigation runs, using less frequent but longer irrigation periods, and careful land leveling. The other methods of irrigation should not produce runoff and therefore do not cause much increased erosion.

QUESTIONS

1. Irrigation would improve crop yields in most humid regions. Why is it not used more there?
2. What difference does it make to an irrigator whether water rights are based on the riparian doctrine or on prior appropriations?
3. How is water delivered from a ditch onto a field?
4. What happens to the salt contained in irrigation water applied by surface irrigation? by trickle irrigation?
5. Why is a sodic soil worse than a saline-sodic soil?
6. What erosion problems may be caused by irrigation?

REFERENCES

Agricultural Research Service, 1974. Attacking salinity on irrigated lands. *Agr. Res.* 23(6):7–10.

Bernstein, L., 1964. *Salt Tolerance of Plants.* USDA Agr. Inf. Bull. 283, 24 p.

Bernstein, L., and L. E. Francois, 1973. Comparisons of drip, furrow, and sprinkler irrigation. *Soil Sci.* 115:73–86.

Booher, L. J., 1974. Surface Irrigation. Agr. Devel. Paper 95. FAO, Rome, 160 p.

Busby, C. E., 1955. Regulation and economic expansion. In *Water,* Yearbook of Agriculture. USDA, Washington, D.C., p. 666–676.

Economic Research Service, 1974. *The World Food Situation and Prospects to 1985.* USDA Foreign Agr. Econ. Rep. 98, 90 p.

El-Ashry, M., and D. C. Gibbons, 1987. Managing the west's water. *J. Soil Water Cons.* 42:8–13.

Gulhati, N. D., and W. C. Smith, 1967. Irrigation agriculture: An historical review. In *Irrigation of Agricultural Lands.* Agronomy Monograph 11. American Society of Agronomy, Madison, Wis., p. 3–11.

Haynes, R. J., 1985. Principles of fertilizer use for trickle irrigated crops. *Fert. Res.* 6:235–255.

Malatic, J. T., and T. B. Hutchings, 1967. Selection and classification of irrigable land. In *Irrigation of Agricultural Lands.* Agronomy Monograph 11. American Society of Agronomy, Madison, Wis., p. 125–173.

McConnell, S. G., and S. S. Waller, 1986. Subirrigated meadow response to application of nitrogen, phosphorus, and Atrazine. *Agron. J.* 78:629–632.

Mengel, D. B., and F. E. Wilson, jr., 1988. Timing of nitrogen fertilizer for rice in relation to paddy flooding. *J. Prod. Agric.* 1:90–92.

Miller, D. E., J. S. Aarstad, and R. G. Evans, 1987. Control of furrow erosion with crop residues and surge flow irrigation. *Soil Sci. Soc. Am. J.* 51:421–425.

Miyamoto, S., 1989. Salt effects on germination, emergence, and seedling mortality of onion. *Agron. J.* 81:202–207.

Proffitt, A. P. B., P. R. Berliner, and D. M. Oosterhuis, 1985. A comparative study of root distribution and water extraction efficiency by wheat grown under high- and low-frequency irrigation. *Agron. J.* 77:655–662.

Richards, L. A., (ed.), 1954. *Diagnosis and Improvement of Saline and Alkali Soils.* Agr. Handbook No. 60, U.S. Department of Agriculture.

Robinson, A. R., and A. S. Humphreys, 1967. Water control and measurement on the farm. In *Irrigation of Agricultural Lands,* Agronomy Monograph 11. American Society of Agronomy, Madison, Wis., p. 828–864.

Russo, D., and D. Bakker, 1987. Crop-water production functions for sweet corn and cotton irrigated with saline waters. *Soil Sci. Soc. Am. J.* 51:1554–1562.

Shoji, K., 1977. Drip irrigation. *Sci. Am.* 237(5):62–68.

Stanley, C. D., J. S. Rogers, J. W. Prevatt, and W. E. Waters, 1981. Subsurface drainage and irrigation for tomatoes. *Soil and Crop Sci. Soc. Fla. Proc.* 40:92–95.

Stone, L. R., R. E. Gwin, jr., P. J. Gallagher, and M. J. Hattendorf, 1987. Dormant-season irrigation: Grain yield, water use, and water loss. *Agron. J.* 79:632–636.

Tadmor, N. H., M. Evenari, and L. Shanan, 1970. Runoff farming in the desert: IV. Survival and yields of perennial range plants. *Agron. J.* 62:695–699.

Thomas, H. E., 1955. Underground sources of our water. In *Water,* Yearbook of Agriculture, USDA, Washington, D.C., p. 62–78.

Thomas, H. E., and D. F. Peterson, jr., 1967. Groundwater supply and development. In *Irrigation of Agricultural Lands.* Agronomy Monograph 11. American Society of Agronomy, Madison, Wis., p. 70–91.

Yaron, D., E. Bresler, H. Bielorai, and B. Harpinist, 1980. A model for optimal irrigation scheduling with saline water. *Water Resour. Res.* 16:257–262.

17

Soil and Water Pollution

Pollution is contamination that makes things unclean or impure. Soil and water are polluted physically, chemically, or biologically. Eroded soil becomes a water pollutant or buries a fertile soil beneath unproductive sediment. Soil may be covered by trash or ruined chemically by contamination with heavy metals or other toxic materials. Poisons sometimes escape from soil or trash into streams and lakes where they kill fish and perhaps birds and animals. The soil may be biologically degraded either by toxic materials or by poor management that exhausts its fertility, depletes its organic matter, and forms clods and crusts that restrict air and water movement.

The rapidly growing world population (Figure 17–1) increases the value of productive soil and clean water. The pollution problem can no longer be ignored because there is no desirable new land to replace that which is "worn out." Earth's resources are a closed system of limited size that is much easier to damage than to improve. Soil and water pollution squander the resources that support life.

17–1 RECENT CONCERN ABOUT POLLUTION

The careless discards of bygone civilizations have yielded much of the available information about ancient people. There was relatively little concern about pollution until recent times, however, because the population was only a fraction of its present size. There was room for both the people and the pollution they caused. The earth is now so fully populated that space restrictions limit the standard of living in many areas. Soil pollution further decreases the standard of living. Water pollution, as shown in Figure 17–2, causes aesthetic, health, and productivity problems.

The damage caused by pollution is difficult to evaluate accurately, but the damage in the United States adds up to many billions of dollars each year. Air

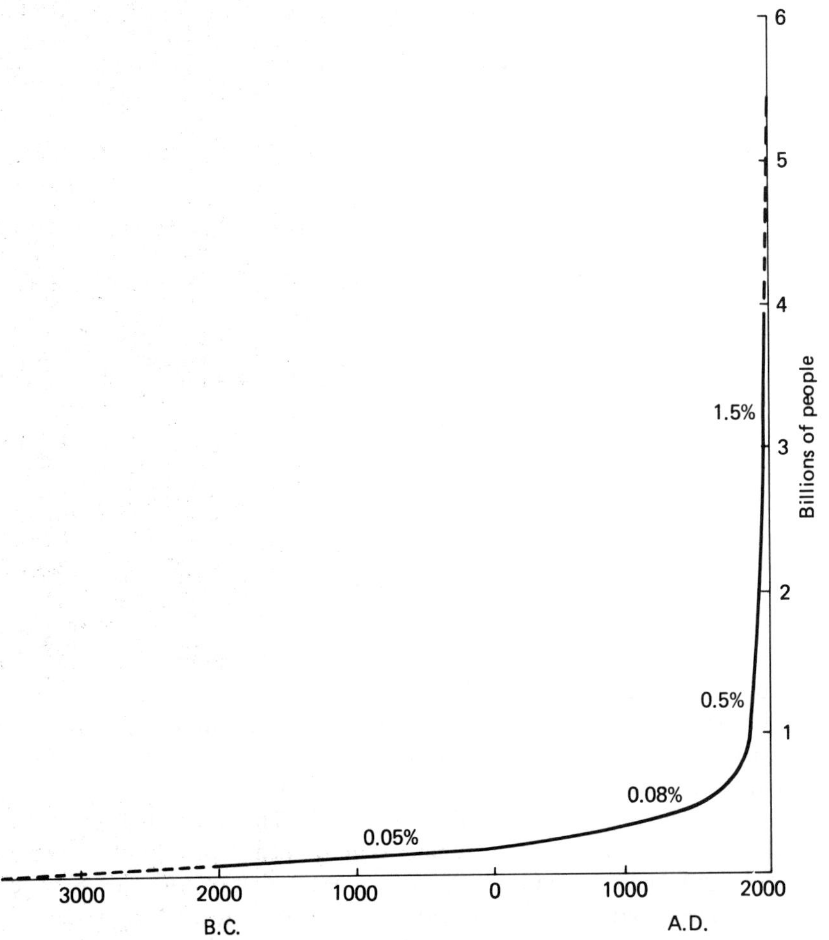

Figure 17-1 The world population growth rate was less than 0.1% per year until about 1600 A.D.; since then the growth rate has increased to about 1.5% per year. The numbers beside the population curve tell the approximate annual increase in population.

pollution alone causes more than half a billion dollars of damage to agricultural crops annually (Shaw, et al., 1971). That loss might double by the year 2000 because increased crop production will be required. Pollution will increase unless billions of dollars are spent to control it.

Another reason for increased concern about pollution is the variety of new types of pollutants. Items made of plant materials and animal products decompose naturally and cause little pollution. The smelting of ores to produce metals has caused a growing amount of pollution for centuries. The wide variety of useful products coming from chemical industries has been accompanied by an equal variety of pollutants. Exotic materials are likely to become pollutants rather than decompose into harmless chemicals. Fortunately, the trend toward increasing chemical pollution is being slowed or reversed by considering decomposition rates when new products are developed.

Figure 17–2 Polluted water is both a hazard and a disappointment for these children. (Courtesy EPA-DOCUMERICA.)

Nuclear wastes cause much concern because of the very long life of many radioactive wastes and the extreme toxicity of some materials, especially plutonium. Safe disposal of such materials is a difficult problem that has yet to be solved on a long-term basis. Also, what should be done with nuclear power plants when they are worn out or obsolete?

The increasing concern about pollution has been accompanied by more sensitive means of detecting pollutants and measuring their concentrations. This increased sensitivity identifies pollutants that would have escaped notice before and raises the question of how much hazard such tiny amounts can cause. The current standard of zero tolerance imposed by the Delaney clause on any chemical that causes cancer in laboratory animals is being questioned. Tolerable levels may need to be defined in some way other than the minimum detectable concentrations.

17–2 SOURCES OF POLLUTANTS

A pollutant is sometimes defined as a resource out of place—much like dirt is soil out of place or a weed is a plant out of place. Most pollutants are either once-useful products that have worn out or are produced as by-products of something useful. The problem is to eliminate the pollution without losing the useful products.

The sources of pollutants can be divided into many types, but only three will be used here: (1) people-related sources, (2) industrial sources, and (3) agricultural sources. People-related wastes come from homes and offices and are proportional to the number of people involved. For example, the amount of sewage produced daily by a city can be estimated by multiplying 0.38 m^3 (13.4 ft^3) by the population

(Thomas and Law, 1977). Industrial wastes are related to products and outputs rather than to the number of people. Agricultural sources are related to land areas, crop production, and livestock numbers. Each of these sources produces its own unique pollutants and needs its own kind of management to control pollution.

17-3 PEOPLE-RELATED WASTES

Population centers must provide means for disposal of solid and liquid wastes. Gaseous wastes are also produced, especially by burning solid wastes, but the resulting air pollution is outside the scope of this book. The solid and liquid wastes will be considered because they are significant pollutants of soil and water.

17-3.1 Solid Wastes

Metal, wood, paper, plastic, glass, and other materials (Table 17-1) are dumped into trash cans and hauled away. The disposal site was once the city dump where piles of trash accumulated and scavengers searched for usable items in the debris. Open dumps had fires that caused air pollution, were havens for rats and other pests, and created health hazards. Dumps were replaced by sanitary landfills where the trash is covered by a layer of soil the same day it is dumped. Sanitation is improved and the hazards are reduced, but satisfactory landfill sites are scarce. Percolating water may pollute the water table, and sight and odor pollution still cause people to protest the location of a landfill site near their residences.

Solid-waste recovery plants are the newest approach to solid-waste disposal. The first municipally owned plant of this type began operation at Ames, Iowa, in 1975. The Ames plant shreds the waste into small pieces and sorts it into combustible

TABLE 17-1 PERCENTAGE COMPOSITION OF SOLID WASTE FROM TWO CITIES AND TWO NEARBY COUNTIES

	City		County	
Solid waste	Oakland, Calif.	Phoenix, Ariz.	Sacramento Co., Calif.	Pima Co., Ariz.
Cans and metals	7.4	7.1	6.4	8.0
Glass	10.1	8.9	9.8	9.7
Paper	38.0	42.5	26.0	39.2
Organics and yard trim	31.0	27.2	29.0	28.5
Plastics	5.0	6.2	1.3	4.8
Textiles (rags)	2.5	3.1	1.1	1.6
Wood	2.5	1.2	0.8	1.0
Tires	2.2	1.0	1.0	1.0
Other (ashes, dirt, etc.)	1.4	2.8	24.6	6.2

Source: Reproduced from *Soil for Management of Organic Wastes and Waste Waters,* Chapter 18, Fuller and Tucker, 1977, p. 472–489 by permission of the American Society of Agronomy, Crop Science Society of America, and Soil Science Society of America; data credited to Benjamin Petrucci, Sacramento, California, and W. H. Fuller, University of Arizona, Tucson.

material, ferrous metal, aluminum, other metals, and reject material, as shown in Figure 17–3. The metals are sold and the combustible material is mixed with coal for electric power production. Another benefit to the city is the low sulfur content of the combustible portion of the waste.

The marketable products may cover the operating costs of solid-waste recovery plants, but probably not the depreciation costs. Such plants are increasing in number, however, because the alternatives are becoming less tenable. Recycling is likely to become more and more important with time.

17–3.2 Liquid Wastes

Sewer systems in the United States transport about 27 billion gallons a day of liquid wastes to sewage plants for treatment. At least, the sewage should be treated. Hundreds of cities and towns routinely dump raw sewage into streams, and about 150 of them dump it into coastal waters, bays, and lakes (Marx 1988). Many more, including some large cities, dump raw sewage during peak flows or plant malfunctions. About half of the sewage treatment plants in the United States provide only *primary treatment,* removing materials that will either float or settle out of quiet water. The effluent enters a nearby stream still carrying dissolved materials, suspended solids, and about two-thirds of the biological oxygen demand (BOD) of the sewage.

The sewage treatment plants of most cities provide *secondary treatment* that uses bacteria to remove about 90% of the solid matter and BOD from the effluent of primary treatment. The bacteria work either in an activated sludge tank through which air is blown to promote microbial activity, or on the surface of stones about 4 in. (10 cm) in diameter that fill trickling-filter tanks. The effluent from secondary

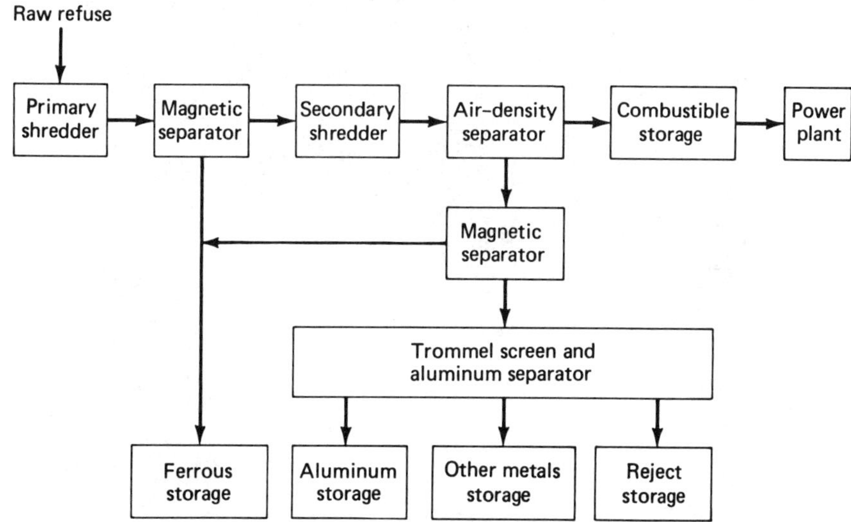

Figure 17–3 A flow diagram for the solid-waste recovery system at Ames, Iowa. (Courtesy City of Ames.)

treatment is usually chlorinated to kill harmful bacteria and then discharged into a stream.

The water pollution from treated effluent is much less serious than it would be without treatment, but the effluent still contains plant nutrients that cause eutrophication. Nitrogen and phosphorus are the most important nutrients because they are the most likely to be deficient enough to prevent algal growth in quiet water. Algae form an unsightly scum on water and then die. Decomposition of the algal mass depletes the water of dissolved O_2 and produces a rotten odor. Eutrophication can be avoided or controlled if the concentration of either nitrogen or phosphorus can be held low enough in the water.

The phosphorus content of streams increases dramatically below sewer outlets and commonly results in large masses of algal growth. Most of this phosphorus comes from laundry detergents and other cleaning agents, so one way to reduce such pollution is to reduce the phosphorus content of detergents. Researchers are seeking alternate ways of producing effective cleaning agents. One reason for optimism is the earlier success in changing detergents from the hard type that produced foam in streams, as shown in Figure 17–4, to the present biodegradable soft type.

Sludge is the solid material removed by primary and secondary treatment of sewage. It represents only about 0.1% of the sewage volume, but that is still a large amount. The wet sludge is usually dried on a sand bed. The dried sludge is a mellow material of variable composition averaging about 4% N, 3% P, and 0.3% K (Sommers, 1977). It can be used to loosen and fertilize garden soils, or applied to fields when the supply is large. Sometimes it is finely ground and mixed with effluent for distribution through a sprinkler irrigation system. Truesdale and Wellings (1983) discuss the use of sludge and the problems associated therewith.

Figure 17–4 Hard detergents once produced masses of foam in streams and even in drinking water. The change from hard to biodegradable detergents in the United States was completed in 1965. (Courtesy USDA Office of Information.)

Tertiary treatment removes dissolved materials from the effluent. Relatively few sewage plants provide tertiary treatment, but the number is increasing because of pollution-control requirements. Two methods are used—chemical treatment and disposal on land by sprinkler irrigation. Chemical treatment requires large quantities of expensive resins to absorb anions and cations. Most interest in tertiary treatment is therefore directed toward disposal on land (Fuller and Warrick, 1984).

The soil to be used for tertiary sewage treatment must be permeable and well drained. High application rates are used to minimize the land area and the size of the irrigation system required. Large droplets result from the large sprinkler nozzles required to avoid clogging problems. A forage crop should be grown on the land to control erosion.

Waste disposal on land usually applies water and nutrients at rates that are much higher than needed for plant growth. The systems should therefore be managed to dispose of water and nutrients. Tile drainage is usually needed to prevent waterlogging. Forage crops should be harvested to remove nutrients. Nitrogen loss by denitrification can be promoted by alternately allowing the soil to dry for several days and then keeping it wet for several days. Excess phosphorus may be permitted to accumulate in the soil as insoluble phosphates of calcium or iron and aluminum, and potassium may be held on cation-exchange sites.

Heavy-metal ions contained in the sewage are usually the factor that limits application amounts or even precludes application to soil. For example, cadmium is toxic to animals if it is present in significant concentrations. Some heavy metals are quite toxic to plant growth. Their toxicity may persist for decades because the metallic ions are held by cation-exchange sites. The zinc equivalent may be used to monitor the problem. It has been defined as the zinc concentration plus double the copper concentration and eight times the nickel concentration. According to Larson et al. (1975), the zinc equivalent added to agricultural soils should not exceed 5 to 10% of the soil's cation-exchange capacity. Typically, a soil with a cation-exchange capacity of 20 meq/100 g can probably accept a total of 200 to 600 tons/acre (500 to 1500 mt/ha) of average sewage sludge (a depth of about 2 to 6 in. or 5 to 15 cm) before being limited by the zinc equivalent. Much larger amounts of effluent can be applied, because the metals tend to be concentrated in the sludge rather than in the effluent.

17-3.3 Rural Home Wastes

Homes not connected to sewer systems still have to dispose of both solid and liquid wastes. Residents of many such homes use their own small version of the old city dump, often by discarding their trash in a gully or on a stony area as shown in Figure 17-5. One advantage many rural homes have is that garbage can be fed to animals and therefore need not be included with the other solid waste.

Septic tanks can be very effective means of disposal for liquid wastes. They provide both settling and bacterial action in the tank, followed by disposal through a tile drain field. A system that functions properly provides the equivalent of primary and secondary sewage treatment in the tank and tertiary treatment in the soil.

Figure 17-5 Trash discarded in a gully is unsightly, may harbor mice and rats, can cause water pollution, and must be removed before the gully can be repaired. (Courtesy F. R. Troeh.)

Problems arise when the tank fills with sediment (it then needs to be pumped out) or when the soil in the drain field will not absorb all of the effluent. Soil permeability is often reduced by bacterial products clogging the pores around the drain lines. Septic tank effluent that reaches the surface from faulty operation causes unpleasant odors and possible health hazards.

17-3.4 Litter

People have a distressing habit of littering wherever they go. Discarded wrappers, containers, and worn-out items fall by the wayside and clutter the landscape. These items injure the appearance of the area, and some of them stifle plant growth by cutting off air, water, and light. Items such as broken glass and sharp pieces of metal can inflict wounds on persons or animals, and some discarded poison containers can be deadly. A small percentage of the population undoubtedly produces most of the litter. The problem seems to be worst when leisure time is involved and people are relaxing.

Cities, towns, and other public bodies spend large sums cleaning up litter. Fines may be levied on "litterbugs," but it seems that few are caught. A newer approach of outlawing disposable bottles and cans and requiring a deposit on all beverage containers has been more successful but cannot solve the whole problem. Changes in attitudes and habits are needed. One approach that has proven helpful is to encourage groups or individuals to "adopt a highway" and keep it clean of litter.

17-4 INDUSTRIAL WASTES

Industries produce a wide variety of solid, liquid, and gaseous wastes. Heat often accompanies the wastes. The solid wastes include slag from smelters, gypsum from phosphate fertilizer plants, sawdust from sawmills, and all kinds of scrap pieces or remnants. The material may be wood, metal, cloth, paper, glass, rubber, plastic, etc. Reactive chemicals are important concerns, especially if they are toxic to people, animals, or plants. Some wastes are dense and some are bulky; some are combustible whereas others are inert and resistant to decomposition.

17-4.1 Solid Industrial Wastes

Disposal methods for solid industrial wastes depend on the nature and amount of the waste. Municipal solid waste disposal systems accept some industrial wastes, and some large industries manage their own landfills. Combustible waste may be burned in high-temperature incinerators. These means dispose of part of the waste, but much still accumulates and pollutes land near factories.

Scrap metals and some other materials can be recycled if they are separated from other wastes. Proper planning coupled with attitude changes resulting in increased recycling could reduce both the waste disposal problem and the consumption of raw materials.

17-4.2 Liquid Industrial Wastes

Most liquid industrial wastes are water-based; petroleum materials are a distant second. According to Shaw, et al. (1971), the more than 300,000 factories in the United States discharge three to four times as much BOD into streams as the human wastes carried by sewers. The water often absorbs acids, bases, or other chemicals as it transports materials, provides a medium in which chemicals react, or serves as a coolant.

Petroleum products, toxic chemicals, and hot water pose difficult disposal problems. Dilution and natural stream processes will purify the water only when the waste flow is small relative to the stream flow. Environmental protection may require that the water be purified or cooled before being emptied into a stream. Sometimes a closed system is needed in which the purified water is reused so pollutants cannot reach a stream. Provision must also be made to reuse, market, or dispose of the materials removed from the water.

17-4.3 Air Pollution

Air pollution will be mentioned briefly here as it relates to soil and water pollution. The atmosphere is sometimes the preferred waste disposal site, as for heat exhausted through a radiator or a cooling tower. Carbon dioxide and water vapor are expelled along with heat when materials are burned. Unfortunately, burning may produce gaseous oxides of sulfur and nitrogen plus fine particles of solid matter that pollute the atmosphere. Such materials often concentrate in droplets of rain, mist, or fog and sometimes react to produce smog. The droplets become soil and water pollutants when they fall.

Oxides of sulfur and nitrogen dissolved in water produce sulfurous, sulfuric, nitrous, and nitric acids. These can acidify rainwater to a pH as low as 2. Acid rain corrodes metals and concrete and virtually eliminates the growth of flowers and many other plants in coal-burning industrial centers. Pollution-control efforts to solve the acid-rain problem need to be targeted at problem sites rather than applied universally. Areas where acid rain is not considered a problem commonly receive free fertilizer benefits amounting to 10 to 15 lb/ac (or kg/ha) of available N and 15 to 20 lb/ac of available S annually.

17-4.4 Nuclear Wastes

Atomic bombs, nuclear-powered ships, and nuclear electric plants inevitably produce nuclear wastes. These wastes are so hazardous and so long-lived that no acceptable long-term means of disposal has yet been found. The disposal problem, the remote but frightening possibility of a nuclear accident, the fearsome prospects of nuclear warfare, and the limited supply of uranium have raised strong opposition to the use of nuclear energy. Equally strong support is based on energy needs, problems and hazards associated with other energy sources, and the military potency of atomic power.

A nuclear reactor uses only a few thousand tons of uranium oxide during its lifetime and produces a comparatively small amount of radioactive wastes. But the twin hazards of long-lasting radioactivity and extreme toxicity of waste components such as plutonium make the storage and disposal methods very important. Corrosion-resistant steel tanks embedded in thick concrete have been used to contain the wastes. Some of these containers rest on the ocean floor where they were dumped several years ago; they are now regarded as potential hazards to fish and other life because the wastes may remain toxic 1000 times as long as the projected life span of the containers.

Consideration is being given to disposal of atomic wastes in deep rock formations. The formations need to be dense and free of earthquake faults and other fractures. There must be a way to form a cavity, place a waste capsule in it, and seal the hole. Preferably, the capsule should be retrievable if the need should arise. Certain salt deposits are regarded as best fulfilling the requirements, but it is difficult to be sure that nothing would ever escape from them.

Obsolete or worn-out nuclear reactors pose another problem. None has yet been dismantled and removed from its site. Removal must be accomplished in a way that protects the workers from radioactivity and leaves the site uncontaminated. Radioactive parts of the plant present a disposal problem similar to that of the spent fuel. Until the problem is solved, old power plants will have to be sealed and guarded to keep out people and animals.

17-5 AGRICULTURAL WASTES

Livestock in the United States produce between 1.5 and 2 million tons of waste per year. Plant residues total hundreds of millions of tons. These materials are generally beneficial when returned to the soil, but some of them get into streams, ponds, and lakes where they cause pollution. In addition, agriculture uses many chemicals, containers, and other potential soil or water pollutants.

The task of reducing agricultural pollution is complicated by the "nonpoint" nature of the sources. Livestock wastes may be deposited anywhere and eventually reach a nearby stream. Similarly, chemicals applied to either soil or plants can be washed into streams by runoff water. Pollution-control efforts must be applied to large areas to reduce significantly the effects of nonpoint sources.

17-5.1 Livestock Wastes

The handling of livestock wastes varies widely. Dried cattle droppings are prized as fuel in India where other fuel is not affordable. However, the manure from a large feedlot in western United States is a disposal problem that accumulates in mammoth piles. Operations that feed tens of thousands of animals seldom have access to enough land to spread the manure as fertilizer. Smaller operations can use their manure on nearby land, but the hauling distance becomes too great for large operations. Attitude is also important—many livestock managers think of the manure as a nuisance rather than as a resource. In fact, in years past, many feedlots such as the one shown in Figure 17-6 were deliberately placed on sloping land next to a stream so that the manure would be washed away.

Much manure has been carelessly handled or ignored because its fertilizer value was deemed to be too low to pay the handling costs. The composition varies

Figure 17-6 Many feedlots are located next to a stream because it was formerly thought to be desirable to let the stream carry the wastes away. (Courtesy USDA Office of Information.)

with types of livestock and management (Table 17-2), but an average ton of wet cattle manure contains about 12 lb of N, 3 lb of P, and 10 lb of K (6 kg of N, 1.5 kg of P, and 5 kg of K per 1000 kg). The commercial fertilizer value of these nutrients was about $2 in 1970, $4 in 1980, and $5 in 1990. These values approximately equal the cost of handling the manure. Given this equal cost option, many people choose to handle a bag of commercial fertilizer instead of a ton of manure. This reasoning ignores three significant factors: (1) cleanup costs should be charged to the livestock operation rather than to fertilizer value; (2) manure contains other nutrients in addition to N, P, and K; and (3) manure is good for the soil structure. These factors added to the value of the N, P, and K make a ton of manure worth much more than its handling cost. Furthermore, manure management would be important to control pollution even if it had no value for crop production (Little, 1989).

Much manure has accumulated in piles behind barns until there was a convenient time to haul and spread it. Such manure usually contains straw or hay used as bedding for the animals. Bedding helps absorb the liquid excrement and the nutrients it contains and thereby increases the tonnage without diluting the nutrient content. Odors from manure piles indicate that nitrogen is volatilizing as ammonia, and sulfur as hydrogen sulfide. Volatilized nitrogen and sulfur are either absorbed by soil or water in the downwind area or circulated in the atmosphere until they are brought down by rain. Airborne ammonia from cattle feedlots may add more nitrogen to nearby lakes and rivers than they receive in runoff and drainage water. Volatilization can be minimized by compacting the manure to keep it anaerobic and by getting the manure to the field and into the soil as soon as possible. Plowing or disking it into the soil is important because aeration accelerates volatilization losses in the field. Lauer et al. (1976) found ammonia losses ranging from 61 to 99% during 5 to 25 days after surface applications.

Manure piles should have a roof over them to keep out rain. A covered area in a feedlot works well because trampling by the animals compacts the manure and helps make the pile anaerobic. Piles that must be in the open should be tall and rounded to shed water. Nutrients are lost if water leaches through a manure pile.

Lagoons are another means of handling livestock wastes. A pipeline may be

TABLE 17-2 AVERAGE WATER AND NUTRIENT CONTENTS OF ANIMAL MANURES

		Nutrients (%)					
Animal	H_2O (%)	N	P	K	S	Ca	Mg
Dairy cattle	79	0.56	0.10	0.50	0.05	0.28	0.11
Fattening cattle	80	0.70	0.20	0.45	0.085	0.12	0.10
Hogs	75	0.50	0.14	0.38	0.135	0.57	0.08
Horse	60	0.69	0.10	0.60	0.07	0.785	0.14
Sheep	65	1.40	0.21	1.00	0.09	0.585	0.185
Broiler	25	1.70	0.81	1.25	–	–	–
Hen	37	1.30	1.20	1.14	–	–	–

Source: Calculated from *Soils for Management of Organic Wastes and Waste Waters,* Chapter 8, Olsen and Barber, 1977, p. 197–215 by permission of the American Society of Agronomy, Crop Science Society of America, and Soil Science Society of America; data credited to R. C. Loehr.

used to carry the wastes to the lagoon since water must be added anyway to dilute them. Most lagoons are anaerobic and therefore produce some odors. Most of the solid matter eventually liquefies by anaerobic digestion; the remainder settles as sludge on the bottom of the lagoon. Much of the organic matter decomposes to CO_2 and H_2O. Half or more of the nitrogen and sulfur may volatilize when long-term retention is practiced. The effluent from a lagoon still contains much organic matter and many plant nutrients that can be applied to land by a sprinkler system or a spray truck but should not be emptied into a stream.

Manure rates up to about 10 tons/ac (22 mt/ha) properly applied and incorporated into the soil are effective for fertilizer purposes and cause little or no pollution. Commercial fertilizers can be used to meet any remaining fertility requirements. Although they represent inefficient use of the nutrients in the manure, rates up to 30 tons/ac (70 mt/ha) have been used in humid regions for at least 40 years without causing harmful buildups of nutrients or soluble salts in the soil (Sommerfeldt et al. 1973).

Manure is sometimes applied to land at rates of 50 to 100 tons/ac (110 to 220 mt/ha) to minimize the amount of land area required for disposal purposes. Such high rates can cause pollution because crops cannot use all of the available nutrients. Nitrates and other soluble salts accumulate in the soil and in drainage water. Runoff water, too, may be contaminated, especially if manure is left on the soil surface. To avoid such pollution, the manure should be used on more land at lower rates. If high rates must be used, luxury consumption and denitrification should be encouraged as discussed for sewage applications in Section 17-3.2.

17-5.2 Plant Residues

Plant residues are usually an asset for controlling soil erosion, retaining plant nutrients, and producing soil organic matter rather than a cause of pollution. Nevertheless, plant residues can cause problems by accumulating as debris either on land or in water. The debris is unsightly and may block a watercourse or plug a screen. Sometimes the residues smother vegetation. Sometimes they cause odors as they rot or produce smoke and soot as they burn.

Tumbleweeds are a common source of debris in arid regions. They accumulate in fences and ditches and against buildings where they may obstruct passage and increase the fire hazard. Broken tree branches and fallen trees also produce litter that can block pathways and even roads, or they may fall into a stream and accumulate in quiet water or next to a dam. The decomposing debris adds to the biological oxygen demand in the water.

Plant residues are so abundant that it is fortunate that they usually cause only minor pollution problems. The usual solution is simply to clean up the offending residues.

17-5.3 Agricultural Chemicals

Thousands of different chemicals are used for agricultural purposes. Very large quantities of many chemicals are spread over the immense areas used for producing crops and livestock. There would certainly be some problems even under ideal conditions. Actually, weather, soil, and animal interactions with chemicals often produce conditions that are far from ideal. Chemical users and their equipment may apply too much chemical in one place and not enough elsewhere. Some users are untrained or perhaps inclined to experiment even in adverse circumstances. A pessimist could easily predict that chemical problems would be much more common and severe than they are.

Most of the concern about agricultural chemicals has involved either fertilizers or pesticides. Other concerns such as the use of nitrates and nitrites as food preservatives and the use of growth stimulants are outside the scope of this book.

Fertilizers. Over 100 million tons of fertilizer N, P, and K are now being applied annually in the world as mineral fertilizers. About 15% of this fertilizer use is in the United States. Fertilizer application rates range from zero to several hundred pounds of nutrients per acre. High-value horticultural crops tend to receive the highest fertilizer rates, but agronomic crops such as corn, cotton, and tobacco also may receive more N, P, and K than is being removed in the harvest. An illustration of the effects of changing cropping and fertilizer practices on soil fertility is shown in Figure 17-7.

The dramatic increase in fertilizer use in this century has improved both the quality and the quantity of crops produced. This trend is likely to continue as an essential element of efforts to provide food and other needs for the world's growing population. Nevertheless, several environmental charges made against fertilizers need to be taken seriously. Three such concerns will be considered here: the effects of fertilizers on water pollution, the effect of denitrification on the ozone layer, and the effects of fertilizers on soil microbes.

Plant nutrients can reach a stream either by overland flow or in drainage water. Overland flow carries nutrients in solution and attached to soil particles in suspension, whereas subsurface drainage water carries only dissolved nutrients. The nutrients attached to eroding soil particles constitute by far the largest of these losses and will be considered in Section 17-6.

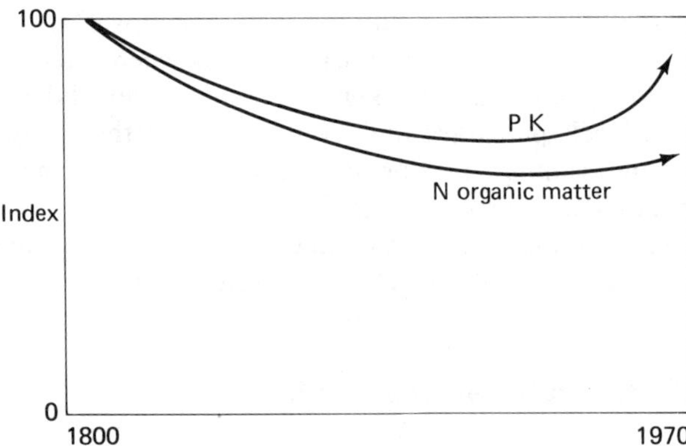

Figure 17-7 A schematic illustration of the general trends of soil fertility in the U.S. Corn Belt from 1800 to 1990. (Courtesy L. M. Thompson.)

Solution losses are proportional to the concentration of the plant nutrients in the water. Nitrate nitrogen (NO_3^-) is a prime concern because it is highly soluble and very mobile in the soil. In contrast, both ammonium and potassium ions (NH_4^+ and K^+) are held by cation exchange, and phosphates ($H_2PO_4^-$ and HPO_4^{--}) have both low solubility and strong attraction to anion-exchange sites.

Leaching losses of nitrate nitrogen are usually small but can be large under certain conditions. Table 17-3 contains data from a nearly level Minnesota soil with tile drainage. The recommended rate for fertilizer nitrogen in this area is about 150 lb/ac (170 kg/ha) for continuous corn. About one-fourth of that nitrogen may be lost by leaching according to this study. Higher fertilizer rates increased the leaching loss; lower rates decreased but did not eliminate the loss. About 16 lb/ac (18 kg/ha) of nitrate nitrogen from decomposing organic matter would have been leached even without any fertilizer.

Drainage makes cropping possible on the Webster soil represented by the data in Table 17-3. Unfortunately, drainage also makes leaching possible (Logan et al., 1980). The leaching of nitrates from well-drained soils in humid regions is usually slower than that indicated in Table 17-3, because the water has farther to go. Longer percolation times give deep-rooted plants time to use more nitrogen. Denitrifying microbes also consume more nitrate and reduce its concentration in the deeper soils. Nitrate leaching is therefore greatest in permeable soils that are shallow to tile drainage or to a gravel layer that drains the water. No leaching occurs from soils of arid regions unless they are irrigated or located in wet positions on the landscape.

Fertilization can increase nitrate leaching if the nitrate concentration in solution is increased at times when leaching losses occur. The losses can be minimized by applying only as much nitrogen as necessary and putting it on as late as possible to meet the crop needs. A 30-year study by the Agricultural Research Service (1970) showed that greatly increased use of fertilizer on nearby land had not increased the nitrate content of the Rio Grande River.

The form of nitrogen fertilizer also makes a difference in leaching rates, especially when the weather is cool. Ammonium and organic forms of nitrogen must be oxidized to nitrate before much nitrogen can be leached from soils that have significant cation-exchange capacities. The nitrification process proceeds slowly at soil temperatures below 50°F (10°C) and stops when the soil freezes. The nitrification rate increases as the soil warms up in the spring, but plant growth should be using the nitrate nitrogen at that time.

TABLE 17-3 NITRATE NITROGEN LOSS IN TILE DRAINAGE WATER FROM VARIOUS RATES OF NITROGEN APPLICATIONS TO CONTINUOUS CORN ON FINE-TEXTURED WEBSTER SOIL IN MINNESOTA

N fertilizer rates				
lb/ac	18	100	200	400
kg/ha	20	112	224	448
NO_3-N in tile drainage water				
lb/ac	17	22	53	107
kg/ha	19	25	59	120

Source: Calculated from data of Gast et al., 1978.

Runoff losses of nitrogen fertilizer range from none to a few percent, rarely exceeding 10% of the amount applied. Dunigan et al. (1976) measured runoff losses in Louisiana on a fertilized silt loam soil on a 5% slope. Less than 3% of the applied nitrogen was lost in the runoff, except when heavy rain on the third day after fertilization carried away 9.5% of the nitrogen from one treatment. Phosphorus and potassium losses were less than 1% of the amounts applied.

Most rains have a significant wetting period before runoff begins. Soluble fertilizer is carried down into the soil during these first few minutes, so little is lost in the runoff. Exceptional losses can occur if intense rain strikes very suddenly or if the rain cannot infiltrate because of frozen or impermeable soil.

Denitrification and ammonia volatilization cause nitrogen to be lost from the soil to the atmosphere. *Ammonia volatilization* can become significant when urea from either commercial fertilizer or manure is applied and left on the soil surface, especially if the soil is alkaline. The urea reacts with water to form ammonium carbonate:

$$CO(NH_2)_2 + 2\ H_2O \rightarrow (NH_4)_2CO_3$$

Reaction with a base under alkaline conditions can then volatilize ammonia:

$$(NH_4)_2CO_3 + 2\ OH^- \rightarrow CO_3{}^{--} + 2\ H_2O + 2\ NH_3$$

Much of the volatilized ammonia is probably carried back to the soil somewhere in rainwater, although some may be oxidized to N_2O or NO.

Denitrification occurs when a soil lacks aeration but contains nitrates. The nitrates may come from fertilizer or from nitrification that occurred in an aerated part of the soil or while the soil was dry enough for air to enter. Increased wetness or movement of nitrate ions to a wetter part of the soil causes anaerobic bacteria to take oxygen from nitrate ions and produce gaseous N_2, N_2O, and NO. The molecular nitrogen is harmless, but the oxides may damage the ozone layer. The atmosphere normally contains small quantities of these oxides formed by lightning and rising from the soil and other sources. The concern is whether increased fertilization might cause higher levels that will decompose too much ozone. Nitrogen oxides from automobile exhausts and other sources add to this problem.

The amounts of nitrogen oxides produced by denitrification are largest where large amounts of nitrate nitrogen occur in soils having alternate wet and dry conditions. This situation is sometimes deliberately created for waste disposal as described in Section 17–3.2. However, denitrification is generally undesirable because it decreases the nitrogen supply for plant growth. The best remedy for these losses is to drain the wet spots and thus improve aeration and reduce denitrification. Undrained wet spots usually should not be cropped and fertilized.

Van Cleemput (1971) showed that under denitrifying conditions an acid medium evolved N_2O and NO, but an alkaline medium produced N_2. Liming of soils where denitrification may occur should therefore reduce the output of nitrogen oxides. Another approach is to inhibit denitrification. Bollag and Henninger (1976) found that fungicides such as captan, maneb, and nabam inhibited denitrification and that the herbicide 2,4–D had a lesser but significant inhibitory effect.

Chemical changes resulting from fertilization can have considerable impact on the microbial population. Some effects show within a few days, as when added nitrogen speeds up the decomposition of organic materials in the soil. Long-term effects may develop over periods of years, as when the acidification effects of ammonium fertilizer cause changes in the microbial population. Fortunately, such changes are normal and reversible. The microbial population is able to adjust to the changing conditions.

Banded fertilizer applications create different conditions in the bands than in the rest of the soil and can have a strong impact on that part. The salt effect may dehydrate and kill microbes in a fertilizer band. Even so, there is a zone around the band where the added nutrients cause microbes to multiply, and the total microbial population is larger than it would be without the fertilizer. Similar effects result from ammonia injection into soil. The pH in the injection zone rises to about 10 and stops all microbial activity, but microbes thrive on the margin of the zone and gradually acidify the soil as they work their way to the center of the zone.

Fertilizers, like most things, can be misused. Low to moderate fertilizer rates cause little or no environmental damage because the nutrients are used by growing plants. In fact, the improved plant growth often reduces pollution by reducing erosion. However, fertilizer nutrients that are not used by plants can contribute to pollution. The excess nutrients may be held by the soil for a while, but eventually they will move into either water or air.

Most fertilizer pollution studies concentrate on nitrogen. Phosphorus and potassium are hard to leach, so not much is lost. Table 17-4 shows what happened to the nitrogen applied to two soils on the North Carolina coastal plain. Crops used about half of the applied nitrogen. Surface runoff removed more than would be expected from the poorly drained soil—it had little runoff but the nitrate concentration was high. The unmeasured nitrogen loss would have included denitrification and any deep percolation that bypassed the tile drains.

Two indirect forms of fertilizer pollution should be mentioned here. One is their manufacture. Processing plants necessarily produce by-products such as gypsum and other materials that may become pollutants. The second form results when

TABLE 17-4 ANNUAL NITROGEN INPUTS AND REMOVALS FROM TWO FERTILIZED COASTAL PLAIN SOILS IN NORTH CAROLINA (TWO-YEAR FIELD AVERAGES)

	Field 1 (moderately well-drained soil)		Field 2 (poorly drained soil)	
	lb/ac	kg/ha	lb/ac	kg/ha
Nitrogen input—fertilizer	143	160	175	196
Nitrogen removal				
Grain harvested	82	92	81	91
Surface runoff	20	22	26	29
Subsurface drains	23	26	14	16
Total removal measured	125	140	121	136
Nitrogen not measured	18	20	54	60

Source: Calculated from data of Gambrell, Gilliam, and Weed, 1975.

mineral fertilizers are substituted for manure. The unused animal wastes cause much more pollution than properly handled manure used to fertilizer fields.

Pesticides. Crop yields are drastically reduced by the combined impact of weeds, insects, and plant diseases. Farmers and gardeners have fought pests with tillage, crop rotations, and selections of resistant crops. Some have gone out against hopeless odds to battle insects in person. The pests may be small but they are exceedingly numerous. A single field may harbor more insects than the human population of the entire nation. The soil in a field almost always holds more weed seed than the farmer would plant of crop seeds.

Chemical warfare against agricultural pests began in the nineteenth century. Two of the earliest pesticides were Paris green—a mixture of arsenic trioxide and copper acetate used as an insecticide since about 1870, and Bordeaux mixture—a copper sulfate and lime mixture used as a fungicide since the 1880s. Bordeaux mixture was originally used to make grapes look poisonous so schoolboys would not steal them. Paris green may have been a by-product of political intrigue, since arsenic compounds were favorite poisons during the Middle Ages.

Highly toxic materials such as arsenic compounds and heavy metals such as copper present serious environmental problems (Kerin, 1983). These problems are amplified by the high application rates required for these materials and the undecomposable nature of their active elements. Furthermore, heavy metals are strongly held by cation exchange in the soil and toxic buildups can last for decades.

The development of DDT as an insecticide in 1940 and of 2,4-D as an herbicide in 1941 opened the way for the metallic pesticides to be replaced by organic materials. The organic pesticides have several advantages—lower rates and fewer applications are needed, more selective toxicity than the metals, and decomposition into simple harmless compounds. Their use, especially that of DDT, expanded rapidly until it was realized that they, too, can cause problems. DDT became highly controversial and was banned after the discovery that it threatened unintended victims by bioaccumulation. Metcalf (1971) cites data from Lake Michigan showing DDT concentrations of 2 parts per trillion in the water increasing progressively through the food chain to 99 parts per million in herring gulls.

Pesticides now go through an elaborate testing procedure to prove that they will work without harming the environment. Their effects on various forms of life are determined, their decomposition rates and tendencies to be adsorbed by soil components are measured, and the specific conditions under which they may be used are defined. Thousands of chemicals are screened to find a few that can be used.

There are still problems with pesticides despite the precautions. Some short-lived pesticides must be applied repeatedly the same season; others last too long and damage the next year's crop. Some need to be applied at different rates on soils that have different organic-matter contents, cation-exchange capacities, or pH. Runoff may carry some chemicals into places where they are harmful. Many grassed waterways, for example, have been killed by atrazine washed from a corn field. Another problem is the tendency of the pests to adapt and develop resistance. New materials are needed to maintain control when the old materials become ineffective.

Pesticides, especially insecticides, applied to the soil can have a significant impact on soil animals ranging in size from earthworms to protozoa. The impact depends on the toxicity and persistence of the chemical and is stronger if the chemical is mixed into the soil than if it remains on the surface. Fortunately, the soil animals can usually recover and repopulate the soil within a few months.

Despite the remaining problems, modern pesticides are making possible several agricultural improvements. They have helped increase crop production during recent decades and are needed to continue that trend in the future. Herbicides save time, energy, and soil by reducing or even eliminating the cultivation of row crops.

Several biological control methods are favored as pesticide alternatives in specific circumstances. Crop breeding to develop resistance to pests is an old, established practice, yet is current enough to send workers all over the world to search for native plants that might carry significant genetic material. Similar searches are conducted for natural predators that can control insect pests. Biological control methods that have been effective against certain insects include the release of large numbers of sterile male insects to interfere with normal insect breeding and the use of synthetic sex attractant compounds to confuse the insects. Such methods are laborious because every situation must be handled separately, but they provide ways to control pests without harming the environment.

17-6 ERODED SOIL AS A POLLUTANT

No other pollutant occurs in amounts comparable to sediment. Streams in the United States carry over 700 times as much eroded soil as sewage. Soil is an important factor in water pollution because of its large volume, the murkiness it produces, the plant nutrients, pesticides, and other polluting chemicals it carries, and the microbes that may be present.

17-6.1 Sediment

Fertile bottomlands are built from thin layers of loamy sediment rich in organic matter. But sediment deposition also occurs in detrimental forms. Some sediment has much lower fertility than the soil it covers. Other sediment is so high in clay that it is unfavorable for plant growth and for tillage operations. Sediment is frequently deposited in such thick layers that plants are smothered and killed, as shown in Figure 17-8. Similar problems can occur with sediment from wind erosion. The sedimentation problems discussed in Chapters 4 and 5 can be considered as a form of land pollution.

Sediment problems usually last longer in water than on land. Sedimentation damage on land is often temporary because new crops can be planted on the sediment or other vegetation will grow and make the land as productive as it was before. Sediment deposited in streams, ponds, and lakes displaces water in ways that can be quite detrimental. Sediment-filled reservoirs no longer serve well for flood control, electric power production, and recreation. Sediment on deltas and riverbeds

Figure 17-8 A heavy spring rain deposited about 18 in. (45 cm) of silt on this Iowa pasture, killing the grass and half burying the fence. (Courtesy USDA Soil Conservation Service.)

raises water levels and increases flood hazards. Sediment in canal and ditch systems requires costly cleanout operations. The progressive and recurring nature of sedimentation problems makes them particularly bothersome in bodies of water.

17-6.2 Muddy Water

A small amount of clay and organic matter will make water cloudy, and some of this effect is natural. Even so, agricultural soil erosion contributes greatly to the opacity of streams and lakes. The nickname "The Big Muddy" given to the Mississippi River indicates what has happened to it. Other human activities also contribute to muddy waters. For example, the Clearwater River in Idaho is fed mostly from forestlands but has nevertheless become murky, largely because of mining operations.

Murky water is obviously objectionable for drinking and cleaning purposes. It may be acceptable for swimming and fishing, but clear water is certainly preferred. The effects on aquatic life are also significant; fewer plant and animal species thrive in muddy water than in clear water, partly because of the dimmer light.

17-6.3 Plant Nutrients in Sediment

Sediment carries much larger quantities of plant nutrients and other chemicals than are dissolved in the water. Several studies have shown that most of the nitrogen and over 90% of the phosphorus moving from fields into streams is carried by sediment.

The phosphorus content of surface waters is important because it is usually the easiest nutrient to control adequately to prevent eutrophication. Sediment and sewage are the two principal sources of phosphorus in water. A combination of soil-conserving practices and sewage treatment therefore is the best way to control eutrophication. Proper fertilization can help reduce pollution by increasing plant growth enough to reduce erosion and the associated nutrient losses.

17-6.4 Pesticides Carried by Sediment

Chemical analyses of water and aquatic life reveal that pesticide residues are widely distributed in streams, lakes, and oceans. Concentrations are usually low, but the occurrence is widespread and many different pesticides are represented. Some pesticides are dissolved in water, but many are adsorbed by soil colloids and carried by the sediment. Sediment gradually releases adsorbed pesticides to the water, thus maintaining a low but significant concentration for months or years.

Insecticides are usually more likely than other pesticides to be harmful to animals and people. One exception was the implication of the herbicide 2,4,5-T as a cause of birth defects after it was widely used to kill trees and brush in Viet Nam. The most troublesome insecticides have been the chlorinated hydrocarbons (DDT and its relatives) because they combine high potency with long persistence and a tendency to accumulate in living things.

Nicholson (1969) lists the principal sources of water pollution by pesticides as (1) runoff from land that has been treated to control pests, (2) industrial wastes from plants that either produce pesticides or use them in producing textiles, (3) accidents and carelessness in using chemicals or disposing of remnants and containers, and (4) the use of pesticides to control aquatic life. Erosion-control practices can reduce the sediment carried in runoff; holding ponds and other waste-treatment practices can reduce the industrial source; and educational and licensing programs are currently aimed at reducing the careless and improper use of pesticides.

SUMMARY

Pollutants contaminate and degrade the environment. People have always caused pollution, but significant concern about pollution is a recent development related to increasing population, new types of pollutants, and increasingly sensitive detection techniques.

People-related wastes are directly related to population. Solid waste has been discarded in dumps or buried but is beginning to be viewed as a resource containing reusable materials. Sewage treatment varies from none to tertiary. Primary treatment removes materials that float or sink, secondary treatment allows bacteria to decompose organic materials, and tertiary treatment removes dissolved ions. Disposal by sprinkler irrigation on land is the favored method of tertiary treatment, but heavy-metal ions can be a problem.

Industrial wastes include scrap and by-product materials, some of which are highly toxic. When feasible, solid materials should be recycled rather than placed in landfills. Liquid industrial wastes include chemicals that must be removed and water that must be cooled before it can be returned to a stream or recycled in a closed system. Air pollution also pollutes soil and water because rain and snow bring sulfur dioxide, nitrogen oxides, and solid particles back to land or water. Nuclear wastes present the most difficult disposal problem of all.

Agricultural waste disposal is complicated by the large amounts of wastes and the large areas involved. Manure has fertilizer value that is often wasted. Losses can be minimized by keeping the manure anaerobic, protecting it from leaching, and working it into the soil as soon as applied. Manure application rates up to 10 tons/ac make effective use of its fertilizer value. Higher rates can be applied for disposal purposes but pollution problems can arise.

Excessive fertilizer rates can raise the nutrient content of both runoff and drainage water above natural levels. Nitrate nitrogen is the nutrient most likely to be lost in large amounts in water. Nitrates may also be lost from wet soil by denitrification. Denitrification can be reduced by draining wet spots or by using certain chemicals.

Accumulations of copper and other heavy metals used in early pesticides are hard to remove from soil. Organic pesticides developed since the 1940s are applied at lower rates than the metal-based materials and have more selective toxicity, but some, such as DDT, cause trouble by bioaccumulation. Some pests can be controlled by biological methods, including crop breeding, natural predators, synthetic sex attractants, and sterile males.

Sediment is the bulkiest pollutant of all. It covers plants and fertile soil, makes water murky, fills reservoirs, and raises river beds. Chemicals carried by sediment commonly produce low but long-lasting contents of nutrients and pesticides in bodies of water.

QUESTIONS

1. What is a pollutant?
2. Why weren't people concerned about pollution centuries ago?
3. How is it possible to dispose of liquid wastes without polluting a stream?
4. What air pollutants can be either helpful or harmful to plant growth?
5. Why is the fertilizer value of manure often ignored?
6. How should manure be handled for maximum benefit and minimum pollution?
7. How can denitrification be reduced?
8. What pollution problems are caused by sediment?

REFERENCES

Agricultural Research Service, 1970. Farm nitrates: No menace to the Rio Grande. *Agr. Res.* 18(10):3–4.

Bollag, J.-M., and N. M. Henninger, 1976. Influence of pesticides on denitrification in soil and with an isolated bacterium. *J. Environ. Qual.* 5:15–18.

BREMNER, J. M., and A. M. BLACKMER, 1978. Nitrous oxide: Emission from soils during nitrification of fertilizer nitrogen. *Science* 9:295–296.

DUNIGAN, E. P., R. A. PHELAN, and C. L. MONDART, JR., 1976. Surface runoff losses of fertilizer elements. *J. Environ. Qual.* 5:339–342.

FULLER, W. H., and T. C. TUCKER, 1977. Land utilization and disposal of organic wastes in arid regions. In *Soils for Management of Organic Wastes and Waste Waters.* Soil Science Society of America, American Society of Agronomy, and Crop Science Society of America, Madison, Wis., p. 471–489.

FULLER, W. H., and A. W. WARRICK, 1984. *Soils in Waste Treatment and Utilization.* CRC Press, Boca Raton, Fla., 288 p.

GAMBRELL, R. P., J. W. GILLIAM, and S. B. WEED, 1975. Nitrogen losses from soils of the North Carolina Coastal Plain as affected by soil drainage. *J. Environ. Qual.* 4:317–323.

GAST, R. G., W. W. NELSON, G. W. RANDALL, 1978. Nitrate accumulation in soils and loss in tile drainage following nitrogen applications to continuous corn. *J. Environ. Qual.* 7:258–261.

HUBBARD, R. K., A. E. ERICKSON, B. G. ELLIS, and A. R. WOLCOTT, 1982. Movement of diffuse source pollutants in small agricultural watersheds of the Great Lakes Basin. *J. Environ. Qual.* 11:117–123.

KERIN, D. D., 1983. Accumulation of some trace elements through the application of fungicides. In *Efficient Use of Fertilizers in Agriculture.* Martinus Nijhoff Publ., The Hague, The Netherlands, p. 351–352.

LARSON, W. E., J. R. GILLEY, and D. R. LINDEN, 1975. Consequences of waste disposal on land. *J. Soil Water Cons.* 30:68–71.

LAUER, D. A., D. R. BOULDIN, and S. D. KLAUSNER, 1976. Ammonia volatilization from dairy manure spread on the soil surface. *J. Environ. Qual.* 5:134–141.

LIKENS, G. E., and F. H. BORMANN, 1974. Acid rain: A serious regional environmental problem. *Science* 184:1176–1179.

LITTLE, C. E., 1989. Annie-Fanny-Mike and the Dunsmore proposition. *J. Soil Water Cons.* 44:16–19.

LOGAN, T. J., G. W. RANDALL, and D. R. TIMMONS, 1980. *Nutrient Content of Tile Drainage from Cropland in the North Central Region.* North Central Region Res. Publ. 268. Ohio Agricultural Research and Development Center, Wooster, Ohio.

LOWRANCE, R. R., R. L. TODD, and L. E. ASMUSSEN, 1983. Waterborne nutrient budgets for the riparian zone of an agricultural watershed. *Agric. Ecosyst. Environ.* 10:371–384.

MARX, W., 1988. Swamped by our own sewage. *Reader's Digest* 132(1):123–128.

METCALF, R. L., 1971. Pesticides. *J. Soil Water Cons.* 26:57–60.

MILLS, W. C., and R. A. LEONARD, 1984. Pesticide pollution probabilities. *Trans. Am. Soc. Agr. Eng.* 27:1704–1710.

NESTEROVA, M. N., and I. A. NEMIROVSKAYA, 1988. Surface pollution of the Pacific Ocean by petrochemicals. *Geojournal* 16:29–34.

NICHOLSON, H. P., 1969. Occurrence and significance of pesticide residues in water. *J. Wash. Acad. Sci.* 59(4):75–85.

PHILLIPS, R. L. (ED.), 1983. *Water Quality Field Guide.* USDA Soil Cons. Serv. Publ. SCS-TP-160, 63 p.

PIPER, S., 1989. Measuring particulate pollution damage from wind erosion in the western United States. *J. Soil Water Cons.* 44:70–75.

SHARPLEY, A. N., S. J. SMITH, and J. W. NANEY, 1987. Environmental impact of agricultural nitrogen and phosphorus use. *J. Agric. Food Chem.* 35:812–817.

SHAW, W. C., H. E. HEGGESTAD, and W. W. HECK, 1971. Pollution poses threat to man, farms, nature. In *A Good Life for More People,* Yearbook of Agriculture. USDA, Washington, D.C., p. 293–299.

SOMMERFELDT, T. G., U. J. PITTMAN, and R. A. MILNE, 1973. Effect of feedlot manure on soil and water quality. *J. Environ. Qual.* 2:423–427.

SOMMERS, L. E., 1977. Chemical composition of sewage sludges and analysis of their potential use as fertilizers. *J. Environ. Qual.* 6:225–232.

THOMAS, R., and J. P. LAW, 1977. Properties of waste waters. In *Soils for Management of Organic Wastes and Waste Waters.* Soil Science Society of America, American Society of Agronomy, and Crop Science Society of America, Madison, Wis., p. 45–72.

TRUESDALE, G. A., AND R. A. WELLINGS, 1983. Organization of sewage and industrial sludge utilization. *Agrochimica* 27:219–222.

VAN CLEEMPUT, O., 1971. Etude de la denitrification dans le sol. *Pedologie* 21:367–376.

WALL, G. J., T. J. LOGAN, and J. L. BALLANTINE, 1989. Pollution control in the Great Lakes Basin: An international effort. *J. Soil Water Cons.* 44:12–15.

YOUNG, C. E., and J. S. SHORTLE, 1989. Benefits and costs of agricultural nonpoint-source pollution controls: The case of St. Albans Bay. *J. Soil Water Cons.* 44:64–67.

18

Economics of Soil Conservation

The costs of soil conservation are usually obvious and therefore seldom overlooked. The returns are less identifiable, especially where conservation merely preserves productive potential that would otherwise be lost. Lowered potential may be masked by weather variations, more fertilizer, new crop varieties, and improved crop management. It takes a perceptive person to properly balance the obscure costs of inaction against the obvious costs of acting to conserve soil. Perception must be followed by decisive action if the soil is to be saved.

Soil-conserving practices often provide long-term benefits in exchange for immediate costs. It is unfortunate but not surprising that the evident needs of the present often win over more important but vague needs of the future. Conservation practices that include short-term benefits are therefore easier to promote than those that are strictly long term. Even so, some practices such as terracing are used in spite of the long time required to recover their costs. Changes in tillage, including contour tillage, reduced tillage, and no-till systems, are usually profitable, but their adoption has been slowed by appearance and convenience factors and pest problems.

Many people may benefit from a landowner's conservation practices. For example, soil that is held on a field neither muddies the water of a stream nor becomes sediment on other land. People living downstream therefore benefit from soil conservation practices upstream. In a broader sense, everyone has a stake in the productive potential of the land. Such interest is represented to some degree by governmental participation in soil conservation through research, education, cost sharing, tax benefits, and legal actions. Such participation is justified by the importance of productive potential as a national asset. Reduced productive potential is the most serious long-term effect of erosion.

Economic emphases of soil conservation have shifted considerably in the last 20 years from the on-farm value of tons of soil to the public cost of sediment. Both aspects are important, but the sediment problem was largely ignored until environmental concerns became a public issue. Emphasis on the on-farm losses has diminished because they can be partly offset by using more fertilizer (Nowak, 1988).

18-1 BENEFITS FROM SOIL CONSERVATION

Soil conservation yields many kinds of benefits. Those to be considered in this section include increases in net returns from land, retention of productive potential, reductions in erosion losses and sediment damage, and environmental benefits.

18-1.1 Increases in Net Returns

Some conservation practices produce an immediate profit, some lead to a delayed profit, and some produce no monetary profit but are used for aesthetic or other nonmonetary reasons. Some practices are usually considered under the heading of good management rather than conservation because they increase profits. Fertilization according to soil tests is such a practice. Fertilizer recommendations are usually based on an economic optimum with little thought for the reduced soil loss resulting from improved plant growth. Fertilization is actually an important soil conservation practice.

Conservation Tillage. The various forms of conservation tillage discussed in Chapter 9 often increase net returns. Most of them reduce the energy input used for tillage and thereby reduce costs. Table 18-1 shows savings of 18% for machinery and 64% for fuel when slot-planted corn was compared to conventionally tilled dryland corn. There was a small increase in pesticide input but it cost only a fraction

TABLE 18-1 ENERGY REQUIRED IN DIESEL FUEL EQUIVALENT (GALLONS/AC) TO PRODUCE CORN IN NEBRASKA BY FOUR TYPES OF TILLAGE UNDER DRYLAND AND IRRIGATED AGRICULTURE

	Dryland				Irrigated			
Input	Conventional	Disk and plant	Tillplant	Slotplant	Conventional	Disk and plant	Tillplant	Slotplant
Machinery	2.55	2.31	2.19	2.10	6.13	5.89	5.76	5.67
Fuel	5.15	2.74	2.60	1.87	5.15	2.74	2.60	1.87
Transport grain	1.81	1.81	1.81	1.81	3.02	3.02	3.02	3.02
Fertilizer	21.67	21.67	21.67	21.67	30.22	30.22	30.22	30.22
Pesticides	1.13	1.13	1.13	1.43	1.13	1.13	1.13	1.43
Drying	8.23	8.23	8.23	8.23	13.70	13.70	13.70	13.70
Irrigation	—	—	—	—	30.87	30.87	30.87	30.87
Total (gal/ac)	40.54	37.89	37.63	37.11	90.22	87.57	87.30	86.78
Total (liters/ha)[1]	379.4	354.5	352.1	347.3	844.3	819.4	816.9	812.1

Source: Calculated from data of Wittmus, et al., 1975.

[1]Gallons/acre × 9.35 = liters/hectare.

of the machinery and fuel savings. Similar fuel savings are indicated in data from Ohio, as shown in Figure 18–1. The Ohio data showed equal average corn yields whether conventional tillage or no-tillage planting was used (Triplett and Van Doren, 1977). There were, however, differences among soils. No-tillage yielded more than conventional tillage on the well-drained Wooster silt loam, but the reverse was true on the less-well-drained Hoytville silty clay loam.

Several studies have shown that average corn yields are insensitive to tillage practices as long as comparable stands and adequate weed control are obtained (Van Doren et al., 1976). Minimum tillage usually shows an advantage on sloping land, where it helps conserve soil and water. Conventional tillage usually yields more than no-tillage where continuous corn is grown on land wet enough to be conducive to root disease. Results with wheat and some other crops have generally been less favorable to no-tillage than corn yields have been.

Fuel and machinery savings from reduced tillage make it possible for producers to make larger profits from equal yields even if they use more pesticides. Rising energy costs and new types of herbicides, insecticides, and fungicides have led to a marked expansion of minimum tillage in recent years. Estimates indicate that minimum tillage was used on 3.8 million acres in the United States in 1963, 34 million acres in 1974, and will be used on 300 million hectares by 1990 (Allen et al., 1977). Fuel savings of $100 million per year could well result from such changes by 1990.

Water Conservation. The importance of water conservation depends on the amount of water already in the soil, the weather, and the plant needs at the time. Water conserved before a dry period can make the difference between success and crop failure. Excess water retained during a wet period can damage the crop and reduce yields, especially in low spots. Good water control sometimes helps even in wet periods, though, by holding water on drier sloping land rather than letting it run onto level areas below.

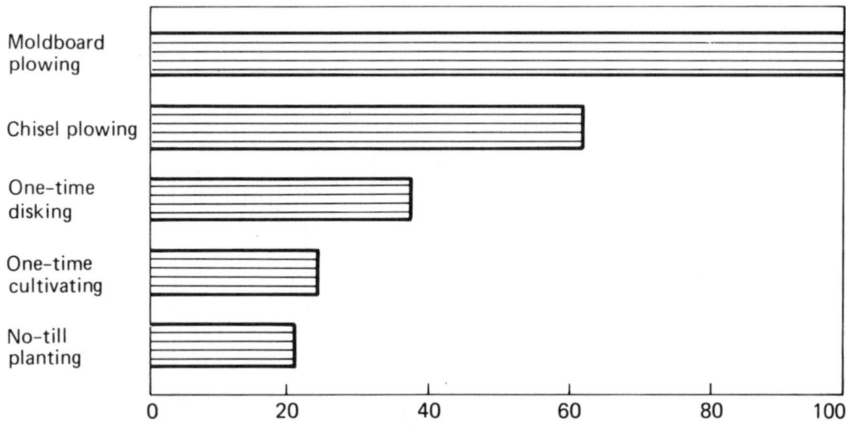

Figure 18–1 Relative fuel requirements for growing corn with five different tillage systems. (From Triplett and Van Doren 1977.)

Times when water conservation will increase yield are common in but not limited to semiarid climates. Subhumid and even humid climates have dry periods during which plant growth suffers. Periods of water deficit are common during the warmest months, as illustrated in Figure 18–2, because water requirements are highest then.

Contour tillage and other water conservation practices described in Chapter 14 might make an average of 2 in. (50 mm) more water available for plant growth on sloping lands during the growing season. This much water would typically increase yields of small grains or soybeans by 7 to 8 bu/ac (5 q/ha), of corn by 20 to 25 bu/ac (15 q/ha), or of lint cotton by 40 to 50 lb/ac (50 kg/ha).

Water conservation on irrigated land is also profitable but in its own way. Any irrigation water conserved can be used to irrigate additional land and thereby increase profits. Individuals may either expand their irrigated land or reduce their water consumption.

Soil Drainage Profits. Soil drainage is another profitable practice associated with soil conservation. Land is seldom drained where it does not add to both profit and convenience. As an example, Bornstein and Fife (1973) calculated 13% and 19% annual returns on an investment in drains spaced 100 ft (30 m) and 200 ft (60 m) apart on poorly drained soils in Vermont.

Irrigation Profits. Irrigation normally increases inputs, yields, and profits. Crop prices that make rainfed agriculture profitable are also likely to make irrigation profitable in many places. Sanghi and Klepper (1977) concluded that exploiting groundwater for irrigation gives too much short-term profit for groundwater conservation to be left to market forces alone. Social costs, future water needs, and the possibility of excessive erosion should also be considered.

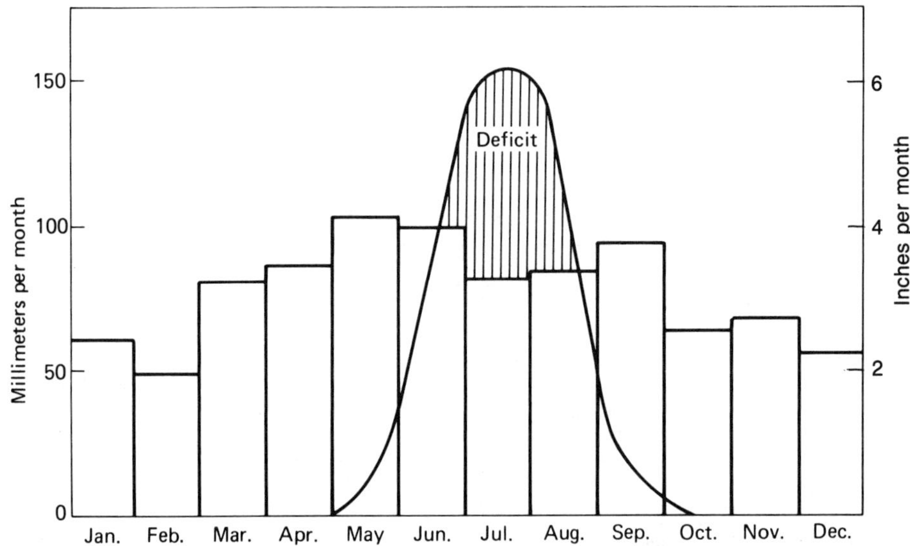

Figure 18–2 Average monthly precipitation in Illinois as compared to the water needs of corn.

Pest-Control Profits. Weeds, insects, and plant diseases can cause increased erosion by reducing the stand of the crop. Controlling these pests can reduce erosion and increase profits at the same time. As an example, Peters (1975) showed that use of aldrin or heptachlor to control insects on Iowa corn increased yields an average of 8 to 10 bu/ac (5 to 6 q/ha) over a 20-year period. Insecticide treatment increased yields on both good and poor soils.

Deferred Profits. Fertilizer, tillage, water management, and pest-control practices should increase profits the same year they are applied. Several years may be required to repay the investment costs of drainage, irrigation, and new machinery but increased returns usually begin with the next harvest. The returns may be delayed longer when practices such as terracing, revegetating grazing land, replanting forests, or soil reclamation are used. These practices must therefore be considered long-term investments.

Terracing is a very effective means of conserving soil, but it is also expensive. To be economical, it must permit yields to be maintained on a long-term basis under more intensive use than would otherwise be feasible. Nonetheless, yields may be reduced for a few years on the areas where topsoil has been removed to build the terraces. The yield reduction can be minimized by stockpiling the topsoil and replacing it after the terraces are built, but this adds to the cost. Often it is more practical to use fertilizers, manure, green manure, and tillage practices to improve the exposed subsoil than to replace topsoil. Reduced soil loss should result eventually in higher yields than would have been obtained without the terraces.

Forage crops and trees conserve soil effectively, but they take time to grow. Range management may require several years of little or no grazing to let desirable grasses become well established. Increased production in later years will make up for the earlier decreased use. A grazing program that maintains productivity should then be established (see Chapter 13). Trees take even longer to grow and become marketable. The value is there, however; the land value increases as the trees grow toward marketable size.

Reclamation of sodic soils is another example of delayed profits. Sodic spots are often so unproductive that *any* plant growth is an improvement. Improving them to where they will not only grow something but will produce a profitable crop takes time (often years) as well as investment (see Chapter 16).

Deferred profits often create a conflict between long-term and short-term values. The need for short-term income can lead to an exploitation of soil and water with maximum removal and as little input as possible. Degraded vegetative cover and serious soil loss can occur under short-term exploitation of land.

18-1.2 Retaining Productive Potential

Nutrient losses and flood damage cause decreases in production for the year in which they occur but they do not always reduce the future productivity of the land. In fact, sediment deposited by a flood may improve the soil's productive potential. However, the area that lost the soil almost surely lost productive potential.

Reduced yield potential resulting from soil loss ranges all the way from 0 to

100%. For example, Olson and Nizeyimana (1988) found corn yield reductions ranging from 5 to 24% on seven loess-derived soils in Illinois. The yield reduction depends greatly on the amount of erosion and the nature of the topsoil, subsoil, and soil parent material. A 2-in. (5-cm) loss from the top of a deep uniform soil may have little long-term impact. A 2-in. loss from another soil may cause clayey subsoil to become part of the plow layer, and productive potential may drop by 10 to 25%. An equal soil loss from a soil that is shallow to bedrock might cause a complete crop failure. The most unfortunate feature of such losses is their permanence. Future yields are decreased along with those of the year when the damage occurs. Colacicco et al. (1989) estimate that a continuation of wind and water erosion at their 1982 rates would cause U.S. yields of corn, soybean, and cotton to decline by an average of 4.6, 3.5, and 4.5%, respectively, over the next 100 years. They estimated that wheat yields would decline 1.6% and that legume hay yields would decline only 0.8%. These estimated declines would have been larger had their model not assumed that fertilizer use will increase.

Soil erosion is seldom uniform across a large area of land. The value of soil conservation for preserving productive potential therefore varies for areas within a field. The most eroded spots may be detected easily by the subsoil color and sparse vegetation. The field as a whole may be producing reasonably well, but these spots are not. Calculation of costs and returns on the eroded spots will frequently show a loss from cropping that reduces the profit obtained from the rest of the field. The damaging effect is sometimes increased by sediment smothering the crop in low areas.

Good management of productive fields containing severely eroded spots is difficult. Using them intensively causes more erosion and sedimentation. Limiting the land use to a system suitable for the problem spots produces little income and fails to use the capability of the rest of the field. Some spots can be protected with contouring or terraces or by the use of minimum tillage. Often it is best to exclude the spots by either relocating the field boundary or going around "patches" in the field. Permanent vegetation on the eroded spots and appropriate crops on the rest maximizes the productivity of the field as a whole. The permanent vegetation may both conserve soil and be useful for wildlife or for a forage crop.

18-1.3 Reduced Erosion Losses

The value of lost soil is an obvious cost of soil erosion. Reductions in soil loss are obvious benefits from soil conservation. The value of each ton of eroded soil varies according to its clay, organic-matter, and nutrient contents. Both wind and water remove fine particles while coarser particles are left behind. Textural sorting combined with the effects of organic-matter accumulation, fertilization, and liming being concentrated in the upper part of the soil usually makes a ton of eroded soil more fertile and therefore more valuable than a ton of average soil.

An approximation of the gross value of the plant nutrients in eroded topsoil can be based on the following assumptions:

1. The commonly used estimate of 4 billion tons (3.6 billion metric tons) of

detrimental soil erosion occurring annually from land in the United States is correct (about 3 billion tons coming from cropland).

2. Each ton of soil has a total nutrient value of $5, totaling $20 billion each year (see Note 18–1).

NOTE 18–1

FERTILITY VALUE OF A TON OF SOIL

The fertility value of a ton of eroded soil can be calculated by using the following assumed values:

1. An average temperate-region topsoil contains about 3% organic matter, but an average ton of sediment contains more colloids so it has about 6% organic matter.
2. The soil organic matter is about 5% N, 0.5% P, and little K apart from that held by cation exchange. The mineral matter contains little N, about as much total P as the organic matter, and about 1.5% K. (Four billion tons of eroded soil contain about the same amount of N and P and more than ten times as much total K as the annual application of commercial fertilizer.)
3. The amounts of these nutrients that will become available annually in a temperate region can be estimated as 3% of the N, 5% of the P, and 1% of the K (these percentages might be as high as 25% of the N in a tropical climate and as low as 1% of the N in a cold climate with the other nutrients in proportion).

Using the figures above and 1990 prices in the United States, an average ton of eroded temperate-region soil has the following fertility value:

	Total content		Available in 1 year	
	Amount (lb/ton)	Value (1990)	Amount (lb/ton)	Value (1990)
Nitrogen	6	$1.20	0.2	$0.04
Phosphorus	1.2	0.30	0.06	0.015
Potassium	28	2.70	0.28	0.025
Other nutrients		0.80		0.02
Total value		$5.00		$0.10

A more realistic but considerably more complex value can be obtained by basing the calculations on available nutrients. This calculation requires computation of a discounted value for all nutrients that will be released in future years. The $5 figure will be used here both for simplicity and because the discount might well be offset by the value of soil components other than plant nutrients.

Soil erosion cannot be completely stopped. Part of it is natural geologic erosion and some accelerated erosion is unavoidable on cropped land. Much land, however, is being eroded at excessive rates. Limiting erosion on all lands in the United States to the tolerable rates specified in Chapter 6 would probably keep about a billion tons of soil annually from entering streams and keep $5 billion worth of plant nutrients from leaving U.S. fields each year.

18-1.4 Reduced Sedimentation Damage

Sedimentation damage occurs both in fields near the source of the sediment and in downstream areas. The soil and water damage caused by floods are inseparable. Estimated amounts of various types of flood damage are shown in Table 18-2. The total flood damage in the United States is approximately $6.5 billion per year. Some damage is unavoidable, but hundreds of millions of dollars per year could be saved through flood-prevention efforts.

About 60% of the flood damage shown in Table 18-2 occurs along small and moderate-sized streams in upstream areas where the drainage area above the site is less than 250,000 ac. One inference is that flood control in the upstream areas can do more good than large downstream structures. Upstream floods typically result from intense rainfall of limited duration. Terraces, contour tillage, and small upstream reservoirs can reduce the magnitude of upstream floods. Protective vegetation and allowing no buildings on floodplains are further means of reducing losses.

Downstream floods result from more widespread and longer-lasting storm systems than upstream floods. The downstream damage is more spectacular because it often occurs in more densely populated areas and is concentrated in occasional

TABLE 18-2 ESTIMATED AVERAGE ANNUAL FLOOD DAMAGE IN THE UNITED STATES (EXCLUDING ALASKA AND HAWAII)

Type of damage	Annual cost in 1988 dollars (millions)	Percentage of total cost
Upstream damage [from drainages <250,000 acres (100,000 ha)]		
Crops and pasture	$1750	26.9
Other agricultural	780	12.0
Sediment	340	5.2
Nonagricultural	700	10.8
Indirect	350	5.4
Total upstream damage	$3920	60.3
Downstream damage		
Metropolitan areas	$1550	23.8
Agricultural	850	13.1
Other	180	2.8
Total downstream damage	$2580	39.7
Total flood damage	$6500	100.0

Source: Calculated from several sources.

large events. There may be enough warning for sandbag levees to be erected and for people to be evacuated. Sometimes the damage is averted, but other times the dikes fail and major damage occurs. Levees provide some containment but they also cause the river to deposit sediment in its bed and thus raise its level to a more hazardous position. The lower reaches of rivers such as the Yellow River in China and the Mississippi River in the United States now flow some tens of feet above their floodplains for long distances, held only by their levees. Unfortunately, many people live on floodplains where a breach in a levee can permit the elevated river to inundate them. The surest way to reduce downstream flood disasters is to avoid building on floodplains.

Agriculture sustains over half of the flood damage, as shown in Table 18–2. Most of the land where flood control practices need to be applied is used for agricultural purposes. Flood control is therefore very significant to farmers and ranchers. Fortunately, soil and water conservation practices also help reduce flooding.

18–1.5 Environmental Benefits From Conservation

The soil conservation movement began out of concern for land that was suffering from erosion. Loss of land and reduced productivity were emphasized. Other environmental damage, including pollution caused by sediment, began to receive attention in the 1960s. Soil erosion damages the land and water where the soil goes as well as where the erosion occurred. The entire process is an environmental concern.

Several types of soil and water pollution can be reduced by soil conservation practices (see Chapter 17). Sediment and the chemicals often associated with it are prime examples. Soil conservation practices can keep most of the soil and chemicals in the fields where they are useful. Landowners benefit from the productive value of soil that is conserved. Downstream benefits occur when sedimentation, eutrophication, and chemical toxicity problems are reduced. Most of these benefits accrue to other landowners and to the general public rather than to the person who built the terraces, changed tillage practices, or planted protective vegetation.

Dollar values can be attached to some but not all of the environmental benefits from conservation. How much is it worth to be able to swim in clean water such as that shown in Figure 18–3?

18–2 COSTS OF CONSERVATION PRACTICES

The costs of conservation practices are almost as hard to evaluate as the benefits. The prices of some practices are variable enough to make it difficult to obtain accurate averages. Furthermore, direct payments do not reflect the management input of the landowner and other persons who provide the required technology. A lot of experience and probably some research were needed to learn how to make the practice feasible.

Opportunity costs are a means of considering many of the less obvious costs of

Figure 18–3 Swimming in Lake Washington after new sewage treatment plants were built and other pollution-control practices established at a cost of $121,000,000. This beach is shown in its earlier, polluted condition in Figure 17–2. (Courtesy EPA-DOCUMERICA.)

conservation. For example, one must forgo the opportunity to grow a crop on the area where a grassed waterway is planted. The opportunity to make a profit is real, even though a gully might destroy it later.

The costs of conservation do not stop when a practice is installed. Opportunity costs remain like a ghost in the background. Someone will surely be tempted to plow up the waterways, fencerows, odd corners, and steep slopes even if the erosion hazard is great. Educational programs are needed to teach new landowners and operators the lessons their predecessors already learned. The cost of the educational programs is also chargeable to conservation.

Maintenance is an obvious continuing cost of conservation. Terrace channels and waterways need to be cleaned and occasionally reshaped. Drainage systems must be kept open. Vegetation must be fertilized, mowed, reestablished, or otherwise tended. It will not last forever without proper care.

18–2.1 Direct and Indirect Costs

Most conservation practices involve both out-of-pocket *direct costs* and less tangible *indirect costs*. Building terraces involves large direct costs, usually in expectation that more intensive use will increase profit and repay the costs. The alternative of less intensive land use involves little or no direct costs but has indirect costs in the form of lower gross returns from the land.

Practices that involve less intensive cropping tend to be used only where necessary because crop value is reduced year after year. Establishing permanent forage crops or other protective vegetation drastically reduces erosion but does not usually produce a high-value crop. Strip cropping and crop rotations have intermediate effects on both erosion and income. None of these practices is too costly to install, but indirect costs sometimes prevent their use.

Large direct costs may not prevent a conservation practice from being extensively used if the costs can be spread over many years. Profit and convenience may justify the investment in a practice that is costly to install but inexpensive to maintain.

Typical direct costs of several conservation practices are shown in Table 18-3. The costs are presented as ranges to allow for variations in the work done and in local charges. Indirect costs are too variable to be generalized and can be estimated only when the circumstances of a specific situation are known.

TABLE 18-3 DIRECT COSTS OF SELECTED CONSERVATION PRACTICES

Practices that produce a net short-term profit (direct costs compensated within a year)		
Basic good management		
Adapted varieties and high-quality seed		
Proper timing of operations		
Optimum plant populations and spacings		
Fertilizing and liming as indicated by a soil test		
Conservation tillage		
Contour tillage		
Reduced tillage		
No tillage		
Practices with indirect costs but little or no direct costs		
Land retirement		
Less intensive cropping		
Crop rotations		
Strip cropping		
Practices with large direct costs		
Water management practices		
Land smoothing	\$100–400/ac	\$250–1000/ha
Tile drainage	\$200–500/ac	\$500–1200/ha
Irrigation	\$500–1000/ac	\$1200–2500/ha
Land reclamation		
Saline soils	\$50–200/ac	\$100–500/ha
Sodic soils	\$300–3000/ac	\$700–7000/ha
Sulfuric soils	\$300–3000/ac	\$700–7000/ha
Smoothing spoil heaps	\$300–600/ac	\$700–1500/ha
Establishing vegetation		
Cover crops	\$50–150/ac	\$100–400/ha
Grassed waterways	\$100–300/ac	\$250–800/ha
Woodland or wildlife plantings	\$100–300/ac	\$250–800/ha
Terracing	\$1000–10,000/mi	\$600–6000/km
Fencing	\$1000–2000/mi	\$600–1200/km

18-2.2 Conservation Practices as Investments

Long-lasting conservation practices are logically considered as investments. A drainage project, for example, is not expected to repay its total cost the first year. Sometimes the installation cost exceeds the gross returns from the crop of any one year. It may take several years to repay the cost and make a net profit.

A conservation practice is a good investment if it produces a satisfactory rate of return over a long enough lifetime. For example, an irrigation system with a lifetime of 20 years could be considered a good investment if the increased profits were as high as the annual payments on a 20-year mortgage with the same principal amount. A $20,000 system must increase the annual profit by $2037 per year to yield an 8% return on the investment and repay its costs in 20 years. Such investments may also be analyzed by comparing their net present value (NPV) to their costs (Note 18-2).

NOTE 18-2
CALCULATION OF NET PRESENT VALUE

A given amount of present benefits is generally preferred over an equal amount of future benefits. Interest rates can be used to determine either the future value of present benefits or the present value of future benefits. The general formula for calculating the present value as a fraction of the future value is

$$\frac{1}{(1 + x)^t}$$

where x is the interest rate in decimal form and t is the number of interest periods (usually years).

A practice with anticipated benefits worth $100 per year for a projected 10-year lifetime will serve as an example. An interest rate of 10% per year will be assumed:

Year	$1/(1 + x)^t$	Anticipated benefits	Net present value of anticipated benefits
0	1.00	$ 100	$100
1	0.91	100	91
2	0.83	100	83
3	0.75	100	75
4	0.68	100	68
5	0.62	100	62
6	0.56	100	56
7	0.51	100	51
8	0.47	100	47
9	0.43	100	43
	Totals	$1000	$676

The percentage of total returns counted as net present value is sensitive to both the interest rate and the time span involved. The method above can be used to calculate the following net present values as percentages of total returns:

Time period (years)	Interest rate (%):					
	4	6	8	10	12	15
5	92.6	89.3	86.2	83.4	80.7	77.1
10	84.4	78.0	72.5	67.6	63.3	57.7
20	70.7	60.8	53.0	46.8	41.8	36.0

Future costs can be discounted and summed in the same manner. Future costs and returns may be handled separately, or their differences may be calculated for each time period and discounted to obtain the net present value.

Most water management, land reclamation, and terracing projects are installed in anticipation of long-term profits. These practices are therefore good investments from economic considerations alone. Some other practices, such as plantings that provide good cover but little income, must be justified on the basis of nonmonetary values such as aesthetic considerations.

18-2.3 Costs of Soil-Loss Restraints

The first mandatory soil and water conservation law was passed in Iowa in 1971. This legislation authorized Iowa soil conservation districts to establish legal limits for rates of soil loss from each type of soil in the state. The U.S. Congress passed the Federal Water Pollution Control Act Amendments in 1972 with the objective of making all possible streams in the nation clean enough for swimming and fishing by 1983. These laws and several other more recent laws place restraints on rates of soil loss. Landowners, taxpayers, and consumers of agricultural products will bear large direct and indirect costs in meeting these legal standards limiting soil loss.

Heady and Nicol (1974) used a computer analysis to estimate the effects of a soil-loss limit of 5 tons/ac (11 mt/ha) on prices in the year 2000. They concluded that if such a limit were enforced, the average annual soil loss from U.S. cropland would be reduced from 10 tons/ac (22 mt/ha) without the limit to 3 tons/ac (6 mt/ha) with the limit (Table 18–4). Crop prices under the 5 tons/ac limit in the year 2000 were estimated to be 7% higher for corn, 3% higher for hay, 4% higher for cattle, and 5% higher for hogs.

The economic effects of soil-loss reductions depend greatly on how and where they are achieved. Taylor (1977) considered the effects that each of three approaches would have on farm income in the High Plains and in the Rolling Plains of western Texas. He concluded that terrace subsidies would increase farm income and reduce

TABLE 18-4 ESTIMATED AVERAGE ANNUAL SOIL LOSS IN REGIONS OF THE UNITED STATES IN THE YEAR 2000 (SOIL LOSS RESTRICTION TO BE MET BY PRACTICES SUCH AS CONTOURING, STRIP CROPPING, TERRACING, AND REDUCED TILLAGE, WITH CHANGES IN LAND USE WHERE REQUIRED)

Region	Estimated average annual soil loss			
	Where loss is unrestricted		Where loss is limited to: 5 tons/ac	(11 mt/ha)
	tons/ac	mt/ha	tons/ac	mt/ha
National	9.9	22.2	2.8	6.3
North Atlantic	9.0	20.2	3.5	7.8
South Atlantic	21.5	48.2	3.3	7.4
North Central	9.2	20.6	2.8	6.3
South Central	15.1	33.8	3.6	8.1
Great Plains	3.2	7.2	1.5	3.4
Northwest	2.3	5.2	1.7	3.8
Southwest	3.3	7.4	2.5	5.8

Source: Calculated from Heady and Nicol, 1974.

soil loss but not enough to meet tolerance limits. A tax on each ton of soil loss would reduce both net returns and soil loss. Legal limits were the only approach projected to reduce soil loss below tolerance value in all places. Such limits would cause much land in the Rolling Plains to be idled. The acreage of cotton and wheat in that area would be reduced by 56% and net returns would be reduced by 63%. The projected effects in the High Plains were less severe—much grain sorghum would be replaced by wheat, and net returns would be reduced by 15%.

Soil-loss limitations applied only to certain areas or states place them at an economic disadvantage. Broader limits that restrict soil loss in the entire nation are likely to increase prices for the crops and may increase the net returns to the producers.

18-3 PAYING FOR SOIL CONSERVATION

People are usually willing to pay for a conservation practice that produces short-term profits. Other practices that require long terms to produce profits are adopted more cautiously, especially if large investments are required. The person paying for the practice must be assured of stable conditions for a long enough time to make the benefits worth more than the costs. An owner-operator is more likely to invest in such practices than an operator with a short-term lease.

Sometimes a group such as a drainage district or an irrigation district can be formed to handle worthwhile practices that are not profitable or practical for individuals. State or federal government may become involved through subsidies or other incentives. Careful planning may be required and detailed analyses made, but the practices may still be justified economically.

Aesthetic, legal, and moral considerations may motivate the use of some practices in spite of unfavorable economics. Some landowners may pay for such practices but group or public action is more common. A park, for example, might be supported by a community and made available to the public at little or no charge.

18–3.1 Payments by Landowners and Operators

Owners and operators pay most of the direct costs of practices that increase profits on their land. Most crop management practices such as the use of clean, viable seed of adapted crop varieties are included. Costs of conservation tillage and of fertilizing and liming also are usually paid by landowners and operators.

Investments in practices with large direct costs that require long terms to become profitable may be shared between landowners and public groups or government agencies. Operators with long-term leases might pay part of the costs, but those with short-term (one- to three-year) leases usually do not pay for long-term investments such as irrigation and drainage systems, land reclamation, and terracing because these require several years to repay their costs.

Owners and operators divide costs in various ways according to lease arrangements. The costs of short-term practices are often shared in the same proportion as the profits from those practices. Owners pay most or all of the cost of long-term practices because these are investments that increase the value of their land.

18–3.2 Payments by Groups

Flood control, drainage projects, and irrigation developments are examples of practices that commonly require group action because they involve many people and properties. Typically, all of the people involved form a district or other legal entity that can act in their behalf. The district authority may include the right to design and apply needed practices, assess the costs to the individual members, obtain assistance from various agencies, borrow money to accomplish its purposes, and, in some cases, levy taxes. Counties or municipalities sometimes act in similar manners.

Groups are sometimes able to obtain assistance that would not be available to individuals. For example, an irrigation district needing to improve its water supply might obtain help from the Bureau of Reclamation. Or a flood-control district might obtain both technical assistance and cost sharing from the small watershed program of the Soil Conservation Service.

Group costs are much like those of individual landowners but on a larger scale. Usually, the costs must be recovered from the land owners by assessments, taxes, or selling of group services.

18–3.3 Government Participation in Soil Conservation

Districts, counties, and municipalities are all local units of government. State and federal governments represent broader areas and more people. Governmental units at any level may want to encourage conservation projects that benefit large numbers of people. The benefits from some projects are so diffuse that they would not likely be installed by individuals or small groups but they may be feasible as government projects. Parks and preserves are examples.

Government has several ways of encouraging the application of soil conservation practices. It can provide technical assistance. It can allow tax credits or other benefits to those who apply the practices. It can provide low-interest loans or pay part or all of the costs itself to finance the practices. Governments also have the option of bypassing economics by establishing legal requirements and enforcing them through the court system.

The U.S. government pays part of the cost of selected conservation practices through the Agricultural Conservation Program. Payments under this program are made by the Agricultural Stabilization and Conservation Service (ASCS) after the Soil Conservation Service (SCS) has certified that the practice was needed, practical, and properly installed. Government payments for group projects, however, are funded through the small watershed program administered by the Soil Conservation Service. For the period from 1933 to 1988, the U.S. government spent about $15 billion on soil conservation practices (Colacicco, et al., 1989).

The most ambitious U.S. soil conservation program to date would be that mandated by the Food Security Act of 1985. This act requires that highly erodible lands be identified from soil maps and that farmers using such lands should have soil conservation plans for them by 1990. The act requires these plans to be in effect so that the soil losses are reduced to tolerable levels by 1995. Models based on 1982 erosion rates indicated that without such action, the United States would lose the productive equivalent of 7.4 million acres of cropland over the next 100 years (Putman, et al., 1988).

The Soil Conservation Service provides technical assistance without charge to farmers and others. This program is designed to conserve soil and water by helping people install conservation practices on their land. The technicians are paid by federal funds that are supplemented in some states by state and local funds.

Environmental concerns have resulted in the passing of several federal and state laws in recent years. The 1972 Federal Water Pollution Control Act, as amended, for example, includes provisions in Section 208 for reducing the sediment load in runoff water. Federal cost sharing is available through the Agricultural Conservation Program and other programs. The Small Business Administration handles a loan program. Various states are developing supplemental programs to help keep pollutants out of streams and lakes.

Some state laws are more stringent than federal laws. The Iowa Soil Conservation Districts Law as amended in 1971 provides means for declaring erosion a "nuisance" and for requiring landowners to limit soil loss to tolerable rates. It also requires that 75% cost sharing be available for mandated soil conservation practices and provides state funds to pay 25% of their cost in addition to the 50% available from the U.S. Agricultural Conservation Program.

18-3.4 Conservation Research and Education

Development and information dissemination must take place before conservation practices can be widely used. Research and education constitute important indirect costs of conservation. Much research is done through government agencies and universities with government support. Foundations, companies, and individuals also have research projects. The Science and Education Administration of the USDA is the principal federal agency involved, and the Hatch Act is one of the main federal sources of agricultural research funds in the universities. State governments also provide substantial funding for research.

Educational activities dealing with soil conservation are part of the curricula of many schools at various grade levels. The educational effort is extended to farmers and others through the Extension Service. The Extension Service is funded from federal, state, and sometimes county sources as a means of disseminating agricultural research findings from the land-grant universities. Educational work is also accomplished by the Soil Conservation Service as a part of its technical assistance program and by such groups as the Soil Conservation Society of America. Various agribusiness companies also have programs that include conservation education. The largest expenditures for educational activities, however, are funded by the federal and state governments.

18-4 CONSERVATION INCENTIVES

People use conservation practices for various monetary, legal, aesthetic, moral, and other reasons. The relative importance of each factor varies from one person and situation to another.

The cost of a soil conservation practice is usually considered even when other factors influence the decision to install a practice. An economic analysis may calculate a *benefit/cost ratio* by dividing probable benefits by estimated costs. A benefit/cost ratio of 1.0 or larger may suffice to cause a practice to be installed. A ratio smaller than 1.0 is likely to end consideration of a project unless there are strong nonmonetary incentives in its favor. Fortunately, strong nonmonetary incentives often cause conservation practices to be installed despite benefit/cost ratios less than 1.0.

Legal requirements mean that a governmental body has decided that individuals must install a certain conservation practice. The legislators believe that important public benefits are involved—benefits that are more decisive for the public interest than for individual decision makers. The polluting effects of soil erosion, for example, are often ignored by the persons losing the soil and have been the basis for the passage of several recent laws. The public benefits might be monetary savings such as not having to remove sediment and other pollutants from water, they might be aesthetic reasons such as the prevention of eutrophication, or they might be based on moral principles.

Convenience factors enter into many decisions. Wet spots, for example, cause inconvenience. The owner may drain the spot even if added returns are unlikely to repay the cost. Rock outcrops have been dynamited at great expense so that the land could be tilled conveniently. Sometimes convenience is a secondary factor influencing the nature of the practice after the need has been established. For example, expensive parallel terraces might be installed for convenience even though cheaper nonparallel terraces could hold the soil equally well.

Aesthetic impressions vary from person to person and may either help or hinder conservation. The feeling that crop residues left on the surface appear "trashy" is a negative effect. The desire for straight rows can make it hard for a person to accept contouring. However, many people see beauty in the patterns of contour strip cropping or in the uniform growth of crops on a field where soil has been reclaimed. Ponds and wildlife plantings are aesthetically appealing to many people and may be built or planted for that reason.

Moral reasons are another incentive for action. It is right to conserve soil rather than let it erode away. It is right to stop pollution even if it is expensive. It is right to provide some areas for wildlife even if crops could be grown there. Soil stewardship programs emphasize morality by suggesting that soil should be conserved for the sake of future generations. The word "conservation" has a strong moral tone that helps to promote its cause.

SUMMARY

Soil conservation costs are usually immediate and obvious, whereas the benefits may be delayed, obscure, and dispersed. Government participation is justified to protect the productive potential of land and represent the interests of many people who are affected by the way soil is treated. Soil conservation emphases have shifted in recent years to include the effects of sedimentation as well as erosion.

Some soil conservation practices produce an immediate profit. Fertilization is so profitable that its conservation effects are often overlooked. Conservation tillage reduces energy input costs. Water conservation increases yields on sloping land. Drainage of wet land and irrigation of dry land produce high returns on the investment. Effective pest control increases yields and reduces erosion.

Practices such as terracing, planting forage crops and trees, and land reclamation result in deferred profits. A conflict may develop between the need for short-term income and the need for long-term protection of the land. Environmental concerns also may conflict with practices that maximize income.

Eroded soil has a total plant nutrient value of about $5 per ton. Effective soil conservation might save $5 billion worth of plant nutrients each year in the United States and also reduce flood damage by hundreds of millions of dollars per year. Soil loss reduces yield potential by any amount from 0 to 100%, depending on the amount of soil lost and the nature of the soil and its underlying material. Eroded spots in a field pose difficult management problems about future use of the field.

Direct costs represent only part of the total costs of conservation. Indirect costs such as research and education provide needed background. Often there are opportunity costs in the form of a profitable crop that could have been grown—reduced income from less intensive cropping may be a stronger deterrent than large direct costs. Conservation practices are a good investment if they produce an adequate annual return over a period of years.

Legal soil-loss limits first became law in the United States in the 1970s. Such laws cause a competitive disadvantage if they apply to only certain areas. Applied to the entire nation, these laws tend to raise prices and increase the producers' income. Subsidies that pay much of the cost of installing conservation practices increase net farm income, whereas taxes on excessive soil loss would reduce it.

Owners and operators often share the costs of practices that produce short-term profits. Owners pay most or all of the costs when long-term profit is anticipated. Groups such as districts or other legal entities become involved when projects are too large for individuals. Governments can encourage the application of soil conservation practices by paying for them directly; by providing technical assistance, low-interest loans, tax credits, or other benefits; by taxing soil loss; or by passing conservancy laws. Governments can also help by providing good research and education programs.

Incentives for installing conservation practices include benefit/cost ratios larger than 1.0, legal requirements, convenience, aesthetic appeal, and moral considerations.

QUESTIONS

1. What are the costs of erosion to a nation?
2. Who suffers most from flood damage?
3. What are the effects of conservation tillage on income and expense for a particular crop?
4. How do direct and indirect costs influence the economic desirability of a conservation practice to a landowner?
5. Which conservation practices are likely to be evaluated on the basis of their suitability as investments?
6. What economic effects would mandatory soil conservation on farms have on a nonfarm family?
7. What conservation costs should be paid by landowners? by operators? by groups? by the general public?

REFERENCES

ALLEN, R. R., B. A. STEWART, and P. W. UNGER, 1977. Conservation tillage and energy. *J. Soil Water Cons.* 32:84–87.

BORNSTEIN, J., and C. L. FIFE, 1973. Economic aspects of sloping land drainage. *J. Soil Water Cons.* 28:76–79.

COLACICCO, D., T. OSBORN, and K. ALT, 1989. Economic damage from soil erosion. *J. Soil Water Cons.* 44:35–39.

FORD, E. C., 1964. Upstream flood damage. *J. Soil Water Cons.* 19:231–234.

FRYE, W. W., and R. L. BLEVINS, 1989. Economically sustainable crop production with legume cover crops and conservation tillage. *J. Soil Water Cons.* 44:57–60.

HEADY, E. O., and V. S. NAGADEVARA, 1975. Economic impacts of state environmental programs in a national framework: The Iowa conservancy law. *J. Soil Water Cons.* 30:272–278.

HEADY, E. O., and K. J. NICOL, 1974. Models and projected results of soil loss restraints for environmental improvement through U.S. agriculture. *Agr. Environ.* 1:355–371.

JACOBS, J. J., and J. F. TIMMONS, 1974. An economic analysis of agricultural land use practices to control water quality. *Am. J. Agr. Econ.* 56:791–798.

MOORE, I. C., B. M. H. SHARP, S. J. BERKOWITZ, and R. R. SCHNEIDER, 1979. Financial incentives to control agricultural nonpoint-source pollution. *J. Soil Water Cons.* 34:60–64.

NOWAK, P. J., 1988. The costs of excessive soil erosion. *J. Soil Water Cons.* 43:307–310.

OLSON, K. R., and E. NIZEYIMANA, 1988. Effects of soil erosion on corn yields of seven Illinois soils. *J. Prod. Agric.* 1:13–19.

PETERS, D. C., 1975. The value of soil insect control in Iowa corn, 1951–70. *J. Econ. Entomol.* 68:483–486.

PUTMAN, J., J. WILLIAMS, and D. SAWYER, 1988. Using the erosion-productivity impact calculator (EPIC) model to estimate the impact of soil erosion for the 1985 RCA appraisal. *J. Soil Water Cons.* 43:321–331.

SANGHI, A. K., and R. KLEPPER, 1977. Economic impact of diminishing groundwater reserves on corn production under center-pivot irrigation. *J. Soil Water Cons.* 32:282–285.

SKOLD, M. D., 1989. Cropland retirement policies and their effects on land use in the Great Plains. *J. Prod. Agric.* 2:197–201.

TAYLOR, C. R., 1977. An analysis of some erosion control policies for the high and rolling plains of Texas. *J. Am. Soc. Farm Mgrs. and Rur. Appr.* 41(1):49–52.

TRIPLETT, G. B., JR., and D. M. VAN DOREN, JR., 1977. Agriculture without tillage. *Sci. Am.* 236:28–33.

VAN DOREN, D. M., JR., G. B. TRIPLETT, JR., and J. E. HENRY, 1976. Influence of long term tillage, crop rotation, and soil type combinations on corn yield. *Soil Sci. Soc. Am. J.* 40:100–105.

WADE, J. C. and E. O. HEADY, 1977. Controlling nonpoint sediment sources with cropland management: A national economic assessment. *Am. J. Agr. Econ.* 59:13–24.

WITTMUS, H., L. OLSON, and D. LANE, 1975. Energy requirements for conventional versus minimum tillage. *J. Soil Water Cons.* 30:72–75.

19 Soil and Water Conservation Agencies in the United States

Conservation is defined as "the official care and protection of natural resources" (Guralnik, 1984). The Conservation Directory (National Wildlife Federation, 1989) lists seven categories of action groups that are concerned with soil and water conservation: U.S. Congress; international, national, and interstate commissions; international, national, and interstate organizations; state and territorial agencies, citizens' groups; Canadian government agencies and national citizens' groups; Canadian provincial territorial agencies and citizens' groups; and colleges and universities in the United States and Canada.

Soil erosion became a matter of national concern in the United States in the 1930s. Four main factors were responsible for this widespread awareness of the erosion problem: results from early field research, a worldwide depression, dust storms, and a dedicated leader. The response of Congress and the people led to the development of a system of soil and water conservation that became a model for countries around the world.

19-1 FIRST FIELD RESEARCH ON SOIL AND WATER CONSERVATION

The first field research on soil and water conservation in the United States was established on the plots shown in Figure 19-1 by M. F. Miller and F. L. Duley at the University of Missouri. They wanted to discover the reasons for declining soil productivity (Note 19-1).

In 1965 the plots were designated by the National Park Service as a Registered National Historic Landmark. The first 14-year summary of the soil and water losses

Figure 19–1 The first soil and water conservation field research plots in the United States were established by M. F. Miller and F. L. Duley on land that is now part of the campus of the University of Missouri at Columbia. The sign reads "Soil Erosion Experiment—Comparison of Different Crops and Methods of Tillage for Preventing Soil Washing. Begun May 1, 1917." The site is now a Registered National Historic Landmark. (Courtesy C. M. Woodruff, University of Missouri.)

from the research plots is presented in Table 4–3. The table shows that the number of years required to erode an average 7-in. (18-cm) plow depth of soil varies from 24 years under fallow to 3043 years with continuous bluegrass. In 1941, 24 years after the erosion plots had been established, the level of the continuous bluegrass plot was 8 in. (20 cm) higher than the continuous fallow.

NOTE 19–1
FIRST FIELD RESEARCH

Inscription on the Monument at the University of Missouri, Columbia, commemorating the first field research plots for studying soil and water conservation:

> SITE OF FIRST PLOTS IN THE UNITED STATES FOR MEASURING RUNOFF AND EROSION AS INFLUENCED BY DIFFERENT CROPS

The study was started in 1917. The first results were published in 1923. They provided the foundation for the Soil Conservation movement. The design of the Experiment served as the prototype for future experiments by the USDA and land grant universities throughout the United States.

The investigations were initiated by M. F. Miller and F. L. Duley in their search for the causes of declining soil productivity. The original plots are being used now to investigate the renovation of eroded soil through the use of legumes, grass, and corn with treatments to supply the nutrients lost through erosion.

19-2 BUCHANAN AMENDMENT

Congress officially recognized soil erosion as a problem when it passed the Buchanan Amendment to the Agricultural Appropriation Bill for fiscal year 1930 (Public Law 70–769, February 16, 1929). The amendment provided $160,000 for establishing 10 soil-erosion experiment stations and 10 plant materials centers throughout the United States (Note 19–2).

NOTE 19–2
EROSION EXPERIMENT STATIONS AND PLANT NURSERIES

The 10 erosion experiment stations were located at Guthrie, Oklahoma; Temple, Texas; Tyler, Texas; Hays, Kansas; Bethany, Missouri; Statesville, North California; Pullman, Washington; Clarinda, Iowa; LaCrosse, Wisconsin; and Zanesville, Ohio.

The 10 plant materials centers were at Mandan, North Dakota; Stillwater, Oklahoma; Cheyenne, Wyoming; Elsberry, Missouri; San Antonio, Texas; Shreveport, Louisiana; Ames, Iowa; Pullman, Washington; Belle Mina, Alabama; and Safford, Arizona. The 10 plant materials centers have been increased to 23 in 22 of the states.

19-3 CIVILIAN CONSERVATION CORPS

The decade of the 1930s was a period of worldwide depression. Millions of people were unemployed and desperate for work. Seeking election as president of the United States, Franklin D. Roosevelt promised to do something about the job situation. He was inaugurated March 4, 1933, and instituted a large government spending program that same month. A law establishing the Emergency Conservation Work Agency was passed by Congress and signed by Roosevelt on March 31, 1933. Work for this and several other agencies was done by the Civilian Conservation Corps, better known as the CCC.

About 3 million persons, mostly young men, were employed in government work programs from the time the Emergency Conservation Work Agency was established until the Civilian Conservation Corps ceased activities in 1942. They were stationed in camps throughout the nation and assigned to work for various government agencies. Many of them worked on soil and water conservation projects.

19-4 SOIL EROSION SERVICE

The Soil Erosion Service was established in the U.S. Department of the Interior as a temporary public works program by a resolution of Congress adopted July 17, 1933. Hugh Hammond Bennett was its director. Five million dollars were appropriated for soil erosion control on both public and private lands. Contracts were signed with local governments and individual landowners that permitted workers from the Civilian Conservation Corps to plant trees, grasses, and legumes on eroding lands and to construct erosion control dams in gullies and in other drainageways, as shown in Figure 19–2.

Forty soil-erosion-control projects were established throughout the United States as part of the growing conservation movement. Each project included an entire watershed for the purpose of making the public aware of soil erosion and how to control it. Landowners signed agreements with the Soil Erosion Service permitting the service to apply soil erosion technology on their lands. All labor, machinery costs, materials costs, and technical assistance were supplied free to the landowners.

The Soil Erosion Service had only a two-year life span before it was replaced by the Soil Conservation Service. Considering that the primary objective was to provide work for the unemployed, it had a tremendous impact on public awareness of the evils of erosion, as well as on erosion-control technology.

19–5 SOIL CONSERVATION SERVICE

Severe droughts during the years 1931 to 1938 coincided with the Great Depression and made the Great Plains of the United States a disaster area. Two giant dust storms made history on May 11, 1934, and March 6, 1935. These storms started in the powder-dry Great Plains, and for several days clouds of dust obscured the sun eastward for a distance of 2000 mi (3000 km). Total silt and clay as particulates in the air masses were estimated at 200 million tons (180 million metric tons). Dust from the Great Plains filtered into the offices and onto the desks of U.S. senators and representatives in Washington, D.C.

Figure 19–2 A masonry drop structure and tile outlet built by the Civilian Conservation Corps to prevent a gully from advancing up this Iowa waterway. (Courtesy USDA Soil Conservation Service.)

At this time Hugh Bennett, Director of the Soil Erosion Service, was trying to have the Service transferred from the Department of Interior to the Department of Agriculture and changed from a temporary works program into a permanent soil conservation agency. The law establishing the Soil Conservation Service was passed on April 27, 1935, 52 days after the start of the second disastrous dust storm, without a dissenting vote. What senator or representative could vote against Public Law 74–46 while brushing the Great Plains dust from his desk? Bennett had won his political battle. He became the chief of the new agency and spent the rest of his professional career as its head.

19–5.1 Legal Mandates

The National Soil Conservation Act of 1935, Public Law 74–46, establishing the Soil Conservation Service, together with subsequent amendments and laws, defines the present activities of the Soil Conservation Service.

The Soil Conservation Service provides direct formal national and indirect informal international leadership in soil and water conservation. Technical assistance on wise land use is given at no charge to individuals, groups, organizations, cities, towns, churches, schools, or county and state governments. The breadth of the assistance given can be judged by the kinds of specialists working for the Soil Conservation Service. These include soil surveyors, soil scientists, soil conservationists, agronomists, foresters, plant materials specialists, land use specialists, biologists, range management specialists, wildlife specialists, geologists, economists, landscape architects, recreation specialists, ecologists, environmentalists, and the following kinds of engineers: agricultural, irrigation, hydraulic, civil, design, drainage, sanitary, and cartographic.

19–5.2 Assistance to Conservation Districts

Under Public Law 74–46 of 1935 and amendments, the Soil Conservation Service administers a broad program of assistance in soil and water conservation on the land in cooperation with Conservation Districts (Section 19–6). Through district organizations, the Soil Conservation Service provides these kinds of assistance at the request of farmers, ranchers, and other landowners:

1. Determining soil suitability guidelines based on soil surveys for agriculture, housing, recreation, waste disposal, and road construction
2. Recommending the best management practices for soil erosion control (Figure 19–3)
3. Designing sediment interception systems
4. Designing water facilities such as farm ponds
5. Planning recreational facilities
6. Designing terrace, irrigation, and drainage systems
7. Developing cropping systems, such as that in Figure 19–4, to reduce erosion
8. Recommending pasture plantings

Figure 19-3 Minimum tillage makes erosion nearly zero in this Illinois field. Weeds were killed by a contact herbicide at the time the corn was seeded in the wheat stubble. (Courtesy USDA Soil Conservation Service.)

Figure 19-4 Terracing, contour strip cropping (eight rows of peanuts alternating with two rows of grain sorghum), winter cover crops, and subsoiling are used in combination to control erosion in this Texas field. (Courtesy USDA-Soil Conservation Service.)

9. Developing range management guidelines
10. Promoting wildlife conservation
11. Promoting woodland conservation
12. Supplying adapted plant materials for conservation plantings
13. Promoting surface mine reclamation guidelines
14. Providing expertise on land use planning

The Soil Conservation Service now has more than 15,000 career employees who provide on-the-land service in stabilizing the soil and water environment for the public good. Most of this service is provided through Conservation Districts.

19-5.3 Assistance to Individual Landowners and Operators

Individual landowners or operators can obtain assistance from Soil Conservation Service personnel by signing an agreement with the local Conservation District. Land use plans and designs for conservation practices recommended by the soil conservation technicians are based on soil maps interpreted according to the information in soil survey reports described in Chapter 7. Plans are made according to decisions of the cooperating landowner or operator in harmony with the capabilities and needs of the soils.

Soil Conservation Service personnel make agronomic and engineering recommendations for each of the 13,000 soil series and map units recognized in the United States. Appropriate combinations of practices are recommended for the particular conditions existing at a specific site. The intent is to conserve soil and water and protect the environment while using the land for the purposes desired by the owner or operator. The Soil Conservation Service provides the technical assistance needed for planning, designing, and guiding the application of conservation practices.

Many types of assistance are available to Conservation District cooperators without charge. Soil and crop specialists will develop cropping- and pasture-management systems to reduce erosion and sedimentation. Engineers design conservation structures, including terraces, diversions, waterways, ponds, irrigation systems, drainage systems, and waste disposal systems. Range conservationists assist ranchers with grazing management techniques for maximizing production with minimum erosion. Foresters recommend tree species and planting and harvesting techniques for woodlands and windbreaks. Plant materials specialists recommend special plant species for use in unusual sites such as acid mine spoils (Chapter 11). Many such plants are distributed each year from the 23 plant materials centers operated in the United States by the Soil Conservation Service.

19-5.4 Surface Mine Spoils Reclamation

Agronomists, soil scientists, plant materials specialists, and engineers work to help stabilize mine spoils. The help is available to mine operators, individuals, groups, or any governmental unit. Four phases of surface mine reclamation are assisted by personnel of the Soil Conservation Service:

1. Planning before mining, including the making of a soil survey
2. Applying conservation practices during mining
3. Applying soil and water conservation practices after mining to establish erosion-resisting perennial vegetation (Figure 19-5)
4. Assistance in reclaiming abandoned mine spoils

19-5.5 Water Resources

Under Public Laws 78-534 passed in 1944 and 83-566 in 1954, the Soil Conservation Service offers assistance to cities, towns, and rural areas in flood reduction, erosion control, reduced siltation, and lower maintenance costs for roads, bridges, and housing developments.

Water impounded in reservoirs provides multiple-use options such as a municipal water supply, fire protection, irrigation, and recreation. River basin studies are also conducted in cooperation with state and other federal agencies. These investigations include flood-hazard analyses of selected streams and salinity-control studies on 550,000 acres (220,000 ha) of land in the Colorado River Basin.

Figure 19-5 This area of coal mine spoils in Kentucky has been vegetated with shortleaf pine and wildlife-food plants such as black cherry. (Courtesy USDA Soil Conservation Service.)

19-5.6 Resource Conservation

Public Law 87-703 of 1962 authorizes the Soil Conservation Service to assist regional (multicounty) areas in aspects of physical resource development. The term "resource conservation" includes conventional soil and water conservation activities plus the development of recreation facilities, fish and wildlife conservation, and the reduction of air and water pollution. Assistance is also offered in land use planning, preservation of scenic and historical sites, and industrial expansion. The goal is to improve the environment, economy, and living standards of people in selected areas. The program involves 1196 counties in all states except Alaska.

19-5.7 Great Plains Conservation Program

As mandated by Public Law 84-1021 in 1956, the Soil Conservation Service administers the Great Plains Conservation Program. This region is subject to severe climatic hazards such as periodic droughts and extremes in temperature. As a consequence, during periods of favorable weather, farmers and ranchers tend to cultivate marginal soils and to overstock ranges that, during dry years, are subject to devastating wind and water erosion.

Additional funds are set aside by Congress for exclusive use in the Great Plains to help intensify and accelerate the normal soil and water conservation activities of the Soil Conservation Service. Special emphasis is being given to making a soils map of the entire Great Plains, converting marginal cropland to permanent pasture and range, and improving rangelands by encouraging more rational grazing management as shown in Figure 19-6.

Figure 19-6 Controlled grazing is emphasized in the Great Plains Conservation Program. The tobosa grass in this Texas range shows the effects of severe overgrazing on the left and proper grazing on the right. (Courtesy USDA Soil Conservation Service.)

19-5.8 Land Use Conversions

Based upon a soil survey, soils are classified into Land Use Capability classes identified by Roman numerals I through VIII. Class I land has the least hazard associated with use, and Class VIII the greatest (Chapter 7). This system helps to identify land that is suffering excessive erosion because of use beyond its long-term capability. For example, the only practical way to reduce erosion and sedimentation on very erodible sloping soils used for continuous row crops is to convert the land use to permanent grassland or woodland, as shown in Figure 19-7. For this reason, the Soil Conservation Service program includes land use conversion. This means persuading thousands of farmers, ranchers, and other land managers to make changes toward less intensive land use. It is also true that smaller but still significant areas of grassland and woodland on Class I and II land could be converted to cropland with little erosion hazard.

19-5.9 International Assistance

Several hundred foreign nationals come each year to the United States to study the organization and field operations of the Soil Conservation Service. These educational experiences are usually financed by the U.S. Agency for International Development or by the Food and Agriculture Organization of the United Nations. Furthermore, many overseas governments request the on-site services of an experienced person from the Soil Conservation Service. While studying the program of the

Figure 19-7 An example of land use conversion. This former wheat field in Wyoming was subject to severe wind erosion until it was seeded to crested wheatgrass and converted to rangeland. (Courtesy USDA Soil Conservation Service.)

Soil Conservation Service, foreign nationals are invariably surprised to learn that much of its success is credited to the service-oriented technique of unpaid farm and ranch officials of the conservation districts and other volunteers.

19-6 CONSERVATION DISTRICTS

When the Soil Conservation Service was established in 1935, its chief, H. H. Bennett, quickly realized that it was a long distance from Washington, D.C. to farmers and ranchers, both geographically and psychologically. Bennett had been raised on a farm in the red Piedmont hills of Anson County, North Carolina. He had witnessed serious sheet and gully erosion and the resultant widespread poverty and decline in crop yields. He became a professional soil scientist and for many years mapped soils in both southern and northern states. This background provided a rare but broad insight. He realized that no agricultural bureaucracy can be effective without major input from farmers and ranchers. As a consequence, he led the development of "A Standard State Soil Conservation Districts Law" to authorize the establishment of districts throughout the United States. For maximum acceptance among the states, Bennett persuaded President Roosevelt to send this model law to all state governors on February 27, 1937. The first Soil Conservation District actually organized was Brown Creek Soil Conservation District in North Carolina; it was approved on August 4, 1937.

Twenty-two states had passed Soil Conservation District laws by the end of 1937, and ten years later all the states plus Puerto Rico and the Virgin Islands had enacted such legislation. Each state modified the model law to fit its land and the wishes of the people, but all these laws included the principle that local citizens have the authority to establish policy and the mandate to accept responsibility for soil and water conservation in each district. During the 1960s several states changed the names of their districts to "Soil and Water Conservation Districts" in recognition of the importance of water management in their programs. More recently, many of the names have been shortened to "Conservation District."

19-6.1 Present Scope

There are 2956 conservation districts in all 50 states, Puerto Rico, and the Virgin Islands comprising 99% of all farms and ranches, 2.6 million cooperators, and 2183 million acres (883 million ha). A typical conservation district coincides with the boundaries of one of the 3197 counties and territories. Each district has an elected governing board of three to five persons who serve without salary. In each state, a board or commission controls state appropriations and serves the conservation districts of the state in administrative, legal, and financial matters. Nationwide, about 18,000 men and women serve on the district governing boards. The National Association of Conservation Districts was organized in 1946; its permanent headquarters is in Washington, D.C. Although the elected conservation district officials serve without pay, the states appropriate funds to be used for official travel, establishing an office, and employing a secretary.

19-6.2 Traditional Activities

Conservation districts are managed by private citizens elected by the residents of the district. Duties of the district supervisors (directors, board members, or commissioners) include the planning and directing of the soil and water conservation programs in the district. This involves the request for use of professional assistance from the USDA-Soil Conservation Service, the USDA-Forest Service, the Land-Grant University Cooperative Extension Service, the Land-Grant Agricultural Experiment Station, the USDA-Bureau of Land Management, the Agricultural Research Service, and other federal and state agencies.

19-7 AGRICULTURAL STABILIZATION AND CONSERVATION SERVICE

The various acts relating to the Agricultural Stabilization and Conservation Service finance soil and water conservation as a joint responsibility of government and landowners. The cost-sharing function is used to encourage cooperators to establish soil and water conservation practices on their land. The federal cost share often pays for about half of the cost of a conservation practice but may pay more or less, depending on the need to encourage the practice. This program provides a means for public funds to pay for public benefits resulting from soil and water conservation.

The Agricultural Stabilization and Conservation Service is entirely a service and action agency. Rather than employing its own technical staff, it seeks and uses the assistance of staff of other agencies in the U.S. Department of Agriculture. Most often used are personnel of the U.S. Soil Conservation Service and the U.S. Forest Service in providing technical program guidance and on-farm assistance. Technical assistance is also supplied by the State Agricultural Extension Service, the State Agricultural Experiment Station, the State Forester, and the personnel of the Farmers Home Administration.

19-8 SCIENCE AND EDUCATION ADMINISTRATION

The Science and Education Administration in the U.S. Department of Agriculture is administered by an assistant secretary. Under the assistant secretary are the Cooperative State Research Service, the Office of Grants and Program Systems, the Agricultural Research Service, the Extension Service, the Forest Service, and the Economic Research Service (U.S. Department of Agriculture, 1987). Most of the research and extension in soil and water conservation is conducted in cooperation with the land-grant agricultural universities in the 50 states.

19-9 UNIVERSITIES AND COLLEGES

The U.S. Congress passed the first Morrill Act in 1862 to assist the states in establishing land-grant colleges to teach agriculture and applied science. Research at these and other institutions was assisted by the Hatch Act of 1887 and the Second Morrill Act of 1890. Statewide informal education from the colleges was authorized and assisted by the Smith-Lever Extension Act of 1914. These agricultural universities and colleges are all intimately involved in soil and water conservation. They conduct research, such as that shown in Figures 19–8, teach, and extend knowledge of soil and water conservation throughout each respective state. Recently, increasing amounts of soil and water conservation research have been conducted at non-land-grant universities and colleges.

Many students are taught principles of soil and water conservation in the agricultural universities before they are employed by such agencies as the USDA–Soil Conservation Service. Research at the universities serves as the basis for the soil and water management practices taught in classes and promoted throughout each state by Extension Service and the Soil Conservation Service. Furthermore, the National Cooperative Soil Survey is usually conducted in cooperation with the Soil Conservation Service and the respective state agricultural university's agricultural experiment station. All 23 plant material centers supervised by the Soil Conservation Service are managed in close cooperation with the agricultural universities.

Many of the agricultural universities teach and conduct research in forestry. Some of this research is conducted in cooperation with the USDA–Forest Service and the state forestry agencies.

19–10 U.S. FOREST SERVICE AND STATE FORESTRY AGENCIES

The U.S. Forest Service has responsibility for managing the 180 million acres (73 million hectares) in the 150 national forests and the 3.7 million acres (1.5 million hectares) of national grasslands. It also cooperates with agricultural universities and state forestry agencies in tree planting, fire protection, and other activities related to soil and water conservation. The Forest Service contact with private land management is usually through cooperative programs with the state forestry agencies and the conservation districts. Federal and state forest nurseries supply forest tree seedlings to plant on eroded and other lands.

The USDA–Forest Service is the principal agency in the United States conducting research on trees-soil-water relationships. This research applies to the 500 million acres (200 million hectares) of commercial forests—over 20% of the area of the United States.

Research relevant to this chapter includes that on the relationship between trees and water yield and erosion. Some precipitation is intercepted by trees and evaporated into the atmosphere without reaching the soil. Another fraction infiltrates the soil, is absorbed by roots, and is transpired into the atmosphere through stomata of the leaves. A third segment becomes surface or subsurface runoff; a final fraction moves downward to replenish the water table.

The Forest Service has established a research project to find ways to increase runoff water yield from a forested watershed. Treatments have included clearcutting the trees and establishing grass as compared to cutting varying percentages of the trees. On some watersheds, an open stand of trees was found to yield more water

a

b

c

Figure 19-8 Research on the use of an aerated pond for cattle waste disposal conducted by Purdue University to minimize air and water pollution while using the waste for increasing pasture production: (a) aeration pond; (b) close-up of floating aerator in operation; (c) effluent being sprayed on pasture. (Courtesy A. C. Dale, Purdue University.)

than an all-grass watershed because the trees held additional snow. The open stand is also better than a clearcut watershed for erosion control.

Research on trees and watershed protection is continuing, especially that relating to establishing a reasonable balance between maximum water runoff for irrigation and soil-erosion losses. Another aspect of research, forest harvest methods and their relationship to erosion, is discussed in Chapter 13.

19-11 OTHER FEDERAL CONSERVATION AGENCIES

Almost all federal agencies have relevance to soil and water conservation; the agencies listed below are statutorily involved (National Wildlife Federation, 1989).

Corps of Engineers, U.S. Department of the Army. The "Corps" manages navigable surface waters and recreation facilities adjacent to public reservoirs, builds dams for water conservation and power generation, conducts research on erosion and sedimentation, and dredges sediment-laden channels.

Bureau of Land Management, U.S. Department of Interior. This agency administers 470 million acres (190 million hectares) of U.S. public lands, mostly in the west. This is about 60% of all public lands. Much of it is in small tracts. The principle of management is multiple-use, including livestock grazing, timber production, watershed protection, industrial mineral development, and outdoor recreation.

Bureau of Reclamation, U.S. Department of Interior. The Bureau of Reclamation builds dams on federal lands in western states for power generation, irrigation, flood control, industrial development, fish and wildlife, and recreation, as shown in Figure 19-9.

Bureau of Indian Affairs, U.S. Department of Interior. The Bureau of Indian Affairs is responsible for soil and water conservation on all Indian lands. Personnel of this bureau advise the Indian land operators on useful and necessary conservation practices. When land is leased to nonreservation operators, the lease contains provisions for the conservation practices required of the lessees.

Environmental Protection Agency. This agency was established to reduce pollution of water and air by solid and liquid residues, toxic substances, pesticides, radiation, and noise. It is an independent agency functioning separately from major departments such as Agriculture and Interior. When eroded soil becomes a sediment pollutant of water or a particulate (dust) pollutant of air, its control is the official concern of this agency. The EPA administers the Water Pollution Control Act of 1972, Public Law 92-500 and amendments.

Tennessee Valley Authority. The Tennessee Valley Authority is an independent agency with headquarters in Knoxville, Tennessee. It was established as an

Figure 19–9 This swimming facility in California was established and is managed by the U.S. Bureau of Reclamation. It is part of a multiple-use reservoir providing irrigation water and outdoor recreation. (Courtesy USDI Bureau of Reclamation.)

areawide organization to develop the natural and human resources of parts of seven states in the watershed of the Tennessee River, an area of 260 million acres (106 million hectares). It conducts research and demonstration projects to reduce erosion and sedimentation by applying all practical conservation measures. This includes a research and demonstration national laboratory for formulating new fertilizers and testing them in the Tennessee Valley and elsewhere, establishing model dams with hydroelectric generation, flood control techniques, and navigation development. Recreation has become one of its most popular uses of water and adjacent lands.

19–12 FOOD AND AGRICULTURE ORGANIZATION

The Food and Agriculture Organization (FAO) is an agency of the United Nations with permanent headquarters in Rome, Italy. The FAO works worldwide but concentrates on helping developing countries. Specific projects of the Food and Agriculture Organization include (Hauck, 1974):

1. Sending consultants on soil and water conservation for specific work in response to government requests
2. Conducting seminars on a regional or country basis
3. Publishing bulletins on soil and water conservation
4. Conducting specific programs as requested in several countries

SUMMARY

In early 1929 the U.S. Congress passed the Buchanan Amendment establishing erosion experiment stations and plant nurseries, in response to critical soil erosion. This was followed in 1933 by the establishment of the Soil Erosion Service, a public works program to provide employment during the Great Depression. Through the effective leadership of H. H. Bennett, assisted by two dust storm episodes, the permanent Soil Conservation Service was established in 1935. The Soil Conservation Service has taken the national and international leadership in all phases of soil and water conservation.

Conservation Districts are nationwide. They are legal subdivisions of state governments and are managed by a governing board elected by private citizens. They call for assistance from technical and other agencies, especially the Soil Conservation Service. The Agricultural Stabilization and Conservation Service has many functions, one of which is to administer a cost-sharing program for soil and water conservation practices adopted by farmers and ranchers.

The Science and Education Administration has three branches. Their assistance to states includes grants to the state extension services and to the state agricultural experiment stations, mostly in cooperation with the land-grant universities. Some of the extension and research grants to the states are used to further soil and water conservation. Nearly all federally funded research is administered by the Science and Education Administration.

Teaching of soil and water conservation in colleges is largely the province of the state agricultural universities. State funds are also used to support off-campus extension teaching and research on soil and water conservation.

The USDA–Forest Service practices and researches soil and water conservation on its National Forests and National Grasslands and offers management advice for private lands. It and the state forestry agencies promote conservation by supplying forest tree seedlings at concessional rates for planting.

Other federal agencies that practice conservation include the Corps of Engineers, Bureau of Land Management, Bureau of Reclamation, Bureau of Indian Affairs, Environmental Protection Agency, and the Tennessee Valley Authority.

The agency with worldwide jurisdiction in soil and water conservation is the Food and Agriculture Organization of the United Nations.

QUESTIONS

1. Explain the factors that led to national awareness of soil erosion in the United States.
2. List the major mandates of the Soil Conservation Service.
3. Enumerate the principal practices promoted by the Soil Conservation Service.
4. Describe the origin and functions of Conservation Districts.
5. Explain cost sharing by the Agricultural Stabilization and Conservation Service.

6. Agricultural universities have three main functions involved in soil and water conservation. Identify and explain their relevant work.
7. Name the other federal agencies that work in soil and water conservation.
8. How does the Food and Agriculture Organization function in soil and water conservation activities?

REFERENCES

AGRICULTURAL RESEARCH SERVICE, 1976. *Soil, Water, Air Sciences Programs.* USDA Agricultural Research Service, Washington, D.C., 63 p.

DAVEY, W. B., 1977. *Conservation Districts and 208 Water Quality Management.* U.S. Environmental Protection Agency and National Association of Soil Conservation Districts, Washington, D.C.

GURALNIK, D. B., (ed.), 1984. *Webster's New World Dictionary of the American Language,* 2nd College ed. Simon and Schuster, New York.

HAUCK, F. W., 1974. Possibilities for assistance by FAO. In *Shifting Cultivation and Soil Conservation in Africa.* Soils Bull. 24. Swedish International Development Authority and FAO, p. 245–247.

LAL, R. (ed.), 1988. *Soil Erosion Research Methods.* Soil and Water Conservation Society, Ankeny, Iowa, 244 p.

MILLER, M. F., and H. H. KRUSEKOPF, 1932. *The Influence of Systems of Cropping and Methods of Culture on Surface Runoff and Soil Erosion.* Mo. Agr. Expt. Sta. Res. Bull. 177, 22 p.

NATIONAL RESEARCH COUNCIL, 1986. *Soil Conservation: Assessing the National Research Inventory.* Vol. 1, 114 p.; Vol. 2, 314 p.

NATIONAL WILDLIFE FEDERATION, 1989. *Conservation Directory,* 34th ed. Washington, D.C., 331 p.

SOIL CONSERVATION SERVICE, 1977. *Employee Handbook.* USDA Publ. SCS-PERS-750 (SI), unpaged.

SOIL SURVEY STAFF, 1975. *Soil Taxonomy: A Basic System of Soil Classification for Making and Interpreting Soil Surveys.* USDA Agric. Handbook 436, 754 p.

U.S. DEPARTMENT OF AGRICULTURE, 1986. *Agricultural Statistics.* USDA, Washington, D.C., 551 p.

U.S. DEPARTMENT OF AGRICULTURE, 1987. *1986–87 Directory of Professional Workers in State Agricultural Experiment Stations and Other Cooperating State Institutions.* Agric. Handbook 305. Cooperative State Research Service.

U.S. DEPARTMENT OF COMMERCE, 1987. *Comparative Climatic Data for the United States through 1986.* National Oceanic and Atmospheric Administration, National Climatic Data Center, Federal Building, Asheville, N.C., 94 p.

20

Soil and Water Conservation around the World

For survival and well-being, governments throughout the world have responded to the challenge of stabilizing erodible soils. Many countries have adopted techniques of organization and practices patterned after those of the USDA–Soil Conservation Service. Most countries have made an effort, however uneven, to conserve soil and water.

20-1 TRANSFER OF CONSERVATION TECHNOLOGY

Some of the most difficult problems facing world development arise from geographic and cultural differences which impede technology transfer from one region to another. The majority of people in developed countries are willing but unable to help people in other countries conserve soil and water. Even the technicians of the USDA-Soil Conservation Service have difficulty adapting effective techniques from the United States to other cultures, especially to situations as different as those in the tropics. The transfer of technology to the tropics will be emphasized because the greatest unsolved problems of soil and water conservation are in this half of the world, where people are in dire need of greater productivity to keep pace with population growth.

Nearly all regions of the world have failed in some conservation efforts, and most countries offering assistance have made many mistakes. Some of the most serious mistakes in technology transfer have involved soil management and have resulted in accelerated erosion, surface crusting, and rapid decline in crop production.

Several years ago, large mechanization projects based on soil-management techniques of continuous cropping were tried in Ghana and Tanzania. Both projects led to a rapid decline in crop yields, owing to irregular topography, small farms, plinthite (laterite) or otherwise fragile soils, crusting of the soil surface, and serious wind and water erosion. The traditional shifting cultivation was a much more satisfactory cropping system than the substitutes that were instituted. More feasible alternatives to shifting cultivation have been found since then. Starting in the 1960s, modern agricultural research centers have been established. There are 22 international agricultural research centers. Thirteen are supported by the Consultative Group on International Agricultural Research and nine are financed through other means. All centers were established primarily to increase food production, but indirectly they are concerned with the most crucial natural resources—soil and water.

20-2 SHIFTING CULTIVATION AND CONSERVATION

Two contrasting kinds of shifting cultivation are used, depending on the soil and its vegetation. The most common type is practiced on humid, forested soils of low fertility on steep slopes with high erodibility. The other type is conducted on humid, grassed, high-based, clay soils with gentle topography and moderate erosion hazard.

20-2.1 Forested Soils in the Tropics

About 250 million farmers in the humid tropical world produce a subsistence living by shifting cultivation. This kind of agriculture is common and sometimes dominant in parts of Asia, Africa, Central America, and South America. The soils are generally permeable, are leached of essential plant nutrients, and are commonly classified as Oxisols or Ultisols.

Shifting cultivation means partially clearing and burning a patch in a forest as shown in Figure 20-1, raising crops mostly by hoe culture and to a lesser extent by animal-powered farming methods for a period of two to three years, then allowing the patch to revert to forest trees for 10 to 20 years while other tracts are cleared and farmed. After a decade or two of soil rejuvenation, the same patch is again cleared and cropped. The cropping period is usually extended for as long as the farmer considers crop yields satisfactory or until there are excessive infestations of weeds, insects, or disease, but this period seldom exceeds five years. Likewise, the period that forest trees are allowed to grow depends on how rapidly and completely trees occupy the cleared patches and how soon the farmer needs the area again for cropping.

Trees are essential during the soil-rejuvenation stage to accelerate the weathering of essential soil minerals, to add organic matter, and to break the cycle of insects, disease, and weeds. Soil productivity is renewed less rapidly where grasses dominate the vegetation during the rejuvenation cycle. This is especially true on soils with low-base status and plinthite. Trees maintain more uniform soil water and temperature conditions, which reduce crystallization of iron and aluminum into plinthite.

Hardened plinthite becomes almost waterproof. The few inches up to three or

Figure 20-1 Shifting cultivation on forested soils requires that a dense stand of trees be cut down and burned. Bulldozers may be used but they cause serious soil deterioration. Much of the work is done with an axe, as in this scene in Ivory Coast. (Courtesy Roy L. Donahue.)

four feet (from a few centimeters to a meter or more) of soil above the plinthite become saturated and easily eroded during heavy rains. Another condition conducive to soil erosion exists on steep slopes when a patch for cropping is cleared and burned. Most soils of the tropics are less fertile, residual organic matter decomposes faster, and precipitation is usually more intense than in temperate regions. The resulting erosion is therefore more rapid than it would be in temperate regions.

It is unfortunate that a workable alternative to shifting cultivation was not developed until recently. That alternative is the use of fertilizers and pesticides combined with minimum tillage to leave organic residues on the surface of the soil. Such a system was researched at Ibadan, Nigeria (in western Africa), by the International Institute of Tropical Agriculture (IITA, 1975). This is a humid forested area and the dominant soils are high in plinthite and ironstone. Traditional shifting cultivation is the predominant cropping system. Research personnel at the Institute hypothesized that modern scientific agriculture could replace shifting cultivation successfully. Field research the Institute used to test this hypothesis included:

1. A surface mulch of crop residues and no-till cultivation to reduce extremes of soil moisture and soil temperature and to control soil erosion
2. Modern insecticides, fungicides, and herbicides to control pests
3. Chemical fertilizers to increase soil fertility and crop productivity

Soybeans grown in this research lost only 1% of the precipitation received, and no soil was eroded. Plowed and cultivated soybeans caused a 15% loss of precipitation and 17 tons/ac (38 mt/ha) of soil loss per year. Loss of water and soil from other crops was much higher.

Unlike industrialized countries where lime and fertilizers are priced relatively low, in many tropical countries it makes more economic sense to improve crop productivity by breeding or discovering plants that are better adapted to forested Oxisols and Ultisols. This approach leads to a "low-input soil management strategy." In the forested tropics, this means pasture grass and legume cultivars tolerant of acid soils high in aluminum saturation, low levels of available phosphorus, and the ability to utilize low-cost rock phosphate. Progress is being made on all of these objectives (Table 20-1).

20-2.2 Grassland Soils in Humid Tropics and Subtropics

Vertisols are the most abundant grassland soils in humid tropical areas. The 5.78 million acres (2.34 million ha) or 1.8% of the land surface of the earth that they occupy is mostly in tropical or subtropical areas with wet and dry seasons. They commonly occur where the annual rainfall is 24 to 40 in. (600 to 1000 mm)—enough to support forest vegetation on other soils, but the Vertisols grow grasses. Two factors favor the grasses—the high base saturation and the high content of montmorillonite clay [at least 30% clay to a depth of 20 in. (50 cm)] that gives Vertisols their self-swallowing action. The shrink-swell potential of the montmorillonite causes deep cracks to open in these soils during dry seasons, as shown in Figure 20-2. Granular surface soil falls into these cracks and causes the soil to shift and "churn" when it gets wet. The churning action distributes organic matter throughout the soil and produces a deep, dark-colored soil. It also can break deep roots of perennial plants and the foundations of buildings.

Traditional crop culture on Vertisols in Ethiopia includes cotton, grain sorghum, and sesame in a shifting cultivation that involves burning the soil. Only

TABLE 20-1 PROMISING GRASSES AND LEGUMES SELECTED/BRED FOR ACID, INFERTILE, TROPICAL, FORESTED OXISOLS AND ULTISOLS.

Grass cultivars	Legume cultivars
Signal grass (*Brachiaria decumbens* 606)	Tick clover (*Desmodium leonii* 3001)
Bluestem (*Andropogon gayanus* 621)	Tick clover (*Desmodium ovalifolium* 350)
Panic grass (*Panicum maximum*)	Zornia (*Zornia latifolia* 883, 728)
Hyparrhenia (*Hyparrhenia rufa*)	Stylosanthes (*Stylosanthes capitata* 1019, 1078)
Crabgrass (*Digitaria decumbens*)	Kudzu (*Pueraria phaseoloides* 9900)

Source: Sanchez, 1986.

Figure 20–2 A Vertisol in northwestern Ethiopia. This soil developed on high-lime materials, is dark colored, has a high percentage of montmorillonite clay, and has wide, deep cracks for at least 90 consecutive days per year. (Courtesy Roy L. Donahue.)

Vertisols are burned—never the adjoining red clay soils. The native tall-grass prairie is plowed with a village-made, tongue-type plow pulled by oxen (bullocks). The plowed rows are crooked, and the seedbed is always cloddy and full of large sod pieces with soil attached. The farmer gathers these sod pieces, puts them in piles, and adds cattle manure in the center of each pile, as shown in Figure 20–3. When the soil and sod pieces have dried, each pile is set on fire and may smolder for several days. Upon cooling, the residues from each burned pile are spread over the field. The soil has improved tilth after burning. After further plowings, seeds of cotton, grain sorghum, or sesame are sown. Field crops are then grown for a period of three to five years, after which the land is abandoned. During abandonment, weeds, annual grasses, and finally perennial native grasses grow over a fallow period of 10 to 20 years; then the burning and cropping cycle is repeated.

During the cropping cycle, the soil becomes weedy, insect and disease populations build up, and soil tilth deteriorates. Soil fertility is decreased by crop removal, soil crust formation becomes more serious, and sheet and gully erosion are increased. By contrast, during the fallow cycle, the grasses improve the physical condition of the soil, pests decrease, fertility increases by weathering of minerals, and erosion is controlled. The native grasses help to develop a fine crumb structure that makes a desirable physical, chemical, and biological seedbed. Burning the black clay soil inside each pile of sod pieces destroys pests, eliminates cloddiness, and transforms the montmorillonitic clay into nonswelling particles that resemble brick

a

b

Figure 20–3 Traditional shifting cultivation on Vertisols in Ethiopia involves (a) plowing the grassland several times with a village-made plow and then (b) gathering sod pieces into piles. Cattle manure is added to the piles and they are allowed to dry; then they are burned and spread back over the field. (Courtesy Roy L. Donahue.)

dust. The surface soil that was a clay loam now acts like a loamy sand. The burning also increases soil pH, available phosphorus, and total carbonates but decreases organic carbon (Donahue, 1972).

Shifting cultivation on burned Vertisols supporting native grasses is a soil conserving practice but is an inefficient land use that will not support rising populations with their increasing demand for land. Replacement of this traditional system awaits field research solutions. Perhaps a solution will be found that is comparable to that for forested areas using minimum tillage, organic surface-residue management, pesticides, and chemical fertilizers. In the meantime, Ethiopian farmers are using a system with no modern inputs that maintains yields and stabilizes the soil against excessive erosion.

20-3 SOIL AND WATER CONSERVATION IN SELECTED AREAS

Specific examples of soil and water conservation are cited here for arid northern Africa and the Middle East, Ghana, Liberia, Greece, the USSR, India, Pakistan, the humid Amazon jungles of Peru, Brazil, and Nicaragua.

20-3.1 Arid Tropical and Subtropical Africa and the Middle East

Soil and water conservation is especially difficult in arid regions. Aridity is common at latitudes between about 15 and 30° north and south of the equator. At these latitudes air masses usually descend, become warmer, and increase their capacity to hold moisture. The result is low precipitation and little plant growth to protect the soil against both water and wind erosion. Also, in areas receiving low precipitation, the annual rain may be received in one or a few storms. The combination of torrential rain and scant vegetation results in excessive erosion.

Desert is commonly defined as an area that receives about 4 in. (100 mm) or less of annual precipitation—not enough to support protective vegetation. However, at an annual precipitation of 6 to 10 in. (150 to 250 mm), many plants can be established to stabilize the soil as well as to supply some forage, firewood, and construction materials.

Special studies of techniques for successful establishment of productive and protective vegetation have been made by the Food and Agriculture Organization of the United Nations (Bensalem, 1977). These activities have been conducted in Tunisia, Morocco, and Algeria. However, the results are considered to be equally applicable to many other countries with similar rainfall. Greater success is assured if the site selected for establishing vegetation is in a swale where additional rainwater collects or if the soils are deep sands where all rainwater infiltrates and plants root deeply.

About 120,000 acres (50,000 ha) of spineless cactus have been planted in Tunisia to stabilize the soil and to provide forage for livestock. Also in Tunisia during a recent five-year period, spineless acacia has been established on about 2500 acres/yr (1000 ha/yr). Windbreaks have been successfully established on fine-textured soil in Tunisia and Algeria by planting native acacia species in mixture with eucalyptus trees from Australia. Two species of pines have proved satisfactory on deep sands—stone pine and cluster pine. New plantations must not be grazed by livestock for a period of two to five years. This restriction requires rigid enforcement by the local government. Trees and shrubs that have been successfully established in the arid and semiarid tropical and subtropical regions as windbreaks or woodlots are listed in Table 20-2.

20-3.2 Ghana and Liberia

Ghana and Liberia are located in the humid part of western Africa about 5 to 10° north of the equator. The Soil Research Institute at Kwadaso-Kumasi in central Ghana has conducted outstanding work relating soils, mechanization, erosion, and

TABLE 20-2 TREE AND SHRUB SPECIES (COMMON ENGLISH NAMES[a]) RECOMMENDED FOR PLANTING AS WOODLOTS, WINDBREAKS, OR SHELTERBELTS IN TROPICAL AND SUBTROPICAL REGIONS WITH ANNUAL PRECIPITATION OF 6 TO 10 IN. (150 TO 250 MM)[b]

Acacia	Mesquite tree
African locust	Mulga
Aleppo pine	Neem tree
Argan tree	Olive tree
Calligonum	Russian olive
Carob tree	Shinus
Eucalyptus	Siris tree
Fourwing saltbush	Sissoo
Horsetail tree	Salsola shrub
Jerusalem thorn	Tamarix
Kassod tree	Tassili cypress

[a]Scientific names are given in Appendix B.

[b]All plants will grow in areas of the lower range of precipitation in swales and on sandy soils.

soil productivity. The Institute made a soil survey of an area where attempts to use mechanized agriculture on soils with plinthite had failed. The survey identified the problem soils and it was recommended that all soils with plinthite be seeded to perennial pasture. Soils without plinthite were recommended for continuous mechanized cultivation. More detailed soil surveys were made after this experience and were used to make a map of Ghana delineating areas suitable for the three kinds of cultivation: tractors, oxen, and hand hoes such as those shown in Figure 20–4.

Liberian agriculture consists mostly of shifting cultivation, with vegetables, upland rainfed rice, and cassava (tapioca) as the main crops. Many commercially successful rubber, cocoa, coffee, and oil palm plantations also exist. Erosion is serious on sloping croplands during extended periods of cropping, especially near large centers of population. Some soils apparently can be cropped without deterioration for five or more years, whereas others cannot support more than two or three crops without a serious decline in yields. To determine suitable soils for the most feasible land resettlement, the government of Liberia requested assistance in establishing a nationwide soil survey.

For three and a half years the U.S. Agency for International Development financed the USDA–Soil Conservation Service to help establish a soil survey in Liberia. The survey is used to aid in scientific land use decisions, including practices to maximize production and minimize erosion and sedimentation (Geiger, 1978).

20–3.3 Greece

Greece has a semitropical climate. Oranges are grown in the warmer parts of the country and olives are grown over a more extensive area. Mean annual precipitation varies from 16 in. (400 mm) at Athens to 33 in. (850 mm) at Kalmia in the Peloponnesus. The dry summer season, ranging from about one month on the island

Figure 20–4 Two kinds of tillage implements used in equatorial Africa. The village-made hoe commonly used in subsistence agriculture seldom disturbs the soil enough to cause serious soil erosion. The disk plow makes it possible to use tractor power in commercial farming and also increases the potential for soil erosion. (Courtesy Roy L. Donahue.)

of Crete to about four months at Athens, is a constraint on production of warm-season plants.

The soils of Greece are dominantly shallow over highly weathered limestone. Nearly all of the topography is hilly to mountainous. Shallow soils on steep slopes are conducive to erosion even though the rains are usually gentle. Soil erosion is a serious handicap to the country because a deep soil is needed to hold sufficient available water for plant growth during the dry summers when temperatures are most favorable for plant growth.

According to a 20-year study by the Athens Soils Institute, serious erosion had occurred on 110,000 acres (45,000 ha) in the Peloponnesus. In another study made by the Land and Water Reclamation Service in two states in northern Greece, Thrace and Macedonia, the loss of agricultural production due to erosion amounted to $8 million per year.

Action programs to control erosion in Greece have consisted of terracing, contour farming, strip cropping, subsoiling, tree planting, grazing control, and gully reclamation. Terraces have been built to protect 22,000 acres (9000 ha) of land.

20-3.4 USSR (Soviet Union)

The Union of Soviet Socialist Republics (Soviet Union) has 560 million acres (226 million ha) under cultivation. Its geographic location parallels that of Canada and northern United States. The USSR cropland has a climate as variable as that from northern Alaska to southern California (Central Intelligence Agency, 1974).

A major part of the arable Soviet farmland is subject to severe wind and water erosion. These natural processes have been accelerated in many areas by agricultural policy stressing production rather than conservation. Plowing of steep slopes, overgrazing, overcutting of trees, and other practices that remove vegetative cover have been particularly damaging in the forest-steppe and forest zones of the European USSR and in the Transcaucasus and central regions. In the dry steppe and semidesert, bare ground is exposed frequently to erosion by strong, dry winds.

Thick loess deposits lead to another problem. Loess is very susceptible to deep gullying even on gentle slopes. Occasional downpours of summer rain produce vast networks of gullies and ravines, particularly in the deep loess deposits that occupy large areas of the Ukraine.

The severity of the erosion problem was acknowledged in a 1967 joint resolution of the USSR Communist Party and the Council of Ministers. The resolution called for increased contour plowing, crop rotation, strip cropping, and sowing grass on steep slopes; the planting and cultivation of forest belts; afforestation of gullies, ravines, and shorelines of rivers and reservoirs; and the construction of erosion-control and flood-control structures.

Windbreaks and shelterbelts are prominent among measures designed to combat both wind and water erosion. Concentrated on the steppe and forest-steppe of European USSR, these forest belts protect against wind erosion, increase the accumulation of snow, and check the erosive action of surface water. Trees and shrubs planted for windbreaks and shelterbelts include: poplar, birch, black locust, Siberian elm, Siberian larch, Scotch pine, English oak, sea buckthorn, golden currant, Russian olive, caragana (Siberian peashrub), tartarian honeysuckle, tamarisk, and willows (Schroeder and Kort, 1989).

Contour plowing, crop rotations, fallowing, stubble mulching, and terracing are used in many areas. Stubble-mulch tillage is a necessity for adequate erosion control in the New Lands area of western Siberia and northern Kazakhstan and in other moisture-deficient areas. Also called trashy fallow, this practice protects the soil from baking, contributes to lower soil temperatures in hot summer weather, decreases the depth of freezing, impedes runoff and evaporation, and enables the soil to absorb more rainfall.

Various types of terraces are used in hilly terrain to reduce the slope gradient.

Found primarily in the mountains of Moldavia, the Caucasus, and Soviet Central Asia, terracing was once considered the basis for mountain agriculture; however, recent research has shown that some mountain soils can be cropped without terraces.

20–3.5 India

About half of the soils in India are subject to deterioration by water and wind erosion, as shown in Figure 20–5. About 16.5% of the land area of India has extremely low productivity because of the following problems (National Commission on Agriculture, India, 1976; Das, 1977): low precipitation, ironstone (hardened plinthite), sandy coastal land, saline and sodic soils, waterlogged soils, and riverine gullies.

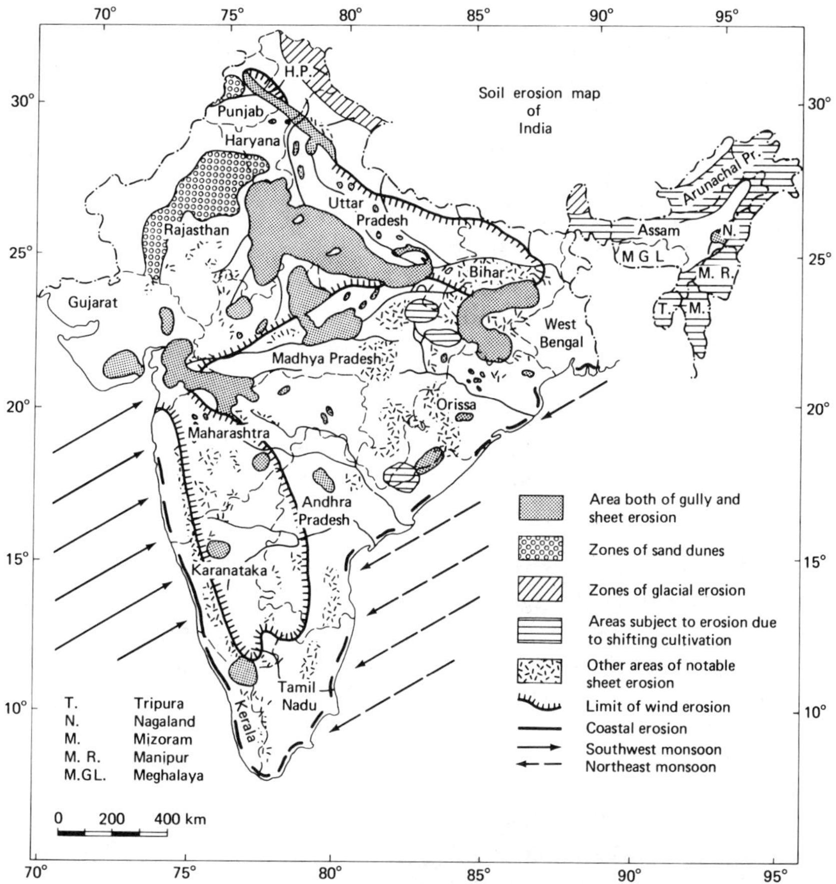

Figure 20–5 Soil erosion in India is a serious constraint for agricultural production. There are large areas of sheet, gully, and wind erosion plus areas of glacial erosion and erosion related to shifting cultivation. (*Source:* Food and Agriculture Organization of the United Nations, *FAO Soils Bull.* 33, D.C. Das, 1977.)

Practices used to control erosion in India include contour cultivation, terracing, and the establishment of protective vegetation. Most of the soil and water conservation works have been concentrated to stabilize shifting sands or to reduce erosion and sedimentation on the watershed of the reservoirs used for hydroelectric power generation and irrigation (Arakeri and Donahue, 1984).

20-3.6 Amazon Jungles of Peru

Research on intensive cropping of corn, peanuts, cowpeas, rice, soybeans, and cassava has been conducted at Yurimaguas, Peru, since 1969 (North Carolina State University, 1976). The soil is classified as a Typic Paleudult, a highly leached, acid soil typical of the humid, lowland, forested tropics in the Amazon River Valley. Shifting cultivation is the dominant kind of traditional agriculture. The research treatments included NPK fertilizers and lime, and mulching with kudzu (surface applied versus incorporated). The results can be summarized in this way:

1. Mulching increased yields of all crops by lowering soil temperatures, lowering bulk density, reducing surface crust formation, controlling weeds, and increasing available soil moisture.
2. Fertilizing with 107 + 54 + 107 lb/ac (120 + 50 + 120 kg/ha) of NPK, plus liming, resulted in yields equal to those of the mulched plots.
3. Leaving the grass and kudzu mulch on the soil surface resulted in higher yields of all crops than when the mulches were incorporated into the soil.

The researchers were not able to explain why the use of mulch alone on the soil surface gave crop-yield increases equal to the best chemical fertilizing and liming practices. Perhaps the chemical fertilizer and lime contained an excess of nutrients or some of the nutrients were not available to the current crops. Another explanation may be that the mulch supplied secondary and micronutrients and stimulated soil organisms to decompose soil minerals and bring slowly available plant nutrients into solution. Also, the mulching would increase infiltration for cultivated crops and be an effective soil and water conservation practice (Lal, 1974). Whatever the cause, surface mulching was very effective for increasing crop yields.

The temperate-region technique of clearing forested land with a bulldozer was tried and declared a failure in tropical Peru. The bulldozer scraped off too much of the most productive topsoil and compacted the remaining soil. The technique of clearing tropical jungle with hand tools and burning was far superior.

20-3.7 Brazil

A soil survey of 200 million acres (82 million hectares) in the principal cropped areas in humid southern and western Brazil classified the soils as Oxisols, Ultisols, and Mollisols (Bloomfield, 1977). It was found that erosion had been accelerated by the rapid increase in soybean production on slopes up to 12%. Soybeans in Brazil had increased 385% from 3.2 to 15.5 million acres (1.3 to 6.3 million hectares) during the period from 1970 to 1976, mostly on land formerly planted to coffee and pasture grasses. Annual precipitation in the region varies from about 48 to 60 in. (1200 to 1500 mm), with a dry season from April to August.

The survey also showed that 52% of the land in the 82-million hectare area had suffered moderate or severe erosion. The severity of past erosion indicated a need for an effective soil and water conservation program in Brazil. A proposal was made that soil and water conservation and soil survey be combined in an organization similar to that of the USDA–Soil Conservation Service.

One study indicated that a soybean field averaged about 9 tons/ac (20 mt/ha) of soil loss annually and water runoff loss was about 7% of the precipitation received. This compared with about 20 tons/ac (42 mt/ha) and 12% of the precipitation for castor beans and 3 tons/ac (7 mt/ha) and 4% for a field planted to sweet potatoes. Fields in 10 other crops had soil and water losses between these extremes.

20–3.8 Australia

Australia, a country about the size of the United States, lies 12 to 44° south of the equator. Whereas only about 10% of the United States is arid, two-thirds of Australia is arid, and there are no perennial streams. The arid lands receive less than 10 in. (250 mm) of rainfall a year, while coastal areas get as much as about 30 in. (750 mm). Temperatures vary from tropical in the north to semitropical in the south. Saline and sodic soils are common in the arid two-thirds of the country.

Wind erosion is a potentially serious problem in the low rainfall, rangeland interior. Control of wind erosion is accomplished by reducing the domestic livestock stocking rate. Fortunately, the stocking rate can be controlled because the rangeland is owned by the central government and is leased to private livestock owners.

Successful water-erosion projects have included terracing, minimum tillage, and improved cropping systems.

One major soil degradation problem has been studied but no solution has been found. It is called "dryland salinity." Extensive areas of soils that were *never irrigated* are becoming salty. The principal theory is that salt is deposited in rainfall. A similar occurrence in *irrigated areas* of North Dakota is known as "saline seeps" (Hallsworth, 1987).

Organizations and agencies concerned with soil and water conservation in Australia include (Hudson, 1986; Gordon and Hannan, 1987):

- Land Conservation Unit, Winnellie, Darwin, N.T.
- Soils Division, CSIRO, Canberra
- Soil Conservation Service, Department of Mineral Resources, and the Department of Environment and Planning.
- Faculty of Resource Management, University of New England, Armidale, New South Wales
- Department of Civil Engineering, University of Melbourne
- School of Earth Science, Macquarie University, New South Wales

20-3.9 The Netherlands

In The Netherlands, where half of the population lives below sea level, it is crucial to reduce contamination of soil and groundwaters. It is very important to be able to prevent, and therefore to predict, excess applications of sewage sludge, animal manures, fertilizers, and pesticides.

Within each soil mapping unit, piezometers (a device for measuring water tables) are established. A representative soil profile is designated for each soil mapping unit. This research measures (1) the travel time for water to move from the soil surface to the mean water table, (2) the soil cation-exchange capacity and (3) the phosphate adsorption capacity of the soil.

The length of time it takes for water to reach the water table is a measure of the amount of soil depth that can adsorb pollutants. The cation-exchange capacity is a measure of the ability of the soil to adsorb heavy metal fertilizer and the pesticide pollutants and thus keep them out of the groundwater. The phosphate adsorption capacity of the soil determines how much phosphate is "tied up" before it reaches surface waters or groundwaters (Breeuwsma et al., 1986).

20-4 ONLY A SAMPLING

This is not the end of the story. Erosion and pollution problems exist in every country, and each country has its own approach to managing and conserving soil and water. This book has sampled only a few of the many examples that could have been cited. Many other problems and solutions could have served as well, but those chosen will convey something of the breadth and magnitude of the need for soil and water conservation in the United States and around the world.

Many things change with time, and the conservation story is no exception. People come and go and they change their ways of doing things. Even small changes may have great impact on the soil and water resources on which everyone depends. Governments and their programs are always limited by earth's finite land base. The human population, however, has never stopped increasing. The pressure on soil and water resources increases with the population numbers and their increasing expectations. Everyone wants a cleaner environment and they want it NOW!

SUMMARY

Soil and water conservation practices are essential in all nations to retain the productive agricultural base needed to support a rapidly increasing population and rising expectations. Most countries have established some kind of conservation agency, often based on the model and assistance of the USDA–Soil Conservation Service. Progress to date, however, has been uneven, partly because the differences in culture, soil, and agriculture are so great that adaptation is necessary but usually has been inadequate. Massive mechanization schemes, as well as most temperate-region techniques of soil management, have failed in the tropics. One reason is that most soils in the tropics, when cropped continuously, form surface crusts and become cloddy, and crop yields soon decline below economic levels.

Shifting cultivation is the traditional technique used in forested tropics to maintain yields and control the loss of soil and water. This consists of two to three years of cultivated crops followed by 10 to 20 years of wild trees and shrubs. Some Vertisols in the tropics are burned and cropped until yields decline, then are "rested in native grass" to rejuvenate them.

Terracing and ridging on the contour have failed in many tropical and subtropical regions because of physical deterioration of the soil. The use of annual cover crops has also failed because the additional tillage they require is conducive to erosion. Perennial crops in rotation with cultivated crops are satisfactory if the perennial crop is killed with an herbicide and the following crop is planted in the crop residue.

The most successful techniques of continuous cropping in the tropics have been these two soil-management systems:

1. Maintain an organic *surface* mulch at all times (no-tillage), or
2. Scientifically determine the major and minor nutrients required for each crop grown and supply them in the amounts needed at the times when the plants can absorb them. This approach must also include the incorporation of enough plant and animal residues to maintain suitable soil tilth.

QUESTIONS

1. Why doesn't the technology of the U.S. Corn Belt work for raising corn in Nigeria?
2. Defend these statements: "Shifting cultivation is a successful technique of agricultural production." "Shifting cultivation is a failure and must be replaced by a more efficient system."
3. Explain how to stabilize the soil in the arid tropics against water and wind and at the same time keep it productive for agriculture.
4. Tell how to control erosion in the humid forested tropics while harvesting continuous agricultural crops.
5. Why does the USSR have so many windbreaks and shelterbelts?

REFERENCES

ARAKERI, H. R., and R. L. DONAHUE, 1984. *Principles of Soil Conservation and Water Management.* Oxford & IBM Publishing Co., New Delhi, Bombay, and Calcutta, India, p. 186–207.

BENSALEM, B., 1977. Examples of soil and water conservation practices in North African Countries, Algeria, Morocco, and Tunisia. In *Soil Conservation and Management in Developing Countries.* Soils Bull. 33. FAO, Rome, p. 151–160.

BLOOMFIELD, N. J., 1977. *An Evaluation of Soil Erosion in Southern Brazil, and a Proposal for an Integrated National Program of Soil Conservation and Soil Survey.* M.S. thesis, Univ. of Wisconsin, Madison, Wis.

BREEUWSMA, A., J. H. M. WOSTEN, J. J. VLEESHOUWER, A. M. VAN SLOBBE, and J. BOUMA, 1986. Derivation of land qualities to assess environmental problems from soil surveys. *Soil Sci. Soc. Am. J.* 50:186–190.

CENTRAL INTELLIGENCE AGENCY, 1974. *USSR Agriculture Atlas.* U.S. Government Printing Office, Washington, D.C.

CONSTANTINESCO, I., 1976. *Soil Conservation for Developing Countries.* Soils Bull. 30. FAO, Rome, 92 p.

COX, M. P., 1977. *On-Farm Management at the Field Level in Pakistan.* Unpublished paper presented at the Seminar on Water Management, Lahore, Pakistan, Nov. 15–17, 1977, 12 p.

DARBY, G. M., 1978. Controlling wind erosion in Nicaragua. *Soil Cons.* 43(11):18–19.

DAS, D. C., 1977. Soil conservation practices and erosion control in India—A case study. In *Soil Conservation and Management in Developing Countries.* Soils Bull. 33. FAO, Rome, p. 11–50.

DONAHUE, R. L., 1972. *Ethiopia: Taxonomy, Cartography, and Ecology of Soils.* Monograph 1. African Studies Center and the Institute of International Agriculture, Michigan State University, East Lansing, Mich., 44 p.

GEIGER, L. C., 1978. Soil survey in Liberia. *Soil Cons.* 43(11):16–17.

GORDON, R. M., and J. C. HANNAN, 1987. Reclamation of surface mines in the Hunter Valley, New South Wales, Australia. In *Innovative Approaches to Mined Land Reclamation,* C. L. Carlson, and J. H. Swisher, (eds.). Southern Illinois Univ. Press, Carbondale and Edwardsville, Ill., p. 525–560.

HALLSWORTH, E. G., 1987. Soil conservation down under. *J. Soil Water Cons.* 42:394–400.

HAMMOND, J., 1988. International activities of the Soil Conservation Service. In *Conservation Farming on Steep Lands,* W. C. Moldenhauer, and N. W. Hudson (eds.). Soil and Water Conservation Society and World Association of Soil and Water Conservation, Ankeny, Iowa, p. 70–74.

HUDSON, N. W., 1986. Soil conservation research and training requirements in developing tropical countries. In *Soil Erosion and Conservation in the Tropics.* Spec. Publ. 43. American Society of Agronomy and Soil Science Society of America, Madison, Wis., p. 121–133.

IITA, 1975. *Annual Report.* International Institute of Tropical Agriculture, Ibadan, Nigeria, 219 p.

IITA, 1978. *IITA Research Highlights, 1977.* International Institute of Tropical Agriculture, Ibadan, Nigeria, 72 p.

LAL, R., 1974. Soil erosion and shifting agriculture. In *Shifting Cultivation and Soil Conservation in Africa.* Soils Bull. 24, Swedish International Development Authority and FAO, Rome, p. 48–71.

LAL, R., (ED.), 1988. *Soil Erosion Research Methods.* Soil and Water Conservation Society, Ankeny, Iowa, and International Society of Soil Science, Wageningen, The Netherlands.

LE HOUÉROU, H. N., 1976. Can desertization be halted? In *Conservation in Arid and Semiarid Zones.* Conservation Guide 3. FAO, Rome, p. 1–15.

MOLDENHAUER, W. C., and N. W. HUDSON (EDS.), 1988. *Conservation Farming on Steep Lands.* Soil and Water Conservation Society, Ankeny, Iowa.

NATIONAL COMMISSION ON AGRICULTURE, INDIA, 1976. *Report of the National Commission on Agriculture:* Part V. Resource Development, Government of India Press, New Delhi, p. 177–322.

NATIONAL WILDLIFE FEDERATION, 1989. *Conservation Directory,* 34th ed. NWF, Washington, D.C., 331 p.

NORTH CAROLINA STATE UNIVERSITY, 1976. *Tropical Soils Research Program, Annual Report for 1975,* Raleigh, N.C., 312 p.

OTHIENO, C. O., and D. H. LAYCOCK, 1977. Factors affecting soil erosion within tea fields. *Trop. Agric.* 54:223–330.

PRESIDENT'S ADVISORY COMMITTEE ON WORLD FOOD SUPPLY, 1967. *The World Food Problem,* Vol. II. Washington, D.C., p. 471–500.

RAPP, A., 1977. Soil erosion and reservoir sedimentation—Case studies in Tanzania. In *Soil Conservation and Management in Developing Countries.* Soils Bull. 33. FAO, Rome, p. 123–131.

SANCHEZ, P. A. (ED.), 1973. *A Review of Soils Research in Tropical Latin America.* N.C. Agr. Exp. Sta. in cooperation with the U.S. Agency for International Development, 197 p.

SANCHEZ, P. A., 1986. A legume-based pasture production strategy for acid infertile soils of tropical America. In *Soil Erosion and Conservation in the Tropics.* Special Publ. 43. American Society of Agronomy and Soil Science Society of America, Madison, Wis., p. 97–120.

SCHROEDER, W. R., and J. KORT, 1989. Shelterbelts in the Soviet Union. *J. Soil Water Cons.* 44:130–134.

U.S. DEPARTMENT OF COMMERCE, 1987. *Comparative Climatic Data for the United States.* National Oceanic and Atmospheric Administration, National Climatic Data Center, Federal Building, Asheville, N.C., 94 p.

VIEWEG, G., and W. WILMS, 1974. Problems associated with a change from shifting cultivation to permanent cultivation of a light soil in the Kilombero Valley, Tanzania. In *Shifting Cultivation and Soil Conservation in Africa.* Soils Bull. 24. Swedish International Development Authority and FAO, Rome, p. 228–229.

WILKINSON, G. E., 1975. Canopy characteristics of maize and the effect on soil erosion in western Nigeria. *Trop. Agr.* 52:289–297.

Appendix A
Conversion Factors

U. S. Public Law 94-168 in 1975 authorized the establishment of a board to plan for voluntary conversion to metric units by 1985. The first edition of this book, published in 1980, used mostly metric units in accord with the intent of the 1975 law. However, since only limited progress has been made on this conversion, the authors decided to use foot-pound-second units as the primary units for this new edition. These are usually supplemented with approximate equivalents in the metric system. Metric units are retained as the primary system or even the only system for some uses where they are in common use in the United States. The intent is to make the book useful for readers both in the United States where foot-pound-second units dominate and in the rest of the world where metric units dominate.

The metric equivalents indicated in parentheses following foot-pound-second units (or occasionally the reverse set of equivalents) are usually only approximate. The degree of precision of matching these equivalents varies according to whether the measurements involved need to be expressed exactly or not. More exact equivalents are provided in this appendix along with many internal relationships for each of these systems of measurement. A few non-related units such as atmospheres also have been used for convenience. The units are grouped according to function.

Length, distance, depth, height (mile, yard, foot, inch, meter and derivatives)

1 mi = 5280 ft = 1609 m = 1.609 km

1 km = 1000 m = 3281 ft = 0.6214 mi

1 m = 100 cm = 1000 mm = 1.094 yd = 3.281 ft = 39.37 in.

1 ft = 12 in. = 30.48 cm = 0.3048 m

1 in. = 2.54 cm = 25.4 mm

1 cm = 10 mm = 0.3937 in.

Area (length squared, acres, hectares)

1 mi^2 = 640 ac = 2.59 km^2 = 259 ha

1 km^2 = 100 ha = 0.3861 mi^2 = 247.1 ac

1 ha = 10,000 m^2 = 2.471 ac

1 ac = 43,560 ft^2 = 0.4047 ha

Volume (length cubed, gallons, quarts, liters)

1 m^3 = 1000 l = 35.31 ft^3 = 264.2 gal (U.S.)

1 ft^3 = 7.48 gal (U.S.) = 28.32 l

1 gal (U.S.) = 4 qt (U.S.) = 3.785 l = 231 $in.^3$

1 l = 1000 ml = 1.057 qt (U.S.) = 61.02 $in.^3$

Weight (tons, pounds, metric tons, quintals, grams and derivatives)

1 mt = 1000 kg = 1.102 short tons = 0.984 long tons = 2204.6 lb

1 ton (short ton) = 2000 lb = 0.9072 mt = 907.2 kg

1 q = 100 kg = 220.46 lb

1 kg = 1000 g = 2.2046 lb

1 lb = 0.4536 kg = 453.6 g = 16 oz (avoirdupois)

Rate, yield (weight per acre or hectare)

1 mt/ha = 10 q/ha = 0.446 short tons/ac = 892 lb/ac

1 ton/ac (short ton) = 2000 lb/ac = 2.2417 mt/ha = 2241.7 kg/ha

1 q/ha = 100 kg/ha = 1.49 bu/ac (wheat at 60 lb/bu)

= 1.59 bu/ac (corn or sorghum at 56 lb/bu)

1 kg/ha = 0.892 lb/ac

1 lb/ac = 1.121 kg/ha

Density (weight per unit volume)

1 g/cm^3 = 62.4 lb/ft^3 = 8.34 lb/gal

Pressure, tension (weight per unit area)

1 atm = 1.013 bars = 1.033 kg/cm^2 = 14.7 $lb/in.^2$

1 kg/cm^2 = 10 m of H_2O = 14.22 $lb/in.^2$ = 0.968 atm

Energy, work (ft lb, kg m, joule, calorie)

1 j = 0.102 kg m = 0.7377 ft lb = 0.239 cal

Velocity, permeability (distance per second, minute, or hour)

1 mi/hr = 1.609 km/hr = 0.447 m/s = 1.4667 ft/s

1 km/hr = 0.6214 mi/hr = 0.27778 m/s = 0.9114 ft/s

1 m/s = 3.281 ft/s = 3.6 km/hr = 2.237 mi/hr

1 ft/s = 0.3048 m/s = 1.097 km/hr = 0.6818 mi/hr

Flow rates (volume per second or hour)

$1\ m^3/s = 1000\ l/s = 35.31\ ft^3/s = 3600\ m^3/hr$

$1\ ft^3/s = 28.32\ l/s = 101.9\ m^3/hr$

Viscosity (poise)

1 p = 0.1 kg/m-sec

Temperature (degrees Fahrenheit, Celsius, Kelvin)

°F = °C x 1.8 + 32

°C = (°F − 32)/1.8 = °K − 273.15

Chemical concentrations (normal, gram-equivalent)

1 *N* = 1 g-eq/l = 1000 meq/l

1 g-eq = gram-weight of 1 mole/valence

1 meq/100 g = 1 mg-eq/100 g

Electrical conductivity (millimho/cm, siemen/cm)

1 mmho/cm = 0.001 mho/cm = 0.001 siemen/cm

Ratios (percent, parts per million)

1/1 = 100% = 1,000,000 ppm

1% = 10,000 ppm

Appendix B
Common and Scientific Names of Plants Mentioned in the Text

The common English names of plants vary widely from one place to another. The following list is supplied to remove any ambiguity that would otherwise arise from the common names used in this book. The equivalent scientific names listed here should have worldwide meaning.

Acacia—*Acacia farnesiana*
Alder, European black—*Alnus glutinosa*
Alfalfa—*Medicago sativa*
Alkaligrass, nuttall—*Puccinellia airoides*
Alkali sacaton—*Sporobolus airoides*
Argan tree—*Argania spinosa*
Ash:
  green—*Fraxinus pennsylvanica*
  white—*Fraxinus americana*
Asparagus—*Asparagus officinalis*
Aspen, trembling—*Populus tremuloides*

Bahiagrass—*Paspalum notatum*
Banana—*Musa* species
Barley—*Hordeum vulgare*
Bayberry—*Myrica cerifera*
Beachgrass:
  American—*Ammophila breviligulata*
  European—*Ammophyila arenaria*
Beachpea—*Lathyrus japonicus*
Bean (bush, climbing, wild)—*Phaseolus* species
  field—*Phaseolus vulgaris*
Beet, red, (garden)—*Beta vulgaris*
Bermudagrass:
  (common and coastal)—*Cynodon dactylon*
  African—*Cynodon transvaalensis*
Birch:
  river—*Betula nigra*
  white—*Betula alba*
  yellow—*Betula allegheniensis*
Birdfoot trefoil—*Lotus corniculatus*
Bitterbrush:
  antelope—*Purshia tridentata*
  desert—*Purshia glandulosa*
Blueberry—*Vaccinium* species
Bluegrass:
  alpine—*Poa* species
  big—*Poa ampla*
  Kentucky—*Poa pratensis*
Bluestem:
  big—*Andropogon gerardi*
  broomsedge—*Andropogon virginicus*
  sand—*Andropogon hallii*
  seacoast—*Andropogon littoralis*
  yellow—*Andropogon ischaemum*
Boxelder—*Acer negundo*
Bromegrass:
  California—*Bromus carinatus*
  mountain—*Bromus marginatus*
  smooth—*Bromus inermis*
Buckthorn—*Rhamnus* species
Buckwheat—*Fagopyrum esculentum*
Buffaloberry, russet—*Shepherdia argentea*
Buffalograss—*Buchloe dactyloides*
Bursage, white—*Franseria dumosa*

Cabbage—*Brassica oleracea*
Cactus—*Cactaea* species
Calligonum—*Calligonum arich*
Camellia—*Camellis japonica*
Caper bush—*Capparis spinosa*
Caragana—*Caragana arborescens*
Carob tree—*Ceratonica siliqua*
Carrot—*Daucus carota*
Cashew—*Anacardium occidentale*
Cassava (tapioca)—*Manihot esculenta*
Cassia—*Cassia* species

Cedar:
- red—*Juniperus virginiana*
- white—*Thuja occidentalis*

Cherry:
- black—*Prunus serotina*
- Nanking—*Prunus tomentosa*
- wild red—*Prunus pennsylvanica*

Chinese silvergrass—*Miscanthus sinensis*
Chokecherry, common—*Prunus virginiana*
Cinquefoil—*Potentilla fruticosa*
Clover:
- alsike—*Trifolium hybridum*
- red—*Trifolium pratense*
- tick—*Desmodium leonii*
- white (Dutch)—*Trifolium repens*

Cocoa—*Cacao nucifera*
Coffee:
- arabica—*Coffea arabica*
- robusta—*Coffea robusta*

Corn, field, pop, or sweet—*Zea mays*
Cotoneaster—*Cotoneaster apiculata*
Cotton, American, Egyptian—*Gossypium barbadense*
Cottonwood—*Populus deltoides*
Crabapple:
- Siberian—*Malus baccata*
- toringo—*Malus sieboldi*

Crabgrass—*Digitaria* species
Cranberry—*Vaccinium macrocarpon*
Creosotebush—*Larrea tridentata*
Crownvetch—*Coronilla varia*
Currant, golden—*Ribes* species
Cypress, bald—*Taxodium distichum*

Dallisgrass—*Paspalum dilatatum*
Deertongue—*Panicum clandestinum*
Dogwood, redosier—*Cornus stolonifera*
Douglas-fir—*Pseudotsuga menziesii*
Elm, Siberian—*Ulmus pumila*
Eucalyptus—*Eucalyptus* species

Fescue:
- red and arctared—*Festuca rubra*
- tall (reed)—*Festuca arundinacea*

Flatpea—*Lathyrus sylvestris*
Flax—*Linum usitatissimum*
Forsythia—*Forsythia* species
Foxtail, creeping—*Alopecurus arundinaceus*

Grama grass:
- black—*Bouteloua eripoda*
- blue—*Bouteloua gracilis*
- sideoats—*Bouteloua curtipendula*

Grape—*Vitus* species

Hackberry—*Celtis* species
Hairgrass, Bering tufted—*Deschampsia caespitosa*
Hanson hedgerose—*Rosa* species
Hardinggrass—*Phalaris tuberosa*
Hawthorne, Arnold—*Crataegus* species
Hemlock:
- eastern—*Tsuga canadensis*
- ground—*Taxus canadensis*

Honeylocust, thornless—*Gledsia triacanthos*
Honeysuckle, tartarian—*Lonicera tartarica*
Horsetail tree (casuarina)—*Casuarina cunninghamia*
Hyparrhenia—*Hyparrhenia rufa*

Indiangrass—*Sorghastrum nutans, S. odorata*
Indigobush—*Amorpha fruticosa,*
Iris, wild—*Iris pseudacorus*

Jerusalem thorn—*Parkinsonia aculeata*
Juniper:
- creeping—*Juniperus horizontalis*
- one-seed—*Juniperus monosperma*
- Rocky Mountain—*Juniperus scopulorum*

Kassod tree—*Cassia siamea*
Kentucky coffeetree—*Gymnocladus dioica*
Kudzu—*Pueraria lobata*

Leadplant—*Amorpha canescens*
Lentil—*Lens culinaris*
Lespedeza:
- common (annual)—*Lespedeza striata*
- sericea (Chinese)—*Lespedeza cuneata*

Lilac—*Syringa vulgaris*
- late—*Syringa villosa*

Locust:
- African—*Parkia clappertoniana*
- black—*Robinia pseudoacacia*

Lovegrass:
- Koran—*Eragrostis ferruginea*
- Lehmann—*Eragrostis lehmanniana*
- sand—*Eragrostis trichodes*
- weeping—*Eragrostis curvula*

Lupine, wild—*Lupinus perennis*

Maple:
- amur—*Acer ginnala*
- red—*Acer rubrum*
- silver (white)—*Acer saccharinum*

Manzanita, pinemat—*Arctostaphylos* species
Mesquite tree—*Prosopis chilensis*
Milkvetch, cicer—*Astragalus cicer*
Millet, German—*Setaria italica*
Mulberry, red—*Morus rubra*
Mulga—*Acacia aneura*

Neem tree—*Azadirachta indica*

Oak:
bur—*Quercus macrocarpa*
English—*Quercus robur*
nothern red—*Quercus rubra*
Oat, common—*Avena sativa*
Olive:
autumn—*Elaegnus umbellata*
Russian—*Elaegnus angustifolia*
tree—*Olea europaea*
Onion—*Allium cepa*
Orange—*Citrus sinensis*
Orchardgrass—*Dactylis glomerata*
Osage-orange—*Maclura pomifera*

Palm:
date—*Phoenix dactylifera*
oil—*Elaeis guineensis*
Panicgrass, coastal—*Panicum amarulum*
Pea, Austrian winter—*Lathyrus hirsutus*
Peanut—*Arachis hypogaea*
Pearl millet—*Pennisetum americanum*
Pea-tree, Siberian—*Caragana arborescens*
Pecan—*Carya illinoensis*
Penstemon—*Penstemon fruticosus*
Pepper, bell—*Capsicum annuum*
Pine:
Aleppo—*Pinus halepensis*
Austrian—*Pinus nigra*
cluster—*Pinus pinaster*
eastern white—*Pinus strobus*
jack—*Pinus banksiana*
loblolly—*Pinus taeda*
lodgepole (shore)—*Pinus contorta latifolia*
longleaf—*Pinus palustris*
Monterey—*Pinus radiata*
mugo (mugho)—*Pinus mugo*
pitch—*Pinus rigida*
ponderosa—*Pinus ponderosa*
red—*Pinus resinosa*
sand—*Pinus clausa*
Scotch (Scots)—*Pinus sylvestris*
shore—*Pinus contorta*
shortleaf—*Pinus echinata*
slash—*Pinus elliottii*
Stone—*Pinus monophylla, P. pinea*
Virginia—*Pinus virginiana*
western white—*Pinus monticola*
Plum:
American—*Prunus americana*
Assyrian—*Cordia myxa*
beach—*Prunus maritima*
chickasaw—*Prunus angustifolia*
Poplar:
northwest, Norway (hybrid)—*Populus sargentii*
robusta (hybrid)—*Populus robusta*
white (silver)—*Populus alba*
yellow (tulip)—*Liriodendron tulipifera*
Potato:
Irish (white)—*Solanum tuberosum*
sweet—*Ipomoea batatas*

Rape—*Brassica napus*
Redbud—*Cercis canadensis*
Redtop grass—*Agrostis alba*
Redwood—*Sequoia sempervirens*
Reed canarygrass—*Phalaris arundinacea*
Rhodesgrass—*Chloris gayana*
Rice—*Oryza sativa*
Rosemary—*Rosmarinus officinalis*
Rosemary, bog—*Andromeda* species
Rose, wild—*Rosa blanda*
Rubber—*Hevea braziliensis*
Russian olive—*Eleagnus angustifolia*
Rye—*Secale* species
Ryegrass:
annual (Italian)—*Lolium multiflorum*
perennial—*Lolium perenne*
Safflower—*Carthamus tinctorius*
Sagebrush—*Artemisia* species
Salsola shrub—*Salsola paletskiana, (S. richteri)*
Saltbush:
Desert—*Atriplex polycarpa*
Fourwing—*Atriplex canescens*
Saltgrass, seashore—*Distichlis spicata*
Sandgrass (purple)—*Triplasis purpurea*
Saskatoon serviceberry—*Amelanchier alnifolia*
Sassafras—*Sassafras albidum*
Scalebroom—*Lepidospartum squamtum*
Scotch-broom—*Cytisus scoparius*
Sea-oats grass—*Uniola paniculata*
Sedges—*Carex* species
Sesame—*Sesamum indicum*
Shinus—*Shinus terebinthifolius, (S. molle)*
Siberian peashrub (caragana)—*Caragana arborescens*
Signal grass—*Brachiaria decumbens*
Silverberry—*Elaeagnus argentea, (E. commutata)*
Siris—*Albizzia lebbek*
Sissoo—*Dalbergia sissoo*
Snowberry—*Symphoricarpos albus*
Snowberry, creeping—*Gaultheria hispidula*
Sorghum, grain—*Sorghum bicolor*
Soybean—*Glycine max*
Spinach—*Spinacia oleracea*
Spruce:
Black Hills—*Picea glauca*
Colorado—*Picea pungens*
Norway—*Picea abies*
white—*Picea glauca*
Squawcarpet—*Ceanothus prostratus*
Strawberry—*Fragaria* species
Stylosanthes—*Stylozanthes capitata*
Sudangrass—*Sorghum sudanense*

Sugar beet—*Beta vulgaris*
Sugarcane—*Saccharum officinarum*
Sunflower—*Helianthus annuus*
Sweetclover:
white—*Melilotus alba*
yellow—*Melilotus officinalis*
Sweetgale—*Myrica gale*
Sweetgum—*Liquidambar styraciflua*
Switchgrass—*Panicum virgatum*
Sycamore (American)—*Platanus occidentalis*

Tamarix (tamarisk)—*Tamarix aphylla, (T. nilotica)*
Tapioca (cassava)—*Manihot esculenta*
Tassili cypress—*Cupressus dupreziana*
Tea—*Camellia sinensis*
Thistle, Russian—*Salsola kali*
Timothy—*Phleum pratense*
Timothy, alpine—*Phleum alpinum*
Tobacco—*Nicotiana* species
Tomato—*Lycopersicon esculentum*
Tumbleweed—*Amaranthus albus*

Veldtgrass—*Ehrharta calycina*
Vetch:
hairy—*Vicia villosa*
reseeding—*Vicia* species
Virginia-creeper—*Parthenocissus quinquefolia*

Wax myrtle—*Myrica cerifera*
Western sandcherry—*Prunus besseyi*
Wheat, common—*Triticum aestivum*
Wheatgrass:
crested—*Agropyron desertorum*
intermediate—*Agropyron intermedium*
pubescent—*Agropyron trichophorum*
slender—*Agropyron trachycaulum*
tall—*Agropyron elongatum*
western—*Agropyron smithii*
Wildbean, trailing—*Strophostyles helvola*
Wildrye:
beardless—*Elymus triticoides*
Canada—*Elymus canadensis*
Russian—*Elymus junceus*
Volga—*Elymus giganteus*
Willow:
crack—*Salix fragilis*
desert—*Chilopsis linearis*
white—*Salix alba*
Wintergreen—*Gaultheria procumbens*

Zornia—*Zornia latifolia*

REFERENCES

ANDERSON, K. L., and C. E. OWENSBY, 1969. *Common Names of a Selected List of Plants,* Tech. Bull. No. 117, Kansas State University, 62 p.

BAILEY, L. H., and E. Z. BAILEY, 1976. *Hortus Third: A Concise Dictionary of Plants Cultivated in the United States and Canada.* Macmillan, New York, 1290 p.

HALLS, L. K., ed., 1977. *Southern Fruit-producing Woody Plants Used by Wildlife.* General Tech. Report SO-16, USDA-Forest Service, 235 p.

HANSON, A. A., 1972. *Grass Varietes in the United States. Agriculture Handbook No. 170, ARS, U.S. Dept. of Agriculture, 124 p.*

SOIL CONSERVATION SERVICE, 1978. *Plant Performance on Surface Coal Mine Spoil in Eastern United States.* TP-155, U.S. Dept. of Agriculture, 76 p.

TERRELL, E. E., 1977. *A Checklist of Names for 3000 Vascular Plants of Economic Importance.* Agriculture Handbook No. 505. ARS, U.S. Dept. of Agriculture, 201 p.

Appendix C Suggested Laboratory Exercises

1. *Soil-Loss Calculations.* The amounts of soil removed by specified amounts of sheet, rill, gully, and wind erosion can be calculated.
2. *Velocity and Energy of Water.* An eaves trough can be used to make an inexpensive water-flow channel. Equipped with an adjustable support, it can be used to measure water velocity on different slope gradients. The water flow rate can be measured by timing how long it takes to fill a container. Kinetic energy can then be calculated. The data can be graphed against slope gradient.
3. *Transporting Power of Water.* Sand grains of a particular size can be placed in an eaves trough and the velocity of water flow increased gradually until the grains begin to move. The water velocity can then be measured. Several sizes can be used and a graph prepared to relate velocity to grain size.
4. *Soil Permeability and Runoff.* Glass tubes an inch or two (a few centimeters) in diameter and perhaps 8 in. (20 cm) long can be used to measure soil permeability and how it changes with time in various soils. The data can be used to calculate how much runoff would occur from a rainstorm of specified intensity and duration on a field of a specified size.
5. *Rainfall and Erosion.* Artificial rainfall can be applied to a tray filled with soil. The time required to produce runoff, the rate of runoff, and the sediment contained in the runoff can all be measured. The type of soil can be varied and the experiment can be done with and without a mulch of plant residues.
6. *Wind Erosion.* An electric fan blowing across a bare sandy soil can produce wind erosion, especially if a small wind tunnel is used to guide the air flow. Saltation height and distance, relative amounts of deposition at various distances, and segregation of particle sizes can be studied with and without wind deflectors that simulate windbreaks.
7. *Soil-Loss Prediction.* The water- and wind-erosion equations can be used to estimate soil loss under various defined circumstances. Alternatives can then be chosen to reduce erosion to specified tolerable levels.
8. *Use of Soil Survey Reports.* An exercise sheet calling for a wide variety of types of soil information on erosion can be used for this exercise. The students obtain the answers from soil survey reports.

9. *Land-Use Capabilities.* Classification theory and soil information can be combined in an exercise to assign land-use capabilities to a group of soils. Each student can be assigned a land-use capability unit to name and describe.
10. *Preparing Interpretive Maps.* A soil map can be used as a base to prepare interpretive maps for land use capabilities, suitability for various types of land use, and usefulness or limitations for various engineering practices.
11. *Planning Land Use and Management.* A soil map of a specific farm or other problem area can be used as a basis for planning the arrangements of field boundaries, lanes, cropping systems, and other land use and management decisions.
12. *Design and Layout.* Topographic maps and soil maps can be used for designing the layout of conservation practices such as strip cropping, terracing, shelterbelt plantings, drainage systems, and irrigation systems.
13. *Calculating Costs and Returns.* An economic analysis can be made of various land use and management alternatives. The costs and returns for each may be related to soil-loss predictions.
14. *Field Trips.* Field trips give the class an opportunity to see various erosion problems and the practices used to control them.
15. *Term Problem.* Several of the preceding exercises can be combined into a comprehensive term problem on soil and water conservation involving the use and management of a specific tract of land.

Index